CORE STATUTES ON INTELLECTUAL PROPERTY 2018–19

Margaret Dowie-Whybrow

 macmillan education  palgrave

The *Palgrave Core Statutes* series

CONTENTS

COPYRIGHT, DESIGNS AND RELATED RIGHTS

UK

EU

INTERNATIONAL

PATENTS

UK

EU

Contents

TRADE MARKS, GEOGRAPHICAL NAMES AND UNFAIR COMPETITION

UK

EU

INTERNATIONAL

INTELLECTUAL PROPERTY ON THE INTERNET

UK

INTERNATIONAL

MULTIDISCIPLINARY LEGISLATION, AGREEMENTS AND TREATIES

ALPHABETICAL LIST OF CONTENTS

PREFACE

This selection represents the core material for any intellectual property law course, whether at undergraduate or postgraduate level.

The passing year has seen many changes in United Kingdom legislation, with some repeals and some previously existing legislation newly in force, making this updated edition an essential component of the studies of any intellectual property law student.

European Union law continues to be applicable and therefore included in this new edition are the European Union Trade Mark Regulation (2017/1001) and Regulation 2017/1128 on cross-border portability of online content. Closer to home, the International Registration of Industrial Designs Order 2018 is included, as well as changes made by the Intellectual Property (Unjustified Threats) Act 2017 and the Digital Economy Act 2017. As in previous editions, this book concentrates on substantive rather than procedural law. The resulting text should satisfy the requirements of most intellectual property law courses and be suitable for examination use.

My thanks must go to both Aléta Bezuidenhout and Nilanjana Sensarkar, for their kind and generous support, and to my husband, Steven, for taking care of other business whilst I concentrated on this book. As always, our children and grandchildren have provided welcome distractions from the law – notably Henry, for wanting piano lessons, and Edward, for always wanting to tell us interesting things. Life is so lively with our many wonderful grandchildren around, and their happiness is infectious. We are blessed. Thanks also must go to Rose, for dragging me away from the screen for exciting excursions, to James and Tommy, for regularly calling me to chat and set the world to rights, and to Sam for continually telling me how lucky I am. He is right.

I have been writing and updating this title for ten years now, and each edition has been dedicated to one or more special people in my life. This year is no exception.

This book is dedicated to Steven, Rose, James, Sam, Tommy, Henry and Edward. They know why.

Margaret Dowie-Whybrow
Kent
June 2018

COPYRIGHT, DESIGNS AND PATENTS ACT 1988
(c. 48)

PART I
COPYRIGHT

CHAPTER I
SUBSISTENCE, OWNERSHIP AND DURATION OF COPYRIGHT

Introductory

1 Copyright and copyright works

(1) Copyright is a property right which subsists in accordance with this Part in the following descriptions of work—
   (a) original literary, dramatic, musical or artistic works,
   (b) sound recordings, films or broadcasts, and
   (c) the typographical arrangement of published editions.

(2) In this Part "copyright work" means a work of any of those descriptions in which copyright subsists.

(3) Copyright does not subsist in a work unless the requirements of this Part with respect to qualification for copyright protection are met (see section 153 and the provisions referred to there).

2 Rights subsisting in copyright works

(1) The owner of the copyright in a work of any description has the exclusive right to do the acts specified in Chapter II as the acts restricted by the copyright in a work of that description.

(2) In relation to certain descriptions of copyright work the following rights conferred by Chapter IV (moral rights) subsist in favour of the author, director or commissioner of the work, whether or not he is the owner of the copyright—
   (a) section 77 (right to be identified as author or director),
   (b) section 80 (right to object to derogatory treatment of work), and
   (c) section 85 (right to privacy of certain photographs and films).

Descriptions of work and related provisions

3 Literary, dramatic and musical works

(1) In this Part—
   "literary work" means any work, other than a dramatic or musical work, which is written, spoken or sung, and accordingly includes—
   (a) a table or compilation, other than a database,
   (b) a computer program,
   (c) preparatory design material for a computer program, and
   (d) a database;
   "dramatic work" includes a work of dance or mime; and
   "musical work" means a work consisting of music, exclusive of any words or action intended to be sung, spoken or performed with the music.

(2) Copyright does not subsist in a literary, dramatic or musical work unless and until it is recorded, in writing or otherwise; and references in this Part to the time at which such a work is made are to the time at which it is so recorded.

(3) It is immaterial for the purposes of subsection (2) whether the work is recorded by or with the permission of the author; and where it is not recorded by the author, nothing in that subsection affects the question whether copyright subsists in the record as distinct from the work recorded.

3A Databases

(1) In this Part "database" means a collection of independent works, data or other materials which—
   (a) are arranged in a systematic or methodical way, and
   (b) are individually accessible by electronic or other means.

(2) For the purposes of this Part a literary work consisting of a database is original if, and only if, by reason of the selection or arrangement of the contents of the database the database constitutes the author's own intellectual creation.

4   Artistic works

(1) In this Part "artistic work" means—
    (a) a graphic work, photograph, sculpture or collage, irrespective of artistic quality,
    (b) a work of architecture being a building or a model for a building, or
    (c) a work of artistic craftsmanship.

(2) In this Part—
"building" includes any fixed structure, and a part of a building or fixed structure;
"graphic work" includes—
    (a) any painting, drawing, diagram, map, chart or plan, and
    (b) any engraving, etching, lithograph, woodcut or similar work;
"photograph" means a recording of light or other radiation on any medium on which an image is produced or from which an image may by any means be produced, and which is not part of a film;
"sculpture" includes a cast or model made for purposes of sculpture.

5A   Sound recordings

(1) In this Part "sound recording" means—
    (a) a recording of sounds, from which the sounds may be reproduced, or
    (b) a recording of the whole or any part of a literary, dramatic or musical work, from which sounds reproducing the work or part may be produced, regardless of the medium on which the recording is made or the method by which the sounds are reproduced or produced.

(2) Copyright does not subsist in a sound recording which is, or to the extent that it is, a copy taken from a previous sound recording.

5B   Films

(1) In this Part "film" means a recording on any medium from which a moving image may by any means be produced.

(2) The sound track accompanying a film shall be treated as part of the film for the purposes of this Part.

(3) Without prejudice to the generality of subsection (2), where that subsection applies—
    (a) references in this Part to showing a film include playing the film sound track to accompany the film,
    (b) references in this Part to playing a sound recording, or to communicating a sound recording to the public, do not include playing or communicating the film sound track to accompany the film,
    (c) references in this Part to copying a work, so far as they apply to a sound recording, do not include copying the film sound track to accompany the film, and
    (d) references in this Part to the issuing, rental or lending of copies of a work, so far as they apply to a sound recording, do not include the issuing, rental or lending of copies of the sound track to accompany the film.

(4) Copyright does not subsist in a film which is, or to the extent that it is, a copy taken from a previous film.

(5) Nothing in this section affects any copyright subsisting in a film sound track as a sound recording.

6   Broadcasts

(1) In this Part a "broadcast" means an electronic transmission of visual images, sounds or other information which—
    (a) is transmitted for simultaneous reception by members of the public and is capable of being lawfully received by them, or
    (b) is transmitted at a time determined solely by the person making the transmission for presentation to members of the public,
and which is not excepted by subsection (1A); and references to broadcasting shall be construed accordingly.

(1A) Excepted from the definition of "broadcast" is any internet transmission unless it is—
- (a) a transmission taking place simultaneously on the internet and by other means,
- (b) a concurrent transmission of a live event, or
- (c) a transmission of recorded moving images or sounds forming part of a programme service offered by the person responsible for making the transmission, being a service in which programmes are transmitted at scheduled times determined by that person.

(2) An encrypted transmission shall be regarded as capable of being lawfully received by members of the public only if decoding equipment has been made available to members of the public by or with the authority of the person making the transmission or the person providing the contents of the transmission.

(3) References in this Part to the person making a broadcast or a transmission which is a broadcast are—
- (a) to the person transmitting the programme, if he has responsibility to any extent for its contents, and
- (b) to any person providing the programme who makes with the person transmitting it the arrangements necessary for its transmission;

and references in this Part to a programme, in the context of broadcasting, are to any item included in a broadcast.

(4) For the purposes of this Part, the place from which a wireless broadcast is made is the place where, under the control and responsibility of the person making the broadcast, the programme-carrying signals are introduced into an uninterrupted chain of communication (including, in the case of a satellite transmission, the chain leading to the satellite and down towards the earth).

(4A) Subsections (3) and (4) have effect subject to section 6A (safeguards in case of certain satellite broadcasts).

(5) References in this Part to the reception of a broadcast include reception of a broadcast relayed by means of a telecommunications system.

(5A) The relaying of a broadcast by reception and immediate re-transmission shall be regarded for the purposes of this Part as a separate act of broadcasting from the making of the broadcast which is so re-transmitted.

(6) Copyright does not subsist in a broadcast which infringes, or to the extent that it infringes, the copyright in another broadcast

6A   Safeguards in relation to certain satellite broadcasts

(1) This section applies where the place from which a broadcast by way of satellite transmission is made is located in a country other than an EEA State and the law of that country fails to provide at least the following level of protection—
- (a) exclusive rights in relation to wireless broadcasting equivalent to those conferred by section 20 (infringement by communication to the public) on the authors of literary, dramatic, musical and artistic works, films and broadcasts;
- (b) a right in relation to live wireless broadcasting equivalent to that conferred on a performer by section 182(1)(b) (consent required for live broadcast of performance); and
- (c) a right for authors of sound recordings and performers to share in a single equitable remuneration in respect of the wireless broadcasting of sound recordings.

(2) Where the place from which the programme-carrying signals are transmitted to the satellite ("the uplink station") is located in an EEA State—
- (a) that place shall be treated as the place from which the broadcast is made, and
- (b) the person operating the uplink station shall be treated as the person making the broadcast.

(3) Where the uplink station is not located in an EEA State but a person who is established in an EEA State has commissioned the making of the broadcast—
- (a) that person shall be treated as the person making the broadcast, and
- (b) the place in which he has his principal establishment in the European Economic Area shall be treated as the place from which the broadcast is made.

8   Published editions

    (1)   In this Part "published edition", in the context of copyright in the typographical arrangement of a published edition, means a published edition of the whole or any part of one or more literary, dramatic or musical works.

    (2)   Copyright does not subsist in the typographical arrangement of a published edition if, or to the extent that, it reproduces the typographical arrangement of a previous edition.

Authorship and ownership of copyright

9   Authorship of work

    (1)   In this Part "author", in relation to a work, means the person who creates it.

    (2)   That person shall be taken to be—

        (aa)   in the case of a sound recording, the producer;

        (ab)   in the case of a film, the producer and the principal director;

        (b)   in the case of a broadcast, the person making the broadcast (see section 6(3)) or, in the case of a broadcast which relays another broadcast by reception and immediate re-transmission, the person making that other broadcast;

        (c)   . . .

        (d)   in the case of the typographical arrangement of a published edition, the publisher.

    (3)   In the case of a literary, dramatic, musical or artistic work which is computer-generated, the author shall be taken to be the person by whom the arrangements necessary for the creation of the work are undertaken.

    (4)   For the purposes of this Part a work is of "unknown authorship" if the identity of the author is unknown or, in the case of a work of joint authorship, if the identity of none of the authors is known.

    (5)   For the purposes of this Part the identity of an author shall be regarded as unknown if it is not possible for a person to ascertain his identity by reasonable inquiry; but if his identity is once known it shall not subsequently be regarded as unknown.

10   Works of joint authorship

    (1)   In this Part a "work of joint authorship" means a work produced by the collaboration of two or more authors in which the contribution of each author is not distinct from that of the other author or authors.

    (1A) A film shall be treated as a work of joint authorship unless the producer and the principal director are the same person.

    (2)   A broadcast shall be treated as a work of joint authorship in any case where more than one person is to be taken as making the broadcast (see section 6(3)).

    (3)   References in this Part to the author of a work shall, except as otherwise provided, be construed in relation to a work of joint authorship as references to all the authors of the work.

10A   Works of co-authorship

    (1)   In this Part a "work of co-authorship" means a work produced by the collaboration of the author of a musical work and the author of a literary work where the two works are created in order to be used together.

    (2)   References in this Part to a work or the author of a work shall, except as otherwise provided, be construed in relation to a work of co-authorship as references to each of the separate musical and literary works comprised in the work of co-authorship and to each of the authors of such works.

11   First ownership of copyright

    (1)   The author of a work is the first owner of any copyright in it, subject to the following provisions.

    (2)   Where a literary, dramatic, musical or artistic work, or a film, is made by an employee in the course of his employment, his employer is the first owner of any copyright in the work subject to any agreement to the contrary.

    (3)   This section does not apply to Crown copyright or Parliamentary copyright (see sections 163 and 165) or to copyright which subsists by virtue of section 168 (copyright of certain international organisations).

Duration of copyright

12   Duration of copyright in literary, dramatic, musical or artistic works

(1)   The following provisions have effect with respect to the duration of copyright in a literary, dramatic, musical or artistic work.

(2)   Copyright expires at the end of the period of 70 years from the end of the calendar year in which the author dies, subject as follows.

(3)   If the work is of unknown authorship, copyright expires—

    (a)   at the end of the period of 70 years from the end of the calendar year in which the work was made, or

    (b)   if during that period the work is made available to the public, at the end of the period of 70 years from the end of the calendar year in which it is first so made available,

subject as follows.

(4)   Subsection (2) applies if the identity of the author becomes known before the end of the period specified in paragraph (a) or (b) of subsection (3).

(5)   For the purposes of subsection (3) making available to the public includes—

    (a)   in the case of a literary, dramatic or musical work—

        (i)   performance in public, or

        (ii)   communication to the public;

    (b)   in the case of an artistic work—

        (i)   exhibition in public,

        (ii)   a film including the work being shown in public, or

        (iii)   communication to the public;

but in determining generally for the purposes of that subsection whether a work has been made available to the public no account shall be taken of any unauthorised act.

(6)   Where the country of origin of the work is not an EEA state and the author of the work is not a national of an EEA state, the duration of copyright is that to which the work is entitled in the country of origin, provided that does not exceed the period which would apply under subsections (2) to (5).

(7)   If the work is computer-generated the above provisions do not apply and copyright expires at the end of the period of 50 years from the end of the calendar year in which the work was made.

(8)   The provisions of this section are adapted as follows in relation to a work of joint authorship or a work of co-authorship—

    (a)   the reference in subsection (2) to the death of the author shall be construed—

        (i)   if the identity of all the authors is known, as a reference to the death of the last of them to die, and

        (ii)   if the identity of one or more of the authors is known and the identity of one or more others is not, as a reference to the death of the last whose identity is known;

    (b)   the reference in subsection (4) to the identity of the author becoming known shall be construed as a reference to the identity of any of the authors becoming known;

    (c)   the reference in subsection (6) to the author not being a national of an EEA state shall be construed as a reference to none of the authors being a national of an EEA state.

(9)   This section does not apply to Crown copyright or Parliamentary copyright (see sections 163 to 166D) or to copyright which subsists by virtue of section 168 (copyright of certain international organisations).

13A   Duration of copyright in sound recordings

(1)   The following provisions have effect with respect to the duration of copyright in a sound recording.

(2)   Subject to subsections (4) and (5) and section 191HA(4), copyright expires—

    (a)   at the end of the period of 50 years from the end of the calendar year in which the recording is made, or

    (b)   if during that period the recording is published, 70 years from the end of the calendar year in which it is first published, or

> (c)   if during that period the recording is not published but is made available to the public by being played in public or communicated to the public, 70 years from the end of the calendar year in which it is first so made available,
>
> but in determining whether a sound recording has been published, played in public or communicated to the public, no account shall be taken of any unauthorised act.

(3)   ...

(4)   Where the author of a sound recording is not a national of an EEA state, the duration of copyright is that to which the sound recording is entitled in the country of which the author is a national, provided that does not exceed the period which would apply under subsection (2).

(5)   If or to the extent that the application of subsection (4) would be at variance with an international obligation to which the United Kingdom became subject prior to 29th October 1993, the duration of copyright shall be as specified in subsection (2).

13B   Duration of copyright in films

(1)   The following provisions have effect with respect to the duration of copyright in a film.

(2)   Copyright expires at the end of the period of 70 years from the end of the calendar year in which the death occurs of the last to die of the following persons—

> (a)   the principal director,
> (b)   the author of the screenplay,
> (c)   the author of the dialogue, or
> (d)   the composer of music specially created for and used in the film;
>
> subject as follows.

(3)   If the identity of one or more of the persons referred to in subsection (2)(a) to (d) is known and the identity of one or more others is not, the reference in that subsection to the death of the last of them to die shall be construed as a reference to the death of the last whose identity is known.

(4)   If the identity of the persons referred to in subsection (2)(a) to (d) is unknown, copyright expires at—

> (a)   the end of the period of 70 years from the end of the calendar year in which the film was made, or
> (b)   if during that period the film is made available to the public, at the end of the period of 70 years from the end of the calendar year in which it is first so made available.

(5)   Subsections (2) and (3) apply if the identity of any of those persons becomes known before the end of the period specified in paragraph (a) or (b) of subsection (4).

(6)   For the purposes of subsection (4) making available to the public includes—

> (a)   showing in public, or
> (b)   communicating to the public;
>
> but in determining generally for the purposes of that subsection whether a film has been made available to the public no account shall be taken of any unauthorised act.

(7)   Where the country of origin is not an EEA state and the author of the film is not a national of an EEA state, the duration of copyright is that to which the work is entitled in the country of origin, provided that does not exceed the period which would apply under subsections (2) to (6).

(8)   In relation to a film of which there are joint authors, the reference in subsection (7) to the author not being a national of an EEA state shall be construed as a reference to none of the authors being a national of an EEA state.

(9)   If in any case there is no person falling within paragraphs (a) to (d) of subsection (2), the above provisions do not apply and copyright expires at the end of the period of 50 years from the end of the calendar year in which the film was made.

(10)   For the purposes of this section the identity of any of the persons referred to in subsection (2)(a) to (d) shall be regarded as unknown if it is not possible for a person to ascertain his identity by reasonable inquiry; but if the identity of any such person is once known it shall not subsequently be regarded as unknown.

14   Duration of copyright in broadcasts

(1)   The following provisions have effect with respect to the duration of copyright in a broadcast.

(2)   Copyright in a broadcast expires at the end of the period of 50 years from the end of the calendar year in which the broadcast was made, subject as follows.

(3)   Where the author of the broadcast is not a national of an EEA state, the duration of copyright in the broadcast is that to which it is entitled in the country of which the author is a national, provided that does not exceed the period which would apply under subsection (2).

(4)   If or to the extent that the application of subsection (3) would be at variance with an international obligation to which the United Kingdom became subject prior to 29th October 1993, the duration of copyright shall be as specified in subsection (2).

(5)   Copyright in a repeat broadcast expires at the same time as the copyright in the original broadcast; and accordingly no copyright arises in respect of a repeat broadcast which is broadcast after the expiry of the copyright in the original broadcast.

(6)   A repeat broadcast means one which is a repeat of a broadcast previously made.

15   Duration of copyright in typographical arrangement of published editions

Copyright in the typographical arrangement of a published edition expires at the end of the period of 25 years from the end of the calendar year in which the edition was first published.

15A   Meaning of country of origin

(1)   For the purposes of the provisions of this Part relating to the duration of copyright the country of origin of a work shall be determined as follows.

(2)   If the work is first published in a Berne Convention country and is not simultaneously published elsewhere, the country of origin is that country.

(3)   If the work is first published simultaneously in two or more countries only one of which is a Berne Convention country, the country of origin is that country.

(4)   If the work is first published simultaneously in two or more countries of which two or more are Berne Convention countries, then—

    (a)   if any of those countries is an EEA state, the country of origin is that country; and

    (b)   if none of those countries is an EEA state, the country of origin is the Berne Convention country which grants the shorter or shortest period of copyright protection.

(5)   If the work is unpublished or is first published in a country which is not a Berne Convention country (and is not simultaneously published in a Berne Convention country), the country of origin is—

    (a)   if the work is a film and the maker of the film has his headquarters in, or is domiciled or resident in a Berne Convention country, that country;

    (b)   if the work is—

       (i)   a work of architecture constructed in a Berne Convention country, or

       (ii)   an artistic work incorporated in a building or other structure situated in a Berne Convention country,

    that country;

    (c)   in any other case, the country of which the author of the work is a national.

(6)   In this section—

    (a)   a "Berne Convention country" means a country which is a party to any Act of the International Convention for the Protection of Literary and Artistic Works signed at Berne on 9th September 1886; and

    (b)   references to simultaneous publication are to publication within 30 days of first publication.

CHAPTER II

RIGHTS OF COPYRIGHT OWNER

The acts restricted by copyright

16   The acts restricted by copyright in a work

(1)   The owner of the copyright in a work has, in accordance with the following provisions of this Chapter, the exclusive right to do the following acts in the United Kingdom—

    (a)   to copy the work (see section 17);

    (b)   to issue copies of the work to the public (see section 18);

       (ba)   to rent or lend the work to the public (see section 18A);

       (c)   to perform, show or play the work in public (see section 19);

       (d)   to communicate the work to the public (see section 20);

       (e)   to make an adaptation of the work or do any of the above in relation to an adaptation (see section 21);

      and those acts are referred to in this Part as the "acts restricted by the copyright".

(2)   Copyright in a work is infringed by a person who without the licence of the copyright owner does, or authorises another to do, any of the acts restricted by the copyright.

(3)   References in this Part to the doing of an act restricted by the copyright in a work are to the doing of it—

       (a)   in relation to the work as a whole or any substantial part of it, and

       (b)   either directly or indirectly;

      and it is immaterial whether any intervening acts themselves infringe copyright.

(4)   This Chapter has effect subject to—

       (a)   the provisions of Chapter III (acts permitted in relation to copyright works), and

       (b)   the provisions of Chapter VII (provisions with respect to copyright licensing).

17   Infringement of copyright by copying

(1)   The copying of the work is an act restricted by the copyright in every description of copyright work; and references in this Part to copying and copies shall be construed as follows.

(2)   Copying in relation to a literary, dramatic, musical or artistic work means reproducing the work in any material form.

This includes storing the work in any medium by electronic means.

(3)   In relation to an artistic work copying includes the making of a copy in three dimensions of a two-dimensional work and the making of a copy in two dimensions of a three-dimensional work.

(4)   Copying in relation to a film or broadcast includes making a photograph of the whole or any substantial part of any image forming part of the film or broadcast.

(5)   Copying in relation to the typographical arrangement of a published edition means making a facsimile copy of the arrangement.

(6)   Copying in relation to any description of work includes the making of copies which are transient or are incidental to some other use of the work.

18   Infringement by issue of copies to the public

(1)   The issue to the public of copies of the work is an act restricted by the copyright in every description of copyright work.

(2)   References in this Part to the issue to the public of copies of a work are to—

       (a)   the act of putting into circulation in the EEA copies not previously put into circulation in the EEA by or with the consent of the copyright owner, or

       (b)   the act of putting into circulation outside the EEA copies not previously put into circulation in the EEA or elsewhere.

(3)   References in this Part to the issue to the public of copies of a work do not include—

       (a)   any subsequent distribution, sale, hiring or loan of copies previously put into circulation (but see section 18A: infringement by rental or lending), or

       (b)   any subsequent importation of such copies into the United Kingdom or another EEA state,

      except so far as paragraph (a) of subsection (2) applies to putting into circulation in the EEA copies previously put into circulation outside the EEA.

(4)   References in this Part to the issue of copies of a work include the issue of the original.

18A   Infringement by rental or lending of work to the public

(1)   The rental or lending of copies of the work to the public is an act restricted by the copyright in—

       (a)   a literary, dramatic or musical work,

       (b)   an artistic work, other than—

           (i)   a work of architecture in the form of a building or a model for a building, or

           (ii)   a work of applied art, or

       (c)   a film or a sound recording.

(2) In this Part, subject to the following provisions of this section—

    (a) "rental" means making a copy of the work available for use, on terms that it will or may be returned, for direct or indirect economic or commercial advantage, and

    (b) "lending" means making a copy of the work available for use, on terms that it will or may be returned, otherwise than for direct or indirect economic or commercial advantage, through an establishment which is accessible to the public.

(3) The expressions "rental" and "lending" do not include—

    (a) making available for the purpose of public performance, playing or showing in public or communication to the public;

    (b) making available for the purpose of exhibition in public; or

    (c) making available for on-the-spot reference use.

(4) The expression "lending" does not include making available between establishments which are accessible to the public.

(5) Where lending by an establishment accessible to the public gives rise to a payment the amount of which does not go beyond what is necessary to cover the operating costs of the establishment, there is no direct or indirect economic or commercial advantage for the purposes of this section.

(6) References in this Part to the rental or lending of copies of a work include the rental or lending of the original.

19 Infringement by performance, showing or playing of work in public

(1) The performance of the work in public is an act restricted by the copyright in a literary, dramatic or musical work.

(2) In this Part "performance", in relation to a work—

    (a) includes delivery in the case of lectures, addresses, speeches and sermons, and

    (b) in general, includes any mode of visual or acoustic presentation, including presentation by means of a sound recording, film or broadcast of the work.

(3) The playing or showing of the work in public is an act restricted by the copyright in a sound recording, film or broadcast.

(4) Where copyright in a work is infringed by its being performed, played or shown in public by means of apparatus for receiving visual images or sounds conveyed by electronic means, the person by whom the visual images or sounds are sent, and in the case of a performance the performers, shall not be regarded as responsible for the infringement.

20 Infringement by communication to the public

(1) The communication to the public of the work is an act restricted by the copyright in—

    (a) a literary, dramatic, musical or artistic work,

    (b) a sound recording or film, or

    (c) a broadcast.

(2) References in this Part to communication to the public are to communication to the public by electronic transmission, and in relation to a work include—

    (a) the broadcasting of the work;

    (b) the making available to the public of the work by electronic transmission in such a way that members of the public may access it from a place and at a time individually chosen by them.

21 Infringement by making adaptation or act done in relation to adaptation

(1) The making of an adaptation of the work is an act restricted by the copyright in a literary, dramatic or musical work.

For this purpose an adaptation is made when it is recorded, in writing or otherwise.

(2) The doing of any of the acts specified in sections 17 to 20, or subsection (1) above, in relation to an adaptation of the work is also an act restricted by the copyright in a literary, dramatic or musical work.

For this purpose it is immaterial whether the adaptation has been recorded, in writing or otherwise, at the time the act is done.

(3)   In this Part "adaptation"—

      (a)   in relation to a literary work, other than a computer program or database, or in relation to a dramatic work, means—

           (i)   a translation of the work;

           (ii)   a version of a dramatic work in which it is converted into a non-dramatic work or, as the case may be, of a non-dramatic work in which it is converted into a dramatic work;

           (iii)   a version of the work in which the story or action is conveyed wholly or mainly by means of pictures in a form suitable for reproduction in a book, or in a newspaper, magazine or similar periodical;

      (ab)   in relation to a computer program, means an arrangement or altered version of the program or a translation of it;

      (ac)   in relation to a database, means an arrangement or altered version of the database or a translation of it;

      (b)   in relation to a musical work, means an arrangement or transcription of the work

(4)   In relation to a computer program a "translation" includes a version of the program in which it is converted into or out of a computer language or code or into a different computer language or code.

(5)   No inference shall be drawn from this section as to what does or does not amount to copying a work.

Secondary infringement of copyright

22   Secondary infringement: importing infringing copy

The copyright in a work is infringed by a person who, without the licence of the copyright owner, imports into the United Kingdom, otherwise than for his private and domestic use, an article which is, and which he knows or has reason to believe is, an infringing copy of the work.

23   Secondary infringement: possessing or dealing with infringing copy

The copyright in a work is infringed by a person who, without the licence of the copyright owner—

      (a)   possesses in the course of a business,

      (b)   sells or lets for hire, or offers or exposes for sale or hire,

      (c)   in the course of a business exhibits in public or distributes, or

      (d)   distributes otherwise than in the course of a business to such an extent as to affect prejudicially the owner of the copyright,

an article which is, and which he knows or has reason to believe is, an infringing copy of the work.

24   Secondary infringement: providing means for making infringing copies

(1)   Copyright in a work is infringed by a person who, without the licence of the copyright owner—

      (a)   makes,

      (b)   imports into the United Kingdom,

      (c)   possesses in the course of a business, or

      (d)   sells or lets for hire, or offers or exposes for sale or hire,

an article specifically designed or adapted for making copies of that work, knowing or having reason to believe that it is to be used to make infringing copies.

(2)   Copyright in a work is infringed by a person who without the licence of the copyright owner transmits the work by means of a telecommunications system (otherwise than by communication to the public), knowing or having reason to believe that infringing copies of the work will be made by means of the reception of the transmission in the United Kingdom or elsewhere.

25   Secondary infringement: permitting use of premises for infringing performance

(1)   Where the copyright in a literary, dramatic or musical work is infringed by a performance at a place of public entertainment, any person who gave permission for that place

to be used for the performance is also liable for the infringement unless when he gave permission he believed on reasonable grounds that the performance would not infringe copyright.

(2) In this section "place of public entertainment" includes premises which are occupied mainly for other purposes but are from time to time made available for hire for the purposes of public entertainment.

26   Secondary infringement: provision of apparatus for infringing performance, etc.

(1) Where copyright in a work is infringed by a public performance of the work, or by the playing or showing of the work in public, by means of apparatus for—
   (a)   playing sound recordings,
   (b)   showing films, or
   (c)   receiving visual images or sounds conveyed by electronic means,
   the following persons are also liable for the infringement.

(2) A person who supplied the apparatus, or any substantial part of it, is liable for the infringement if when he supplied the apparatus or part—
   (a)   he knew or had reason to believe that the apparatus was likely to be so used as to infringe copyright, or
   (b)   in the case of apparatus whose normal use involves a public performance, playing or showing, he did not believe on reasonable grounds that it would not be so used as to infringe copyright.

(3) An occupier of premises who gave permission for the apparatus to be brought onto the premises is liable for the infringement if when he gave permission he knew or had reason to believe that the apparatus was likely to be so used as to infringe copyright.

(4) A person who supplied a copy of a sound recording or film used to infringe copyright is liable for the infringement if when he supplied it he knew or had reason to believe that what he supplied, or a copy made directly or indirectly from it, was likely to be so used as to infringe copyright.

Infringing copies

27   Meaning of "infringing copy"

(1) In this Part "infringing copy", in relation to a copyright work, shall be construed in accordance with this section.

(2) An article is an infringing copy if its making constituted an infringement of the copyright in the work in question.

(3) An article is also an infringing copy if—
   (a)   it has been or is proposed to be imported into the United Kingdom, and
   (b)   its making in the United Kingdom would have constituted an infringement of the copyright in the work in question, or a breach of an exclusive licence agreement relating to that work.

(4) Where in any proceedings the question arises whether an article is an infringing copy and it is shown—
   (a)   that the article is a copy of the work, and
   (b)   that copyright subsists in the work or has subsisted at any time,
   it shall be presumed until the contrary is proved that the article was made at a time when copyright subsisted in the work.

(5) Nothing in subsection (3) shall be construed as applying to an article which may lawfully be imported into the United Kingdom by virtue of any enforceable EU right within the meaning of section 2(1) of the European Communities Act 1972.

(6) In this Part "infringing copy" includes a copy falling to be treated as an infringing copy by virtue of any of the following provisions—
   section 29A(3) (copies for text and data analysis for non-commercial research),
   section 31A(5) and (6) (disabled persons: copies of works for personal use),
   section 31B(11) (making and supply of accessible copies by authorised bodies),
   section 35(5) (recording by educational establishments of broadcasts),
   section 36(8) (copying and use of extracts of works by educational establishments),
   section 42A(5)(b) (copying by librarians: single copies of published works),
   section 43(5)(b) (copying by librarians or archivists: single copies of unpublished works),

section 56(2) (further copies, adaptations, &c of work in electronic form retained on transfer of principal copy),

section 61(6)(b) (recordings of folksongs),

section 63(2) (copies made for purpose of advertising artistic work for sale),

section 68(4) (copies made for purpose of broadcast,

section 70(2) (recording for the purposes of time-shifting),

section 71(2) (photographs of broadcasts), or

any provision of an order under section 141 (statutory licence for certain reprographic copying by educational establishments).

CHAPTER III

ACTS PERMITTED IN RELATION TO COPYRIGHT WORKS

Introductory

28   Introductory provisions

(1) The provisions of this Chapter specify acts which may be done in relation to copyright works notwithstanding the subsistence of copyright; they relate only to the question of infringement of copyright and do not affect any other right or obligation restricting the doing of any of the specified acts.

(2) Where it is provided by this Chapter that an act does not infringe copyright, or may be done without infringing copyright, and no particular description of copyright work is mentioned, the act in question does not infringe the copyright in a work of any description.

(3) No inference shall be drawn from the description of any act which may by virtue of this Chapter be done without infringing copyright as to the scope of the acts restricted by the copyright in any description of work.

(4) The provisions of this Chapter are to be construed independently of each other, so that the fact that an act does not fall within one provision does not mean that it is not covered by another provision.

28A   Making of temporary copies

Copyright in a literary work, other than a computer program or a database, or in a dramatic, musical or artistic work, the typographical arrangement of a published edition, a sound recording or a film, is not infringed by the making of a temporary copy which is transient or incidental, which is an integral and essential part of a technological process and the sole purpose of which is to enable—

(a) a transmission of the work in a network between third parties by an intermediary; or

(b) a lawful use of the work;

and which has no independent economic significance.

General

29   Research and private study

(1) Fair dealing with a work for the purposes of research for a non-commercial purpose does not infringe any copyright in the work provided that it is accompanied by a sufficient acknowledgement.

(1B) No acknowledgement is required in connection with fair dealing for the purposes mentioned in subsection (1) where this would be impossible for reasons of practicality or otherwise.

(1C) Fair dealing with a work for the purposes of private study does not infringe any copyright in the work.

(2) . . .

(3) Copying by a person other than the researcher or student himself is not fair dealing if—

    (a) in the case of a librarian, or a person acting on behalf of a librarian, that person does anything which is not permitted under section 42A (copying by librarians: single copies of published works), or

    (b) in any other case, the person doing the copying knows or has reason to believe that it will result in copies of substantially the same material being provided to more than one person at substantially the same time and for substantially the same purpose.

(4) It is not fair dealing—
  (a) to convert a computer program expressed in a low level language into a version expressed in a higher level language, or
  (b) incidentally in the course of so converting the program, to copy it,
  (these acts being permitted if done in accordance with section 50B (decompilation)).
(4A) It is not fair dealing to observe, study or test the functioning of a computer program in order to determine the ideas and principles which underlie any element of the program (these acts being permitted if done in accordance with section 50BA (observing, studying and testing)).
(4B) To the extent that a term of a contract purports to prevent or restrict the doing of any act which, by virtue of this section, would not infringe copyright, that term is unenforceable.
(5) . . .

29A Copies for text and data analysis for non-commercial research

(1) The making of a copy of a work by a person who has lawful access to the work does not infringe copyright in the work provided that—
  (a) the copy is made in order that a person who has lawful access to the work may carry out a computational analysis of anything recorded in the work for the sole purpose of research for a non-commercial purpose, and
  (b) the copy is accompanied by a sufficient acknowledgement (unless this would be impossible for reasons of practicality or otherwise).
(2) Where a copy of a work has been made under this section, copyright in the work is infringed if—
  (a) the copy is transferred to any other person, except where the transfer is authorised by the copyright owner, or
  (b) the copy is used for any purpose other than that mentioned in subsection (1)(a), except where the use is authorised by the copyright owner.
(3) If a copy made under this section is subsequently dealt with—
  (a) it is to be treated as an infringing copy for the purposes of that dealing, and
  (b) if that dealing infringes copyright, it is to be treated as an infringing copy for all subsequent purposes.
(4) In subsection (3) "dealt with" means sold or let for hire, or offered or exposed for sale or hire.
(5) To the extent that a term of a contract purports to prevent or restrict the making of a copy which, by virtue of this section, would not infringe copyright, that term is unenforceable.

30 Criticism, review, quotation and news reporting

(1) Fair dealing with a work for the purpose of criticism or review, of that or another work or of a performance of a work, does not infringe any copyright in the work provided that it is accompanied by a sufficient acknowledgement (unless this would be impossible for reasons of practicality or otherwise) and provided that the work has been made available to the public.
(1ZA) Copyright in a work is not infringed by the use of a quotation from the work (whether for criticism or review or otherwise) provided that—
  (a) the work has been made available to the public,
  (b) the use of the quotation is fair dealing with the work,
  (c) the extent of the quotation is no more than is required by the specific purpose for which it is used, and
  (d) the quotation is accompanied by a sufficient acknowledgement (unless this would be impossible for reasons of practicality or otherwise).
(1A) For the purposes of subsections (1) and (1ZA) a work has been made available to the public if it has been made available by any means, including—
  (a) the issue of copies to the public;
  (b) making the work available by means of an electronic retrieval system;
  (c) the rental or lending of copies of the work to the public;
  (d) the performance, exhibition, playing or showing of the work in public;
  (e) the communication to the public of the work,
  but in determining generally for the purposes of those subsections whether a work has been made available to the public no account shall be taken of any unauthorised act.

(2) Fair dealing with a work (other than a photograph) for the purpose of reporting current events does not infringe any copyright in the work provided that (subject to subsection (3)) it is accompanied by a sufficient acknowledgement.

(3) No acknowledgement is required in connection with the reporting of current events by means of a sound recording, film or broadcast where this would be impossible for reasons of practicality or otherwise.

(4) To the extent that a term of a contract purports to prevent or restrict the doing of any act which, by virtue of subsection (1ZA), would not infringe copyright, that term is unenforceable.

30A   Caricature, parody or pastiche

(1) Fair dealing with a work for the purposes of caricature, parody or pastiche does not infringe copyright in the work.

(2) To the extent that a term of a contract purports to prevent or restrict the doing of any act which, by virtue of this section, would not infringe copyright, that term is unenforceable.

31   Incidental inclusion of copyright material

(1) Copyright in a work is not infringed by its incidental inclusion in an artistic work, sound recording, film, or broadcast.

(2) Nor is the copyright infringed by the issue to the public of copies, or the playing, showing or communication to the public, of anything whose making was, by virtue of subsection(1), not an infringement of the copyright.

(3) A musical work, words spoken or sung with music, or so much of a sound recording or broadcast as includes a musical work or such words, shall not be regarded as incidentally included in another work if it is deliberately included.

Disability

31A   Disabled persons: copies of works for personal use

(1) This section applies if—
(a) a disabled person has lawful possession or lawful use of a copy of the whole or part of a work, and
(b) the person's disability prevents the person from enjoying the work to the same degree as a person who does not have that disability.

(2) The making of an accessible copy of the copy of the work referred to in subsection (1)(a) does not infringe copyright if—
(a) the copy is made by the disabled person or by a person acting on behalf of the disabled person,
(b) the copy is made for the disabled person's personal use, and
(c) the same kind of accessible copies of the work are not commercially available on reasonable terms by or with the authority of the copyright owner.

(3) If a person makes an accessible copy under this section on behalf of a disabled person and charges the disabled person for it, the sum charged must not exceed the cost of making and supplying the copy.

(4) Copyright is infringed by the transfer of an accessible copy of a work made under this section to any person other than—
(a) a person by or for whom an accessible copy of the work may be made under this section, or
(b) a person who intends to transfer the copy to a person falling within paragraph (a), except where the transfer is authorised by the copyright owner.

(5) An accessible copy of a work made under this section is to be treated for all purposes as an infringing copy if it is held by a person at a time when the person does not fall within subsection (4)(a) or (b).

(6) If an accessible copy made under this section is subsequently dealt with—
(a) it is to be treated as an infringing copy for the purposes of that dealing, and
(b) if that dealing infringes copyright, it is to be treated as an infringing copy for all subsequent purposes.

(7) In this section "dealt with" means sold or let for hire or offered or exposed for sale or hire.

31B Making and supply of accessible copies by authorised bodies

(1) If an authorised body has lawful possession of a copy of the whole or part of a published work, the body may, without infringing copyright, make and supply accessible copies of the work for the personal use of disabled persons.

(2) But subsection (1) does not apply if the same kind of accessible copies of the work are commercially available on reasonable terms by or with the authority of the copyright owner.

(3) If an authorised body has lawful access to or lawful possession of the whole or part of a broadcast or a copy of a broadcast, the body may, without infringing copyright—
    (a) in the case of a broadcast, make a recording of the broadcast, and make and supply accessible copies of the recording or of any work included in the broadcast, and
    (b) in the case of a copy of a broadcast, make and supply accessible copies of that copy or of any work included in the broadcast,
for the personal use of disabled persons.

(4) But subsection (3) does not apply if the same kind of accessible copies of the broadcast, or of any work included in it, are commercially available on reasonable terms by or with the authority of the copyright owner.

(5) For the purposes of subsections (1) and (3), supply *"for the personal use of disabled persons"* includes supply to a person acting on behalf of a disabled person.

(6) An authorised body which is an educational establishment conducted for profit must ensure that any accessible copies which it makes under this section are used only for its educational purposes.

(7) An accessible copy made under this section must be accompanied by—
    (a) a statement that it is made under this section, and
    (b) a sufficient acknowledgement (unless this would be impossible for reasons of practicality or otherwise).

(8) If an accessible copy is made under this section of a work which is in copy-protected electronic form, the accessible copy must, so far as is reasonably practicable, incorporate the same or equally effective copy protection (unless the copyright owner agrees otherwise).

(9) An authorised body which has made an accessible copy of a work under this section may supply it to another authorised body which is entitled to make accessible copies of the work under this section for the purposes of enabling that other body to make accessible copies of the work.

(10) If an authorised body supplies an accessible copy it has made under this section to a person or authorised body as permitted by this section and charges the person or body for it, the sum charged must not exceed the cost of making and supplying the copy.

(11) If an accessible copy made under this section is subsequently dealt with—
    (a) it is to be treated as an infringing copy for the purposes of that dealing, and
    (b) if that dealing infringes copyright, it is to be treated as an infringing copy for all subsequent purposes.

(12) In this section *"dealt with"* means sold or let for hire or offered or exposed for sale or hire.

31BA Making and supply of intermediate copies by authorised bodies

(1) An authorised body which is entitled to make an accessible copy of a work under section 31B may, without infringing copyright, make a copy of the work ("an intermediate copy") if this is necessary in order to make the accessible copy.

(2) An authorised body which has made an intermediate copy of a work under this section may supply it to another authorised body which is entitled to make accessible copies of the work under section 31B for the purposes of enabling that other body to make accessible copies of the work.

(3) Copyright is infringed by the transfer of an intermediate copy made under this section to a person other than another authorised body as permitted by subsection (2), except where the transfer is authorised by the copyright owner.

(4)   If an authorised body supplies an intermediate copy to an authorised body under subsection (2) and charges the body for it, the sum charged must not exceed the cost of making and supplying the copy.

31BB   Accessible and intermediate copies: records and notification

(1)   An authorised body must keep a record of—

     (a)   accessible copies it makes under section 31B,

     (b)   intermediate copies it makes under section 31BA, and

     (c)   the persons to whom such copies are supplied.

(2)   An authorised body must allow the copyright owner or a person acting for the copyright owner, on giving reasonable notice, to inspect at any reasonable time—

     (a)   records kept under subsection (1), and

     (b)   records of copies made under sections 31B and 31C as those sections were in force before the coming into force of these Regulations.

(3)   Within a reasonable time of making an accessible copy under section 31B, an authorised body must—

     (a)   notify any body which—

         (i)   represents particular copyright owners or owners of copyright in the type of work concerned, and

         (ii)   has given notice to the Secretary of State of the copyright owners, or the classes of copyright owner, represented by it, or

     (b)   if there is no such body, notify the copyright owner (unless it is not reasonably possible to ascertain the name and address of the copyright owner).

31F   Sections 31A to 31BB: interpretation and general

(1)   This section supplements sections 31A to 31BB and includes definitions.

(2)   "Disabled person" means a person who has a physical or mental impairment which prevents the person from enjoying a copyright work to the same degree as a person who does not have that impairment, and "disability" is to be construed accordingly.

(3)   But a person is not to be regarded as disabled by reason only of an impairment of visual function which can be improved, by the use of corrective lenses, to a level that is normally acceptable for reading without a special level or kind of light.

(4)   An "accessible copy" of a copyright work means a version of the work which enables the fuller enjoyment of the work by disabled persons.

(5)   An accessible copy—

     (a)   may include facilities for navigating around the version of the work, but

     (b)   must not include any changes to the work which are not necessary to overcome the problems suffered by the disabled persons for whom the accessible copy is intended.

(6)   "Authorised body" means—

     (a)   an educational establishment, or

     (b)   a body that is not conducted for profit.

(7)   The "supply" of a copy includes making it available for use, otherwise than for direct or indirect economic or commercial advantage, on terms that it will or may be returned.

(8)   To the extent that a term of a contract purports to prevent or restrict the doing of any act which, by virtue of section 31A, 31B or 31BA, would not infringe copyright, that term is unenforceable.

Education

32   Illustration for instruction

(1)   Fair dealing with a work for the sole purpose of illustration for instruction does not infringe copyright in the work provided that the dealing is—

     (a)   for a non-commercial purpose,

     (b)   by a person giving or receiving instruction (or preparing for giving or receiving instruction), and

     (c)   accompanied by a sufficient acknowledgement (unless this would be impossible for reasons of practicality or otherwise).

(2)   For the purposes of subsection (1), "giving or receiving instruction" includes setting examination questions, communicating the questions to pupils and answering the questions.

(3)   To the extent that a term of a contract purports to prevent or restrict the doing of any act which, by virtue of this section, would not infringe copyright, that term is unenforceable.

33   Anthologies for educational use

(1)   The inclusion of a short passage from a published literary or dramatic work in a collection which—

    (a)   is intended for use in educational establishments and is so described in its title, and in any advertisements issued by or on behalf of the publisher, and

    (b)   consists mainly of material in which no copyright subsists,

    does not infringe the copyright in the work if the work itself is not intended for use in such establishments and the inclusion is accompanied by a sufficient acknowledgement.

(2)   Subsection (1) does not authorise the inclusion of more than two excerpts from copyright works by the same author in collections published by the same publisher over any period of five years.

(3)   In relation to any given passage the reference in subsection (2) to excerpts from works by the same author—

    (a)   shall be taken to include excerpts from works by him in collaboration with another, and

    (b)   if the passage in question is from such a work, shall be taken to include excerpts from works by any of the authors, whether alone or in collaboration with another.

(4)   References in this section to the use of a work in an educational establishment are to any use for the educational purposes of such an establishment.

34   Performing, playing or showing work in course of activities of educational establishment

(1)   The performance of a literary, dramatic or musical work before an audience consisting of teachers and pupils at an educational establishment and other persons directly connected with the activities of the establishment—

    (a)   by a teacher or pupil in the course of the activities of the establishment, or

    (b)   at the establishment by any person for the purposes of instruction,

    is not a public performance for the purposes of infringement of copyright.

(2)   The playing or showing of a sound recording, film or broadcast before such an audience at an educational establishment for the purposes of instruction is not a playing or showing of the work in public for the purposes of infringement of copyright.

(3)   A person is not for this purpose directly connected with the activities of the educational establishment simply because he is the parent of a pupil at the establishment.

35   Recording by educational establishments of broadcasts

(1)   A recording of a broadcast, or a copy of such a recording, may be made by or on behalf of an educational establishment for the educational purposes of that establishment without infringing copyright in the broadcast, or in any work included in it, provided that—

    (a)   the educational purposes are non-commercial, and

    (b)   the recording or copy is accompanied by a sufficient acknowledgement (unless this would be impossible for reasons of practicality or otherwise).

(2)   Copyright is not infringed where a recording of a broadcast or a copy of such a recording, made under subsection (1), is communicated by or on behalf of the educational establishment to its pupils or staff for the non-commercial educational purposes of that establishment.

(3)   Subsection (2) only applies to a communication received outside the premises of the establishment if that communication is made by means of a secure electronic network accessible only by the establishment's pupils and staff.

(4)   Acts which would otherwise be permitted by this section are not permitted if, or to the extent that, licences are available authorising the acts in question and the educational establishment responsible for those acts knew or ought to have been aware of that fact.

(5) If a copy made under this section is subsequently dealt with—
   (a) it is to be treated as an infringing copy for the purposes of that dealing, and
   (b) if that dealing infringes copyright, it is to be treated as an infringing copy for all subsequent purposes.

(6) In this section "dealt with" means—
   (a) sold or let for hire,
   (b) offered or exposed for sale or hire, or
   (c) communicated otherwise than as permitted by subsection (2).

36 Copying and use of extracts of works by educational establishments

(1) The copying of extracts of a relevant work by or on behalf of an educational establishment does not infringe copyright in the work, provided that—
   (a) the copy is made for the purposes of instruction for a non-commercial purpose, and
   (b) the copy is accompanied by a sufficient acknowledgement (unless this would be impossible for reasons of practicality or otherwise).

(2) Copyright is not infringed where a copy of an extract made under subsection (1) is communicated by or on behalf of the educational establishment to its pupils or staff for the purposes of instruction for a non-commercial purpose.

(3) Subsection (2) only applies to a communication received outside the premises of the establishment if that communication is made by means of a secure electronic network accessible only by the establishment's pupils and staff.

(4) In this section *"relevant work"* means a copyright work other than—
   (a) a broadcast, or
   (b) an artistic work which is not incorporated into another work.

(5) Not more than 5% of a work may be copied under this section by or on behalf of an educational establishment in any period of 12 months, and for these purposes a work which incorporates another work is to be treated as a single work.

(6) Acts which would otherwise be permitted by this section are not permitted if, or to the extent that, licences are available authorising the acts in question and the educational establishment responsible for those acts knew or ought to have been aware of that fact.

(7) The terms of a licence granted to an educational establishment authorising acts permitted by this section are of no effect so far as they purport to restrict the proportion of a work which may be copied (whether on payment or free of charge) to less than that which would be permitted by this section.

(8) If a copy made under this section is subsequently dealt with—
   (a) it is to be treated as an infringing copy for the purposes of that dealing, and
   (b) if that dealing infringes copyright, it is to be treated as an infringing copy for all subsequent purposes.

(9) In this section *"dealt with"* means—
   (a) sold or let for hire,
   (b) offered or exposed for sale or hire, or
   (c) communicated otherwise than as permitted by subsection (2).

36A Lending of copies by educational establishments

Copyright in a work is not infringed by the lending of copies of the work by an educational establishment.

Libraries and archives

40A Lending of copies by libraries or archives

(1) Copyright in a work of any description is not infringed by the following acts by a public library in relation to a book within the public lending right scheme—
   (a) lending the book;
   (b) in relation to an audio-book or e-book, copying or issuing a copy of the book as an act incidental to lending it.

(1ZA) *Subsection (1) applies to an e-book or an e-audio-book only if—*
   (a) *the book has been lawfully acquired by the library, and*
   (b) *the lending is in compliance with any purchase or licensing terms to which the book is subject.*

(1A) In subsections (1) *and (1ZA)*—
- (a) "book", "audio-book" and "e-book" have the meanings given in section 5 of the Public Lending Right Act 1979,
- (aa) *"e-audio-book" means an audio-book (as defined in paragraph (a)) in a form enabling lending of the book by electronic transmission,*
- (b) "the public lending right scheme" means the scheme in force under section 1 of that Act,
- (c) a book is within the public lending right scheme if it is a book within the meaning of the provisions of the scheme relating to eligibility, whether or not it is in fact eligible, and
- (d) "lending" is to be read in accordance with the definition of "lent out" in section 5 of that Act (and section 18A of this Act does not apply).
- (2) Copyright in a work is not infringed by the lending of copies of the work by a library or archive (other than a public library) which is not conducted for profit. Italicised text is inserted by Digital Economy Act 2017 s31 and is not yet in force.

40B Libraries and educational establishments etc: making works available through dedicated terminals
- (1) Copyright in a work is not infringed by an institution specified in subsection (2) communicating the work to the public or making it available to the public by means of a dedicated terminal on its premises, if the conditions in subsection (3) are met.
- (2) The institutions are—
  - (a) a library,
  - (b) an archive,
  - (c) a museum, and
  - (d) an educational establishment.
- (3) The conditions are that the work or a copy of the work—
  - (a) has been lawfully acquired by the institution,
  - (b) is communicated or made available to individual members of the public for the purposes of research or private study, and
  - (c) is communicated or made available in compliance with any purchase or licensing terms to which the work is subject.

41 Copying by librarians: supply of single copies to other libraries
- (1) A librarian may, if the conditions in subsection (2) are met, make a single copy of the whole or part of a published work and supply it to another library, without infringing copyright in the work.
- (2) The conditions are—
  - (a) the copy is supplied in response to a request from a library which is not conducted for profit, and
  - (b) at the time of making the copy the librarian does not know, or could not reasonably find out, the name and address of a person entitled to authorise the making of a copy of the work.
- (3) The condition in subsection (2)(b) does not apply where the request is for a copy of an article in a periodical.
- (4) Where a library makes a charge for supplying a copy under this section, the sum charged must be calculated by reference to the costs attributable to the production of the copy.
- (5) To the extent that a term of a contract purports to prevent or restrict the doing of any act which, by virtue of this section, would not infringe copyright, that term is unenforceable.

42 Copying by librarians etc. replacement copies of works
- (1) A librarian, archivist or curator of a library, archive or museum may, without infringing copyright, make a copy of an item in that institution's permanent collection—
  - (a) in order to preserve or replace that item in that collection, or
  - (b) where an item in the permanent collection of another library, archive or museum has been lost, destroyed or damaged, in order to replace the item in the collection of that other library, archive or museum,
  provided that the conditions in subsections (2) and (3) are met.

(2)   The first condition is that the item is—
     (a)   included in the part of the collection kept wholly or mainly for the purposes of reference on the institution's premises,
     (b)   included in a part of the collection not accessible to the public, or
     (c)   available on loan only to other libraries, archives or museums.

(3)   The second condition is that it is not reasonably practicable to purchase a copy of the item to achieve either of the purposes mentioned in subsection (1).

(4)   The reference in subsection (1)(b) to a library, archive or museum is to a library, archive or museum which is not conducted for profit.

(5)   Where an institution makes a charge for supplying a copy to another library, archive or museum under subsection (1)(b), the sum charged must be calculated by reference to the costs attributable to the production of the copy.

(6)   In this section "item" means a work or a copy of a work.

(7)   To the extent that a term of a contract purports to prevent or restrict the doing of any act which, by virtue of this section, would not infringe copyright, that term is unenforceable.

42A   Copying by librarians: single copies of published works

(1)   A librarian of a library which is not conducted for profit may, if the conditions in subsection (2) are met, make and supply a single copy of—
     (a)   one article in any one issue of a periodical, or
     (b)   a reasonable proportion of any other published work,
     without infringing copyright in the work.

(2)   The conditions are—
     (a)   the copy is supplied in response to a request from a person who has provided the librarian with a declaration in writing which includes the information set out in subsection (3), and
     (b)   the librarian is not aware that the declaration is false in a material particular.

(3)   The information which must be included in the declaration is—
     (a)   the name of the person who requires the copy and the material which that person requires,
     (b)   a statement that the person has not previously been supplied with a copy of that material by any library,
     (c)   a statement that the person requires the copy for the purposes of research for a non-commercial purpose or private study, will use it only for those purposes and will not supply the copy to any other person, and
     (d)   a statement that to the best of the person's knowledge, no other person with whom the person works or studies has made, or intends to make, at or about the same time as the person's request, a request for substantially the same material for substantially the same purpose.

(4)   Where a library makes a charge for supplying a copy under this section, the sum charged must be calculated by reference to the costs attributable to the production of the copy.

(5)   Where a person ("P") makes a declaration under this section that is false in a material particular and is supplied with a copy which would have been an infringing copy if made by P—
     (a)   P is liable for infringement of copyright as if P had made the copy, and
     (b)   the copy supplied to P is to be treated as an infringing copy for all purposes.

(6)   To the extent that a term of a contract purports to prevent or restrict the doing of any act which, by virtue of this section, would not infringe copyright, that term is unenforceable.

43   Copying by librarians or archivists: single copies of unpublished works

(1)   A librarian or archivist may make and supply a single copy of the whole or part of a work without infringing copyright in the work, provided that—
     (a)   the copy is supplied in response to a request from a person who has provided the librarian or archivist with a declaration in writing which includes the information set out in subsection (2), and
     (b)   the librarian or archivist is not aware that the declaration is false in a material particular.

(2) The information which must be included in the declaration is—
  (a) the name of the person who requires the copy and the material which that person requires,
  (b) a statement that the person has not previously been supplied with a copy of that material by any library or archive, and
  (c) a statement that the person requires the copy for the purposes of research for a non-commercial purpose or private study, will use it only for those purposes and will not supply the copy to any other person.
(3) But copyright is infringed if—
  (a) the work had been published or communicated to the public before the date it was deposited in the library or archive, or
  (b) the copyright owner has prohibited the copying of the work,
  and at the time of making the copy the librarian or archivist is, or ought to be, aware of that fact.
(4) Where a library or archive makes a charge for supplying a copy under this section, the sum charged must be calculated by reference to the costs attributable to the production of the copy.
(5) Where a person ("P") makes a declaration under this section that is false in a material particular and is supplied with a copy which would have been an infringing copy if made by P—
  (a) P is liable for infringement of copyright as if P had made the copy, and
  (b) the copy supplied to P is to be treated as an infringing copy for all purposes.

43A Sections 40A to 43: interpretation

(1) The following definitions have effect for the purposes of sections 40A to 43.
(2) "Library" means—
  (a) a library which is publicly accessible, or
  (b) a library of an educational establishment.
(3) "Museum" includes a gallery.
(4) "Conducted for profit", in relation to a library, archive or museum, means a body of that kind which is established or conducted for profit or which forms part of, or is administered by, a body established or conducted for profit.
(5) References to a librarian, archivist or curator include a person acting on behalf of a librarian, archivist or curator.

44 Copy of work required to be made as condition of export

If an article of cultural or historical importance or interest cannot lawfully be exported from the United Kingdom unless a copy of it is made and deposited in an appropriate library or archive, it is not an infringement of copyright to make that copy.

44A Legal deposit libraries

(1) Copyright is not infringed by the copying of a work from the internet by a deposit library or person acting on its behalf if—
  (a) the work is of a description prescribed by regulations under section 10(5) of the 2003 Act,
  (b) its publication on the internet, or a person publishing it there, is connected with the United Kingdom in a manner so prescribed, and
  (c) the copying is done in accordance with any conditions so prescribed.
(2) Copyright is not infringed by the doing of anything in relation to relevant material permitted to be done under regulations under section 7 of the 2003 Act.
(3) The Secretary of State may by regulations make provision excluding, in relation to prescribed activities done in relation to relevant material, the application of such of the provisions of this Chapter as are prescribed.
(4) Regulations under subsection (3) may in particular make provision prescribing activities—
  (a) done for a prescribed purpose,
  (b) done by prescribed descriptions of reader,
  (c) done in relation to prescribed descriptions of relevant material,
  (d) done other than in accordance with prescribed conditions.

(5)   Regulations under this section may make different provision for different purposes.

(6)   Regulations under this section shall be made by statutory instrument which shall be subject to annulment in pursuance of a resolution of either House of Parliament.

(7)   In this section—

(a)   "the 2003 Act" means the Legal Deposit Libraries Act 2003;

(b)   "deposit library", "reader" and "relevant material" have the same meaning as in section 7 of the 2003 Act;

(c)   "prescribed" means prescribed by regulations made by the Secretary of State.

Orphan works

44B   Permitted uses of orphan works

(1)   Copyright in an orphan work is not infringed by a relevant body in the circumstances set out in paragraph 1(1) of Schedule ZA1 (subject to paragraph 6 of that Schedule).

(2)   "Orphan work" and "relevant body" have the meanings given by that Schedule.

Public administration

45   Parliamentary and judicial proceedings

(1)   Copyright is not infringed by anything done for the purposes of parliamentary or judicial proceedings.

(2)   Copyright is not infringed by anything done for the purposes of reporting such proceedings; but this shall not be construed as authorising the copying of a work which is itself a published report of the proceedings.

46   Royal Commissions and statutory inquiries

(1)   Copyright is not infringed by anything done for the purposes of the proceedings of a Royal Commission or statutory inquiry.

(2)   Copyright is not infringed by anything done for the purpose of reporting any such proceedings held in public; but this shall not be construed as authorising the copying of a work which is itself a published report of the proceedings.

(3)   Copyright in a work is not infringed by the issue to the public of copies of the report of a Royal Commission or statutory inquiry containing the work or material from it.

(4)   In this section—

"Royal Commission" includes a Commission appointed for Northern Ireland by the Secretary of State in pursuance of the prerogative powers of Her Majesty delegated to him under section 7(2) of the Northern Ireland Constitution Act 1973; and "statutory inquiry" means an inquiry held or investigation conducted in pursuance of a duty imposed or power conferred by or under an enactment.

47   Material open to public inspection or on official register

(1)   Where material is open to public inspection pursuant to a statutory requirement, or is on a statutory register, any copyright in the material as a literary work is not infringed by the copying of so much of the material as contains factual information of any description, by or with the authority of the appropriate person, for a purpose which does not involve the issuing of copies to the public.

(2)   Where material is open to public inspection pursuant to a statutory requirement, copyright in the material is not infringed by an act to which subsection (3A) applies provided that—

(a)   the act is done by or with the authority of the appropriate person,

(b)   the purpose of the act is—

(i)   to enable the material to be inspected at a more convenient time or place, or

(ii)   to otherwise facilitate the exercise of any right for the purpose of which the statutory requirement is imposed, and

(c)   in the case of the act specified in subsection (3A)(c), the material is not commercially available to the public by or with the authority of the copyright owner.

(3)　Where material which contains information about matters of general scientific, technical, commercial or economic interest is on a statutory register or is open to public inspection pursuant to a statutory requirement, copyright in the material is not infringed by an act to which subsection (3A) applies provided that—

(a)　the act is done by or with the authority of the appropriate person,

(b)　the purpose of the act is to disseminate that information, and

(c)　in the case of the act specified in subsection (3A)(c), the material is not commercially available to the public by or with the authority of the copyright owner.

(3A)　This subsection applies to any of the following acts—

(a)　copying the material,

(b)　issuing copies of the material to the public, and

(c)　making the material (or a copy of it) available to the public by electronic transmission in such a way that members of the public may access it from a place and at a time individually chosen by them.

(4)　The Secretary of State may by order provide that subsection (1), (2) or (3) shall, in such cases as may be specified in the order, apply only to copies marked in such manner as may be so specified.

(5)　The Secretary of State may by order provide that subsections (1) to (3) apply, to such extent and with such modifications as may be specified in the order—

(a)　to material made open to public inspection by—

(i)　an international organisation specified in the order, or

(ii)　a person so specified who has functions in the United Kingdom under an inter-national agreement to which the United Kingdom is party, or

(b)　to a register maintained by an international organisation specified in the order,

as they apply in relation to material open to public inspection pursuant to a statutory requirement or to a statutory register.

(6)　In this section—

"appropriate person" means the person required to make the material open to public inspection or, as the case may be, the person maintaining the register;

"statutory register" means a register maintained in pursuance of a statutory requirement; and

"statutory requirement" means a requirement imposed by provision made by or under an enactment.

(7)　An order under this section shall be made by statutory instrument which shall be subject to annulment in pursuance of a resolution of either House of Parliament.

48　Material communicated to the Crown in the course of public business

(1)　This section applies where a literary, dramatic, musical or artistic work has in the course of public business been communicated to the Crown for any purpose, by or with the licence of the copyright owner and a document or other material thing recording or embodying the work is owned by or in the custody or control of the Crown.

(2)　The Crown may, without infringing copyright in the work, do an act specified in subsection (3) provided that—

(a)　the act is done for the purpose for which the work was communicated to the Crown, or any related purpose which could reasonably have been anticipated by the copyright owner, and

(b)　the work has not been previously published otherwise than by virtue of this section.

(3)　The acts referred to in subsection (2) are—

(a)　copying the work,

(b)　issuing copies of the work to the public, and

(c)　making the work (or a copy of it) available to the public by electronic transmission in such a way that members of the public may access it from a place and at a time individually chosen by them.

(4)　In subsection (1) "public business" includes any activity carried on by the Crown.

(5)　This section has effect subject to any agreement to the contrary between the Crown and the copyright owner.

(6)   In this section "the Crown" includes a health service body, as defined in section 60(7) of the National Health Service and Community Care Act 1990, the National Health Service Commissioning Board, a clinical commissioning group established under section 14D of the National Health Service Act 2006, the Care Quality Commission, Health Education England, the Health Research Authority and a National Health Service trust established under *section 25 of the National Health Service Act 2006,* section 18 of the National Health Service (Wales) Act 2006 or the National Health Service (Scotland) Act 1978 and an NHS foundation trust and also includes a health and social services body, as defined in Article 7(6) of the Health and Personal Social Services (Northern Ireland) Order 1991, and a Health and Social Services trust established under that Order; and the reference in subsection (1) above to public business shall be construed accordingly.

Note: The words in italics in subsection (6) will be repealed when Health and Social Care Act 2012, s 306(4) brings the Health and Social Care Act 2012, s 179(6), Sch 14, Pt 2, para 52 into force.

49   Public records

Material which is comprised in public records within the meaning of the Public Records Act 1958, the Public Records (Scotland) Act 1937 or the Public Records Act (Northern Ireland) 1923, or in Welsh public records (as defined in the Government of Wales Act 2006), which are open to public inspection in pursuance of that Act, may be copied, and a copy may be supplied to any person, by or with the authority of any officer appointed under that Act, without infringement of copyright.

50   Acts done under statutory authority

(1)   Where the doing of a particular act is specifically authorised by an Act of Parliament, whenever passed, then, unless the Act provides otherwise, the doing of that act does not infringe copyright.

(2)   Subsection (1) applies in relation to an enactment contained in Northern Ireland legislation as it applies in relation to an Act of Parliament.

(3)   Nothing in this section shall be construed as excluding any defence of statutory authority otherwise available under or by virtue of any enactment.

Computer programs: lawful users

50A   Back up copies

(1)   It is not an infringement of copyright for a lawful user of a copy of a computer program to make any back up copy of it which it is necessary for him to have for the purposes of his lawful use.

(2)   For the purposes of this section and sections 50B, 50BA and 50C a person is a lawful user of a computer program if (whether under a licence to do any acts restricted by the copyright in the program or otherwise), he has a right to use the program.

(3)   Where an act is permitted under this section, it is irrelevant whether or not there exists any term or condition in an agreement which purports to prohibit or restrict the act (such terms being, by virtue of section 296A, void).

50B   Decompilation

(1)   It is not an infringement of copyright for a lawful user of a copy of a computer program expressed in a low level language—

(a)   to convert it into a version expressed in a higher level language, or

(b)   incidentally in the course of so converting the program, to copy it,

(that is, to "decompile" it), provided that the conditions in subsection (2) are met.

(2)   The conditions are that—

(a)   it is necessary to decompile the program to obtain the information necessary to create an independent program which can be operated with the program decompiled or with another program ("the permitted objective"); and

(b)   the information so obtained is not used for any purpose other than the permitted objective.

(3)   In particular, the conditions in subsection (2) are not met if the lawful user—

(a)   has readily available to him the information necessary to achieve the permitted objective;

      (b)   does not confine the decompiling to such acts as are necessary to achieve the permitted objective;

      (c)   supplies the information obtained by the decompiling to any person to whom it is not necessary to supply it in order to achieve the permitted objective; or

      (d)   uses the information to create a program which is substantially similar in its expression to the program decompiled or to do any act restricted by copyright.

(4)   Where an act is permitted under this section, it is irrelevant whether or not there exists any term or condition in an agreement which purports to prohibit or restrict the act (such terms being, by virtue of section 296A, void).

50BA   Observing, studying and testing of computer programs

(1)   It is not an infringement of copyright for a lawful user of a copy of a computer program to observe, study or test the functioning of the program in order to determine the ideas and principles which underlie any element of the program if he does so while performing any of the acts of loading, displaying, running, transmitting or storing the program which he is entitled to do.

(2)   Where an act is permitted under this section, it is irrelevant whether or not there exists any term or condition in an agreement which purports to prohibit or restrict the act (such terms being, by virtue of section 296A, void).

50C   Other acts permitted to lawful users

(1)   It is not an infringement of copyright for a lawful user of a copy of a computer program to copy or adapt it, provided that the copying or adapting—

      (a)   is necessary for his lawful use; and

      (b)   is not prohibited under any term or condition of an agreement regulating the circumstances in which his use is lawful.

(2)   It may, in particular, be necessary for the lawful use of a computer program to copy it or adapt it for the purpose of correcting errors in it.

(3)   This section does not apply to any copying or adapting permitted under section 50A, 50B or 50BA.

Databases: permitted acts

50D   Acts permitted in relation to databases

(1)   It is not an infringement of copyright in a database for a person who has a right to use the database or any part of the database, (whether under a licence to do any of the acts restricted by the copyright in the database or otherwise) to do, in the exercise of that right, anything which is necessary for the purposes of access to and use of the contents of the database or of that part of the database.

(2)   Where an act which would otherwise infringe copyright in a database is permitted under this section, it is irrelevant whether or not there exists any term or condition in any agreement which purports to prohibit or restrict the act (such terms being, by virtue of section 296B, void).

Designs

51   Design documents and models

(1)   It is not an infringement of any copyright in a design document or model recording or embodying a design for anything other than an artistic work or a typeface to make an article to the design or to copy an article made to the design.

(2)   Nor is it an infringement of the copyright to issue to the public, or include in a film, or communicate to the public, anything the making of which was, by virtue of subsection (1), not an infringement of that copyright.

(3)   In this section—

"design" means the design of the shape or configuration (whether internal or external) of the whole or part of an article, other than surface decoration; and "design document" means any record of a design, whether in the form of a drawing, a written description, a photograph, data stored in a computer or otherwise.

52   . . .

53   Things done in reliance on registration of design

(1) The copyright in an artistic work is not infringed by anything done—

    (a) in pursuance of an assignment or licence made or granted by a person registered—

        (i) under the Registered Designs Act 1949 as the proprietor of a corresponding design, or

        (ii) under the Community Design Regulation as the right holder of a corresponding registered Community design, and

    (b) in good faith in reliance on the registration and without notice of any proceedings for the cancellation or invalidation of the registration or, in a case of registration under the 1949 Act, for rectifying the relevant entry in the register of designs;

and this is so notwithstanding that the person registered as the proprietor was not the proprietor of the design for the purposes of the 1949 Act or, in a case of registration under the Community Design Regulation, that the person registered as the right holder was not the right holder of the design for the purposes of the Regulation.

(2) In subsection (1) a "corresponding design", in relation to an artistic work, means a design within the meaning of the 1949 Act which if applied to an article would produce something which would be treated for the purposes of this Part as a copy of the artistic work.

(3) In subsection (1), a "corresponding registered Community design", in relation to an artistic work, means a design within the meaning of the Community Design Regulation which if applied to an article would produce something which would be treated for the purposes of this Part as a copy of the artistic work.

(4) In this section, "the Community Design Regulation" means Council Regulation (EC) No 6/2002 of 12 December 2001 on Community designs.

Typefaces

54   Use of typeface in ordinary course of printing

(1) It is not an infringement of copyright in an artistic work consisting of the design of a typeface—

    (a) to use the typeface in the ordinary course of typing, composing text, typesetting or printing,

    (b) to possess an article for the purpose of such use, or

    (c) to do anything in relation to material produced by such use;

and this is so notwithstanding that an article is used which is an infringing copy of the work.

(2) However, the following provisions of this Part apply in relation to persons making, importing or dealing with articles specifically designed or adapted for producing material in a particular typeface, or possessing such articles for the purpose of dealing with them, as if the production of material as mentioned in subsection (1) did infringe copyright in the artistic work consisting of the design of the typeface—

section 24 (secondary infringement: making, importing, possessing or dealing with article for making infringing copy),

sections 99 and 100 (order for delivery up and right of seizure),

section 107(2) (offence of making or possessing such an article), and

section 108 (order for delivery up in criminal proceedings).

(3) The references in subsection (2) to "dealing with" an article are to selling, letting for hire, or offering or exposing for sale or hire, exhibiting in public, or distributing.

55   Articles for producing material in particular typeface

(1) This section applies to the copyright in an artistic work consisting of the design of a typeface where articles specifically designed or adapted for producing material in that typeface have been marketed by or with the licence of the copyright owner.

(2) After the period of 25 years from the end of the calendar year in which the first such articles are marketed, the work may be copied by making further such articles, or doing anything for the purpose of making such articles, and anything may be done in relation to articles so made, without infringing copyright in the work.

(3) In subsection (1) "marketed" means sold, let for hire or offered or exposed for sale or hire, in the United Kingdom or elsewhere.

Works in electronic form

56   Transfers of copies of works in electronic form

(1)   This section applies where a copy of a work in electronic form has been purchased on terms which, expressly or impliedly or by virtue of any rule of law, allow the purchaser to copy the work, or to adapt it or make copies of an adaptation, in connection with his use of it.

(2)   If there are no express terms—

    (a)   prohibiting the transfer of the copy by the purchaser, imposing obligations which continue after a transfer, prohibiting the assignment of any licence or terminating any licence on a transfer, or

    (b)   providing for the terms on which a transferee may do the things which the purchaser was permitted to do,

    anything which the purchaser was allowed to do may also be done without infringement of copyright by a transferee; but any copy, adaptation or copy of an adaptation made by the purchaser which is not also transferred shall be treated as an infringing copy for all purposes after the transfer.

(3)   The same applies where the original purchased copy is no longer usable and what is transferred is a further copy used in its place.

(4)   The above provisions also apply on a subsequent transfer, with the substitution for references in subsection (2) to the purchaser of references to the subsequent transferor.

Miscellaneous: literary, dramatic, musical and artistic works

57   Anonymous or pseudonymous works: acts permitted on assumptions as to expiry of copyright or death of author

(1)   Copyright in a literary, dramatic, musical or artistic work is not infringed by an act done at a time when, or in pursuance of arrangements made at a time when—

    (a)   it is not possible by reasonable inquiry to ascertain the identity of the author, and

    (b)   it is reasonable to assume—

        (i)   that copyright has expired, or

        (ii)   that the author died 70 years or more before the beginning of the calendar year in which the act is done or the arrangements are made.

(2)   Subsection (1)(b)(ii) does not apply in relation to—

    (a)   a work in which Crown copyright subsists, or

    (b)   a work in which copyright originally vested in an international organisation by virtue of section 168 and in respect of which an Order under that section specifies a copyright period longer than 70 years.

(3)   In relation to a work of joint authorship—

    (a)   the reference in subsection (1) to its being possible to ascertain the identity of the author shall be construed as a reference to its being possible to ascertain the identity of any of the authors, and

    (b)   the reference in subsection (1)(b)(ii) to the author having died shall be construed as a reference to all the authors having died.

58   Use of notes or recordings of spoken words in certain cases

(1)   Where a record of spoken words is made, in writing or otherwise, for the purpose—

    (a)   of reporting current events, or

    (b)   of communicating to the public the whole or part of the work,

    it is not an infringement of any copyright in the words as a literary work to use the record or material taken from it (or to copy the record, or any such material, and use the copy) for that purpose, provided the following conditions are met.

(2)   The conditions are that—

    (a)   the record is a direct record of the spoken words and is not taken from a previous record or from a broadcast;

    (b)   the making of the record was not prohibited by the speaker and, where copyright already subsisted in the work, did not infringe copyright;

    (c)   the use made of the record or material taken from it is not of a kind prohibited by or on behalf of the speaker or copyright owner before the record was made; and

    (d)   the use is by or with the authority of a person who is lawfully in possession of the record.

59   Public reading or recitation

(1)   The reading or recitation in public by one person of a reasonable extract from a published literary or dramatic work does not infringe any copyright in the work if it is accompanied by a sufficient acknowledgement.

(2)   Copyright in a work is not infringed by the making of a sound recording, or the communication to the public, of a reading or recitation which by virtue of subsection (1) does not infringe copyright in the work, provided that the recording, or communication to the public consists mainly of material in relation to which it is not necessary to rely on that subsection.

60   Abstracts of scientific or technical articles

(1)   Where an article on a scientific or technical subject is published in a periodical accompanied by an abstract indicating the contents of the article, it is not an infringement of copyright in the abstract, or in the article, to copy the abstract or issue copies of it to the public.

(2)   This section does not apply if or to the extent that there is a licensing scheme certified for the purposes of this section under section 143 providing for the grant of licences.

61   Recordings of folksongs

(1)   A sound recording of a performance of a song may be made for the purpose of including it in an archive maintained by a body not established or conducted for profit without infringing any copyright in the words as a literary work or in the accompanying musical work, provided the conditions in subsection (2) below are met.

(2)   The conditions are that—

    (a)   the words are unpublished and of unknown authorship at the time the recording is made,

    (b)   the making of the recording does not infringe any other copyright, and

    (c)   its making is not prohibited by any performer.

(3)   A single copy of a sound recording made in reliance on subsection (1) and included in an archive referred to in that subsection may be made and supplied by the archivist without infringing copyright in the recording or the works included in it, provided that—

    (a)   the copy is supplied in response to a request from a person who has provided the archivist with a declaration in writing which includes the information set out in subsection (4), and

    (b)   the archivist is not aware that the declaration is false in a material particular.

(4)   The information which must be included in the declaration is—

    (a)   the name of the person who requires the copy and the sound recording which is the subject of the request,

    (b)   a statement that the person has not previously been supplied with a copy of that sound recording by any archivist, and

    (c)   a statement that the person requires the copy for the purposes of research for a non-commercial purpose or private study, will use it only for those purposes and will not supply the copy to any other person.

(5)   Where an archive makes a charge for supplying a copy under this section, the sum charged must be calculated by reference to the costs attributable to the production of the copy.

(6)   Where a person ("P") makes a declaration under this section that is false in a material particular and is supplied with a copy which would have been an infringing copy if made by P—

    (a)   P is liable for infringement of copyright as if P had made the copy, and

    (b)   the copy supplied to P is to be treated as an infringing copy for all purposes.

(7)   In this section references to an archivist include a person acting on behalf of an archivist.

62   Representation of certain artistic works on public display

(1)   This section applies to—
    (a)   buildings, and
    (b)   sculptures, models for buildings and works of artistic craftsmanship, if permanently situated in a public place or in premises open to the public.

(2)   The copyright in such a work is not infringed by—
    (a)   making a graphic work representing it,
    (b)   making a photograph or film of it, or
    (c)   making a broadcast of a visual image of it.

(3)   Nor is the copyright infringed by the issue to the public of copies, or the communication to the public, of anything whose making was, by virtue of this section, not an infringement of the copyright.

63   Advertisement of sale of artistic work

(1)   It is not an infringement of copyright in an artistic work to copy it, or to issue copies to the public, for the purpose of advertising the sale of the work.

(2)   Where a copy which would otherwise be an infringing copy is made in accordance with this section but is subsequently dealt with for any other purpose, it shall be treated as an infringing copy for the purposes of that dealing, and if that dealing infringes copyright for all subsequent purposes.
For this purpose "dealt with" means sold or let for hire, offered or exposed for sale or hire, exhibited in public, distributed or communicated to the public.

64   Making of subsequent works by same artist

Where the author of an artistic work is not the copyright owner, he does not infringe the copyright by copying the work in making another artistic work, provided he does not repeat or imitate the main design of the earlier work.

65   Reconstruction of buildings

Anything done for the purposes of reconstructing a building does not infringe any copyright—
(a)   in the building, or
(b)   in any drawings or plans in accordance with which the building was, by or with the licence of the copyright owner, constructed.

Miscellaneous: lending of works and playing of sound recordings

66   Lending to public of copies of certain works

(1)   The Secretary of State may by order provide that in such cases as may be specified in the order the lending to the public of copies of literary, dramatic, musical or artistic works, sound recordings or films shall be treated as licensed by the copyright owner subject only to the payment of such reasonable royalty or other payment as may be agreed or determined in default of agreement by the Copyright Tribunal.

(2)   No such order shall apply if, or to the extent that, there is a licensing scheme certified for the purposes of this section under section 143 providing for the grant of licences.

(3)   An order may make different provision for different cases and may specify cases by reference to any factor relating to the work, the copies lent, the lender or the circumstances of the lending.

(4)   An order shall be made by statutory instrument; and no order shall be made unless a draft of it has been laid before and approved by a resolution of each House of Parliament.

(5)   Nothing in this section affects any liability under section 23 (secondary infringement: possessing or dealing with infringing copy) in respect of the lending of infringing copies.

Miscellaneous: films and sound recordings

66A　Films: acts permitted on assumptions as to expiry of copyright, etc.

(1) Copyright in a film is not infringed by an act done at a time when, or in pursuance of arrangements made at a time when—

　　(a)　it is not possible by reasonable inquiry to ascertain the identity of any of the persons referred to in section 13B(2)(a) to (d) (persons by reference to whose life the copyright period is ascertained), and

　　(b)　it is reasonable to assume—

　　　　(i)　that copyright has expired, or

　　　　(ii)　that the last to die of those persons died 70 years or more before the beginning of the calendar year in which the act is done or the arrangements are made.

(2) Subsection (1)(b)(ii) does not apply in relation to—

　　(a)　a film in which Crown copyright subsists, or

　　(b)　a film in which copyright originally vested in an international organisation by virtue of section 168 and in respect of which an Order under that section specifies a copyright period longer than 70 years.

Miscellaneous: broadcasts

68　Incidental recording for purposes of broadcast

(1) This section applies where by virtue of a licence or assignment of copyright a person is authorised to broadcast—

　　(a)　a literary, dramatic or musical work, or an adaptation of such a work,

　　(b)　an artistic work, or

　　(c)　a sound recording or film.

(2) He shall by virtue of this section be treated as licensed by the owner of the copyright in the work to do or authorise any of the following for the purposes of the broadcast—

　　(a)　in the case of a literary, dramatic or musical work, or an adaptation of such a work, to make a sound recording or film of the work or adaptation;

　　(b)　in the case of an artistic work, to take a photograph or make a film of the work;

　　(c)　in the case of a sound recording or film, to make a copy of it.

(3) That licence is subject to the condition that the recording, film, photograph or copy in question—

　　(a)　shall not be used for any other purpose, and

　　(b)　shall be destroyed within 28 days of being first used for broadcasting the work.

(4) A recording, film, photograph or copy made in accordance with this section shall be treated as an infringing copy—

　　(a)　for the purposes of any use in breach of the condition mentioned in subsection (3)(a), and

　　(b)　for all purposes after that condition or the condition mentioned in subsection (3)(b) is broken.

69　Recording for purposes of supervision and control of broadcasts and other services

(1) Copyright is not infringed by the making or use by the British Broadcasting Corporation, for the purpose of maintaining supervision and control over programmes broadcast by them, or included in any on-demand programme service provided by them, of recordings of those programmes.

(2) Copyright is not infringed by anything done in pursuance of—

　　(a)　section 167(1) of the Broadcasting Act 1990, section 115(4) or (6) or 117 of the Broadcasting Act 1996 or paragraph 20 of Schedule 12 to the Communications Act 2003;

　　(b)　a condition which, by virtue of section 334(1) of the Communications Act 2003, is included in a licence granted under Part I or III of that Act or Part I or II of the Broadcasting Act 1996;

　　(c)　a direction given under section 109(2) of the Broadcasting Act 1990 (power of OFCOM to require production of recordings etc);

　　(d)　section 334(3) of the Communications Act 2003.

(3)   Copyright is not infringed by the use by OFCOM in connection with the performance of any of their functions under the Broadcasting Act 1990, the Broadcasting Act 1996 or the Communications Act 2003 of—

  (a)   any recording, script or transcript which is provided to them under or by virtue of any provision of those Acts; or

  (b)   any existing material which is transferred to them by a scheme made under section 30 of the Communications Act 2003.

(4)   In subsection (3), "existing material" means—

  (a)   any recording, script or transcript which was provided to the Independent Television Commission or the Radio Authority under or by virtue of any provision of the Broadcasting Act 1990 or the Broadcasting Act 1996; and

  (b)   any recording or transcript which was provided to the Broadcasting Standards Commission under section 115(4) or (6) or 116(5) of the Broadcasting Act 1996.

(5)   Copyright is not infringed by the use by an appropriate regulatory authority designated under section 368B of the Communications Act 2003, in connection with the performance of any of their functions under that Act, of any recording, script or transcript which is provided to them under or by virtue of any provision of that Act.

(6)   In this section "on-demand programme service" has the same meaning as in the Communications Act 2003 (see section 368A of that Act).

70   Recording for purposes of time-shifting

(1)   The making in domestic premises for private and domestic use of a recording of a broadcast solely for the purpose of enabling it to be viewed or listened to at a more convenient time does not infringe any copyright in the broadcast or in any work included in it.

(2)   Where a copy which would otherwise be an infringing copy is made in accordance with this section but is subsequently dealt with—

  (a)   it shall be treated as an infringing copy for the purposes of that dealing; and

  (b)   if that dealing infringes copyright, it shall be treated as an infringing copy for all subsequent purposes.

(3)   In subsection (2), "dealt with" means sold or let for hire, offered or exposed for sale or hire or communicated to the public.

71   Photographs of broadcasts

(1)   The making in domestic premises for private and domestic use of a photograph of the whole or any part of an image forming part of a broadcast, or a copy of such a photograph, does not infringe any copyright in the broadcast or in any film included in it.

(2)   Where a copy which would otherwise be an infringing copy is made in accordance with this section but is subsequently dealt with—

  (a)   it shall be treated as an infringing copy for the purposes of that dealing; and

  (b)   if that dealing infringes copyright, it shall be treated as an infringing copy for all subsequent purposes.

(3)   In subsection (2), "dealt with" means sold or let for hire, offered or exposed for sale or hire or communicated to the public.

72   Free public showing or playing of broadcast

(1)   The showing or playing in public of a broadcast to an audience who have not paid for admission to the place where the broadcast is to be seen or heard does not infringe any copyright in—

  (a)   the broadcast; or

  (b)   any sound recording (except so far as it is an excepted sound recording) included in it.

(1A)   For the purposes of this Part an "excepted sound recording" is a sound recording—

  (a)   whose author is not the author of the broadcast in which it is included; and

  (b)   which is a recording of music with or without words spoken or sung.

(1B)   Where by virtue of subsection (1) the copyright in a broadcast shown or played in public is not infringed, copyright in any film or excepted sound recording included in it is not infringed if the playing or showing of that broadcast in public—

  (a)   . . .

      (b)   is necessary for the purposes of—
          (i)   repairing equipment for the reception of broadcasts;
          (ii)   demonstrating that a repair to such equipment has been carried out; or
          (iii) demonstrating such equipment which is being sold or let for hire or offered or exposed for sale or hire.

(2)   The audience shall be treated as having paid for admission to a place—
    (a)   if they have paid for admission to a place of which that place forms part; or
    (b)   if goods or services are supplied at that place (or a place of which it forms part)—
        (i)   at prices which are substantially attributable to the facilities afforded for seeing or hearing the broadcast, or
        (ii)   at prices exceeding those usually charged there and which are partly attributable to those facilities.

(3)   The following shall not be regarded as having paid for admission to a place—
    (a)   persons admitted as residents or inmates of the place;
    (b)   persons admitted as members of a club or society where the payment is only for membership of the club or society and the provision of facilities for seeing or hearing broadcasts is only incidental to the main purposes of the club or society.

(4)   Where the making of the broadcast was an infringement of the copyright in a sound recording or film, the fact that it was heard or seen in public by the reception of the broadcast shall be taken into account in assessing the damages for that infringement.

73–74 . . .

75   Recording of broadcast for archival purposes

(1)   A recording of a broadcast or a copy of such a recording may be made for the purpose of being placed in an archive maintained by a body which is not established or conducted for profit without infringing any copyright in the broadcast or in any work included in it.

(2)   To the extent that a term of a contract purports to prevent or restrict the doing of any act which, by virtue of this section, would not infringe copyright, that term is unenforceable.

Adaptations

76   Adaptations

An act which by virtue of this Chapter may be done without infringing copyright in a literary, dramatic or musical work does not, where that work is an adaptation, infringe any copyright in the work from which the adaptation was made.

CHAPTER IIIA
CERTAIN PERMITTED USES OF ORPHAN WORKS

76A   Certain permitted uses of orphan works

Schedule ZA1 makes provision about the use by relevant bodies of orphan works.

CHAPTER IV
MORAL RIGHTS

Right to be identified as author or director

77   Right to be identified as author or director

(1)   The author of a copyright literary, dramatic, musical or artistic work, and the director of a copyright film, has the right to be identified as the author or director of the work in the circumstances mentioned in this section; but the right is not infringed unless it has been asserted in accordance with section 78.

(2)   The author of a literary work (other than words intended to be sung or spoken with music) or a dramatic work has the right to be identified whenever—
    (a)   the work is published commercially, performed in public, or communicated to the public; or
    (b)   copies of a film or sound recording including the work are issued to the public; and that right includes the right to be identified whenever any of those events

occur in relation to an adaptation of the work as the author of the work from which the adaptation was made.

(3) The author of a musical work, or a literary work consisting of words intended to be sung or spoken with music, has the right to be identified whenever—

  (a)   the work is published commercially;

  (b)   copies of a sound recording of the work are issued to the public; or

  (c)   a film of which the sound-track includes the work is shown in public or copies of such a film are issued to the public;

and that right includes the right to be identified whenever any of those events occur in relation to an adaptation of the work as the author of the work from which the adaptation was made.

(4) The author of an artistic work has the right to be identified whenever—

  (a)   the work is published commercially or exhibited in public, or a visual image of it is communicated to the public;

  (b)   a film including a visual image of the work is shown in public or copies of such a film are issued to the public; or

  (c)   in the case of a work of architecture in the form of a building or a model for a building, a sculpture or a work of artistic craftsmanship, copies of a graphic work representing it, or of a photograph of it, are issued to the public.

(5) The author of a work of architecture in the form of a building also has the right to be identified on the building as constructed or, where more than one building is constructed to the design, on the first to be constructed.

(6) The director of a film has the right to be identified whenever the film is shown in public, or communicated to the public, or copies of the film are issued to the public.

(7) The right of the author or director under this section is—

  (a)   in the case of commercial publication or the issue to the public of copies of a film or sound recording, to be identified in or on each copy or, if that is not appropriate, in some other manner likely to bring his identity to the notice of a person acquiring a copy,

  (b)   in the case of identification on a building, to be identified by appropriate means visible to persons entering or approaching the building, and

  (c)   in any other case, to be identified in a manner likely to bring his identity to the attention of a person seeing or hearing the performance, exhibition, showing, or communication to the public in question;

and the identification must in each case be clear and reasonably prominent.

(8) If the author or director in asserting his right to be identified specifies a pseudonym, initials or some other particular form of identification, that form shall be used; otherwise any reasonable form of identification may be used.

(9) This section has effect subject to section 79 (exceptions to right).

78   Requirement that right be asserted

(1) A person does not infringe the right conferred by section 77 (right to be identified as author or director) by doing any of the acts mentioned in that section unless the right has been asserted in accordance with the following provisions so as to bind him in relation to that act.

(2) The right may be asserted generally, or in relation to any specified act or description of acts—

  (a)   on an assignment of copyright in the work, by including in the instrument effecting the assignment a statement that the author or director asserts in relation to that work his right to be identified, or

  (b)   by instrument in writing signed by the author or director.

(3) The right may also be asserted in relation to the public exhibition of an artistic work—

  (a)   by securing that when the author or other first owner of copyright parts with possession of the original, or of a copy made by him or under his direction or control, the author is identified on the original or copy, or on a frame, mount or other thing to which it is attached, or

  (b)   by including in a licence by which the author or other first owner of copyright authorises the making of copies of the work a statement signed by or on behalf of the person granting the licence that the author asserts his right to be identified in the event of the public exhibition of a copy made in pursuance of the licence.

(4) The persons bound by an assertion of the right under subsection (2) or (3) are—

    (a)   in the case of an assertion under subsection (2)(a), the assignee and anyone claiming through him, whether or not he has notice of the assertion;

    (b)   in the case of an assertion under subsection (2)(b), anyone to whose notice the assertion is brought;

    (c)   in the case of an assertion under subsection (3)(a), anyone into whose hands that original or copy comes, whether or not the identification is still present or visible;

    (d)   in the case of an assertion under subsection (3)(b), the licensee and anyone into whose hands a copy made in pursuance of the licence comes, whether or not he has notice of the assertion.

(5) In an action for infringement of the right the court shall, in considering remedies, take into account any delay in asserting the right.

79   Exceptions to right

(1) The right conferred by section 77 (right to be identified as author or director) is subject to the following exceptions.

(2) The right does not apply in relation to the following descriptions of work—

    (a)   a computer program;

    (b)   the design of a typeface;

    (c)   any computer-generated work.

(3) The right does not apply to anything done by or with the authority of the copyright owner where copyright in the work originally vested in the author's or director's employer by virtue of section 11(2) (works produced in the course of employment).

(4) The right is not infringed by an act which by virtue of any of the following provisions would not infringe copyright in the work—

    (a)   section 30 (fair dealing for certain purposes), so far as it relates to the reporting of current events by means of a sound recording, film or broadcast;

    (b)   section 31 (incidental inclusion of work in an artistic work, sound recording, film or broadcast);

    . . .

    (d)   section 45 (parliamentary and judicial proceedings);

    (e)   section 46(1) or (2) (Royal Commissions and statutory inquiries);

    (f)   section 51 (use of design documents and models);

    . . .

    (h)   section 57 or 66A (acts permitted on assumptions as to expiry of copyright, etc.).

(4A) The right is also not infringed by any act done for the purposes of an examination which by virtue of any provision of Chapter 3 of Part 1 would not infringe copyright.

(5) The right does not apply in relation to any work made for the purpose of reporting current events.

(6) The right does not apply in relation to the publication in—

    (a)   a newspaper, magazine or similar periodical, or

    (b)   an encyclopaedia, dictionary, yearbook or other collective work of reference,

of a literary, dramatic, musical or artistic work made for the purposes of such publication or made available with the consent of the author for the purposes of such publication.

(7) The right does not apply in relation to—

    (a)   a work in which Crown copyright or Parliamentary copyright subsists, or

    (b)   a work in which copyright originally vested in an international organisation by virtue of section 168,

unless the author or director has previously been identified as such in or on published copies of the work.

Right to object to derogatory treatment of work

80   Right to object to derogatory treatment of work

(1) The author of a copyright literary, dramatic, musical or artistic work, and the director of a copyright film, has the right in the circumstances mentioned in this section not to have his work subjected to derogatory treatment.

(2) For the purposes of this section—

    (a) "treatment" of a work means any addition to, deletion from or alteration to or adaptation of the work, other than—

        (i) a translation of a literary or dramatic work, or

        (ii) an arrangement or transcription of a musical work involving no more than a change of key or register; and

    (b) the treatment of a work is derogatory if it amounts to distortion or mutilation of the work or is otherwise prejudicial to the honour or reputation of the author or director;

and in the following provisions of this section references to a derogatory treatment of a work shall be construed accordingly.

(3) In the case of a literary, dramatic or musical work the right is infringed by a person who—

    (a) publishes commercially, performs in public or communicates to the public a derogatory treatment of the work; or

    (b) issues to the public copies of a film or sound recording of, or including, a derogatory treatment of the work.

(4) In the case of an artistic work the right is infringed by a person who—

    (a) publishes commercially or exhibits in public a derogatory treatment of the work, or communicates to the public a visual image of a derogatory treatment of the work,

    (b) shows in public a film including a visual image of a derogatory treatment of the work or issues to the public copies of such a film, or

    (c) in the case of—

        (i) a work of architecture in the form of a model for a building,

        (ii) a sculpture, or

        (iii) a work of artistic craftsmanship,

    issues to the public copies of a graphic work representing, or of a photograph of, a derogatory treatment of the work.

(5) Subsection (4) does not apply to a work of architecture in the form of a building; but where the author of such a work is identified on the building and it is the subject of derogatory treatment he has the right to require the identification to be removed.

(6) In the case of a film, the right is infringed by a person who—

    (a) shows in public or communicates to the public a derogatory treatment of the film; or

    (b) issues to the public copies of a derogatory treatment of the film.

(7) The right conferred by this section extends to the treatment of parts of a work resulting from a previous treatment by a person other than the author or director, if those parts are attributed to, or are likely to be regarded as the work of, the author or director.

(8) This section has effect subject to sections 81 and 82 (exceptions to and qualifications of right).

81 Exceptions to right

(1) The right conferred by section 80 (right to object to derogatory treatment of work) is subject to the following exceptions.

(2) The right does not apply to a computer program or to any computer-generated work.

(3) The right does not apply in relation to any work made for the purpose of reporting current events.

(4) The right does not apply in relation to the publication in—

    (a) a newspaper, magazine or similar periodical, or

    (b) an encyclopaedia, dictionary, yearbook or other collective work of reference,

of a literary, dramatic, musical or artistic work made for the purposes of such publication or made available with the consent of the author for the purposes of such publication. Nor does the right apply in relation to any subsequent exploitation elsewhere of such a work without any modification of the published version.

(5) The right is not infringed by an act which by virtue of section 57 or 66A (acts permitted on assumptions as to expiry of copyright etc.) would not infringe copyright.

(6) The right is not infringed by anything done for the purpose of—

    (a) avoiding the commission of an offence,

    (b) complying with a duty imposed by or under an enactment, or

(c)   in the case of the British Broadcasting Corporation, avoiding the inclusion in a programme broadcast by them of anything which offends against good taste or decency or which is likely to encourage or incite to crime or to lead to disorder or to be offensive to public feeling,

provided, where the author or director is identified at the time of the relevant act or has previously been identified in or on published copies of the work, that there is a sufficient disclaimer.

82   Qualification of right in certain cases

(1)   This section applies to—

    (a)   works in which copyright originally vested in the author's or director's employer by virtue of section 11(2) (works produced in course of employment),

    (b)   works in which Crown copyright or Parliamentary copyright subsists, and

    (c)   works in which copyright originally vested in an international organisation by virtue of section 168.

(2)   The right conferred by section 80 (right to object to derogatory treatment of work) does not apply to anything done in relation to such a work by or with the authority of the copyright owner unless the author or director—

    (a)   is identified at the time of the relevant act, or

    (b)   has previously been identified in or on published copies of the work;

and where in such a case the right does apply, it is not infringed if there is a sufficient disclaimer.

83   Infringement of right by possessing or dealing with infringing article

(1)   The right conferred by section 80 (right to object to derogatory treatment of work) is also infringed by a person who—

    (a)   possesses in the course of a business, or

    (b)   sells or lets for hire, or offers or exposes for sale or hire, or

    (c)   in the course of a business exhibits in public or distributes, or

    (d)   distributes otherwise than in the course of a business so as to affect prejudicially the honour or reputation of the author or director,

an article which is, and which he knows or has reason to believe is, an infringing article.

(2)   An "infringing article" means a work or a copy of a work which—

    (a)   has been subjected to derogatory treatment within the meaning of section 80, and

    (b)   has been or is likely to be the subject of any of the acts mentioned in that section in circumstances infringing that right.

False attribution of work

84   False attribution of work

(1)   A person has the right in the circumstances mentioned in this section—

    (a)   not to have a literary, dramatic, musical or artistic work falsely attributed to him as author, and

    (b)   not to have a film falsely attributed to him as director;

and in this section an "attribution", in relation to such a work, means a statement (express or implied) as to who is the author or director.

(2)   The right is infringed by a person who—

    (a)   issues to the public copies of a work of any of those descriptions in or on which there is a false attribution, or

    (b)   exhibits in public an artistic work, or a copy of an artistic work, in or on which there is a false attribution.

(3)   The right is also infringed by a person who—

    (a)   in the case of a literary, dramatic or musical work, performs the work in public or communicates it to the public as being the work of a person, or

    (b)   in the case of a film, shows it in public or communicates it to the public as being directed by a person,

knowing or having reason to believe that the attribution is false.

(4)   The right is also infringed by the issue to the public or public display of material containing a false attribution in connection with any of the acts mentioned in subsection (2) or (3).

(5) The right is also infringed by a person who in the course of a business—

    (a) possesses or deals with a copy of a work of any of the descriptions mentioned in subsection (1) in or on which there is a false attribution, or

    (b) in the case of an artistic work, possesses or deals with the work itself when there is a false attribution in or on it,

knowing or having reason to believe that there is such an attribution and that it is false.

(6) In the case of an artistic work the right is also infringed by a person who in the course of a business—

    (a) deals with a work which has been altered after the author parted with possession of it as being the unaltered work of the author, or

    (b) deals with a copy of such a work as being a copy of the unaltered work of the author, knowing or having reason to believe that that is not the case.

(7) References in this section to dealing are to selling or letting for hire, offering or exposing for sale or hire, exhibiting in public, or distributing.

(8) This section applies where, contrary to the fact—

    (a) a literary, dramatic or musical work is falsely represented as being an adaptation of the work of a person, or

    (b) a copy of an artistic work is falsely represented as being a copy made by the author of the artistic work,

as it applies where the work is falsely attributed to a person as author.

Right to privacy of certain photographs and films

85 Right to privacy of certain photographs and films

(1) A person who for private and domestic purposes commissions the taking of a photograph or the making of a film has, where copyright subsists in the resulting work, the right not to have—

    (a) copies of the work issued to the public,

    (b) the work exhibited or shown in public, or

    (c) the work communicated to the public;

and, except as mentioned in subsection (2), a person who does or authorises the doing of any of those acts infringes that right.

(2) The right is not infringed by an act which by virtue of any of the following provisions would not infringe copyright in the work—

    (a) section 31 (incidental inclusion of work in an artistic work, film or broadcast);

    (b) section 45 (parliamentary and judicial proceedings);

    (c) section 46 (Royal Commissions and statutory inquiries);

    (d) section 50 (acts done under statutory authority);

    (e) section 57 or 66A (acts permitted on assumptions as to expiry of copyright, etc.).

Supplementary

86 Duration of rights

(1) The rights conferred by section 77 (right to be identified as author or director), section 80 (right to object to derogatory treatment of work) and section 85 (right to privacy of certain photographs and films) continue to subsist so long as copyright subsists in the work.

(2) The right conferred by section 84 (false attribution) continues to subsist until 20 years after a person's death.

87 Consent and waiver of rights

(1) It is not an infringement of any of the rights conferred by this Chapter to do any act to which the person entitled to the right has consented.

(2) Any of those rights may be waived by instrument in writing signed by the person giving up the right.

(3) A waiver—

    (a) may relate to a specific work, to works of a specified description or to works generally, and may relate to existing or future works, and

    (b) may be conditional or unconditional and may be expressed to be subject to revocation;

and if made in favour of the owner or prospective owner of the copyright in the work or works to which it relates, it shall be presumed to extend to his licensees and successors in title unless a contrary intention is expressed.

(4) Nothing in this Chapter shall be construed as excluding the operation of the general law of contract or estoppel in relation to an informal waiver or other transaction in relation to any of the rights mentioned in subsection (1).

88   Application of provisions to joint works

(1) The right conferred by section 77 (right to be identified as author or director) is, in the case of a work of joint authorship, a right of each joint author to be identified as a joint author and must be asserted in accordance with section 78 by each joint author in relation to himself.

(2) The right conferred by section 80 (right to object to derogatory treatment of work) is, in the case of a work of joint authorship, a right of each joint author and his right is satisfied if he consents to the treatment in question.

(3) A waiver under section 87 of those rights by one joint author does not affect the rights of the other joint authors.

(4) The right conferred by section 84 (false attribution) is infringed, in the circumstances mentioned in that section—

(a) by any false statement as to the authorship of a work of joint authorship, and

(b) by the false attribution of joint authorship in relation to a work of sole authorship; and such a false attribution infringes the right of every person to whom authorship of any description is, whether rightly or wrongly, attributed.

(5) The above provisions also apply (with any necessary adaptations) in relation to a film which was, or is alleged to have been, jointly directed, as they apply to a work which is, or is alleged to be, a work of joint authorship.

A film is "jointly directed" if it is made by the collaboration of two or more directors and the contribution of each director is not distinct from that of the other director or directors.

(6) The right conferred by section 85 (right to privacy of certain photographs and films) is, in the case of a work made in pursuance of a joint commission, a right of each person who commissioned the making of the work, so that—

(a) the right of each is satisfied if he consents to the act in question, and

(b) a waiver under section 87 by one of them does not affect the rights of the others.

89   Application of provisions to parts of works

(1) The rights conferred by section 77 (right to be identified as author or director) and section 85 (right to privacy of certain photographs and films) apply in relation to the whole or any substantial part of a work.

(2) The rights conferred by section 80 (right to object to derogatory treatment of work) and section 84 (false attribution) apply in relation to the whole or any part of a work.

CHAPTER V
DEALINGS WITH RIGHTS IN COPYRIGHT WORKS

Copyright

90   Assignment and licences

(1) Copyright is transmissible by assignment, by testamentary disposition or by operation of law, as personal or moveable property.

(2) An assignment or other transmission of copyright may be partial, that is, limited so as to apply—

(a) to one or more, but not all, of the things the copyright owner has the exclusive right to do;

(b) to part, but not the whole, of the period for which the copyright is to subsist.

(3) An assignment of copyright is not effective unless it is in writing signed by or on behalf of the assignor.

(4) A licence granted by a copyright owner is binding on every successor in title to his interest in the copyright, except a purchaser in good faith for valuable consideration and without notice (actual or constructive) of the licence or a person deriving title from

such a purchaser; and references in this Part to doing anything with, or without, the licence of the copyright owner shall be construed accordingly.

91 Prospective ownership of copyright

(1) Where by an agreement made in relation to future copyright, and signed by or on behalf of the prospective owner of the copyright, the prospective owner purports to assign the future copyright (wholly or partially) to another person, then if, on the copyright coming into existence, the assignee or another person claiming under him would be entitled as against all other persons to require the copyright to be vested in him, the copyright shall vest in the assignee or his successor in title by virtue of this subsection.

(2) In this Part—

"future copyright" means copyright which will or may come into existence in respect of a future work or class of works or on the occurrence of a future event; and

"prospective owner" shall be construed accordingly, and includes a person who is prospectively entitled to copyright by virtue of such an agreement as is mentioned in subsection (1).

(3) A licence granted by a prospective owner of copyright is binding on every successor in title to his interest (or prospective interest) in the right, except a purchaser in good faith for valuable consideration and without notice (actual or constructive) of the licence or a person deriving title from such a purchaser; and references in this Part to doing anything with, or without, the licence of the copyright owner shall be construed accordingly.

92 Exclusive licences

(1) In this Part an "exclusive licence" means a licence in writing signed by or on behalf of the copyright owner authorising the licensee to the exclusion of all other persons, including the person granting the licence, to exercise a right which would otherwise be exercisable exclusively by the copyright owner.

(2) The licensee under an exclusive licence has the same rights against a successor in title who is bound by the licence as he has against the person granting the licence.

93 Copyright to pass under will with unpublished work

Where under a bequest (whether specific or general) a person is entitled, beneficially or otherwise, to—

(a) an original document or other material thing recording or embodying a literary, dramatic, musical or artistic work which was not published before the death of the testator, or

(b) an original material thing containing a sound recording or film which was not published before the death of the testator,

the bequest shall, unless a contrary intention is indicated in the testator's will or a codicil to it, be construed as including the copyright in the work in so far as the testator was the owner of the copyright immediately before his death.

93A Presumption of transfer of rental right in case of film production agreement

(1) Where an agreement concerning film production is concluded between an author and a film producer, the author shall be presumed, unless the agreement provides to the contrary, to have transferred to the film producer any rental right in relation to the film arising by virtue of the inclusion of a copy of the author's work in the film.

(2) In this section "author" means an author, or prospective author, of a literary, dramatic, musical or artistic work.

(3) Subsection (1) does not apply to any rental right in relation to the film arising by virtue of the inclusion in the film of the screenplay, the dialogue or music specifically created for and used in the film.

(4) Where this section applies, the absence of signature by or on behalf of the author does not exclude the operation of section 91(1) (effect of purported assignment of future copyright).

(5) The reference in subsection (1) to an agreement concluded between an author and a film producer includes any agreement having effect between those persons, whether made by them directly or through intermediaries.

(6)   Section 93B (right to equitable remuneration on transfer of rental right) applies where there is a presumed transfer by virtue of this section as in the case of an actual transfer.

Right to equitable remuneration where rental right transferred

93B   Right to equitable remuneration where rental right transferred

(1)   Where an author to whom this section applies has transferred his rental right concerning a sound recording or a film to the producer of the sound recording or film, he retains the right to equitable remuneration for the rental.
The authors to whom this section applies are—
(a)   the author of a literary, dramatic, musical or artistic work, and
(b)   the principal director of a film.

(2)   The right to equitable remuneration under this section may not be assigned by the author except to a collecting society for the purpose of enabling it to enforce the right on his behalf.
The right is, however, transmissible by testamentary disposition or by operation of law as personal or moveable property; and it may be assigned or further transmitted by any person into whose hands it passes.

(3)   Equitable remuneration under this section is payable by the person for the time being entitled to the rental right, that is, the person to whom the right was transferred or any successor in title of his.

(4)   The amount payable by way of equitable remuneration is as agreed by or on behalf of the persons by and to whom it is payable, subject to section 93C (reference of amount to Copyright Tribunal).

(5)   An agreement is of no effect in so far as it purports to exclude or restrict the right to equitable remuneration under this section.

(6)   References in this section to the transfer of rental right by one person to another include any arrangement having that effect, whether made by them directly or through intermediaries.

(7)   In this section a "collecting society" means a society or other organisation which has as its main object, or one of its main objects, the exercise of the right to equitable remuneration under this section on behalf of more than one author.

93C   Equitable remuneration: reference of amount to Copyright Tribunal

(1)   In default of agreement as to the amount payable by way of equitable remuneration under section 93B, the person by or to whom it is payable may apply to the Copyright Tribunal to determine the amount payable.

(2)   A person to or by whom equitable remuneration is payable under that section may also apply to the Copyright Tribunal—
(a)   to vary any agreement as to the amount payable, or
(b)   to vary any previous determination of the Tribunal as to that matter;
but except with the special leave of the Tribunal no such application may be made within twelve months from the date of a previous determination.
An order made on an application under this subsection has effect from the date on which it is made or such later date as may be specified by the Tribunal.

(3)   On an application under this section the Tribunal shall consider the matter and make such order as to the method of calculating and paying equitable remuneration as it may determine to be reasonable in the circumstances, taking into account the importance of the contribution of the author to the film or sound recording.

(4)   Remuneration shall not be considered inequitable merely because it was paid by way of a single payment or at the time of the transfer of the rental right.

(5)   An agreement is of no effect in so far as it purports to prevent a person questioning the amount of equitable remuneration or to restrict the powers of the Copyright Tribunal under this section.

Moral rights

94   Moral rights not assignable

The rights conferred by Chapter IV (moral rights) are not assignable.

95   Transmission of moral rights on death

(1)   On the death of a person entitled to the right conferred by section 77 (right to identification of author or director), section 80 (right to object to derogatory treatment of work) or section 85 (right to privacy of certain photographs and films)—

    (a)   the right passes to such person as he may by testamentary disposition specifically direct,

    (b)   if there is no such direction but the copyright in the work in question forms part of his estate, the right passes to the person to whom the copyright passes, and

    (c)   if or to the extent that the right does not pass under paragraph (a) or (b) it is exercisable by his personal representatives.

(2)   Where copyright forming part of a person's estate passes in part to one person and in part to another, as for example where a bequest is limited so as to apply—

    (a)   to one or more, but not all, of the things the copyright owner has the exclusive right to do or authorise, or

    (b)   to part, but not the whole, of the period for which the copyright is to subsist,

    any right which passes with the copyright by virtue of subsection (1) is correspondingly divided.

(3)   Where by virtue of subsection (1)(a) or (b) a right becomes exercisable by more than one person—

    (a)   it may, in the case of the right conferred by section 77 (right to identification of author or director), be asserted by any of them;

    (b)   it is, in the case of the right conferred by section 80 (right to object to derogatory treatment of work) or section 85 (right to privacy of certain photographs and films), a right exercisable by each of them and is satisfied in relation to any of them if he consents to the treatment or act in question; and

    (c)   any waiver of the right in accordance with section 87 by one of them does not affect the rights of the others.

(4)   A consent or waiver previously given or made binds any person to whom a right passes by virtue of subsection (1).

(5)   Any infringement after a person's death of the right conferred by section 84 (false attribution) is actionable by his personal representatives.

(6)   Any damages recovered by personal representatives by virtue of this section in respect of an infringement after a person's death shall devolve as part of his estate as if the right of action had subsisted and been vested in him immediately before his death.

CHAPTER VI
REMEDIES FOR INFRINGEMENT

Rights and remedies of copyright owner

96   Infringement actionable by copyright owner

(1)   An infringement of copyright is actionable by the copyright owner.

(2)   In an action for infringement of copyright all such relief by way of damages, injunctions, accounts or otherwise is available to the plaintiff as is available in respect of the infringement of any other property right.

(3)   This section has effect subject to the following provisions of this Chapter.

97   Provisions as to damages in infringement action

(1)   Where in an action for infringement of copyright it is shown that at the time of the infringement the defendant did not know, and had no reason to believe, that copyright subsisted in the work to which the action relates, the plaintiff is not entitled to damages against him, but without prejudice to any other remedy.

(2)   The court may in an action for infringement of copyright having regard to all the circumstances, and in particular to—

    (a)   the flagrancy of the infringement, and

    (b)   any benefit accruing to the defendant by reason of the infringement,

    award such additional damages as the justice of the case may require.

97A   Injunctions against service providers

(1) The High Court (in Scotland, the Court of Session) shall have power to grant an injunction against a service provider, where that service provider has actual knowledge of another person using their service to infringe copyright.

(2) In determining whether a service provider has actual knowledge for the purpose of this section, a court shall take into account all matters which appear to it in the particular circumstances to be relevant and, amongst other things, shall have regard to—

    (a) whether a service provider has received a notice through a means of contact made available in accordance with regulation 6(1)(c) of the Electronic Commerce (EC Directive) Regulations 2002; and

    (b) the extent to which any notice includes—

        (i) the full name and address of the sender of the notice;

        (ii) details of the infringement in question.

(3) In this section "service provider" has the meaning given to it by regulation 2 of the Electronic Commerce (EC Directive) Regulations 2002.

98   Undertaking to take licence of right in infringement proceedings

(1) If in proceedings for infringement of copyright in respect of which a licence is available as of right under section 144 (powers exercisable in consequence of report of Competition and Markets Authority) the defendant undertakes to take a licence on such terms as may be agreed or, in default of agreement, settled by the Copyright Tribunal under that section—

    (a) no injunction shall be granted against him,

    (b) no order for delivery up shall be made under section 99, and

    (c) the amount recoverable against him by way of damages or on an account of profits shall not exceed double the amount which would have been payable by him as licensee if such a licence on those terms had been granted before the earliest infringement.

(2) An undertaking may be given at any time before final order in the proceedings, without any admission of liability.

(3) Nothing in this section affects the remedies available in respect of an infringement committed before licences of right were available.

99   Order for delivery up

(1) Where a person—

    (a) has an infringing copy of a work in his possession, custody or control in the course of a business, or

    (b) has in his possession, custody or control an article specifically designed or adapted for making copies of a particular copyright work, knowing or having reason to believe that it has been or is to be used to make infringing copies,

the owner of the copyright in the work may apply to the court for an order that the infringing copy or article be delivered up to him or to such other person as the court may direct.

(2) An application shall not be made after the end of the period specified in section 113 (period after which remedy of delivery up not available); and no order shall be made unless the court also makes, or it appears to the court that there are grounds for making, an order under section 114 (order as to disposal of infringing copy or other article).

(3) A person to whom an infringing copy or other article is delivered up in pursuance of an order under this section shall, if an order under section 114 is not made, retain it pending the making of an order, or the decision not to make an order, under that section.

(4) Nothing in this section affects any other power of the court.

100   Right to seize infringing copies and other articles

(1) An infringing copy of a work which is found exposed or otherwise immediately available for sale or hire, and in respect of which the copyright owner would be entitled to apply for an order under section 99, may be seized and detained by him or a person authorised by him.

The right to seize and detain is exercisable subject to the following conditions and is subject to any decision of the court under section 114.

(2) Before anything is seized under this section notice of the time and place of the proposed seizure must be given to a local police station.

(3) A person may for the purpose of exercising the right conferred by this section enter premises to which the public have access but may not seize anything in the possession, custody or control of a person at a permanent or regular place of business of his, and may not use any force.

(4) At the time when anything is seized under this section there shall be left at the place where it was seized a notice in the prescribed form containing the prescribed particulars as to the person by whom or on whose authority the seizure is made and the grounds on which it is made.

(5) In this section—
"premises" includes land, buildings, moveable structures, vehicles, vessels, aircraft and hovercraft; and "prescribed" means prescribed by order of the Secretary of State.

(6) An order of the Secretary of State under this section shall be made by statutory instrument which shall be subject to annulment in pursuance of a resolution of either House of Parliament.

Rights and remedies of exclusive licensee

101 Rights and remedies of exclusive licensee

(1) An exclusive licensee has, except against the copyright owner, the same rights and remedies in respect of matters occurring after the grant of the licence as if the licence had been an assignment.

(2) His rights and remedies are concurrent with those of the copyright owner; and references in the relevant provisions of this Part to the copyright owner shall be construed accordingly.

(3) In an action brought by an exclusive licensee by virtue of this section a defendant may avail himself of any defence which would have been available to him if the action had been brought by the copyright owner.

101A Certain infringements actionable by a non-exclusive licensee

(1) A non-exclusive licensee may bring an action for infringement of copyright if—
   (a) the infringing act was directly connected to a prior licensed act of the licensee; and
   (b) the licence—
      (i) is in writing and is signed by or on behalf of the copyright owner; and
      (ii) expressly grants the non-exclusive licensee a right of action under this section.

(2) In an action brought under this section, the non-exclusive licensee shall have the same rights and remedies available to him as the copyright owner would have had if he had brought the action.

(3) The rights granted under this section are concurrent with those of the copyright owner and references in the relevant provisions of this Part to the copyright owner shall be construed accordingly.

(4) In an action brought by a non-exclusive licensee by virtue of this section a defendant may avail himself of any defence which would have been available to him if the action had been brought by the copyright owner.

(5) Subsections (1) to (4) of section 102 shall apply to a non-exclusive licensee who has a right of action by virtue of this section as it applies to an exclusive licensee.

(6) In this section a "non-exclusive licensee" means the holder of a licence authorising the licensee to exercise a right which remains exercisable by the copyright owner.

102 Exercise of concurrent rights

(1) Where an action for infringement of copyright brought by the copyright owner or an exclusive licensee relates (wholly or partly) to an infringement in respect of which they have concurrent rights of action, the copyright owner or, as the case may be, the exclusive licensee may not, without the leave of the court, proceed with the action unless the other is either joined as a plaintiff or added as a defendant.

(2)   A copyright owner or exclusive licensee who is added as a defendant in pursuance of subsection (1) is not liable for any costs in the action unless he takes part in the proceedings.

(3)   The above provisions do not affect the granting of interlocutory relief on an application by a copyright owner or exclusive licensee alone.

(4)   Where an action for infringement of copyright is brought which relates (wholly or partly) to an infringement in respect of which the copyright owner and an exclusive licensee have or had concurrent rights of action—

     (a)   the court shall in assessing damages take into account—

         (i)   the terms of the licence, and

         (ii)   any pecuniary remedy already awarded or available to either of them in respect of the infringement;

     (b)   no account of profits shall be directed if an award of damages has been made, or an account of profits has been directed, in favour of the other of them in respect of the infringement; and

     (c)   the court shall if an account of profits is directed apportion the profits between them as the court considers just, subject to any agreement between them;

   and these provisions apply whether or not the copyright owner and the exclusive licensee are both parties to the action.

(5)   The copyright owner shall notify any exclusive licensee having concurrent rights before applying for an order under section 99 (order for delivery up) or exercising the right conferred by section 100 (right of seizure); and the court may on the application of the licensee make such order under section 99 or, as the case may be, prohibiting or permitting the exercise by the copyright owner of the right conferred by section 100, as it thinks fit having regard to the terms of the licence.

Remedies for infringement of moral rights

103   Remedies for infringement of moral rights

(1)   An infringement of a right conferred by Chapter IV (moral rights) is actionable as a breach of statutory duty owed to the person entitled to the right.

(2)   In proceedings for infringement of the right conferred by section 80 (right to object to derogatory treatment of work) the court may, if it thinks it is an adequate remedy in the circumstances, grant an injunction on terms prohibiting the doing of any act unless a disclaimer is made, in such terms and in such manner as may be approved by the court, dissociating the author or director from the treatment of the work.

Presumptions

104   Presumptions relevant to literary, dramatic, musical and artistic works

(1)   The following presumptions apply in proceedings brought by virtue of this Chapter with respect to a literary, dramatic, musical or artistic work.

(2)   Where a name purporting to be that of the author appeared on copies of the work as published or on the work when it was made, the person whose name appeared shall be presumed, until the contrary is proved—

     (a)   to be the author of the work;

     (b)   to have made it in circumstances not falling within section 11(2), 163, 165 or 168 (works produced in course of employment, Crown copyright, Parliamentary copyright or copyright of certain international organisations).

(3)   In the case of a work alleged to be a work of joint authorship, subsection (2) applies in relation to each person alleged to be one of the authors.

(4)   Where no name purporting to be that of the author appeared as mentioned in subsection (2) but—

     (a)   the work qualifies for copyright protection by virtue of section 155 (qualification by reference to country of first publication), and

     (b)   a name purporting to be that of the publisher appeared on copies of the work as first published,

   the person whose name appeared shall be presumed, until the contrary is proved, to have been the owner of the copyright at the time of publication.

(5) If the author of the work is dead or the identity of the author cannot be ascertained by reasonable inquiry, it shall be presumed, in the absence of evidence to the contrary —

    (a) that the work is an original work, and

    (b) that the plaintiff's allegations as to what was the first publication of the work and as to the country of first publication are correct.

105 Presumptions relevant to sound recordings and films

(1) In proceedings brought by virtue of this Chapter with respect to a sound recording, where copies of the recording as issued to the public bear a label or other mark stating —

    (a) that a named person was the owner of copyright in the recording at the date of issue of the copies, or

    (b) that the recording was first published in a specified year or in a specified country,

the label or mark shall be admissible as evidence of the facts stated and shall be presumed to be correct until the contrary is proved.

(2) In proceedings brought by virtue of this Chapter with respect to a film, where copies of the film as issued to the public bear a statement —

    (a) that a named person was the director or producer of the film,

    (aa) that a named person was the principal director, the author of the screenplay, the author of the dialogue or the composer of music specifically created for and used in the film,

    (b) that a named person was the owner of copyright in the film at the date of issue of the copies, or

    (c) that the film was first published in a specified year or in a specified country,

the statement shall be admissible as evidence of the facts stated and shall be presumed to be correct until the contrary is proved.

(3) In proceedings brought by virtue of this Chapter with respect to a computer program, where copies of the program are issued to the public in electronic form bearing a statement —

    (a) that a named person was the owner of copyright in the program at the date of issue of the copies, or

    (b) that the program was first published in a specified country or that copies of it were first issued to the public in electronic form in a specified year,

the statement shall be admissible as evidence of the facts stated and shall be presumed to be correct until the contrary is proved.

(4) The above presumptions apply equally in proceedings relating to an infringement alleged to have occurred before the date on which the copies were issued to the public.

(5) In proceedings brought by virtue of this Chapter with respect to a film, where the film as shown in public, or communicated to the public bears a statement —

    (a) that a named person was the director or producer of the film, or

    (aa) that a named person was the principal director of the film, the author of the screenplay, the author of the dialogue or the composer of music specifically created for and used in the film, or,

    (b) that a named person was the owner of copyright in the film immediately after it was made,

the statement shall be admissible as evidence of the facts stated and shall be presumed to be correct until the contrary is proved.

This presumption applies equally in proceedings relating to an infringement alleged to have occurred before the date on which the film was shown in public or communicated to the public.

(6) For the purposes of this section, a statement that a person was the director of a film shall be taken, unless a contrary indication appears, as meaning that he was the principal director of the film.

106 Presumptions relevant to works subject to Crown copyright

In proceedings brought by virtue of this Chapter with respect to a literary, dramatic or musical work in which Crown copyright subsists, where there appears on printed copies of the work a statement of the year in which the work was first published commercially, that statement shall be admissible as evidence of the fact stated and shall be presumed to be correct in the absence of evidence to the contrary.

Offences

107   Criminal liability for making or dealing with infringing articles, etc.

(1)   A person commits an offence who, without the licence of the copyright owner—

    (a)   makes for sale or hire, or

    (b)   imports into the United Kingdom otherwise than for his private and domestic use, or

    (c)   possesses in the course of a business with a view to committing any act infringing the copyright, or

    (d)   in the course of a business—

        (i)   sells or lets for hire, or

        (ii)   offers or exposes for sale or hire, or

        (iii)   exhibits in public, or

        (iv)   distributes, or

    (e)   distributes otherwise than in the course of a business to such an extent as to affect prejudicially the owner of the copyright,

an article which is, and which he knows or has reason to believe is, an infringing copy of a copyright work.

(2)   A person commits an offence who—

    (a)   makes an article specifically designed or adapted for making copies of a particular copyright work, or

    (b)   has such an article in his possession,

knowing or having reason to believe that it is to be used to make infringing copies for sale or hire or for use in the course of a business.

(2A)   A person ("P") who infringes copyright in a work by communicating the work to the public commits an offence if P—

    (a)   knows or has reason to believe that P is infringing copyright in the work, and

    (b)   either—

        (i)   intends to make a gain for P or another person, or

        (ii)   knows or has reason to believe that communicating the work to the public will cause loss to the owner of the copyright, or will expose the owner of the copyright to a risk of loss.

(2B)   For the purposes of subsection (2A)—

    (a)   "gain" and "loss"—

        (i)   extend only to gain or loss in money, and

        (ii)   include any such gain or loss whether temporary or permanent, and

    (b)   "loss" includes a loss by not getting what one might get.

(3)   Where copyright is infringed (otherwise than by reception of a communication to the public)—

    (a)   by the public performance of a literary, dramatic or musical work, or

    (b)   by the playing or showing in public of a sound recording or film,

any person who caused the work to be so performed, played or shown is guilty of an offence if he knew or had reason to believe that copyright would be infringed.

(4)   A person guilty of an offence under subsection (1)(a), (b), (d)(iv) or (e) is liable—

    (a)   on summary conviction to imprisonment for a term not exceeding six months or a fine, or both;

    (b)   on conviction on indictment to a fine or imprisonment for a term not exceeding ten years, or both.

(4A)   A person guilty of an offence under subsection (2A) is liable—

    (a)   on summary conviction to imprisonment for a term not exceeding three months or a fine, or both;

    (b)   on conviction on indictment to a fine or imprisonment for a term not exceeding ten years, or both.

(5)   A person guilty of any other offence under this section is liable on summary conviction to imprisonment for a term not exceeding three months or a fine not exceeding level 5 on the standard scale, or both.

(6)   Sections 104 to 106 (presumptions as to various matters connected with copyright) do not apply to proceedings for an offence under this section; but without prejudice to their application in proceedings for an order under section 108 below.

107A Enforcement by local weights and measures authority

(1) It is the duty of every local weights and measures authority to enforce within their area the provisions of section 107.

(3) Subsection (1) above does not apply in relation to the enforcement of section 107 in Northern Ireland, but it is the duty of the Department of Economic Development to enforce that section in Northern Ireland.

(3A) For the investigatory powers available to a local weights and measures authority or the Department of Enterprise, Trade and Investment in Northern Ireland for the purposes of the duties in this section, see Schedule 5 to the Consumer Rights Act 2015.

(4) Any enactment which authorises the disclosure of information for the purpose of facilitating the enforcement of the Trade Descriptions Act 1968 shall apply as if section 107 were contained in that Act and as if the functions of any person in relation to the enforcement of that section were functions under that Act.

(5) Nothing in this section shall be construed as authorising a local weights and measures authority to bring proceedings in Scotland for an offence.

108 Order for delivery up in criminal proceedings

(1) The court before which proceedings are brought against a person for an offence under section 107 may, if satisfied that at the time of his arrest or charge—

(a) he had in his possession, custody or control in the course of a business an infringing copy of a copyright work, or

(b) he had in his possession, custody or control an article specifically designed or adapted for making copies of a particular copyright work, knowing or having reason to believe that it had been or was to be used to make infringing copies,

order that the infringing copy or article be delivered up to the copyright owner or to such other person as the court may direct.

. . .

(3) An order may be made by the court of its own motion or on the application of the prosecutor (or, in Scotland, the Lord Advocate or procurator-fiscal), and may be made whether or not the person is convicted of the offence, but shall not be made—

(a) after the end of the period specified in section 113 (period after which remedy of delivery up not available), or

(b) if it appears to the court unlikely that any order will be made under section 114 (order as to disposal of infringing copy or other article).

(4) An appeal lies from an order made under this section by a magistrates' court—

(a) in England and Wales, to the Crown Court, and

(b) in Northern Ireland, to the county court;

and in Scotland, where an order has been made under this section, the person from whose possession, custody or control the infringing copy or article has been removed may, without prejudice to any other form of appeal under any rule of law, appeal against that order in the same manner as against sentence.

(5) A person to whom an infringing copy or other article is delivered up in pursuance of an order under this section shall retain it pending the making of an order, or the decision not to make an order, under section 114.

(6) Nothing in this section affects the powers of the court under section 143 of the Powers of Criminal Courts (Sentencing) Act 2000, Part II of the Proceeds of Crime (Scotland) Act 1995 or Article 11 of the Criminal Justice (Northern Ireland) Order 1994 (general provisions as to forfeiture in criminal proceedings).

109 Search warrants

(1) Where a justice of the peace (in Scotland, a sheriff or justice of the peace) is satisfied by information on oath given by a constable (in Scotland, by evidence on oath) that there are reasonable grounds for believing—

(a) that an offence under section 107(1), (2) or (2A) has been or is about to be committed in any premises, and

(b) that evidence that such an offence has been or is about to be committed is in those premises,

he may issue a warrant authorising a constable to enter and search the premises, using such reasonable force as is necessary.

(2)   The power conferred by subsection (1) does not, in England and Wales, extend to authorising a search for material of the kinds mentioned in section 9(2) of the Police and Criminal Evidence Act 1984 (certain classes of personal or confidential material).

(3)   A warrant under this section—
  (a)   may authorise persons to accompany any constable executing the warrant, and
  (b)   remains in force for three months from the date of its issue.

(4)   In executing a warrant issued under this section a constable may seize an article if he reasonably believes that it is evidence that any offence under section 107(1), (2) or (2A) has been or is about to be committed.

(5)   In this section "premises" includes land, buildings, fixed or moveable structures, vehicles, vessels, aircraft and hovercraft.

110   Offence by body corporate: liability of officers

(1)   Where an offence under section 107 committed by a body corporate is proved to have been committed with the consent or connivance of a director, manager, secretary or other similar officer of the body, or a person purporting to act in any such capacity, he as well as the body corporate is guilty of the offence and liable to be proceeded against and punished accordingly.

(2)   In relation to a body corporate whose affairs are managed by its members "director" means a member of the body corporate.

Provision for preventing importation of infringing copies

111   Infringing copies may be treated as prohibited goods

(1)   The owner of the copyright in a published literary, dramatic or musical work may give notice in writing to the Commissioners of Customs and Excise—
  (a)   that he is the owner of the copyright in the work, and
  (b)   that he requests the Commissioners, for a period specified in the notice, to treat as prohibited goods printed copies of the work which are infringing copies.

(2)   The period specified in a notice under subsection (1) shall not exceed five years and shall not extend beyond the period for which copyright is to subsist.

(3)   The owner of the copyright in a sound recording or film may give notice in writing to the Commissioners of Customs and Excise—
  (a)   that he is the owner of the copyright in the work,
  (b)   that infringing copies of the work are expected to arrive in the United Kingdom at a time and a place specified in the notice, and
  (c)   that he requests the Commissioners to treat the copies as prohibited goods.

(3A)   The Commissioners may treat as prohibited goods only infringing copies of works which arrive in the United Kingdom—
  (a)   from outside the European Economic Area, or
  (b)   from within that Area but not having been entered for free circulation.

(3B)   This section does not apply to goods placed in, or expected to be placed in, one of the situations referred to in Article 1(1), in respect of which an application may be made under Article 5(1), of Council Regulation (EC) No 1383/2003 concerning customs action against goods suspected of infringing certain intellectual property rights and the measures to be taken against goods found to have infringed such rights.

(4)   When a notice is in force under this section the importation of goods to which the notice relates, otherwise than by a person for his private and domestic use, is prohibited; but a person is not by reason of the prohibition liable to any penalty other than forfeiture of the goods.

112   Power of Commissioners of Customs and Excise to make regulations

(1)   The Commissioners of Customs and Excise may make regulations prescribing the form in which notice is to be given under section 111 and requiring a person giving notice—
  (a)   to furnish the Commissioners with such evidence as may be specified in the regulations, either on giving notice or when the goods are imported, or at both those times, and
  (b)   to comply with such other conditions as may be specified in the regulations.

. . .

Supplementary

113   Period after which remedy of delivery up not available

(1)   An application for an order under section 99 (order for delivery up in civil proceedings) may not be made after the end of the period of six years from the date on which the infringing copy or article in question was made, subject to the following provisions.

(2)   If during the whole or any part of that period the copyright owner—
 (a)   is under a disability, or (b) is prevented by fraud or concealment from discovering the facts entitling him to apply for an order,
an application may be made at any time before the end of the period of six years from the date on which he ceased to be under a disability or, as the case may be, could with reasonable diligence have discovered those facts.

. . .

(4)   An order under section 108 (order for delivery up in criminal proceedings) shall not, in any case, be made after the end of the period of six years from the date on which the infringing copy or article in question was made.

114   Order as to disposal of infringing copy or other article

(1)   An application may be made to the court for an order that an infringing copy or other article delivered up in pursuance of an order under section 99 or 108, or seized and detained in pursuance of the right conferred by section 100, shall be—
 (a)   forfeited to the copyright owner, or
 (b)   destroyed or otherwise dealt with as the court may think fit,
or for a decision that no such order should be made.

(2)   In considering what order (if any) should be made, the court shall consider whether other remedies available in an action for infringement of copyright would be adequate to compensate the copyright owner and to protect his interests.

(3)   Provision shall be made by rules of court as to the service of notice on persons having an interest in the copy or other articles, and any such person is entitled—
 (a)   to appear in proceedings for an order under this section, whether or not he was served with notice, and
 (b)   to appeal against any order made, whether or not he appeared;
and an order shall not take effect until the end of the period within which notice of an appeal may be given or, if before the end of that period notice of appeal is duly given, until the final determination or abandonment of the proceedings on the appeal.

(4)   Where there is more than one person interested in a copy or other article, the court shall make such order as it thinks just and may (in particular) direct that the article be sold, or otherwise dealt with, and the proceeds divided.

(5)   If the court decides that no order should be made under this section, the person in whose possession, custody or control the copy or other article was before being delivered up or seized is entitled to its return.

(6)   References in this section to a person having an interest in a copy or other article include any person in whose favour an order could be made in respect of it—
 (a)   under this section or under section 204 or 231 of this Act;
 (b)   under section 24D of the Registered Designs Act 1949;
 (c)   under section 19 of Trade Marks Act 1994 (including that section as applied by regulation 4 of the Community Trade Mark Regulations 2006; or
 (d)   under regulation 1C of the Community Design Regulations 2005.

114A Forfeiture of infringing copies, etc.: England and Wales or Northern Ireland

(1)   In England and Wales or Northern Ireland where there have come into the possession of any person in connection with the investigation or prosecution of a relevant offence—
 (a)   infringing copies of a copyright work, or
 (b)   articles specifically designed or adapted for making copies of a particular copyright work,
that person may apply under this section for an order for the forfeiture of the infringing copies or articles.

(2) For the purposes of this section "relevant offence" means—

    (a) an offence under section 107(1), (2) or (2A) (criminal liability for making or dealing with infringing articles, etc),

    (b) an offence under the Trade Descriptions Act 1968,

    (ba) an offence under the Business Protection from Misleading Marketing Regulations 2008,

    (bb) an offence under the Consumer Protection from Unfair Trading Regulations 2008, or

    (c) an offence involving dishonesty or deception.

(3) An application under this section may be made—

    (a) where proceedings have been brought in any court for a relevant offence relating to some or all of the infringing copies or articles, to that court, or

    (b) where no application for the forfeiture of the infringing copies or articles has been made under paragraph (a), by way of complaint to a magistrates' court.

(4) On an application under this section, the court shall make an order for the forfeiture of any infringing copies or articles only if it is satisfied that a relevant offence has been committed in relation to the infringing copies or articles.

(5) A court may infer for the purposes of this section that such an offence has been committed in relation to any infringing copies or articles if it is satisfied that such an offence has been committed in relation to infringing copies or articles which are representative of the infringing copies or articles in question (whether by reason of being of the same design or part of the same consignment or batch or otherwise).

(6) Any person aggrieved by an order made under this section by a magistrates' court, or by a decision of such a court not to make such an order, may appeal against that order or decision—

    (a) in England and Wales, to the Crown Court, or

    (b) in Northern Ireland, to the county court.

(7) An order under this section may contain such provision as appears to the court to be appropriate for delaying the coming into force of the order pending the making and determination of any appeal (including any application under section 111 of the Magistrates' Courts Act 1980 or Article 146 of the Magistrates' Courts (Northern Ireland) Order 1981 (statement of case)).

(8) Subject to subsection (9), where any infringing copies or articles are forfeited under this section they shall be destroyed in accordance with such directions as the court may give.

(9) On making an order under this section the court may direct that the infringing copies or articles to which the order relates shall (instead of being destroyed) be forfeited to the owner of the copyright in question or dealt with in such other way as the court considers appropriate.

114B Forfeiture of infringing copies, etc.: Scotland

(1) In Scotland the court may make an order under this section for the forfeiture of any—

    (a) infringing copies of a copyright work, or

    (b) articles specifically designed or adapted for making copies of a particular copyright work.

(2) An order under this section may be made—

    (a) on an application by the procurator-fiscal made in the manner specified in section 134 of the Criminal Procedure (Scotland) Act 1995, or

    (b) where a person is convicted of a relevant offence, in addition to any other penalty which the court may impose.

(3) On an application under subsection (2)(a), the court shall make an order for the forfeiture of any infringing copies or articles only if it is satisfied that a relevant offence has been committed in relation to the infringing copies or articles.

(4) The court may infer for the purposes of this section that such an offence has been committed in relation to any infringing copies or articles if it is satisfied that such an offence has been committed in relation to infringing copies or articles which are representative of the infringing copies or articles in question (whether by reason of being of the same design or part of the same consignment or batch or otherwise).

(5) The procurator-fiscal making the application under subsection (2)(a) shall serve on any person appearing to him to be the owner of, or otherwise to have an interest in, the infringing copies or articles to which the application relates a copy of the application, together with a notice giving him the opportunity to appear at the hearing of the application to show cause why the infringing copies or articles should not be forfeited.

(6) Service under subsection (5) shall be carried out, and such service may be proved, in the manner specified for citation of an accused in summary proceedings under the Criminal Procedure (Scotland) Act 1995.

(7) Any person upon whom notice is served under subsection (5) and any other person claiming to be the owner of, or otherwise to have an interest in, infringing copies or articles to which an application under this section relates shall be entitled to appear at the hearing of the application to show cause why the infringing copies or articles should not be forfeited.

(8) The court shall not make an order following an application under subsection (2)(a)—
  (a) if any person on whom notice is served under subsection (5) does not appear, unless service of the notice on that person is proved, or
  (b) if no notice under subsection (5) has been served, unless the court is satisfied that in the circumstances it was reasonable not to serve such notice.

(9) Where an order for the forfeiture of any infringing copies or articles is made following an application under subsection (2)(a), any person who appeared, or was entitled to appear, to show cause why infringing copies or articles should not be forfeited may, within 21 days of the making of the order, appeal to the High Court by Bill of Suspension.

(10) Section 182(5)(a) to (e) of the Criminal Procedure (Scotland) Act 1995 shall apply to an appeal under subsection (9) as it applies to a stated case under Part 2 of that Act.

(11) An order following an application under subsection (2)(a) shall not take effect—
  (a) until the end of the period of 21 days beginning with the day after the day on which the order is made, or
  (b) if an appeal is made under subsection (9) above within that period, until the appeal is determined or abandoned.

(12) An order under subsection (2)(b) shall not take effect—
  (a) until the end of the period within which an appeal against the order could be brought under the Criminal Procedure (Scotland) Act 1995, or
  (b) if an appeal is made within that period, until the appeal is determined or abandoned.

(13) Subject to subsection (14), infringing copies or articles forfeited under this section shall be destroyed in accordance with such directions as the court may give.

(14) On making an order under this section the court may direct that the infringing copies or articles to which the order relates shall (instead of being destroyed) be forfeited to the owner of the copyright in question or dealt with in such other way as the court considers appropriate.

(15) For the purposes of this section—
  "relevant offence" means—
  (a) an offence under section 107(1), (2) or (2A) (criminal liability for making or dealing with infringing articles, etc),
  (b) an offence under the Trade Descriptions Act 1968,
  (c) an offence under the Business Protection from Misleading Marketing Regulations 2008,
  (d) an offence under the Consumer Protection from Unfair Trading Regulations 2008, or
  (e) any offence involving dishonesty or deception;
  "the court" means—
  (a) in relation to an order made on an application under subsection (2)(a), the sheriff, and
  (b) in relation to an order made under subsection (2)(b), the court which imposed the penalty.

115   Jurisdiction of county court and sheriff court

(1)   In England and Wales the county court and in Northern Ireland a county court may entertain proceedings under—

section 99 (order for delivery up of infringing copy or other article),

section 102(5) (order as to exercise of rights by copyright owner where exclusive licensee has concurrent rights), or

section 114 (order as to disposal of infringing copy or other article),

save that, in Northern Ireland, a county court may entertain such proceedings only where the value of the infringing copies and other articles in question does not exceed the county court limit for actions in tort.

(2)   In Scotland proceedings for an order under any of those provisions may be brought in the sheriff court.

(3)   Nothing in this section shall be construed as affecting the jurisdiction of the High Court or, in Scotland, the Court of Session.

CHAPTER VII
COPYRIGHT LICENSING

Licensing schemes and licensing bodies

116   Licensing schemes and licensing bodies

(1)   In this Part a "licensing scheme" means a scheme setting out—

   (a)   the classes of case in which the operator of the scheme, or the person on whose behalf he acts, is willing to grant copyright licences, and

   (b)   the terms on which licences would be granted in those classes of case;

and for this purpose a "scheme" includes anything in the nature of a scheme, whether described as a scheme or as a tariff or by any other name.

(2)   In this Chapter a "licensing body" means—

   (a)   a society or other organisation which has as its main object, or one of its main objects, the negotiation or granting, either as owner or prospective owner of copyright or as agent for him, of copyright licences, and whose objects include the granting of licences covering works of more than one author, or

   (b)   any other organisation which is a collective management organisation as defined by regulation 2 of the Collective Management of Copyright (EU Directive) Regulations 2016.

(3)   In this section "copyright licences" means licences to do, or authorise the doing of, any of the acts restricted by copyright.

(4)   References in this Chapter to licences or licensing schemes covering works of more than one author do not include licences or schemes covering only—

   (a)   a single collective work or collective works of which the authors are the same, or

   (b)   works made by, or by employees of or commissioned by, a single individual, firm, company or group of companies.

For this purpose a group of companies means a holding company and its subsidiaries, within the meaning of section 1159 of the Companies Act 2006.

(5)   Schedule A1 confers powers to provide for the regulation of licensing bodies.

Orphan works licensing and extended collective licensing

116A Power to provide for licensing of orphan works

(1)   The Secretary of State may by regulations provide for the grant of licences in respect of works that qualify as orphan works under the regulations.

(2)   The regulations may—

   (a)   specify a person or a description of persons authorised to grant licences, or

   (b)   provide for a person designated in the regulations to specify a person or a description of persons authorised to grant licences.

(3)   The regulations must provide that, for a work to qualify as an orphan work, it is a requirement that the owner of copyright in it has not been found after a diligent search made in accordance with the regulations.

(4) The regulations may provide for the granting of licences to do, or authorise the doing of, any act restricted by copyright that would otherwise require the consent of the missing owner.

(5) The regulations must provide for any licence—
  (a) to have effect as if granted by the missing owner;
  (b) not to give exclusive rights;
  (c) not to be granted to a person authorised to grant licences.

(6) The regulations may apply to a work although it is not known whether copyright subsists in it, and references to a missing owner and a right or interest of a missing owner are to be read as including references to a supposed owner and a supposed right or interest.

116B Extended collective licensing

(1) The Secretary of State may by regulations provide for a licensing body that applies to the Secretary of State under the regulations to be authorised to grant copyright licences in respect of works in which copyright is not owned by the body or a person on whose behalf the body acts.

(2) An authorisation must specify—
  (a) the types of work to which it applies, and
  (b) the acts restricted by copyright that the licensing body is authorised to license.

(3) The regulations must provide for the copyright owner to have a right to limit or exclude the grant of licences by virtue of the regulations.

(4) The regulations must provide for any licence not to give exclusive rights.

(5) In this section "copyright licences" has the same meaning as in section 116.

(6) Nothing in this section applies in relation to Crown copyright or Parliamentary copyright.

116C General provision about licensing under sections 116A and 116B

(1) This section and section 116D apply to regulations under sections 116A and 116B.

(2) The regulations may provide for a body to be or remain authorised to grant licences only if specified requirements are met, and for a question whether they are met to be determined by a person, and in a manner, specified in the regulations.

(3) The regulations may specify other matters to be taken into account in any decision to be made under the regulations as to whether to authorise a person to grant licences.

(4) The regulations must provide for the treatment of any royalties or other sums paid in respect of a licence, including—
  (a) the deduction of administrative costs;
  (b) the period for which sums must be held;
  (c) the treatment of sums after that period (as bona vacantia or otherwise).

(5) The regulations must provide for circumstances in which an authorisation to grant licences may be withdrawn, and for determining the rights and obligations of any person if an authorisation is withdrawn.

(6) The regulations may include other provision for the purposes of authorisation and licensing, including in particular provision—
  (a) for determining the rights and obligations of any person if a work ceases to qualify as an orphan work (or ceases to qualify by reference to any copyright owner), or if a rights owner exercises the right referred to in section 116B(3), while a licence is in force;
  (b) about maintenance of registers and access to them;
  (c) permitting the use of a work for incidental purposes including an application or search;
  (d) for a right conferred by section 77 to be treated as having been asserted in accordance with section 78;
  (e) for the payment of fees to cover administrative expenses.

116D Regulations under sections 116A and 116B

(1) The power to make regulations includes power—
  (a) to make incidental, supplementary or consequential provision, including provision extending or restricting the jurisdiction of the Copyright Tribunal or conferring powers on it;

   (b)　to make transitional, transitory or saving provision;
   (c)　to make different provision for different purposes.
(2)　Regulations under any provision may amend this Part, or any other enactment or subordinate legislation passed or made before that provision comes into force, for the purpose of making consequential provision or extending or restricting the jurisdiction of the Copyright Tribunal or conferring powers on it.
(3)　Regulations may make provision by reference to guidance issued from time to time by any person.
(4)　The power to make regulations is exercisable by statutory instrument.
(5)　A statutory instrument containing regulations may not be made unless a draft of the instrument has been laid before and approved by a resolution of each House of Parliament.

References and applications with respect to licensing schemes

117　Licensing schemes to which following sections apply

Sections 118 to 123 (references and applications with respect to licensing schemes) apply to licensing schemes which are operated by licensing bodies and cover works of more than one author, so far as they relate to licences for—
(a)　copying the work,
(b)　rental or lending of copies of the work to the public,
(c)　performing, showing or playing the work in public, or
(d)　communicating the work to the public;
and references in those sections to a licensing scheme shall be construed accordingly.

118　Reference of proposed licensing scheme to tribunal

(1)　The terms of a licensing scheme proposed to be operated by a licensing body may be referred to the Copyright Tribunal by an organisation claiming to be representative of persons claiming that they require licences in cases of a description to which the scheme would apply, either generally or in relation to any description of case.
(2)　The Tribunal shall first decide whether to entertain the reference, and may decline to do so on the ground that the reference is premature.
(3)　If the Tribunal decides to entertain the reference it shall consider the matter referred and make such order, either confirming or varying the proposed scheme, either generally or so far as it relates to cases of the description to which the reference relates, as the Tribunal may determine to be reasonable in the circumstances.
(4)　The order may be made so as to be in force indefinitely or for such period as the Tribunal may determine.

119　Reference of licensing scheme to tribunal

(1)　If while a licensing scheme is in operation a dispute arises between the operator of the scheme and—
   (a)　a person claiming that he requires a licence in a case of a description to which the scheme applies, or
   (b)　an organisation claiming to be representative of such persons,
   that person or organisation may refer the scheme to the Copyright Tribunal in so far as it relates to cases of that description.
(2)　A scheme which has been referred to the Tribunal under this section shall remain in operation until proceedings on the reference are concluded.
(3)　The Tribunal shall consider the matter in dispute and make such order, either confirming or varying the scheme so far as it relates to cases of the description to which the reference relates, as the Tribunal may determine to be reasonable in the circumstances.
(4)　The order may be made so as to be in force indefinitely or for such period as the Tribunal may determine.

120　Further reference of scheme to tribunal

(1)　Where the Copyright Tribunal has on a previous reference of a licensing scheme under section 118 or 119 or 128A, or under this section, made an order with respect to the scheme, then, while the order remains in force—

(a)   the operator of the scheme,

(b)   a person claiming that he requires a licence in a case of the description to which the order applies, or

(c)   an organisation claiming to be representative of such persons,

may refer the scheme again to the Tribunal so far as it relates to cases of that description.

(2)   A licensing scheme shall not, except with the special leave of the Tribunal, be referred again to the Tribunal in respect of the same description of cases—

(a)   within twelve months from the date of the order on the previous reference, or

(b)   if the order was made so as to be in force for 15 months or less, until the last three months before the expiry of the order.

(3)   A scheme which has been referred to the Tribunal under this section shall remain in operation until proceedings on the reference are concluded.

(4)   The Tribunal shall consider the matter in dispute and make such order, either confirming, varying or further varying the scheme so far as it relates to cases of the description to which the reference relates, as the Tribunal may determine to be reasonable in the circumstances.

(5)   The order may be made so as to be in force indefinitely or for such period as the Tribunal may determine.

121   Application for grant of licence in connection with licensing scheme

(1)   A person who claims, in a case covered by a licensing scheme, that the operator of the scheme has refused to grant him or procure the grant to him of a licence in accordance with the scheme, or has failed to do so within a reasonable time after being asked, may apply to the Copyright Tribunal.

(2)   A person who claims, in a case excluded from a licensing scheme, that the operator of the scheme either—

(a)   has refused to grant him a licence or procure the grant to him of a licence, or has failed to do so within a reasonable time of being asked, and that in the circumstances it is unreasonable that a licence should not be granted, or

(b)   proposes terms for a licence which are unreasonable, may apply to the Copyright Tribunal.

(3)   A case shall be regarded as excluded from a licensing scheme for the purposes of subsection (2) if—

(a)   the scheme provides for the grant of licences subject to terms excepting matters from the licence and the case falls within such an exception, or

(b)   the case is so similar to those in which licences are granted under the scheme that it is unreasonable that it should not be dealt with in the same way.

(4)   If the Tribunal is satisfied that the claim is well-founded, it shall make an order declaring that, in respect of the matters specified in the order, the applicant is entitled to a licence on such terms as the Tribunal may determine to be applicable in accordance with the scheme or, as the case may be, to be reasonable in the circumstances.

(5)   The order may be made so as to be in force indefinitely or for such period as the Tribunal may determine.

122   Application for review of order as to entitlement to licence

(1)   Where the Copyright Tribunal has made an order under section 121 that a person is entitled to a licence under a licensing scheme, the operator of the scheme or the original applicant may apply to the Tribunal to review its order.

(2)   An application shall not be made, except with the special leave of the Tribunal—

(a)   within twelve months from the date of the order, or of the decision on a previous application under this section, or

(b)   if the order was made so as to be in force for 15 months or less, or as a result of the decision on a previous application under this section is due to expire within 15 months of that decision, until the last three months before the expiry date.

(3)   The Tribunal shall on an application for review confirm or vary its order as the Tribunal may determine to be reasonable having regard to the terms applicable in accordance with the licensing scheme or, as the case may be, the circumstances of the case.

123 Effect of order of tribunal as to licensing scheme

(1) A licensing scheme which has been confirmed or varied by the Copyright Tribunal—
    (a)   under section 118 (reference of terms of proposed scheme), or
    (b)   under section 119 or 120 (reference of existing scheme to Tribunal),
shall be in force or, as the case may be, remain in operation, so far as it relates to the description of case in respect of which the order was made, so long as the order remains in force.

(2) While the order is in force a person who in a case of a class to which the order applies—
    (a)   pays to the operator of the scheme any charges payable under the scheme in respect of a licence covering the case in question or, if the amount cannot be ascertained, gives an undertaking to the operator to pay them when ascertained, and
    (b)   complies with the other terms applicable to such a licence under the scheme,
shall be in the same position as regards infringement of copyright as if he had at all material times been the holder of a licence granted by the owner of the copyright in question in accordance with the scheme.

(3) The Tribunal may direct that the order, so far as it varies the amount of charges payable, has effect from a date before that on which it is made, but not earlier than the date on which the reference was made or, if later, on which the scheme came into operation.
If such a direction is made—
    (a)   any necessary repayments, or further payments, shall be made in respect of charges already paid, and
    (b)   the reference in subsection (2)(a) to the charges payable under the scheme shall be construed as a reference to the charges so payable by virtue of the order.
No such direction may be made where subsection (4) below applies.

(4) An order of the Tribunal under section 119 or 120 made with respect to a scheme which is certified for any purpose under section 143 has effect, so far as it varies the scheme by reducing the charges payable for licences, from the date on which the reference was made to the Tribunal.

(5) Where the Tribunal has made an order under section 121 (order as to entitlement to licence under licensing scheme) and the order remains in force, the person in whose favour the order is made shall if he—
    (a)   pays to the operator of the scheme any charges payable in accordance with the order or, if the amount cannot be ascertained, gives an undertaking to pay the charges when ascertained, and
    (b)   complies with the other terms specified in the order,
be in the same position as regards infringement of copyright as if he had at all material times been the holder of a licence granted by the owner of the copyright in question on the terms specified in the order.

References and applications with respect to licensing by licensing bodies

124 Licences to which following sections apply

Sections 125 to 128 (references and applications with respect to licensing by licensing bodies) apply to licences which are granted by a licensing body otherwise than in pursuance of a licensing scheme and cover works of more than one author, so far as they authorise—
(a) copying the work,
(b) rental or lending of copies of the work to the public,
(c) performing, showing or playing the work in public, or
(d) communicating the work to the public;
and references in those sections to a licence shall be construed accordingly.

125 Reference to tribunal of proposed licence

(1) The terms on which a licensing body proposes to grant a licence may be referred to the Copyright Tribunal by the prospective licensee.

(2) The Tribunal shall first decide whether to entertain the reference, and may decline to do so on the ground that the reference is premature.

(3) If the Tribunal decides to entertain the reference it shall consider the terms of the proposed licence and make such order, either confirming or varying the terms, as it may determine to be reasonable in the circumstances.

(4) The order may be made so as to be in force indefinitely or for such period as the Tribunal may determine.

126 Reference to tribunal of expiring licence

(1) A licensee under a licence which is due to expire, by effluxion of time or as a result of notice given by the licensing body, may apply to the Copyright Tribunal on the ground that it is unreasonable in the circumstances that the licence should cease to be in force.

(2) Such an application may not be made until the last three months before the licence is due to expire.

(3) A licence in respect of which a reference has been made to the Tribunal shall remain in operation until proceedings on the reference are concluded.

(4) If the Tribunal finds the application well-founded, it shall make an order declaring that the licensee shall continue to be entitled to the benefit of the licence on such terms as the Tribunal may determine to be reasonable in the circumstances.

(5) An order of the Tribunal under this section may be made so as to be in force indefinitely or for such period as the Tribunal may determine.

127 Application for review of order as to licence

(1) Where the Copyright Tribunal has made an order under section 125, 126 or 128B (where that order did not relate to a licensing scheme), the licensing body or the person entitled to the benefit of the order may apply to the Tribunal to review its order.

(2) An application shall not be made, except with the special leave of the Tribunal—
   (a) within twelve months from the date of the order or of the decision on a previous application under this section, or
   (b) if the order was made so as to be in force for 15 months or less, or as a result of the decision on a previous application under this section is due to expire within 15 months of that decision, until the last three months before the expiry date.

(3) The Tribunal shall on an application for review confirm or vary its order as the Tribunal may determine to be reasonable in the circumstances.

128 Effect of order of tribunal as to licence

(1) Where the Copyright Tribunal has made an order under section 125 or 126 and the order remains in force, the person entitled to the benefit of the order shall if he—
   (a) pays to the licensing body any charges payable in accordance with the order or, if the amount cannot be ascertained, gives an undertaking to pay the charges when ascertained, and
   (b) complies with the other terms specified in the order,
   be in the same position as regards infringement of copyright as if he had at all material times been the holder of a licence granted by the owner of the copyright in question on the terms specified in the order.

(2) The benefit of the order may be assigned—
   (a) in the case of an order under section 125, if assignment is not prohibited under the terms of the Tribunal's order; and
   (b) in the case of an order under section 126, if assignment was not prohibited under the terms of the original licence.

(3) The Tribunal may direct that an order under section 125 or 126, or an order under section 127 varying such an order, so far as it varies the amount of charges payable, has effect from a date before that on which it is made, but not earlier than the date on which the reference or application was made or, if later, on which the licence was granted or, as the case may be, was due to expire.
   If such a direction is made—
   (a) any necessary repayments, or further payments, shall be made in respect of charges already paid, and
   (b) the reference in subsection (1)(a) to the charges payable in accordance with the order shall be construed, where the order is varied by a later order, as a reference to the charges so payable by virtue of the later order.

Factors to be taken into account in certain classes of case

129   General considerations: unreasonable discrimination

In determining what is reasonable on a reference or application under this Chapter relating to a licensing scheme or licence, the Copyright Tribunal shall have regard to—

(a)   the availability of other schemes, or the granting of other licences, to other persons in similar circumstances, and

(b)   the terms of those schemes or licences,

and shall exercise its powers so as to secure that there is no unreasonable discrimination between licensees, or prospective licensees, under the scheme or licence to which the reference or application relates and licensees under other schemes operated by, or other licences granted by, the same person.

130   Licences for reprographic copying

Where a reference or application is made to the Copyright Tribunal under this Chapter relating to the licensing of reprographic copying of published literary, dramatic, musical or artistic works, or the typographical arrangement of published editions, the Tribunal shall have regard to—

(a)   the extent to which published editions of the works in question are otherwise available,

(b)   the proportion of the work to be copied, and

(c)   the nature of the use to which the copies are likely to be put.

133   Licences to reflect payments in respect of underlying rights

(1)   In considering what charges should be paid for a licence—

(a)   on a reference or application under this Chapter relating to licences for the rental or lending of copies of a work, or

(b)   on an application under section 142 (royalty or other sum payable for lending of certain works),

the Copyright Tribunal shall take into account any reasonable payments which the owner of the copyright in the work is liable to make in consequence of the granting of the licence, or of the acts authorised by the licence, to owners of copyright in works included in that work.

(2)   On any reference or application under this Chapter relating to licensing in respect of the copyright in sound recordings, films or broadcasts, the Copyright Tribunal shall take into account, in considering what charges should be paid for a licence, any reasonable payments which the copyright owner is liable to make in consequence of the granting of the licence, or of the acts authorised by the licence, in respect of any performance included in the recording, film or broadcast.

134   Licences in respect of works included in re-transmissions

(1)   This section applies to references or applications under this Chapter relating to licences to include in a broadcast—

(a)   literary, dramatic, musical or artistic works, or,

(b)   sound recordings or films,

where one broadcast ("the first transmission") is, by reception and immediate re-transmission, to be further broadcast ("the further transmission").

(2)   So far as the further transmission is to the same area as the first transmission, the Copyright Tribunal shall, in considering what charges (if any) should be paid for licences for either transmission, have regard to the extent to which the copyright owner has already received, or is entitled to receive, payment for the other transmission which adequately remunerates him in respect of transmissions to that area.

(3)   So far as the further transmission is to an area outside that to which the first transmission was made, the Tribunal shall leave the further transmission out of account in considering what charges (if any) should be paid for licences for the first transmission.

135   Mention of specific matters not to exclude other relevant considerations

The mention in sections 129 to 134 of specific matters to which the Copyright Tribunal is to have regard in certain classes of case does not affect the Tribunal's general obligation in any case to have regard to all relevant considerations.

Use as of right of sound recordings in broadcasts

135A Circumstances in which right available

(1) Section 135C applies to the inclusion in a broadcast of any sound recordings if—

    (a) a licence to include those recordings in the broadcast could be granted by a licensing body or such a body could procure the grant of a licence to do so,

    (b) the condition in subsection (2) or (3) applies, and

    (c) the person including those recordings in the broadcast has complied with section 135B.

(2) Where the person including the recordings in the broadcast does not hold a licence to do so, the condition is that the licensing body refuses to grant, or procure the grant of, such a licence, being a licence—

    (a) whose terms as to payment for including the recordings in the broadcast would be acceptable to him or comply with an order of the Copyright Tribunal under section 135D relating to such a licence or any scheme under which it would be granted, and

    (b) allowing unlimited needletime or such needletime as he has demanded.

(3) Where he holds a licence to include the recordings in the broadcast, the condition is that the terms of the licence limit needletime and the licensing body refuses to substitute or procure the substitution of terms allowing unlimited needletime or such needletime as he has demanded, or refuses to do so on terms that fall within subsection (2)(a).

(4) The references in subsection (2) to refusing to grant, or procure the grant of, a licence, and in subsection (3) to refusing to substitute or procure the substitution of terms, include failing to do so within a reasonable time of being asked.

(5) In the group of sections from this section to section 135G—

"broadcast" does not include any broadcast which is a transmission of the kind specified in section 6(1A)(b) or (c);

"needletime" means the time in any period (whether determined as a number of hours in the period or a proportion of the period, or otherwise) in which any proceedings may be included in a broadcast;

"sound recording" does not include a film sound track when accompanying a film.

(6) In sections 135B to 135G, "terms of payment" means terms as to payment for including sound recordings in a broadcast.

135B Notice of intention to exercise right

(1) A person intending to avail himself of the right conferred by section 135C must—

    (a) give notice to the licensing body of his intention to exercise the right, asking the body to propose terms of payment, and

    (b) after receiving the proposal or the expiry of a reasonable period, give reasonable notice to the licensing body of the date on which he proposes to begin exercising that right, and the terms of payment in accordance with which he intends to do so.

(2) Where he has a licence to include the recordings in a broadcast, the date specified in a notice under subsection (1)(b) must not be sooner than the date of expiry of that licence except in a case falling within section 135A(3).

(3) Before the person intending to avail himself of the right begins to exercise it, he must—

    (a) give reasonable notice to the Copyright Tribunal of his intention to exercise the right, and of the date on which he proposes to begin to do so, and

    (b) apply to the Tribunal under section 135D to settle the terms of payment.

135C Conditions for exercise of right

(1) A person who, on or after the date specified in a notice under section 135B(1)(b), includes in a broadcast any sound recordings in circumstances in which this section applies, and who—

    (a) complies with any reasonable condition, notice of which has been given to him by the licensing body, as to inclusion in the broadcasting of those recordings,

    (b) provides that body with such information about their inclusion in the broadcast as it may reasonably require, and

(c)   makes the payments to the licensing body that are required by this section,

shall be in the same position as regards infringement of copyright as if he had at all material times been the holder of a licence granted by the owner of the copyright in question.

(2)   Payments are to be made at not less than quarterly intervals in arrears.

(3)   The amount of any payment is that determined in accordance with any order of the Copyright Tribunal under section 135D or, if no such order has been made—

(a)   in accordance with any proposal for terms of payment made by the licensing body pursuant to a request under section 135B, or

(b)   where no proposal has been so made or the amount determined in accordance with the proposal so made is unreasonably high, in accordance with the terms of payment notified to the licensing body under section 135B(1)(b).

(4)   Where this section applies to the inclusion in a broadcast of any sound recordings, it does so in place of any licence.

135D Applications to settle payments

(1)   On an application to settle the terms of payment, the Copyright Tribunal shall consider the matter and make such order as it may determine to be reasonable in the circumstances.

(2)   An order under subsection (1) has effect from the date the applicant begins to exercise the right conferred by section 135C and any necessary repayments, or further payments, shall be made in respect of amounts that have fallen due.

135E References etc. about conditions, information and other terms

(1)   A person exercising the right conferred by section 135C, or who has given notice to the Copyright Tribunal of his intention to do so, may refer to the Tribunal—

(a)   any question whether any condition as to the inclusion in a broadcast of sound recordings, notice of which has been given to him by the licensing body in question, is a reasonable condition, or

(b)   any question whether any information is information which the licensing body can reasonably require him to provide.

(2)   On a reference under this section, the Tribunal shall consider the matter and make such order as it may determine to be reasonable in the circumstances.

135F Application for review of order

(1)   A person exercising the right conferred by section 135C or the licensing body may apply to the Copyright Tribunal to review any order under section 135D or 135E.

(2)   An application shall not be made, except with the special leave of the Tribunal—

(a)   within twelve months from the date of the order, or of the decision on a previous application under this section, or

(b)   if the order was made so as to be in force for fifteen months or less, or as a result of a decision on a previous application is due to expire within fifteen months of that decision, until the last three months before the expiry date.

(3)   On the application the Tribunal shall consider the matter and make such order confirming or varying the original order as it may determine to be reasonable in the circumstances.

(4)   An order under this section has effect from the date on which it is made or such later date as may be specified by the Tribunal.

135G Factors to be taken into account

(1)   In determining what is reasonable on an application or reference under section 135D or 135E, or on reviewing any order under section 135F, the Copyright Tribunal shall—

(a)   have regard to the terms of any orders which it has made in the case of persons in similar circumstances exercising the right conferred by section 135C, and

(b)   exercise its powers so as to secure that there is no unreasonable discrimination between persons exercising that right against the same licensing body.

(2)   In settling the terms of payment under section 135D, the Tribunal shall not be guided by any order it has made under any enactment other than that section.

(3)   Section 134 (factors to be taken into account: retransmissions) applies on an application or reference under sections 135D to 135F as it applies on an application or reference relating to a licence.

135H Power to amend sections 135A to 135G

(1) The Secretary of State may by order, subject to such transitional provision as appears to him to be appropriate, amend sections 135A to 135G so as—

  (a) to include in any reference to sound recordings any works of a description specified in the order; or

  (b) to exclude from any reference to a broadcast any broadcast of a description so specified.

(2) An order shall be made by statutory instrument; and no order shall be made unless a draft of it has been laid before and approved by resolution of each House of Parliament.

Implied indemnity in schemes or licences for reprographic copying

136 Implied indemnity in certain schemes and licences for reprographic copying

(1) This section applies to—

  (a) schemes for licensing reprographic copying of published literary, dramatic, musical or artistic works, or the typographical arrangement of published editions, and

  (b) licences granted by licensing bodies for such copying,

  where the scheme or licence does not specify the works to which it applies with such particularity as to enable licensees to determine whether a work falls within the scheme or licence by inspection of the scheme or licence and the work.

(2) There is implied—

  (a) in every scheme to which this section applies an undertaking by the operator of the scheme to indemnify a person granted a licence under the scheme, and

  (b) in every licence to which this section applies an undertaking by the licensing body to indemnify the licensee,

  against any liability incurred by him by reason of his having infringed copyright by making or authorising the making of reprographic copies of a work in circumstances within the apparent scope of his licence.

(3) The circumstances of a case are within the apparent scope of a licence if—

  (a) it is not apparent from inspection of the licence and the work that it does not fall within the description of works to which the licence applies; and

  (b) the licence does not expressly provide that it does not extend to copyright of the description infringed.

(4) In this section "liability" includes liability to pay costs; and this section applies in relation to costs reasonably incurred by a licensee in connection with actual or contemplated proceedings against him for infringement of copyright as it applies to sums which he is liable to pay in respect of such infringement.

(5) A scheme or licence to which this section applies may contain reasonable provision—

  (a) with respect to the manner in which, and time within which, claims under the undertaking implied by this section are to be made;

  (b) enabling the operator of the scheme or, as the case may be, the licensing body to take over the conduct of any proceedings affecting the amount of his liability to indemnify.

Reprographic copying by educational establishments

137 Power to extend coverage of scheme or licence

(1) This section applies to—

  (a) a licensing scheme to which sections 118 to 123 apply (see section 117) and which is operated by a licensing body, or

  (b) a licence to which sections 125 to 128 apply (see section 124),

  so far as it provides for the grant of licences, or is a licence, authorising the making by or on behalf of educational establishments for the purposes of instruction of reprographic copies of published literary, dramatic, musical or artistic works, or of the typographical arrangement of published editions.

(2) If it appears to the Secretary of State with respect to a scheme or licence to which this section applies that—

    (a)   works of a description similar to those covered by the scheme or licence are unreasonably excluded from it, and

    (b)   making them subject to the scheme or licence would not conflict with the normal exploitation of the works or unreasonably prejudice the legitimate interests of the copyright owners,

he may by order provide that the scheme or licence shall extend to those works.

(3)   Where he proposes to make such an order, the Secretary of State shall give notice of the proposal to—

    (a)   the copyright owners,

    (b)   the licensing body in question, and \

    (c)   such persons or organisations representative of educational establishments, and such other persons or organisations, as the Secretary of State thinks fit.

(4)   The notice shall inform those persons of their right to make written or oral representations to the Secretary of State about the proposal within six months from the date of the notice; and if any of them wishes to make oral representations, the Secretary of State shall appoint a person to hear the representations and report to him.

(5)   In considering whether to make an order the Secretary of State shall take into account any representations made to him in accordance with subsection (4), and such other matters as appear to him to be relevant.

138   Variation or discharge of order extending scheme or licence

(1)   The owner of the copyright in a work in respect of which an order is in force under section 137 may apply to the Secretary of State for the variation or discharge of the order, stating his reasons for making the application.

(2)   The Secretary of State shall not entertain an application made within two years of the making of the original order, or of the making of an order on a previous application under this section, unless it appears to him that the circumstances are exceptional.

(3)   On considering the reasons for the application the Secretary of State may confirm the order forthwith; if he does not do so, he shall give notice of the application to—

    (a)   the licensing body in question, and

    (b)   such persons or organisations representative of educational establishments, and such other persons or organisations, as he thinks fit.

(4)   The notice shall inform those persons of their right to make written or oral representations to the Secretary of State about the application within the period of two months from the date of the notice; and if any of them wishes to make oral representations, the Secretary of State shall appoint a person to hear the representations and report to him.

(5)   In considering the application the Secretary of State shall take into account the reasons for the application, any representations made to him in accordance with subsection (4), and such other matters as appear to him to be relevant.

(6)   The Secretary of State may make such order as he thinks fit confirming or discharging the order (or, as the case may be, the order as previously varied), or varying (or further varying) it so as to exclude works from it.

139   Appeals against orders

(1)   The owner of the copyright in a work which is the subject of an order under section 137 (order extending coverage of scheme or licence) may appeal to the Copyright Tribunal which may confirm or discharge the order, or vary it so as to exclude works from it, as it thinks fit having regard to the considerations mentioned in subsection (2) of that section.

(2)   Where the Secretary of State has made an order under section 138 (order confirming, varying or discharging order extending coverage of scheme or licence)—

    (a)   the person who applied for the order, or

    (b)   any person or organisation representative of educational establishments who was given notice of the application for the order and made representations in accordance with subsection (4) of that section,

may appeal to the Tribunal which may confirm or discharge the order or make any other order which the Secretary of State might have made.

(3)   An appeal under this section shall be brought within six weeks of the making of the order or such further period as the Tribunal may allow.

(4) An order under section 137 or 138 shall not come into effect until the end of the period of six weeks from the making of the order or, if an appeal is brought before the end of that period, until the appeal proceedings are disposed of or withdrawn.

(5) If an appeal is brought after the end of that period, any decision of the Tribunal on the appeal does not affect the validity of anything done in reliance on the order appealed against before that decision takes effect.

140 Inquiry whether new scheme or general licence required

(1) The Secretary of State may appoint a person to inquire into the question whether new provision is required (whether by way of a licensing scheme or general licence) to authorise the making by or on behalf of educational establishments for the purposes of instruction of reprographic copies of—

(a) published literary, dramatic, musical or artistic works, or

(b) the typographical arrangement of published editions,

of a description which appears to the Secretary of State not to be covered by an existing licensing scheme or general licence and not to fall within the power conferred by section 137 (power to extend existing schemes and licences to similar works).

(2) The procedure to be followed in relation to an inquiry shall be such as may be prescribed by regulations made by the Secretary of State.

(3) The regulations shall, in particular, provide for notice to be given to—

(a) persons or organisations appearing to the Secretary of State to represent the owners of copyright in works of that description, and

(b) persons or organisations appearing to the Secretary of State to represent educational establishments,

and for the making of written or oral representations by such persons; but without prejudice to the giving of notice to, and the making of representations by, other persons and organisations.

(4) The person appointed to hold the inquiry shall not recommend the making of new provision unless he is satisfied—

(a) that it would be of advantage to educational establishments to be authorised to make reprographic copies of the works in question, and

(b) that making those works subject to a licensing scheme or general licence would not conflict with the normal exploitation of the works or unreasonably prejudice the legitimate interests of the copyright owners.

(5) If he does recommend the making of new provision he shall specify any terms, other than terms as to charges payable, on which authorisation under the new provision should be available.

(6) Regulations under this section shall be made by statutory instrument which shall be subject to annulment in pursuance of a resolution of either House of Parliament.

(7) In this section (and section 141) a "general licence" means a licence granted by a licensing body which covers all works of the description to which it applies.

141 Statutory licence where recommendation not implemented

(1) The Secretary of State may, within one year of the making of a recommendation under section 140 by order provide that if, or to the extent that, provision has not been made in accordance with the recommendation, the making by or on behalf of an educational establishment, for the purposes of instruction, of reprographic copies of the works to which the recommendation relates shall be treated as licensed by the owners of the copyright in the works.

(2) For that purpose provision shall be regarded as having been made in accordance with the recommendation if—

(a) a certified licensing scheme has been established under which a licence is available to the establishment in question, or

(b) a general licence has been—

(i) granted to or for the benefit of that establishment, or

(ii) referred by or on behalf of that establishment to the Copyright Tribunal under section 125 (reference of terms of proposed licence), or

(iii) offered to or for the benefit of that establishment and refused without such a reference,

and the terms of the scheme or licence accord with the recommendation.

(3) The order shall also provide that any existing licence authorising the making of such copies (not being a licence granted under a certified licensing scheme or a general licence) shall cease to have effect to the extent that it is more restricted or more onerous than the licence provided for by the order.

(4) The order shall provide for the licence to be free of royalty but, as respects other matters, subject to any terms specified in the recommendation and to such other terms as the Secretary of State may think fit.

(5) The order may provide that where a copy which would otherwise be an infringing copy is made in accordance with the licence provided by the order but is subsequently dealt with, it shall be treated as an infringing copy for the purposes of that dealing, and if that dealing infringes copyright for all subsequent purposes.
In this subsection "dealt with" means sold or let for hire, offered or exposed for sale or hire, or exhibited in public.

(6) The order shall not come into force until at least six months after it is made.

(7) An order may be varied from time to time, but not so as to include works other than those to which the recommendation relates or remove any terms specified in the recommendation, and may be revoked.

(8) An order under this section shall be made by statutory instrument which shall be subject to annulment in pursuance of a resolution of either House of Parliament.

(9) In this section a "certified licensing scheme" means a licensing scheme certified for the purposes of this section under section 143.

Royalty or other sum payable for rental of certain works

142   Royalty or other sum payable for lending of certain works

(1) An application to settle the royalty or other sum payable in pursuance of section 66 (lending of copies of certain copyright works) may be made to the Copyright Tribunal by the copyright owner or the person claiming to be treated as licensed by him.

(2) The Tribunal shall consider the matter and make such order as it may determine to be reasonable in the circumstances.

(3) Either party may subsequently apply to the Tribunal to vary the order, and the Tribunal shall consider the matter and make such order confirming or varying the original order as it may determine to be reasonable in the circumstances.

(4) An application under subsection (3) shall not, except with the special leave of the Tribunal, be made within twelve months from the date of the original order or of the order on a previous application under that subsection.

(5) An order under subsection (3) has effect from the date on which it is made or such later date as may be specified by the Tribunal.

Certification of licensing schemes

143   Certification of licensing schemes

(1) A person operating or proposing to operate a licensing scheme may apply to the Secretary of State to certify the scheme for the purposes of—
. . .
(b) section 60 (abstracts of scientific or technical articles),
(c) section 66 (lending to public of copies of certain works), or
. . .
(e) section 141 (reprographic copying of published works by educational establishments).

(2) The Secretary of State shall by order made by statutory instrument certify the scheme if he is satisfied that it—
(a) enables the works to which it relates to be identified with sufficient certainty by persons likely to require licences, and
(b) sets out clearly the charges (if any) payable and the other terms on which licences will be granted.

(3) The scheme shall be scheduled to the order and the certification shall come into operation for the purposes of section 60, 66 or 141, as the case may be—

(a)   on such date, not less than eight weeks after the order is made, as may be specified in the order, or

(b)   if the scheme is the subject of a reference under section 118 (reference of proposed scheme), any later date on which the order of the Copyright Tribunal under that section comes into force or the reference is withdrawn.

(4)   A variation of the scheme is not effective unless a corresponding amendment of the order is made; and the Secretary of State shall make such an amendment in the case of a variation ordered by the Copyright Tribunal on a reference under section 118, 119 or 120, and may do so in any other case if he thinks fit.

(5)   The order shall be revoked if the scheme ceases to be operated and may be revoked if it appears to the Secretary of State that it is no longer being operated according to its terms.

Powers exercisable in consequence of competition report

144   Powers exercisable in consequence of report of Competition and Markets Authority

(1)   Subsection (1A) applies where whatever needs to be remedied, mitigated or prevented by the Secretary of State or (as the case may be) the Competition and Markets Authority under section 12(5) of the Competition Act 1980 or section 41(2), 55(2), 66(6), 75(2), 83(2), 138(2), 147(2) or 160(2) of, or paragraph 5(2) or 10(2) of Schedule 7 to, the Enterprise Act 2002 (powers to take remedial action following references to the Competition and Markets Authority in connection with public bodies and certain other persons, mergers or market investigations) consists of or includes—

(a)   conditions in licences granted by the owner of copyright in a work restricting the use of the work by the licensee or the right of the copyright owner to grant other licences; or

(b)   a refusal of a copyright owner to grant licences on reasonable terms.

(1A) The powers conferred by Schedule 8 to the Enterprise Act 2002 include power to cancel or modify those conditions and, instead or in addition, to provide that licences in respect of the copyright shall be available as of right.

(2)   The references to anything permitted by Schedule 8 to the Enterprise Act 2002 in section 12(5A) of the Competition Act 1980 and in sections 75(4)(a), 83(4)(a), 84(2)(a), 89(1), 160(4)(a), 161(3)(a) and 164(1) of, and paragraphs 5, 10 and 11 of Schedule 7 to, the Act of 2002 shall be construed accordingly.

(3)   The Secretary of State or (as the case may be) the Competition and Markets Authority shall only exercise the powers available by virtue of this section if he or it is satisfied that to do so does not contravene any Convention relating to copyright to which the United Kingdom is a party.

(4)   The terms of a licence available by virtue of this section shall, in default of agreement, be settled by the Copyright Tribunal on an application by the person requiring the licence; and terms so settled shall authorise the licensee to do everything in respect of which a licence is so available.

(5)   Where the terms of a licence are settled by the Tribunal, the licence has effect from the date on which the application to the Tribunal was made.

Compulsory collective administration of certain rights

144A Collective exercise of certain rights in relation to cable re-transmission

(1)   This section applies to the right of the owner of copyright in a literary, dramatic, musical or artistic work, sound recording or film to grant or refuse authorisation for cable re-transmission of a wireless broadcast from another EEA state in which the work is included. That right is referred to below as "cable re-transmission right".

(2)   Cable re-transmission right may be exercised against a cable operator only through a licensing body.

(3)   Where a copyright owner has not transferred management of his cable re-transmission right to a licensing body, the licensing body which manages rights of the same category shall be deemed to be mandated to manage his right.

Where more than one licensing body manages rights of that category, he may choose which of them is deemed to be mandated to manage his right.

(4) A copyright owner to whom subsection (3) applies has the same rights and obligations resulting from any relevant agreement between the cable operator and the licensing body as have copyright owners who have transferred management of their cable re-transmission right to that licensing body.

(5) Any rights to which a copyright owner may be entitled by virtue of subsection (4) must be claimed within the period of three years beginning with the date of the cable re-transmission concerned.

(6) This section does not affect any rights exercisable by the maker of the broadcast, whether in relation to the broadcast or a work included in it.

(7) In this section—

"cable operator" means a person responsible for cable re-transmission of a wireless broadcast; and

"cable re-transmission" means the reception and immediate re-transmission by cable, including the transmission of microwave energy between terrestrial fixed points, of a wireless broadcast.

CHAPTER VIII
THE COPYRIGHT TRIBUNAL

The Tribunal

145   The Copyright Tribunal

(1) The Tribunal established under section 23 of the Copyright Act 1956 is renamed the Copyright Tribunal.

(2) The Tribunal shall consist of a chairman and two deputy chairmen appointed by the Lord Chancellor, after consultation with the Secretary of State, and not less than two or more than eight ordinary members appointed by the Secretary of State.

(3) A person is not eligible for appointment as chairman or deputy chairman unless—
    (a) he satisfies the judicial-appointment eligibility condition on a 5-year basis;
    (b) he is an advocate or solicitor in Scotland of at least 5 years' standing;
    (c) he is a member of the Bar of Northern Ireland or solicitor of the Court of Judicature of Northern Ireland of at least 5 years' standing; or
    (d) he has held judicial office.

Jurisdiction and procedure

149   Jurisdiction of the Tribunal

The Copyright Tribunal has jurisdiction under this Part to hear and determine proceedings under—

(zb) section 93C (application to determine amount of equitable remuneration under section 93B);

(a) section 118, 119 or 120 (reference of licensing scheme);

(b) section 121 or 122 (application with respect to entitlement to licence under licensing scheme);

(c) section 125, 126 or 127 (reference or application with respect to licensing by licensing body);

(ca) section 128B (reference by the Secretary of State under section 128A);

(cc) section 135D or 135E (application or reference with respect to use as of right of sound recordings in broadcasts);

(d) section 139 (appeal against order as to coverage of licensing scheme or licence);

(e) section 142 (application to settle royalty or other sum payable for lending of certain works);

(f) section 144(4) (application to settle terms of copyright licence available as of right);

(fa) paragraph 7 of Schedule ZA1 (application to determine compensation for use of orphan works).

Appeals

152 Appeal to the court on point of law

(1) An appeal lies on any point of law arising from a decision of the Copyright Tribunal to the High Court or, in the case of proceedings of the Tribunal in Scotland, to the Court of Session.

(2) Provision shall be made by rules under section 150 limiting the time within which an appeal may be brought.

(3) Provision may be made by rules under that section—

    (a) for suspending, or authorising or requiring the Tribunal to suspend, the operation of orders of the Tribunal in cases where its decision is appealed against;

    (b) for modifying in relation to an order of the Tribunal whose operation is suspended the operation of any provision of this Act as to the effect of the order;

    (c) for the publication of notices or the taking of other steps for securing that persons affected by the suspension of an order of the Tribunal will be informed of its suspension.

CHAPTER IX
QUALIFICATION FOR AND EXTENT OF COPYRIGHT PROTECTION

Qualification for copyright protection

153 Qualification for copyright protection

(1) Copyright does not subsist in a work unless the qualification requirements of this Chapter are satisfied as regards—

    (a) the author (see section 154), or

    (b) the country in which the work was first published (see section 155), or

    (c) in the case of a broadcast, the country from which the broadcast was made (see section 156).

(2) Subsection (1) does not apply in relation to Crown copyright or Parliamentary copyright (see sections 163 to 166D) or to copyright subsisting by virtue of section 168 (copyright of certain international organisations).

(3) If the qualification requirements of this Chapter, or section 163, 165 or 168, are once satisfied in respect of a work, copyright does not cease to subsist by reason of any subsequent event.

154 Qualification by reference to author

(1) A work qualifies for copyright protection if the author was at the material time a qualifying person, that is—

    (a) a British citizen, a national of another EEA state, a British overseas territories citizen, a British National (Overseas), a British Overseas citizen, a British subject or a British protected person within the meaning of the British Nationality Act 1981, or

    (b) an individual domiciled or resident in the United Kingdom or another EEA state or in the Channel Islands, the Isle of Man or Gibraltar or in a country to which the relevant provisions of this Part extend, or

    (c) a body incorporated under the law of a part of the United Kingdom or another EEA state or of the Channel Islands, the Isle of Man or Gibraltar or of a country to which the relevant provisions of this Part extend.

(2) Where, or so far as, provision is made by Order under section 159 (application of this Part to countries to which it does not extend), a work also qualifies for copyright protection if at the material time the author was a citizen or subject of, an individual domiciled or resident in, or a body incorporated under the law of, a country to which the Order relates.

(3) A work of joint authorship qualifies for copyright protection if at the material time any of the authors satisfies the requirements of subsection (1) or (2); but where a work qualifies for copyright protection only under this section, only those authors who satisfy those requirements shall be taken into account for the purposes of—

section 11(1) and (2) (first ownership of copyright; entitlement of author or author's employer),

section 12 (duration of copyright), and section 9(4) (meaning of "unknown authorship") so far as it applies for the purposes of section 12, and

section 57 (anonymous or pseudonymous works: acts permitted on assumptions as to expiry of copyright or death of author).

(4) The material time in relation to a literary, dramatic, musical or artistic work is—
  (a) in the case of an unpublished work, when the work was made or, if the making of the work extended over a period, a substantial part of that period;
  (b) in the case of a published work, when the work was first published or, if the author had died before that time, immediately before his death.

(5) The material time in relation to other descriptions of work is as follows—
  (a) in the case of a sound recording or film, when it was made;
  (b) in the case of a broadcast, when the broadcast was made;
  (c) . . .
  (d) in the case of the typographical arrangement of a published edition, when the edition was first published.

155 Qualification by reference to country of first publication

(1) A literary, dramatic, musical or artistic work, a sound recording or film, or the typographical arrangement of a published edition, qualifies for copyright protection if it is first published—
  (a) in the United Kingdom, another EEA state, the Channel Islands, the Isle of Man or Gibraltar or
  (b) in a country to which the relevant provisions of this Part extend.

(2) Where, or so far as, provision is made by Order under section 159 (application of this Part to countries to which it does not extend), such a work also qualifies for copyright protection if it is first published in a country to which the Order relates.

(3) For the purposes of this section, publication in one country shall not be regarded as other than the first publication by reason of simultaneous publication elsewhere; and for this purpose publication elsewhere within the previous 30 days shall be treated as simultaneous.

156 Qualification by reference to place of transmission

(1) A broadcast qualifies for copyright protection if it is made from a place in—
  (a) the United Kingdom, another EEA state, the Channel Islands, the Isle of Man or Gibraltar or
  (b) in a country to which the relevant provisions of this Part extend.

(2) Where, or so far as, provision is made by Order under section 159 (application of this Part to countries to which it does not extend), a broadcast also qualifies for copyright protection if it is made from a place in a country to which the Order relates.

Extent and application of this Part

157 Countries to which this Part extends

(1) This Part extends to England and Wales, Scotland and Northern Ireland.

(2) Her Majesty may by Order in Council direct that this Part shall extend, subject to such exceptions and modifications as may be specified in the Order, to—
  (a) any of the Channel Islands,
  (b) the Isle of Man, or
  (c) any colony.

(3) That power includes power to extend, subject to such exceptions and modifications as may be specified in the Order, any Order in Council made under the following provisions of this Chapter.

(4) The legislature of a country to which this Part has been extended may modify or add to the provisions of this Part, in their operation as part of the law of that country, as the legislature may consider necessary to adapt the provisions to the circumstances of that country—
  (a) as regards procedure and remedies, or

(b)　as regards works qualifying for copyright protection by virtue of a connection with that country.

(5)　Nothing in this section shall be construed as restricting the extent of paragraph 36 of Schedule 1 (transitional provisions: dependent territories where the Copyright Act 1956 or the Copyright Act 1911 remains in force) in relation to the law of a dependent territory to which this Part does not extend.

159　Application of this Part to countries to which it does not extend

(1)　Where a country is a party to the Berne Convention or a member of the World Trade Organisation, this Part, so far as it relates to literary, dramatic, musical and artistic works, films and typographical arrangements of published editions—

(a)　applies in relation to a citizen or subject of that country or a person domiciled or resident there as it applies in relation to a person who is a British citizen or is domiciled or resident in the United Kingdom,

(b)　applies in relation to a body incorporated under the law of that country as it applies in relation to a body incorporated under the law of a part of the United Kingdom, and

(c)　applies in relation to a work first published in that country as it applies in relation to a work first published in the United Kingdom.

(2)　Where a country is a party to the Rome Convention, this Part, so far as it relates to sound recordings and broadcasts—

(a)　applies in relation to that country as mentioned in paragraphs (a), (b) and (c) of subsection (1), and

(b)　applies in relation to a broadcast made from that country as it applies to a broadcast made from the United Kingdom.

(3)　Where a country is a party to the WPPT, this Part, so far as relating to sound recordings, applies in relation to that country as mentioned in paragraphs (a), (b) and (c) of subsection (1).

(4)　Her Majesty may by Order in Council—

(a)　make provision for the application of this Part to a country by subsection (1), (2) or (3) to be subject to specified restrictions;

(b)　make provision for applying this Part, or any of its provisions, to a specified country;

(c)　make provision for applying this Part, or any of its provisions, to any country of a specified description;

(d)　make provision for the application of legislation to a country under paragraph (b) or (c) to be subject to specified restrictions.

(5)　Provision made under subsection (4) may apply generally or in relation to such classes of works, or other classes of case, as are specified.

(6)　Her Majesty may not make an Order in Council containing provision under subsection (4)(b) or (c) unless satisfied that provision has been or will be made under the law of the country or countries in question, in respect of the classes to which the provision under subsection (4)(b) or (c) relates, giving adequate protection to the owners of copyright under this Part.

(7)　Application under subsection (4)(b) or (c) is in addition to application by subsections (1) to (3).

(8)　Provision made under subsection (4)(c) may cover countries that become (or again become) of the specified description after the provision comes into force.

(9)　In this section—

"the Berne Convention" means any Act of the International Convention for the Protection of Literary and Artistic Works signed at Berne on 9 September 1886;

"the Rome Convention" means the International Convention for the Protection of Performers, Producers of Phonograms and Broadcasting Organisations done at Rome on 26 October 1961;

"the WPPT" means the World Intellectual Property Organisation Performances and Phonograms Treaty adopted in Geneva on 20 December 1996.

(10)　A statutory instrument containing an Order in Council under this section is subject to annulment in pursuance of a resolution of either House of Parliament.

160   Denial of copyright protection to citizens of countries not giving adequate protection to British works

(1)   If it appears to Her Majesty that the law of a country fails to give adequate protection to British works to which this section applies, or to one or more classes of such works, Her Majesty may make provision by Order in Council in accordance with this section restricting the rights conferred by this Part in relation to works of authors connected with that country.

(2)   An Order in Council under this section shall designate the country concerned and provide that, for the purposes specified in the Order, works first published after a date specified in the Order shall not be treated as qualifying for copyright protection by virtue of such publication if at that time the authors are—

(a)   citizens or subjects of that country (not domiciled or resident in the United Kingdom or another country to which the relevant provisions of this Part extend), or

(b)   bodies incorporated under the law of that country;

and the Order may make such provision for all the purposes of this Part or for such purposes as are specified in the Order, and either generally or in relation to such class of cases as are specified in the Order, having regard to the nature and extent of that failure referred to in subsection (1).

(3)   This section applies to literary, dramatic, musical and artistic works, sound recordings and films; and "British works" means works of which the author was a qualifying person at the material time within the meaning of section 154.

(4)   A statutory instrument containing an Order in Council under this section shall be subject to annulment in pursuance of a resolution of either House of Parliament.

Supplementary

161   Territorial waters and the continental shelf

(1)   For the purposes of this Part the territorial waters of the United Kingdom shall be treated as part of the United Kingdom.

(2)   This Part applies to things done in the United Kingdom sector of the continental shelf on a structure or vessel which is present there for purposes directly connected with the exploration of the sea bed or subsoil or the exploitation of their natural resources as it applies to things done in the United Kingdom.

(3)   The United Kingdom sector of the continental shelf means the areas designated by order under section 1(7) of the Continental Shelf Act 1964.

162   British ships, aircraft and hovercraft

(1)   This Part applies to things done on a British ship, aircraft or hovercraft as it applies to things done in the United Kingdom.

(2)   In this section—

"British ship" means a ship which is a British ship for the purposes of the Merchant Shipping Acts 1995 otherwise than by virtue of registration in a country outside the United Kingdom; and

"British aircraft" and "British hovercraft" mean an aircraft or hovercraft registered in the United Kingdom.

CHAPTER X
MISCELLANEOUS AND GENERAL

Crown and Parliamentary copyright

163   Crown copyright

(1)   Where a work is made by Her Majesty or by an officer or servant of the Crown in the course of his duties—

(a)   the work qualifies for copyright protection notwithstanding section 153(1) (ordinary requirement as to qualification for copyright protection), and

(b)   Her Majesty is the first owner of any copyright in the work.

(2) Copyright in such a work is referred to in this Part as "Crown copyright", notwithstanding that it may be, or have been, assigned to another person.

(3) Crown copyright in a literary, dramatic, musical or artistic work continues to subsist—

(a) until the end of the period of 125 years from the end of the calendar year in which the work was made, or

(b) if the work is published commercially before the end of the period of 75 years from the end of the calendar year in which it was made, until the end of the period of 50 years from the end of the calendar year in which it was first so published.

(4) In the case of a work of joint authorship where one or more but not all of the authors are persons falling within subsection (1), this section applies only in relation to those authors and the copyright subsisting by virtue of their contribution to the work.

(5) Except as mentioned above, and subject to any express exclusion elsewhere in this Part, the provisions of this Part apply in relation to Crown copyright as to other copyright.

(6) This section does not apply to a work if, or to the extent that, Parliamentary copyright subsists in the work (see sections 165 to 166D).

164 Copyright in Acts and Measures

(1) Her Majesty is entitled to copyright in every Act of Parliament, Act of the Scottish Parliament, Measure of the National Assembly for Wales, Act of the National Assembly for Wales, Act of the Northern Ireland Assembly or Measure of the General Synod of the Church of England.

(2) The copyright subsists—

(a) in the case of an Act or a Measure of the General Synod of the Church of England, until the end of the period of 50 years from the end of the calendar year in which Royal Assent was given, and

(b) in the case of a Measure of the National Assembly for Wales, until the end of the period of 50 years from the end of the calendar year in which the Measure was approved by Her Majesty in Council.

(3) References in this Part to Crown copyright (except in section 163) include copyright under this section; and, except as mentioned above, the provisions of this Part apply in relation to copyright under this section as to other Crown copyright.

(4) No other copyright, or right in the nature of copyright, subsists in an Act or Measure.

165 Parliamentary copyright

(1) Where a work is made by or under the direction or control of the House of Commons or the House of Lords—

(a) the work qualifies for copyright protection notwithstanding section 153(1) (ordinary requirement as to qualification for copyright protection), and

(b) the House by whom, or under whose direction or control, the work is made is the first owner of any copyright in the work, and if the work is made by or under the direction or control of both Houses, the two Houses are joint first owners of copyright.

(2) Copyright in such a work is referred to in this Part as "Parliamentary copyright", notwithstanding that it may be, or have been, assigned to another person.

(3) Parliamentary copyright in a literary, dramatic, musical or artistic work continues to subsist until the end of the period of 50 years from the end of the calendar year in which the work was made.

(4) For the purposes of this section, works made by or under the direction or control of the House of Commons or the House of Lords include—

(a) any work made by an officer or employee of that House in the course of his duties, and

(b) any sound recording, film, or live broadcast of the proceedings of that House; but a work shall not be regarded as made by or under the direction or control of either House by reason only of its being commissioned by or on behalf of that House.

(5) In the case of a work of joint authorship where one or more but not all of the authors are acting on behalf of, or under the direction or control of, the House of Commons or the House of Lords, this section applies only in relation to those authors and the copyright subsisting by virtue of their contribution to the work.

(6)   Except as mentioned above, and subject to any express exclusion elsewhere in this Part, the provisions of this Part apply in relation to Parliamentary copyright as to other copyright.

(7)   The provisions of this section also apply, subject to any exceptions or modifications specified by Order in Council, to works made by or under the direction or control of any other legislative body of a country to which this Part extends; and references in this Part to "Parliamentary copyright" shall be construed accordingly.

(8)   A statutory instrument containing an Order in Council under subsection (7) shall be subject to annulment in pursuance of a resolution of either House of Parliament.

166   Copyright in Parliamentary Bills

(1)   Copyright in every Bill introduced into Parliament belongs, in accordance with the following provisions, to one or both of the Houses of Parliament.

(2)   Copyright in a public Bill belongs in the first instance to the House into which the Bill is introduced, and after the Bill has been carried to the second House to both Houses jointly, and subsists from the time when the text of the Bill is handed in to the House in which it is introduced.

(3)   Copyright in a private Bill belongs to both Houses jointly and subsists from the time when a copy of the Bill is first deposited in either House.

(4)   Copyright in a personal Bill belongs in the first instance to the House of Lords, and after the Bill has been carried to the House of Commons to both Houses jointly, and subsists from the time when it is given a First Reading in the House of Lords.

(5)   Copyright under this section ceases—
(a)   on Royal Assent, or
(b)   if the Bill does not receive Royal Assent, on the withdrawal or rejection of the Bill or the end of the Session:
Provided that, copyright in a Bill continues to subsist notwithstanding its rejection in any Session by the House of Lords if, by virtue of the Parliament Acts 1911 and 1949, it remains possible for it to be presented for Royal Assent in that Session.

(6)   References in this Part to Parliamentary copyright (except in section 165) include copyright under this section; and, except as mentioned above, the provisions of this Part apply in relation to copyright under this section as to other Parliamentary copyright.

(7)   No other copyright, or right in the nature of copyright, subsists in a Bill after copyright has once subsisted under this section; but without prejudice to the subsequent operation of this section in relation to a Bill which, not having passed in one Session, is reintroduced in a subsequent Session.

166A   Copyright in Bills of the Scottish Parliament

(1)   Copyright in every Bill introduced into the Scottish Parliament belongs to the Scottish Parliamentary Corporate Body.

(2)   Copyright under this section subsists from the time when the text of the Bill is handed in to the Parliament for introduction—
(a)   until the Bill receives Royal Assent, or
(b)   if the Bill does not receive Royal Assent, until it is withdrawn or rejected or no further parliamentary proceedings may be taken in respect of it.

(3)   References in this Part to Parliamentary copyright (except in section 165) include copyright under this section; and, except as mentioned above, the provisions of this Part apply in relation to copyright under this section as to other Parliamentary copyright.

(4)   No other copyright, or right in the nature of copyright, subsists in a Bill after copyright has once subsisted under this section; but without prejudice to the subsequent operation of this section in relation to a Bill which, not having received Royal Assent, is later reintroduced into the Parliament.

166B   Copyright in Bills of the Northern Ireland Assembly

(1)   Copyright in every Bill introduced into the Northern Ireland Assembly belongs to the Northern Ireland Assembly Commission.

(2)   Copyright under this section subsists from the time when the text of the Bill is handed in to the Assembly for introduction—
(a)   until the Bill receives Royal Assent, or

    (b)   if the Bill does not receive Royal Assent, until it is withdrawn or rejected or no further proceedings of the Assembly may be taken in respect of it.

(3)   References in this Part to Parliamentary copyright (except in section 165) include copyright under this section; and, except as mentioned above, the provisions of this Part apply in relation to copyright under this section as to other Parliamentary copyright.

(4)   No other copyright, or right in the nature of copyright, subsists in a Bill after copyright has once subsisted under this section; but without prejudice to the subsequent operation of this section in relation to a Bill which, not having received Royal Assent, is later reintroduced into the Assembly.

166C Copyright in proposed Measures of the National Assembly for Wales

(1)   Copyright in every proposed Assembly Measure introduced into the National Assembly for Wales belongs to the National Assembly for Wales Commission.

(2)   Copyright under this section subsists from the time when the text of the proposed Assembly Measure is handed in to the Assembly for introduction—
    (a)   until the proposed Assembly Measure is approved by Her Majesty in Council, or
    (b)   if the proposed Assembly Measure is not approved by Her Majesty in Council, until it is withdrawn or rejected or no further proceedings of the Assembly may be taken in respect of it.

(3)   References in this Part to Parliamentary copyright (except in section 165) include copyright under this section; and, except as mentioned above, the provisions of this Part apply in relation to copyright under this section as to other Parliamentary copyright.

(4)   No other copyright, or right in the nature of copyright, subsists in a proposed Assembly Measure after copyright has once subsisted under this section; but without prejudice to the subsequent operation of this section in relation to a proposed Assembly Measure which, not having been approved by Her Majesty in Council, is later reintroduced into the Assembly.

166D Copyright in Bills of the National Assembly for Wales

(1)   Copyright in every Bill introduced into the National Assembly for Wales belongs to the National Assembly for Wales Commission.

(2)   Copyright under this section subsists from the time when the text of the Bill is handed in to the Assembly for introduction—
    (a)   until the Bill receives Royal Assent, or
    (b)   if the Bill does not receive Royal Assent, until it is withdrawn or rejected or no further proceedings of the Assembly may be taken in respect of it.

(3)   References in this Part to Parliamentary copyright (except in section 165) include copyright under this section; and, except as mentioned above, the provisions of this Part apply in relation to copyright under this section as to other Parliamentary copyright.

(4)   No other copyright, or right in the nature of copyright, subsists in a Bill after copyright has once subsisted under this section; but without prejudice to the subsequent operation of this section in relation to a Bill which, not having received Royal Assent, is later reintroduced into the Assembly.

167 Houses of Parliament: supplementary provisions with respect to copyright

(1)   For the purposes of holding, dealing with and enforcing copyright, and in connection with all legal proceedings relating to copyright, each House of Parliament shall be treated as having the legal capacities of a body corporate, which shall not be affected by a prorogation or dissolution.

(2)   The functions of the House of Commons as owner of copyright shall be exercised by the Speaker on behalf of the House; and if so authorised by the Speaker, or in case of a vacancy in the office of Speaker, those functions may be discharged by the Chairman of Ways and Means or a Deputy Chairman.

(3)   For this purpose a person who on the dissolution of Parliament was Speaker of the House of Commons, Chairman of Ways and Means or a Deputy Chairman may continue to act until the corresponding appointment is made in the next Session of Parliament.

(4)   The functions of the House of Lords as owner of copyright shall be exercised by the Clerk of the Parliaments on behalf of the House; and if so authorised by him, or in case of a vacancy in the office of Clerk of the Parliaments, those functions may be discharged by the Clerk Assistant or the Reading Clerk.

(5)   Legal proceedings relating to copyright—
        (a)   shall be brought by or against the House of Commons in the name of "The Speaker of the House of Commons"; and
        (b)   shall be brought by or against the House of Lords in the name of "The Clerk of the Parliaments".

Other miscellaneous provisions

168   Copyright vesting in certain international organisations

(1)   Where an original literary, dramatic, musical or artistic work—
        (a)   is made by an officer or employee of, or is published by, an international organisation to which this section applies, and
        (b)   does not qualify for copyright protection under section 154 (qualification by reference to author) or section 155 (qualification by reference to country of first publication),
        copyright nevertheless subsists in the work by virtue of this section and the organisation is first owner of that copyright.

(2)   The international organisations to which this section applies are those as to which Her Majesty has by Order in Council declared that it is expedient that this section should apply.

(3)   Copyright of which an international organisation is first owner by virtue of this section continues to subsist until the end of the period of 50 years from the end of the calendar year in which the work was made or such longer period as may be specified by Her Majesty by Order in Council for the purpose of complying with the international obligations of the United Kingdom.

(4)   An international organisation to which this section applies shall be deemed to have, and to have had at all material times, the legal capacities of a body corporate for the purpose of holding, dealing with and enforcing copyright and in connection with all legal proceedings relating to copyright.

(5)   A statutory instrument containing an Order in Council under this section shall be subject to annulment in pursuance of a resolution of either House of Parliament.

169   Folklore, etc.: anonymous unpublished works

(1)   Where in the case of an unpublished literary, dramatic, musical or artistic work of unknown authorship there is evidence that the author (or, in the case of a joint work, any of the authors) was a qualifying individual by connection with a country outside the United Kingdom, it shall be presumed until the contrary is proved that he was such a qualifying individual and that copyright accordingly subsists in the work, subject to the provisions of this Part.

(2)   If under the law of that country a body is appointed to protect and enforce copyright in such works, Her Majesty may by Order in Council designate that body for the purposes of this section.

(3)   A body so designated shall be recognised in the United Kingdom as having authority to do in place of the copyright owner anything, other than assign copyright, which it is empowered to do under the law of that country; and it may, in particular, bring proceedings in its own name.

(4)   A statutory instrument containing an Order in Council under this section shall be subject to annulment in pursuance of a resolution of either House of Parliament.

(5)   In subsection (1) a "qualifying individual" means an individual who at the material time (within the meaning of section 154) was a person whose works qualified under that section for copyright protection.

(6)   This section does not apply if there has been an assignment of copyright in the work by the author of which notice has been given to the designated body; and nothing in this section affects the validity of an assignment of copyright made, or licence granted, by the author or a person lawfully claiming under him.

Transitional provisions and savings

170   Transitional provisions and savings

(1)   Schedule 1 contains transitional provisions and savings relating to works made, and acts or events occurring, before the commencement of this Part, and otherwise with respect to the operation of the provisions of this Part.

(2)   The Secretary of State may by regulations amend Schedule 1 to reduce the duration of copyright in existing works which are unpublished, other than photographs or films.

(3)   The regulations may provide for the copyright to expire—

   (a)   with the end of the term of protection of copyright laid down by Directive 2006/116/ EC or at any later time;

   (b)   subject to that, on the commencement of the regulations or at any later time.

(4)   "Existing works" has the same meaning as in Schedule 1.

(5)   Regulations under subsection (2) may—

   (a)   make different provision for different purposes;

   (b)   make supplementary or transitional provision;

   (c)   make consequential provision, including provision amending any enactment or subordinate legislation passed or made before that subsection comes into force.

(6)   The power to make regulations under subsection (2) is exercisable by statutory instrument.

(7)   A statutory instrument containing regulations under subsection (2) may not be made unless a draft of the instrument has been laid before and approved by resolution of each House of Parliament.

171   Rights and privileges under other enactments or the common law

(1)   Nothing in this Part affects—

   (a)   any right or privilege of any person under any enactment (except where the enactment is expressly repealed, amended or modified by this Act);

   (b)   any right or privilege of the Crown subsisting otherwise than under an enactment;

   (c)   any right or privilege of either House of Parliament;

   (d)   the right of the Crown or any person deriving title from the Crown to sell, use or otherwise deal with articles forfeited under the laws relating to customs and excise;

   (e)   the operation of any rule of equity relating to breaches of trust or confidence.

(2)   Subject to those savings, no copyright or right in the nature of copyright shall subsist otherwise than by virtue of this Part or some other enactment in that behalf.

(3)   Nothing in this Part affects any rule of law preventing or restricting the enforcement of copyright, on grounds of public interest or otherwise.

(4)   Nothing in this Part affects any right of action or other remedy, whether civil or criminal, available otherwise than under this Part in respect of acts infringing any of the rights conferred by Chapter IV (moral rights).

(5)   The savings in subsection (1) have effect subject to section 164(4) and section 166(7) (copyright in Acts, Measures and Bills: exclusion of other rights in the nature of copyright).

Interpretation

172   General provisions as to construction

(1)   This Part restates and amends the law of copyright, that is, the provisions of the Copyright Act 1956, as amended.

(2)   A provision of this Part which corresponds to a provision of the previous law shall not be construed as departing from the previous law merely because of a change of expression.

(3)   Decisions under the previous law may be referred to for the purpose of establishing whether a provision of this Part departs from the previous law, or otherwise for establishing the true construction of this Part.

172A Meaning of EEA and related expressions

(1) In this Part—
"the EEA" means the European Economic Area; and
"EEA state" means a member State, Iceland, Liechtenstein or Norway.

(2) References in this Part to a person being a national of an EEA State shall be construed in relation to a body corporate as references to its being incorporated under the law of an EEA state.

173 Construction of references to copyright owner

(1) Where different persons are (whether in consequence of a partial assignment or otherwise) entitled to different aspects of copyright in a work, the copyright owner for any purpose of this Part is the person who is entitled to the aspect of copyright relevant for that purpose.

(2) Where copyright (or any aspect of copyright) is owned by more than one person jointly, references in this Part to the copyright owner are to all the owners, so that, in particular, any requirement of the licence of the copyright owner requires the licence of all of them.

174 Meaning of "educational establishment" and related expressions

(1) The expression "educational establishment" in a provision of this Part means—
(a) any school, and
(b) any other description of educational establishment specified for the purposes of this Part, or that provision, by order of the Secretary of State.

(2) The Secretary of State may by order provide that the provisions of this Part relating to educational establishments shall apply, with such modifications and adaptations as may be specified in the order, in relation to teachers who are employed by a local authority (as defined in section 579(1) of the Education Act 1996) or (in Northern Ireland) a local education authority, to give instruction elsewhere to pupils who are unable to attend an educational establishment.

(3) In subsection (1)(a) "school"—
(a) in relation to England and Wales, has the same meaning as in the Education Act 1996;
(b) in relation to Scotland, has the same meaning as in the Education (Scotland) Act 1962, except that it includes an approved school within the meaning of the Social Work (Scotland) Act 1968; and
(c) in relation to Northern Ireland, has the same meaning as in the Education and Libraries (Northern Ireland) Order 1986.

(4) An order under subsection (1)(b) may specify a description of educational establishment by reference to the instruments from time to time in force under any enactment specified in the order.

(5) In relation to an educational establishment the expressions "teacher" and "pupil" in this Part include, respectively, any person who gives and any person who receives instruction.

(6) References in this Part to anything being done "on behalf of" an educational establishment are to its being done for the purposes of that establishment by any person.

(7) An order under this section shall be made by statutory instrument which shall be subject to annulment in pursuance of a resolution of either House of Parliament.

175 Meaning of publication and commercial publication

(1) In this Part "publication", in relation to a work—
(a) means the issue of copies to the public, and
(b) includes, in the case of a literary, dramatic, musical or artistic work, making it available to the public by means of an electronic retrieval system;
and related expressions shall be construed accordingly.

(2) In this Part "commercial publication", in relation to a literary, dramatic, musical or artistic work means—
(a) issuing copies of the work to the public at a time when copies made in advance of the receipt of orders are generally available to the public, or

(b)   making the work available to the public by means of an electronic retrieval system; and related expressions shall be construed accordingly.

(3)   In the case of a work of architecture in the form of a building, or an artistic work incorporated in a building, construction of the building shall be treated as equivalent to publication of the work.

(4)   The following do not constitute publication for the purposes of this Part and references to commercial publication shall be construed accordingly—

(a)   in the case of a literary, dramatic or musical work—
(i)   the performance of the work, or
(ii)   the communication to the public of the work (otherwise than for the purposes of an electronic retrieval system);

(b)   in the case of an artistic work—
(i)   the exhibition of the work,
(ii)   the issue to the public of copies of a graphic work representing, or of photographs of, a work of architecture in the form of a building or a model for a building, a sculpture or a work of artistic craftsmanship,
(iii)   the issue to the public of copies of a film including the work, or
(iv)   the communication to the public of the work (otherwise than for the purposes of an electronic retrieval system);

(c)   in the case of a sound recording or film—
(i)   the work being played or shown in public, or
(ii)   the communication to the public of the work.

(5)   References in this Part to publication or commercial publication do not include publication which is merely colourable and not intended to satisfy the reasonable requirements of the public.

(6)   No account shall be taken for the purposes of this section of any unauthorised act.

176   Requirement of signature: application in relation to body corporate

(1)   The requirement in the following provisions that an instrument be signed by or on behalf of a person is also satisfied in the case of a body corporate by the affixing of its seal—

section 78(3)(b) (assertion by licensor of right to identification of author in case of public exhibition of copy made in pursuance of the licence),
section 90(3) (assignment of copyright),
section 91(1) (assignment of future copyright),
section 92(1) (grant of exclusive licence).

(2)   The requirement in the following provisions that an instrument be signed by a person is satisfied in the case of a body corporate by signature on behalf of the body or by the affixing of its seal—

section 78(2)(b) (assertion by instrument in writing of right to have author identified),
section 87(2) (waiver of moral rights).

177   Adaptation of expressions for Scotland

In the application of this Part to Scotland—
"account of profits" means accounting and payment of profits; "accounts" means count, reckoning and payment; "assignment" means assignation;
"costs" means expenses;
"defendant" means defender;
"delivery up" means delivery;
"estoppel" means personal bar;
"injunction" means interdict;
"interlocutory relief" means interim remedy; and
"plaintiff" means pursuer.

178   Minor definitions

In this Part—
"article", in the context of an article in a periodical, includes an item of any description;
"business" includes a trade or profession;
"collective work" means—
(a)   a work of joint authorship, or

(b)   a work in which there are distinct contributions by different authors or in which works or parts of works of different authors are incorporated;

"computer-generated", in relation to a work, means that the work is generated by computer in circumstances such that there is no human author of the work;

"country" includes any territory;

"the Crown" includes the Crown in right of the Scottish Administration, of the Welsh Government or of Her Majesty's Government in Northern Ireland or in any country outside the United Kingdom to which this Part extends;

"electronic" means actuated by electric, magnetic, electro-magnetic, electro-chemical or electro-mechanical energy, and "in electronic form" means in a form usable only by electronic means;

"employed", "employee", "employer" and "employment" refer to employment under a contract of service or of apprenticeship;

"facsimile copy" includes a copy which is reduced or enlarged in scale;

"international organisation" means an organisation the members of which include one or more states;

"judicial proceedings" includes proceedings before any court, tribunal or person having authority to decide any matter affecting a person's legal rights or liabilities;

"parliamentary proceedings" includes proceedings of the Northern Ireland Assembly, of the Scottish Parliament or of the European Parliament and Assembly proceedings within the meaning of section 1(5) of the Government of Wales Act 2006;

"private study" does not include any study which is directly or indirectly for a commercial purpose;

"producer" in relation to a sound recording or a film, means the person by whom the arrangements necessary for the sound recording or film are undertaken.

"public library" means a library administered by or on behalf of—

(a)   in England and Wales, a library authority within the meaning of the Public Libraries and Museums Act 1964;

(b)   in Scotland, a statutory library authority within the meaning of the Public Libraries (Scotland) Act 1955;

(c)   in Northern Ireland, an Education or Library Board within the meaning of the Education and Libraries (Northern Ireland) Order 1986;

"rental right" means the right of a copyright owner to authorise or prohibit the rental of copies of the work (see section 18A);

"reprographic copy" and "reprographic copying" refer to copying by means of a reprographic process;

"reprographic process" means a process—

(a)   for making facsimile copies, or

(b)   involving the use of an appliance for making multiple copies,

and includes, in relation to a work held in electronic form, any copying by electronic means, but does not include the making of a film or sound recording;

"sufficient acknowledgement" means an acknowledgement identifying the work in question by its title or other description, and identifying the author unless—

(a)   in the case of a published work, it is published anonymously;

(b)   in the case of an unpublished work, it is not possible for a person to ascertain the identity of the author by reasonable inquiry;

"sufficient disclaimer", in relation to an act capable of infringing the right conferred by section 80 (right to object to derogatory treatment of work), means a clear and reasonably prominent indication—

(a)   given at the time of the act, and

(b)   if the author or director is then identified, appearing along with the identification,

that the work has been subjected to treatment to which the author or director has not consented;

"telecommunications system" means a system for conveying visual images, sounds or other information by electronic means;

"typeface" includes an ornamental motif used in printing;

"unauthorised", as regards anything done in relation to a work, means done otherwise than—

(a)   by or with the licence of the copyright owner, or

(b)　if copyright does not subsist in the work, by or with the licence of the author or, in a case where section 11(2) would have applied, the author's employer or, in either case, persons lawfully claiming under him, or

(c)　in pursuance of section 48 (copying, etc. of certain material by the Crown);

"wireless broadcast" means a broadcast by means of wireless telegraphy;

"wireless telegraphy" means the sending of electro-magnetic energy over paths not provided by a material substance constructed or arranged for that purpose, but does not include the transmission of microwave energy between terrestrial fixed points;

"writing" includes any form of notation or code, whether by hand or otherwise and regardless of the method by which, or medium in or on which, it is recorded, and "written" shall be construed accordingly.

179　Index of defined expressions

The following Table shows provisions defining or otherwise explaining expressions used in this Part (other than provisions defining or explaining an expression used only in the same section)—

accessible copy (in sections 31A to 31F)	section 31F(4)
account of profits and accounts (in Scotland)	section 177
acts restricted by copyright	section 16(1)
adaptation	section 21(3)
approved body	section 31B(12)
archivist (in sections 40A to 43)	section 43A(5)
article (in a periodical)	section 178
artistic work	section 4(1)
assignment (in Scotland)	section 177
author	sections 9 and 10(3)
authorised body (in sections 31B to 31BB)	section 31F(6)
broadcast (and related expressions)	section 6
building	section 4(2)
business	section 178
. . .	
collective work	section 178
commencement (in Schedule 1)	paragraph 1(2) of that Schedule
commercial publication	section 175
communication to the public	section 20
computer-generated	section 178
conducted for profit (in sections 40A to 43)	section 43A(4)
copy and copying	section 17
copyright (generally)	section 1
copyright (in Schedule 1)	paragraph 2(2) of that Schedule
copyright owner	section 101(2) and 173
Copyright Tribunal	section 145
copyright work	section 1(2)
costs (in Scotland)	section 177
country	section 178
country of origin	section 15A
the Crown	section 178
Crown copyright	sections 163(2) and 164(3)
curator (in sections 40A to 43)	section 43A(5)
Database	section 3A(1)
defendant (in Scotland)	section 177
delivery up (in Scotland)	section 177
disabled person (in sections 31A to 31F)	section 31F(2) and (3)
dramatic work	section 3(1)
educational establishment	sections 174(1) to (4)
the EEA, EEA state and national of an EEA state	section 172A
electronic and electronic form	section 178
employed, employee, employer and employment	section 178
excepted sound recording	section 72(1A)

exclusive licence	section 92(1)
existing works (in Schedule 1)	paragraph 1(3) of that Schedule
facsimile copy	section 178
film	section 5B
future copyright	section 91(2)
general licence (in sections 140 and 141)	section 140(7)
graphic work	section 4(2)
infringing copy	section 27
injunction (in Scotland)	section 177
interlocutory relief (in Scotland)	section 177
international organization	section 178
issue of copies to the public	section 18
joint authorship (work of)	sections 10(1) and (2)
judicial proceedings	section 178
lawful user (in sections 50A to 50C)	section 50A(2)
lending	section 18A(2) to (6)
librarian (in sections 40A to 43)	section 43A(5)
library (in sections 40A to 43)	section 43A(2)
licence (in sections 125 to 128)	section 124
licence of copyright owner	sections 90(4), 91(3) and 173
licensing body (in Chapter VII)	section 116(2)
licensing scheme (generally)	section 116(1)
licensing scheme (in sections 118 to 121)	section 117
literary work	section 3(1)
made (in relation to a literary, dramatic or musical work)	section 3(2)
museum (in sections 40A to 43)	section 43A(3)
musical work	section 3(1)
needletime	section 135A
the new copyright provisions (in Schedule 1)	paragraph 1(1) of that Schedule
the 1911 Act (in Schedule 1)	paragraph 1(1) of that Schedule
the 1956 Act (in Schedule 1)	paragraph 1(1) of that Schedule
on behalf of (in relation to an educational establishment)	section 174(5)
original (in relation to a database)	section 3A(2)
Parliamentary copyright	sections 165(2) and (7) and 166(6), 166A(3), 166B(3), 166C(3) and 166D(3)
parliamentary proceedings	section 178
performance	section 19(2)
photograph	section 4(2)
plaintiff (in Scotland)	section 177
private study	section 178
producer (in relation to a sound recording or film)	section 178
programme (in the context of broadcasting)	section 6(3)
prospective owner (of copyright)	section 91(2)
publication and related expressions	section 175
public library	section 178
published edition (in the context of copyright in the typographical arrangement)	section 8
pupil	section 174(5)
rental	section 18A(2) to (6)
rental right	section 178
reprographic copies and reprographic copying	section 178
reprographic process	section 178
sculpture	section 4(2)
signed	section 176
sound recording	section 5A and 135A
sufficient acknowledgement	section 178
sufficient disclaimer	section 178

supply (in sections 31B to 31BB)	section 31F(7)
teacher	section 174(5)
telecommunications system	section 178
terms of payment	section 135A
typeface	section 178
unauthorised (as regards things done in relation to a work)	section 178
unknown (in relation to the author of a work)	section 9(5)
unknown authorship (work of)	section 9(4)
wireless broadcast	section 178
wireless telegraphy	section 178
work (in Schedule 1)	paragraph 2(1) of that Schedule
work of more than one author (in Chapter VII)	section 116(4)
writing and written	section 178

PART II

RIGHTS IN PERFORMANCES

CHAPTER 1

INTRODUCTORY

180　Rights conferred on performers and persons having recording rights

(1)　Chapter 2 of this Part (economic rights) confers rights—

(a)　on a performer, by requiring his consent to the exploitation of his performances (see sections 181 to 184), and

(b)　on a person having recording rights in relation to a performance, in relation to recordings made without his consent or that of the performer (see sections 185 to 188),

and creates offences in relation to dealing with or using illicit recordings and certain other related acts (see sections 198 and 201).

(1A)　Rights are also conferred on a performer by the following provisions of Chapter 3 of this Part (moral rights)—

(a)　section 205C (right to be identified);

(b)　section 205F (right to object to derogatory treatment of performance).

(2)　In this Part—

"performance" means—

(a)　a dramatic performance (which includes dance and mime),

(b)　a musical performance,

(c)　a reading or recitation of a literary work, or

(d)　a performance of a variety act or any similar presentation,

which is, or so far as it is, a live performance given by one or more individuals; and "recording", in relation to a performance, means a film or sound recording—

(a)　made directly from the live performance,

(b)　made from a broadcast of the performance, or

(c)　made, directly or indirectly, from another recording of the performance.

(3)　The rights conferred by this Part apply in relation to performances taking place before the commencement of this Part; but no act done before commencement, or in pursuance of arrangements made before commencement, shall be regarded as infringing those rights.

(4)　The rights conferred by this Part are independent of—

(a)　any copyright in, or moral rights relating to, any work performed or any film or sound recording of, or broadcast including, the performance, and

(b)　any other right or obligation arising otherwise than under this Part.

181　Qualifying performances

A performance is a qualifying performance for the purposes of the provisions of this Part relating to performers' rights if it is given by a qualifying individual (as defined in section 206) or takes place in a qualifying country (as so defined).

CHAPTER 2
ECONOMIC RIGHTS

Performers' rights

182   Consent required for recording, etc. of live performance

(1)   A performer's rights are infringed by a person who, without his consent—

    (a)   makes a recording of the whole or any substantial part of a qualifying performance directly from the live performance,

    (b)   broadcasts live the whole or any substantial part of a qualifying performance,

    (c)   makes a recording of the whole or any substantial part of a qualifying performance directly from a broadcast of the live performance.

(2)   . . .

(3)   In an action for infringement of a performer's rights brought by virtue of this section damages shall not be awarded against a defendant who shows that at the time of the infringement he believed on reasonable grounds that consent had been given.

182A Consent required for copying of recording

(1)   A performer's rights are infringed by a person who, without his consent, makes a copy of a recording of the whole or any substantial part of a qualifying performance.

(1A) In subsection (1), making a copy of a recording includes making a copy which is transient or is incidental to some other use of the original recording.

(2)   It is immaterial whether the copy is made directly or indirectly.

(3)   The right of a performer under this section to authorise or prohibit the making of such copies is referred to in this Chapter as "reproduction right".

182B Consent required for issue of copies to public

(1)   A performer's rights are infringed by a person who, without his consent, issues to the public copies of a recording of the whole or any substantial part of a qualifying performance.

(2)   References in this Part to the issue to the public of copies of a recording are to—

    (a)   the act of putting into circulation in the EEA copies not previously put into circulation in the EEA by or with the consent of the performer, or

    (b)   the act of putting into circulation outside the EEA copies not previously put into circulation in the EEA or elsewhere.

(3)   References in this Part to the issue to the public of copies of a recording do not include—

    (a)   any subsequent distribution, sale, hiring or loan of copies previously put into circulation (but see section 182C: consent required for rental or lending), or

    (b)   any subsequent importation of such copies into the United Kingdom or another EEA state,

except so far as paragraph (a) of subsection (2) applies to putting into circulation in the EEA copies previously put into circulation outside the EEA.

(4)   References in this Part to the issue of copies of a recording of a performance include the issue of the original recording of the live performance.

(5)   The right of a performer under this section to authorise or prohibit the issue of copies to the public is referred to in this Chapter as "distribution right".

182C Consent required for rental or lending of copies to public

(1)   A performer's rights are infringed by a person who, without his consent, rents or lends to the public copies of a recording of the whole or any substantial part of a qualifying performance.

(2)   In this Chapter, subject to the following provisions of this section—

    (a)   "rental" means making a copy of a recording available for use, on terms that it will or may be returned, for direct or indirect economic or commercial advantage, and

    (a)   "lending" means making a copy of a recording available for use, on terms that it will or may be returned, otherwise than for direct or indirect economic or commercial advantage, through an establishment which is accessible to the public.

(3) The expressions "rental" and "lending" do not include—
    (a) making available for the purpose of public performance, playing or showing in public or communication to the public;
    (b) making available for the purpose of exhibition in public; or
    (c) making available for on-the-spot reference use

(4) The expression "lending" does not include making available between establishments which are accessible to the public.

(5) Where lending by an establishment accessible to the public gives rise to a payment the amount of which does not go beyond what is necessary to cover the operating costs of the establishment, there is no direct or indirect economic or commercial advantage for the purposes of this section.

(6) References in this Chapter to the rental or lending of copies of a recording of a performance include the rental or lending of the original recording of the live performance.

(7) In this Chapter—
"rental right" means the right of a performer under this section to authorise or prohibit the rental of copies to the public, and
"lending right" means the right of a performer under this section to authorise or prohibit the lending of copies to the public.

182CA Consent required for making available to the public

(1) A performer's rights are infringed by a person who, without his consent, makes available to the public a recording of the whole or any substantial part of a qualifying performance by electronic transmission in such a way that members of the public may access the recording from a place and at a time individually chosen by them.

(2) The right of a performer under this section to authorise or prohibit the making available to the public of a recording is referred to in this Chapter as "making available right".

182D Right to equitable remuneration for exploitation of sound recording

(1) Where a commercially published sound recording of the whole or any substantial part of a qualifying performance—
    (a) is played in public, or
    (b) is communicated to the public otherwise than by its being made available to the public in the way mentioned in section 182CA(1),
the performer is entitled to equitable remuneration from the owner of the copyright in the sound recording or, where copyright in the sound recording has expired pursuant to section 191HA(4), from a person who plays the sound recording in public or communicates the sound recording to the public.

(1A) In subsection (1), the reference to publication of a sound recording includes making it available to the public by electronic transmission in such a way that members of the public may access it from a place and at a time individually chosen by them.

(2) The right to equitable remuneration under this section may not be assigned by the performer except to a collecting society for the purpose of enabling it to enforce the right on his behalf.
The right is, however, transmissible by testamentary disposition or by operation of law as personal or moveable property; and it may be assigned or further transmitted by any person into whose hands it passes.

(3) The amount payable by way of equitable remuneration is as agreed by or on behalf of the persons by and to whom it is payable, subject to the following provisions.

(4) In default of agreement as to the amount payable by way of equitable remuneration, the person by or to whom it is payable may apply to the Copyright Tribunal to determine the amount payable.

(5) A person to or by whom equitable remuneration is payable may also apply to the Copyright Tribunal—
    (a) to vary any agreement as to the amount payable, or
    (b) to vary any previous determination of the Tribunal as to that matter;
but except with the special leave of the Tribunal no such application may be made within twelve months from the date of a previous determination.
An order made on an application under this subsection has effect from the date on which it is made or such later date as may be specified by the Tribunal.

(6)   On an application under this section the Tribunal shall consider the matter and make such order as to the method of calculating and paying equitable remuneration as it may determine to be reasonable in the circumstances, taking into account the importance of the contribution of the performer to the sound recording.

(7)   An agreement is of no effect in so far as it purports—

(a)   to exclude or restrict the right to equitable remuneration under this section, or

(a)   to prevent a person questioning the amount of equitable remuneration or to restrict the powers of the Copyright Tribunal under this section.

(8)   In this section "collecting society" means a society or other organisation which has as its main object, or one of its main objects, the exercise of the right to equitable remuneration on behalf of more than one performer.

183   Infringement of performer's rights by use of recording made without consent

A performer's rights are infringed by a person who, without his consent—

(a)   shows or plays in public the whole or any substantial part of a qualifying performance, or

(b)   communicates to the public the whole or any substantial part of a qualifying performance,

by means of a recording which was, and which that person knows or has reason to believe was, made without the performer's consent.

184   Infringement of performer's rights by importing, possessing or dealing with illicit recording

(1)   A performer's rights are infringed by a person who, without his consent—

(a)   imports into the United Kingdom otherwise than for his private and domestic use, or

(b)   in the course of a business possesses, sells or lets for hire, offers or exposes for sale or hire, or distributes,

a recording of a qualifying performance which is, and which that person knows or has reason to believe is, an illicit recording.

(2)   Where in an action for infringement of a performer's rights brought by virtue of this section a defendant shows that the illicit recording was innocently acquired by him or a predecessor in title of his, the only remedy available against him in respect of the infringement is damages not exceeding a reasonable payment in respect of the act complained of.

(3)   In subsection (2) "innocently acquired" means that the person acquiring the recording did not know and had no reason to believe that it was an illicit recording.

Rights of person having recording rights

185   Exclusive recording contracts and persons having recording rights

(1)   In this Chapter an "exclusive recording contract" means a contract between a performer and another person under which that person is entitled to the exclusion of all other persons (including the performer) to make recordings of one or more of his performances with a view to their commercial exploitation.

(2)   References in this Chapter to a "person having recording rights", in relation to a performance, are (subject to subsection (3)) to a person—

(a)   who is party to and has the benefit of an exclusive recording contract to which the performance is subject, or

(b)   to whom the benefit of such a contract has been assigned,

and who is a qualifying person.

(3)   If a performance is subject to an exclusive recording contract but the person mentioned in subsection (2) is not a qualifying person, references in this Chapter to a "person having recording rights" in relation to the performance are to any person—

(a)   who is licensed by such a person to make recordings of the performance with a view to their commercial exploitation, or

(b)   to whom the benefit of such a licence has been assigned,

and who is a qualifying person.

(4)   In this section "with a view to commercial exploitation" means with a view to the recordings being sold or let for hire, or shown or played in public.

186   Consent required for recording of performance subject to exclusive contract

(1)   A person infringes the rights of a person having recording rights in relation to a performance who, without his consent or that of the performer, makes a recording of the whole or any substantial part of the performance.

(2)   In an action for infringement of those rights brought by virtue of this section damages shall not be awarded against a defendant who shows that at the time of the infringement he believed on reasonable grounds that consent had been given.

187   Infringement of recording rights by use of recording made without consent

(1)   A person infringes the rights of a person having recording rights in relation to a performance who, without his consent or, in the case of a qualifying performance, that of the performer—

(a)   shows or plays in public the whole or any substantial part of the performance, or

(b)   communicates to the public the whole or any substantial part of the performance,

by means of a recording which was, and which that person knows or has reason to believe was, made without the appropriate consent.

(2)   The reference in subsection (1) to "the appropriate consent" is to the consent of—

(a)   the performer, or

(b)   the person who at the time the consent was given had recording rights in relation to the performance (or, if there was more than one such person, of all of them).

188   Infringement of recording rights by importing, possessing or dealing with illicit recording

(1)   A person infringes the rights of a person having recording rights in relation to a performance who, without his consent or, in the case of a qualifying performance, that of the performer—

(a)   imports into the United Kingdom otherwise than for his private and domestic use, or

(b)   in the course of a business possesses, sells or lets for hire, offers or exposes for sale or hire, or distributes,

a recording of the performance which is, and which that person knows or has reason to believe is, an illicit recording.

(2)   Where in an action for infringement of those rights brought by virtue of this section a defendant shows that the illicit recording was innocently acquired by him or a predecessor in title of his, the only remedy available against him in respect of the infringement is damages not exceeding a reasonable payment in respect of the act complained of.

(3)   In subsection (2) "innocently acquired" means that the person acquiring the recording did not know and had no reason to believe that it was an illicit recording.

Exceptions to rights conferred

189   Acts permitted notwithstanding rights conferred by this Chapter

The provisions of Schedule 2 specify acts which may be done notwithstanding the rights conferred by this Chapter, being acts which correspond broadly to certain of those specified in Chapter III of Part I (acts permitted notwithstanding copyright).

190   Power of tribunal to give consent on behalf of performer in certain cases

(1)   The Copyright Tribunal may, on the application of a person wishing to make a copy of a recording of a performance, give consent in a case where the identity or whereabouts of the person entitled to the reproduction right cannot be ascertained by reasonable inquiry.

(2)   Consent given by the Tribunal has effect as consent of the person entitled to the reproduction right for the purposes of—

(a)   the provisions of this Chapter relating to performers' rights, and

(b)   section 198(3)(a) (criminal liability: sufficient consent in relation to qualifying performances),

and may be given subject to any conditions specified in the Tribunal's order.

(3)   The Tribunal shall not give consent under subsection (1)(a) except after the service or publication of such notices as may be required by rules made under section 150 (general procedural rules) or as the Tribunal may in any particular case direct.

(4)   . . .

(5)   In any case the Tribunal shall take into account the following factors—

(a)   whether the original recording was made with the performer's consent and is lawfully in the possession or control of the person proposing to make the further recording;

(a)   whether the making of the further recording is consistent with the obligations of the parties to the arrangements under which, or is otherwise consistent with the purposes for which, the original recording was made.

(6)   Where the Tribunal gives consent under this section it shall, in default of agreement between the applicant and the performer, make such order as it thinks fit as to the payment to be made to that person in consideration of consent being given.

Duration rights

191   Duration of rights

(1)   The following provisions have effect with respect to the duration of the rights conferred by this Chapter.

(2)   The rights conferred by this Chapter in relation to a performance expire—

(a)   at the end of the period of 50 years from the end of the calendar year in which the performance takes place, or

(b)   if during that period a recording of the performance, other than a sound recording, is released, 50 years from the end of the calendar year in which it is released, or

(c)   if during that period a sound recording of the performance is released, 70 years from the end of the calendar year in which it is released,

subject as follows.

(3)   For the purposes of subsection (2) a recording is "released" when it is first published, played or shown in public or communicated to the public; but in determining whether a recording has been released no account shall be taken of any unauthorised act.

(4)   Where a performer is not a national of an EEA state, the duration of the rights conferred by this Chapter in relation to his performance is that to which the performance is entitled in the country of which he is a national, provided that does not exceed the period which would apply under subsections (2) and (3).

(5)   If or to the extent that the application of subsection (4) would be at variance with an international obligation to which the United Kingdom became subject prior to 29th October 1993, the duration of the rights conferred by this Chapter shall be as specified in subsections (2) and (3).

Performers' property rights

191A Performers' property rights

(1)   The following rights conferred by this Chapter on a performer—

reproduction right (section 182A),

distribution right (section 182B),

rental right and lending right (section 182C),

making available right (section 182CA),

are property rights ("performer's property rights").

(2)   References in this Chapter to the consent of the performer shall be construed in relation to a performer's property rights as references to the consent of the rights owner.

(3)   Where different persons are (whether in consequence of a partial assignment or otherwise) entitled to different aspects of a performer's property rights in relation to a performance, the rights owner for any purpose of this Chapter is the person who is entitled to the aspect of those rights relevant for that purpose.

(4)   Where a performer's property rights (or any aspect of them) is owned by more than one person jointly, references in this Chapter to the rights owner are to all the owners, so that, in particular, any requirement of the licence of the rights owner requires the licence of all of them.

191B Assignment and licences

(1) A performer's property rights are transmissible by assignment, by testamentary disposition or by operation of law, as personal or moveable property

(2) An assignment or other transmission of a performer's property rights may be partial, that is, limited so as to apply—

 (a) to one or more, but not all, of the things requiring the consent of the rights owner;

 (b) to part, but not the whole, of the period for which the rights are to subsist.

(3) An assignment of a performer's property rights is not effective unless it is in writing signed by or on behalf of the assignor.

(4) A licence granted by the owner of a performer's property rights is binding on every successor in title to his interest in the rights, except a purchaser in good faith for valuable consideration and without notice (actual or constructive) of the licence or a person deriving title from such a purchaser; and references in this Chapter to doing anything with, or without, the licence of the rights owner shall be construed accordingly.

191C Prospective ownership of a performer's property rights

(1) This section applies where by an agreement made in relation to a future recording of a performance, and signed by or on behalf of the performer, the performer purports to assign his performer's property rights (wholly or partially) to another person.

(2) If on the rights coming into existence the assignee or another person claiming under him would be entitled as against all other persons to require the rights to be vested in him, they shall vest in the assignee or his successor in title by virtue of this subsection.

(3) A licence granted by a prospective owner of a performer's property rights is binding on every successor in title to his interest (or prospective interest) in the rights, except a purchaser in good faith for valuable consideration and without notice (actual or constructive) of the licence or a person deriving title from such a purchaser. References in this Chapter to doing anything with, or without, the licence of the rights owner shall be construed accordingly.

(4) In subsection (3) "prospective owner" in relation to a performer's property rights means a person who is prospectively entitled to those rights by virtue of such an agreement as is mentioned in subsection (1).

191D Exclusive licences

(1) In this Chapter an "exclusive licence" means a licence in writing signed by or on behalf of the owner of a performer's property rights authorising the licensee to the exclusion of all other persons, including the person granting the licence, to do anything requiring the consent of the rights owner.

(2) The licensee under an exclusive licence has the same rights against a successor in title who is bound by the licence as he has against the person granting the licence.

191E Performer's property right to pass under will with unpublished original recording

Where under a bequest (whether general or specific) a person is entitled beneficially or otherwise to any material thing containing an original recording of a performance which was not published before the death of the testator, the bequest shall, unless a contrary intention is indicated in the testator's will or a codicil to it, be construed as including any performer's rights in relation to the recording to which the testator was entitled immediately before his death.

191F Presumption of transfer of rental right in case of film production agreement

(1) Where an agreement concerning film production is concluded between a performer and a film producer, the performer shall be presumed, unless the agreement provides to the contrary, to have transferred to the film producer any rental right in relation to the film arising from the inclusion of a recording of his performance in the film.

(2) Where the section applies, the absence of signature by or on behalf of the performer does not exclude the operation of section 191C (effect of purported assignment of future rights).

(3)   The reference in subsection (1) to an agreement concluded between a performer and a film producer includes any agreement having effect between those persons, whether made by them directly or through intermediaries.

(4)   Section 191G (right to equitable remuneration on transfer of rental right) applies where there is a presumed transfer by virtue of this section as in the case of an actual transfer.

191G   Right to equitable remuneration where rental right transferred

(1)   Where a performer has transferred his rental right concerning a sound recording or a film to the producer of the sound recording or film, he retains the right to equitable remuneration for the rental.

The reference above to the transfer of rental right by one person to another includes any arrangement having that effect, whether made by them directly or through intermediaries.

(2)   The right to equitable remuneration under this section may not be assigned by the performer except to a collecting society for the purpose of enabling it to enforce the right on his behalf.

The right is, however, transmissible by testamentary disposition or by operation of law as personal or moveable property; and it may be assigned or further transmitted by any person into whose hands it passes.

(3)   Equitable remuneration under this section is payable by the person for the time being entitled to the rental right, that is, the person to whom the right was transferred or any successor in title of his.

(4)   The amount payable by way of equitable remuneration is as agreed by or on behalf of the persons by and to whom it is payable, subject to section 191H (reference of amount to Copyright Tribunal).

(5)   An agreement is of no effect in so far as it purports to exclude or restrict the right to equitable remuneration under this section.

(6)   In this section a "collecting society" means a society or other organisation which has as its main object, or one of its main objects, the exercise of the right to equitable remuneration on behalf of more than one performer.

191H   Equitable remuneration: reference of amount to Copyright Tribunal

(1)   In default of agreement as to the amount payable by way of equitable remuneration under section 191G, the person by or to whom it is payable may apply to the Copyright Tribunal to determine the amount payable.

(2)   A person to or by whom equitable remuneration is payable may also apply to the Copyright Tribunal—

(a)   to vary any agreement as to the amount payable, or

(b)   to vary any previous determination of the Tribunal as to that matter;

but except with the special leave of the Tribunal no such application may be made within twelve months from the date of a previous determination.

An order made on an application under this subsection has effect from the date on which it is made or such later date as may be specified by the Tribunal.

(3)   On an application under this section the Tribunal shall consider the matter and make such order as to the method of calculating and paying equitable remuneration as it may determine to be reasonable in the circumstances, taking into account the importance of the contribution of the performer to the film or sound recording.

(4)   Remuneration shall not be considered inequitable merely because it was paid by way of a single payment or at the time of the transfer of the rental right.

(5)   An agreement is of no effect in so far as it purports to prevent a person questioning the amount of equitable remuneration or to restrict the powers of the Copyright Tribunal under this section.

191HA   Assignment of performer's property rights in a sound recording

(1)   This section applies where a performer has by an agreement assigned the following rights concerning a sound recording to the producer of the sound recording—

(a)   reproduction, distribution and making available rights, or

(b)   performer's property rights.

(2) If, at the end of the 50-year period, the producer has failed to meet one or both of the following conditions, the performer may give a notice in writing to the producer of the performer's intention to terminate the agreement—

    (a) condition 1 is to issue to the public copies of the sound recording in sufficient quantities;

    (b) condition 2 is to make the sound recording available to the public by electronic transmission in such a way that a member of the public may access the recording from a place and at a time chosen by him or her.

(3) If, at any time after the end of the 50-year period, the producer, having met one or both of the conditions referred to in subsection (2), fails to do so, the performer may give a notice in writing to the producer of the performer's intention to terminate the agreement.

(4) If at the end of the period of 12 months beginning with the date of the notice, the producer has not met the conditions referred to in subsection (2), the agreement terminates and the copyright in the sound recording expires with immediate effect.

(5) An agreement is of no effect in so far as it purports to exclude or restrict the right to give a notice under subsection (2) or (3).

(6) A reference in this section to the assignment of rights includes any arrangement having that effect, whether made directly between the parties or through intermediaries.

(7) In this section—

    "50-year period" means

    (a) where the sound recording is published during the initial period, the period of 50 years from the end of the calendar year in which the sound recording is first published, or

    (b) where during the initial period the sound recording is not published but is made available to the public by being played in public or communicated to the public, the period of 50 years from the end of the calendar year in which it was first made available to the public,

    but in determining whether a sound recording has been published, played in public or communicated to the public, no account shall be taken of any unauthorised act,

    "initial period" means the period beginning on the date the recording is made and ending 50 years from the end of the calendar year in which the sound recording is made,

    "producer" means the person for the time being entitled to the copyright in the sound recording,

    "sufficient quantities" means such quantity as to satisfy the reasonable requirements of the public for copies of the sound recording,

    "unauthorised act" has the same meaning as in section 178.

191HB Payment in consideration of assignment

(1) A performer who, under an agreement relating to the assignment of rights referred to in section 191HA(1) (an "assignment agreement"), is entitled to a non-recurring payment in consideration of the assignment, is entitled to an annual payment for each relevant period from—

    (a) the producer, or

    (b) where the producer has granted an exclusive licence of the copyright in the sound recording, the licensee under the exclusive licence (the "exclusive licensee").

(2) In this section, *"relevant period"* means—

    (a) the period of 12 months beginning at the end of the 50-year period, and

    (b) each subsequent period of 12 months beginning with the end of the previous period, until the date on which copyright in the sound recording expires.

(3) The producer or, where relevant, the exclusive licensee gives effect to the entitlement under subsection (1) by remitting to a collecting society for distribution to the performer in accordance with its rules an amount for each relevant period equal to 20% of the gross revenue received during that period in respect of—

    (a) the reproduction and issue to the public of copies of the sound recording, and

    (b) the making available to the public of the sound recording by electronic transmission in such a way that members of the public may access it from a place and at a time individually chosen by them.

(4) The amount required to be remitted under subsection (3) is payable within 6 months of the end of each relevant period and is recoverable by the collecting society as a debt.

(5) Subsection (6) applies where—

    (a) the performer makes a written request to the producer or, where relevant, the exclusive licensee for information in that person's possession or under that person's control to enable the performer—

        (i) to ascertain the amount of the annual payment to which the performer is entitled under subsection (1), or

        (ii) to secure its distribution by the collecting society, and

    (b) the producer or, where relevant, the exclusive licensee does not supply the information within the period of 90 days beginning with the date of the request.

(6) The performer may apply to the county court, or in Scotland to the sheriff, for an order requiring the producer or, where relevant, the exclusive licensee to supply the information.

(7) An agreement is of no effect in so far as it purports to exclude or restrict the entitlement under subsection (1).

(8) In the event of any dispute as to the amount required to be remitted under subsection (3), the performer may apply to the Copyright Tribunal to determine the amount payable.

(9) Where a performer is entitled under an assignment agreement to recurring payments in consideration of the assignment, the payments must, from the end of the 50-year period, be made in full, regardless of any provision in the agreement which entitles the producer to withhold or deduct sums from the amounts payable.

(10) In this section—

    "producer" and *"50-year period"* each has the same meaning as in section 191HA,

    "exclusive licence" has the same meaning as in section 92, and

    "collecting society" has the same meaning as in section 191G.

191I Infringement actionable by rights owner

(1) An infringement of a performer's property rights is actionable by the rights owner.

(2) In an action for infringement of a performer's property rights all such relief by way of damages, injunctions, accounts or otherwise is available to the plaintiff as is available in respect of the infringement of any other property right.

(3) This section has effect subject to the following provisions of this Chapter.

191J Provisions as to damages in infringement action

(1) Where in an action for infringement of a performer's property rights it is shown that at the time of the infringement the defendant did not know and had no reason to believe, that the rights subsisted in the recording to which the action relates, the plaintiff is not entitled to damages against him, but without prejudice to any other remedy.

(2) The court may in an action for infringement of a performer's property rights having regard to all the circumstances, and in particular to—

    (a) the flagrancy of the infringement, and

    (b) any benefit accruing to the defendant by reason of the infringement,

    award such additional damages as the justice of the case may require.

191JA Injunctions against service providers

(1) The High Court (in Scotland, the Court of Session) shall have power to grant an injunction against a service provider, where that service provider has actual knowledge of another person using their service to infringe a performer's property right.

(2) In determining whether a service provider has actual knowledge for the purpose of this section, a court shall take into account all matters which appear to it in the particular circumstances to be relevant and, amongst other things, shall have regard to—

    (a) whether a service provider has received a notice through a means of contact made available in accordance with regulation 6(1)(c) of the Electronic Commerce (EC Directive) Regulations 2002; and

    (b) the extent to which any notice includes—

        (i) the full name and address of the sender of the notice;

        (ii) details of the infringement in question.

(3) In this section "service provider" has the meaning given to it by regulation 2 of the Electronic Commerce (EC Directive) Regulations 2002.

(4) Section 177 applies in respect of this section as it applies in respect of Part 1.

191K Undertaking to take licence of right in infringement proceedings

(1) If in proceedings for infringement of a performer's property rights in respect of which a licence is available as of right under paragraph 17 of Schedule 2A (powers exercisable in consequence of competition report) the defendant undertakes to take a licence on such terms as may be agreed or, in default of agreement, settled by the Copyright Tribunal under that paragraph—

    (a) no injunction shall be granted against him,

    (b) no order for delivery up shall be made under section 195, and

    (c) the amount recoverable against him by way of damages or on an account of profits shall not exceed double the amount which would have been payable by him as licensee if such a licence on those terms had been granted before the earliest infringement.

(2) An undertaking may be given at any time before final order in the proceedings, without any admission of liability.

(3) Nothing in this section affects the remedies available in respect of an infringement committed before licences of right were available.

191L Rights and remedies for exclusive licensee

(1) An exclusive licensee has, except against the owner of a performer's property rights, the same rights and remedies in respect of matters occurring after the grant of the licence as if the licence had been an assignment.

(2) His rights and remedies are concurrent with those of the rights owner; and references in the relevant provisions of this Chapter to the rights owner shall be construed accordingly.

(3) In an action brought by an exclusive licensee by virtue of this section a defendant may avail himself of any defence which would have been available to him if the action had been brought by the rights owner.

191M Exercise of concurrent rights

(1) Where an action for infringement of a performer's property rights brought by the rights owner or an exclusive licensee relates (wholly or partly) to an infringement in respect of which they have concurrent rights of action, the rights owner or, as the case may be, the exclusive licensee may not, without the leave of the court, proceed with the action unless the other is either joined as plaintiff or added as a defendant.

(2) A rights owner or exclusive licensee who is added as a defendant in pursuance of subsection (1) is not liable for any costs in the action unless he takes part in the proceedings.

(3) The above provisions do not affect the granting of interlocutory relief on an application by the rights owner or exclusive licensee alone.

(4) Where an action for infringement of a performer's property rights is brought which relates (wholly or partly) to an infringement in respect of which the rights owner and an exclusive licensee have or had concurrent rights of action—

    (a) the court shall in assessing damages take into account—

        (i) the terms of the licence, and

        (ii) any pecuniary remedy already awarded or available to either of them in respect of the infringement;

    (b) no account of profits shall be directed if an award of damages has been made, or an account of profits has been directed, in favour of the other of them in respect of the infringement; and

    (c) the court shall if an account of profits is directed apportion the profits between them as the court considers just, subject to any agreement between them;

and these provisions apply whether or not the rights owner and the exclusive licensee are both parties to the action.

(5) The owner of a performer's property rights shall notify any exclusive licensee having concurrent rights before applying for an order under section 195 (order for delivery up) or exercising the right conferred by section 196 (right of seizure); and the court

may on the application of the licensee make such order under section 195 or, as the case may be, prohibiting or permitting the exercise by the rights owner of the right conferred by section 196, as it thinks fit having regard to the terms of the licence.

Non-property rights

192A Performers' non-property rights

(1) the rights conferred on a performer by—

section 182 (consent required for recording, etc. of live performance),

section 183 (infringement of performer's rights by use of recording made without consent),

section 184 (infringement of performer's rights importing, possessing or dealing with illicit recording),

section 191HA (assignment of performer's property rights in a sound recording), and

section 191HB (payment in consideration of assignment),

are not assignable or transmissible, except to the following extent.

They are referred to in this Chapter as "performer's non-property rights".

(2) On the death of a person entitled to any such right—

(a) the right passes to such person as he may by testamentary disposition specifically direct, and

(b) if or to the extent that there is no such direction, the right is exercisable by his personal representatives.

(3) References in this Chapter to the performer, in the context of the person having any such right, shall be construed as references to the person for the time being entitled to exercise those rights.

(4) Where by virtue of subsection (2)(a) a right becomes exercisable by more than one person, it is exercisable by each of them independently of the other or others.

(5) Any damages recovered by personal representatives by virtue of this section in respect of an infringement after a person's death shall devolve as part of his estate as if the right of action had subsisted and been vested in him immediately before his death.

192B Transmissibility of rights of person having recording rights

(1) The rights conferred by this Chapter on a person having recording rights are not assignable or transmissible.

(2) This does not affect section 185(2)(b) or (3)(b), so far as those provisions confer rights under this Chapter on a person to whom the benefit of a contract or licence is assigned.

193 Consent

(1) Consent for the purposes of this Chapter, by a person having a performer's non-property rights, or by a person having recording rights, may be given in relation to a specific performance, a specified description of performances or performances generally, and may relate to past or future performances.

(2) A person having recording rights in a performance is bound by any consent given by a person through whom he derives his rights under the exclusive recording contract or licence in question, in the same way as if the consent had been given by him.

(3) Where a performer's non-property right passes to another person, any consent binding on the person previously entitled binds the person to whom the right passes in the same way as if the consent had been given by him.

194 Infringement actionable as breach of statutory duty

An infringement of—

(a) a performer's non-property rights, or

(b) any right conferred by this Chapter on a person having recording rights, is actionable by the person entitled to the right as a breach of statutory duty.

Delivery up or seizure of illicit recordings

195 Order for delivery up

(1) Where a person has in his possession, custody or control in the course of a business an illicit recording of a performance, a person having performer's rights or recording

rights in relation to the performance under this Chapter may apply to the court for an order that the recording be delivered up to him or to such other person as the court may direct.

(2) An application shall not be made after the end of the period specified in section 203; and no order shall be made unless the court also makes, or it appears to the court that there are grounds for making, an order under section 204 (order as to disposal of illicit recording).

(3) A person to whom a recording is delivered up in pursuance of an order under this section shall, if an order under section 204 is not made, retain it pending the making of an order, or the decision not to make an order, under that section.

(4) Nothing in this section affects any other power of the court.

196 Right to seize illicit recordings

(1) An illicit recording of a performance which is found exposed or otherwise immediately available for sale or hire, and in respect of which a person would be entitled to apply for an order under section 195, may be seized and detained by him or a person authorised by him.

The right to seize and detain is exercisable subject to the following conditions and is subject to any decision of the court under section 204 (order as to disposal of illicit recording).

(2) Before anything is seized under this section notice of the time and place of the proposed seizure must be given to a local police station.

(3) A person may for the purpose of exercising the right conferred by this section enter premises to which the public have access but may not seize anything in the possession, custody or control of a person at a permanent or regular place of business of his and may not use any force.

(4) At the time when anything is seized under this section there shall be left at the place where it was seized a notice in the prescribed form containing the prescribed particulars as to the person by whom or on whose authority the seizure is made and the grounds on which it is made.

(5) In this section—

"premises" includes land, buildings, fixed or moveable structures, vehicles, vessels, aircraft and hovercraft; and

"prescribed" means prescribed by order of the Secretary of State.

(6) An order of the Secretary of State under this section shall be made by statutory instrument which shall be subject to annulment in pursuance of a resolution of either House of Parliament.

197 Meaning of "illicit recording"

(1) In this Chapter "illicit recording", in relation to a performance, shall be construed in accordance with this section.

(2) For the purposes of a performer's rights, a recording of the whole or any substantial part of a performance of his is an illicit recording if it is made, otherwise than for private purposes, without his consent.

(3) For the purposes of the rights of a person having recording rights, a recording of the whole or any substantial part of a performance subject to the exclusive recording contract is an illicit recording if it is made, otherwise than for private purposes, without his consent or that of the performer.

(4) For the purposes of sections 198 and 199 (offences and orders for delivery up in criminal proceedings), a recording is an illicit recording if it is an illicit recording for the purposes mentioned in subsection (2) or subsection (3).

(5) In this Chapter "illicit recording" includes a recording falling to be treated as an illicit recording by virtue of any of the following provisions of Schedule 2—

paragraph 1D(3) (copies for text and data analysis for non-commercial research),

paragraph 3A(5) or (6) or 3B(10) (accessible copies of recordings made for disabled persons)

. . .

paragraph 6(5) (recording by educational establishments of broadcasts),

paragraph 6ZA(7) (copying and use of extracts of recordings by educational establishments),

paragraph 6F(5)(b) (copying by librarians: single copies of published recordings),
paragraph 6G(5)(b) (copying by librarians or archivists: single copies of unpublished recordings),
paragraph 12(2) (recordings of performance in electronic form retained on transfer of principal recording), . . .
paragraph 14(6)(b) (recordings of folksongs),
paragraph 16(3) (recordings made for purposes of broadcast),
paragraph 17A(2) (recording for the purposes of time-shifting), or
paragraph 17B(2) (photographs of broadcasts),
but otherwise does not include a recording made in accordance with any of the provisions of that Schedule.

(6) It is immaterial for the purposes of this section where the recording was made.

197A Presumptions relevant to recordings of performances

(1) In proceedings brought by virtue of this Part with respect to the rights in a performance, where copies of a recording of the performance as issued to the public bear a statement that a named person was the performer, the statement shall be admissible as evidence of the fact stated and shall be presumed to be correct until the contrary is proved.

(2) Subsection (1) does not apply to proceedings for an offence under section 198 (criminal liability for making etc illicit recordings); but without prejudice to its application in proceedings for an order under section 199 (order for delivery up in criminal proceedings).

Offences

198 Criminal liability for making, dealing with or using illicit recordings

(1) A person commits an offence who without sufficient consent—
  (a) makes for sale or hire, or
  (b) imports into the United Kingdom otherwise than for his private and domestic use, or
  (c) possesses in the course of a business with a view to committing any act infringing the rights conferred by this Chapter, or
  (d) in the course of a business—
    (i) sells or lets for hire, or
    (ii) offers or exposes for sale or hire, or
    (iii) distributes,
a recording which is, and which he knows or has reason to believe is, an illicit recording.

(1A) A person ("P") who infringes copyright in a work by communicating the work to the public commits an offence if P—
  (a) knows or has reason to believe that P is infringing copyright in the work, and
  (b) either—
    (i) intends to make a gain for P or another person, or
    (ii) knows or has reason to believe that communicating the work to the public will cause loss to the owner of the copyright, or will expose the owner of the copyright to a risk of loss.

(1B) For the purposes of subsection (1A)—
  (a) "gain" and "loss"—
    (i) extend only to gain or loss in money, and
    (ii) include any such gain or loss whether temporary or permanent, and
  (b) "loss" includes a loss by not getting what one might get.

(2) A person commits an offence who causes a recording of a performance made without sufficient consent to be—
  (a) shown or played in public, or
  (b) communicated to the public,
thereby infringing any of the rights conferred by this Chapter, if he knows or has reason to believe that those rights are thereby infringed.

(3) In subsections (1) and (2) "sufficient consent" means—
  (a) in the case of a qualifying performance, the consent of the performer, and
  (b) in the case of a non-qualifying performance subject to an exclusive recording contract—
    (i) for the purposes of subsection (1)(a) (making of recording), the consent of the performer or the person having recording rights, and

(ii)   for the purposes of subsection (1)(b), (c) and (d) and subsection (2) (dealing with or using recording), the consent of the person having recording rights. The references in this subsection to the person having recording rights are to the person having those rights at the time the consent is given or, if there is more than one such person, to all of them.

(4)   No offence is committed under subsection (1) or (2) by the commission of an act which by virtue of any provision of Schedule 2 may be done without infringing the rights conferred by this Chapter.

(5)   A person guilty of an offence under subsection (1)(a), (b) or (d)(iii) is liable—
   (a)   on summary conviction to imprisonment for a term not exceeding six months or a fine or both;
   (b)   on conviction on indictment to a fine or imprisonment for a term not exceeding ten years, or both.

(5A)   A person guilty of an offence under subsection (1A) is liable—
   (a)   on summary conviction to imprisonment for a term not exceeding three months or a fine or both;
   (b)   on conviction on indictment to a fine or imprisonment for a term not exceeding ten years, or both.

(6)   A person guilty of any other offence under this section is liable on summary conviction to a fine not exceeding level 5 on the standard scale or imprisonment for a term not exceeding six months, or both.

198A Enforcement by local weights and measures authority

(1)   It is the duty of every local weights and measures authority to enforce within their area the provisions of section 198.

(2)   . . .

(3)   Subsection (1) above does not apply in relation to the enforcement of section 198 in Northern Ireland, but it is the duty of the Department of Economic Development to enforce that section in Northern Ireland.

. . .

(3A)   For the investigatory powers available to a local weights and measures authority or the Department of Enterprise, Trade and Investment in Northern Ireland for the purposes of the duties in this section, see Schedule 5 to the Consumer Rights Act 2015.

(4)   Any enactment which authorises the disclosure of information for the purpose of facilitating the enforcement of the Trade Descriptions Act 1968 shall apply as if section 198 were contained in that Act and as if the functions of any person in relation to the enforcement of that section were functions under that Act.

(5)   Nothing in this section shall be construed as authorising a local weights and measures authority to bring proceedings in Scotland for an offence.

199 Order for delivery up in criminal proceedings

(1)   The court before which proceedings are brought against a person for an offence under section 198 may, if satisfied that at the time of his arrest or charge he had in his possession, custody or control in the course of a business an illicit recording of a performance, order that it be delivered up to a person having performers' rights or recording rights in relation to the performance or to such other person as the court may direct.

(2)   For this purpose a person shall be treated as charged with an offence—
   (a)   in England, Wales and Northern Ireland, when he is orally charged or is served with a summons or indictment;
   (b)   in Scotland, when he is cautioned, charged or served with a complaint or indictment.

(3)   An order may be made by the court of its own motion or on the application of the prosecutor (or, in Scotland, the Lord Advocate or procurator-fiscal), and may be made whether or not the person is convicted of the offence, but shall not be made—
   (a)   after the end of the period specified in section 203 (period after which remedy of delivery up not available), or
   (b)   if it appears to the court unlikely that any order will be made under section 204 (order as to disposal of illicit recording).

(4)   An appeal lies from an order made under this section by a magistrates' court—
    (a)   in England and Wales, to the Crown Court, and
    (b)   in Northern Ireland, to the county court;
and in Scotland, where an order has been made under this section, the person from whose possession, custody or control the illicit recording has been removed may, without prejudice to any other form of appeal under any rule of law, appeal against that order in the same manner as against sentence.

(5)   A person to whom an illicit recording is delivered up in pursuance of an order under this section shall retain it pending the making of an order, or the decision not to make an order, under section 204.

(6)   Nothing in in this section affects the powers of the court under section 143 of the Powers of Criminal Courts (Sentencing) Act 2000, Part II of the Proceeds of Crime (Scotland) Act 1995 or Article 11 of the Criminal Justice (Northern Ireland) Order 1994 (general provisions as to forfeiture in criminal proceedings).

200   Search warrants

(1)   Where a justice of the peace (in Scotland, a sheriff or justice of the peace) is satisfied by information on oath given by a constable (in Scotland, by evidence on oath) that there are reasonable grounds for believing—
    (a)   that an offence under section 198(1) or (1A) (offences of making, importing, possessing, selling etc. or distributing illicit recordings) has been or is about to be committed in any premises, and
    (b)   that evidence that such an offence has been or is about to be committed is in those premises,
he may issue a warrant authorising a constable to enter and search the premises, using such reasonable force as is necessary.

(2)   The power conferred by subsection (1) does not, in England and Wales, extend to authorising a search for material of the kinds mentioned in section 9(2) of the Police and Criminal Evidence Act 1984 (certain classes of personal or confidential material).

(3)   A warrant under subsection (1)—
    (a)   may authorise persons to accompany any constable executing the warrant, and
    (b)   remains in force for 28 days from the date of its issue.

(3A) In executing a warrant issued under subsection (1) a constable may seize an article if he reasonably believes that it is evidence that any offence under section 198(1) or (1A) has been or is about to be committed.

(4)   In this section "premises" includes land, buildings, fixed or moveable structures, vehicles, vessels, aircraft and hovercraft.

201   False representation of authority to give consent

(1)   It is an offence for a person to represent falsely that he is authorised by any person to give consent for the purposes of this Chapter in relation to a performance, unless he believes on reasonable grounds that he is so authorised.

(2)   A person guilty of an offence under this section is liable on summary conviction to imprisonment for a term not exceeding six months or a fine not exceeding level 5 on the standard scale or both.

202   Offence by body corporate: liability of officers

(1)   Where an offence under this Chapter committed by a body corporate is proved to have been committed with the consent or connivance of a director, manager, secretary or other similar officer of the body, or a person purporting to act in any such capacity, he as well as the body corporate is guilty of the offence and liable to be proceeded against and punished accordingly.

(2)   In relation to a body corporate whose affairs are managed by its members "director" means a member of the body corporate.

Supplementary provisions with respect to delivery up and seizure

203   Period after which remedy of delivery up not available

(1)   An application for an order under section 195 (order for delivery up in civil proceedings) may not be made after the end of the period of six years from the date on which the illicit recording in question was made, subject to the following provisions.

(2) If during the whole or any part of that period a person entitled to apply for an order—
    (a) is under a disability, or
    (b) is prevented by fraud or concealment from discovering the facts entitling him to apply,
an application may be made by him at any time before the end of the period of six years from the date on which he ceased to be under a disability or, as the case may be, could with reasonable diligence have discovered those facts.

(3) In subsection (2) "disability"—
    (a) in England and Wales, has the same meaning as in the Limitation Act 1980;
    (b) in Scotland, means legal disability within the meaning of the Prescription and Limitations (Scotland) Act 1973;
    (c) in Northern Ireland, has the same meaning as in the Statute of Limitation (Northern Ireland) 1958.

(4) An order under section 199 (order for delivery up in criminal proceedings) shall not, in any case, be made after the end of the period of six years from the date on which the illicit recording in question was made.

204 Order as to disposal of illicit recording

(1) An application may be made to the court for an order that an illicit recording of a performance delivered up in pursuance of an order under section 195 or 199, or seized and detained in pursuance of the right conferred by section 196, shall be—
    (a) forfeited to such person having performer's rights or recording rights in relation to the performance as the court may direct, or
    (b) destroyed or otherwise dealt with as the court may think fit,
or for a decision that no such order should be made.

(2) In considering what order (if any) should be made, the court shall consider whether other remedies available in an action for infringement of the rights conferred by this Chapter would be adequate to compensate the person or persons entitled to the rights and to protect their interests.

(3) Provision shall be made by rules of court as to the service of notice on persons having an interest in the recording, and any such person is entitled—
    (a) to appear in proceedings for an order under this section, whether or not he was served with notice, and
    (b) to appeal against any order made, whether or not he appeared;
and an order shall not take effect until the end of the period within which notice of an appeal may be given or, if before the end of that period notice of appeal is duly given, until the final determination or abandonment of the proceedings on the appeal.

(4) Where there is more than one person interested in a recording, the court shall make such order as it thinks just and may (in particular) direct that the recording be sold, or otherwise dealt with, and the proceeds divided.

(5) If the court decides that no order should be made under this section, the person in whose possession, custody or control the recording was before being delivered up or seized is entitled to its return.

(6) References in this section to a person having an interest in a recording include any person in whose favour an order could be made in respect of the recording—
    (a) under this section or under section 114 or 231 of this Act;
    (b) under section 24D of the Registered Designs Act 1949;
    (c) under section 19 of Trade Marks Act 1994 (including that section as applied by regulation 4 of the Community Trade Mark Regulations 2006); or
    (d) under regulation 1C of the Community Design Regulations 2005.

204A Forfeiture of illicit recordings: England and Wales or Northern Ireland

(1) In England and Wales or Northern Ireland where illicit recordings of a performance have come into the possession of any person in connection with the investigation or prosecution of a relevant offence, that person may apply under this section for an order for the forfeiture of the illicit recordings.

(2) For the purposes of this section "relevant offence" means—
    (a) an offence under section 198(1) or (1A) (criminal liability for making or dealing with illicit recordings),
    (b) an offence under the Trade Descriptions Act 1968,

       (ba)   an offence under the Business Protection from Misleading Marketing Regulations 2008,

       (bb)   an offence under the Consumer Protection from Unfair Trading Regulations 2008, or

       (c)   an offence involving dishonesty or deception.

(3)   An application under this section may be made—

       (a)   where proceedings have been brought in any court for a relevant offence relating to some or all of the illicit recordings, to that court, or

       (b)   where no application for the forfeiture of the illicit recordings has been made under paragraph (a), by way of complaint to a magistrates' court.

(4)   On an application under this section, the court shall make an order for the forfeiture of any illicit recordings only if it is satisfied that a relevant offence has been committed in relation to the illicit recordings.

(5)   A court may infer for the purposes of this section that such an offence has been committed in relation to any illicit recordings if it is satisfied that such an offence has been committed in relation to illicit recordings which are representative of the illicit recordings in question (whether by reason of being part of the same consignment or batch or otherwise).

(6)   Any person aggrieved by an order made under this section by a magistrates' court, or by a decision of such a court not to make such an order, may appeal against that order or decision—

       (a)   in England and Wales, to the Crown Court, or

       (b)   in Northern Ireland, to the county court.

(7)   An order under this section may contain such provision as appears to the court to be appropriate for delaying the coming into force of the order pending the making and determination of any appeal (including any application under section 111 of the Magistrates' Courts Act 1980 or Article 146 of the Magistrates' Courts (Northern Ireland) Order 1981 (statement of case)).

(8)   Subject to subsection (9), where any illicit recordings are forfeited under this section they shall be destroyed in accordance with such directions as the court may give.

(9)   On making an order under this section the court may direct that the illicit recordings to which the order relates shall (instead of being destroyed) be forfeited to the person having the performers' rights or recording rights in question or dealt with in such other way as the court considers appropriate.

204B Forfeiture: Scotland

(1)   In Scotland the court may make an order under this section for the forfeiture of any illicit recordings.

(2)   An order under this section may be made—

       (a)   on an application by the procurator-fiscal made in the manner specified in section 134 of the Criminal Procedure (Scotland) Act 1995, or

       (b)   where a person is convicted of a relevant offence, in addition to any other penalty which the court may impose.

(3)   On an application under subsection (2)(a), the court shall make an order for the forfeiture of any illicit recordings only if it is satisfied that a relevant offence has been committed in relation to the illicit recordings.

(4)   The court may infer for the purposes of this section that such an offence has been committed in relation to any illicit recordings if it is satisfied that such an offence has been committed in relation to illicit recordings which are representative of the illicit recordings in question (whether by reason of being part of the same consignment or batch or otherwise).

(5)   The procurator-fiscal making the application under subsection (2)(a) shall serve on any person appearing to him to be the owner of, or otherwise to have an interest in, the illicit recordings to which the application relates a copy of the application, together with a notice giving him the opportunity to appear at the hearing of the application to show cause why the illicit recordings should not be forfeited.

(6)   Service under subsection (5) shall be carried out, and such service may be proved, in the manner specified for citation of an accused in summary proceedings under the Criminal Procedure (Scotland) Act 1995.

(7) Any person upon whom notice is served under subsection (5) and any other person claiming to be the owner of, or otherwise to have an interest in, illicit recordings to which an application under this section relates shall be entitled to appear at the hearing of the application to show cause why the illicit recordings should not be forfeited.

(8) The court shall not make an order following an application under subsection (2)(a)—

  (a) if any person on whom notice is served under subsection (5) does not appear, unless service of the notice on that person is proved, or

  (b) if no notice under subsection (5) has been served, unless the court is satisfied that in the circumstances it was reasonable not to serve such notice.

(9) Where an order for the forfeiture of any illicit recordings is made following an application under subsection (2)(a), any person who appeared, or was entitled to appear, to show cause why the illicit recordings should not be forfeited may, within 21 days of the making of the order, appeal to the High Court by Bill of Suspension.

(10) Section 182(5)(a) to (e) of the Criminal Procedure (Scotland) Act 1995 shall apply to an appeal under subsection (9) as it applies to a stated case under Part 2 of that Act.

(11) An order following an application under subsection (2)(a) shall not take effect—

  (a) until the end of the period of 21 days beginning with the day after the day on which the order is made, or

  (b) if an appeal is made under subsection (9) above within that period, until the appeal is determined or abandoned.

(12) An order under subsection (2)(b) shall not take effect—

  (a) until the end of the period within which an appeal against the order could be brought under the Criminal Procedure (Scotland) Act 1995, or

  (b) if an appeal is made within that period, until the appeal is determined or abandoned.

(13) Subject to subsection (14), illicit recordings forfeited under this section shall be destroyed in accordance with such directions as the court may give.

(14) On making an order under this section the court may direct that the illicit recordings to which the order relates shall (instead of being destroyed) be forfeited to the person having the performers' rights or recording rights in question or dealt with in such other way as the court considers appropriate.

(15) For the purposes of this section—

  "relevant offence" means—

  (a) an offence under section 198(1) or (1A) (criminal liability for making or dealing with illicit recordings),

  (b) an offence under the Trade Descriptions Act 1968,

  (c) an offence under the Business Protection from Misleading Marketing Regulations 2008,

  (d) an offence under the Consumer Protection from Unfair Trading Regulations 2008, or

  (e) any offence involving dishonesty or deception;

  "the court" means—

  (a) in relation to an order made on an application under subsection (2)(a), the sheriff, and

  (b) in relation to an order made under subsection (2)(b), the court which imposed the penalty.

205 Jurisdiction of county court and sheriff court

(1) In England and Wales the county court and in Northern Ireland a county court may entertain proceedings under—

  section 195 (order for delivery up of illicit recording), or

  section 204 (order as to disposal of illicit recording),

  save that, in Northern Ireland, a county court may entertain such proceedings only where the value of the illicit recordings in question does not exceed the county court limit for actions in tort.

(2) In Scotland proceedings for an order under either of those provisions may be brought in the sheriff court.

(3) Nothing in this section shall be construed as affecting the jurisdiction of the High Court or, in Scotland, the Court of Session.

Licensing of performers' rights

205A Licensing of performers' rights

The provisions of Schedule 2A have effect with respect to the licensing of performers' rights.

205B Jurisdiction of Copyright Tribunal

(1) The Copyright Tribunal has jurisdiction under this Chapter to hear and determine proceedings under—

    (a) section 182D (amount of equitable remuneration for exploitation of commercial sound recording);

    (b) section 190 (application to give consent on behalf of owner of reproduction right);

    (c) section 191H (amount of equitable remuneration on transfer of rental right);

    (d) paragraph 3,4 or 5 of Schedule 2A (reference of licensing scheme);

    (e) paragraph 6 or 7 of that Schedule (application with respect to licence under licensing scheme);

    (f) paragraph 10, 11 or 12 of that Schedule (reference or application with respect to licensing by licensing body);

    (g) paragraph 15 of that Schedule (application to settle royalty for certain lending);

    (h) paragraph 17 of that Schedule (application to settle terms of licence available as of right).

(2) The provisions of Chapter VIII of Part I (general provisions relating to the Copyright Tribunal) apply in relation to the Tribunal when exercising any jurisdiction under this Chapter.

(3) Provision shall be made by rules under section 150 prohibiting the Tribunal from entertaining a reference under paragraph 3,4 or 5 of Schedule 2A (reference of licensing scheme) by a representative organisation unless the Tribunal is satisfied that the organisation is reasonably representative of the class of persons which it claims to represent.

CHAPTER 3

MORAL RIGHTS

Right to be identified as performer

205C Right to be identified as performer

(1) Whenever a person—

    (a) produces or puts on a qualifying performance that is given in public,

    (b) broadcasts live a qualifying performance,

    (c) communicates to the public a sound recording of a qualifying performance, or

    (d) issues to the public copies of such a recording,

the performer has the right to be identified as such.

(2) The right of the performer under this section is—

    (a) in the case of a performance that is given in public, to be identified in any programme accompanying the performance or in some other manner likely to bring his identity to the notice of a person seeing or hearing the performance,

    (b) in the case of a performance that is broadcast, to be identified in a manner likely to bring his identity to the notice of a person seeing or hearing the broadcast,

    (c) in the case of a sound recording that is communicated to the public, to be identified in a manner likely to bring his identity to the notice of a person hearing the communication,

    (d) in the case of a sound recording that is issued to the public, to be identified in or on each copy or, if that is not appropriate, in some other manner likely to bring his identity to the notice of a person acquiring a copy,

or (in any of the above cases) to be identified in such other manner as may be agreed between the performer and the person mentioned in subsection (1).

(3) The right conferred by this section in relation to a performance given by a group (or so much of a performance as is given by a group) is not infringed—

(a) in a case falling within paragraph (a), (b) or (c) of subsection (2), or

(b) in a case falling within paragraph (d) of that subsection in which it is not reasonably practicable for each member of the group to be identified,

if the group itself is identified as specified in subsection (2).

(4) In this section "group" means two or more performers who have a particular name by which they may be identified collectively.

(5) If the assertion under section 205D specifies a pseudonym, initials or some other particular form of identification, that form shall be used; otherwise any reasonable form of identification may be used.

(6) This section has effect subject to section 205E (exceptions to right).

205D Requirement that right be asserted

(1) A person does not infringe the right conferred by section 205C (right to be identified as performer) by doing any of the acts mentioned in that section unless the right has been asserted in accordance with the following provisions so as to bind him in relation to that act.

(2) The right may be asserted generally, or in relation to any specified act or description of acts—

(a) by instrument in writing signed by or on behalf of the performer, or

(b) on an assignment of a performer's property rights, by including in the instrument effecting the assignment a statement that the performer asserts in relation to the performance his right to be identified.

(3) The persons bound by an assertion of the right under subsection (2) are—

(a) in the case of an assertion under subsection (2)(a), anyone to whose notice the assertion is brought;

(b) in the case of an assertion under subsection (2)(b), the assignee and anyone claiming through him, whether or not he has notice of the assertion.

(4) In an action for infringement of the right the court shall, in considering remedies, take into account any delay in asserting the right.

205E Exceptions to right

(1) The right conferred by section 205C (right to be identified as performer) is subject to the following exceptions.

(2) The right does not apply where it is not reasonably practicable to identify the performer (or, where identification of a group is permitted by virtue of section 205C(3), the group).

(3) The right does not apply in relation to any performance given for the purposes of reporting current events.

(4) The right does not apply in relation to any performance given for the purposes of advertising any goods or services.

(5) The right is not infringed by an act which by virtue of any of the following provisions of Schedule 2 would not infringe any of the rights conferred by Chapter 2—

(a) paragraph 2(1A) (news reporting);

(b) paragraph 3 (incidental inclusion of a performance or recording);

(c) paragraph 4(2) (things done for the purposes of examination);

(d) paragraph 8 (parliamentary and judicial proceedings);

(e) paragraph 9 (Royal Commissions and statutory inquiries).

Right to object to derogatory treatment

205F Right to object to derogatory treatment of performance

(1) The performer of a qualifying performance has a right which is infringed if—

(a) the performance is broadcast live, or

(b) by means of a sound recording the performance is played in public or communicated to the public,

with any distortion, mutilation or other modification that is prejudicial to the reputation of the performer.

(2) This section has effect subject to section 205G (exceptions to right).

205G   Exceptions to right

(1)   The right conferred by section 205F (right to object to derogatory treatment of performance) is subject to the following exceptions.

(2)   The right does not apply in relation to any performance given for the purposes of reporting current events.

(3)   The right is not infringed by modifications made to a performance which are consistent with normal editorial or production practice.

(4)   Subject to subsection (5), the right is not infringed by anything done for the purpose of—

     (a)   avoiding the commission of an offence,

     (b)   complying with a duty imposed by or under an enactment, or

     (c)   in the case of the British Broadcasting Corporation, avoiding the inclusion in a programme broadcast by them of anything which offends against good taste or decency or which is likely to encourage or incite crime or lead to disorder or to be offensive to public feeling.

(5)   Where—

     (a)   the performer is identified in a manner likely to bring his identity to the notice of a person seeing or hearing the performance as modified by the act in question; or

     (b)   he has previously been identified in or on copies of a sound recording issued to the public,

    subsection (4) applies only if there is sufficient disclaimer.

(6)   In subsection (5) "sufficient disclaimer", in relation to an act capable of infringing the right, means a clear and reasonably prominent indication—

     (a)   given in a manner likely to bring it to the notice of a person seeing or hearing the performance as modified by the act in question, and

     (b)   if the performer is identified at the time of the act, appearing along with the identification,

    that the modifications were made without the performer's consent.

205H   Infringement of right by possessing or dealing with infringing article

(1)   The right conferred by section 205F (right to object to derogatory treatment of performance) is also infringed by a person who—

     (a)   possesses in the course of business, or

     (b)   sells or lets for hire, or offers or exposes for sale or hire, or

     (c)   distributes,

    an article which is, and which he knows or has reason to believe is, an infringing article.

(2)   An "infringing article" means a sound recording of a qualifying performance with any distortion, mutilation or other modification that is prejudicial to the reputation of the performer.

Supplementary

205I   Duration of rights

(1)   A performer's rights under this Chapter in relation to a performance subsist so long as that performer's rights under Chapter 2 subsist in relation to the performance.

(2)   In subsection (1) "performer's rights" includes rights of a performer that are vested in a successor of his.

205J   Consent and waiver of rights

(1)   It is not an infringement of the rights conferred by this Chapter to do any act to which consent has been given by or on behalf of the person entitled to the right.

(2)   Any of those rights may be waived by instrument in writing signed by or on behalf of the person giving up the right.

(3)   A waiver—

     (a)   may relate to a specific performance, to performances of a specified description or to performances generally, and may relate to existing or future performances, and

     (b)   may be conditional or unconditional and may be expressed to be subject to revocation, and if made in favour of the owner or prospective owner of a performer's property rights in the performance or performances to which it relates, it shall be presumed to extend to his licensees and successors in title unless a contrary intention is expressed.

(4) Nothing in this Chapter shall be construed as excluding the operation of the general law of contract or estoppel in relation to an informal waiver or other transaction in relation to either of the rights conferred by this Chapter.

205K Application of provisions to parts of performances

(1) The right conferred by section 205C (right to be identified as performer) applies in relation to the whole or any substantial part of a performance.

(2) The right conferred by section 205F (right to object to derogatory treatment of performance) applies in relation to the whole or any part of a performance.

205L Moral rights not assignable

The rights conferred by this Chapter are not assignable.

205M Transmission of moral rights on death

(1) On the death of a person entitled to a right conferred by this Chapter—

(a) the right passes to such person as he may by testamentary disposition specifically direct,

(b) if there is no such direction but the performer's property rights in respect of the performance in question form part of his estate, the right passes to the person to whom the property rights pass,

(c) if or to the extent that the right does not pass under paragraph (a) or (b) it is exercisable by his personal representatives.

(2) Where a performer's property rights pass in part to one person and in part to another, as for example where a bequest is limited so as to apply—

(a) to one or more, but not all, of the things to which the owner has the right to consent, or

(b) to part, but not the whole, of the period for which the rights subsist,

any right which by virtue of subsection (1) passes with the performer's property rights is correspondingly divided.

(3) Where by virtue of subsection (1)(a) or (1)(b) a right becomes exercisable by more than one person—

(a) it is, in the case of the right conferred by section 205F (right to object to derogatory treatment of performance), a right exercisable by each of them and is satisfied in relation to any of them if he consents to the treatment or act in question, and

(b) any waiver of the right in accordance with section 205J by one of them does not affect the rights of the others.

(4) A consent or waiver previously given or made binds any person to whom a right passes by virtue of subsection (1).

(5) Any damages recovered by personal representatives by virtue of this section in respect of an infringement after a person's death shall devolve as part of his estate as if the right of action had subsisted and been vested in him immediately before his death.

205N Remedies for infringement of moral rights

(1) An infringement of a right conferred by this Chapter is actionable as a breach of statutory duty owed to the person entitled to the right.

(2) Where—

(a) there is an infringement of a right conferred by this Chapter,

(b) a person falsely claiming to act on behalf of a performer consented to the relevant conduct or purported to waive the right, and

(c) there would have been no infringement if he had been so acting,

that person shall be liable, jointly and severally with any person liable in respect of the infringement by virtue of subsection (1), as if he himself had infringed the right.

(3) Where proceedings for infringement of the right conferred on a performer by this Chapter, it shall be a defence to prove—

    (a)   that a person claiming to act on behalf of the performer consented to the defendant's conduct or purported to waive the right, and

    (b)   that the defendant reasonably believed that the person was acting on behalf of the performer.

(4)   In proceedings for infringement of the right conferred by section 205F the court may, if it thinks it an adequate remedy in the circumstances, grant an injunction on terms prohibiting the doing of any act unless a disclaimer is made, in such terms and in such manner as may be approved by the court, dissociating the performer from the broadcast or sound recording of the performance.

CHAPTER 4

QUALIFICATION FOR PROTECTION, EXTENT AND INTERPRETATION

Qualification for protection and extent

206   Qualifying countries, individuals and persons

(1)   In this Part—

"qualifying country" means—

    (a)   the United Kingdom,

    (b)   another EEA state,

    (ba)   the Channel Islands, the Isle of Man or Gibraltar,

    (bb)   a country which is a party to the Rome Convention, or

    (c)   to the extent that an Order under section 208 so provides, a country designated under that section as enjoying reciprocal protection;

"qualifying individual" means a citizen or subject of, or an individual resident in, a qualifying country; and

"qualifying person" means a qualifying individual or a body corporate or other body having legal personality which—

    (a)   is formed under the law of a part of the United Kingdom or another qualifying country, and

    (b)   has in any qualifying country a place of business at which substantial business activity is carried on.

(2)   The reference in the definition of "qualifying individual" to a person's being a citizen or subject of a qualifying country shall be construed—

    (a)   in relation to the United Kingdom, as a reference to his being a British citizen, and

    (b)   in relation to a colony of the United Kingdom, as a reference to his being a British overseas territories' citizen by connection with that colony.

(3)   In determining for the purpose of the definition of "qualifying person" whether substantial business activity is carried on at a place of business in any country, no account shall be taken of dealings in goods which are at all material times outside that country.

(4)   Her Majesty may by Order in Council—

    (a)   make provision for the application of this Part to a country by virtue of paragraph (bb) or (c) of the definition of "qualifying country" in subsection (1) to be subject to specified restrictions;

    (b)   amend the definition of "qualifying country" in subsection (1) so as to add a country which is not a party to the Rome Convention;

    (c)   make provision for the application of this Part to a country added under paragraph (b) to be subject to specified restrictions.

(5)   A statutory instrument containing an Order in Council under this section is subject to annulment in pursuance of a resolution of either House of Parliament.

(6)   In this section, "the Rome Convention" means the International Convention for the Protection of Performers, Producers of Phonograms and Broadcasting Organisations done at Rome on 26 October 1961.

207   Countries to which this Part extends

This Part extends to England and Wales, Scotland and Northern Ireland.

208 Countries enjoying reciprocal protection

(1) Her Majesty may by Order in Council designate as enjoying reciprocal protection under this Part—

(a) a Convention country, or

(b) a country as to which Her Majesty is satisfied that provision has been or will be made under its law giving adequate protection for British performances.

(2) A "Convention country" means a country which is a party to a Convention relating to performers' rights to which the United Kingdom is also a party.

(3) A "British performance" means a performance—

(a) given by an individual who is a British citizen or resident in the United Kingdom, or

(b) taking place in the United Kingdom.

(4) If the law of that country provides adequate protection only for certain descriptions of performance, an Order under subsection (1)(b) designating that country shall contain provision limiting to a corresponding extent the protection afforded by this Part in relation to performances connected with that country.

(5) The power conferred by subsection (1)(b) is exercisable in relation to any colony of the United Kingdom, as in relation to a foreign country.

(6) A statutory instrument containing an Order in Council under this section shall be subject to annulment in pursuance of a resolution of either House of Parliament.

209 Territorial waters and the continental shelf

(1) For the purposes of this Part the territorial waters of the United Kingdom shall be treated as part of the United Kingdom.

(2) This Part applies to things done in the United Kingdom sector of the continental shelf on a structure or vessel which is present there for purposes directly connected with the exploration of the sea bed or subsoil or the exploitation of their natural resources as it applies to things done in the United Kingdom.

(3) The United Kingdom sector of the continental shelf means the areas designated by order under section 1(7) of the Continental Shelf Act 1964.

210 British ships, aircraft and hovercraft

(1) This Part applies to things done on a British ship, aircraft or hovercraft as it applies to things done in the United Kingdom.

(2) In this section—

"British ship" means a ship which is a British ship for the purposes of the Merchant Shipping Act 1995 otherwise than by virtue of registration in a country outside the United Kingdom; and

"British aircraft" and "British hovercraft" mean an aircraft or hovercraft registered in the United Kingdom.

210A Requirement of signature: application in relation to body corporate

(1) The requirement in the following provisions that an instrument be signed by or on behalf of a person is also satisfied in the case of a body corporate by the affixing of its seal—

section 191B(3) (assignment of performer's property rights);

section 191C(1) (assignment of future performer's property rights);

section 191D(1) (grant of exclusive licence).

(2) The requirement in the following provisions that an instrument be signed by a person is also satisfied in the case of a body corporate by signature on behalf of the body or by the affixing of its seal—

section 205D(2)(a) (assertion of performer's moral rights);

section 205J(2) (waiver of performer's moral rights).

Interpretation

211 Expressions having same meaning as in copyright provisions

(1) The following expressions have the same meaning in this Part as in Part I (copyright)—

assignment (in Scotland),

　　　　broadcast,
　　　　business,
　　　　communication to the public,
　　　　country,
　　　　defendant (in Scotland),
　　　　delivery up (in Scotland),
　　　　the EEA,
　　　　EEA State,
　　　　film,
　　　　injunction (in Scotland),
　　　　literary work,
　　　　published,
　　　　signed,
　　　　sound recording, and
　　　　wireless broadcast.

(2)　The provisions of—

(a)　section 5B(2) and (3) (supplementary provisions relating to films), and

(b)　section 6(3) to (5A) and section 19(4) (supplementary provisions relating to broadcasting),

apply for the purposes of this Part, and in relation to an infringement of the rights conferred by this Part, as they apply for the purposes of Part I and in relation to an infringement of copyright.

212　Index of defined expressions

The following Table shows provisions defining or otherwise explaining expressions used in this Part (other than provisions defining or explaining an expression used only in the same section)—

accessible copy (in paragraphs 3A to 3E of Schedule 2)	paragraph 3E(4) of Schedule 2
assignment (in Scotland)	section 211(1) (and section 177)
broadcast (and related expressions)	section 211 (and section 6)
business	section 211(1) (and section 178)
communication to the public	section 211(1) and section 20
consent of performer (in relation to performer's property right)	section 191A(2)
country	section 211(1) (and section 178)
defendant (in Scotland)	section 211(1) (and section 177)
delivery up (in Scotland)	section 211(1) (and section 177)
disabled person (in paragraphs 3A to 3E of Schedule 2)	paragraph 3E(2) and (3) of Schedule 2
distribution right	section 182B(5)
the EEA and EEA state	section 211(1) and section 172A
exclusive recording contract	section 185(1)
film	section 211(1) (and section 5)
group	section 205C(4)
illicit recording	section 197
injunction (in Scotland)	section 211(1) (and section 177)
issue to the public	section 182B
lending right	section 182C(7)
literary work	section 211(1) (and section 3(1))
making available right	section 182CA
performance	section 180(2)
performer's non-property rights	section 192A(1)
performer's property rights	section 191A(1)
published	section 211(1) (and section 175)
qualifying country	section 206(1)
qualifying individual	section 206(1) and (2)
qualifying performance	section 181
qualifying person	section 206(1) and (3)
recording (of a performance)	section 180(2)

recording rights (person having)   section 185(2) and (3)
rental right   section 182C(7)
reproduction right   section 182A(3)
rights owner (in relation to performer's property rights)   section 191A(3) and (4)
signed   section 211(1) (and section 176)
sound recording   section 211(1) (and section 5A)
wireless broadcast   section 211(1) (and section 178)

212A Power to amend in consequence of changes to international law

(1) The Secretary of State may by order amend this Part in consequence of changes to international law in the area of performance rights.

(2) An order under this section must be made by statutory instrument; and no order may be made unless a draft of it has been laid before and approved by a resolution of each House of Parliament.

PART III
DESIGN RIGHT

CHAPTER I
DESIGN RIGHT IN ORIGINAL DESIGNS

Introductory

213 Design right

(1) Design right is a property right which subsists in accordance with this Part in an original design.

(2) In this Part "design" means the design of the shape or configuration (whether internal or external) of the whole or part of an article.

(3) Design right does not subsist in—
   (a) a method or principle of construction,
   (b) features of shape or configuration of an article which—
      (i) enable the article to be connected to, or placed in, around or against, another article so that either article may perform its function, or
      (ii) are dependent upon the appearance of another article of which the article is intended by the designer to form an integral part, or
   (c) surface decoration.

(4) A design is not "original" for the purposes of this Part if it is commonplace in a qualifying country in the design field in question at the time of its creation; and "qualifying country" has the meaning given in section 217(3).

(5) Design right subsists in a design only if the design qualifies for design right protection by reference to—
   (a) the designer or the person by whom the designer was employed (see sections 218 and 219), or
   (b) the person by whom and country in which articles made to the design were first marketed (see section 220),
   or in accordance with any Order under section 221 (power to make further provision with respect to qualification).

(5A) Design right does not subsist in a design which consists of or contains a controlled representation within the meaning of the Olympic Symbol etc. (Protection) Act 1995.

(6) Design right does not subsist unless and until the design has been recorded in a design document or an article has been made to the design.

(7) Design right does not subsist in a design which was so recorded, or to which an article was made, before the commencement of this Part.

214 The designer

(1) In this Part the "designer", in relation to a design, means the person who creates it.

(2) In the case of a computer-generated design the person by whom the arrangements necessary for the creation of the design are undertaken shall be taken to be the designer.

215   Ownership of design right

(1)   The designer is the first owner of any design right in a design which is not created in the course of employment.

. . .

(3)   Where a design is created by an employee in the course of his employment, his employer is the first owner of any design right in the design.

(4)   If a design qualifies for design right protection by virtue of section 220 (qualification by reference to first marketing of articles made to the design), the above rules do not apply and the person by whom the articles in question are marketed is the first owner of the design right.

216   Duration of design right

(1)   Design right expires—

(a)   fifteen years from the end of the calendar year in which the design was first recorded in a design document or an article was first made to the design, whichever first occurred, or

(b)   if articles made to the design are made available for sale or hire within five years from the end of that calendar year, ten years from the end of the calendar year in which that first occurred.

(2)   The reference in subsection (1) to articles being made available for sale or hire is to their being made so available anywhere in the world by or with the licence of the design right owner.

Qualification for design right protection

217   Qualifying individuals and qualifying persons

(1)   In this Part—

"qualifying person" means—

(a)   an individual habitually resident in a qualifying country, or

(b)   a body corporate or other body having legal personality which—

(i)   is formed under the law of a part of the United Kingdom or another qualifying country, and

(ii)   has in any qualifying country a place of business at which substantial business activity is carried on.

(2)   References in this Part to a qualifying person include the Crown and the government of any other qualifying country.

(3)   In this section "qualifying country" means—

(a)   the United Kingdom,

(b)   a country to which this Part extends by virtue of an Order under section 255,

(c)   another member State of the European Economic Community, or

(d)   to the extent that an Order under section 256 so provides, a country designated under that section as enjoying reciprocal protection.

. . .

(5)   In determining for the purpose of the definition of "qualifying person" whether substantial business activity is carried on at a place of business in any country, no account shall be taken of dealings in goods which are at all material times outside that country.

218   Qualification by reference to designer

(1)   This section applies to a design which is not created in the course of employment.

(2)   A design to which this section applies qualifies for design right protection if the designer is a qualifying person.

(3)   A joint design to which this section applies qualifies for design right protection if any of the designers is a qualifying person.

(4)   Where a joint design qualifies for design right protection under this section, only those designers who are qualifying persons are entitled to design right under section 215(1) (first ownership of design right: entitlement of designer).

219   Qualification by reference to employer

(1)   A design qualifies for design right protection if it is created in the course of employment with a qualifying person.

(2)   In the case of joint employment a design qualifies for design right protection if any of the employers is a qualifying person.

(3)   Where a design which is created in the course of joint employment qualifies for design right protection under this section, only those employers who are qualifying persons are entitled to design right under section 215(3) (first ownership of design right: entitlement of employer).

220   Qualification by reference to first marketing

(1)   A design which does not qualify for design right protection under section 218 or 219 (qualification by reference to designer or employer) qualifies for design right protection if the first marketing of articles made to the design—

(a)   is by a qualifying person, and

(b)   takes place in the United Kingdom, another country to which this Part extends by virtue of an Order under section 255, or another member State of the European Economic Community.

(2)   If the first marketing of articles made to the design is done jointly by two or more persons, the design qualifies for design right protection if any of those persons meets the requirement specified in subsection (1)(a).

(3)   In such a case only the persons who meet that requirement are entitled to design right under section 215(4) (first ownership of design right: entitlement of first marketer of articles made to the design).

. . .

221   Power to make further provision as to qualification

(1)   Her Majesty may, with a view to fulfilling an international obligation of the United Kingdom, by Order in Council provide that a design qualifies for design right protection if such requirements as are specified in the Order are met.

(2)   An Order may make different provision for different descriptions of design or article; and may make such consequential modifications of the operation of sections 215 (ownership of design right) and sections 218 to 220 (other means of qualification) as appear to Her Majesty to be appropriate.

(3)   A statutory instrument containing an Order in Council under this section shall be subject to annulment in pursuance of a resolution of either House of Parliament.

Dealings with design right

222   Assignment and licences

(1)   Design right is transmissible by assignment, by testamentary disposition or by operation of law, as personal or moveable property.

(2)   An assignment or other transmission of design right may be partial, that is, limited so as to apply—

(a)   to one or more, but not all, of the things the design right owner has the exclusive right to do;

(b)   to part, but not the whole, of the period for which the right is to subsist.

(3)   An assignment of design right is not effective unless it is in writing signed by or on behalf of the assignor.

(4)   A licence granted by the owner of design right is binding on every successor in title to his interest in the right, except a purchaser in good faith for valuable consideration and without notice (actual or constructive) of the licence or a person deriving title from such a purchaser; and references in this Part to doing anything with, or without, the licence of the design right owner shall be construed accordingly.

223   Prospective ownership of design right

(1)   Where by an agreement made in relation to future design right, and signed by or on behalf of the prospective owner of the design right, the prospective owner purports to assign the future design right (wholly or partially) to another person, then if, on the right

coming into existence, the assignee or another person claiming under him would be entitled as against all other persons to require the right to be vested in him, the right shall vest in him by virtue of this section.

(2)   In this section—

"future design right" means design right which will or may come into existence in respect of a future design or class of designs or on the occurrence of a future event; and "prospective owner" shall be construed accordingly, and includes a person who is prospectively entitled to design right by virtue of such an agreement as is mentioned in subsection (1).

(3)   A licence granted by a prospective owner of design right is binding on every successor in title to his interest (or prospective interest) in the right, except a purchaser in good faith for valuable consideration and without notice (actual or constructive) of the licence or a person deriving title from such a purchaser; and references in this Part to doing anything with, or without, the licence of the design right owner shall be construed accordingly.

224   Assignment of right in registered design presumed to carry with it design right

Where a design consisting of a design in which design right subsists is registered under the Registered Designs Act 1949 and the proprietor of the registered design is also the design right owner, an assignment of the right in the registered design shall be taken to be also an assignment of the design right, unless a contrary intention appears.

225   Exclusive licences

(1)   In this Part an "exclusive licence" means a licence in writing signed by or on behalf of the design right owner authorising the licensee to the exclusion of all other persons, including the person granting the licence, to exercise a right which would otherwise be exercisable exclusively by the design right owner.

(2)   The licensee under an exclusive licence has the same rights against any successor in title who is bound by the licence as he has against the person granting the licence.

CHAPTER II
RIGHTS OF DESIGN RIGHT OWNER AND REMEDIES

Infringement of design right

226   Primary infringement of design right

(1)   The owner of design right in a design has the exclusive right to reproduce the design for commercial purposes—
    (a)   by making articles to that design, or
    (b)   by making a design document recording the design for the purpose of enabling such articles to be made.

(2)   Reproduction of a design by making articles to the design means copying the design so as to produce articles exactly or substantially to that design, and references in this Part to making articles to a design shall be construed accordingly.

(3)   Design right is infringed by a person who without the licence of the design right owner does, or authorises another to do, anything which by virtue of this section is the exclusive right of the design right owner.

(4)   For the purposes of this section reproduction may be direct or indirect, and it is immaterial whether any intervening acts themselves infringe the design right.

(5)   This section has effect subject to the provisions of Chapter III (exceptions to rights of design right owner).

227   Secondary infringement: importing or dealing with infringing article

(1)   Design right is infringed by a person who, without the licence of the design right owner—
    (a)   imports into the United Kingdom for commercial purposes, or
    (b)   has in his possession for commercial purposes, or
    (c)   sells, lets for hire, or offers or exposes for sale or hire, in the course of a business,
    an article which is, and which he knows or has reason to believe is, an infringing article.

(2)   This section has effect subject to the provisions of Chapter III (exceptions to rights of design right owner).

228   Meaning of "infringing article"

(1)   In this Part "infringing article", in relation to a design, shall be construed in accordance with this section.

(2)   An article is an infringing article if its making to that design was an infringement of design right in the design.

(3)   An article is also an infringing article if—
   (a)   it has been or is proposed to be imported into the United Kingdom, and
   (b)   its making to that design in the United Kingdom would have been an infringement of design right in the design or a breach of an exclusive licence agreement relating to the design.

(4)   Where it is shown that an article is made to a design in which design right subsists or has subsisted at any time, it shall be presumed until the contrary is proved that the article was made at a time when design right subsisted.

(5)   Nothing in subsection (3) shall be construed as applying to an article which may lawfully be imported into the United Kingdom by virtue of any enforceable EU right within the meaning of section 2(1) of the European Communities Act 1972.

(6)   The expression "infringing article" does not include a design document, notwithstanding that its making was or would have been an infringement of design right.

Remedies for infringement

229   Rights and remedies of design right owner

(1)   An infringement of design right is actionable by the design right owner.

(2)   In an action for infringement of design right all such relief by way of damages, injunctions, accounts or otherwise is available to the plaintiff as is available in respect of the infringement of any other property right.

(3)   The court may in an action for infringement of design right, having regard to all the circumstances and in particular to—
   (a)   the flagrancy of the infringement, and
   (b)   any benefit accruing to the defendant by reason of the infringement,
   award such additional damages as the justice of the case may require.

(4)   This section has effect subject to section 233 (innocent infringement).

230   Order for delivery up

(1)   Where a person—
   (a)   has in his possession, custody or control for commercial purposes an infringing article, or
   (b)   has in his possession, custody or control anything specifically designed or adapted for making articles to a particular design, knowing or having reason to believe that it has been or is to be used to make an infringing article,
   the owner of the design right in the design in question may apply to the court for an order that the infringing article or other thing be delivered up to him or to such other person as the court may direct.

(2)   An application shall not be made after the end of the period specified in the following provisions of this section; and no order shall be made unless the court also makes, or it appears to the court that there are grounds for making, an order under section 231 (order as to disposal of infringing article, etc.).

(3)   An application for an order under this section may not be made after the end of the period of six years from the date on which the article or thing in question was made, subject to subsection (4).

(4)   If during the whole or any part of that period the design right owner—
   (a)   is under a disability, or
   (b)   is prevented by fraud or concealment from discovering the facts entitling him to apply for an order,
   an application may be made at any time before the end of the period of six years from the date on which he ceased to be under a disability or, as the case may be, could with reasonable diligence have discovered those facts.

(5)   In subsection (4) "disability"—
   (a)   in England and Wales, has the same meaning as in the Limitation Act 1980;
   (b)   in Scotland, means legal disability within the meaning of the Prescription and Limitation (Scotland) Act 1973;
   (c)   in Northern Ireland, has the same meaning as in the Statute of Limitations (Northern Ireland) 1958.
(6)   A person to whom an infringing article or other thing is delivered up in pursuance of an order under this section shall, if an order under section 231 is not made, retain it pending the making of an order, or the decision not to make an order, under that section.
(7)   Nothing in this section affects any other power of the court.

231   Order as to disposal of infringing articles, etc.

(1)   An application may be made to the court for an order that an infringing article or other thing delivered up in pursuance of an order under section 230 shall be—
   (a)   forfeited to the design right owner, or
   (b)   destroyed or otherwise dealt with as the court may think fit,
   or for a decision that no such order should be made.
(2)   In considering what order (if any) should be made, the court shall consider whether other remedies available in an action for infringement of design right would be adequate to compensate the design right owner and to protect his interests.
(3)   Provision shall be made by rules of court as to the service of notice on persons having an interest in the article or other thing, and any such person is entitled—
   (a)   to appear in proceedings for an order under this section, whether or not he was served with notice, and
   (b)   to appeal against any order made, whether or not he appeared;
   and an order shall not take effect until the end of the period within which notice of an appeal may be given or, if before the end of that period notice of appeal is duly given, until the final determination or abandonment of the proceedings on the appeal.
(4)   Where there is more than one person interested in an article or other thing, the court shall make such order as it thinks just and may (in particular) direct that the thing be sold, or otherwise dealt with, and the proceeds divided.
(5)   If the court decides that no order should be made under this section, the person in whose possession, custody or control the article or other thing was before being delivered up is entitled to its return.

   . . .

233   Innocent infringement

(1)   Where in an action for infringement of design right brought by virtue of section 226 (primary infringement) it is shown that at the time of the infringement the defendant did not know, and had no reason to believe, that design right subsisted in the design to which the action relates, the plaintiff is not entitled to damages against him, but without prejudice to any other remedy.
(2)   Where in an action for infringement of design right brought by virtue of section 227 (secondary infringement) a defendant shows that the infringing article was innocently acquired by him or a predecessor in title of his, the only remedy available against him in respect of the infringement is damages not exceeding a reasonable royalty in respect of the act complained of.
(3)   In subsection (2) "innocently acquired" means that the person acquiring the article did not know and had no reason to believe that it was an infringing article.

234   Rights and remedies of exclusive licensee

(1)   An exclusive licensee has, except against the design right owner, the same rights and remedies in respect of matters occurring after the grant of the licence as if the licence had been an assignment.
(2)   His rights and remedies are concurrent with those of the design right owner; and references in the relevant provisions of this Part to the design right owner shall be construed accordingly.

(3)   In an action brought by an exclusive licensee by virtue of this section a defendant may avail himself of any defence which would have been available to him if the action had been brought by the design right owner.

235   Exercise of concurrent rights

(1)   Where an action for infringement of design right brought by the design right owner or an exclusive licensee relates (wholly or partly) to an infringement in respect of which they have concurrent rights of action, the design right owner or, as the case may be, the exclusive licensee may not, without the leave of the court, proceed with the action unless the other is either joined as a plaintiff or added as a defendant.

(2)   A design right owner or exclusive licensee who is added as a defendant in pursuance of subsection (1) is not liable for any costs in the action unless he takes part in the proceedings.

(3)   The above provisions do not affect the granting of interlocutory relief on the application of the design right owner or an exclusive licensee.

(4)   Where an action for infringement of design right is brought which relates (wholly or partly) to an infringement in respect of which the design right owner and an exclusive licensee have concurrent rights of action—

(a)   the court shall, in assessing damages, take into account—
(i)   the terms of the licence, and
(ii)   any pecuniary remedy already awarded or available to either of them in respect of the infringement;

(b)   no account of profits shall be directed if an award of damages has been made, or an account of profits has been directed, in favour of the other of them in respect of the infringement; and

(c)   the court shall if an account of profits is directed apportion the profits between them as the court considers just, subject to any agreement between them;

and these provisions apply whether or not the design right owner and the exclusive licensee are both parties to the action.

(5)   The design right owner shall notify any exclusive licensee having concurrent rights before applying for an order under section 230 (order for delivery up of infringing article, &c.); and the court may on the application of the licensee make such order under that section as it thinks fit having regard to the terms of the licence.

CHAPTER III
EXCEPTIONS TO RIGHTS OF DESIGN RIGHT OWNERS

Infringement of copyright

236   Infringement of copyright

Where copyright subsists in a work which consists of or includes a design in which design right subsists, it is not an infringement of design right in the design to do anything which is an infringement of the copyright in that work.

Availability of licences of right

237   Licences available in last five years of design right

(1)   Any person is entitled as of right to a licence to do in the last five years of the design right term anything which would otherwise infringe the design right.

(2)   The terms of the licence shall, in default of agreement, be settled by the comptroller.

(3)   The Secretary of State may if it appears to him necessary in order to—
(a)   comply with an international obligation of the United Kingdom, or
(b)   secure or maintain reciprocal protection for British designs in other countries,
by order exclude from the operation of subsection (1) designs of a description specified in the order or designs applied to articles of a description so specified.

(4)   An order shall be made by statutory instrument; and no order shall be made unless a draft of it has been laid before and approved by a resolution of each House of Parliament.

238   Powers exercisable for protection of the public interest

(1)   Subsection (1A) applies where whatever needs to be remedied, mitigated or prevented by the Secretary of State or (as the case may be) the Competition and Markets Authority under section 12(5) of the Competition Act 1980 or section 41(2), 55(2), 66(6), 75(2), 83(2), 138(2), 147(2), 147A(2) or 160(2) of, or paragraph 5(2) or 10(2) of Schedule 7 to, the Enterprise Act 2002 (powers to take remedial action following references to the Competition and Markets Authority in connection with public bodies and certain other persons, mergers or market investigations etc) consists of or includes—

(a)   conditions in licences granted by a design right owner restricting the use of the design by the licensee or the right of the design right owner to grant other licences, or

(b)   a refusal of a design right owner to grant licences on reasonable terms.

(1A) The powers conferred by Schedule 8 to the Enterprise Act 2002 include power to cancel or modify those conditions and, instead or in addition, to provide that licences in respect of the design right shall be available as of right.

(2)   The references to anything permitted by Schedule 8 to the Enterprise Act 2002 in section 12(5A) of the Competition Act 1980 and in sections 75(4)(a), 83(4)(a), 84(2)(a), 89(1), 160(4)(a), 161(3)(a) and 164(1) of, and paragraphs 5, 10 and 11 of Schedule 7 to, the Act of 2002 shall be construed accordingly.

(3)   The terms of a licence available by virtue of this section shall, in default of agreement, be settled by the comptroller.

239   Undertaking to take licence of right in infringement proceedings

(1)   If in proceedings for infringement of design right in a design in respect of which a licence is available as of right under section 237 or 238 the defendant undertakes to take a licence on such terms as may be agreed or, in default of agreement, settled by the comptroller under that section—

(a)   no injunction shall be granted against him,

(b)   no order for delivery up shall be made under section 230, and

(c)   the amount recoverable against him by way of damages or on an account of profits shall not exceed double the amount which would have been payable by him as licensee if such a licence on those terms had been granted before the earliest infringement.

(2)   An undertaking may be given at any time before final order in the proceedings, without any admission of liability.

(3)   Nothing in this section affects the remedies available in respect of an infringement committed before licences of right were available.

Crown use of designs

240   Crown use of designs

(1)   A government department, or a person authorised in writing by a government department, may without the licence of the design right owner—

(a)   do anything for the purpose of supplying articles for the services of the Crown, or

(b)   dispose of articles no longer required for the services of the Crown;

and nothing done by virtue of this section infringes the design right.

(2)   References in this Part to "the services of the Crown" are to—

(a)   the defence of the realm,

(b)   foreign defence purposes, and

(c)   health service purposes.

(3)   The reference to the supply of articles for "foreign defence purposes" is to their supply—

(a)   for the defence of a country outside the realm in pursuance of an agreement or arrangement to which the government of that country and Her Majesty's Government in the United Kingdom are parties; or

(b)   for use by armed forces operating in pursuance of a resolution of the United Nations or one of its organs.

(4) The reference to the supply of articles for "health service purposes" are to their supply for the purpose of providing—

(za) primary medical services or primary dental services under the National Health Service Act 2006 or the National Health Service (Wales) Act 2006, or primary medical services under Part 1 of the National Health Service (Scotland) Act 1978,

(a) pharmaceutical services, general medical services or general dental services under—

(i) Chapter 1 of Part 7 of the National Health Service Act 2006, or Chapter 1 of Part 7 of the National Health Service (Wales) Act 2006 (in the case of pharmaceutical services),

(ii) Part II of the National Health Service (Scotland) Act 1978 (in the case of pharmaceutical services or general dental services), or

(iii) the corresponding provisions of the law in force in Northern Ireland; or

(b) personal medical services or personal dental services in accordance with arrangements made under—

(i) . . .

(ii) section 17C of the 1978 Act (in the case of personal dental services), or

(iii) the corresponding provisions of the law in force in Northern Ireland, or

(c) local pharmaceutical services provided under the National Health Service Act 2006 or the National Health Service (Wales) Act 2006.

(5) In this Part—

"Crown use", in relation to a design, means the doing of anything by virtue of this section which would otherwise be an infringement of design right in the design; and

"the government department concerned", in relation to such use, means the government department by whom or on whose authority the act was done.

(6) The authority of a government department in respect of Crown use of a design may be given to a person either before or after the use and whether or not he is authorised, directly or indirectly, by the design right owner to do anything in relation to the design.

(7) A person acquiring anything sold in the exercise of powers conferred by this section, and any person claiming under him, may deal with it in the same manner as if the design right were held on behalf of the Crown.

243 Crown use: compensation for loss of profit

(1) Where Crown use is made of a design, the government department concerned shall pay—

(a) to the design right owner, or

(b) if there is an exclusive licence in force in respect of the design, to the exclusive licensee,

compensation for any loss resulting from his not being awarded a contract to supply the articles made to the design.

. . .

244 Special provision for Crown use during emergency

(1) During a period of emergency the powers exercisable in relation to a design by virtue of section 240 (Crown use) include power to do any act which would otherwise be an infringement of design right for any purpose which appears to the government department concerned necessary or expedient—

(a) for the efficient prosecution of any war in which Her Majesty may be engaged;

(b) for the maintenance of supplies and services essential to the life of the community;

(c) for securing a sufficiency of supplies and services essential to the well-being of the community;

(d) for promoting the productivity of industry, commerce and agriculture;

(e) for fostering and directing exports and reducing imports, or imports of any classes, from all or any countries and for redressing the balance of trade;

(f) generally for ensuring that the whole resources of the community are available for use, and are used, in a manner best calculated to serve the interests of the community; or

(g)   for assisting the relief of suffering and the restoration and distribution of essential supplies and services in any country outside the United Kingdom which is in grave distress as the result of war.

. . .

Miscellaneous

244A   Exception for private acts, experiments and teaching

Design right is not infringed by—

(a)   an act which is done privately and for purposes which are not commercial;

(b)   an act which is done for experimental purposes; or

(c)   an act of reproduction for teaching purposes or for the purpose of making citations provided that—

      (i)   the act of reproduction is compatible with fair trade practice and does not unduly prejudice the normal exploitation of the design, and

      (ii)   mention is made of the source.

244B   Exception for overseas ships and aircraft

Design right is not infringed by—

(a)   the use of equipment on ships or aircraft which are registered in another country but which are temporarily in the United Kingdom;

(b)   the importation into the United Kingdom of spare parts or accessories for the purpose of repairing such ships or aircraft; or

(c)   the carrying out of repairs on such ships or aircraft.

General

245   Power to provide for further exceptions

(1)   The Secretary of State may if it appears to him necessary in order to—

      (a)   comply with an international obligation of the United Kingdom, or

      (b)   secure or maintain reciprocal protection for British designs in other countries,

    by order provide that acts of a description specified in the order do not infringe design right.

(2)   An order may make different provision for different descriptions of design or article.

(3)   An order shall be made by statutory instrument and no order shall be made unless a draft of it has been laid before and approved by a resolution of each House of Parliament.

CHAPTER IV
JURISDICTION OF THE COMPTROLLER AND THE COURT

Jurisdiction of the comptroller

246   Jurisdiction to decide matters relating to design right

(1)   A party to a dispute as to any of the following matters may refer the dispute to the comptroller for his decision—

      (a)   the subsistence of design right,

      (b)   the term of design right, or

      (c)   the identity of the person in whom design right first vested;

    and the comptroller's decision on the reference is binding on the parties to the dispute.

(2)   No other court or tribunal shall decide any such matter except—

      (a)   on a reference or appeal from the comptroller,

      (b)   in infringement or other proceedings in which the issue arises incidentally, or

      (c)   in proceedings brought with the agreement of the parties or the leave of the comptroller.

(3)   The comptroller has jurisdiction to decide any incidental question of fact or law arising in the course of a reference under this section.

247 Application to settle terms of licence of right

(1) A person requiring a licence which is available as of right by virtue of—

    (a) section 237 (licences available in last five years of design right), or

    (b) an order under section 238 (licences made available in the public interest),

    may apply to the comptroller to settle the terms of the licence.

(2) No application for the settlement of the terms of a licence available by virtue of section 237 may be made earlier than one year before the earliest date on which the licence may take effect under that section.

(3) The terms of a licence settled by the comptroller shall authorise the licensee to do—

    (a) in the case of licence available by virtue of section 237, everything which would be an infringement of the design right in the absence of a licence;

    (b) in the case of a licence available by virtue of section 238, everything in respect of which a licence is so available.

(4) In settling the terms of a licence the comptroller shall have regard to such factors as may be prescribed by the Secretary of State by order made by statutory instrument.

. . .

248 Settlement of terms where design right owner unknown

(1) This section applies where a person making an application under section 247 (settlement of terms of licence of right) is unable on reasonable inquiry to discover the identity of the design right owner.

(2) The comptroller may in settling the terms of the licence order that the licence shall be free of any obligation as to royalties or other payments.

(3) If such an order is made the design right owner may apply to the comptroller to vary the terms of the licence with effect from the date on which his application is made.

(4) If the terms of a licence are settled by the comptroller and it is subsequently established that a licence was not available as of right, the licensee shall not be liable in damages for, or for an account of profits in respect of, anything done before he was aware of any claim by the design right owner that a licence was not available.

CHAPTER V

MISCELLANEOUS AND GENERAL

Unjustified threats

253 Threats of infringement proceedings

(1) A communication contains a "threat of infringement proceedings" if a reasonable person in the position of a recipient would understand from the communication that—

    (a) design right subsists in a design, and

    (b) a person intends to bring proceedings (whether in a court in the United Kingdom or elsewhere) against another person for infringement of the design right by—

        (i) an act done in the United Kingdom, or

        (ii) an act which, if done, would be done in the United Kingdom.

(2) References in this section and in section 253C to a "recipient" include, in the case of a communication directed to the public or a section of the public, references to a person to whom the communication is directed.

253A Actionable threats

(1) Subject to subsections (2) to (5), a threat of infringement proceedings made by any person is actionable by any person aggrieved by the threat.

(2) A threat of infringement proceedings is not actionable if the infringement is alleged to consist of—

    (a) making an article for disposal, or

    (b) importing an article for disposal.

(3) A threat of infringement proceedings is not actionable if the infringement is alleged to consist of an act which, if done, would constitute an infringement of a kind mentioned in subsection (2)(a) or (b).

(4) A threat of infringement proceedings is not actionable if the threat—
   (a) is made to a person who has done, or intends to do, an act mentioned in subsection (2)(a) or (b) in relation to an article, and
   (b) is a threat of proceedings for an infringement alleged to consist of doing anything else in relation to that article.
(5) A threat of infringement proceedings which is not an express threat is not actionable if it is contained in a permitted communication.
(6) In sections 253C and 253D an "actionable threat" means a threat of infringement proceedings that is actionable in accordance with this section.

253B Permitted communications

(1) For the purposes of section 253A(5), a communication containing a threat of infringement proceedings is a "permitted communication" if—
   (a) the communication, so far as it contains information that relates to the threat, is made for a permitted purpose;
   (b) all of the information that relates to the threat is information that—
      (i) is necessary for that purpose (see subsection (5)(a) to (c) for some examples of necessary information), and
      (ii) the person making the communication reasonably believes is true.
(2) Each of the following is a "permitted purpose"—
   (a) giving notice that design right subsists in a design;
   (b) discovering whether, or by whom, design right in a design has been infringed by an act mentioned in section 253A(2)(a) or (b);
   (c) giving notice that a person has a right in or under the design right in a design, where another person's awareness of the right is relevant to any proceedings that may be brought in respect of the design right in the design.
(3) The court may, having regard to the nature of the purposes listed in subsection (2)(a) to (c), treat any other purpose as a "permitted purpose" if it considers that it is in the interests of justice to do so.
(4) But the following may not be treated as a "permitted purpose"—
   (a) requesting a person to cease doing, for commercial purposes, anything in relation to an article made to a design,
   (b) requesting a person to deliver up or destroy an article made to a design, or
   (c) requesting a person to give an undertaking relating to an article made to a design.
(5) If any of the following information is included in a communication made for a permitted purpose, it is information that is "necessary for that purpose" (see subsection (1)(b)(i))—
   (a) a statement that design right subsists in a design;
   (b) details of the design, or of a right in or under the design right in the design, which—
      (i) are accurate in all material respects, and
      (ii) are not misleading in any material respect; and
   (c) information enabling the identification of articles that are alleged to be infringing articles in relation to the design.

253C Remedies and defences

(1) Proceedings in respect of an actionable threat may be brought against the person who made the threat for—
   (a) a declaration that the threat is unjustified;
   (b) an injunction against the continuance of the threat;
   (c) damages in respect of any loss sustained by the aggrieved person by reason of the threat.
(2) It is a defence for the person who made the threat to show that the act in respect of which proceedings were threatened constitutes (or if done would constitute) an infringement of design right.
(3) It is a defence for the person who made the threat to show—
   (a) that, despite having taken reasonable steps, the person has not identified anyone who has done an act mentioned in section 253A(2)(a) or (b) in relation to the article which is the subject of the threat, and

(b)   that the person notified the recipient, before or at the time of making the threat, of the steps taken.

253D Professional advisers

(1)   Proceedings in respect of an actionable threat may not be brought against a professional adviser (or any person vicariously liable for the actions of that professional adviser) if the conditions in subsection (3) are met.

(2)   In this section "professional adviser" means a person who, in relation to the making of the communication containing the threat—

(a)   is acting in a professional capacity in providing legal services or the services of a trade mark attorney or a patent attorney, and

(b)   is regulated in the provision of legal services, or the services of a trade mark attorney or a patent attorney, by one or more regulatory bodies (whether through membership of a regulatory body, the issue of a licence to practise or any other means).

(3)   The conditions are that—

(a)   in making the communication the professional adviser is acting on the instructions of another person, and

(b)   when the communication is made the professional adviser identifies the person on whose instructions the adviser is acting.

(4)   This section does not affect any liability of the person on whose instructions the professional adviser is acting.

(5)   It is for a person asserting that subsection (1) applies to prove (if required) that at the material time—

(a)   the person concerned was acting as a professional adviser, and

(b)   the conditions in subsection (3) were met.

253E Supplementary: proceedings for delivery up etc.

In section 253(1)(b) the reference to proceedings for infringement of design right includes a reference to—

(a)   proceedings for an order under section 230 (order for delivery up), and

(b)   proceedings for an order under section 231 (order as to disposal of infringing articles).

Licensee under licence of right not to claim connection with design right owner

254 Licensee under licence of right not to claim connection with design right owner

(1)   A person who has a licence in respect of a design by virtue of section 237 or 238 (licences of right) shall not, without the consent of the design right owner—

(a)   apply to goods which he is marketing, or proposes to market, in reliance on that licence a trade description indicating that he is the licensee of the design right owner, or

(b)   use any such trade description in an advertisement in relation to such goods.

(2)   A contravention of subsection (1) is actionable by the design right owner.

(3)   In this section "trade description", the reference to applying a trade description to goods and "advertisement" have the same meaning as in the Trade Descriptions Act 1968.

Extent of operation of this Part

255 Countries to which this Part extends

(1)   This Part extends to England and Wales, Scotland and Northern Ireland.

(2)   Her Majesty may by Order in Council direct that this Part shall extend, subject to such exceptions and modifications as may be specified in the Order, to—

(a)   any of the Channel Islands,

(b)   the Isle of Man, or

(c)   any colony.

(3)   That power includes power to extend, subject to such exceptions and modifications as may be specified in the Order, any Order in Council made under section 221 (further

provision as to qualification for design right protection) or section 256 (countries enjoying reciprocal protection).

(4)   The legislature of a country to which this Part has been extended may modify or add to the provisions of this Part, in their operation as part of the law of that country, as the legislature may consider necessary to adapt the provisions to the circumstances of that country; but not so as to deny design right protection in a case where it would otherwise exist.

. . .

256   Countries enjoying reciprocal protection

(1)   Her Majesty may, if it appears to Her that the law of a country provides adequate protection for British designs, by Order in Council designate that country as one enjoying reciprocal protection under this Part.

(2)   If the law of a country provides adequate protection only for certain classes of British design, or only for designs applied to certain classes of article, any Order designating that country shall contain provision limiting, to a corresponding extent, the protection afforded by this Part in relation to designs connected with that country.

(3)   An Order under this section shall be subject to annulment in pursuance of a resolution of either House of Parliament.

257   Territorial waters and the continental shelf

(1)   For the purposes of this Part the territorial waters of the United Kingdom shall be treated as part of the United Kingdom.

. . .

Interpretation

258   Construction of references to design right owner

(1)   Where different persons are (whether in consequence of a partial assignment or otherwise) entitled to different aspects of design right in a work, the design right owner for any purpose of this Part is the person who is entitled to the right in the respect relevant for that purpose.

(2)   Where design right (or any aspect of design right) is owned by more than one person jointly, references in this Part to the design right owner are to all the owners, so that, in particular, any requirement of the licence of the design right owner requires the licence of all of them.

259   Joint designs

(1)   In this Part a "joint design" means a design produced by the collaboration of two or more designers in which the contribution of each is not distinct from that of the other or others.

(2)   References in this Part to the designer of a design shall, except as otherwise provided, be construed in relation to a joint design as references to all the designers of the design.

260   Application of provisions to articles in kit form

(1)   The provisions of this Part apply in relation to a kit, that is, a complete or substantially complete set of components intended to be assembled into an article, as they apply in relation to the assembled article.

(2)   Subsection (1) does not affect the question whether design right subsists in any aspect of the design of the components of a kit as opposed to the design of the assembled article.

261   Requirement of signature: application in relation to body corporate

The requirement in the following provisions that an instrument be signed by or on behalf of a person is also satisfied in the case of a body corporate by the affixing of its seal—
section 222(3) (assignment of design right),
section 223(1) (assignment of future design right),
section 225(1) (grant of exclusive licence).

262 Adaptation of expressions in relation to Scotland

In the application of this Part to Scotland—

"account of profits" means accounting and payment of profits; "accounts" means count, reckoning and payment; "assignment" means assignation;

"costs" means expenses;

"declaration" means declarator;

"defendant" means defender;

"delivery up" means delivery;

"injunction" means interdict;

"interlocutory relief" means interim remedy; and

"plaintiff" means pursuer.

263 Minor definitions

(1) In this Part—

"British design" means a design which qualifies for design right protection by reason of a connection with the United Kingdom of the designer or the person by whom the designer is employed;

"business" includes a trade or profession;

"the comptroller" means the Comptroller-General of Patents, Designs and Trade Marks;

"computer-generated", in relation to a design, means that the design is generated by computer in circumstances such that there is no human designer,

"country" includes any territory;

"the Crown" includes the Crown in right of Her Majesty's Government in Northern Ireland and the Crown in right of the Scottish Administration and the Crown in right of the Welsh Assembly Government;

"design document" means any record of a design, whether in the form of a drawing, a written description, a photograph, data stored in a computer or otherwise;

"employee", "employment" and "employer" refer to employment under a contract of service or of apprenticeship;

"government department" includes a Northern Ireland department and any part of the Scottish Administration and any part of the Welsh Assembly Government.

(2) References in this Part to "marketing", in relation to an article, are to its being sold or let for hire, or offered or exposed for sale or hire, in the course of a business, and related expressions shall be construed accordingly; but no account shall be taken for the purposes of this Part of marketing which is merely colourable and not intended to satisfy the reasonable requirements of the public.

(3) References in this Part to an act being done in relation to an article for "commercial purposes" are to its being done with a view to the article in question being sold or hired in the course of a business.

PART VII

MISCELLANEOUS AND GENERAL

Circumvention of protection measures

296 Circumvention of technical devices applied to computer programs

(1) This section applies where—

(a) a technical device has been applied to a computer program; and

(b) a person (A) knowing or having reason to believe that it will be used to make infringing copies—

(i) manufactures for sale or hire, imports, distributes, sells or lets for hire, offers or exposes for sale or hire, advertises for sale or hire or has in his possession for commercial purposes any means the sole intended purpose of which is to facilitate the unauthorised removal or circumvention of the technical device; or

(ii) publishes information intended to enable or assist persons to remove or circumvent the technical device.

(2) The following persons have the same rights against A as a copyright owner has in respect of an infringement of copyright—

    (a) a person—

        (i) issuing to the public copies of, or

        (ii) communicating to the public,

        the computer program to which the technical device has been applied;

    (b) the copyright owner or his exclusive licensee, if he is not the person specified in paragraph (a);

    (c) the owner or exclusive licensee of any intellectual property right in the technical device applied to the computer program.

(3) The rights conferred by subsection (2) are concurrent, and sections 101(3) and 102(1) to (4) apply, in proceedings under this section, in relation to persons with concurrent rights as they apply, in proceedings mentioned in those provisions, in relation to a copyright owner and exclusive licensee with concurrent rights.

(4) Further, the persons in subsection (2) have the same rights under section 99 or 100 (delivery up or seizure of certain articles) in relation to any such means as is referred to in subsection (1) which a person has in his possession, custody or control with the intention that it should be used to facilitate the unauthorised removal or circumvention of any technical device which has been applied to a computer program, as a copyright owner has in relation to an infringing copy.

(5) The rights conferred by subsection (4) are concurrent, and section 102(5) shall apply, as respects anything done under section 99 or 100 by virtue of subsection (4), in relation to persons with concurrent rights as it applies, as respects anything done under section 99 or 100, in relation to a copyright owner and exclusive licensee with concurrent rights.

(6) In this section references to a technical device in relation to a computer program are to any device intended to prevent or restrict acts that are not authorised by the copyright owner of that computer program and are restricted by copyright.

(7) The following provisions apply in relation to proceedings under this section as in relation to proceedings under Part 1 (copyright)—

    (a) sections 104 to 106 of this Act (presumptions as to certain matters relating to copyright); and

    (b) section 72 of the Senior Courts Act 1981, section 15 of the Law Reform (Miscellaneous Provisions) (Scotland) Act 1985 and section 94A of the Judicature (Northern Ireland) Act 1978 (withdrawal of privilege against self-incrimination in certain proceedings relating to intellectual property);

    and section 114 of this Act applies, with the necessary modifications, in relation to the disposal of anything delivered up or seized by virtue of subsection (4).

(8) Expressions used in this section which are defined for the purposes of Part 1 of this Act (copyright) have the same meaning as in that Part.

296ZA Circumvention of technological measures

(1) This section applies where—

    (a) effective technological measures have been applied to a copyright work other than a computer program; and

    (b) a person (B) does anything which circumvents those measures knowing, or with reasonable grounds to know, that he is pursuing that objective.

(2) This section does not apply where a person, for the purposes of research into cryptography, does anything which circumvents effective technological measures unless in so doing, or in issuing information derived from that research, he affects prejudicially the rights of the copyright owner.

(3) The following persons have the same rights against B as a copyright owner has in respect of an infringement of copyright—

    (a) a person—

        (i) issuing to the public copies of, or

        (ii) communicating to the public,

        the work to which effective technological measures have been applied; and

    (b) the copyright owner or his exclusive licensee, if he is not the person specified in paragraph (a).

(4) The rights conferred by subsection (3) are concurrent, and sections 101(3) and 102(1) to (4) apply, in proceedings under this section, in relation to persons with concurrent rights as they apply, in proceedings mentioned in those provisions, in relation to a copyright owner and exclusive licensee with concurrent rights.

(5) The following provisions apply in relation to proceedings under this section as in relation to proceedings under Part 1 (copyright)—

(a) sections 104 to 106 of this Act (presumptions as to certain matters relating to copyright); and

(b) section 72 of the Senior Courts Act 1981, section 15 of the Law Reform (Miscellaneous Provisions) (Scotland) Act 1985 and section 94A of the Judicature (Northern Ireland) Act 1978 (withdrawal of privilege against self-incrimination in certain proceedings relating to intellectual property).

(6) Subsections (1) to (4) and (5)(b) and any other provision of this Act as it has effect for the purposes of those subsections apply, with any necessary adaptations, to rights in performances, publication right and database right.

(7) The provisions of regulation 22 (presumptions relevant to database right) of the Copyright and Rights in Databases Regulations 1997 (SI 1997/3032) apply in proceedings brought by virtue of this section in relation to database right.

296ZB Devices and services designed to circumvent technological measures

(1) A person commits an offence if he—

(a) manufactures for sale or hire, or

(b) imports otherwise than for his private and domestic use, or

(c) in the course of a business—

(i) sells or lets for hire, or

(ii) offers or exposes for sale or hire, or

(iii) advertises for sale or hire, or

(iv) possesses, or

(v) distributes, or

(d) distributes otherwise than in the course of a business to such an extent as to affect prejudicially the copyright owner,

any device, product or component which is primarily designed, produced, or adapted for the purpose of enabling or facilitating the circumvention of effective technological measures.

(2) A person commits an offence if he provides, promotes, advertises or markets—

(a) in the course of a business, or

(b) otherwise than in the course of a business to such an extent as to affect prejudicially the copyright owner,

a service the purpose of which is to enable or facilitate the circumvention of effective technological measures.

(3) Subsections (1) and (2) do not make unlawful anything done by, or on behalf of, law enforcement agencies or any of the intelligence services—

(a) in the interests of national security; or

(b) for the purpose of the prevention or detection of crime, the investigation of an offence, or the conduct of a prosecution,

and in this subsection "intelligence services" has the meaning given in section 81 of the Regulation of Investigatory Powers Act 2000.

(4) A person guilty of an offence under subsection (1) or (2) is liable—

(a) on summary conviction, to imprisonment for a term not exceeding three months, or to a fine not exceeding the statutory maximum, or both;

(b) on conviction on indictment to a fine or imprisonment for a term not exceeding two years, or both.

(5) It is a defence to any prosecution for an offence under this section for the defendant to prove that he did not know, and had no reasonable ground for believing, that—

(a) the device, product or component; or

(b) the service,

enabled or facilitated the circumvention of effective technological measures.

296ZC Devices and services designed to circumvent technological measures: search warrants and forfeiture

(1) The provisions of sections 297B (search warrants), 297C (forfeiture of unauthorised decoders: England and Wales or Northern Ireland) and 297D (forfeiture of unauthorised decoders: Scotland) apply to offences under section 296ZB with the following modifications.

(2) In section 297B the reference to an offence under section 297A(1) shall be construed as a reference to an offence under section 296ZB(1) or (2).

(3) In sections 297C(2)(a) and 297D(15) the references to an offence under section 297A(1) shall be construed as a reference to an offence under section 296ZB(1).

(4) In sections 297C and 297D references to unauthorised decoders shall be construed as references to devices, products or components for the purpose of circumventing effective technological measures.

296ZD Rights and remedies in respect of devices and services designed to circumvent technological measures

(1) This section applies where—

(a) effective technological measures have been applied to a copyright work other than a computer program; and

(b) a person (C) manufactures, imports, distributes, sells or lets for hire, offers or exposes for sale or hire, advertises for sale or hire, or has in his possession for commercial purposes any device, product or component, or provides services which—

(i) are promoted, advertised or marketed for the purpose of the circumvention of, or

(ii) have only a limited commercially significant purpose or use other than to circumvent, or

(iii) are primarily designed, produced, adapted or performed for the purpose of enabling or facilitating the circumvention of,

those measures.

(2) The following persons have the same rights against C as a copyright owner has in respect of an infringement of copyright—

(a) a person—

(i) issuing to the public copies of, or

(ii) communicating to the public,

the work to which effective technological measures have been applied;

(b) the copyright owner or his exclusive licensee, if he is not the person specified in paragraph (a); and

(c) the owner or exclusive licensee of any intellectual property right in the effective technological measures applied to the work.

(3) The rights conferred by subsection (2) are concurrent, and sections 101(3) and 102(1) to (4) apply, in proceedings under this section, in relation to persons with concurrent rights as they apply, in proceedings mentioned in those provisions, in relation to a copyright owner and exclusive licensee with concurrent rights.

(4) Further, the persons in subsection (2) have the same rights under section 99 or 100 (delivery up or seizure of certain articles) in relation to any such device, product or component which a person has in his possession, custody or control with the intention that it should be used to circumvent effective technological measures, as a copyright owner has in relation to any infringing copy.

(5) The rights conferred by subsection (4) are concurrent, and section 102(5) shall apply, as respects anything done under section 99 or 100 by virtue of subsection (4), in relation to persons with concurrent rights as it applies, as respects anything done under section 99 or 100, in relation to a copyright owner and exclusive licensee with concurrent rights.

(6) The following provisions apply in relation to proceedings under this section as in relation to proceedings under Part 1 (copyright)—

(a) sections 104 to 106 of this Act (presumptions as to certain matters relating to copyright); and

(b)   section 72 of the Senior Courts Act 1981, section 15 of the Law Reform (Miscellaneous Provisions) (Scotland) Act 1985 and section 94A of the Judicature (Northern Ireland) Act 1978 (withdrawal of privilege against self-incrimination in certain proceedings relating to intellectual property);

and section 114 of this Act applies, with the necessary modifications, in relation to the disposal of anything delivered up or seized by virtue of subsection (4).

(7)   In section 97(1) (innocent infringement of copyright) as it applies to proceedings for infringement of the rights conferred by this section, the reference to the defendant not knowing or having reason to believe that copyright subsisted in the work shall be construed as a reference to his not knowing or having reason to believe that his acts enabled or facilitated an infringement of copyright.

(8)   Subsections (1) to (5), (6)(b) and (7) and any other provision of this Act as it has effect for the purposes of those subsections apply, with any necessary adaptations, to rights in performances, publication right and database right.

(9)   The provisions of regulation 22 (presumptions relevant to database right) of the Copyright and Rights in Databases Regulations 1997 apply in proceedings brought by virtue of this section in relation to database right.

296ZE Remedy where effective technological measures prevent permitted acts

(1)   In this section—

"permitted act" means an act which may be done in relation to copyright works, notwithstanding the subsistence of copyright, by virtue of a provision of this Act listed in Part 1 of Schedule 5A;

"voluntary measure or agreement" means—

(a)   any measure taken voluntarily by a copyright owner, his exclusive licensee or a person issuing copies of, or communicating to the public, a work other than a computer program, or

(b)   any agreement between a copyright owner, his exclusive licensee or a person issuing copies of, or communicating to the public, a work other than a computer program and another party,

the effect of which is to enable a person to carry out a permitted act.

(2)   Where the application of any effective technological measure to a copyright work other than a computer program prevents a person from carrying out a permitted act in relation to that work then that person or a person being a representative of a class of persons prevented from carrying out a permitted act may issue a notice of complaint to the Secretary of State.

(3)   Following receipt of a notice of complaint, the Secretary of State may give to the owner of that copyright work or an exclusive licensee such directions as appear to the Secretary of State to be requisite or expedient for the purpose of—

(a)   establishing whether any voluntary measure or agreement relevant to the copyright work the subject of the complaint subsists; or

(b)   (where it is established there is no subsisting voluntary measure or agreement) ensuring that the owner or exclusive licensee of that copyright work makes available to the complainant the means of carrying out the permitted act the subject of the complaint to the extent necessary to so benefit from that permitted act.

(4)   The Secretary of State may also give directions—

(a)   as to the form and manner in which a notice of complaint in subsection (2) may be delivered to him;

(b)   as to the form and manner in which evidence of any voluntary measure or agreement may be delivered to him; and

(c)   generally as to the procedure to be followed in relation to a complaint made under this section;

and shall publish directions given under this subsection in such manner as in his opinion will secure adequate publicity for them.

(5)   It shall be the duty of any person to whom a direction is given under subsection (3)(a) or (b) to give effect to that direction.

(6) The obligation to comply with a direction given under subsection (3)(b) is a duty owed to the complainant or, where the complaint is made by a representative of a class of persons, to that representative and to each person in the class represented; and a breach of the duty is actionable accordingly (subject to the defences and other incidents applying to actions for breach of statutory duty).

(7) Any direction under this section may be varied or revoked by a subsequent direction under this section.

(8) Any direction given under this section shall be in writing.

(9) This section does not apply to copyright works made available to the public on agreed contractual terms in such a way that members of the public may access them from a place and at a time individually chosen by them.

(10) This section applies only where a complainant has lawful access to the protected copyright work, or where the complainant is a representative of a class of persons, where the class of persons have lawful access to the work.

(11) Subsections (1) to (10) apply with any necessary adaptations to—

    (a) rights in performances, and in this context the expression "permitted act" refers to an act that may be done by virtue of a provision of this Act listed in Part 2 of Schedule 5A;

    (b) database right, and in this context the expression "permitted act" refers to an act that may be done by virtue of a provision of this Act listed in Part 3 of Schedule 5A; and

    (c) publication right.

296ZF Interpretation of sections 296ZA to 296ZE

(1) In sections 296ZA to 296ZE, "technological measures" are any technology, device or component which is designed, in the normal course of its operation, to protect a copyright work other than a computer program.

(2) Such measures are "effective" if the use of the work is controlled by the copyright owner through—

    (a) an access control or protection process such as encryption, scrambling or other transformation of the work, or

    (b) a copy control mechanism,

which achieves the intended protection.

(3) In this section, the reference to—

    (a) protection of a work is to the prevention or restriction of acts that are not authorised by the copyright owner of that work and are restricted by copyright; and

    (b) use of a work does not extend to any use of the work that is outside the scope of the acts restricted by copyright.

(4) Expressions used in sections 296ZA to 296ZE which are defined for the purposes of Part 1 of this Act (copyright) have the same meaning as in that Part.

Rights management information

296ZG Electronic rights management information

(1) This section applies where a person (D), knowingly and without authority, removes or alters electronic rights management information which—

    (a) is associated with a copy of a copyright work, or

    (b) appears in connection with the communication to the public of a copyright work, and where D knows, or has reason to believe, that by so doing he is inducing, enabling, facilitating or concealing an infringement of copyright.

(2) This section also applies where a person (E), knowingly and without authority, distributes, imports for distribution or communicates to the public copies of a copyright work from which electronic rights management information—

    (a) associated with the copies, or

    (b) appearing in connection with the communication to the public of the work, has been removed or altered without authority and where E knows, or has reason to believe, that by so doing he is inducing, enabling, facilitating or concealing an infringement of copyright.

(3) A person issuing to the public copies of, or communicating, the work to the public, has the same rights against D and E as a copyright owner has in respect of an infringement of copyright.

(4) The copyright owner or his exclusive licensee, if he is not the person issuing to the public copies of, or communicating, the work to the public, also has the same rights against D and E as he has in respect of an infringement of copyright.

(5) The rights conferred by subsections (3) and (4) are concurrent, and sections 101(3) and 102(1) to (4) apply, in proceedings under this section, in relation to persons with concurrent rights as they apply, in proceedings mentioned in those provisions, in relation to a copyright owner and exclusive licensee with concurrent rights.

(6) The following provisions apply in relation to proceedings under this section as in relation to proceedings under Part 1 (copyright)—

   (a) sections 104 to 106 of this Act (presumptions as to certain matters relating to copyright); and

   (b) section 72 of the Senior Courts Act 1981, section 15 of the Law Reform (Miscellaneous Provisions) (Scotland) Act 1985 and section 94A of the Judicature (Northern Ireland) Act 1978 (withdrawal of privilege against self-incrimination in certain proceedings relating to intellectual property).

(7) In this section—

   (a) expressions which are defined for the purposes of Part 1 of this Act (copyright) have the same meaning as in that Part; and

   (b) "rights management information" means any information provided by the copyright owner or the holder of any right under copyright which identifies the work, the author, the copyright owner or the holder of any intellectual property rights, or information about the terms and conditions of use of the work, and any numbers or codes that represent such information.

(8) Subsections (1) to (5) and (6)(b), and any other provision of this Act as it has effect for the purposes of those subsections, apply, with any necessary adaptations, to rights in performances, publication right and database right.

(9) The provisions of regulation 22 (presumptions relevant to database right) of the Copyright and Rights in Databases Regulations 1997 apply in proceedings brought by virtue of this section in relation to database right.

Computer programs

296A Avoidance of certain terms

(1) Where a person has the use of a computer program under an agreement, any term or condition in the agreement shall be void in so far as it purports to prohibit or restrict—

   (a) the making of any back up copy of the program which it is necessary for him to have for the purposes of the agreed use;

   (b) where the conditions in section 50B(2) are met, the decompiling of the program; or

   (c) the observing, studying or testing of the functioning of the program in accordance with section 50BA.

(2) In this section, decompile, in relation to a computer program, has the same meaning as in section 50B.

Databases

296B Avoidance of certain terms relating to databases

Where under an agreement a person has a right to use a database or part of a database, any term or condition in the agreement shall be void in so far as it purports to prohibit or restrict the performance of any act which would but for section 50D infringe the copyright in the database.

Fraudulent reception of transmissions

297   Offence of fraudulently receiving programmes

(1)   A person who dishonestly receives a programme included in a broadcasting or cable programme service provided from a place in the United Kingdom with intent to avoid payment of any charge applicable to the reception of the programme commits an offence and is liable on summary conviction to a fine not exceeding level 5 on the standard scale.

(2)   Where an offence under this section committed by a body corporate is proved to have been committed with the consent or connivance of a director, manager, secretary or other similar officer of the body, or a person purporting to act in any such capacity, he as well as the body corporate is guilty of the offence and liable to be proceeded against and punished accordingly.

In relation to a body corporate whose affairs are managed by its members "director" means a member of the body corporate.

297A   Unauthorised decoders

(1)   A person commits an offence if he—

(a)   makes, imports, distributes, sells or lets for hire or offers or exposes for sale or hire any unauthorised decoder;

(b)   has in his possession for commercial purposes any unauthorised decoder;

(c)   instals, maintains or replaces for commercial purposes any unauthorised decoder;

or

(d)   advertises any unauthorised decoder for sale or hire or otherwise promotes any unauthorised decoder by means of commercial communications.

(2)   A person guilty of an offence under subsection (1) is liable—

(a)   on summary conviction, to imprisonment for a term not exceeding six months, or to a fine not exceeding the statutory maximum, or to both;

(b)   on conviction on indictment, to imprisonment for a term not exceeding ten years, or to a fine, or to both.

(3)   It is a defence to any prosecution for an offence under this section for the defendant to prove that he did not know, and had no reasonable ground for believing, that the decoder was an unauthorised decoder.

(4)   In this section—

"apparatus" includes any device, component or electronic data (including software); "conditional access technology" means any technical measure or arrangement whereby access to encrypted transmissions in an intelligible form is made conditional on prior individual authorisation; "decoder" means any apparatus which is designed or adapted to enable (whether on its own or with any other apparatus) an encrypted transmission to be decoded; "encrypted" includes subjected to scrambling or the operation of cryptographic envelopes, electronic locks, passwords or any other analogous application; "transmission" means—

(a)   any programme included in a broadcasting . . . service which is provided from a place in the United Kingdom or any other member State; or

(b)   an information society service (within the meaning of Directive 98/34/EC of the European Parliament and of the Council of 22nd June 1998, as amended by Directive 98/48/EC of the European Parliament and of the Council of 20th July 1998) which is provided from a place in the United Kingdom or any other member State; and

"unauthorised", in relation to a decoder, means that the decoder is designed or adapted to enable an encrypted transmission, or any service of which it forms part, to be accessed in an intelligible form without payment of the fee (however imposed) which the person making the transmission, or on whose behalf it is made, charges for accessing the transmission or service (whether by the circumvention of any conditional access technology related to the transmission or service or by any other means).

297B Search warrants

(1)   Where a justice of the peace (in Scotland, a sheriff or justice of the peace) is satisfied by information on oath given by a constable (in Scotland, by evidence on oath) that there are reasonable grounds for believing—

(a)   that an offence under section 297A(1) has been or is about to be committed in any premises, and

(b)   that evidence that such an offence has been or is about to be committed is in those premises,

he may issue a warrant authorising a constable to enter and search the premises, using such reasonable force as is necessary.

(2)   The power conferred by subsection (1) does not, in England and Wales, extend to authorising a search for material of the kinds mentioned in section 9(2) of the Police and Criminal Evidence Act 1984 (certain classes of personal or confidential material).

(3)   A warrant under subsection (1)—

(a)   may authorise persons to accompany any constable executing the warrant, and

(b)   remains in force for three months from the date of its issue.

(4)   In executing a warrant issued under subsection (1) a constable may seize an article if he reasonably believes that it is evidence that any offence under section 297A(1) has been or is about to be committed.

(5)   In this section "premises" includes land, buildings, fixed or moveable structures, vehicles, vessels, aircraft and hovercraft.

297C Forfeiture of unauthorised decoders: England and Wales or Northern Ireland

(1)   In England and Wales or Northern Ireland where unauthorised decoders have come into the possession of any person in connection with the investigation or prosecution of a relevant offence, that person may apply under this section for an order for the forfeiture of the unauthorised decoders.

(2)   For the purposes of this section "relevant offence" means—

(a)   an offence under section 297A(1) (criminal liability for making, importing, etc unauthorised decoders),

(b)   an offence under the Trade Descriptions Act 1968,

(ba) an offence under the Business Protection from Misleading Marketing Regulations 2008,

(bb) an offence under the Consumer Protection from Unfair Trading Regulations 2008, or

(c)   an offence involving dishonesty or deception.

(3)   An application under this section may be made—

(a)   where proceedings have been brought in any court for a relevant offence relating to some or all of the unauthorised decoders, to that court, or

(b)   where no application for the forfeiture of the unauthorised decoders has been made under paragraph (a), by way of complaint to a magistrates' court.

(4)   On an application under this section, the court shall make an order for the forfeiture of any unauthorised decoders only if it is satisfied that a relevant offence has been committed in relation to the unauthorised decoders.

(5)   A court may infer for the purposes of this section that such an offence has been committed in relation to any unauthorised decoders if it is satisfied that such an offence has been committed in relation to unauthorised decoders which are representative of the unauthorised decoders in question (whether by reason of being of the same design or part of the same consignment or batch or otherwise).

(6)   Any person aggrieved by an order made under this section by a magistrates' court, or by a decision of such a court not to make such an order, may appeal against that order or decision—

(a)   in England and Wales, to the Crown Court, or

(b)   in Northern Ireland, to the county court.

(7)   An order under this section may contain such provision as appears to the court to be appropriate for delaying the coming into force of the order pending the making and determination of any appeal (including any application under section 111 of the

Magistrates' Courts Act 1980 or Article 146 of the Magistrates' Courts (Northern Ireland) Order 1981 (statement of case)).

(8) Subject to subsection (9), where any unauthorised decoders are forfeited under this section they shall be destroyed in accordance with such directions as the court may give.

(9) On making an order under this section the court may direct that the unauthorised decoders to which the order relates shall (instead of being destroyed) be forfeited to a person who has rights or remedies under section 298 in relation to the unauthorised decoders in question, or dealt with in such other way as the court considers appropriate.

297D Forfeiture of unauthorised decoders: Scotland

(1) In Scotland the court may make an order under this section for the forfeiture of unauthorised decoders.

(2) An order under this section may be made—
   (a) on an application by the procurator-fiscal made in the manner specified in section 134 of the Criminal Procedure (Scotland) Act 1995, or
   (b) where a person is convicted of a relevant offence, in addition to any other penalty which the court may impose.

(3) On an application under subsection (2)(a), the court shall make an order for the forfeiture of any unauthorised decoders only if it is satisfied that a relevant offence has been committed in relation to the unauthorised decoders.

(4) The court may infer for the purposes of this section that such an offence has been committed in relation to any unauthorised decoders if it is satisfied that such an offence has been committed in relation to unauthorised decoders which are representative of the unauthorised decoders in question (whether by reason of being of the same design or part of the same consignment or batch or otherwise).

(5) The procurator-fiscal making the application under subsection (2)(a) shall serve on any person appearing to him to be the owner of, or otherwise to have an interest in, the unauthorised decoders to which the application relates a copy of the application, together with a notice giving him the opportunity to appear at the hearing of the application to show cause why the unauthorised decoders should not be forfeited.

(6) Service under subsection (5) shall be carried out, and such service may be proved, in the manner specified for citation of an accused in summary proceedings under the Criminal Procedure (Scotland) Act 1995.

(7) Any person upon whom notice is served under subsection (5) and any other person claiming to be the owner of, or otherwise to have an interest in, unauthorised decoders to which an application under this section relates shall be entitled to appear at the hearing of the application to show cause why the unauthorised decoders should not be forfeited.

(8) The court shall not make an order following an application under subsection (2)(a)—
   (a) if any person on whom notice is served under subsection (5) does not appear, unless service of the notice on that person is proved, or
   (b) if no notice under subsection (5) has been served, unless the court is satisfied that in the circumstances it was reasonable not to serve such notice.

(9) Where an order for the forfeiture of any unauthorised decoders is made following an application under subsection (2)(a), any person who appeared, or was entitled to appear, to show cause why the unauthorised decoders should not be forfeited may, within 21 days of the making of the order, appeal to the High Court by Bill of Suspension.

(10) Section 182(5)(a) to (e) of the Criminal Procedure (Scotland) Act 1995 shall apply to an appeal under subsection (9) as it applies to a stated case under Part 2 of that Act.

(11) An order following an application under subsection (2)(a) shall not take effect—
   (a) until the end of the period of 21 days beginning with the day after the day on which the order is made, or
   (b) if an appeal is made under subsection (9) above within that period, until the appeal is determined or abandoned.

(12) An order under subsection (2)(b) shall not take effect—
   (a) until the end of the period within which an appeal against the order could be brought under the Criminal Procedure (Scotland) Act 1995, or
   (b) if an appeal is made within that period, until the appeal is determined or abandoned.

(13) Subject to subsection (14), where any unauthorised decoders are forfeited under this section they shall be destroyed in accordance with such directions as the court may give.

(14) On making an order under this section the court may direct that the unauthorised decoders to which the order relates shall (instead of being destroyed) be forfeited to a person who has rights or remedies under section 298 in relation to the unauthorised decoders in question, or dealt with in such other way as the court considers appropriate.

(15) For the purposes of this section—

"relevant offence" means—

(a) an offence under section 297A(1) (criminal liability for making, importing, etc. unauthorised decoders),

(b) an offence under the Trade Descriptions Act 1968,

(c) an offence under the Business Protection from Misleading Marketing Regulations 2008,

(d) an offence under the Consumer Protection from Unfair Trading Regulations 2008, or

(e) any offence involving dishonesty or deception;

"the court" means—

(a) in relation to an order made on an application under subsection (2)(a), the sheriff, and

(b) in relation to an order made under subsection (2)(b), the court which imposed the penalty.

298 Rights and remedies in respect of apparatus, etc. for unauthorised reception of transmissions

(1) A person who—

(a) makes charges for the reception of programmes included in a broadcasting service provided from a place in the United Kingdom or any other member State,

(b) sends encrypted transmissions of any other description from a place in the United Kingdom or any other member State, or

(c) provides conditional access services from a place in the United Kingdom or any other member State,

is entitled to the following rights and remedies.

(2) He has the same rights and remedies against a person—

(a) who—

(i) makes, imports, distributes, sells or lets for hire, offers or exposes for sale or hire, or advertises for sale or hire,

(ii) has in his possession for commercial purposes, or

(iii) instals, maintains or replaces for commercial purposes,

any apparatus designed or adapted to enable or assist persons to access the programmes or other transmissions or circumvent conditional access technology related to the programmes or other transmissions when they are not entitled to do so, or

(b) who publishes or otherwise promotes by means of commercial communications any information which is calculated to enable or assist persons to access the programmes or other transmissions or circumvent conditional access technology related to the programmes or other transmissions when they are not entitled to do so,

as a copyright owner has in respect of an infringement of copyright.

(3) Further, he has the same rights under section 99 or 100 (delivery up or seizure of certain articles) in relation to any such apparatus as a copyright owner has in relation to an infringing copy.

(4) Section 72 of the Senior Courts Act 1981, section 15 of the Law Reform (Miscellaneous Provisions) (Scotland) Act 1985 and section 94A of the Judicature (Northern Ireland) Act 1978 (withdrawal of privilege against self-incrimination in certain proceedings relating to intellectual property) apply to proceedings under this section as to proceedings under Part I of this Act (copyright).

(5) In section 97(1) (innocent infringement of copyright) as it applies to proceedings for infringement of the rights conferred by this section, the reference to the defendant

not knowing or having reason to believe that copyright subsisted in the work shall be construed as a reference to his not knowing or having reason to believe that his acts infringed the rights conferred by this section.

(6) Section 114 applies, with the necessary modifications, in relation to the disposal of anything delivered up or seized by virtue of subsection (3) above.

(7) In this section "apparatus", "conditional access technology" and "encrypted" have the same meanings as in section 297A, "transmission" includes transmissions as defined in that section and "conditional access services" means services comprising the provision of conditional access technology.

299   Supplementary provisions as to fraudulent reception

(1) Her Majesty may by Order in Council—

    (a) provide that section 297 applies in relation to programmes included in services provided from a country or territory outside the United Kingdom, and

    (b) provide that section 298 applies in relation to such programmes and to encrypted transmissions sent from such a country or territory.

(2) . . .

(3) A statutory instrument containing an Order in Council under subsection (1) shall be subject to annulment in pursuance of a resolution of either House of Parliament.

(4) Where sections 297 and 298 apply in relation to a broadcasting service, they also apply to any service run for the person providing that service, or a person providing programmes for that service, which consists wholly or mainly in the sending by means of a telecommunications system of sounds or visual images, or both.

(5) In sections 297, 297A and 298, and this section, "programme", and "broadcasting", and related expressions, have the same meaning as in Part I (copyright).

Provisions for the benefit of the Hospital for Sick Children

301   Provisions for the benefit of the Hospital for Sick Children

The provisions of Schedule 6 have effect for conferring on GOSH Children's Charity for the benefit of Great Ormond Street Hospital for Children a right to a royalty in respect of the public performance, commercial publication, or communication to the public of the play "Peter Pan" by Sir James Matthew Barrie, or of any adaptation of that work, notwithstanding that copyright in the work expired on 31st December 1987.

General

304   Extent

(1) Provision as to the extent of Part I (copyright), Part II (rights in performances) and Part III (design right) is to be found in sections 157, 207 and 255 respectively; the extent of the other provisions of this Act is as follows.

(2) Parts IV to VII extend to England and Wales, Scotland and Northern Ireland, except that—

    (a) sections 287 to 292 (patents county courts) extend to England and Wales only,

    . . .

SCHEDULE 2
RIGHTS IN PERFORMANCES: PERMITTED ACTS

Introductory

1.   (1) The provisions of this Schedule specify acts which may be done in relation to a performance or recording notwithstanding the rights conferred by this Chapter; they relate only to the question of infringement of those rights and do not affect any other right or obligation restricting the doing of any of the specified acts.

    (2) No inference shall be drawn from the description of any act which may by virtue of this Schedule be done without infringing the rights conferred by this Chapter as to the scope of those rights.

    (3) The provisions of this Schedule are to be construed independently of each other, so that the fact that an act does not fall within one provision does not mean that it is not covered by another provision.

Making of temporary copies

1A.   The rights conferred by this Chapter are not infringed by the making of a temporary copy of a recording of a performance which is transient or incidental, which is an integral and essential part of a technological process and the sole purpose of which is to enable—

(a)   a transmission of the recording in a network between third parties by an intermediary; or

(b)   a lawful use of the recording;

and which has no independent economic significance.

1C.   (1)   Fair dealing with a performance or a recording of a performance for the purposes of research for a non-commercial purpose does not infringe the rights conferred by this Chapter.

(2)   Fair dealing with a performance or recording of a performance for the purposes of private study does not infringe the rights conferred by this Chapter.

(3)   Copying of a recording by a person other than the researcher or student is not fair dealing if—

(a)   in the case of a librarian, or a person acting on behalf of a librarian, that person does anything which is not permitted under paragraph 6F (copying by librarians: single copies of published recordings), or

(b)   in any other case, the person doing the copying knows or has reason to believe that it will result in copies of substantially the same material being provided to more than one person at substantially the same time and for substantially the same purpose.

(4)   To the extent that a term of a contract purports to prevent or restrict the doing of any act which, by virtue of this paragraph, would not infringe any right conferred by this Chapter, that term is unenforceable.

(5)   Expressions used in this paragraph have the same meaning as in section 29.

1D.   (1)   The making of a copy of a recording of a performance by a person who has lawful access to the recording does not infringe any rights conferred by this Chapter provided that the copy is made in order that a person who has lawful access to the recording may carry out a computational analysis of anything recorded in the recording for the sole purpose of research for a non-commercial purpose.

(2)   Where a copy of a recording has been made under this paragraph, the rights conferred by this Chapter are infringed if—

(a)   the copy is transferred to any other person, except where the transfer is authorised by the rights owner, or

(b)   the copy is used for any purpose other than that mentioned in sub-paragraph (1), except where the use is authorised by the rights owner.

(3)   If a copy of a recording made under this paragraph is subsequently dealt with—

(a)   it is to be treated as an illicit recording for the purposes of that dealing, and

(b)   if that dealing infringes any right conferred by this Chapter, it is to be treated as an illicit recording for all subsequent purposes.

(4)   To the extent that a term of a contract purports to prevent or restrict the making of a copy which, by virtue of this paragraph, would not infringe any right conferred by this Chapter, that term is unenforceable.

(5)   Expressions used in this paragraph have the same meaning as in section 29A.

Criticism, reviews and news reporting

2.   (1)   Fair dealing with a performance or recording for the purpose of criticism or review, of that or another performance or recording, or of a work, does not infringe any of the rights conferred by this Chapter provided that the performance or recording has been made available to the public.

(1ZA)   The rights conferred by this Chapter in a performance or a recording of a performance are not infringed by the use of a quotation from the performance or recording (whether for criticism or review or otherwise) provided that—

(a)   the performance or recording has been made available to the public,

(b)   the use of the quotation is fair dealing with the performance or recording, and

(c)   the extent of the quotation is no more than is required by the specific purpose for which it is used.

(1A) Fair dealing with a performance or recording for the purpose of reporting current events does not infringe any of the rights conferred by this Chapter.

(1B) To the extent that a term of a contract purports to prevent or restrict the doing of any act which, by virtue of sub-paragraph (1ZA), would not infringe any right conferred by this Chapter, that term is unenforceable.

(2) Expressions used in this paragraph have the same meaning as in section 30.

Caricature, parody or pastiche

2A. (1) Fair dealing with a performance or a recording of a performance for the purposes of caricature, parody or pastiche does not infringe the rights conferred by this Chapter in the performance or recording.

(2) To the extent that a term of a contract purports to prevent or restrict the doing of any act which, by virtue of this paragraph, would not infringe any right conferred by this Chapter, that term is unenforceable.

(3) Expressions used in this paragraph have the same meaning as in section 30A.

Incidental inclusion of performance or recording

3. (1) The rights conferred by this Chapter are not infringed by the incidental inclusion of a performance or recording in a sound recording, film, or broadcast.

(2) Nor are those rights infringed by anything done in relation to copies of, or the playing, showing, or communication to the public of, anything whose making was, by virtue of sub-paragraph (1), not an infringement of those rights.

(3) A performance or recording so far as it consists of music, or words spoken or sung with music, shall not be regarded as incidentally included in a sound recording or broadcast if it is deliberately included.

(4) Expressions used in this paragraph have the same meaning as in section 31.

Disabled persons: copies of recordings for personal use

3A. (1) This paragraph applies if—

(a) a disabled person has lawful possession or lawful use of a copy of the whole or part of a recording of a performance, and

(b) the person's disability prevents the person from enjoying the recording to the same degree as a person who does not have that disability.

(2) The making of an accessible copy of the copy of the recording referred to in sub-paragraph (1)(a) does not infringe the rights conferred by this Chapter if—

(a) the copy is made by the disabled person or by a person acting on behalf of the disabled person,

(b) the copy is made for the disabled person's personal use, and

(c) the same kind of accessible copies of the recording are not commercially available on reasonable terms by or with the authority of the rights owner.

(3) If a person makes an accessible copy under this paragraph on behalf of a disabled person and charges the disabled person for it, the sum charged must not exceed the cost of making and supplying the copy.

(4) The rights conferred by this Chapter are infringed by the transfer of an accessible copy of a recording made under this paragraph to any person other than—

(a) a person by or for whom an accessible copy of the recording may be made under this paragraph, or

(b) a person who intends to transfer the copy to a person falling within paragraph (a), except where the transfer is authorised by the rights owner.

(5) An accessible copy of a recording made under this paragraph is to be treated for all purposes as an illicit recording if it is held by a person at a time when the person does not fall within sub-paragraph (4)(a) or (b).

(6) If an accessible copy of a recording made under this paragraph is subsequently dealt with—

(a) it is to be treated as an illicit recording for the purposes of that dealing, and

(b) if that dealing infringes any right conferred by this Chapter, it is to be treated as an illicit recording for all subsequent purposes.

Making and supply of accessible copies by authorised bodies

3B.   (1)   If an authorised body has lawful possession of or lawful access to a copy of the whole or part of a recording of a performance (including a recording of a performance included in a broadcast), the body may, without infringing the rights conferred by this Chapter, make and supply accessible copies of the recording for the personal use of disabled persons.

     (2)   If an authorised body has lawful access to the whole or part of a broadcast, the body may, without infringing the rights conferred by this Chapter, make a recording of the broadcast, and make and supply accessible copies of the recording, for the personal use of disabled persons.

     (3)   But sub-paragraphs (1) and (2) do not apply if the same kind of accessible copies of the recording, or of the broadcast, are commercially available on reasonable terms by or with the consent of the rights owner.

     (4)   For the purposes of sub-paragraphs (1) and (2), supply "for the personal use of disabled persons" includes supply to a person acting on behalf of a disabled person.

     (5)   An authorised body which is an educational establishment conducted for profit must ensure that any accessible copies which it makes under this paragraph are used only for its educational purposes.

     (6)   An accessible copy made under this paragraph must be accompanied by a statement that it is made under this paragraph, unless it is accompanied by an equivalent statement in accordance with section 31B(7).

     (7)   If an accessible copy is made under this paragraph of a recording which is in copy-protected electronic form, the accessible copy must, so far as is reasonably practicable, incorporate the same or equally effective copy protection (unless the rights owner agrees otherwise).

     (8)   An authorised body which has made an accessible copy of a recording under this paragraph may supply it to another authorised body which is entitled to make accessible copies of the recording under this paragraph for the purposes of enabling that other body to make accessible copies of the recording.

     (9)   If an authorised body supplies an accessible copy it has made under this paragraph to a person or authorised body as permitted by this paragraph and charges the person or body for it, the sum charged must not exceed the cost of making and supplying the copy.

    (10) If an accessible copy of a recording made under this paragraph is subsequently dealt with —

        (a)   it is to be treated as an illicit recording for the purposes of that dealing, and

        (b)   if that dealing infringes any right conferred by this Chapter, it is to be treated as an illicit recording for all subsequent purposes.

Making and supply of intermediate copies by authorised bodies

3C.   (1)   An authorised body which is entitled to make an accessible copy of a recording of a performance under paragraph 3B may, without infringing the rights conferred by this Chapter, make a copy of the recording ("an intermediate copy") if this is necessary in order to make the accessible copy.

     (2)   An authorised body which has made an intermediate copy of a recording under this paragraph may supply it to another authorised body which is entitled to make accessible copies of the recording under paragraph 3B for the purposes of enabling that other body to make accessible copies of the recording.

     (3)   The rights conferred by this Chapter are infringed by the transfer of an intermediate copy made under this paragraph to a person other than another authorised body as permitted by sub-paragraph (2), except where the transfer is authorised by the rights owner.

     (4)   If an authorised body supplies an intermediate copy to an authorised body under sub-paragraph (2) and charges the body for it, the sum charged must not exceed the cost of making and supplying the copy.

Accessible and intermediate copies: records

3D.   (1)   An authorised body must keep a record of—
           (a)   accessible copies it makes under paragraph 3B,
           (b)   intermediate copies it makes under paragraph 3C, and
           (c)   the persons to whom such copies are supplied.
      (2)   An authorised body must allow the rights owner or a person acting for the rights owner, on giving reasonable notice, to inspect the records at any reasonable time.

Paragraphs 3A to 3D: interpretation and general

3E.   (1)   This paragraph supplements paragraphs 3A to 3D and includes definitions.
      (2)   "Disabled person" means a person who has a physical or mental impairment which prevents the person from enjoying a recording of a performance to the same degree as a person who does not have that impairment, and "disability" is to be construed accordingly.
      (3)   But a person is not to be regarded as disabled by reason only of an impairment of visual function which can be improved, by the use of corrective lenses, to a level that is normally acceptable for reading without a special level or kind of light.
      (4)   An "accessible copy" of a recording of a performance means a version of the recording which enables the fuller enjoyment of the recording by disabled persons.
      (5)   An accessible copy—
           (a)   may include facilities for navigating around the version of the recording, but
           (b)   must not include any changes to the recording which are not necessary to overcome the problems suffered by the disabled persons for whom the accessible copy is intended.
      (6)   To the extent that a term of a contract purports to prevent or restrict the doing of any act which, by virtue of paragraph 3A, 3B or 3C, would not infringe any right conferred by this Chapter, that term is unenforceable.
      (7)   "Authorised body" and "supply" have the meaning given in section 31F, and other expressions used in paragraphs 3A to 3D but not defined in this paragraph have the same meaning as in sections 31A to 31BB.

Illustration for instruction

4.   (1)   Fair dealing with a performance or a recording of a performance for the sole purpose of illustration for instruction does not infringe the rights conferred by this Chapter provided that the dealing is—
           (a)   for a non-commercial purpose, and
           (b)   by a person giving or receiving instruction (or preparing for giving or receiving instruction).
      (2)   To the extent that a term of a contract purports to prevent or restrict the doing of any act which, by virtue of this paragraph, would not infringe any right conferred by this Chapter, that term is unenforceable.
      (3)   Expressions used in this paragraph have the same meaning as in section 32.

Playing or showing sound recording, film or broadcast at educational establishment

5.   (1)   The playing or showing of a sound recording, film or broadcast at an educational establishment for the purposes of instruction before an audience consisting of teachers and pupils at the establishment and other persons directly connected with the activities of the establishment is not a playing or showing of a performance in public for the purposes of infringement of the rights conferred by this Chapter.
      (2)   A person is not for this purpose directly connected with the activities of the educational establishment simply because he is the parent of a pupil at the establishment.
      (3)   Expressions used in this paragraph have the same meaning as in section 34 and any provision made under section 174(2) with respect to the application of that section also applies for the purposes of this paragraph.

Recording by educational establishments of broadcasts

6. (1) A recording of a broadcast, or a copy of such a recording, may be made by or on behalf of an educational establishment for the educational purposes of that establishment without infringing any of the rights conferred by this Chapter in relation to any performance or recording included in it, provided that the educational purposes are non-commercial.

(2) The rights conferred by this Chapter are not infringed where a recording of a broadcast or a copy of such a recording, made under sub-paragraph (1), is communicated by or on behalf of the educational establishment to its pupils or staff for the non-commercial educational purposes of that establishment.

(3) Sub-paragraph (2) only applies to a communication received outside the premises of the establishment if that communication is made by means of a secure electronic network accessible only by the establishment's pupils and staff.

(4) Acts which would otherwise be permitted by this paragraph are not permitted if, or to the extent that, licences are available authorising the acts in question and the educational establishment responsible for those acts knew or ought to have been aware of that fact.

(5) If a recording made under this paragraph is subsequently dealt with—
 (a) it is to be treated as an illicit recording for the purposes of that dealing, and
 (b) if that dealing infringes any right conferred by this Chapter, it is to be treated as an illicit recording for all subsequent purposes.

(6) In this paragraph "dealt with" means—
 (a) sold or let for hire,
 (b) offered or exposed for sale or hire, or
 (c) communicated otherwise than as permitted by sub-paragraph (2).

(7) Expressions used in this paragraph (other than "dealt with") have the same meaning as in section 35 and any provision made under section 174(2) with respect to the application of that section also applies for the purposes of this paragraph.

Copying and use of extracts of recordings by educational establishments

6ZA. (1) The copying of extracts of a recording of a performance by or on behalf of an educational establishment does not infringe any of the rights conferred by this Chapter in the recording provided that the copy is made for the purposes of instruction for a non-commercial purpose.

(2) The rights conferred by this Chapter are not infringed where an extract of a recording of a performance, made under sub-paragraph (1), is communicated by or on behalf of the educational establishment to its pupils or staff for the purposes of instruction for a non-commercial purpose.

(3) Sub-paragraph (2) only applies to a communication received outside the premises of the establishment if that communication is made by means of a secure electronic network accessible only by the establishment's pupils and staff.

(4) Not more than 5% of a recording may be copied under this paragraph by or on behalf of an educational establishment in any period of 12 months.

(5) Acts which would otherwise be permitted by this paragraph are not permitted if, or to the extent that, licences are available authorising the acts in question and the educational establishment responsible for those acts knew or ought to have been aware of that fact.

(6) The terms of a licence granted to an educational establishment authorising acts permitted by this paragraph are of no effect so far as they purport to restrict the proportion of a recording which may be copied (whether on payment or free of charge) to less than that which would be permitted by this paragraph.

(7) If a recording made under this paragraph is subsequently dealt with—
 (a) it is to be treated as an illicit recording for the purposes of that dealing, and
 (b) if that dealing infringes any right conferred by this Chapter, it is to be treated as an illicit recording for all subsequent purposes.

(8)　In this paragraph "dealt with" means—
    (a)　sold or let for hire,
    (b)　offered or exposed for sale or hire, or
    (c)　communicated otherwise than as permitted by sub-paragraph (2).

(9)　Expressions used in this paragraph (other than "dealt with") have the same meaning as in section 36 and any provision made under section 174(2) with respect to the application of that section also applies for the purposes of this paragraph.

Lending of copies by educational establishments

6A.　(1)　The rights conferred by this Chapter are not infringed by the lending of copies of a recording of a performance by an educational establishment.

(2)　Expressions used in this paragraph have the same meaning as in section 36A; and any provision with respect to the application of that section made under section 174(2) (instruction given elsewhere than an educational establishment) applies also for the purposes of this paragraph.

Lending of copies by libraries or archives

6B.　(A1)　The rights conferred by this Chapter are not infringed by the following acts by a public library in relation to a book within the public lending right scheme—
    (a)　lending the book;
    (b)　in relation to an audio-book or e-book, copying or issuing a copy of the book as an act incidental to lending it.

(A2)　Expressions used in sub-paragraph (A1) have the same meaning as in section 40A(1).

(1)　The rights conferred by this Chapter are not infringed by the lending of copies of a recording of a performance by a library or archive (other than a public library) which is not conducted for profit.

Libraries and educational establishments etc: making recordings of performances available through dedicated terminals

6C.　(1)　The rights conferred by this Chapter in a recording of a performance are not infringed by an institution specified in sub-paragraph (2) communicating the recording to the public or making it available to the public by means of a dedicated terminal on its premises, if the conditions in sub-paragraph (3) are met.

(2)　The institutions are—
    (a)　a library,
    (b)　an archive,
    (c)　a museum, and
    (d)　an educational establishment.

(3)　The conditions are that the recording or a copy of the recording—
    (a)　has been lawfully acquired by the institution,
    (b)　is communicated or made available to individual members of the public for the purposes of research or private study, and
    (c)　is communicated or made available in compliance with any purchase or licensing terms to which the recording is subject.

Copying by librarians: supply of single copies to other libraries

6D.　(1)　A librarian may, if the conditions in sub-paragraph (2) are met, make a single copy of the whole or part of a published recording of a performance and supply it to another library, without infringing any rights conferred by this Chapter in the recording.

(2)　The conditions are—
    (a)　the copy is supplied in response to a request from a library which is not conducted for profit, and
    (b)　at the time of making the copy the librarian does not know, or could not reasonably find out, the name and address of a person entitled to authorise the making of a copy of the recording.

(3) Where a library makes a charge for supplying a copy under this paragraph, the sum charged must be calculated by reference to the costs attributable to the production of the copy.

(4) To the extent that a term of a contract purports to prevent or restrict the doing of any act which, by virtue of this paragraph, would not infringe any right conferred by this Chapter, that term is unenforceable.

Copying by librarians etc: replacement copies of recordings

6E. (1) A librarian, archivist or curator of a library, archive or museum may, without infringing any rights conferred by this Chapter, make a copy of a recording of a performance in that institution's permanent collection—
  (a) in order to preserve or replace that recording in that collection, or
  (b) where a recording in the permanent collection of another library, archive or museum has been lost, destroyed or damaged, in order to replace the recording in the collection of that other library, archive or museum,
  provided that the conditions in sub-paragraphs (2) and (3) are met.

(2) The first condition is that the recording is—
  (a) included in the part of the collection kept wholly or mainly for the purposes of reference on the institution's premises,
  (b) included in a part of the collection not accessible to the public, or
  (c) available on loan only to other libraries, archives or museums.

(3) The second condition is that it is not reasonably practicable to purchase a copy of the recording to achieve either of the purposes mentioned in sub-paragraph (1).

(4) The reference in sub-paragraph (1)(b) to a library, archive or museum is to a library, archive or museum which is not conducted for profit.

(5) Where an institution makes a charge for supplying a copy to another library, archive or museum under sub-paragraph (1)(b), the sum charged must be calculated by reference to the costs attributable to the production of the copy.

(6) To the extent that a term of a contract purports to prevent or restrict the doing of any act which, by virtue of this paragraph, would not infringe any right conferred by this Chapter, that term is unenforceable.

Copying by librarians: single copies of published recordings

6F. (1) A librarian of a library which is not conducted for profit may, if the conditions in sub-paragraph (2) are met, make and supply a single copy of a reasonable proportion of a published recording without infringing any of the rights in the recording conferred by this Chapter.

(2) The conditions are—
  (a) the copy is supplied in response to a request from a person who has provided the librarian with a declaration in writing which includes the information set out in sub-paragraph (3), and
  (b) the librarian is not aware that the declaration is false in a material particular.

(3) The information which must be included in the declaration is—
  (a) the name of the person who requires the copy and the material which that person requires,
  (b) a statement that the person has not previously been supplied with a copy of that material by any library,
  (c) a statement that the person requires the copy for the purposes of research for a non-commercial purpose or private study, will use it only for those purposes and will not supply the copy to any other person, and
  (d) a statement that to the best of the person's knowledge, no other person with whom the person works or studies has made, or intends to make, at or about the same time as the person's request, a request for substantially the same material for substantially the same purpose.

(4) Where a library makes a charge for supplying a copy under this paragraph, the sum charged must be calculated by reference to the costs attributable to the production of the copy.

(5) Where a person ("P") makes a declaration under this paragraph that is false in a material particular and is supplied with a copy of a recording which would have been an illicit recording if made by P—

    (a) P is liable for infringement of the rights conferred by this Chapter as if P had made the copy, and

    (b) the copy supplied to P is to be treated as an illicit recording for all purposes.

(6) To the extent that a term of a contract purports to prevent or restrict the doing of any act which, by virtue of this paragraph, would not infringe any right conferred by this Chapter, that term is unenforceable.

Copying by librarians or archivists: single copies of unpublished recordings

6G. (1) A librarian or archivist may make and supply a single copy of the whole or part of a recording without infringing any of the rights conferred by this Chapter in the recording, provided that—

    (a) the copy is supplied in response to a request from a person who has provided the librarian or archivist with a declaration in writing which includes the information set out in sub-paragraph (2), and

    (b) the librarian or archivist is not aware that the declaration is false in a material particular.

(2) The information which must be included in the declaration is—

    (a) the name of the person who requires the copy and the material which that person requires,

    (b) a statement that the person has not previously been supplied with a copy of that material by any library or archive, and

    (c) a statement that the person requires the copy for the purposes of research for a non-commercial purpose or private study, will use it only for those purposes and will not supply the copy to any other person.

(3) But the rights conferred by this Chapter are infringed if—

    (a) the recording had been published or communicated to the public before the date it was deposited in the library or archive, or

    (b) the rights owner has prohibited the copying of the recording,

and at the time of making the copy the librarian or archivist is, or ought to be, aware of that fact.

(4) Where a library or archive makes a charge for supplying a copy under this paragraph, the sum charged must be calculated by reference to the costs attributable to the production of the copy.

(5) Where a person ("P") makes a declaration under this paragraph that is false in a material particular and is supplied with a copy of a recording which would have been an illicit recording if made by P—

    (a) P is liable for infringement of the rights conferred by this Chapter as if P had made the copy, and

    (b) the copy supplied to P is to be treated as an illicit recording for all purposes.

Paragraphs 6B to 6G: interpretation

6H. Expressions used in paragraphs 6B to 6G have the same meaning as in sections 40A to 43.

Certain permitted uses of orphan works

6I. (1) The rights conferred by this Chapter are not infringed by a relevant body in the circumstances set out in paragraph 1(2) of Schedule ZA1 (subject to paragraph 6 of that Schedule).

(2) "Relevant body" has the meaning given by that Schedule.

Copy of work required to be made as condition of export

7. (1) If an article of cultural or historical importance or interest cannot lawfully be exported from the United Kingdom unless a copy of it is made and deposited in an appropriate library or archive, it is not an infringement of any right conferred by this Chapter to make that copy.

(2) Expressions used in this paragraph have the same meaning as in section 44.

Parliamentary and judicial proceedings

8.   (1)   The rights conferred by this Chapter are not infringed by anything done for the purposes of parliamentary or judicial proceedings or for the purpose of reporting such proceedings.

      (2)   Expressions used in this paragraph have the same meaning as in section 45.

Royal Commissions and statutory inquiries

9.   (1)   The rights conferred by this Chapter are not infringed by anything done for the purposes of the proceedings of a Royal Commission or statutory inquiry or for the purpose of reporting any such proceedings held in public.

      (2)   Expressions used in this paragraph have the same meaning as in section 46.

Public records

10.   (1)   Material which is comprised in public records within the meaning of the Public Records Act 1958, the Public Records (Scotland) Act 1937 or the Public Records Act (Northern Ireland) 1923, or in Welsh public records (as defined in the Government of Wales Act 2006), which are open to public inspection in pursuance of that Act, may be copied, and a copy may be supplied to any person, by or with the authority of any officer appointed under that Act, without infringing any right conferred by this Chapter.

      (2)   Expressions used in this paragraph have the same meaning as in section 49.

Acts done under statutory authority

11.   (1)   Where the doing of a particular act is specifically authorised by an Act of Parliament, whenever passed, then, unless the Act provides otherwise, the doing of that act does not infringe the rights conferred by this Chapter.

      (2)   Sub-paragraph (1) applies in relation to an enactment contained in Northern Ireland legislation as it applies to an Act of Parliament.

      (3)   Nothing in this paragraph shall be construed as excluding any defence of statutory authority otherwise available under or by virtue of any enactment.

      (4)   Expressions used in this paragraph have the same meaning as in section 50.

Transfer of copies of works in electronic form

12.   (1)   This paragraph applies where a recording of a performance in electronic form has been purchased on terms which, expressly or impliedly or by virtue of any rule of law, allow the purchaser to make further recordings in connection with his use of the recording.

      (2)   If there are no express terms—

             (a)   prohibiting the transfer of the recording by the purchaser, imposing obligations which continue after a transfer, prohibiting the assignment of any consent or terminating any consent on a transfer, or

             (b)   providing for the terms on which a transferee may do the things which the purchaser was permitted to do,

             anything which the purchaser was allowed to do may also be done by a transferee without infringement of the rights conferred by this Chapter, but any recording made by the purchaser which is not also transferred shall be treated as an illicit recording for all purposes after the transfer.

      (3)   The same applies where the original purchased recording is no longer usable and what is transferred is a further copy used in its place.

      (4)   The above provisions also apply on a subsequent transfer, with the substitution for references in sub-paragraph (2) to the purchaser of references to the subsequent transferor.

      (5)   This paragraph does not apply in relation to a recording purchased before the commencement of this Chapter.

      (6)   Expressions used in this paragraph have the same meaning as in section 56.

Use of recordings of spoken works in certain cases

13.   (1)   Where a recording of the reading or recitation of a literary work is made for the purpose—
               (a)   of reporting current events, or
               (b)   of communicating to the public the whole or part of the reading or recitation,
               it is not an infringement of the rights conferred by this Chapter to use the recording (or to copy the recording and use the copy) for that purpose, provided the following conditions are met.
        (2)   The conditions are that—
               (a)   the recording is a direct recording of the reading or recitation and is not taken from a previous recording or from a broadcast;
               (b)   the making of the recording was not prohibited by or on behalf of the person giving the reading or recitation;
               (c)   the use made of the recording is not of a kind prohibited by or on behalf of that person before the recording was made; and
               (d)   the use is by or with the authority of a person who is lawfully in possession of the recording.
        (3)   Expressions used in this paragraph have the same meaning as in section 58.

Recordings of folksongs

14.   (1)   A recording of a performance of a song may be made for the purpose of including it in an archive maintained by a body not established or conducted for profit without infringing any of the rights conferred by this Chapter, provided the conditions in sub-paragraph (2) below are met.
        (2)   The conditions are that—
               (a)   the words are unpublished and of unknown authorship at the time the recording is made,
               (b)   the making of the recording does not infringe any copyright, and
               (c)   its making is not prohibited by any performer.
        (3)   A single copy of a recording made in reliance on sub-paragraph (1) and included in an archive referred to in that sub-paragraph may be made and supplied by the archivist without infringing any right conferred by this Chapter, provided that—
               (a)   the copy is supplied in response to a request from a person who has provided the archivist with a declaration in writing which includes the information set out in sub-paragraph (4), and
               (b)   the archivist is not aware that the declaration is false in a material particular.
        (4)   The information which must be included in the declaration is—
               (a)   the name of the person who requires the copy and the recording which is the subject of the request,
               (b)   a statement that the person has not previously been supplied with a copy of that recording by any archivist, and
               (c)   a statement that the person requires the copy for the purposes of research for a non-commercial purpose or private study, will use it only for those purposes and will not supply the copy to any other person.
        (5)   Where an archive makes a charge for supplying a copy under this paragraph, the sum charged must be calculated by reference to the costs attributable to the production of the copy.
        (6)   Where a person ("P") makes a declaration under this paragraph that is false in a material particular and is supplied with a copy of a recording which would have been an illicit recording if made by P—
               (a)   P is liable for infringement of the rights conferred by this Chapter as if P had made the copy, and
               (b)   the copy supplied to P is to be treated as an illicit recording for all purposes.
        (7)   In this paragraph references to an archivist include a person acting on behalf of an archivist.
        (8)   Expressions used in this paragraph have the same meaning as in section 61.

Lending of certain recordings

14A. (1) The Secretary of State may by order provide that in such cases as may be specified in the order the lending to the public of copies of films or sound recordings shall be treated as licensed by the performer subject only to the payment of such reasonable royalty or other payment as may be agreed or determined in default of agreement by the Copyright Tribunal.

(2) No such order shall apply if, or to the extent that, there is a licensing scheme certified for the purposes of this paragraph under paragraph 16 of Schedule 2A providing for the grant of licences.

(3) An order may make different provision for different cases and may specify cases by reference to any factor relating to the work, the copies lent, the lender or the circumstances of the lending.

(4) An order shall be made by statutory instrument; and no order shall be made unless a draft of it has been laid before and approved by a resolution of each House of Parliament.

(5) Nothing in this section affects any liability under section 184(1)(b) (secondary infringement: possessing or dealing with illicit recording) in respect of the lending of illicit recordings.

(6) Expressions used in this paragraph have the same meaning as in section 66.

Incidental recording for purposes of broadcast

16. (1) A person who proposes to broadcast a recording of a performance in circumstances not infringing the rights conferred by this Chapter shall be treated as having consent for the purposes of the broadcast.

(2) That consent is subject to the condition that the further recording—

(a) shall not be used for any other purpose, and

(b) shall be destroyed within 28 days of being first used for broadcasting the performance.

(3) A recording made in accordance with this paragraph shall be treated as an illicit recording—

(a) for the purposes of any use in breach of the condition mentioned in sub-paragraph (2)(a), and

(b) for all purposes after that condition or the condition mentioned in sub-paragraph (2)(b) is broken.

(4) Expressions used in this paragraph have the same meaning as in section 68.

Recordings for purposes of supervision and control of broadcasts and other services

17. (1) The rights conferred by this Chapter are not infringed by the making or use by the British Broadcasting Corporation, for the purpose of maintaining supervision and control over programmes broadcast by them, or included in any on-demand programme service provided by them, of recordings of those programmes.

(2) The rights conferred by this Chapter are not infringed by anything done in pursuance of—

(a) section 167(1) of the Broadcasting Act 1990, section 115(4) or (6) or 117 of the Broadcasting Act 1996 or paragraph 20 of Schedule 12 to the Communications Act 2003;

(b) a condition which, by virtue of section 334(1) of the Communications Act 2003, is included in a licence granted under Part I or III of that Act or Part I or II of the Broadcasting Act 1996;

(c) a direction given under section 109(2) of the Broadcasting Act 1990 (power of OFCOM to require production of recordings etc.);

(d) section 334(3), 368O(1) or (3) of the Communications Act 2003.

(3) The rights conferred by this Chapter are not infringed by the use by OFCOM in connection with the performance of any of their functions under the Broadcasting Act 1990, the Broadcasting Act 1996 or the Communications Act 2003 of—

(a) any recording, script or transcript which is provided to them under or by virtue of any provision of those Acts; or

    (b)   any existing material which is transferred to them by a scheme made under section 30 of the Communications Act 2003.

(4)   In subsection (3), "existing material" means—

    (a)   any recording, script or transcript which was provided to the Independent Television Commission or the Radio Authority under or by virtue of any provision of the Broadcasting Act 1990 or the Broadcasting Act 1996; and

    (b)   any recording or transcript which was provided to the Broadcasting Standards Commission under section 115(4) or (6) or 116(5) of the Broadcasting Act 1996.

(5)   The rights conferred by this Chapter are not infringed by the use by the appropriate regulatory authority designated under section 368B of the Communications Act 2003, in connection with the performance of any of their functions under that Act, of any recording, script or transcript which is provided to them under or by virtue of any provision of that Act.

(6)   In this paragraph "on-demand programme service" has the same meaning as in the Communications Act 2003 (see section 368A of that Act).

Recording for the purposes of time-shifting

17A.   (1)   The making in domestic premises for private and domestic use of a recording of a broadcast solely for the purpose of enabling it to be viewed or listened to at a more convenient time does not infringe any right conferred by this Chapter in relation to a performance or recording included in the broadcast.

    (2)   Where a recording which would otherwise be an illicit recording is made in accordance with this paragraph but is subsequently dealt with—

        (a)   it shall be treated as an illicit recording for the purposes of that dealing; and

        (b)   if that dealing infringes any right conferred by this Chapter, it shall be treated as an illicit recording for all subsequent purposes.

    (3)   In sub-paragraph (2), "dealt with" means sold or let for hire, offered or exposed for sale or hire or communicated to the public.

    (4)   Expressions used in this paragraph have the same meaning as in section 70.

Photographs of broadcasts

17B.   (1)   The making in domestic premises for private and domestic use of a photograph of the whole or any part of an image forming part of a broadcast, or a copy of such a photograph, does not infringe any right conferred by this Chapter in relation to a performance or recording included in the broadcast.

    (2)   Where a recording which would otherwise be an illicit recording is made in accordance with this paragraph but is subsequently dealt with—

        (a)   it shall be treated as an illicit recording for the purposes of that dealing; and

        (b)   if that dealing infringes any right conferred by this Chapter, it shall be treated as an illicit recording for all subsequent purposes.

    (3)   In sub-paragraph (2), "dealt with" means sold or let for hire, offered or exposed for sale or hire or communicated to the public.

    (4)   Expressions used in this paragraph have the same meaning as in section 71.

Free public showing or playing of broadcast

18.   (1)   The showing or playing in public of a broadcast to an audience who have not paid for admission to the place where the broadcast is to be seen or heard does not infringe any right conferred by this Chapter in relation to a performance or recording included in—

    (a)   the broadcast, or

    (b)   any sound recording (except so far as it is an excepted sound recording) or film which is played or shown in public by reception of the broadcast.

(1A)   The showing or playing in public of a broadcast to an audience who have not paid for admission to the place where the broadcast is to be seen or heard does not infringe any right conferred by this Chapter in relation to a performance or recording included in any excepted sound recording which is played in public by reception of the broadcast, if the playing or showing of that broadcast in public—

    (a)   . . .

    (b)   is necessary for the purposes of —
        (i)   repairing equipment for the reception of broadcasts;
        (ii)   demonstrating that a repair to such equipment has been carried out; or
        (iii)   demonstrating such equipment which is being sold or let for hire or offered or exposed for sale or hire.

(2)   The audience shall be treated as having paid for admission to a place —
    (a)   if they have paid for admission to a place of which that place forms part; or
    (b)   if goods or services are supplied at that place (or a place of which it forms part) —
        (i)   at prices which are substantially attributable to the facilities afforded for seeing or hearing the broadcast, or
        (ii)   at prices exceeding those usually charged there and which are partly attributable to those facilities.

(3)   The following shall not be regarded as having paid for admission to a place —
    (a)   persons admitted as residents or inmates of the place;
    (b)   persons admitted as members of a club or society where the payment is only for membership of the club or society and the provision of facilities for seeing or hearing broadcasts is only incidental to the main purposes of the club or society.

(4)   Where the making of the broadcast was an infringement of the rights conferred by this Chapter in relation to a performance or recording, the fact that it was heard or seen in public by the reception of the broadcast shall be taken into account in assessing the damages for that infringement.

(5)   Expressions used in this paragraph have the same meaning as in section 72.

. . .

Recording of broadcast for archival purposes

21.   (1)   A recording of a broadcast of a designated class, or a copy of such a recording, may be made for the purpose of being placed in an archive maintained by a body which is not established or conducted for profit without infringing any right conferred by this Chapter in relation to a performance or recording included in the broadcast.

    (2)   To the extent that a term of a contract purports to prevent or restrict the doing of any act which, by virtue of this paragraph, would not infringe any right conferred by this Chapter, that term is unenforceable.

    (3)   Expressions used in this paragraph have the same meaning as in section 75.

SCHEDULE 2A
LICENSING OF PERFORMERS' RIGHTS

Licensing schemes and licensing bodies

1.   (1)   In this Chapter a "licensing scheme" means a scheme setting out —
    (a)   the classes of case in which the operator of the scheme, or the person on whose behalf he acts, is willing to grant performers' property right licences, and
    (b)   the terms on which licences would be granted in those classes of case;
    and for this purpose a "scheme" includes anything in the nature of a scheme, whether described as a scheme or as a tariff or by any other name.

    (2)   In this Chapter a "licensing body" means a society or other organisation which has as its main object, or one of its main objects, the negotiating or granting, whether as owner or prospective owner of a performer's property rights or as agent for him, of performers' property right licences, and whose objects include the granting of licences covering the performances of more than one performer.

    (3)   In this paragraph "performers' property right licences" means licences to do, or authorise the doing of, any of the things for which consent is required under section 182A, 182B, 182C or 182CA.

    (4)   References in this Chapter to licences or licensing schemes covering the performances of more than one performer do not include licences or schemes covering only —
    (a)   performances recorded in a single recording,
    (b)   performances recorded in more than one recording where —
        (i)   the performers giving the performances are the same, or
        (ii)   the recordings are made by, or by employees of or commissioned by, a single individual, firm, company or group of companies.

For purpose a group of companies means a holding company and its subsidiaries within the meaning of section 1159 of the Companies Act 2006.

(5) Schedule A1 confers powers to provide for the regulation of licensing bodies.

Power to provide for licensing of orphan rights

1A. (1) The Secretary of State may by regulations provide for the grant of licences to do, or authorise the doing of, acts to which section 182, 182A, 182B, 182C, 182CA, 183 or 184 applies in respect of a performance, where—
(a) the performer's consent would otherwise be required under that section, but
(b) the right to authorise or prohibit the act qualifies as an orphan right under the regulations.

(2) The regulations may—
(a) specify a person or a description of persons authorised to grant licences, or
(b) provide for a person designated in the regulations to specify a person or a description of persons authorised to grant licences.

(3) The regulations must provide that, for a right to qualify as an orphan right, it is a requirement that the owner of the right has not been found after a diligent search made in accordance with the regulations.

(4) The regulations must provide for any licence—
(a) to have effect as if granted by the missing owner;
(b) not to give exclusive rights;
(c) not to be granted to a person authorised to grant licences.

(5) The regulations may apply in a case where it is not known whether a performer's right subsists, and references to a right, to a missing owner and to an interest of a missing owner are to be read as including references to a supposed right, owner or interest.

Extended collective licensing

1B. (1) The Secretary of State may by regulations provide for a licensing body that applies to the Secretary of State under the regulations to be authorised to grant licences to do, or authorise the doing of, acts to which section 182, 182A, 182B, 182C, 182CA, 183 or 184 applies in respect of a performance, where the right to authorise or prohibit the act is not owned by the body or a person on whose behalf the body acts.

(2) An authorisation must specify the acts to which any of those sections applies that the licensing body is authorised to license.

(3) The regulations must provide for the rights owner to have a right to limit or exclude the grant of licences by virtue of the regulations.

(4) The regulations must provide for any licence not to give exclusive rights.

. . .

References and applications with respect to licensing schemes

2. Paragraphs 3 to 8 (references and applications with respect to licensing schemes) apply to licensing schemes operated by licensing bodies in relation to a performer's property rights which cover the performances of more than one performer, so far as they relate to licences for—
(a) copying a recording of the whole or any substantial part of a qualifying performance,
(aa) making such a recording available to the public in the way mentioned in section 182CA(1), or
(b) renting or lending copies of a recording to the public;
and in those paragraphs "licensing scheme" means a licensing scheme of any of those descriptions.

Reference of proposed licensing scheme to tribunal

3. (1) The terms of a licensing scheme proposed to be operated by a licensing body may be referred to the Copyright Tribunal by an organisation claiming to be representative of persons claiming that they require licences in cases of a description to which the scheme would apply, either generally or in relation to any description of case.

(2) The Tribunal shall first decide whether to entertain the reference, and may decline to do so on the ground that the reference is premature.

(3) If the Tribunal decides to entertain the reference it shall consider the matter referred and make such order, either confirming or varying the proposed scheme, either generally or so far as it relates to cases of the description to which the reference relates, as the Tribunal may determine to be reasonable in the circumstances.

(4) The order may be made so as to be in force indefinitely or for such period as the Tribunal may determine.

Reference of licensing scheme to tribunal

4. (1) If while a licensing scheme is in operation a dispute arises between the operator of the scheme and —

   (a) a person claiming that he requires a licence in a case of a description to which the scheme applies, or

   (b) an organisation claiming to be representative of such persons,

   that person or organisation may refer the scheme to the Copyright Tribunal in so far as it relates to cases of that description.

   (2) A scheme which has been referred to the Tribunal under this paragraph shall remain in operation until proceedings on the reference are concluded.

   (3) The Tribunal shall consider the matter in dispute and make such order, either confirming or varying the scheme so far as it relates to cases of the description to which the reference relates, as the Tribunal may determine to be reasonable in the circumstances.

   (4) The order may be made so as to be in force indefinitely or for such period as the Tribunal may determine.

Further reference of scheme to tribunal

5. (1) Where the Copyright Tribunal has on a previous reference of a licensing scheme under paragraph 3 or 4, or under this paragraph, made an order with respect to the scheme, then, while the order remains in force —

   (a) the operator of the scheme,

   (b) a person claiming that he requires a licence in a case of the description to which the order applies, or

   (c) an organisation claiming to be representative of such persons,

   may refer the scheme again to the Tribunal so far as it relates to cases of that description.

   (2) A licensing scheme shall not, except with the special leave of the Tribunal, be referred again to the Tribunal in respect of the same description of cases —

   (a) within twelve months from the date of the order on the previous reference, or

   (b) if the order was made so as to be in force for 15 months or less, until the last three months before the expiry of the order.

   (3) A scheme which has been referred to the Tribunal under this paragraph shall remain in operation until proceedings on the reference are concluded.

   (4) The Tribunal shall consider the matter in dispute and make such order, either confirming, varying or further varying the scheme so far as it relates to cases of the description to which the reference relates, as the Tribunal may determine to be reasonable in the circumstances.

   (5) The order may be made so as to be in force indefinitely or for such period as the Tribunal may determine.

Application for grant of licence in connection with licensing scheme

6. (1) A person who claims, in a case covered by a licensing scheme, that the operator of the scheme has refused to grant him or procure the grant to him of a licence in accordance with the scheme, or has failed to do so within a reasonable time after being asked, may apply to the Copyright Tribunal.

(2)   A person who claims, in a case excluded from a licensing scheme, that the operator of the scheme either—

    (a)   has refused to grant him a licence or procure the grant to him of a licence, or has failed to do so within a reasonable time of being asked, and that in the circumstances it is unreasonable that a licence should not be granted, or

    (b)   proposes terms for a licence which are unreasonable, may apply to the Copyright Tribunal.

(3)   A case shall be regarded as excluded from a licensing scheme for the purposes of sub-paragraph (2) if—

    (a)   the scheme provides for the grant of licences subject to terms excepting matters from the licence and the case falls within such an exception, or

    (b)   the case is so similar to those in which licences are granted under the scheme that it is unreasonable that it should not be dealt with in the same way.

(4)   If the Tribunal is satisfied that the claim is well-founded, it shall make an order declaring that, in respect of the matters specified in the order, the applicant is entitled to a licence on such terms as the Tribunal may determine to be applicable in accordance with the scheme or, as the case may be, to be reasonable in the circumstances.

(5)   The order may be made so as to be in force indefinitely or for such period as the Tribunal may determine.

Application for review of order as to entitlement to licence

7.   (1)   Where the Copyright Tribunal has made an order under paragraph 6 that a person is entitled to a licence under a licensing scheme, the operator of the scheme or the original applicant may apply to the Tribunal to review its order.

       (2)   An application shall not be made, except with the special leave of the Tribunal—

    (a)   within twelve months from the date of the order, or of the decision on a previous application under this paragraph, or

    (b)   if the order was made so as to be in force for 15 months or less, or as a result of the decision on a previous application under this paragraph is due to expire within 15 months of that decision, until the last three months before the expiry date.

       (3)   The Tribunal shall on an application for review confirm or vary its order as the Tribunal may determine to be reasonable having regard to the terms applicable in accordance with the licensing scheme or, as the case may be, the circumstances of the case.

Effect of order of tribunal as to licensing scheme

8.   (1)   A licensing scheme which has been confirmed or varied by the Copyright Tribunal—

    (a)   under paragraph 3 (reference of terms of proposed scheme), or

    (b)   under paragraph 4 or 5 (reference of existing scheme to Tribunal),

         shall be in force or, as the case may be, remain in operation, so far as it relates to the description of case in respect of which the order was made, so long as the order remains in force.

       (2)   While the order is in force a person who in a case of a class to which the order applies—

    (a)   pays to the operator of the scheme any charges payable under the scheme in respect of a licence covering the case in question or, if the amount cannot be ascertained, gives an undertaking to the operator to pay them when ascertained, and

    (b)   complies with the other terms applicable to such a licence under the scheme, shall be in the same position as regards infringement of performers' property rights as if he had at all material times been the holder of a licence granted by the rights owner in question in accordance with the scheme.

       (3)   The Tribunal may direct that the order, so far as it varies the amount of charges payable, has effect from a date before that on which it is made, but not earlier than the date on which the reference was made or, if later, on which the scheme came into operation. If such a direction is made—

    (a)   any necessary repayments, or further payments, shall be made in respect of charges already paid, and

(b)   the reference in sub-paragraph (2)(a) to the charges payable under the scheme shall be construed as a reference to the charges so payable by virtue of the order.

No such direction may be made where sub-paragraph (4) below applies.

(4)   An order of the Tribunal under paragraph 4 or 5 made with respect to a scheme which is certified for any purpose under paragraph 16 has effect, so far as it varies the scheme by reducing the charges payable for licences, from the date on which the reference was made to the Tribunal.

(5)   Where the Tribunal has made an order under paragraph 6 (order as to entitlement to licence under licensing scheme) and the order remains in force, the person in whose favour the order is made shall if he—

(a)   pays to the operator of the scheme any charges payable in accordance with the order or, if the amount cannot be ascertained, gives an undertaking to pay the charges when ascertained, and

(b)   complies with the other terms specified in the order,

be in the same position as regards infringement of performers' property rights as if he had at all material times been the holder of a licence granted by the rights owner in question on the terms specified in the order.

References and applications with respect to licensing by licensing bodies

9.   Paragraphs 10 to 13 (references and applications with respect to licensing by licensing bodies) apply to licences relating to a performer's property rights which cover the performance of more than one performer granted by a licensing body otherwise than in pursuance of a licensing scheme, so far as the licences authorise—

(a)   copying a recording of the whole or any substantial part of a qualifying performance, . . .

(aa) making such a recording available to the public in the way mentioned in section 182CA(1), or

(b)   renting or lending copies of a recording to the public;

and references in those paragraphs to a licence shall be construed accordingly.

Reference to tribunal of proposed licence

10.   (1)   The terms on which a licensing body proposes to grant a licence may be referred to the Copyright Tribunal by the prospective licensee.

(2)   The Tribunal shall first decide whether to entertain the reference, and may decline to do so on the ground that the reference is premature.

(3)   If the Tribunal decides to entertain the reference it shall consider the terms of the proposed licence and make such order, either confirming or varying the terms as it may determine to be reasonable in the circumstances.

(4)   The order may be made so as to be in force indefinitely or for such period as the Tribunal may determine.

Reference to tribunal of expiring licence

11.   (1)   A licensee under a licence which is due to expire, by effluxion of time or as a result of notice given by the licensing body, may apply to the Copyright Tribunal on the ground that it is unreasonable in the circumstances that the licence should cease to be in force.

(2)   Such an application may not be made until the last three months before the licence is due to expire.

(3)   A licence in respect of which a reference has been made to the Tribunal shall remain in operation until proceedings on the reference are concluded.

(4)   If the Tribunal finds the application well-founded, it shall make an order declaring that the licensee shall continue to be entitled to the benefit of the licence on such terms as the Tribunal may determine to be reasonable in the circumstances.

(5)   An order of the Tribunal under this paragraph may be made so as to be in force indefinitely or for such period as the Tribunal may determine.

Application for review of order as to licence

12.   (1)   Where the Copyright Tribunal has made an order under paragraph 10 or 11, the licensing body or the person entitled to the benefit of the order may apply to the Tribunal to review its order.

       (2)   An application shall not be made, except with the special leave of the Tribunal—
              (a)   within twelve months from the date of the order or of the decision on a previous application under this paragraph, or
              (b)   if the order was made so as to be in force for 15 months or less, or as a result of the decision on a previous application under this paragraph is due to expire within 15 months of that decision, until the last three months before the expiry date.

       (3)   The Tribunal shall on an application for review confirm or vary its order as the Tribunal may determine to be reasonable in the circumstances.

Effect of order of tribunal as to licence

13.   (1)   Where the Copyright Tribunal has made an order under paragraph 10 or 11 and the order remains in force, the person entitled to the benefit of the order shall if he—
              (a)   pays to the licensing body any charges payable in accordance with the order or, if the amount cannot be ascertained, gives an undertaking to pay the charges when ascertained, and
              (b)   complies with the other terms specified in the order,
              be in the same position as regards infringement of performers' property rights as if he had at all material times been the holder of a licence granted by the rights owner in question on the terms specified in the order.

       (2)   The benefit of the order may be assigned—
              (a)   in the case of an order under paragraph 10, if assignment is not prohibited under the terms of the Tribunal's order; and
              (b)   in the case of an order under paragraph 11, if assignment was not prohibited under the terms of the original licence.

       (3)   The Tribunal may direct that an order under paragraph 10 or 11, or an order under paragraph 12 varying such an order, so far as it varies the amount of charges payable, has effect from a date before that on which it is made, but not earlier than the date on which the reference or application was made or, if later, on which the licence was granted or, as the case may be, was due to expire.
              If such a direction is made—
              (a)   any necessary repayments, or further payments, shall be made in respect of charges already paid, and
              (b)   the reference in sub-paragraph (1)(a) to the charges payable in accordance with the order shall be construed, where the order is varied by a later order, as a reference to the charges so payable by virtue of the later order.

General considerations: unreasonable discrimination

14.   (1)   In determining what is reasonable on a reference or application under this Schedule relating to a licensing scheme or licence, the Copyright Tribunal shall have regard to—
              (a)   the availability of other schemes, or the granting of other licences, to other persons in similar circumstances, and
              (b)   the terms of those schemes or licences,
              and shall exercise its powers so as to secure that there is no unreasonable discrimination between licensees, or prospective licensees, under the scheme or licence to which the reference or application relates and licensees under other schemes operated by, or other licences granted by, the same person.

       (2)   This does not affect the Tribunal's general obligation in any case to have regard to all relevant circumstances.

Application to settle royalty or other sum payable for lending

15.   (1)   An application to settle the royalty or other sum payable in pursuance of paragraph 14A of Schedule 2 (lending of certain recordings) may be made to the Copyright Tribunal by the owner of a performer's property rights or the person claiming to be treated as licensed by him.

(2) The Tribunal shall consider the matter and make such order as it may determine to be reasonable in the circumstances.

(3) Either party may subsequently apply to the Tribunal to vary the order, and the Tribunal shall consider the matter and make such order confirming or varying the original order as it may determine to be reasonable in the circumstances.

(4) An application under sub-paragraph (3) shall not, except with the special leave of the Tribunal, be made within twelve months from the date of the original order or of the order on a previous application under that sub-paragraph.

(5) An order under sub-paragraph (3) has effect from the date on which it is made or such later date as may be specified by the Tribunal

Certification of licensing schemes

16. (1) A person operating or proposing to operate a licensing scheme may apply to the Secretary of State to certify the scheme for the purposes of paragraph 6, 14A or 20 of Schedule 2 (recording of broadcasts by educational establishments, lending of certain recordings, provision of sub-titled copies of broadcast).

(2) The Secretary of State shall by order made by statutory instrument certify the scheme if he is satisfied that it—
   (a) enables the works to which it relates to be identified with sufficient certainty by persons likely to require licences, and
   (b) sets out clearly the charges (if any) payable and the other terms on which licences will be granted.

(3) The scheme shall be scheduled to the order and the certification shall come into operation for the purposes of the relevant paragraph of Schedule 2—
   (a) on such date, not less than eight weeks after the order is made, as may be specified in the order, or
   (b) if the scheme is the subject of a reference under paragraph 3 (reference of proposed scheme), any later date on which the order of the Copyright Tribunal under that paragraph comes into force or the reference is withdrawn.

(4) A variation of the scheme is not effective unless a corresponding amendment of the order is made; and the Secretary of State shall make such an amendment in the case of a variation ordered by the Copyright Tribunal on a reference under paragraph 3,4 or 5, and may do so in any other case if he thinks fit.

(5) The order shall be revoked if the scheme ceases to be operated and may be revoked if it appears to the Secretary of State that it is no longer being operated according to its terms.

Powers exercisable in consequence of competition report

17. (1) Sub-paragraph (1A) applies where whatever needs to be remedied, mitigated or prevented by the Secretary of State, or (as the case may be) the Competition and Markets Authority under section 12(5) of the Competition Act 1980 or section 41(2), 55(2), 66(6), 75(2), 83(2), 138(2), 147(2) or 160(2) of, or paragraph 5(2) or 10(2) of Schedule 7 to, the Enterprise Act 2002 (powers to take remedial action following references to the Competition and Markets Authority in connection with public bodies and certain other persons, mergers or market investigations etc) consists of or includes—
   (a) conditions in licences granted by the owner of a performer's property rights restricting the use to which a recording may be put by the licensee or the right of the owner to grant other licenses, or
   (b) a refusal of an owner of a performer's property rights to grant licences on reasonable terms.

(1A) The powers conferred by Schedule 8 to the Enterprise Act 2002 include power to cancel or modify those conditions and, instead or in addition, to provide that licences in respect of the performer's property rights shall be available as of right.

(2) The references to anything permitted by Schedule 8 to the Enterprise Act 2002 in section 12(5A) of the Competition Act 1980 and in sections 75(4)(a), 83(4)(a), 84(2)(a), 89(1), 160(4)(a), 161(3)(a) and 164(1) of, and paragraphs 5, 10 and 11 of Schedule 7 to, the Act of 2002 shall be construed accordingly.

(3) The Secretary of State or (as the case may be) the Competition and Markets Authority shall only exercise the powers available by virtue of this paragraph if he or it is satisfied

that to do so does not contravene any Convention relating to performers' rights to which the United Kingdom is a party.

(4)   The terms of a licence available by virtue of this paragraph shall, in default of agreement, be settled by the Copyright Tribunal on an application by the person requiring the licence; and terms so settled shall authorise the licensee to do everything in respect of which a licence is so available.

(5)   Where the terms of a licence are settled by the Tribunal, the licence has effect from the date on which the application to the Tribunal was made.

. . .

SCHEDULE 5A
PERMITTED ACTS TO WHICH SECTION 296ZE APPLIES

PART 1
COPYRIGHT EXCEPTIONS

section 29 (research and private study)
section 29A (copies for text and data analysis for non-commercial research)
section 31A (disabled persons: copies of works for personal use)
section 31B (making and supply of accessible copies by authorised bodies)
section 31BA (making and supply of intermediate copies by authorised bodies)
section 32 (illustration for instruction)
section 35 (recording by educational establishments of broadcasts)
section 36 (copying and use of extracts of works by educational establishments)
section 41 (copying by librarians: supply of single copies to other libraries)
section 42 (copying by librarians etc: replacement copies of works)
section 42A (copying by librarians: single copies of published works)
section 43 (copying by librarians or archivists: single copies of unpublished works)
section 44 (copy of work required to be made as condition of export)
section 45 (Parliamentary and judicial proceedings)
section 46 (Royal Commissions and statutory inquiries)
section 47 (material open to public inspection or on official register)
section 48 (material communicated to the Crown in the course of public business)
section 49 (public records)
section 50 (acts done under statutory authority)
section 61 (recordings of folksongs)
section 68 (incidental recording for purposes of broadcast)
section 69 (recording for purposes of supervision and control of broadcasts)
section 70 (recording for purposes of time-shifting)
section 71 (photographs of broadcasts)
section 75 (recording of broadcast for archival purposes)

PART 2
RIGHTS IN PERFORMANCES EXCEPTIONS

paragraph 1C of Schedule 2 (research and private study)
paragraph 1D of Schedule 2 (copies for text and data analysis for non-commercial research)
paragraph 3A of Schedule 2 (disabled persons: copies of recordings for personal use)
paragraph 3B of Schedule 2 (making and supply of accessible copies by authorised bodies)
paragraph 3C of Schedule 2 (making and supply of intermediate copies by authorised bodies)
paragraph 4 of Schedule 2 (illustration for instruction)
paragraph 6 of Schedule 2 (recording by educational establishments of broadcasts)
paragraph 6ZA of Schedule 2 (copying and use of extracts of recordings by educational establishments)
paragraph 6D of Schedule 2 (copying by librarians: supply of single copies to other libraries)
paragraph 6E of Schedule 2 (copying by librarians etc: replacement copies of recordings)
paragraph 6F of Schedule 2 (copying by librarians: single copies of published recordings)

paragraph 6G of Schedule 2 (copying by librarians or archivists: single copies of unpublished recordings)

paragraph 7 of Schedule 2 (copy of work required to be made as condition of export)

paragraph 8 of Schedule 2 (Parliamentary and judicial proceedings)

paragraph 9 of Schedule 2 (Royal Commissions and statutory inquiries)

paragraph 10 of Schedule 2 (public records)

paragraph 11 of Schedule 2 (acts done under statutory authority)

paragraph 14 of Schedule 2 (recordings of folksongs)

paragraph 16 of Schedule 2 (incidental recording for purposes of broadcast)

paragraph 17 of Schedule 2 (recordings for purposes of supervision and control of broadcasts)

paragraph 17A of Schedule 2 (recording for the purposes of time-shifting)

paragraph 17B of Schedule 2 (photographs of broadcasts)

paragraph 21 of Schedule 2 (recording of broadcast for archival purposes)

PART 3
DATABASE RIGHT EXCEPTIONS

regulation 20 of and Schedule 1 to the Copyright and Rights in Databases Regulations 1997

REGISTERED DESIGNS ACT 1949
(c. 88)

1   Registration of designs

(1)   A design may, subject to the following provisions of this Act, be registered under this Act on the making of an application for registration.

(2)   In this Act "design" means the appearance of the whole or a part of a product resulting from the features of, in particular, the lines, contours, colours, shape, texture or materials of the product or its ornamentation.

(3)   In this Act—

"complex product" means a product which is composed of at least two replaceable component parts permitting disassembly and reassembly of the product; and

"product" means any industrial or handicraft item other than a computer program; and, in particular, includes packaging, get-up, graphic symbols, typographic type-faces and parts intended to be assembled into a complex product.

1B   Requirement of novelty and individual character

(1)   A design shall be protected by a right in a registered design to the extent that the design is new and has individual character.

(2)   For the purposes of subsection (1) above, a design is new if no identical design or no design whose features differ only in immaterial details has been made available to the public before the relevant date.

(3)   For the purposes of subsection (1) above, a design has individual character if the overall impression it produces on the informed user differs from the overall impression produced on such a user by any design which has been made available to the public before the relevant date.

(4)   In determining the extent to which a design has individual character, the degree of freedom of the author in creating the design shall be taken into consideration.

(5)   For the purposes of this section, a design has been made available to the public before the relevant date if—

(a)   it has been published (whether following registration or otherwise), exhibited, used in trade or otherwise disclosed before that date; and

(b)   the disclosure does not fall within subsection (6) below.

(6)   A disclosure falls within this subsection if—

(a)   it could not reasonably have become known before the relevant date in the normal course of business to persons carrying on business in the European Economic Area and specialising in the sector concerned;

(b) it was made to a person other than the designer, or any successor in title of his, under conditions of confidentiality (whether express or implied);

(c) it was made by the designer, or any successor in title of his, during the period of 12 months immediately preceding the relevant date;

(d) it was made by a person other than the designer, or any successor in title of his, during the period of 12 months immediately preceding the relevant date in consequence of information provided or other action taken by the designer or any successor in title of his; or

(e) it was made during the period of 12 months immediately preceding the relevant date as a consequence of an abuse in relation to the designer or any successor in title of his.

(7) In subsections (2), (3), (5) and (6) above "the relevant date" means the date on which the application for the registration of the design was made or is treated by virtue of section 3B(2), (3) or (5) or 14(2) of this Act as having been made.

(8) For the purposes of this section, a design applied to or incorporated in a product which constitutes a component part of a complex product shall only be considered to be new and to have individual character—

(a) if the component part, once it has been incorporated into the complex product, remains visible during normal use of the complex product; and

(b) to the extent that those visible features of the component part are in themselves new and have individual character.

(9) In subsection (8) above "normal use" means use by the end user; but does not include any maintenance, servicing or repair work in relation to the product.

1C Designs dictated by their technical function

(1) A right in a registered design shall not subsist in features of appearance of a product which are solely dictated by the product's technical function.

(2) A right in a registered design shall not subsist in features of appearance of a product which must necessarily be reproduced in their exact form and dimensions so as to permit the product in which the design is incorporated or to which it is applied to be mechanically connected to, or placed in, around or against, another product so that either product may perform its function.

(3) Subsection (2) above does not prevent a right in a registered design subsisting in a design serving the purpose of allowing multiple assembly or connection of mutually interchangeable products within a modular system.

1D Designs contrary to public policy or morality

A right in a registered design shall not subsist in a design which is contrary to public policy or to accepted principles of morality.

2 Proprietorship of designs

(1) The author of a design shall be treated for the purposes of this Act as the original proprietor of the design, subject to the following provisions.

. . .

(1B) Where a design is created by an employee in the course of his employment, his employer shall be treated as the original proprietor of the design.

(2) Where a design becomes vested, whether by assignment, transmission or operation of law, in any person other than the original proprietor, either alone or jointly with the original proprietor, that other person, or as the case may be the original proprietor and that other person, shall be treated for the purposes of this Act as the proprietor of the design.

(3) In this Act the "author" of a design means the person who creates it.

(4) In the case of a design generated by computer in circumstances such that there is no human author, the person by whom the arrangements necessary for the creation of the design are made shall be taken to be the author.

3 Applications for registration

(1) An application for the registration of a design or designs shall be filed at the Patent Office in the prescribed manner.

. . .

(3) An application for the registration of a design or designs in which national unregistered design right subsists shall be made by the person claiming to be the design right owner.

(4) . . .

(5) An application for the registration of a design which, owing to any default or neglect on the part of the applicant, has not been completed so as to enable registration to be effected within such time as may be prescribed shall be deemed to be abandoned.

3A Determination of applications for registration

(1) Subject as follows, the registrar shall not refuse to register a design included in an application under this Act.

(2) If it appears to the registrar that an application for the registration of a design or designs has not been made in accordance with any rules made under this Act, he may refuse to register any design included in it.

(3) If it appears to the registrar that the applicant is not under section 3(2) or (3) or 14 entitled to apply for the registration of a design included in the application, he shall refuse to register that design.

(4) If it appears to the registrar that the application for registration includes—

(a) something which does not fulfil the requirements of section 1(2) of this Act;

(b) a design that does not fulfil the requirements of section 1C or 1D of this Act; or

(c) a design to which a ground of refusal mentioned in Schedule A1 to this Act applies,

he shall refuse to register that thing or that design.

3B Modification of applications for registration

(1) The registrar may, at any time before an application for the registration of a design or designs is determined, permit the applicant to make such modifications of the application as the registrar thinks fit.

(2) Where an application for the registration of a design or designs has been modified before it has been determined in such a way that any design included in the application has been altered significantly, the registrar may, for the purpose of deciding whether and to what extent the design is new or has individual character, direct that the application so far as relating to that design shall be treated as having been made on the date on which it was so modified.

(3) Where—

(a) an application for the registration of more than one design has been modified before it has been determined to exclude one or more designs from the application; and

(b) a subsequent application for the registration of a design so excluded has, within such period (if any) as has been prescribed for such applications, been made by the person who made the earlier application or his successor in title,

the registrar may, for the purpose of deciding whether and to what extent the design is new or has individual character, direct that the subsequent application shall be treated as having been made on the date on which the earlier application was, or is treated as having been, made.

(4) Where the registration of a design has been refused on any ground mentioned in section 3A(4)(b) or (c) of this Act, the application for the design may be modified by the applicant if it appears to the registrar that—

(a) the identity of the design is retained; and

(b) the modifications have been made in accordance with any rules made under this Act.

(5) An application modified under subsection (4) above shall be treated as the original application and, in particular, as made on the date on which the original application was made or is treated as having been made.

(6) Any modification under this section may, in particular, be effected by making a partial disclaimer in relation to the application.

3C Date of registration of designs

(1) Subject as follows, a design, when registered, shall be registered as of the date on which the application was made or is treated as having been made.

(2) Subsection (1) above shall not apply to an application which is treated as having been made on a particular date by section 14(2) of this Act or by virtue of the operation of section 3B(3) or (5) of this Act by reference to section 14(2) of this Act.

(3) A design, when registered, shall be registered as of—

(a) in the case of an application which is treated as having been made on a particular date by section 14(2) of this Act, the date on which the application was made;

(b) in the case of an application which is treated as having been made on a particular date by virtue of the operation of section 3B(3) of this Act by reference to section 14(2) of this Act, the date on which the earlier application was made;

(c) in the case of an application which is treated as having been made on a particular date by virtue of the operation of section 3B(5) of this Act by reference to section 14(2) of this Act, the date on which the original application was made.

3D Appeals in relation to applications for registration

An appeal lies from any decision of the registrar under section 3A or 3B of this Act.

5 Provisions for secrecy of certain designs

(1) Where, either before or after the commencement of this Act, an application for the registration of a design has been made, and it appears to the registrar that the design is one of a class notified to him by the Secretary of State as relevant for defence purposes, he may give directions for prohibiting or restricting the publication of information with respect to the design, or the communication of such information to any person or class of persons specified in the directions.

(2) The Secretary of State shall by rules make provision for securing that where such directions are given—

(a) the representation or specimen of the design,

(b) ...

shall not be open to public inspection at the Patent Office during the continuance in force of the directions.

(3) Where the registrar gives any such directions as aforesaid, he shall give notice of the application and of the directions to the Secretary of State, and thereupon the following provisions shall have effect, that is to say—

(a) the Secretary of State shall, upon receipt of such notice, consider whether the publication of the design would be prejudicial to the defence of the realm and unless a notice under paragraph (c) of this subsection has previously been given by that authority to the registrar, shall reconsider that question before the expiration of nine months from the date of filing of the application for registration of the design and at least once in every subsequent year;

(b) for the purpose aforesaid, the Secretary of State may, at any time after the design has been registered or, with the consent of the applicant, at any time before the design has been registered, inspect the representation or specimen of the design filed in pursuance of the application;

(c) if upon consideration of the design at any time it appears to the Secretary of State that the publication of the design would not, or would no longer, be prejudicial to the defence of the realm, he shall give notice to the registrar to that effect;

(d) on the receipt of any such notice the registrar shall revoke the directions and may, subject to such conditions, if any, as he thinks fit, extend the time for doing anything required or authorised to be done by or under this Act in connection with the application or registration, whether or not that time has previously expired.

(4) No person resident in the United Kingdom shall, except under the authority of a written permit granted by or on behalf of the registrar, make or cause to be made any application outside the United Kingdom for the registration of a design of any class prescribed for the purposes of this subsection unless—

(a) an application for registration of the same design has been made in the United Kingdom not less than six weeks before the application outside the United Kingdom; and

(b) either no directions have been given under subsection (1) of this section in relation to the application in the United Kingdom or all such directions have been revoked:

Provided that this subsection shall not apply in relation to a design for which an application for protection has first been filed in a country outside the United Kingdom by a person resident outside the United Kingdom.

Effect of registration, etc

7 Right given by registration

(1) The registration of a design under this Act gives the registered proprietor the exclusive right to use the design and any design which does not produce on the informed user a different overall impression.

(2) For the purposes of subsection (1) above and section 7A of this Act any reference to the use of a design includes a reference to—

(a) the making, offering, putting on the market, importing, exporting or using of a product in which the design is incorporated or to which it is applied; or

(b) stocking such a product for those purposes.

(3) In determining for the purposes of subsection (1) above whether a design produces a different overall impression on the informed user, the degree of freedom of the author in creating his design shall be taken into consideration.

(4) The right conferred by subsection (1) above is subject to any limitation attaching to the registration in question (including, in particular, any partial disclaimer or any declaration by the registrar or a court of partial invalidity).

7A Infringements of rights in registered designs

(1) Subject as follows, the right in a registered design is infringed by a person who, without the consent of the registered proprietor, does anything which by virtue of section 7 of this Act is the exclusive right of the registered proprietor.

(2) The right in a registered design is not infringed by—

(a) an act which is done privately and for purposes which are not commercial;

(b) an act which is done for experimental purposes;

(c) an act of reproduction for teaching purposes or for the purpose of making citations provided that the conditions mentioned in subsection (3) below are satisfied;

(d) the use of equipment on ships or aircraft which are registered in another country but which are temporarily in the United Kingdom;

(e) the importation into the United Kingdom of spare parts or accessories for the purpose of repairing such ships or aircraft; or

(f) the carrying out of repairs on such ships or aircraft.

(3) The conditions mentioned in this subsection are—

(a) the act of reproduction is compatible with fair trade practice and does not unduly prejudice the normal exploitation of the design; and

(b) mention is made of the source.

(4) The right in a registered design is not infringed by an act which relates to a product in which any design protected by the registration is incorporated or to which it is applied if the product has been put on the market in the European Economic Area by the registered proprietor or with his consent.

(5) The right in a registered design of a component part which may be used for the purpose of the repair of a complex product so as to restore its original appearance is not infringed by the use for that purpose of any design protected by the registration.

(6) No proceedings shall be taken in respect of an infringement of the right in a registered design committed before the date on which the certificate of registration of the design under this Act is granted.

7B Right of prior use

(1) A person who, before the application date, used a registered design in good faith or made serious and effective preparations to do so may continue to use the design for the purposes for which, before that date, the person had used it or made the preparations to use it.

(2) In subsection (1), the "application date", in relation to a registered design, means—

(a) the date on which an application for the registration was made under section 3, or

(b)   where an application for the registration was treated as having been made by virtue of section 14(2), the date on which it was treated as having been so made.

(3)   Subsection (1) does not apply if the design which the person used, or made preparations to use, was copied from the design which was subsequently registered.

(4)   The right conferred on a person by subsection (1) does not include a right to licence another person to use the design.

(5)   Nor may the person on whom the right under subsection (1) is conferred assign the right, or transmit it on death (or in the case of a body corporate on its dissolution), unless—

(a)   the design was used, or the preparations for its use were made, in the course of a business, and

(b)   the right is assigned or transmitted with the part of the business in which the design was used or the preparations for its use were made.

8   Duration of right in registered design

(1)   The right in a registered design subsists in the first instance for a period of five years from the date of the registration of the design.

(2)   The period for which the right subsists may be extended for a second, third, fourth and fifth period of five years, by applying to the registrar for an extension and paying the prescribed renewal fee.

(3)   If the first, second, third or fourth period expires without such application and payment being made, the right shall cease to have effect; and the registrar shall, in accordance with rules made by the Secretary of State, notify the proprietor of that fact.

(4)   If during the period of six months immediately following the end of that period an application for extension is made and the prescribed renewal fee and any prescribed additional fee is paid, the right shall be treated as if it had never expired, with the result that—

(a)   anything done under or in relation to the right during that further period shall be treated as valid,

(b)   an act which would have constituted an infringement of the right if it had not expired shall be treated as an infringement, and

(c)   an act which would have constituted use of the design for the services of the Crown if the right had not expired shall be treated as such use.

8A   Restoration of lapsed right in design

(1)   Where the right in a registered design has expired by reason of a failure to extend, in accordance with section 8(2) or (4), the period for which the right subsists, an application for the restoration of the right in the design may be made to the registrar within the prescribed period.

(2)   The application may be made by the person who was the registered proprietor of the design or by any other person who would have been entitled to the right in the design if it had not expired; and where the design was held by two or more persons jointly, the application may, with the leave of the registrar, be made by one or more of them without joining the others.

(3)   Notice of the application shall be published by the registrar in the prescribed manner.

(4)   If the registrar is satisfied that the failure of the proprietor to see that the period for which the right subsisted was extended in accordance with section 8(2) or (4) was unintentional, he shall, on payment of any unpaid renewal fee and any prescribed additional fee, order the restoration of the right in the design.

(5)   The order may be made subject to such conditions as the registrar thinks fit, and if the proprietor of the design does not comply with any condition the registrar may revoke the order and give such consequential directions as he thinks fit.

(6)   Rules altering the period prescribed for the purposes of subsection (1) may contain such transitional provisions and savings as appear to the Secretary of State to be necessary or expedient.

8B   Effect of order for restoration of right

(1)   The effect of an order under section 8A for the restoration of the right in a registered design is as follows.

(2)   Anything done under or in relation to the right during the period between expiry and restoration shall be treated as valid.

(3)   Anything done during that period which would have constituted an infringement if the right had not expired shall be treated as an infringement—

(a)   if done at a time when it was possible for an application for extension to be made under section 8(4); or

(b)   if it was a continuation or repetition of an earlier infringing act.

(4)   If, after it was no longer possible for such an application for extension to be made and before publication of notice of the application for restoration, a person—

(a)   began in good faith to do an act which would have constituted an infringement of the right in the design if it had not expired, or

(b)   made in good faith effective and serious preparations to do such an act,

he has the right to continue to do the act or, as the case may be, to do the act, notwithstanding the restoration of the right in the design; but this does not extend to granting a licence to another person to do the act.

(5)   If the act was done, or the preparations were made, in the course of a business, the person entitled to the right conferred by subsection (4) may—

(a)   authorise the doing of that act by any partners of his for the time being in that business, and

(b)   assign that right, or transmit it on death (or in the case of a body corporate on its dissolution), to any person who acquires that part of the business in the course of which the act was done or the preparations were made.

(6)   Where a product is disposed of to another in exercise of the rights conferred by subsection (4) or subsection (5), that other and any person claiming through him may deal with the product in the same way as if it had been disposed of by the registered proprietor of the design.

(7)   The above provisions apply in relation to the use of a registered design for the services of the Crown as they apply in relation to infringement of the right in the design.

11   Cancellation of registration

The registrar may, upon a request made in the prescribed manner by the registered proprietor, cancel the registration of a design.

11ZA   Grounds for invalidity of registration

(1)   The registration of a design may be declared invalid—

(a)   on the ground that it does not fulfil the requirements of section 1(2) of this Act;

(b)   on the ground that it does not fulfil the requirements of sections 1B to 1D of this Act; or

(c)   where any ground of refusal mentioned in Schedule A1 to this Act applies.

(1A) The registration of a design ("the later design") may be declared invalid if it is not new or does not have individual character when compared to a design which—

(a)   has been made available to the public on or after the relevant date; but

(b)   is protected as from a date prior to the relevant date—

(i)   by virtue of registration under this Act or the Community Design Regulation or an application for such registration, or

(ii)   by virtue of an international registration (within the meaning of Articles 106a to 106f of that Regulation) designating the Community.

(1B) In subsection (1A) "the relevant date" means the date on which the application for the registration of the later design was made or is treated by virtue of section 3B(2), (3) or (5) or 14(2) of this Act as having been made.

(2)   The registration of a design may be declared invalid on the ground of the registered proprietor not being the proprietor of the design and the proprietor of the design objecting.

(3)   The registration of a design involving the use of an earlier distinctive sign may be declared invalid on the ground of an objection by the holder of rights to the sign which include the right to prohibit in the United Kingdom such use of the sign.

(4)   The registration of a design constituting an unauthorised use of a work protected by the law of copyright in the United Kingdom may be declared invalid on the ground of an objection by the owner of the copyright.

(5)   In this section and sections 11ZB, 11ZC and 11ZE of this Act (other than section 11ZE(1)) references to the registration of a design include references to the former registration of a design; and these sections shall apply, with necessary modifications, in relation to such former registrations.

11ZB   Applications for declaration of invalidity

(1)   Any person interested may make an application to the registrar for a declaration of invalidity under section 11ZA(1)(a) or (b) of this Act.

(2)   Any person concerned by the use in question may make an application to the registrar for a declaration of invalidity under section 11ZA(1)(c) of this Act.

(3)   The relevant person may make an application to the registrar for a declaration of invalidity under section 11ZA(1A) of this Act.

(4)   In subsection (3) above "the relevant person" means, in relation to an earlier design protected by virtue of registration under this Act or the Community Design Regulation or an application for such registration, the registered proprietor of the design, the holder of the registered Community design or (as the case may be) the applicant.

(5)   The person able to make an objection under subsection (2), (3) or (4) of section 11ZA of this Act may make an application to the registrar for a declaration of invalidity under that subsection.

(6)   An application may be made under this section in relation to a design at any time after the design has been registered.

11ZC   Determination of applications for declaration of invalidity

(1)   This section applies where an application has been made to the registrar for a declaration of invalidity in relation to a registration.

(2)   If it appears to the registrar that the application has not been made in accordance with any rules made under this Act, he may refuse the application.

(3)   If it appears to the registrar that the application has not been made in accordance with section 11ZB of this Act, he shall refuse the application.

(4)   Subject to subsections (2) and (3) above, the registrar shall make a declaration of invalidity if it appears to him that the ground of invalidity specified in the application has been established in relation to the registration.

(5)   Otherwise the registrar shall refuse the application.

(6)   A declaration of invalidity may be a declaration of partial invalidity.

11ZD   Modification of registration

(1)   Subsections (2) and (3) below apply where the registrar intends to declare the registration of a design invalid under section 11ZA(1)(b) or (c), (1A), (3) or (4) of this Act.

(2)   The registrar shall inform the registered proprietor of that fact.

(3)   The registered proprietor may make an application to the registrar for the registrar to make such modifications to the registration of the design as the registered proprietor specifies in his application.

(4)   Such modifications may, in particular, include the inclusion on the register of a partial disclaimer by the registered proprietor.

(5)   If it appears to the registrar that the application has not been made in accordance with any rules made under this Act, the registrar may refuse the application.

(6)   If it appears to the registrar that the identity of the design is not retained or the modified registration would be invalid by virtue of section 11ZA of this Act, the registrar shall refuse the application.

(7)   Otherwise the registrar shall make the specified modifications.

(8)   A modification of a registration made under this section shall have effect, and be treated always to have had effect, from the grant of registration.

11ZE   Effect of cancellation or invalidation of registration

(1)   A cancellation of registration under section 11 of this Act takes effect from the date of the registrar's decision or from such other date as the registrar may direct.

(2)   Where the registrar declares the registration of a design invalid to any extent, the registration shall to that extent be treated as having been invalid from the date of registration or from such other date as the registrar may direct.

11ZF Appeals in relation to cancellation or invalidation
An appeal lies from any decision of the registrar under section 11 to 11ZE of this Act.

11A Powers exercisable for protection of the public interest
(1) Where a report of the Competition and Markets Authority has been laid before Parliament containing conclusions to the effect—

(a), (b) . . .

(c) on a competition reference, that a person was engaged in an anti-competitive practice which operated or may be expected to operate against the public interest, or

(d) on a reference under section 11 of the Competition Act 1980 (reference of public bodies and certain other persons), that a person is pursuing a course of conduct which operates against the public interest,

the appropriate Minister or Ministers may apply to the registrar to take action under this section.

(2) Before making an application the appropriate Minister or Ministers shall publish, in such a manner as he or they think appropriate, a notice describing the nature of the proposed application and shall consider any representations which may be made within 30 days of such publication by persons whose interests appear to him or them to be affected.

(3) If on an application under this section it appears to the registrar that the matters specified in the Commission's report as being those which in the Commission's opinion operate or operated or may be expected to operate against the public interest include—

(a) conditions in licences granted in respect of a registered design by its proprietor restricting the use of the design by the licensee or the right of the proprietor to grant other licences, he may by order cancel or modify any such condition.

(4), (5) . . .

(6) An appeal lies from any order of the registrar under this section.

(7) In this section "the appropriate Minister or Ministers" means the Minister or Ministers to whom the report of the Competition and Markets Authority was made.

11AB Powers exercisable following merger and market investigations
(1) Subsection (2) below applies where—

(a) section 41(2), 55(2), 66(6), 75(2), 83(2), 138(2), 147(2) or 160(2) of, or paragraph 5(2) or 10(2) of Schedule 7 to, the Enterprise Act 2002 (powers to take remedial action following merger or market investigations) applies;

(b) the Competition and Markets Authority or (as the case may be) the Secretary of State considers that it would be appropriate to make an application under this section for the purpose of remedying, mitigating or preventing a matter which cannot be dealt with under the enactment concerned; and

(c) the matter concerned involves conditions in licences granted in respect of a registered design by its proprietor restricting the use of the design by the licensee or the right of the proprietor to grant other licences.

(2) The Competition and Markets Authority or (as the case may be) the Secretary of State may apply to the registrar to take action under this section.

(3) Before making an application the Competition and Markets Authority or (as the case may be) the Secretary of State shall publish, in such manner as it or he thinks appropriate, a notice describing the nature of the proposed application and shall consider any representations which may be made within 30 days of such publication by persons whose interests appear to it or him to be affected.

(4) The registrar may, if it appears to him on an application under this section that the application is made in accordance with this section, by order cancel or modify any condition concerned of the kind mentioned in subsection (1)(c) above.

(5) An appeal lies from any order of the registrar under this section.

(6) References in this section to the Competition and Markets Authority are references to a CMA group except where—

(a) section 75(2) of the Enterprise Act 2002 applies; or

(b)   any other enactment mentioned in subsection (1)(a) above applies and the functions of the Competition and Markets Authority under that enactment are being performed by the CMA Board by virtue of section 34(3)C or 133A(2) of the Enterprise Act 2002.

(7)   References in section 35, 36, 47, 63, 134 or 141 of the Enterprise Act 2002 (questions to be decided by the Competition and Markets Authority in its reports) to taking action under section 41(2), 55, 66, 138 or 147 shall include references to taking action under subsection (2) above.

(8)   An order made by virtue of this section in consequence of action under subsection (2) above where an enactment mentioned in subsection (1)(a) above applies shall be treated, for the purposes of sections 91(3), 92(1)(a), 162(1) and 166(3) of the Enterprise Act 2002 (duties to register and keep under review enforcement orders etc), as if it were made under the relevant power in Part 3 or (as the case may be) 4 of that Act to make an enforcement order (within the meaning of the Part concerned).

(9)   In subsection (6) "CMA Board" and "CMA group" have the same meaning as in Schedule 4 to the Enterprise and Regulatory Reform Act 2013.

12   Use for services of the Crown

The provisions of the First Schedule to this Act shall have effect with respect to the use of registered designs for the services of the Crown and the rights of third parties in respect of such use.

International arrangements

13   Orders in Council as to convention countries

(1)   His Majesty may, with a view to the fulfilment of a treaty, convention, arrangement or engagement, by Order in Council declare that any country specified in the Order is a convention country for the purposes of this Act:

Provided that a declaration may be made as aforesaid for the purposes either of all or of some only of the provisions of this Act, and a country in the case of which a declaration made for the purposes of some only of the provisions of this Act is in force shall be deemed to be a convention country for the purposes of those provisions only.

(2)   His Majesty may by Order in Council direct that any of the Channel Islands, any colony shall be deemed to be a convention country for the purposes of all or any of the provisions of this Act; and an Order made under this subsection may direct that any such provisions shall have effect, in relation to the territory in question, subject to such conditions or limitations, if any, as may be specified in the Order.

(3)   For the purposes of subsection (1) of this section, every colony, protectorate, territory subject to the authority or under the suzerainty of another country, and territory administered by another country under the trusteeship system of the United Nations, shall be deemed to be a country in the case of which a declaration may be made under that subsection.

14   Registration of design where application for protection in convention country has been made

(1)   An application for registration of a design or designs in respect of which protection has been applied for in a convention country may be made in accordance with the provisions of this Act by the person by whom the application for protection was made or his personal representative or assignee:

Provided that no application shall be made by virtue of this section after the expiration of six months from the date of the application for protection in a convention country or, where more than one such application for protection has been made, from the date of the first application.

(2)   Where an application for registration of a design or designs is made by virtue of this section, the application shall be treated, for the purpose of determining whether (and to what extent) that or any other design is new or has individual character, as made on the date of the application for protection in the convention country or, if more than one such application was made, on the date of the first such application.

(3) Subsection (2) shall not be construed as excluding the power to give directions under section 3B(2) or (3) of this Act in relation to an application made by virtue of this section.

(4) Where a person has applied for protection for a design by an application which—

(a) in accordance with the terms of a treaty subsisting between two or more convention countries, is equivalent to an application duly made in any one of those convention countries; or

(b) in accordance with the law of any convention country, is equivalent to an application duly made in that convention country,

he shall be deemed for the purposes of this section to have applied in that convention country.

15 Extension of time for applications under s. 14 in certain cases

(1) If the Secretary of State is satisfied that provision substantially equivalent to the provision to be made by or under this section has been or will be made under the law of any convention country, he may make rules empowering the registrar to extend the time for making application under subsection (1) of section fourteen of this Act for registration of a design in respect of which protection has been applied for in that country in any case where the period specified in the proviso to that subsection expires during a period prescribed by the rules.

(2) Rules made under this section—

(a) may, where any agreement or arrangement has been made between His Majesty's Government in the United Kingdom and the government of the convention country for the supply or mutual exchange of information or products, provide, either generally or in any class of case specified in the rules, that an extension of time shall not be granted under this section unless the design has been communicated in accordance with the agreement or arrangement;

(b) may, either generally or in any class of case specified in the rules, fix the maximum extension which may be granted under this section;

(c) may prescribe or allow any special procedure in connection with applications made by virtue of this section;

(d) may empower the registrar to extend, in relation to an application made by virtue of this section, the time limited by or under the foregoing provisions of this Act for doing any act, subject to such conditions, if any, as may be imposed by or under the rules;

(e) may provide for securing that the rights conferred by registration on an application made by virtue of this section shall be subject to such restrictions or conditions as may be specified by or under the rules and in particular to restrictions and conditions for the protection of persons (including persons acting on behalf of His Majesty) who, otherwise than as the result of a communication made in accordance with such an agreement or arrangement as is mentioned in paragraph (a) of this subsection, and before the date of the application in question or such later date as may be allowed by the rules, may have imported or made products to which the design is applied or in which it is incorporated or may have made an application for registration of the design.

15ZA Accession to the Hague Agreement

(1) The Secretary of State may by order make provision for giving effect in the United Kingdom to the provisions of the Geneva Act of the Hague Agreement Concerning the International Registration of Industrial Designs adopted by the Diplomatic Conference on 2 July 1999.

(2) An order under this section may, in particular, make provision about—

(a) the making of applications for international registrations at the Patent Office;

(b) the procedures to be followed where an international registration designates the United Kingdom;

(c) the effect of an international registration which designates the United Kingdom;

(d) the communication of information to the International Bureau;

(e) the payment of fees.

(3) An order under this section may—
   (a) amend this Act;
   (b) apply specified provisions of this Act with such modifications as may be specified.

(4) An expression used in subsection (2) and in the Agreement referred to in subsection (1) has the same meaning in that subsection as it has in the Agreement.

15B Assignment, &c of registered designs and applications for registered designs

(1) A registered design or an application for a registered design is transmissible by assignment, testamentary disposition or operation of law in the same way as other personal or moveable property, subject to the following provisions of this section.

(2) Any transmission of a registered design or an application for a registered design is subject to any rights vested in any other person of which notice is entered in the register of designs, or in the case of applications, notice is given to the registrar.

(3) An assignment of, or an assent relating to, a registered design or application for a registered design is not effective unless it is in writing signed by or on behalf of the assignor or, as the case may be, a personal representative.

(4) Except in Scotland, the requirement in subsection (3) may be satisfied in a case where the assignor or personal representative is a body corporate by the affixing of its seal.

(5) Subsections (3) and (4) apply to assignment by way of security as in relation to any other assignment.

(6) A registered design or application for a registered design may be the subject of a charge (in Scotland, security) in the same way as other personal or moveable property.

(7) The proprietor of a registered design may grant a licence to use that registered design.

(8) Any equities (in Scotland, rights) in respect of a registered design or an application for a registered design may be enforced in like manner as in respect of any other personal or moveable property.

15C Exclusive licences

(1) In this Act an *"exclusive licence"* means a licence in writing signed by or on behalf of the proprietor of the registered design authorising the licensee to the exclusion of all other persons, including the person granting the licence, to exercise a right which would otherwise be exercisable exclusively by the proprietor of the registered design.

(2) The licensee under an exclusive licence has the same rights against any successor in title who is bound by the licence as he has against the person granting the licence.

17 Register of designs, etc.

(1) The registrar shall maintain the register of designs, in which shall be entered—
   (a) the names and addresses of proprietors of registered designs;
   (b) notices of assignments and of transmissions of registered designs; and
   (c) such other matters as may be prescribed or as the registrar may think fit.

(2) No notice of any trust, whether express, implied or constructive, shall be entered in the register of designs, and the registrar shall not be affected by any such notice.

(3) The register need not be kept in documentary form.

(4) Subject to the provisions of this Act and to rules made by the Secretary of State under it, the public shall have a right to inspect the register at the Patent Office at all convenient times.

. . .

18 Certificate of registration

(1) The registrar shall grant a certificate of registration in the prescribed form to the registered proprietor of a design when the design is registered.

(2) The registrar may, in a case where he is satisfied that the certificate of registration has been lost or destroyed, or in any other case in which he thinks it expedient, furnish one or more copies of the certificate.

19   Registration of assignments, etc.

(1)   Where any person becomes entitled by assignment, transmission or operation of law to a registered design or to a share in a registered design, or becomes entitled as mortgagee, licensee or otherwise to any other interest in a registered design, he shall apply to the registrar in the prescribed manner for the registration of his title as proprietor or co-proprietor or, as the case may be, of notice of his interest, in the register of designs.

(2)   Without prejudice to the provisions of the foregoing subsection, an application for the registration of the title of any person becoming entitled by assignment to a registered design or a share in a registered design, or becoming entitled by virtue of a mortgage, licence or other instrument to any other interest in a registered design, may be made in the prescribed manner by the assignor, mortgagor, licensor or other party to that instrument, as the case may be.

(3)   Where application is made under this section for the registration of the title of any person, the registrar shall, upon proof of title to his satisfaction—

   (a)   where that person is entitled to a registered design or a share in a registered design, register him in the register of designs as proprietor or co-proprietor of the design, and enter in that register particulars of the instrument or event by which he derives title; or

   (b)   where that person is entitled to any other interest in the registered design, enter in that register notice of his interest, with particulars of the instrument (if any) creating it.

. . .

(3B) Where national unregistered design right subsists in a registered design and the proprietor of the registered design is also the design right owner, an assignment of the national unregistered design right shall be taken to be also an assignment of the right in the registered design, unless a contrary intention appears.

(4)   . . .

(5)   Except for the purposes of an application to rectify the register under the following provisions of this Act, a document in respect of which no entry has been made in the register of designs under subsection (3) of this section shall not be admitted in any court as evidence of the title of any person to a registered design or share of or interest in a registered design unless the court otherwise directs.

20   Rectification of register

(1)   The court may, on the application of the relevant person, order the register of designs to be rectified by the making of any entry therein or the variation or deletion of any entry therein.

(1A) In subsection (1) above "the relevant person" means—

   (a)   in the case of an application invoking any ground referred to in section 11ZA(1) (c) of this Act, any person concerned by the use in question;

   (b)   in the case of an application invoking the ground mentioned in section 11ZA(1A) of this Act, the appropriate person;

   (c)   in the case of an application invoking any ground mentioned in section 11ZA(2), (3) or (4) of this Act, the person able to make the objection;

   (d)   in any other case, any person aggrieved.

(1B) In subsection (1A) above "the appropriate person" means, in relation to an earlier design protected by virtue of registration under this Act or the Community Design Regulation or an application for such registration, the registered proprietor of the design, the holder of the registered Community design or (as the case may be) the applicant.

. . .

21   Power to correct clerical errors

(1)   The registrar may, in accordance with the provisions of this section, correct any error in an application for the registration or in the representation of a design, or any error in the register of designs.

. . .

22   Inspection of registered designs [and associated documents]

(1)   Where a design has been registered under this Act, there shall be open to inspection at the Patent Office on and after the day on which the certificate of registration is granted—

(a)   the representation or specimen of the design.

[and

(aa)   every document kept at the Patent Office in connection with that design.]

This subsection has effect subject to *subsection (4)* [subsections (4) to (7)] and to any rules made under section 5(2) of this Act.

. . .

(4)   Where registration of a design has been refused pursuant to an application under this Act, or an application under this Act has been abandoned in relation to any design—

(a)   the application, so far as relating to that design, and

(b)   any representation, specimen or other document which has been filed and relates to that design,

shall not at any time be open to inspection at the Patent Office or be published by the registrar.

[(5)   For the purposes of subsection (1), a document is not to be regarded as open for inspection unless (in addition to being open for inspection in hard copy) it is made available by electronic transmission in such a way that members of the public may access it at a place and time individually chosen by them.

(6)   The Secretary of State may by rules specify cases or circumstances in which a document kept at the Patent Office in connection with a registered design may not be inspected.

(7)   Rules made under subsection (6) may confer a discretion on the registrar.]

Note: Words in italics will be repealed and words in square brackets will be added when the Intellectual Property Act 2014, s 9 comes fully into force.

23   Information as to existence of right in registered design

On the request of a person furnishing such information as may enable the registrar to identify the design, and on payment of the prescribed fee, the registrar shall inform him—

(a)   whether the design is registered, and

(b)   whether any extension of the period of the right in the registered design has been granted, and shall state the date of registration and the name and address of the registered proprietor.

Legal proceedings: general

24A   Action for infringement

(1)   An infringement of the right in a registered design is actionable by the registered proprietor.

(2)   In an action for infringement all such relief by way of damages, injunctions, accounts or otherwise is available to him as is available in respect of the infringement of any other property right.

(3)   This section has effect subject to section 24B of this Act (exemption of innocent infringer from liability).

24B   Exemption of innocent infringer from liability

(1)   In proceedings for the infringement of the right in a registered design damages shall not be awarded against a defendant who proves that at the date of the infringement he was not aware, and had no reasonable ground for supposing, that the design was registered.

(2)   For the purposes of subsection (1), a person shall not be deemed to have been aware or to have had reasonable grounds for supposing that the design was registered by reason only of the marking of a product with—

(a)   the word "registered" or any abbreviation thereof, or

(b)   any word or words expressing or implying that the design applied to, or incorporated in, the product has been registered,

unless the number of the design or a relevant internet link accompanied the word or words or the abbreviation in question.

(2A) The reference in subsection (2) to a relevant internet link is a reference to an address of a posting on the internet—
    (a)   which is accessible to the public free of charge, and
    (b)   which clearly associates the product with the number of the design.
(3)   Nothing in this section shall affect the power of the court to grant an injunction in any proceedings for infringement of the right in a registered design.

24C Order for delivery up

(1)   Where a person—
    (a)   has in his possession, custody or control for commercial purposes an infringing article, or
    (b)   has in his possession, custody or control anything specifically designed or adapted for making articles to a particular design which is a registered design, knowing or having reason to believe that it has been or is to be used to make an infringing article,
the registered proprietor in question may apply to the court for an order that the infringing article or other thing be delivered up to him or to such other person as the court may direct.
(2)   An application shall not be made after the end of the period specified in the following provisions of this section; and no order shall be made unless the court also makes, or it appears to the court that there are grounds for making, an order under section 24D of this Act (order as to disposal of infringing article, etc.).
(3)   An application for an order under this section may not be made after the end of the period of six years from the date on which the article or thing in question was made, subject to subsection (4).
(4)   If during the whole or any part of that period the registered proprietor—
    (a)   is under a disability, or
    (b)   is prevented by fraud or concealment from discovering the facts entitling him to apply for an order,
an application may be made at any time before the end of the period of six years from the date on which he ceased to be under a disability or, as the case may be, could with reasonable diligence have discovered those facts.
(5)   . . .
(6)   A person to whom an infringing article or other thing is delivered up in pursuance of an order under this section shall, if an order under section 24D of this Act is not made, retain it pending the making of an order, or the decision not to make an order, under that section.
(7)   The reference in subsection (1) to an act being done in relation to an article for "commercial purposes" are to its being done with a view to the article in question being sold or hired in the course of a business.
(8)   Nothing in this section affects any other power of the court.

24D Order as to disposal of infringing articles, etc.

(1)   An application may be made to the court for an order that an infringing article or other thing delivered up in pursuance of an order under section 24C of this Act shall be—
    (a)   forfeited to the registered proprietor, or
    (b)   destroyed or otherwise dealt with as the court may think fit,
or for a decision that no such order should be made.
(2)   In considering what order (if any) should be made, the court shall consider whether other remedies available in an action for infringement of the right in a registered design would be adequate to compensate the registered proprietor and to protect his interests.
(3)   Where there is more than one person interested in an article or other thing, the court shall make such order as it thinks just and may (in particular) direct that the thing be sold, or otherwise dealt with, and the proceeds divided.
(4)   If the court decides that no order should be made under this section, the person in whose possession, custody or control the article or other thing was before being delivered up is entitled to its return.

(5)   References in this section to a person having an interest in an article or other thing include any person in whose favour an order could be made in respect of it—

(a)   under this section;

(b)   under section 19 of Trade Marks Act 1994 (including that section as applied by regulation 4 of the Community Trade Mark Regulations 2006);

(c)   under section 114, 204 or 231 of the Copyright, Designs and Patents Act 1988; or

(d)   under regulation 1C of the Community Design Regulations 2005.

24F   Rights and remedies of exclusive licensee

(1)   In relation to a registered design, an exclusive licensee has, except against the registered proprietor, the same rights and remedies in respect of matters occurring after the grant of the licence as if the licence had been an assignment.

(2)   His rights and remedies are concurrent with those of the registered proprietor; and references to the registered proprietor in the provisions of this Act relating to infringement shall be construed accordingly.

(3)   In an action brought by an exclusive licensee by virtue of this section a defendant may avail himself of any defence which would have been available to him if the action had been brought by the registered proprietor.

(4)   Where an action for infringement of the right in a registered design brought by the registered proprietor or an exclusive licensee relates (wholly or partly) to an infringement in respect of which they have concurrent rights of action, the proprietor or, as the case may be, the exclusive licensee may not, without the leave of the court, proceed with the action unless the other is either joined as a claimant or added as a defendant.

(5)   A registered proprietor or exclusive licensee who is added as a defendant in pursuance of subsection (4) is not liable for any costs in the action unless he takes part in the proceedings.

(6)   Subsections (4) and (5) do not affect the granting of interlocutory relief on the application of the registered proprietor or an exclusive licensee.

(7)   Where an action for infringement of the right in a registered design is brought which relates (wholly or partly) to an infringement in respect of which the registered proprietor and an exclusive licensee have concurrent rights of action—

(a)   the court shall, in assessing damages, take into account—

(i)   the terms of the licence, and

(ii)   any pecuniary remedy already awarded or available to either of them in respect of the infringement;

(b)   no account of profits shall be directed if an award of damages has been made, or an account of profits has been directed, in favour of the other of them in respect of the infringement; and

(c)   the court shall if an account of profits is directed apportion the profits between them as the court considers just, subject to any agreement between them; and

these provisions apply whether or not the proprietor and the exclusive licensee are both parties to the action.

(8)   The registered proprietor shall notify any exclusive licensee having concurrent rights before applying for an order under section 24C of this Act (order for delivery up of infringing article, etc.); and the court may on the application of the licensee make such order under that section as it thinks fit having regard to the terms of the licence.

24G   Meaning of "infringing article"

(1)   In this Act "infringing article", in relation to a design, shall be construed in accordance with this section.

(2)   An article is an infringing article if its making to that design was an infringement of the right in a registered design.

(3)   An article is also an infringing article if—

(a)   it has been or is proposed to be imported into the United Kingdom, and

(b)   its making to that design in the United Kingdom would have been an infringement of the right in a registered design or a breach of an exclusive licensing agreement relating to that registered design.

(4) Where it is shown that an article is made to a design which is or has been a registered design, it shall be presumed until the contrary is proved that the article was made at a time when the right in the registered design subsisted.

(5) Nothing in subsection (3) shall be construed as applying to an article which may be lawfully imported into the United Kingdom by virtue of an enforceable EU right within the meaning of section 2(1) of the European Communities Act 1972.

Legal proceedings and appeals

25 Certificate of contested validity of registration

(1) If in any proceedings before the court the validity of the registration of a design is contested, and it is found by the court that the design is, to any extent, validly registered, the court may certify that the validity of the registration of the design was contested in those proceedings.

(2) Where any such certificate has been granted, then if in any subsequent proceedings before the court for infringement of the right in the registered design or for invalidation of the registration of the design, a final order or judgment is made or given in favour of the registered proprietor, he shall, unless the court otherwise directs, be entitled to his costs as between solicitor and client:

Provided that this subsection shall not apply to the costs of any appeal in any such proceedings as aforesaid.

Unjustified threats

26 Threats of infringement proceedings

(1) A communication contains a "threat of infringement proceedings" if a reasonable person in the position of a recipient would understand from the communication that—
   (a) a registered design exists, and
   (b) a person intends to bring proceedings (whether in a court in the United Kingdom or elsewhere) against another person for infringement of the right in the registered design by—
      (i) an act done in the United Kingdom, or
      (ii) an act which, if done, would be done in the United Kingdom.

(2) References in this section and in section 26C to a "recipient" include, in the case of a communication directed to the public or a section of the public, references to a person to whom the communication is directed.

26A Actionable threats

(1) Subject to subsections (2) to (5), a threat of infringement proceedings made by any person is actionable by any person aggrieved by the threat.

(2) A threat of infringement proceedings is not actionable if the infringement is alleged to consist of—
   (a) making a product for disposal, or
   (b) importing a product for disposal.

(3) A threat of infringement proceedings is not actionable if the infringement is alleged to consist of an act which, if done, would constitute an infringement of a kind mentioned in subsection (2)(a) or (b).

(4) A threat of infringement proceedings is not actionable if the threat—
   (a) is made to a person who has done, or intends to do, an act mentioned in subsection (2)(a) or (b) in relation to a product, and
   (b) is a threat of proceedings for an infringement alleged to consist of doing anything else in relation to that product.

(5) A threat of infringement proceedings which is not an express threat is not actionable if it is contained in a permitted communication.

(6) In sections 26C and 26D an "actionable threat" means a threat of infringement proceedings that is actionable in accordance with this section.

26B Permitted communications

(1) For the purposes of section 26A(5), a communication containing a threat of infringement proceedings is a "permitted communication" if—

    (a) the communication, so far as it contains information that relates to the threat, is made for a permitted purpose;

    (b) all of the information that relates to the threat is information that—

        (i) is necessary for that purpose (see subsection (5)(a) to (c) for some examples of necessary information), and

        (ii) the person making the communication reasonably believes is true.

(2) Each of the following is a "permitted purpose"—

    (a) giving notice that a registered design exists;

    (b) discovering whether, or by whom, the right in a registered design has been infringed by an act mentioned in section 26A(2)(a) or (b);

    (c) giving notice that a person has a right in or under a registered design, where another person's awareness of the right is relevant to any proceedings that may be brought in respect of the registered design.

(3) The court may, having regard to the nature of the purposes listed in subsection (2)(a) to (c), treat any other purpose as a "permitted purpose" if it considers that it is in the interests of justice to do so.

(4) But the following may not be treated as a "permitted purpose"—

    (a) requesting a person to cease doing, for commercial purposes, anything in relation to a product in which a design is incorporated or to which it is applied,

    (b) requesting a person to deliver up or destroy a product in which a design is incorporated or to which it is applied, or

    (c) requesting a person to give an undertaking relating to a product in which a design is incorporated or to which it is applied.

(5) If any of the following information is included in a communication made for a permitted purpose, it is information that is "necessary for that purpose" (see subsection (1)(b)(i))—

    (a) a statement that a right in a registered design exists and is in force or that an application for registration of a design has been made;

    (b) details of the registered design, or of a right in or under the right in the registered design, which—

        (i) are accurate in all material respects, and

        (ii) are not misleading in any material respect; and

    (c) information enabling the identification of the products in which the registered design is allegedly incorporated or to which the registered design is allegedly applied.

26C Remedies and defences

(1) Proceedings in respect of an actionable threat may be brought against the person who made the threat for—

    (a) a declaration that the threat is unjustified;

    (b) an injunction against the continuance of the threat;

    (c) damages in respect of any loss sustained by the aggrieved person by reason of the threat.

(2) It is a defence for the person who made the threat to show that the act in respect of which proceedings were threatened constitutes (or if done would constitute) an infringement of the right in the registered design.

(3) It is a defence for the person who made the threat to show—

    (a) that, despite having taken reasonable steps, the person has not identified anyone who has done an act mentioned in section 26A(2)(a) or (b) in relation to the product which is the subject of the threat, and

    (b) that the person notified the recipient, before or at the time of making the threat, of the steps taken.

26D Professional advisers

(1) Proceedings in respect of an actionable threat may not be brought against a professional adviser (or any person vicariously liable for the actions of that professional adviser) if the conditions in subsection (3) are met.

(2) In this section "professional adviser" means a person who, in relation to the making of the communication containing the threat—

    (a) is acting in a professional capacity in providing legal services or the services of a trade mark attorney or a patent attorney, and

    (b) is regulated in the provision of legal services, or the services of a trade mark attorney or a patent attorney, by one or more regulatory bodies (whether through membership of a regulatory body, the issue of a licence to practise or any other means).

(3) The conditions are that—

    (a) in making the communication the professional adviser is acting on the instructions of another person, and

    (b) when the communication is made the professional adviser identifies the person on whose instructions the adviser is acting.

(4) This section does not affect any liability of the person on whose instructions the professional adviser is acting.

(5) It is for a person asserting that subsection (1) applies to prove (if required) that at the material time—

    (a) the person concerned was acting as a professional adviser, and

    (b) the conditions in subsection (3) were met.

26E Supplementary: pending registration

(1) In sections 26 and 26B references to a registered design include references to a design in respect of which an application for registration has been made under section 3.

(2) Where the threat of infringement proceedings is made after an application for registration has been made (but before registration) the reference in section 26C(2) to "the registered design" is to be treated as a reference to the design registered in pursuance of that application.

26F Supplementary: proceedings for delivery up etc.

In section 26(1)(b) the reference to proceedings for infringement of the right in a registered design includes a reference to—

(a) proceedings for an order under section 24C (order for delivery up), and

(b) proceedings for an order under section 24D (order as to disposal of infringing articles).

Meaning of "the court" and appeals

27 The court

(1) In this Act "the court" means—

    (a) in England and Wales the High Court (subject to section 27A(6)),

    (b) in Scotland, the Court of Session, and

    (c) in Northern Ireland, the High Court.

. . .

27A Appeals from decisions of registrar

(1) An appeal against a decision of the registrar under this Act may be made to—

    (a) a person appointed by the Lord Chancellor (an "appointed person"), or

    (b) the court.

(2) On an appeal under this section to an appointed person, the appointed person may refer the appeal to the court if—

    (a) it appears to the appointed person that a point of general legal importance is involved,

    (b) the registrar requests that the appeal be so referred, or

    (c) such a request is made by any party to the proceedings before the registrar in which the decision appealed against was made.

(3) Before referring an appeal to the court under subsection (2), the appointed person must give the appellant and any other party to the appeal an opportunity to make representations as to whether it should be so referred.

(4)   Where, on an appeal under this section to an appointed person, the appointed person does not refer the appeal to the court—
      (a)   the appointed person must hear and determine the appeal, and
      (b)   the appointed person's decision is final.

(5)   Sections 30 and 31 (costs, evidence) apply to proceedings before an appointed person as they apply to proceedings before the registrar.

(6)   In the application of this section to England and Wales, *"the court"* means the High Court.

Offences

33   Offences under s 5

(1)   If any person fails to comply with any direction given under section five of this Act or makes or causes to be made an application for the registration of a design in contravention of that section, he shall be guilty of an offence and liable—
      (a)   on conviction on indictment to imprisonment for a term not exceeding two years or a fine, or both;
      (b)   on summary conviction to imprisonment for a term not exceeding six months or a fine not exceeding the statutory maximum, or both.

35   Fine for falsely representing a design as registered

(1)   If any person falsely represents that a design applied to, or incorporated in, any product sold by him is registered, he shall be liable on summary conviction to a fine not exceeding level 3 on the standard scale; and for the purposes of this provision a person who sells a product having stamped, engraved or impressed thereon or otherwise applied thereto the word "registered", or any other word expressing or implying that the design applied to, or incorporated in, the product is registered, shall be deemed to represent that the design applied to, or incorporated in, the product is registered.

(2)   If any person, after the right in a registered design has expired, marks any product to which the design has been applied or in which it has been incorporated with the word "registered", or any word or words implying that there is a subsisting right in the design under this Act, or causes any such product to be so marked, he shall be liable on summary conviction to a fine not exceeding level 1 on the standard scale.

(3)   For the purposes of this section, the use in the United Kingdom in relation to a design—
      (a)   of the word "registered", or
      (b)   of any other word or symbol importing a reference (express or implied) to registration,
shall be deemed to be a representation as to registration under this Act unless it is shown that the reference is to registration elsewhere than in the United Kingdom and that the design is in fact so registered.

35ZA   Offence of unauthorised copying etc. of design in course of business

(1)   A person commits an offence if—
      (a)   in the course of a business, the person intentionally copies a registered design so as to make a product—
          (i)   exactly to that design, or
          (ii)   with features that differ only in immaterial details from that design, and
      (b)   the person does so—
          (i)   knowing, or having reason to believe, that the design is a registered design, and
          (ii)   without the consent of the registered proprietor of the design.

(2)   Subsection (3) applies in relation to a product where a registered design has been intentionally copied so as to make the product—
      (a)   exactly to the design, or
      (b)   with features that differ only in immaterial details from the design.

(3)   A person commits an offence if—
      (a)   in the course of a business, the person offers, puts on the market, imports, exports or uses the product, or stocks it for one or more of those purposes,

    (b)   the person does so without the consent of the registered proprietor of the design, and

    (c)   the person does so knowing, or having reason to believe, that—

        (i)   a design has been intentionally copied without the consent of the registered proprietor so as to make the product exactly to the design or with features that differ only in immaterial details from the design, and

        (ii)   the design is a registered design.

(4)   It is a defence for a person charged with an offence under this section to show that the person reasonably believed that the registration of the design was invalid.

(5)   It is also a defence for a person charged with an offence under this section to show that the person—

    (a)   did not infringe the right in the design, or

    (b)   reasonably believed that the person did not do so.

(6)   The reference in subsection (3) to using a product in the course of a business does not include a reference to using it for a purpose which is merely incidental to the carrying on of the business.

(7)   In this section "registered design" includes a registered Community design; and a reference to the registered proprietor is, in the case of a registered Community design, to be read as a reference to the holder.

(8)   A person guilty of an offence under this section is liable—

    (a)   on conviction on indictment, to imprisonment for a term not exceeding ten years or to a fine or to both;

    (b)   on summary conviction in England and Wales or Northern Ireland, to imprisonment for a term not exceeding six months or to a fine not exceeding the statutory maximum or to both;

    (c)   on summary conviction in Scotland, to imprisonment for a term not exceeding 12 months or to a fine not exceeding the statutory maximum or to both.

35ZB Section 35ZA: enforcement

(1A)   For the investigatory powers available to a local weights and measures authority or the Department of Enterprise, Trade and Investment in Northern Ireland for the purposes of the enforcement of section 35ZA, see Schedule 5 to the Consumer Rights Act 2015.

(2)   Any enactment which authorises the disclosure of information for the purpose of facilitating the enforcement of the Trade Descriptions Act 1968 applies—

    (a)   as if section 35ZA were a provision of that Act, and

    (b)   as if the functions of any person in relation to the enforcement of that section were functions under that Act.

(3)   Nothing in this section is to be construed as authorising a local weights and measures authority to bring proceedings in Scotland.

35ZC Section 35ZA: forfeiture in England and Wales or Northern Ireland

(1)   In England and Wales or Northern Ireland, a person who, in connection with the investigation or prosecution of an offence under section 35ZA, has come into the possession of relevant products or articles may apply under this section for an order for the forfeiture of the products or articles.

(2)   "Relevant product" means a product which is made exactly to a registered design, or with features that differ only in immaterial details from a registered design, by copying that design intentionally.

(3)   "Relevant article" means an article which is specifically designed or adapted for making copies of a registered design intentionally.

(4)   An application under this section may be made—

    (a)   where proceedings have been brought in any court for an offence under section 35ZA relating to some or all of the products or articles, to that court;

    (b)   where no application for the forfeiture of the products or articles has been made under paragraph (a), by way of complaint to a magistrates' court.

(5)   On an application under this section, the court may make an order for the forfeiture of products or articles only if it is satisfied that an offence under section 35ZA has been committed in relation to the products or articles.

(6)   A court may infer for the purposes of this section that such an offence has been committed in relation to any products or articles if it is satisfied that such an offence has been committed in relation to products or articles which are representations of them (whether by reason of being of the same design or part of the same consignment or batch or otherwise).

(7)   Any person aggrieved by an order made under this section by a magistrates' court, or by a decision of such a court not to make such an order, may appeal against that order or decision—
   (a)   in England and Wales, to the Crown Court;
   (b)   in Northern Ireland, to the county court.

(8)   An order so made may contain such provision as appears to the court to be appropriate for delaying the coming into force of the order pending the making and determination of any appeal (including any application under section 111 of the Magistrates' Courts Act 1980 or Article 146 of the Magistrates' Courts (Northern Ireland) Order 1981).

(9)   Subject to subsection (10), any products or articles forfeited under this section are to be destroyed in accordance with such directions as the court may give.

(10) On making an order under this section, the court may, if it considers it appropriate to do so, direct that the products or articles to which the order relates shall (instead of being destroyed) be released to such person and on such conditions as the court may specify.

35ZD Section 35ZA: forfeiture in Scotland

(1)   In Scotland, the court may make an order for the forfeiture of any relevant products or articles (as defined by section 35ZC).

(2)   An order under this section may be made—
   (a)   on an application by the procurator fiscal made in the manner specified in section 134 of the Criminal Procedure (Scotland) Act 1995, or
   (b)   where a person is convicted of an offence under section 35ZA, in addition to any other penalty which the court may impose.

(3)   On an application under subsection (2)(a), the court may make an order for the forfeiture of relevant products or articles only if it is satisfied that an offence under section 35ZA has been committed in relation to the relevant products or articles.

(4)   The court may infer for the purposes of this section that such an offence has been committed in relation to any relevant products or articles which are representative of them (whether by reason of being of the same design or part of the same consignment or batch or otherwise).

. . .

35A Offence by body corporate: liability of officers

(1)   Where an offence under this Act committed by a body corporate is proved to have been committed with the consent or connivance of a director, manager, secretary or other similar officer of the body, or a person purporting to act in any such capacity, he as well as the body corporate is guilty of the offence and liable to be proceeded against and punished accordingly.

(2)   In relation to a body corporate whose affairs are managed by its members "director" means a member of the body corporate.

(3)   Proceedings for an offence under this Act alleged to have been committed by a partnership are to be brought against the partnership in the name of the firm and not in that of the partners; but without prejudice to any liability of the partners under subsection (6) or (7).

. . .

(5)   A fine imposed on a partnership (other than a Scottish partnership) on its conviction in such proceedings must be paid out of the partnership assets.

(6)   Where a partnership (other than a Scottish partnership) is guilty of an offence under this Act, every partner, other than a partner who is proved to have been ignorant of or to have attempted to prevent the commission of the offence, is also guilty of the offence and liable to be proceeded against and punished accordingly.

(7)   Where an offence under this Act committed by a Scottish partnership is proved to have been committed with the consent or connivance of a partner in the partnership, or a person purporting to act in that capacity, he as well as the partnership is guilty of the offence and liable to be proceeded against and punished accordingly.

43   Savings

(1)   . . .

(2)   Nothing in this Act shall affect the right of the Crown or of any person deriving title directly or indirectly from the Crown to sell or use products forfeited under the laws relating to customs or excise.

44   Interpretation

(1)   In this Act, except where the context otherwise requires, the following expressions have the meanings hereby respectively assigned by them, that is to say—

"assignee" includes the personal representative of a deceased assignee, and references to the assignee of any person include references to the assignee of the personal representative or assignee of that person;

"author" in relation to a design, has the meaning given by section 2(3) and (4);

"Community Design Regulation" means Council Regulation (EC) 6/2002 of 12th December 2001 on Community Designs;

"complex product" has the meaning assigned to it by section 1(3) of this Act;

"the court" shall be construed in accordance with section 27 of this Act;

"design" has the meaning assigned to it by section 1(2) of this Act;

"electronic communication" has the same meaning as in the Electronic Communications Act 2000;

"employee", "employment" and "employer" refer to employment under a contract of service or of apprenticeship,

"national unregistered design right" means design right within the meaning of Part III of the Copyright, Designs and Patents Act 1988;

"prescribed" means prescribed by rules made by the Secretary of State under this Act;

"product" has the meaning assigned to it by section 1(3) of this Act;

"proprietor" has the meaning assigned to it by section two of this Act;

"registered Community design" means a design that complies with the conditions contained in, and is registered in the manner provided for in, the Community Design Regulation;

"registered proprietor" means the person or persons for the time being entered in the register of designs as proprietor of the design;

"registrar" means the Comptroller-General of Patents Designs and Trade Marks;

. . .

(4)   For the purposes of subsection (1) of section 14 of this Act, the expression "personal representative", in relation to a deceased person, includes the legal representative of the deceased appointed in any country outside the United Kingdom.

45   Application to Scotland

(1)   In the application of this Act to Scotland—

"account of profits" means accounting and payment of profits;

"accounts" means count, reckoning and payment;

"arbitrator" means arbiter;

"assignment" means assignation;

"claimant" means pursuer;

"costs" means expenses;

"defendant" means defender;

"delivery up" means delivery;

"injunction" means interdict;

"interlocutory relief" means interim remedy.

(1A) In the application of section 26C(1)(a) (remedy for unjustified threat of infringement proceedings) to Scotland, "declaration" means "declarator".

(2)   References to the Crown shall be construed as including references to the Crown in right of the Scottish Administration.

46   Application to Northern Ireland
In the application of this Act to Northern Ireland
(1), (2) . . .
(3)   References to enactments include enactments comprised in Northern Ireland legislation:
(3A) References to the Crown include the Crown in right of Her Majesty's Government in Northern Ireland:
(4)   References to a Government department shall be construed as including references to a Northern Ireland department and in relation to a Northern Ireland department references to the Treasury shall be construed as references to the Department of Finance and Personnel:
(4A) Any reference to a claimant includes a reference to a plaintiff.

47   Application to Isle of Man
This Act extends to the Isle of Man, subject to any modifications contained in an Order made by Her Majesty in Council, and accordingly, subject to any such Order, references in this Act to the United Kingdom shall be construed as including the Isle of Man.

47A   Territorial waters and the continental shelf
(1)   For the purposes of this Act the territorial waters of the United Kingdom shall be treated as part of the United Kingdom.
(2)   This Act applies to things done in the United Kingdom sector of the continental shelf on a structure or vessel which is present there for purposes directly connected with the exploration of the sea bed or subsoil or the exploitation of their natural resources as it applies to things done in the United Kingdom.
(3)   The United Kingdom sector of the continental shelf means the areas designated by order under section 1(7) of the Continental Shelf Act 1964.
. . .

SCHEDULE A1

Grounds for refusal of registration in relation to emblems etc.

1.   (1)   A design shall be refused registration under this Act if it involves the use of—
        (a)   the Royal arms, or any of the principal armorial bearings of the Royal arms, or any insignia or device so nearly resembling the Royal arms or any such armorial bearing as to be likely to be mistaken for them or it;
        (b)   a representation of the Royal crown or any of the Royal flags;
        (c)   a representation of Her Majesty or any member of the Royal family, or any colourable imitation thereof; or
        (d)   words, letters or devices likely to lead persons to think that the applicant either has or recently has had Royal patronage or authorisation;
        unless it appears to the registrar that consent for such use has been given by or on behalf of Her Majesty or (as the case may be) the relevant member of the Royal family.
        (2)   A design shall be refused registration under this Act if it involves the use of—
        (a)   the national flag of the United Kingdom (commonly known as the Union Jack); or
        (b)   the flag of England, Wales, Scotland, Northern Ireland or the Isle of Man,
        and it appears to the registrar that the use would be misleading or grossly offensive.
        (3)   A design shall be refused registration under this Act if it involves the use of—
        (a)   arms to which a person is entitled by virtue of a grant of arms by the Crown; or
        (b)   insignia so nearly resembling such arms as to be likely to be mistaken for them;
              unless it appears to the registrar that consent for such use has been given by or on behalf of the person concerned and the use is not in any way contrary to the law of arms.
        (4)   A design shall be refused registration under this Act if it involves the use of a controlled representation within the meaning of the Olympic Symbol etc (Protection) Act 1995 unless it appears to the registrar that—
        (a)   the application is made by the person for the time being appointed under section 1(2) of the Olympic Symbol etc (Protection) Act 1995 (power of Secretary of State to appoint a person as the proprietor of the Olympics association right); or

      (b)   consent for such use has been given by or on behalf of the person mentioned in paragraph (a) above.

Grounds for refusal in relation to emblems etc. of Paris Convention countries

2.   (1)   A design shall be refused registration under this Act if it involves the use of the flag of a Paris Convention country unless—
        (a)   the authorisation of the competent authorities of that country has been given for the registration; or
        (b)   it appears to the registrar that the use of the flag in the manner proposed is permitted without such authorisation.

    (2)   A design shall be refused registration under this Act if it involves the use of the armorial bearings or any other state emblem of a Paris Convention country which is protected under the Paris Convention unless the authorisation of the competent authorities of that country has been given for the registration.

    (3)   A design shall be refused registration under this Act if—
        (a)   the design involves the use of an official sign or hallmark adopted by a Paris Convention country and indicating control and warranty;
        (b)   the sign or hallmark is protected under the Paris Convention; and
        (c)   the design could be applied to or incorporated in goods of the same, or a similar, kind as those in relation to which the sign or hallmark indicates control and warranty;
        unless the authorisation of the competent authorities of that country has been given for the registration.

    (4)   The provisions of this paragraph as to national flags and other state emblems, and official signs or hallmarks, apply equally to anything which from a heraldic point of view imitates any such flag or other emblem, or sign or hallmark.

    (5)   Nothing in this paragraph prevents the registration of a design on the application of a national of a country who is authorised to make use of a state emblem, or official sign or hallmark, of that country, notwithstanding that it is similar to that of another country.

Grounds for refusal in relation to emblems etc. of certain international organisations

3.   (1)   This paragraph applies to—
        (a)   the armorial bearings, flags or other emblems; and
        (b)   the abbreviations and names,
        of international intergovernmental organisations of which one or more Paris Convention countries are members.

    (2)   A design shall be refused registration under this Act if it involves the use of any such emblem, abbreviation or name which is protected under the Paris Convention unless—
        (a)   the authorisation of the international organisation concerned has been given for the registration; or
        (b)   it appears to the registrar that the use of the emblem, abbreviation or name in the manner proposed—
            (i)   is not such as to suggest to the public that a connection exists between the organisation and the design; or
            (ii)   is not likely to mislead the public as to the existence of a connection between the user and the organisation.

    (3)   The provisions of this paragraph as to emblems of an international organisation apply equally to anything which from a heraldic point of view imitates any such emblem.

    (4)   Nothing in this paragraph affects the rights of a person whose bona fide use of the design in question began before 4th January 1962 (when the relevant provisions of the Paris Convention entered into force in relation to the United Kingdom).

Paragraphs 2 and 3: supplementary

4.   (1)   For the purposes of paragraph 2 above state emblems of a Paris Convention country (other than the national flag), and official signs or hallmarks, shall be regarded as protected under the Paris Convention only if, or to the extent that—
        (a)   the country in question has notified the United Kingdom in accordance with Article 6*ter*(3) of the Convention that it desires to protect that emblem, sign or hallmark;

    (b)   the notification remains in force; and

    (c)   the United Kingdom has not objected to it in accordance with Article 6*ter*(4) or any such objection has been withdrawn.

(2)   For the purposes of paragraph 3 above the emblems, abbreviations and names of an international organisation shall be regarded as protected under the Paris Convention only if, or to the extent that—

    (a)   the organisation in question has notified the United Kingdom in accordance with Article 6*ter*(3) of the Convention that it desires to protect that emblem, abbreviation or name;

    (b)   the notification remains in force; and

    (c)   the United Kingdom has not objected to it in accordance with Article 6*ter*(4) or any such objection has been withdrawn.

(3)   Notification under Article 6*ter*(3) of the Paris Convention shall have effect only in relation to applications for the registration of designs made more than two months after the receipt of the notification.

Interpretation

5.   In this Schedule—

"a Paris Convention country" means a country, other than the United Kingdom, which is a party to the Paris Convention; and

"the Paris Convention" means the Paris Convention for the Protection of Industrial Property of 20th March 1883.

FIRST SCHEDULE
PROVISIONS AS TO THE USE OF REGISTERED DESIGNS FOR THE SERVICES OF THE CROWN AND AS TO THE RIGHTS OF THIRD PARTIES IN RESPECT OF SUCH USE

Use of registered designs for services of the Crown

1.   (1)   Notwithstanding anything in this Act, any Government department, and any person authorised in writing by a Government department, may use any registered design for the services of the Crown in accordance with the following provisions of this paragraph.

    (2)   If and so far as the design has before the date of registration thereof been duly recorded by or applied by or on behalf of a Government department otherwise than in consequence of the communication of the design directly or indirectly by the registered proprietor or any person from whom he derives title, any use of the design by virtue of this paragraph may be made free of any royalty or other payment to the registered proprietor.

    (3)   If and so far as the design has not been so recorded or applied as aforesaid, any use of the design made by virtue of this paragraph at any time after the date of registration thereof, or in consequence of any such communication as aforesaid, shall be made upon such terms as may be agreed upon, either before or after the use, between the Government department and the registered proprietor with the approval of the Treasury, or as may in default of agreement be determined by the court on a reference under paragraph 3 of this Schedule.

    (4)   The authority of a Government department in respect of a design may be given under this paragraph either before or after the design is registered and either before or after the acts in respect of which the authority is given are done, and may be given to any person whether or not he is authorised directly or indirectly by the registered proprietor to use the design.

    (5)   Where any use of a design is made by or with the authority of a Government department under this paragraph, then, unless it appears to the department that it would be contrary to the public interest so to do, the department shall notify the registered proprietor as soon as practicable after the use is begun, and furnish him with such information as to the extent of the use as he may from time to time require.

    (6)   For the purposes of this and the next following paragraph "the services of the Crown" shall be deemed to include—

(a) the supply to the government of any country outside the United Kingdom, in pursuance of an agreement or arrangement between Her Majesty's Government in the United Kingdom and the government of that country, of products required —

(i) for the defence of that country; or

(ii) for the defence of any other country whose government is party to any agreement or arrangement with Her Majesty's said Government in respect of defence matters;

(b) the supply to the United Nations, or to the government of any country belonging to that organisation, in pursuance of an agreement or arrangement between Her Majesty's Government and that organisation or government, of products required for any armed forces operating in pursuance of a resolution of that organisation or any organ of that organisation;

and the power of a Government department or a person authorised by a Government department under this paragraph to use a design shall include power to sell to any such government or to the said organisation any products the supply of which is authorised by this sub-paragraph, and to sell to any person any products made in the exercise of the powers conferred by this paragraph which are no longer required for the purpose for which they were made.

(7) The purchaser of any products sold in the exercise of powers conferred by this paragraph, and any person claiming through him, shall have power to deal with them in the same manner as if the rights in the registered design were held on behalf of His Majesty.

Rights of third parties in respect of Crown use

2. (1) In relation to any use of a registered design, or a design in respect of which an application for registration is pending, made for the services of the Crown —

(a) by a Government department or a person authorised by a Government department under the last foregoing paragraph; or

(b) by the registered proprietor or applicant for registration to the order of a Government department,

the provisions of any licence, assignment or agreement made, whether before or after the commencement of this Act, between the registered proprietor or applicant for registration or any person who derives title from him or from whom he derives title and any person other than a Government department shall be of no effect so far as those provisions restrict or regulate the use of the design, or any model, document or information relating thereto, or provide for the making of payments in respect of any such use, or calculated by reference thereto; and the reproduction or publication of any model or document in connection with the said use shall not be deemed to be an infringement of any copyright or national unregistered design right subsisting in the model or document.

(2) Where an exclusive licence granted otherwise than for royalties or other benefits determined by reference to the use of the design is in force under the registered design then —

(a) in relation to any use of the design which, but for the provisions of this and the last foregoing paragraph, would constitute an infringement of the rights of the licensee, sub-paragraph (3) of the last foregoing paragraph shall have effect as if for the reference to the registered proprietor there were substituted a reference to the licensee; and

(b) in relation to any use of the design by the licensee by virtue of an authority given under the last foregoing paragraph, that paragraph shall have effect as if the said sub-paragraph (3) were omitted.

(3) Subject to the provisions of the last foregoing sub-paragraph, where the registered design or the right to apply for or obtain registration of the design has been assigned to the registered proprietor in consideration of royalties or other benefits determined by reference to the use of the design, then —

(a) in relation to any use of the design by virtue of paragraph 1 of this Schedule, sub-paragraph (3) of that paragraph shall have effect as if the reference to the registered proprietor included a reference to the assignor, and any sum payable by virtue of that sub-paragraph shall be divided between the registered proprietor and the assignor in such proportion as may be agreed upon between them or as may in default of agreement be determined by the court on a reference under the next following paragraph; and

(b)   in relation to any use of the design made for the services of the Crown by the registered proprietor to the order of a Government department, sub-paragraph (3) of paragraph 1 of this Schedule shall have effect as if that use were made by virtue of an authority given under that paragraph.

(4)   Where, under sub-paragraph (3) of paragraph 1 of this Schedule, payments are required to be made by a Government department to a registered proprietor in respect of any use of a design, any person being the holder of an exclusive licence under the registered design (not being such a licence as is mentioned in sub-paragraph (2) of this paragraph) authorising him to make that use of the design shall be entitled to recover from the registered proprietor such part (if any) of those payments as may be agreed upon between that person and the registered proprietor, or as may in default of agreement be determined by the court under the next following paragraph to be just having regard to any expenditure incurred by that person—

(a)   in developing the said design; or

(b)   in making payments to the registered proprietor, other than royalties or other payments determined by reference to the use of the design, in consideration of the licence;

and if, at any time before the amount of any such payment has been agreed upon between the Government department and the registered proprietor, that person gives notice in writing of his interest to the department, any agreement as to the amount of that payment shall be of no effect unless it is made with his consent.

(5)   In this paragraph "exclusive licence" means a licence from a registered proprietor which confers on the licensee, or on the licensee and persons authorised by him, to the exclusion of all other persons (including the registered proprietor), any right in respect of the registered design.

Compensation for loss of profit

2A.   (1)   Where Crown use is made of a registered design, the government department concerned shall pay—

(a)   to the registered proprietor, or

(b)   if there is an exclusive licence in force in respect of the design, to the exclusive licensee,

compensation for any loss resulting from his not being awarded a contract to supply the products to which the design is applied or in which it is incorporated.

(2)   Compensation is payable only to the extent that such a contract could have been fulfilled from his existing manufacturing capacity; but is payable notwithstanding the existence of circumstances rendering him ineligible for the award of such a contract.

(3)   In determining the loss, regard shall be had to the profit which would have been made on such a contract and to the extent to which any manufacturing capacity was underused.

(4)   No compensation is payable in respect of any failure to secure contracts for the supply of products to which the design is applied or in which it is incorporated otherwise than for the services of the Crown.

(5)   The amount payable under this paragraph shall, if not agreed between the registered proprietor or licensee and the government department concerned with the approval of the Treasury, be determined by the court on a reference under paragraph 3; and it is in addition to any amount payable under paragraph 1 or 2 of this Schedule.

(6)   In this paragraph—

"Crown use", in relation to a design, means the doing of anything by virtue of paragraph 1 which would otherwise be an infringement of the right in the design; and

"the government department concerned", in relation to such use, means the government department by whom or on whose authority the act was done.

Reference of disputes as to Crown use

3.　(1)　Any dispute as to—

(a)　the exercise by a Government department, or a person authorised by a Government department, of the powers conferred by paragraph 1 of this Schedule,

(b)　terms for the use of a design for the services of the Crown under that paragraph,

(c)　the right of any person to receive any part of a payment made under paragraph 1(3), or

(d)　the right of any person to receive a payment under paragraph 2A,

may be referred to the court by either party to the dispute.

(2)　In any proceedings under this paragraph to which a Government department are a party, the department may—

(a)　if the registered proprietor is a party to the proceedings and the department are a relevant person within the meaning of section 20 of this Act, apply for invalidation of the registration of the design upon any ground upon which the registration of a design may be declared invalid on an application to the court under section twenty of this Act;

(b)　in any case and provided that the department would be the relevant person within the meaning of section 20 of this Act if they had made an application on the grounds for invalidity being raised, put in issue the validity of the registration of the design without applying for its invalidation.

(3)　If in such proceedings as aforesaid any question arises whether a design has been recorded or applied as mentioned in paragraph 1 of this Schedule, and the disclosure of any document recording the design, or of any evidence of the application thereof, would in the opinion of the department be prejudicial to the public interest, the disclosure may be made confidentially to counsel for the other party or to an independent expert mutually agreed upon.

(4)　In determining under this paragraph any dispute between a Government department and any person as to terms for the use of a design for the services of the Crown, the court shall have regard to any benefit or compensation which that person or any person from whom he derives title may have received, or may be entitled to receive, directly or indirectly from any Government department in respect of the design in question.

(5)　In any proceedings under this paragraph the court may at any time order the whole proceedings or any question or issue of fact arising therein to be referred to a special or official referee or an arbitrator on such terms as the court may direct; and references to the court in the foregoing provisions of this paragraph shall be construed accordingly.

Special provisions as to Crown use during emergency

4.　(1)　During any period of emergency within the meaning of this paragraph, the powers exercisable in relation to a design by a Government department, or a person authorised by a Government department under paragraph 1 of this Schedule shall include power to use the design for any purpose which appears to the department necessary or expedient—

(a)　for the efficient prosecution of any war in which His Majesty may be engaged;

(b)　for the maintenance of supplies and services essential to the life of the community;

(c)　for securing a sufficiency of supplies and services essential to the well-being of the community;

(d)　for promoting the productivity of industry, commerce and agriculture;

(e)　for fostering and directing exports and reducing imports, or imports of any classes, from all or any countries and for redressing the balance of trade;

(f)　generally for ensuring that the whole resources of the community are available for use, and are used, in a manner best calculated to serve the interests of the community; or

(g)　for assisting the relief of suffering and the restoration and distribution of essential supplies and services in any part of His Majesty's dominions or any foreign countries that are in grave distress as the result of war;

and any reference in this Schedule to the services of the Crown shall be construed as including a reference to the purposes aforesaid.

. . .

DURATION OF COPYRIGHT AND RIGHTS IN PERFORMANCES REGULATIONS 1995
(SI 1995 No. 3297)

PART I
INTRODUCTORY PROVISIONS

1   Citation, commencement and extent
(1) These Regulations may be cited as the Duration of Copyright and Rights in Performances Regulations 1995.
(2) These Regulations come into force on 1st January 1996.
(3) These Regulations extend to the whole of the United Kingdom.

2   Interpretation
In these Regulations—
"EEA Agreement" means the Agreement on the European Economic Area signed at Oporto on 2nd May 1992, as adjusted by the Protocol signed at Brussels on 17th March 1993; and
"EEA state" means a member state, Iceland, Liechtenstein or Norway.

3   Implementation of Directive, etc.
These Regulations make provision for the purpose of implementing—
(a) the main provisions of Council Directive No. 93/98/EEC of 29th October 1993 harmonizing the term of protection of copyright and certain related rights; and
(b) certain obligations of the United Kingdom created by or arising under the EEA Agreement so far as relevant to the implementation of that Directive.

4   Scheme of the regulations
The Copyright, Designs and Patents Act 1988 is amended in accordance with the provisions of Part II of these Regulations, subject to the savings and transitional provisions in Part III of these Regulations.

PART III
SAVINGS AND TRANSITIONAL PROVISIONS

Introductory

12   Introductory
(1) References in this Part to "commencement", without more, are to the date on which these Regulations come into force.
(2) In this Part—
"the 1988 Act" means the Copyright, Designs and Patents Act 1988;
"the 1988 provisions" means the provisions of that Act as they stood immediately before commencement (including the provisions of Schedule 1 to that Act continuing the effect of earlier enactments); and
"the new provisions" means the provisions of that Act as amended by these Regulations.
(3) Expressions used in this Part which are defined for the purposes of Part I or II of the 1988 Act, in particular references to the copyright owner, have the same meaning as in that Part.

13   Films not protected as such
In relation to a film in which copyright does not or did not subsist as such but which is or was protected—
(a) as an original dramatic work, or
(b) by virtue of the protection of the photographs forming part of the film,
references in the new provisions, and in this Part, to copyright in a film are to any copyright in the film as an original dramatic work or, as the case may be, in photographs forming part of the film.

Copyright

14   Copyright: interpretation

(1)   In the provisions of this Part relating to copyright—
    (a)   "existing", in relation to a work, means made before commencement; and
    (b)   "existing copyright work" means a work in which copyright subsisted immediately before commencement.

(2)   For the purposes of those provisions a work of which the making extended over a period shall be taken to have been made when its making was completed.

(3)   References in those provisions to "moral rights" are to the rights conferred by Chapter IV of Part I of the 1988 Act.

15   Duration of copyright: general saving

(1)   Copyright in an existing copyright work shall continue to subsist until the date on which it would have expired under the 1988 provisions if that date is later than the date on which copyright would expire under the new provisions.

(2)   Where paragraph (1) has effect, section 57 of the 1988 Act (anonymous or pseudonymous works: acts permitted on assumptions as to expiry of copyright or death of author) applies as it applied immediately before commencement (that is, without the amendments made by Regulation 5(2)).

16   Duration of copyright: application of new provisions

The new provisions relating to duration of copyright apply—
(a)   to copyright works made after commencement;
(b)   to existing works which first qualify for copyright protection after commencement;
(c)   to existing copyright works, subject to Regulation 15 (general saving for any longer period applicable under 1988 provisions);
(d)   to existing works in which copyright expired before 31st December 1995 but which were on 1st July 1995 protected in another EEA state under legislation relating to copyright or related rights; and
(e)   to existing works which qualify for copyright protection as a result of the disapplication of paragraph 6(1) of Schedule 1 to the 1988 Act by sub-paragraph (1A) of paragraph 6 of Schedule 1 to the 1988 Act.

17   Extended and revived copyright

In the following provisions of this Part—
"extended copyright" means any copyright which subsists by virtue of the new provisions after the date on which it would have expired under the 1988 provisions; and
"revived copyright" means any copyright which subsists by virtue of the new provisions after having expired under the 1988 provisions or any earlier enactment relating to copyright.

18   Ownership of extended copyright

(1)   The person who is the owner of the copyright in a work immediately before commencement is as from commencement the owner of any extended copyright in the work, subject as follows.

(2)   If he is entitled to copyright for a period less than the whole of the copyright period under the 1988 provisions, any extended copyright is part of the reversionary interest expectant on the termination of that period.

19   Ownership of revived copyright

(1)   The person who was the owner of the copyright in a work immediately before it expired (the "former copyright owner") is as from commencement the owner of any revived copyright in the work, subject as follows.

(2)   If the former copyright owner has died before commencement, or in the case of a legal person has ceased to exist before commencement, the revived copyright shall vest—
    (a)   in the case of a film, in the principal director of the film or his personal representatives, and
    (b)   in any other case, in the author of the work or his personal representatives.

(3)   Where revived copyright vests in personal representatives by virtue of paragraph (2), it shall be held by them for the benefit of the person who would have been entitled to it had it been vested in the principal director or author immediately before his death and had devolved as part of his estate.

20   Prospective ownership of extended or revived copyright

(1)   Where by an agreement made before commencement in relation to extended or revived copyright, and signed by or on behalf of the prospective owner of the copyright, the prospective owner purports to assign the extended or revived copyright (wholly or partially) to another person, then if, on commencement the assignee or another person claiming under him would be entitled as against all other persons to require the copyright to be vested in him, the copyright shall vest in the assignee or his successor in title by virtue of this paragraph.

(2)   A licence granted by a prospective owner of extended or revived copyright is binding on every successor in title to his interest (or prospective interest) in the right, except a purchaser in good faith for valuable consideration and without notice (actual or constructive) of the licence or a person deriving title from such a purchaser; and references in Part I of the 1988 Act to doing anything with, or without, the licence of the copyright owner shall be construed accordingly.

(3)   In paragraph (2) "prospective owner" includes a person who is prospectively entitled to extended or revived copyright by virtue of such an agreement as is mentioned in paragraph (1).

21   Extended copyright: existing licences, agreement, etc.

(1)   Any copyright licence, any term or condition of an agreement relating to the exploitation of a copyright work, or any waiver or assertion of moral rights, which—

     (a)   subsists immediately before commencement in relation to an existing copyright work, and

     (b)   is not to expire before the end of the copyright period under the 1988 provisions,

   shall continue to have effect during the period of any extended copyright, subject to any agreement to the contrary.

(2)   Any copyright licence, or term or condition relating to the exploitation of a copyright work, imposed by order of the Copyright Tribunal which—

     (a)   subsists immediately before commencement in relation to an existing copyright work, and

     (b)   is not to expire before the end of the copyright period under the 1988 provisions,

   shall continue to have effect during the period of any extended copyright, subject to any further order of the Tribunal.

22   Revived copyright: exercise of moral rights

(1)   The following provisions have effect with respect to the exercise of moral rights in relation to a work in which there is revived copyright.

(2)   Any waiver or assertion of moral rights which subsisted immediately before the expiry of copyright shall continue to have effect during the period of revived copyright.

(3)   Moral rights are exercisable after commencement by the author of a work or, as the case may be, the director of a film in which revived copyright subsists, as with any other copyright work.

(4)   Where the author or director died before commencement—

     (a)   the rights conferred by—

        section 77 (right to identification as author or director),

        section 80 (right to object to derogatory treatment of work), or

        section 85 (right to privacy of certain photographs and films),

        are exercisable after commencement by his personal representatives, and

     (b)   any infringement after commencement of the right conferred by section 84 (false attribution) is actionable by his personal representatives.

(5)   Any damages recovered by personal representatives by virtue of this Regulation in respect of an infringement after a person's death shall devolve as part of his estate as if the right of action had subsisted and been vested in him immediately before his death.

(6)   Nothing in these Regulations shall be construed as causing a moral right to be exercisable if, or to the extent that, the right was excluded by virtue of paragraph 23 or 24 of Schedule 1 on the commencement of the 1988 Act or would have been so excluded if copyright had not previously expired.

23   Revived copyright: saving for acts of exploitation when work in public domain, etc.

(1)   No act done before commencement shall be regarded as infringing revived copyright in a work.

(2)   It is not an infringement of revived copyright in a work—

   (a)   to do anything after commencement in pursuance of arrangements made before 1st January 1995 at a time when copyright did not subsist in the work, or

   (b)   to issue to the public after commencement copies of the work made before 1st July 1995 at a time when copyright did not subsist in the work.

(3)   It is not an infringement of revived copyright in a work to do anything after commencement in relation to a literary, dramatic, musical or artistic work or a film made before commencement, or made in pursuance of arrangements made before commencement, which contains a copy of that work or is an adaptation of that work if—

   (a)   the copy or adaptation was made before 1st July 1995 at a time when copyright did not subsist in the work in which revived copyright subsists, or

   (b)   the copy or adaptation was made in pursuance of arrangements made before 1st July 1995 at a time when copyright did not subsist in the work in which revived copyright subsists.

(4)   It is not an infringement of revived copyright in a work to do after commencement anything which is a restricted act in relation to the work if the act is done at a time when, or is done in pursuance of arrangements made at a time when, the name and address of a person entitled to authorise the act cannot by reasonable inquiry be ascertained.

(5)   In this Regulation "arrangements" means arrangements for the exploitation of the work in question.

(6)   It is not an infringement of any moral right to do anything which by virtue of this Regulation is not an infringement of copyright.

. . .

26   Film sound tracks: application of new provisions

(1)   The new provisions relating to the treatment of film sound tracks apply to existing sound tracks as from commencement.

(2)   The owner of any copyright in a film has as from commencement corresponding rights as copyright owner in any existing sound track treated as part of the film; but without prejudice to any rights of the owner of the copyright in the sound track as a sound recording.

(3)   Anything done before commencement under or in relation to the copyright in the sound recording continues to have effect and shall have effect, so far as concerns the sound track, in relation to the film as in relation to the sound recording.

(4)   It is not an infringement of the copyright in the film (or of any moral right in the film) to do anything after commencement in pursuance of arrangements for the exploitation of the sound recording made before commencement.

Rights in performances

27   Rights in performances: interpretation

(1)   In the provisions of this Part relating to rights in performances—

   (a)   "existing", in relation to a performance, means given before commencement; and

(b)   "existing protected performance" means a performance in relation to which rights under Part II of the 1988 act (rights in performances) subsisted immediately before commencement.

(2)   References in this Part to performers' rights are to the rights given by section 180(1)(a) of the 1988 Act and references to recording rights are to the rights given by section 180(1)(b) of that Act.

28   Duration of rights in performances: general saving

Any rights under Part II of the 1988 Act in an existing protected performance shall continue to subsist until the date on which they would have expired under the 1988 provisions if that date is later than the date on which the rights would expire under the new provisions.

29   Duration of rights in performances: application of new provisions

The new provisions relating to the duration of rights under Part II of the 1988 Act apply—

(a)   to performances taking place after commencement;

(b)   to existing performances which first qualify for protection under Part II of the 1988 Act after commencement;

(c)   to existing protected performances, subject to Regulation 28 (general saving for any longer period applicable under 1988 provisions); and

(d)   to existing performances—

(i)   in which rights under Part II of the 1988 Act expired after the commencement of that Part and before 31st December 1995, or

(ii)   which were protected by earlier enactments relating to the protection of performers and in which rights under that Part did not arise by reason only that the performance was given at a date such that the rights would have ceased to subsist before the commencement of that Part,

but which were on 1st July 1995 protected in another EEA state under legislation relating to copyright or related rights.

30   Extended and revived performance rights

In the following provisions of this Part—

"extended performance rights" means rights under Part II of the 1988 Act which subsist by virtue of the new provisions after the date on which they would have expired under the 1988 provisions; and

"revived performance rights" means rights under Part II of the 1988 Act which subsist by virtue of the new provisions—

(a)   after having expired under the 1988 provisions, or

(b)   in relation to a performance which was protected by earlier enactments relating to the protection of performers and in which rights under that Part did not arise by reason only that the performance was given at a date such that the rights would have ceased to subsist before the commencement of that Part.

References in the following provisions of this Part to "revived pre-1988 rights" are to revived performance rights within paragraph (b) of the above definition.

31   Entitlement to extended or revived performance rights

(1)   Any extended performance rights are exercisable as from commencement by the person who was entitled to exercise those rights immediately before commencement, that is—

(a)   in the case of performers' rights, the performer or (if he has died) the person entitled by virtue of section 192(2) of the 1988 Act to exercise those rights;

(b)   in the case of recording rights, the person who was within the meaning of section 185 of the 1988 Act the person having those rights.

(2)   Any revived performance rights are exercisable as from commencement—

(a)   in the case of rights which expired after the commencement of the 1988 Act, by the person who was entitled to exercise those rights immediately before they expired;

(b)   in the case of revived pre-1988 performers' rights, by the performer or his personal representatives;

(c)   in the case of revived pre-1988 recording rights, by the person who would have been the person having those rights immediately before the commencement of the 1988 Act or, if earlier, immediately before the death of the performer, applying the provisions of section 185 of that Act to the circumstances then obtaining.

(3)   Any remuneration or damages received by a person's personal representatives by virtue of a right conferred on them by paragraph (1) or (2) shall devolve as part of that person's estate as if the right had subsisted and been vested in him immediately before his death.

32   Extended performance rights: existing consents, agreement, etc.

Any consent, or any term or condition of an agreement, relating to the exploitation of an existing protected performance which—

(a)   subsists immediately before commencement, and

(b)   is not to expire before the end of the period for which rights under Part II of the 1988 Act subsist in relation to that performance,

shall continue to subsist during the period of any extended performance rights, subject to any agreement to the contrary.

33   Revived performance rights: saving for acts of exploitation when performance in public domain, etc.

(1)   No act done before commencement shall be regarded as infringing revived performance rights in a performance.

(2)   It is not an infringement of revived performance rights in a performance—

(a)   to do anything after commencement in pursuance of arrangements made before 1st January 1995 at a time when the performance was not protected, or

(b)   to issue to the public after commencement a recording of a performance made before 1st July 1995 at a time when the performance was not protected.

(3)   It is not an infringement of revived performance rights in a performance to do anything after commencement in relation to a sound recording or film made before commencement, or made in pursuance of arrangements made before commencement, which contains a recording of the performance if—

(a)   the recording of the performance was made before 1st July 1995 at a time when the performance was not protected, or

(b)   the recording of the performance was made in pursuance of arrangements made before 1st July 1995 at a time when the performance was not protected.

(4)   It is not an infringement of revived performance rights in a performance to do after commencement anything at a time when, or in pursuance of arrangements made at a time when, the name and address of a person entitled to authorise the act cannot by reasonable inquiry be ascertained.

(5)   In this Regulation "arrangements" means arrangements for the exploitation of the performance in question.

(6)   References in this Regulation to a performance being protected are—

(a)   in relation to the period after the commencement of the 1988 Act, to rights under Part II of that Act subsisting in relation to the performance, and

(b)   in relation to earlier periods, to the consent of the performer being required under earlier enactments relating to the protection of performers.

. . .

Supplementary

36   Construction of references to EEA states

(1)   For the purpose of the new provisions relating to the term of copyright protection applicable to a work of which the country of origin is not an EEA state and of which the author is not a national of an EEA state—

(a)   a work first published before 1st July 1995 shall be treated as published in an EEA state if it was on that date regarded under the law of the United Kingdom or another EEA state as having been published in that state;

   (b)   an unpublished film made before 1st July 1995 shall be treated as originating in an EEA state if it was on that date regarded under the law of the United Kingdom or another EEA state as a film whose maker had his headquarters in, or was domiciled or resident in, that state; and

   (c)   the author of a work made before 1st July 1995 shall be treated as an EEA national if he was on that date regarded under the law of the United Kingdom or another EEA state as a national of that state.

The references above to the law of another EEA state are to the law of that state having effect for the purposes of rights corresponding to those provided for in Part I of the 1988 Act.

(2)   For the purposes of the new provisions relating to the term of protection applicable to a performance where the performer is not a national of an EEA state, the performer of a performance given before 1st July 1995 shall be treated as an EEA national if he was on that date regarded under the law of the United Kingdom or another EEA state as a national of that state.

The reference above to the law of another EEA state is to the law of that state having effect for the purposes of rights corresponding to those provided for in Part II of the 1988 Act.

(3)   In this Regulation "another EEA state" means an EEA state other than the United Kingdom.

COPYRIGHT AND RELATED RIGHTS REGULATIONS 1996
(SI 1996 No. 2967)

PART I
INTRODUCTORY PROVISIONS

1   Citation, commencement and extent

(1)   These Regulations may be cited as the Copyright and Related Rights Regulations 1996.

(2)   These Regulations come into force on 1st December 1996.

(3)   These Regulations extend to the whole of the United Kingdom.

2   Interpretation

In these Regulations—

"EEA Agreement" means the Agreement on the European Economic Area signed at Oporto on 2nd May 1992, as adjusted by the Protocol signed at Brussels on 17th March 1993; and

"EEA state" means a member state, Iceland, Liechtenstein or Norway.

3   Implementation of Directives, etc.

These Regulations make provision for the purpose of implementing—

(a)   Council Directive No. 92/100/EEC of 19 November 1992 on rental right and lending right and on certain rights related to copyright in the field of intellectual property;

(b)   Council Directive No. 93/83/EEC of 27 September 1993 on the coordination of certain rules concerning copyright and rights related to copyright applicable to satellite broadcasting and cable retransmission;

(c)   the provisions of Council Directive No. 93/98/EEC of 29 October 1993 harmonizing the term of protection of copyright and certain related rights, so far as not implemented by the Duration of Copyright and Rights in Performances Regulations 1995; and

(d)   certain obligations of the United Kingdom created by or arising under the EEA Agreement so far as relevant to the implementation of those Directives.

4   Scheme of the regulations

The Copyright, Designs, and Patents Act 1988 is amended in accordance with the provisions of Part II of these Regulations, subject to the savings and transitional provisions in Part III of these Regulations.

PART II

AMENDMENTS OF THE COPYRIGHT, DESIGNS AND PATENTS ACT 1988

Publication right

16 Publication right

(1) A person who after the expiry of copyright protection, publishes for the first time a previously unpublished work has, in accordance with the following provisions, a property right ("publication right") equivalent to copyright.

(2) For this purpose publication includes any making available to the public, in particular—

    (a) the issue of copies to the public;

    (b) making the work available by means of an electronic retrieval system;

    (c) the rental or lending of copies of the work to the public;

    (d) the performance, exhibition or showing of the work in public; or

    (e) communicating the work to the public.

(3) No account shall be taken for this purpose of any unauthorised act.

In relation to a time when there is no copyright in the work, an unauthorised act means an act done without the consent of the owner of the physical medium in which the work is embodied or on which it is recorded.

(4) A work qualifies for publication right protection only if—

    (a) first publication is in the European Economic Area, and

    (b) the publisher of the work is at the time of first publication a national of an EEA state. Where two or more persons jointly publish the work, it is sufficient for the purposes of paragraph (b) if any of them is a national of an EEA state.

(5) No publication right arises from the publication of a work in which Crown copyright or Parliamentary copyright subsisted.

(6) Publication right expires at the end of the period of 25 years from the end of the calendar year in which the work was first published.

(7) In this regulation and regulation 17A a "work" means a literary, dramatic, musical or artistic work or a film.

(8) Expressions used in this regulation (other than "publication") have the same meaning as in Part I.

17 Application of copyright provisions to publication right

(1) The substantive provisions of Part I relating to copyright (but not moral rights in copyright works), that is, the relevant provisions of—

Chapter II (rights of copyright owner),

Chapter III (acts permitted in relation to copyright works),

Chapter V (dealings with rights in copyright works),

Chapter VII (remedies for infringement), and

Chapter VII (copyright licensing),

apply in relation to publication right as in relation to copyright, subject to the following exceptions and modifications.

(2) The following provisions do not apply—

    (a) in Chapter III (acts permitted in relation to copyright works), sections 57, 64, 66A and 67;

    (b) in Chapter VI (remedies for infringement), sections 104 to 106;

    (c) in Chapter VII (copyright licensing), section 116(4).

(3) The following provisions have effect with the modifications indicated—

    (a) in section 107(4) and (5) (offences of making or dealing in infringing articles, etc.), the maximum punishment on summary conviction is imprisonment for a term not exceeding three months or a fine not exceeding level 5 on the standard scale, or both;

    (b) in sections 116(2), 117 and 124 for "works of more than one author" substitute "works of more than one publisher".

(4) The other relevant provisions of Part I, that is—

in Chapter I, provisions defining expressions used generally in Part I

Chapter VIII (the Copyright Tribunal),

in Chapter IX—

    section 161 (territorial waters and the continental shelf), and

    sections 162 (British ships, aircraft and hovercraft), and in Chapter X—

section 171(1) and (3) (savings for other rules of law, etc.), and

sections 172 to 179 (general interpretation provisions),

apply, with any necessary adaptations, for the purposes of supplementing the substantive provisions of that Part as applied by this regulation.

(5) Except where the context otherwise requires, any other enactment relating to copyright (whether passed or made before or after these regulations) applies in relation to publication right as in relation to copyright.

In this paragraph "enactment" includes an enactment contained in subordinate legislation with the meaning of the Interpretation Act 1978.

17A Presumptions relevant to works subject to publication right

In proceedings brought by virtue of Chapter 6 of Part 1 of the Copyright, Designs and Patents Act 1988, as applied to publication right by regulation 17, with respect to a work, where copies of the work as issued to the public bear a statement that a named person was the owner of publication right in the work at the date of issue of the copies, the statement shall be admissible as evidence of the fact stated and shall be presumed to be correct until the contrary is proved.

17B Application of presumptions in relation to an order for delivery up in criminal proceedings

Regulation 17A does not apply to proceedings for an offence under section 107 of the Copyright, Designs and Patents Act 1988 as applied and modified by regulation 17 in relation to publication right; but without prejudice to its application in proceedings for an order under section 108 of the Copyright, Designs and Patents Act 1988 as that section applies to publication right by virtue of regulation 17.

PART III

TRANSITIONAL PROVISIONS AND SAVINGS

General provisions

25 Introductory

(1) In this Part—

"commencement" means the commencement of these Regulations; and

"existing", in relation to a work or performance, means made or given before commencement.

(2) For the purposes of this Part a work of which the making extended over a period shall be taken to have been made when its making was completed.

(3) In this Part a "new right" means a right arising by virtue of these Regulations, in relation to a copyright work or a qualifying performance, to authorise or prohibit an act.

The expression does not include—

(a) a right corresponding to a right which existed immediately before commencement, or

(b) a right to remuneration arising by virtue of these Regulations.

(4) Expressions used in this Part have the same meaning in relation to copyright as they have in Part I of the Copyright, Designs and Patents Act 1988 , and in relation to performances as in Part II of that Act.

26 General rules

(1) Subject to anything in regulations 28 to 36 (special transitional provisions and savings), these regulations apply to copyright works made, and to performances given, before or after commencement.

(2) No act done before commencement shall be regarded as an infringement of any new right, or as giving rise to any right to remuneration arising by virtue of these Regulations.

27 Saving for certain existing agreements

(1) Except as otherwise expressly provided, nothing in these Regulations affects an agreement made before 19th November 1992.

(2)   No act done in pursuance of any such agreement after commencement shall be regarded as an infringement of any new right.

Special provisions

28   Broadcasts

The provisions of—

regulation 5 (place where broadcast treated as made) and

regulation 6 (safeguards in relation to certain satellite broadcasts),

have effect in relation to broadcasts made after commencement.

29   Satellite broadcasting: international co-production agreements

(1)   This regulation applies to an agreement concluded before 1st January 1995—

    (a)   between two or more co-producers of a film, one of whom is a national of an EEA state, and

    (b)   the provisions of which grant to the parties exclusive rights to exploit all communication to the public of the film in separate geographical areas.

(2)   Where such an agreement giving such exclusive exploitation rights in relation to the United Kingdom does not expressly or by implication address satellite broadcasting from the United Kingdom, the person to whom those exclusive rights have been granted shall not make any such broadcast without the consent of any other party to the agreement whose language-related exploitation rights would be adversely affected by that broadcast.

30   New rights: exercise of rights in relation to performances

(1)   Any new right conferred by these Regulations in relation to a qualifying performance is exercisable as from commencement by the performer or (if he has died) by the person who immediately before commencement was entitled by virtue of section 192(2) to exercise the rights conferred on the performer by Part II in relation to that performance.

(2)   Any remuneration or damages received by a person's personal representatives by virtue of a right conferred on them by paragraph (1) shall devolve as part of that person's estate as if the right had subsisted and been vested in him immediately before his death.

31   New rights: effect of pre-commencement authorisation of copying

Where before commencement—

(a)   the owner or prospective owner of copyright in a literary, dramatic, musical or artistic work has authorised a person to make a copy of the work, or

(b)   the owner or prospective owner of performers' rights in a performance has authorised a person to make a copy of a recording of the performance, any new right in relation to that copy shall vest on commencement in the person so authorised, subject to any agreement to the contrary.

32   New rights: effect of pre-commencement film production agreement

(1)   Sections 93A and 191F (presumption of transfer of rental right in case of production agreement) apply in relation to an agreement concluded before commencement. As section 93A so applies, the restriction in subsection (3) of that section shall be omitted (exclusion of presumption in relation to screenplay, dialogue or music specifically created for the film).

(2)   Sections 93B and 191G (right to equitable remuneration where rental right transferred) have effect accordingly, but subject to regulation 33 (right to equitable remuneration applicable to rental after 1st April 1997).

33   Right to equitable remuneration applicable to rental after 1st April 1997

No right to equitable remuneration under section 93B or 191G (right to equitable remuneration where rental right transferred) arises—

(a)   in respect of any rental of a sound recording or film before 1st April 1997, or

(b)   in respect of any rental after that date of a sound recording or film made in pursuance of an agreement entered into before 1st July 1994, unless the author or performer (or a successor in title of his) has before 1st January 1997 notified the person by whom the remuneration would be payable that he intends to exercise that right.

34   Savings for existing stocks

(1)   Any new right in relation to a copyright work does not apply to a copy of the work acquired by a person before commencement for the purpose of renting or lending it to the public.

(2)   Any new right in relation to a qualifying performance does not apply to a copy of a recording of the performance acquired by a person before commencement for the purpose of renting or lending it to the public .

35   Lending of copies by libraries or archives

Until the making of regulations under section 37 of the Copyright, Designs and Patents Act 1988 for the purposes of section 40A(2) of that Act (lending of copies by libraries or archives), the reference in section 40A(2) (and in paragraph 6B of Schedule 2) to a prescribed library or archive shall be construed as a reference to any library or archive in the United Kingdom prescribed by paragraphs 2 to 6 of Part A of Schedule 1 to the Copyright (Librarians and Archivists) (Copying of Copyright Material) Regulations 1989 .

36   Authorship of films

(1)   Regulation 18 (authorship of films) applies as from commencement in relation to films made on or after 1st July 1994.

(2)   It is not an infringement of any right which the principal director has by virtue of these Regulations to do anything after commencement in pursuance of arrangements for the exploitation of the film made before 19th November 1992.

This does not affect any right of his to equitable remuneration under section 93B.

COMMUNITY DESIGN REGULATIONS 2005
(SI 2005 No. 2339)

1   Introductory and interpretation

(1)   These Regulations may be cited as the Community Design Regulations 2005 . . .

(2)   In these Regulations—

"Community design court" means a court designated as such by the Community Designs (Designation of Community Design Courts) Regulations 2005;

"the Community Design Regulation" means Council Regulation (EC) 6/2002 of 12th December 2001 on Community Designs;

"Community design", "registered Community design" and "unregistered Community design" have the same meanings as in the Community Design Regulation; and

"international registration" has the same meaning as in Articles 106a to 106f of the Community Design Regulation.

(3)   In addition, references to a Community design and a registered Community design include a reference to a design protected by virtue of an international registration designating the European Union.

1A   Infringement proceedings

(1)   . . .

(2)   Subject to paragraphs (3) to (5), in an action for infringement of a Community design all such relief by way of damages, injunctions, accounts or otherwise is available to the holder of the Community design as is available in respect of the infringement of any other property right.

(3)   In an action for the infringement of the right in a registered Community design damages shall not be awarded against a person who proves that at the date of the infringement they were not aware, and had no reasonable ground for supposing, that the design was registered.

(4)   For the purpose of paragraph (3), a person shall not be deemed to have been aware or to have had reasonable grounds for supposing that the design was registered by reason only of the marking of a product with—

(a)   the word "registered" or any abbreviation of that word, or

(b)   any word or words expressing or implying that the design applied to, or incorporated in, the product has been registered, unless the number of the design accompanied the word or words or the abbreviation in question.

(5)   In an action for the infringement of an unregistered Community design, damages shall not be awarded against a person who proves that at the date of the infringement that they were not aware, and had no reason to believe, that the design to which the action relates was protected as an unregistered Community design.

1B   Order for delivery up

(1)   Where a person—

    (a)   has in his possession, custody or control for commercial purposes an infringing article, or

    (b)   has in his possession, custody or control anything specifically designed or adapted for making articles to a particular design which is a Community design, knowing or having reason to believe that it has been or is to be used to make an infringing article,

the holder of the Community design in question may apply to the Community design court for an order that the infringing article or other thing be delivered up to him or to such other person as the court may direct.

. . .

(3)   An application for an order under this regulation may not be made after the end of the period of six years from the date on which the article or thing in question was made, subject to paragraph (4).

(4)   If during the whole or any part of that period the holder of the Community design—

    (a)   is under a disability, or

    (b)   is prevented by fraud or concealment from discovering the facts entitling him to apply for an order,

an application may be made at any time before the end of the period of six years from the date on which he ceased to be under a disability or, as the case may be, could with reasonable diligence have discovered those facts.

. . .

(6)   A person to whom an infringing article or other thing is delivered up in pursuance of an order under this regulation shall, if an order under regulation 1C is not made, retain it pending the making of an order, or the decision not to make an order, under that regulation.

(7)   The reference in paragraph (1) to an act being done in relation to an article for "commercial purposes" are to its being done with a view to the article in question being sold or hired in the course of a business.

1C   Order as to disposal of infringing articles, &c

(1)   An application may be made to the Community design court for an order that an infringing article or other thing delivered up in pursuance of an order under regulation 1B shall be—

    (a)   forfeited to the holder of the Community design, or

    (b)   destroyed or otherwise dealt with as the court may think fit,

or for a decision that no such order should be made.

(2)   In considering what order (if any) should be made, the court shall consider whether other remedies available in an action for infringement of the right in a Community design would be adequate to compensate the holder and to protect his interests.

(3)   Where there is more than one person interested in an article or other thing, the court shall make such order as it thinks just and may (in particular) direct that the thing be sold, or otherwise dealt with, and the proceeds divided.

(4)   If the court decides that no order should be made under this regulation, the person in whose possession, custody or control the article or other thing was before being delivered up is entitled to its return.

. . .

1D   Meaning of "infringing article"

(1)   In these Regulations "infringing article", in relation to a design, shall be construed in accordance with this regulation.

(2) An article is an infringing article if its making to that design was an infringement of a Community design.

(3) An article is also an infringing article if—

    (a) it has been or is proposed to be imported into the United Kingdom, and

    (b) its making to that design in the United Kingdom would have been an infringement of a Community design or a breach of an exclusive licensing agreement relating to that Community design.

(4) Where it is shown that an article is made to a design which is or has been a Community design, it shall be presumed until the contrary is proved that the article was made at a time when the right in the Community design subsisted.

(5) Nothing in paragraph (3) shall be construed as applying to an article which may be lawfully imported into the United Kingdom by virtue of an enforceable EU right within the meaning of section 2(1) of the European Communities Act 1972.

2 Unjustified threats: threats of infringement proceedings

(1) A communication contains a "threat of infringement proceedings" if a reasonable person in the position of a recipient would understand from the communication that—

    (a) a Community design exists, and

    (b) a person intends to bring proceedings (whether in a court in the United Kingdom or elsewhere) against another person for infringement of the Community design by—

        (i) an act done in the United Kingdom, or

        (ii) an act which, if done, would be done in the United Kingdom.

(2) References in this regulation and in regulation 2C to a "recipient" include, in the case of a communication directed to the public or a section of the public, references to a person to whom the communication is directed.

2A Unjustified threats: actionable threats

(1) Subject to paragraphs (2) to (5), a threat of infringement proceedings made by any person is actionable by any person aggrieved by the threat.

(2) A threat of infringement proceedings is not actionable if the infringement is alleged to consist of—

    (a) making an article for disposal, or

    (b) importing an article for disposal.

(3) A threat of infringement proceedings is not actionable if the infringement is alleged to consist of an act which, if done, would constitute an infringement of a kind mentioned in paragraph (2)(a) or (b).

(4) A threat of infringement proceedings is not actionable if the threat—

    (a) is made to a person who has done, or intends to do, an act mentioned in paragraph (2)(a) or (b) in relation to an article, and

    (b) is a threat of proceedings for an infringement alleged to consist of doing anything else in relation to that article.

(5) A threat of infringement proceedings which is not an express threat is not actionable if it is contained in a permitted communication.

(6) In regulations 2C and 2D an "actionable threat" means a threat of infringement proceedings that is actionable in accordance with this regulation.

2B Unjustified threats: permitted communications

(1) For the purposes of regulation 2A(5), a communication containing a threat of infringement proceedings is a "permitted communication" if—

    (a) the communication, so far as it contains information that relates to the threat, is made for a permitted purpose;

    (b) all of the information that relates to the threat is information that—

        (i) is necessary for that purpose (see paragraph (5)(a) to (c) for some examples of necessary information), and

        (ii) the person making the communication reasonably believes is true.

(2) Each of the following is a "permitted purpose"—

    (a) giving notice that a Community design exists;

    (b) discovering whether, or by whom, a Community design has been infringed by an act mentioned in regulation 2A(2)(a) or (b);

(c)　giving notice that a person has a right in or under a Community design, where another person's awareness of the right is relevant to any proceedings that may be brought in respect of the Community design.

(3)　The court may, having regard to the nature of the purposes listed in paragraph (2)(a) to (c), treat any other purpose as a "permitted purpose" if it considers that it is in the interests of justice to do so.

(4)　But the following may not be treated as a "permitted purpose"—

(a)　requesting a person to cease doing, for commercial purposes, anything in relation to an article made to a design, in which a design is incorporated or to which it is applied,

(b)　requesting a person to deliver up or destroy an article made to a design, in which a design is incorporated or to which it is applied, or

(c)　requesting a person to give an undertaking relating to an article made to a design, in which a design is incorporated or to which it is applied.

(5)　If any of the following information is included in a communication made for a permitted purpose, it is information that is "necessary for that purpose" (see paragraph (1)(b)(i))—

(a)　a statement—

(i)　that a design is a registered Community design and the registration is in force,

(ii)　that an application for a registered Community design has been made, or

(iii)　that a design is protected as an unregistered Community design;

(b)　details of the Community design, or of a right in or under the Community design, which—

(i)　are accurate in all material respects, and

(ii)　are not misleading in any material respect; and

(c)　information enabling the identification of the article that is alleged to be infringing an article in relation to the design.

2C　Unjustified threats: remedies and defences

(1)　Proceedings in respect of an actionable threat may be brought against the person who made the threat for—

(a)　a declaration that the threat is unjustified;

(b)　an injunction against the continuance of the threat;

(c)　damages in respect of any loss sustained by the aggrieved person by reason of the threat.

(2)　It is a defence for the person who made the threat to show that the act in respect of which proceedings were threatened constitutes (or if done would constitute) an infringement of the Community design.

(3)　It is a defence for the person who made the threat to show—

(a)　that, despite having taken reasonable steps, the person has not identified anyone who has done an act mentioned in regulation 2A(2)(a) or (b) in relation to the article which is the subject of the threat, and

(b)　that the person notified the recipient, before or at the time of making the threat, of the steps taken.

2D　Unjustified threats: professional advisers

(1)　Proceedings in respect of an actionable threat may not be brought against a professional adviser (or any person vicariously liable for the actions of that professional adviser) if the conditions in paragraph (3) are met.

(2)　In this section "professional adviser" means a person who, in relation to the making of the communication containing the threat—

(a)　is acting in a professional capacity in providing legal services or the services of a trade mark attorney or a patent attorney, and

(b)　is regulated in the provision of legal services, or the services of a trade mark attorney or a patent attorney, by one or more regulatory bodies (whether through membership of a regulatory body, the issue of a licence to practise or any other means).

(3)　The conditions are that—

(a)　in making the communication the professional adviser is acting on the instructions of another person, and

(b)   when the communication is made the professional adviser identifies the person on whose instructions the adviser is acting.

(4)   This section does not affect any liability of the person on whose instructions the professional adviser is acting.

(5)   It is for a person asserting that paragraph (1) applies to prove (if required) that at the material time—

(a)   the person concerned was acting as a professional adviser, and

(b)   the conditions in paragraph (3) were met.

2E   Unjustified threats: supplementary: pending registration

(1)   In the application of regulations 2 and 2B in relation to a registered Community design, references to a Community design include references to a Community design in respect of which an application for registration has been filed in accordance with Article 35 of the Community Design Regulation.

(2)   Where the threat of infringement proceedings is made after an application for registration has been filed (but before registration) the reference in regulation 2C(2) to "the Community design" is to be treated as a reference to the design registered in pursuance of that application.

2F   Unjustified threats: supplementary: proceedings for delivery up etc.

In regulation 2(1)(b) the reference to proceedings for infringement of the Community design includes a reference to—

(a)   proceedings for an order under regulation 1B (order for delivery up), and

(b)   proceedings for an order under regulation 1C (order as to disposal of infringing articles).

3   Falsely representing a design as a registered Community design

(1)   It is an offence for a person falsely to represent that a design applied to, or incorporated in, any product sold by him is a registered Community design.

(2)   It is an offence for a person, after a registered Community design has expired, to represent (expressly or by implication) that a design applied to, or incorporated in, any product sold is still registered in the manner provided for in the Community Design Regulation.

(3)   A person guilty of an offence under paragraph (1) is liable on summary conviction to a fine not exceeding level 3 on the standard scale.

(4)   A person guilty of an offence under paragraph (2) is liable on summary conviction to a fine not exceeding level 1 on the standard scale.

4   Privilege for communications with those on the special list of professional design representatives

(1)   This regulation applies to communications as to any matter relating to the protection of any design.

(2)   Any such communication—

(a)   between a person and his professional designs representative, or

(b)   for the purposes of obtaining, or in response to a request for, information which a person is seeking for the purpose of instructing his professional designs representative,

is privileged from, or in Scotland protected against, disclosure in legal proceedings in the same way as a communication between a person and his solicitor or, as the case may be, a communication for the purpose of obtaining, or in response to a request for, information which a person is seeking for the purpose of instructing his solicitor.

(3)   In paragraph (2) "professional designs representative" means a person who is on the special list of professional representatives for design matters referred to in Article 78 of the Community Design Regulation.

5   Use of Community design for services of the Crown

The provisions of the Schedule to these Regulations shall have effect with respect to the use of registered Community designs and unregistered Community designs for the services of the Crown and the rights of third parties in respect of such use.

INTELLECTUAL PROPERTY (ENFORCEMENT, ETC.) REGULATIONS 2006
(SI 2006 No. 1028)

3   Assessment of damages

(1)   Where in an action for infringement of an intellectual property right the defendant knew, or had reasonable grounds to know, that he engaged in infringing activity, the damages awarded to the claimant shall be appropriate to the actual prejudice he suffered as a result of the infringement.

(2)   When awarding such damages—

    (a)   all appropriate aspects shall be taken into account, including in particular—

        (i)   the negative economic consequences, including any lost profits, which the claimant has suffered, and any unfair profits made by the defendant; and

        (ii)   elements other than economic factors, including the moral prejudice caused to the claimant by the infringement; or

    (b)   where appropriate, they may be awarded on the basis of the royalties or fees which would have been due had the defendant obtained a licence.

(3)   This regulation does not affect the operation of any enactment or rule of law relating to remedies for the infringement of intellectual property rights except to the extent that it is inconsistent with the provisions of this regulation.

(4)   In the application of this regulation to—

    (a)   Scotland, "claimant" includes pursuer; "defendant" includes defender; and "enactment" includes an enactment comprised in, or an instrument made under, an Act of the Scottish Parliament; and

    (b)   Northern Ireland, "claimant" includes plaintiff.

COPYRIGHT AND RIGHTS IN PERFORMANCES (LICENSING OF ORPHAN WORKS) REGULATIONS 2014
(SI 2014 No. 2863)

2   Interpretation

In these Regulations—

"the Act" means the Copyright, Designs and Patents Act 1988;

. . .

"diligent search" has the meaning set out in regulation 4;

"identified right holder" is a right holder of the type referred to in regulation 12(1);

"orphan licence" is a licence authorising the use of an orphan work;

"orphan licensee" means a person who either wishes to be granted or has been granted an orphan licence;

"orphan work" has the meaning set out in regulation 3;

"relevant work" has the meaning set out in regulation 3;

"restricted acts" means the acts in relation to a performance to which sections 182, 182A, 182B, 182C, 182CA, 183 or 184 of the Act apply;

"right holder" has the meaning set out in regulation 3.

3   Relevant work, right holder and orphan work

(1)   "Relevant work" means a work which is protected by copyright or a performance in respect of which certain acts constitute restricted acts.

(2)   A reference to a "relevant work" includes a reference to a work or a performance, which itself falls within the definition of "relevant work" and is embedded in or incorporated in, or constitutes an integral part of, another relevant work.

(3)   "Right holder" in relation to a relevant work means—

    (a)   an owner of the copyright in the relevant work;

    (b)   a licensee under an exclusive licence in relation to the relevant work;

    (c)   a person with rights to permit or prohibit one or more of the restricted acts in relation to a performance recorded by the relevant work and, in the case of a performance, which is embedded or incorporated in or constitutes an integral part of another relevant work, a person with rights to permit or prohibit one or more of the restricted acts in relation to the performance; and

    (d)   a licensee under an exclusive licence in relation to those rights.

(4)   A relevant work is an orphan work where, after a diligent search made in accordance with regulation 4, one or more of the right holders in the relevant work have either not been identified or, if identified, have not been located.

(5)   Where a relevant work has more than one right holder and, after a diligent search made in accordance with regulation 4, one or more of the right holders have either not been identified or, if identified, have not been located, then the relevant work is an orphan work to the extent that the rights of those right holders are either not identified or not located.

(6)   In these Regulations, a reference to an orphan work includes a relevant work in which it is not known whether copyright or the right to permit or prohibit the restricted acts subsists, and references to a right holder who has not been identified or located are to be read as including references to a supposed right holder.

(7)   A relevant work ceases to be an orphan work to the extent that a right holder is identified in accordance with regulation 12.

4   Diligent search

(1)   An orphan licensee shall, before applying for an orphan licence, carry out a diligent search or refer to an existing diligent search which is valid and, in either case, is appropriate to the orphan work which is the proposed subject matter of the orphan licence and relates to the rights in the relevant work which the orphan licensee proposes to use.

(2)   A diligent search must comprise a reasonable search of the relevant sources to identify and locate the right holders of the relevant work.

(3)   The sources that are relevant for the relevant work must, as a minimum, include—

    (a)   the relevant register maintained by the authorising body and the relevant databases maintained by the Office for Harmonization in the Internal Market; and

    (b)   where there is no record that the relevant work is an orphan work in the register or databases referred to in paragraph (a), any relevant sources listed for that category of work in Part 2 of Schedule ZA1 to the Act.

(4)   The authorising body may issue guidance on what sources may additionally be relevant in the case of different relevant works.

(5)   A diligent search is valid, for the purposes of paragraph (1), for seven years from the earlier of the date—

    (a)   on which an orphan licence of the orphan work was first granted by the authorising body; or

    (b)   that the record of a diligent search undertaken in respect of a relevant work was first made public by the Office for Harmonization in the Internal Market.

(6)   An orphan licensee shall provide the authorising body with such information concerning—

    (a)   the diligent search; and

    (b)   the use that the orphan licensee proposes to make of the orphan work,

as the authorising body may require in connection with the application for an orphan licence.

(7)   The orphan licensee shall, when applying for an orphan licence, provide the authorising body with an application in the form required by the authorising body, including in electronic form, and the application shall—

    (a)   demonstrate that a diligent search has been carried out; and

    (b)   contain a declaration in writing by the orphan licensee stating that the information provided in the application is correct.

(8)   Where an orphan licensee makes a declaration under sub-paragraph (7)(b) that the orphan licensee knows or has reason to believe is false and the orphan licensee is granted an orphan licence and carries out any of the acts restricted by copyright or the restricted acts, the orphan licensee is liable for infringement of copyright or sections 182, 182A, 182B, 182C, 182CA, 183 or 184 of the Act as appropriate.

(9)   The authorising body shall take reasonable steps to ensure that the search relied upon by the orphan licensee satisfies the requirements for a diligent search.

5   Record and register of orphan works

(1)   The authorising body shall maintain and update a register which sets out the details of the orphan works in respect of which—

    (a)   a diligent search has been carried out and an application, for the grant of an orphan licence, has been made to and is being considered by the authorising body;

    (b)   orphan licences have been granted together with the permitted uses of the relevant works; and

    (c)   orphan licences have been refused.

(2)   The authorising body shall make the register available to the public by electronic means and free of charge.

6   Licensing of orphan works

(1)   Once the authorising body has received the information set out in regulations 4(6) and (7), it may grant an orphan licence.

(2)   The authorising body may only grant an orphan licence which—

    (a)   permits non-exclusive use of an orphan work in the United Kingdom;

    (b)   permits acts restricted by the copyright or sections 182, 182A, 182B, 182C, 182CA, 183 or 184 of the Act in an orphan work for a term not exceeding 7 years;

    (c)   prohibits the grant of sub-licences;

    (d)   has effect as if granted by the right holder of the relevant work; and

    (e)   provides that the use of an orphan work does not affect the moral rights of an author under Chapter IV of Part 1 of the Act or the moral rights of a performer under Chapter 3 of Part 2 of the Act and treats those moral rights as having been asserted.

(3)   Subject to the requirements set out in paragraph (2), the authorising body may grant a licence subject to conditions.

(4)   An orphan licence may not be granted to a person authorised to grant licences.

(5)   The authorising body may refuse to grant a licence—

    (a)   on the ground that, in its reasonable opinion, a proposed use or adaptation is not appropriate having regard to the circumstances of the case, including whether the proposed adaptation constitutes derogatory treatment of the work; or

    (b)   on any other reasonable ground.

(6)   Subject to the requirements set out in paragraph (2), the authorising body may, during the term of a licence, vary the terms of an orphan licence.

7   Use for incidental purposes

Any person may, without infringing copyright or sections 182, 182A, 182B, 182C, 182CA, 183 or 184 of the Act, make reasonable use of an orphan work for purposes which are incidental to—

(a)   the application for the grant of an orphan licence; and

(b)   the processing of the application and the maintenance of the register referred to in regulation 5(1).

8   Renewal of orphan licence

(1)   Upon the request of the orphan licensee, submitted in the form required not less than six months before the expiration of the orphan licence, the authorising body may renew an orphan licence for a further term not exceeding 7 years.

(2)   A request for a renewal of an orphan licence shall be accompanied by evidence of a diligent search carried out in accordance with regulation 4 together with the information set out in regulations 4(6) and (7).

. . .

12   Rights of identified right holder

(1)   This regulation applies where the right holder in an orphan work identifies themselves to the authorising body and satisfies the authorising body of their identity and of their ownership of relevant rights in the orphan work either—

    (a)   in the period between the receipt by the authorising body of an application for the grant of an orphan licence and the grant by the authorising body of that licence; or

(b)   within eight years or less of the date on which the authorising body has granted an orphan licence of the orphan work.

(2)   If the authorising body has verified the diligent search but has not granted an orphan licence then the work shall, to the extent of the rights of the identified right holder, cease to be an orphan work.

(3)   If the authorising body has granted an orphan licence then the orphan licence shall continue for the remainder of its unexpired term or until the expiration of the notice period which is set out in the orphan licence notwithstanding the fact that the right holder is identified.

(4)   The authorising body shall within two months of being satisfied that the right holder has been identified—

(a)   notify the orphan licensee that the right holder has been identified;

(b)   pay to the right holder a sum equal to the licence fee paid by the orphan licensee in respect of the orphan work.

. . .

DESIGNS (INTERNATIONAL REGISTRATION OF INDUSTRIAL DESIGNS) ORDER 2018
(SI 2018 No. 23)

1   Citation, commencement and extent

(1)   This Order may be cited as the Designs (International Registration of Industrial Designs) Order 2018.

(2)   This Order comes into force on the date on which the United Kingdom becomes bound by the Geneva Act of the Hague Agreement concerning the International Registration of Industrial Designs pursuant to article 28(3)(b) of that Act.

(3)   This Order extends to England and Wales, Scotland, Northern Ireland and the Isle of Man.

2   Interpretation

In this Order—

"the 2006 Rules" means the Registered Design Rules 2006;

"the Act" means the Registered Designs Act 1949 and "section" means a section of that Act;

"Common Regulations" means the regulations adopted under Article 24 of the Geneva Act with effect from 1st January 2017;

"Geneva Act" means the Geneva Act of the Hague Agreement concerning the international registration of industrial designs adopted by the diplomatic conference on 2nd July 1999;

"holder", in relation to an international registration, means the person in whose name an international registration is recorded in the International Register;

"International Bureau" means the International Bureau of the World Intellectual Property Organisation;

"International Register" means the register of industrial designs maintained by the International Bureau for the purposes of the Geneva Act;

"international registration" means a registration of a design in the International Register for the purpose of the Geneva Act and the Common Regulations;

"protected international registration (UK)" means a grant of protection under Rule 18bis of the Common Regulations for a design which is the subject of a request for international registration (UK), and references to "protection" and "protected" are construed accordingly;

"request for international registration (UK)" means a request for international registration made in pursuance of Article 5(1) of the Geneva Act in respect of which the United Kingdom is a designated Contracting Party.

3   International registration

The provisions of the Act (except those listed in Part 1 of Schedule 1) and the 2006 Rules (except those listed in Part 2 of Schedule 1) apply to a design which is the subject of a protected international registration (UK) and a request for international registration (UK) with the following modifications—

(a)   references to a registered design are to include references to a design which is the subject of a protected international registration (UK);

(b)   references to a registered proprietor are to include references to a holder of an international registration in respect of which a protected international registration (UK) applies;

(c)   references to an application for registration of a design are to include references to a request for international registration (UK);

(d)   references to an applicant for registration are to include references to the holder of an international registration making a request for an international registration (UK);

(e)   references to registration of a design are to include the conferring of protection for a design so that it becomes a protected international registration (UK) and include any changes to the registration;

(f)   references to the register are to the International Register;

(g)   the modifications to the Act and the 2006 Rules set out in Schedule 2; and

(h)   such further modifications as the context requires for the purpose of giving effect to those provisions as applied by this Order.

4   Communication of information to the International Bureau

Notwithstanding any other enactment or rule of law, the registrar may communicate to the International Bureau any information which the registrar is required to communicate under the Act (as it has effect by virtue of this Order) or pursuant to the Geneva Act or Common Regulations.

SCHEDULE 1
LEGISLATIVE DISAPPLICATIONS

PART 1
PROVISIONS OF THE ACT WHICH DO NOT APPLY TO
PROTECTED INTERNATIONAL REGISTRATIONS (UK) OR REQUESTS
FOR INTERNATIONAL REGISTRATION (UK)

section 3 (application for registration)
section 3A(2) (determination of applications for registration)
section 3B (modification of applications for registration)
section 3C(2) and (3) (date of registrations of designs)
section 5 (provisions for secrecy of certain designs)
section 8A (restoration of lapsed right in design)
section 8B (effect of order for restoration of right)
section 11 (cancellation of registration)
section 11ZD (modification of registration)
section 14(1) and (3) (registration of design where application for protection in a convention country has been made)
section 15 (extension of time for application under s. 14 in certain cases)
section 15B(2) (assignment, &c. of registered designs and applications for registered designs)
section 17 (register of designs etc.) except section 17(8)
section 18 (certificate of registration)
section 19 (registration of assignments, etc.)
section 20 (rectification of register)
section 21 (power to correct clerical errors)
section 22 (inspection of registered designs)
section 31A(1)(a) (power to require to use forms)
section 33 (offences under s. 5)
section 36(1A)(ab) and (d) (general power of Secretary of State to make rules, etc.)

PART 2
PROVISIONS OF THE 2006 RULES WHICH DO NOT APPLY TO
PROTECTED INTERNATIONAL REGISTRATIONS (UK) OR REQUESTS
FOR INTERNATIONAL REGISTRATION (UK)

rule 4 (applications)
rule 5 (formal requirements)

rule 6 (partial disclaimers)

rule 7(2) and (5) (convention applications)

rule 9 (representation of design for publication)

rule 10 (time limits under section 3(5) and section 3B)

rule 11 (publication)

rule 12 (extension of duration of right in registered design)

rule 13 (restoration of a lapsed right in a design under section 8A)

rule 14 (cancellation of registration)

rule 26 (certificate of registration)

rule 27 (registration of interests) (except paragraph (4) of rule 27)

rule 28 (inspection of register, representations and specimens)

rule 31 (information about rights in registered designs)

rule 32 (copies of entries in, or extracts from, the register)

rule 33 (copies of representations and specimens)

rule 34 (alteration of name or address)

rule 35 (notice of rectification of the register)

SCHEDULE 2

PART 1
MODIFICATIONS TO PROVISIONS OF THE ACT APPLIED TO PROTECTED INTERNATIONAL REGISTRATIONS (UK) AND REQUESTS FOR INTERNATIONAL REGISTRATION (UK)

1.   The Act is modified as follows.

2.   Section 1B (requirement of novelty and individual character) applies with the omission in subsection (7) of "3B(2), (3) or (5) or".

3.   Section 3A (determination of applications for registration) applies —

   (a)   with the substitution for subsection (3) of —

      "(3) If it appears to the registrar that the holder of an international registration making a request for international registration (UK) of a design in respect of which protection has been applied for in a convention country is not the person who applied for protection in that country (or that person's personal representative), he shall refuse the request";

   (b)   with the substitution in subsection (4) for "register that thing or that design" of "confer protection for that design or thing so that it becomes a protected international registration (UK).";

   (c)   with the insertion after subsection (4) of —

      "(5) Where the registrar —

     (a)   refuses a request for international registration (UK); or

     (b)   proceeds with the grant of a request for international registration (UK) on consideration of the applicant's observations or representations or successful appeal of a decision to refuse a request for international registration (UK), the registrar must notify the International Bureau in accordance with Article 12 of the Geneva Act and Rule 18 of the Common Regulations.".

4.   Section 3C (date of registrations of designs) applies with the substitution for subsection (1) of —

"(1) A design which is the subject of a request for international registration (UK) shall be protected from and including the date on which the international registration produces the effect as a grant of protection under this Act notified in the statement of grant of protection under Rule 18bis of the Common Regulations.".

5.   Section 3D (appeals in relation to applications for registration) applies with the reference to section 3A as modified under paragraph 3 and the omission of the reference to section 3B.

6.   Section 7A (infringement of rights in registered design) applies with the substitution for subsection (6) of —

"(6) No proceedings shall be taken in respect of an infringement of the right in a design which is the subject of a protected international registration (UK) committed before the date of issue of the statement of grant of protection under Rule 18bis of the Common Regulations.".

7.   Subsection (2) of section 7B (right of prior use) applies —

   (a)   with the omission in paragraph (a) of "under section 3";

(b)   with the substitution for paragraph (b) of—

"(b) where a request was made for international registration (UK) for a design in respect of which protection has been applied for in a convention country, the date on which it was treated as having been so made.".

8.   Section 8 (duration of right in registered design) applies with the substitution for subsections (2) and (3) of—

"(2) The period for which the right subsists may be extended for a second, third, fourth and fifth period of five years, by applying to the International Bureau, in accordance with Article 17 of the Geneva Act and subject to the payment of the fees specified under the Common Regulations.

(3) If the first, second, third or fourth period expires without such application and payment being made, the protected international registration (UK) shall cease to have effect.".

9.   Section 11ZA(1B) (grounds for invalidity of registration) applies, with the omission of "3B(2), (3) or (5) or".

10.   Section 11ZB (applications for declarations of invalidity) applies—

(a)   with the insertion in subsection (2) of "or the court" after "registrar";

(b)   with the insertion in subsection (3) of "or the court" after "registrar";

(c)   with the insertion in subsection (5) of "or the court" after "registrar".

11.   Section 11ZE (effect of cancellation or invalidation of registration) applies—

(a)   with the omission of subsection (1);

(b)   with the insertion in subsection (2) of "or the court" after "registrar".

12.   Section 11ZF (appeals in relation to cancellation or invalidation) applies with substitution for "11 to 11ZE" of "11ZA, 11ZB, 11ZC and 11ZE".

13.   Section 14 (registration of design where application for protection in convention country has been made) applies with the reference in subsection (2) to an application for registration of a design made by virtue of section 14 being read as a request for international registration (UK) for a design in respect of which protection has been applied for in a convention country.

14.   Section 15B (assignment, &c. of registered designs and applications for registered designs), applies, with the substitution for subsection (1) of—

"(1) A protected international registration (UK) is transmissible by assignment, testamentary disposition or operation of law in the same way as other personal or moveable property.".

15.   Section 40 (fees) applies with the omission of the words "the registration of designs and applications therefore, and in respect of other".

16.   Section 44 (interpretation) applies with the insertion after paragraph (4) of—

"(5) Any expression defined for the purposes of the Designs (International Registration of Industrial Designs) Order 2018 which is used in this Act as modified by that Order has the same meaning as in that Order.".

. . .

COUNCIL DIRECTIVE 93/83/EEC

on the coordination of certain rules concerning copyright and rights related to copyright applicable to satellite broadcasting and cable retransmission

. . .

CHAPTER I
DEFINITIONS

Article 1 Definitions

1.   For the purpose of this Directive, "fsatellitef" means any satellite operating on frequency bands which, under telecommunications law, are reserved for the broadcast of signals for reception by the public or which are reserved for closed, point-to-point communication. In the latter case, however, the circumstances in which individual reception of the signals takes place must be comparable to those which apply in the first case.

2.   (a)   For the purpose of this Directive, "communication to the public by satellite" means the act of introducing, under the control and responsibility of the broadcasting organization, the programme-carrying signals intended for reception by the public into an uninterrupted chain of communication leading to the satellite and down towards the earth.

(b) The act of communication to the public by satellite occurs solely in the Member State where, under the control and responsibility of the broadcasting organization, the programme-carrying signals are introduced into an uninterrupted chain of communication leading to the satellite and down towards the earth.

(c) If the programme-carrying signals are encrypted, then there is communication to the public by satellite on condition that the means for decrypting the broadcast are provided to the public by the broadcasting organization or with its consent.

(d) Where an act of communication to the public by satellite occurs in a non-Community State which does not provide the level of protection provided for under Chapter II,

    (i) if the programme-carrying signals are transmitted to the satellite from an uplink situation situated in a Member State, that act of communication to the public by satellite shall be deemed to have occurred in that Member State and the rights provided for under Chapter II shall be exercisable against the person operating the uplink station; or

    (ii) if there is no use of an uplink station situated in a Member State but a broadcasting organization established in a Member State has commissioned the act of communication to the public by satellite, that act shall be deemed to have occurred in the Member State in which the broadcasting organization has its principal establishment in the Community and the rights provided for under Chapter II shall be exercisable against the broadcasting organization.

3. For the purposes of this Directive, "cable retransmission" means the simultaneous, unaltered and unabridged retransmission by a cable or microwave system for reception by the public of an initial transmission from another Member State, by wire or over the air, including that by satellite, of television or radio programmes intended for reception by the public.

4. For the purposes of this Directive "collecting society" means any organization which manages or administers copyright or rights related to copyright as its sole purpose or as one of its main purposes.

5. For the purposes of this Directive, the principal director of a cinematographic or audiovisual work shall be considered as its author or one of its authors. Member States may provide for others to be considered as its co-authors.

CHAPTER II
BROADCASTING OF PROGRAMMES BY SATELLITE

Article 2 Broadcasting right

Member States shall provide an exclusive right for the author to authorize the communication to the public by satellite of copyright works, subject to the provisions set out in this chapter.

Article 3 Acquisition of broadcasting rights

1. Member States shall ensure that the authorization referred to in Article 2 may be acquired only be agreement.

2. A Member State may provide that a collective agreement between a collecting society and a broadcasting organization concerning a given category of works may be extended to rightholders of the same category who are not represented by the collecting society, provided that :

— the communication to the public by satellite simulcasts a terrestrial broadcast by the same broadcaster, and

— the unrepresented rightholder shall, at any time, have the possibility of excluding the extension of the collective agreement to his works and of exercising his rights either individually or collectively.

3. Paragraph 2 shall not apply to cinematographic works, including works created by a process analogous to cinematography.

4. Where the law of a Member State provides for the extension of a collective agreement in accordance with the provisions of paragraph 2, that Member States shall inform the Commission which broadcasting organizations are entitled to avail themselves of that law. The Commission shall publish this information in the *Official Journal of the European Communities* (C series).

Article 4 Rights of performers, phonogram producers and broadcasting organizations

1.   For the purposes of communication to the public by satellite, the rights of performers, phonogram producers and broadcasting organizations shall be protected in accordance with the provisions of Articles 6, 7, 8 and 10 of Directive 92/100/EEC.
2.   For the purposes of paragraph 1, "broadcasting by wireless means" in Directive 92/100/EEC shall be understood as including communication to the public by satellite.
3.   With regard to the exercise of the rights referred to in paragraph 1, Articles 2 (7) and 12 of Directive 92/100/EEC shall apply.

Article 5 Relation between copyright and related rights

Protection of copyright-related rights under this Directive shall leave intact and shall in no way affect the protection of copyright.

Article 6 Minimum protection

1.   Member States may provide for more far-reaching protection for holders of rights related to copyright than that required by Article 8 of Directive 92/100/EEC.
2.   In applying paragraph 1 Member States shall observe the definitions contained in Article 1 (1) and (2).

Article 7 Transitional provisions

1.   With regard to the application in time of the rights referred to in Article 4 (1) of this Directive, Article 13 (1), (2), (6) and (7) of Directive 92/100/EEC shall apply. Article 13 (4) and (5) of Directive 92/100/EEC shall apply *mutatis mutandis*.
2.   Agreements concerning the exploitation of works and other protected subject matter which are in force on the date mentioned in Article 14 (1) shall be subject to the provisions of Articles 1 (2), 2 and 3 as from 1 January 2000 if they expire after that date.
3.   When an international co-production agreement concluded before the date mentioned in Article 14 (1) between a co-producer from a Member State and one or more co-producers from other Member States or third countries expressly provides for a system of division of exploitation rights between the co-producers by geographical areas for all means of communication to the public, without distinguishing the arrangement applicable to communication to the public by satellite from the provisions applicable to the other means of communication, and where communication to the public by satellite of the co-production would prejudice the exclusivity, in particular the language exclusivity, of one of the co-producers or his assignees in a given territory, the authorization by one of the co-producers or his assignees for a communication to the public by satellite shall require the prior consent of the holder of that exclusivity, whether co-producer or assignee.

CHAPTER III
CABLE RETRANSMISSION

Article 8 Cable retransmission right

1.   Member States shall ensure that when programmes from other Member States are retransmitted by cable in their territory the applicable copyright and related rights are observed and that such retransmission takes place on the basis of individual or collective contractual agreements between copyright owners, holders of related rights and cable operators.
2.   Notwithstanding paragraph 1, Member States may retain until 31 December 1997 such statutory licence systems which are in operation or expressly provided for by national law on 31 July 1991.

Article 9 Exercise of the cable retransmission right

1.   Member States shall ensure that the right of copyright owners and holders or related rights to grant or refuse authorization to a cable operator for a cable retransmission may be exercised only through a collecting society.
2.   Where a rightholder has not transferred the management of his rights to a collecting society, the collecting society which manages rights of the same category shall be deemed to be mandated to manage his rights. Where more than one collecting society manages rights of that category, the rightholder shall be free to choose which of those collecting societies is

deemed to be mandated to manage his rights. A rightholder referred to in this paragraph shall have the same rights and obligations resulting from the agreement between the cable operator and the collecting society which is deemed to be mandated to manage his rights as the rightholders who have mandated that collecting society and he shall be able to claim those rights within a period, to be fixed by the Member State concerned, which shall not be shorter than three years from the date of the cable retransmission which includes his work or other protected subject matter.

3. A Member State may provide that, when a right-holder authorizes the initial transmission within its territory of a work or other protected subject matter, he shall be deemed to have agreed not to exercise his cable retransmission rights on an individual basis but to exercise them in accordance with the provisions of this Directive.

Article 10 Exercise of the cable retransmission right by broadcasting organizations

Member States shall ensure that Article 9 does not apply to the rights exercised by a broadcasting organization in respect of its own transmission, irrespective of whether the rights concerned are its own or have been transferred to it by other copyright owners and/or holders of related rights.

Article 11 Mediators

1. Where no agreement is concluded regarding authorization of the cable retransmission of a broadcast. Member States shall ensure that either party may call upon the assistance of one or more mediators.
2. The task of the mediators shall be to provide assistance with negotiation. They may also submit proposals to the parties.
3. It shall be assumed that all the parties accept a proposal as referred to in paragraph 2 if none of them expresses its opposition within a period of three months. Notice of the proposal and of any opposition thereto shall be served on the parties concerned in accordance with the applicable rules concerning the service of legal documents.
4. The mediators shall be so selected that their independence and impartiality are beyond reasonable doubt.

Article 12 Prevention of the abuse of negotiating positions

1. Member States shall ensure by means of civil or administrative law, as appropriate, that the parties enter and conduct negotiations regarding authorization for cable retransmission in good faith and do not prevent or hinder negotiation without valid justification.
2. A Member State which, on the date mentioned in Article 14 (1), has a body with jurisdiction in its territory over cases where the right to retransmit a programme by cable to the public in that Member State has been unreasonably refused or offered on unreasonable terms by a broadcasting organization may retain that body.
3. Paragraph 2 shall apply for a transitional period of eight years from the date mentioned in Article 14 (1).

CHAPTER IV

GENERAL PROVISIONS

Article 13 Collective administration of rights

This Directive shall be without prejudice to the regulation of the activities of collecting societies by the Member States.

Article 14 Final provisions

1. Member States shall bring into force the laws, regulations and administrative provisions necessary to comply with this Directive before 1 January 1995. They shall immediately inform the Commission thereof.

    When Member States adopt these measures, the latter shall contain a reference to this Directive or shall be accompanied by such reference at the time of their official publication. The methods of making such a reference shall be laid down by the Member States.
2. Member States shall communicate to the Commission the provisions of national law which they adopt in the field covered by this Directive.

3.   Not later than 1 January 2000, the Commission shall submit to the European Parliament, the Council and the Economic and Social Committee a report on the application of this Directive and, if necessary, make further proposals to adapt it to developments in the audio and audiovisual sector.

COUNCIL DIRECTIVE 96/9/EC
(legal protection of databases)

. . .

CHAPTER I
SCOPE

Article 1 Scope
1.   This Directive concerns the legal protection of databases in any form.
2.   For the purposes of this Directive, "database" shall mean a collection of independent works, data or other materials arranged in a systematic or methodical way and individually accessible by electronic or other means.
3.   Protection under this Directive shall not apply to computer programs used in the making or operation of databases accessible by electronic means.

Article 2 Limitations on the scope
This Directive shall apply without prejudice to Community provisions relating to:
(a)   the legal protection of computer programs;
(b)   rental right, lending right and certain rights related to copyright in the field of intellectual property;
(c)   the term of protection of copyright and certain related rights.

CHAPTER II
COPYRIGHT

Article 3 Object of protection
1.   In accordance with this Directive, databases which, by reason of the selection or arrangement of their contents, constitute the author's own intellectual creation shall be protected as such by copyright. No other criteria shall be applied to determine their eligibility for that protection.
2.   The copyright protection of databases provided for by this Directive shall not extend to their contents and shall be without prejudice to any rights subsisting in those contents themselves.

Article 4 Database authorship
1.   The author of a database shall be the natural person or group of natural persons who created the base or, where the legislation of the Member States so permits, the legal person designated as the rightholder by that legislation.
2.   Where collective works are recognized by the legislation of a Member State, the economic rights shall be owned by the person holding the copyright.
3.   In respect of a database created by a group of natural persons jointly, the exclusive rights shall be owned jointly.

Article 5 Restricted acts
In respect of the expression of the database which is protectable by copyright, the author of a database shall have the exclusive right to carry out or to authorize:
(a)   temporary or permanent reproduction by any means and in any form, in whole or in part;
(b)   translation, adaptation, arrangement and any other alteration;
(c)   any form of distribution to the public of the database or of copies thereof. The first sale in the Community of a copy of the database by the rightholder or with his consent shall exhaust the right to control resale of that copy within the Community;

(d)   any communication, display or performance to the public;

(e)   any reproduction, distribution, communication, display or performance to the public of the results of the acts referred to in (b).

Article 6 Exceptions to restricted acts

1.   The performance by the lawful user of a database or of a copy thereof of any of the acts listed in Article 5 which is necessary for the purposes of access to the contents of the databases and normal use of the contents by the lawful user shall not require the authorization of the author of the database. Where the lawful user is authorized to use only part of the database, this provision shall apply only to that part.

2.   Member States shall have the option of providing for limitations on the rights set out in Article 5 in the following cases:

    (a)   in the case of reproduction for private purposes of a non-electronic database;

    (b)   where there is use for the sole purpose of illustration for teaching or scientific research, as long as the source is indicated and to the extent justified by the non-commercial purpose to be achieved;

    (c)   where there is use for the purposes of public security of for the purposes of an administrative or judicial procedure;

    (d)   where other exceptions to copyright which are traditionally authorized under national law are involved, without prejudice to points (a), (b) and (c).

3.   In accordance with the Berne Convention for the protection of Literary and Artistic Works, this Article may not be interpreted in such a way as to allow its application to be used in a manner which unreasonably prejudices the rightholder's legitimate interests or conflicts with normal exploitation of the database.

CHAPTER III
SUI GENERIS RIGHT

Article 7 Object of protection

1.   Member States shall provide for a right for the maker of a database which shows that there has been qualitatively and/or quantitatively a substantial investment in either the obtaining, verification or presentation of the contents to prevent extraction and/or re-utilization of the whole or of a substantial part, evaluated qualitatively and/or quantitatively, of the contents of that database.

2.   For the purposes of this Chapter:

    (a)   "extraction" shall mean the permanent or temporary transfer of all or a substantial part of the contents of a database to another medium by any means or in any form;

    (b)   "re-utilization" shall mean any form of making available to the public all or a substantial part of the contents of a database by the distribution of copies, by renting, by on-line or other forms of transmission. The first sale of a copy of a database within the Community by the rightholder or with his consent shall exhaust the right to control resale of that copy within the Community;

    Public lending is not an act of extraction or re-utilization.

3.   The right referred to in paragraph 1 may be transferred, assigned or granted under contractual licence.

4.   The right provided for in paragraph 1 shall apply irrespective of the eligibility of that database for protection by copyright or by other rights. Moreover, it shall apply irrespective of eligibility of the contents of that database for protection by copyright or by other rights. Protection of databases under the right provided for in paragraph 1 shall be without prejudice to rights existing in respect of their contents.

5.   The repeated and systematic extraction and/or re-utilization of insubstantial parts of the contents of the database implying acts which conflict with a normal exploitation of that database or which unreasonably prejudice the legitimate interests of the maker of the database shall not be permitted.

Article 8 Rights and obligations of lawful users

1.   The maker of a database which is made available to the public in whatever manner may not prevent a lawful user of the database from extracting and/or re-utilizing insubstantial parts of its contents, evaluated qualitatively and/or quantitatively, for any purposes whatsoever.

Where the lawful user is authorized to extract and/or re-utilize only part of the database, this paragraph shall apply only to that part.

2.   A lawful user of a database which is made available to the public in whatever manner may not perform acts which conflict with normal exploitation of the database or unreasonably prejudice the legitimate interests of the maker of the database.

3.   A lawful user of a database which is made available to the public in any manner may not cause prejudice to the holder of a copyright or related right in respect of the works or subject matter contained in the database.

Article 9 Exceptions to the sui generis right

Member States may stipulate that lawful users of a database which is made available to the public in whatever manner may, without the authorization of its maker, extract or re-utilize a substantial part of its contents:

(a)   in the case of extraction for private purposes of the contents of a non-electronic database;

(b)   in the case of extraction for the purposes of illustration for teaching or scientific research, as long as the source is indicated and to the extent justified by the non-commercial purpose to be achieved;

(c)   in the case of extraction and/or re-utilization for the purposes of public security or an administrative or judicial procedure.

Article 10 Term of protection

1.   The right provided for in Article 7 shall run from the date of completion of the making of the database. It shall expire fifteen years from the first of January of the year following the date of completion.

2.   In the case of a database which is made available to the public in whatever manner before expiry of the period provided for in paragraph 1, the term of protection by that right shall expire fifteen years from the first of January of the year following the date when the database was first made available to the public.

3.   Any substantial change, evaluated qualitatively or quantitatively, to the contents of a database, including any substantial change resulting from the accumulation of successive additions, deletions or alterations, which would result in the database being considered to be a substantial new investment, evaluated qualitatively or quantitatively, shall qualify the database resulting from that investment for its own term of protection.

Article 11 Beneficiaries of protection under the sui generis right

1.   The right provided for in Article 7 shall apply to database whose makers or rightholders are nationals of a Member State or who have their habitual residence in the territory of the Community.

2.   Paragraph 1 shall also apply to companies and firms formed in accordance with the law of a Member State and having their registered office, central administration or principal place of business within the Community; however, where such a company or firm has only its registered office in the territory of the Community, its operations must be genuinely linked on an ongoing basis with the economy of a Member State.

3.   Agreements extending the right provided for in Article 7 to databases made in third countries and falling outside the provisions of paragraphs 1 and 2 shall be concluded by the Council acting on a proposal from the Commission. The term of any protection extended to databases by virtue of that procedure shall not exceed that available pursuant to Article 10.

CHAPTER IV
COMMON PROVISIONS

Article 12 Remedies

Member States shall provide appropriate remedies in respect of infringements of the rights provided for in this Directive.

Article 13 Continued application of other legal provisions

This Directive shall be without prejudice to provisions concerning in particular copyright, rights related to copyright or any other rights or obligations subsisting in the data, works or other materials incorporated into a database, patent rights, trade marks, design rights, the protection of national treasures, laws on restrictive practices and unfair competition, trade secrets, security, confidentiality, data protection and privacy, access to public documents, and the law of contract.

Article 14 Application over time

1.   Protection pursuant to this Directive as regards copyright shall also be available in respect of databases created prior to the date referred to Article 16(1) which on that date fulfil the requirements laid down in this Directive as regards copyright protection of databases.

2.   Notwithstanding paragraph 1, where a database protected under copyright arrangements in a Member State on the date of publication of this Directive does not fulfil the eligibility criteria for copyright protection laid down in Article 3(1), this Directive shall not result in any curtailing in that Member State of the remaining term of protection afforded under those arrangements.

3.   Protection pursuant to the provisions of this Directive as regards the right provided for in Article 7 shall also be available in respect of databases the making of which was completed not more than fifteen years prior to the date referred to in Article 16(1) and which on that date fulfil the requirements laid down in Article 7.

4.   The protection provided for in paragraphs 1 and 3 shall be without prejudice to any acts concluded and rights acquired before the date referred to in those paragraphs.

5.   In the case of a database the making of which was completed not more than fifteen years prior to the date referred to in Article 16(1), the term of protection by the right provided for in Article 7 shall expire fifteen years from the first of January following that date.

Article 15 Binding nature of certain provisions

Any contractual provision contrary to Articles 6(1) and 8 shall be null and void.

. . .

COUNCIL DIRECTIVE 98/71/EC
(legal protection of designs)

. . .

Article 1 Definitions

For the purpose of this Directive:

(a)   "design" means the appearance of the whole or a part of a product resulting from the features of, in particular, the lines, contours, colours, shape, texture and/or materials of the product itself and/or its ornamentation;

(b)   "product" means any industrial or handicraft item, including inter alia parts intended to be assembled into a complex product, packaging, get-up, graphic symbols and typographic typefaces, but excluding computer programs;

(c)   "complex product" means a product which is composed of multiple components which can be replaced permitting disassembly and reassembly of the product.

Article 2 Scope of application

1.   This Directive shall apply to:
  (a)   design rights registered with the central industrial property offices of the Member States;
  (b)   design rights registered at the Benelux Design Office;
  (c)   design rights registered under international arrangements which have effect in a Member State;
  (d)   applications for design rights referred to under (a), (b) and (c).

2.   For the purpose of this Directive, design registration shall also comprise the publication following filing of the design with the industrial property office of a Member State in which such publication has the effect of bringing a design right into existence.

Article 3 Protection requirements

1.   Member States shall protect designs by registration, and shall confer exclusive rights upon their holders in accordance with the provisions of this Directive.

2.   A design shall be protected by a design right to the extent that it is new and has individual character.

3.   A design applied to or incorporated in a product which constitutes a component part of a complex product shall only be considered to be new and to have individual character:

(a) if the component part, once it has been incorporated into the complex product, remains visible during normal use of the latter, and

(b) to the extent that those visible features of the component part fulfil in themselves the requirements as to novelty and individual character.

4.   "Normal use" within the meaning of paragraph (3)(a) shall mean use by the end user, excluding maintenance, servicing or repair work.

Article 4 Novelty

A design shall be considered new if no identical design has been made available to the public before the date of filing of the application for registration or, if priority is claimed, the date of priority. Designs shall be deemed to be identical if their features differ only in immaterial details.

Article 5 Individual character

1.   A design shall be considered to have individual character if the overall impression it produces on the informed user differs from the overall impression produced on such a user by any design which has been made available to the public before the date of filing of the application for registration or, if priority is claimed, the date of priority.

2.   In assessing individual character, the degree of freedom of the designer in developing the design shall be taken into consideration.

Article 6 Disclosure

1.   For the purpose of applying Articles 4 and 5, a design shall be deemed to have been made available to the public if it has been published following registration or otherwise, or exhibited, used in trade or otherwise disclosed, except where these events could not reasonably have become known in the normal course of business to the circles specialised in the sector concerned, operating within the Community, before the date of filing of the application for registration or, if priority is claimed, the date of priority. The design shall not, however, be deemed to have been made available to the public for the sole reason that it has been disclosed to a third person under explicit or implicit conditions of confidentiality.

2.   A disclosure shall not be taken into consideration for the purpose of applying Articles 4 and 5 if a design for which protection is claimed under a registered design right of a Member State has been made available to the public:

(a) by the designer, his successor in title, or a third person as a result of information provided or action taken by the designer, or his successor in title; and

(b) during the 12-month period preceding the date of filing of the application or, if priority is claimed, the date of priority.

3.   Paragraph 2 shall also apply if the design has been made available to the public as a consequence of an abuse in relation to the designer or his successor in title.

Article 7 Designs dictated by their technical function and designs of interconnections

1.   A design right shall not subsist in features of appearance of a product which are solely dictated by its technical function.

2.   A design right shall not subsist in features of appearance of a product which must necessarily be reproduced in their exact form and dimensions in order to permit the product in which the design is incorporated or to which it is applied to be mechanically connected to or placed in, around or against another product so that either product may perform its function.

3.   Notwithstanding paragraph 2, a design right shall, under the conditions set out in Articles 4 and 5, subsist in a design serving the purpose of allowing multiple assembly or connection of mutually interchangeable products within a modular system.

Article 8 Designs contrary to public policy or morality

A design right shall not subsist in a design which is contrary to public policy or to accepted principles of morality.

Article 9 Scope of protection

1.   The scope of the protection conferred by a design right shall include any design which does not produce on the informed user a different overall impression.

2.   In assessing the scope of protection, the degree of freedom of the designer in developing his design shall be taken into consideration.

Article 10 Term of protection

Upon registration, a design which meets the requirements of Article 3(2) shall be protected by a design right for one or more periods of five years from the date of filing of the application. The right holder may have the term of protection renewed for one or more periods of five years each, up to a total term of 25 years from the date of filing.

Article 11 Invalidity or refusal of registration

1.   A design shall be refused registration, or, if the design has been registered, the design right shall be declared invalid:

   (a) if the design is not a design within the meaning of Article 1(a); or

   (b) if it does not fulfil the requirements of Articles 3 to 8; or

   (c) if the applicant for or the holder of the design right is not entitled to it under the law of the Member State concerned; or

   (d) if the design is in conflict with a prior design which has been made available to the public after the date of filing of the application or, if priority is claimed, the date of priority, and which is protected from a date prior to the said date by a registered Community design or an application for a registered Community design or by a design right of the Member State concerned, or by an application for such a right.

2.   Any Member State may provide that a design shall be refused registration, or, if the design has been registered, that the design right shall be declared invalid:

   (a) if a distinctive sign is used in a subsequent design, and Community law or the law of the Member State concerned governing that sign confers on the right holder of the sign the right to prohibit such use; or

   (b) if the design constitutes an unauthorised use of a work protected under the copyright law of the Member State concerned; or

   (c) if the design constitutes an improper use of any of the items listed in Article 6b of the Paris Convention for the Protection of Industrial Property, or of badges, emblems and escutcheons other than those covered by Article 6b of the said Convention which are of particular public interest in the Member State concerned.

3.   The ground provided for in paragraph 1(c) may be invoked solely by the person who is entitled to the design right under the law of the Member State concerned.

4.   The grounds provided for in paragraph 1(d) and in paragraph 2(a) and (b) may be invoked solely by the applicant for or the holder of the conflicting right.

5.   The ground provided for in paragraph 2(c) may be invoked solely by the person or entity concerned by the use.

6.   Paragraphs 4 and 5 shall be without prejudice to the freedom of Member States to provide that the grounds provided for in paragraphs 1(d) and 2(c) may also be invoked by the appropriate authority of the Member State in question on its own initiative.

7.   When a design has been refused registration or a design right has been declared invalid pursuant to paragraph 1(b) or to paragraph 2, the design may be registered or the design right maintained in an amended form, if in that form it complies with the requirements for protection and the identity of the design is retained. Registration or maintenance in an amended form may include registration accompanied by a partial disclaimer by the holder of the design right or entry in the design Register of a court decision declaring the partial invalidity of the design right.

8.   Any Member State may provide that, by way of derogation from paragraphs 1 to 7, the grounds for refusal of registration or for invalidation in force in that State prior to the date on which the provisions necessary to comply with this Directive enter into force shall apply to design applications which have been made prior to that date and to resulting registrations.

9.   A design right may be declared invalid even after it has lapsed or has been surrendered.

Article 12 Rights conferred by the design right

1.   The registration of a design shall confer on its holder the exclusive right to use it and to prevent any third party not having his consent from using it. The aforementioned use shall cover, in particular, the making, offering, putting on the market, importing, exporting or using of a product in which the design is incorporated or to which it is applied, or stocking such a product for those purposes.

2.   Where, under the law of a Member State, acts referred to in paragraph 1 could not be prevented before the date on which the provisions necessary to comply with this Directive entered into force, the rights conferred by the design right may not be invoked to prevent continuation of such acts by any person who had begun such acts prior to that date.

Article 13 Limitation of the rights conferred by the design right

1.   The rights conferred by a design right upon registration shall not be exercised in respect of:
   (a)   acts done privately and for non-commercial purposes;
   (b)   acts done for experimental purposes;
   (c)   acts of reproduction for the purposes of making citations or of teaching, provided that such acts are compatible with fair trade practice and do not unduly prejudice the normal exploitation of the design, and that mention is made of the source.
2.   In addition, the rights conferred by a design right upon registration shall not be exercised in respect of:
   (a)   the equipment on ships and aircraft registered in another country when these temporarily enter the territory of the Member State concerned;
   (b)   the importation in the Member State concerned of spare parts and accessories for the purpose of repairing such craft;
   (c)   the execution of repairs on such craft.

Article 14 Transitional provision

Until such time as amendments to this Directive are adopted on a proposal from the Commission in accordance with the provisions of Article 18, Member States shall maintain in force their existing legal provisions relating to the use of the design of a component part used for the purpose of the repair of a complex product so as to restore its original appearance and shall introduce changes to those provisions only if the purpose is to liberalise the market for such parts.

Article 15 Exhaustion of rights

The rights conferred by a design right upon registration shall not extend to acts relating to a product in which a design included within the scope of protection of the design right is incorporated or to which it is applied, when the product has been put on the market in the Community by the holder of the design right or with his consent.

Article 16 Relationship to other forms of protection

The provisions of this Directive shall be without prejudice to any provisions of Community law or of the law of the Member State concerned relating to unregistered design rights, trade marks or other distinctive signs, patents and utility models, typefaces, civil liability or unfair competition.

Article 17 Relationship to copyright

A design protected by a design right registered in or in respect of a Member State in accordance with this Directive shall also be eligible for protection under the law of copyright of that State as from the date on which the design was created or fixed in any form. The extent to which, and the conditions under which, such a protection is conferred, including the level of originality required, shall be determined by each Member State.

. . .

DIRECTIVE 2001/29/EC
(copyright and related rights in the information society)

CHAPTER I
OBJECTIVE AND SCOPE

Article 1 Scope

1.   This Directive concerns the legal protection of copyright and related rights in the framework of the internal market, with particular emphasis on the information society.

2.   Except in the cases referred to in Article 11, this Directive shall leave intact and shall in no way affect existing Community provisions relating to:
(a)   the legal protection of computer programs;
(b)   rental right, lending right and certain rights related to copyright in the field of intellectual property;
(c)   copyright and related rights applicable to broadcasting of programmes by satellite and cable retransmission;
(d)   the term of protection of copyright and certain related rights;
(e)   the legal protection of databases.

CHAPTER II
RIGHTS AND EXCEPTIONS

Article 2 Reproduction right

Member States shall provide for the exclusive right to authorise or prohibit direct or indirect, temporary or permanent reproduction by any means and in any form, in whole or in part:
(a)   for authors, of their works;
(b)   for performers, of fixations of their performances;
(c)   for phonogram producers, of their phonograms;
(d)   for the producers of the first fixations of films, in respect of the original and copies of their films;
(e)   for broadcasting organisations, of fixations of their broadcasts, whether those broadcasts are transmitted by wire or over the air, including by cable or satellite.

Article 3 Right of communication to the public of works and right of making available to the public other subject-matter

1.   Member States shall provide authors with the exclusive right to authorise or prohibit any communication to the public of their works, by wire or wireless means, including the making available to the public of their works in such a way that members of the public may access them from a place and at a time individually chosen by them.
2.   Member States shall provide for the exclusive right to authorise or prohibit the making available to the public, by wire or wireless means, in such a way that members of the public may access them from a place and at a time individually chosen by them:
(a)   for performers, of fixations of their performances;
(b)   for phonogram producers, of their phonograms;
(c)   for the producers of the first fixations of films, of the original and copies of their films;
(d)   for broadcasting organisations, of fixations of their broadcasts, whether these broadcasts are transmitted by wire or over the air, including by cable or satellite.
3.   The rights referred to in paragraphs 1 and 2 shall not be exhausted by any act of communication to the public or making available to the public as set out in this Article.

Article 4 Distribution right

1.   Member States shall provide for authors, in respect of the original of their works or of copies thereof, the exclusive right to authorise or prohibit any form of distribution to the public by sale or otherwise.
2.   The distribution right shall not be exhausted within the Community in respect of the original or copies of the work, except where the first sale or other transfer of ownership in the Community of that object is made by the rightholder or with his consent.

Article 5 Exceptions and limitations

1.   Temporary acts of reproduction referred to in Article 2, which are transient or incidental, which are an integral and essential part of a technological process and whose sole purpose is to enable:
(a)   a transmission in a network between third parties by an intermediary, or
(b)   a lawful use
of a work or other subject-matter to be made, and which have no independent economic significance, shall be exempted from the reproduction right provided for in Article 2.
2.   Member States may provide for exceptions or limitations to the reproduction right provided for in Article 2 in the following cases:

(a) in respect of reproductions on paper or any similar medium, effected by the use of any kind of photographic technique or by some other process having similar effects, with the exception of sheet music, provided that the rightholders receive fair compensation;

(b) in respect of reproductions on any medium made by a natural person for private use and for ends that are neither directly nor indirectly commercial, on condition that the rightholders receive fair compensation which takes account of the application or non-application of technological measures referred to in Article 6 to the work or subject-matter concerned;

(c) in respect of specific acts of reproduction made by publicly accessible libraries, educational establishments or museums, or by archives, which are not for direct or indirect economic or commercial advantage;

(d) in respect of ephemeral recordings of works made by broadcasting organisations by means of their own facilities and for their own broadcasts; the preservation of these recordings in official archives may, on the grounds of their exceptional documentary character, be permitted;

(e) in respect of reproductions of broadcasts made by social institutions pursuing non-commercial purposes, such as hospitals or prisons, on condition that the rightholders receive fair compensation.

3. Member States may provide for exceptions or limitations to the rights provided for in Articles 2 and 3 in the following cases:

(a) use for the sole purpose of illustration for teaching or scientific research, as long as the source, including the author's name, is indicated, unless this turns out to be impossible and to the extent justified by the non-commercial purpose to be achieved;

(b) uses, for the benefit of people with a disability, which are directly related to the disability and of a non-commercial nature, to the extent required by the specific disability;

(c) reproduction by the press, communication to the public or making available of published articles on current economic, political or religious topics or of broadcast works or other subject-matter of the same character, in cases where such use is not expressly reserved, and as long as the source, including the author's name, is indicated, or use of works or other subject-matter in connection with the reporting of current events, to the extent justified by the informatory purpose and as long as the source, including the author's name, is indicated, unless this turns out to be impossible;

(d) quotations for purposes such as criticism or review, provided that they relate to a work or other subject-matter which has already been lawfully made available to the public, that, unless this turns out to be impossible, the source, including the author's name, is indicated, and that their use is in accordance with fair practice, and to the extent required by the specific purpose;

(e) use for the purposes of public security or to ensure the proper performance or reporting of administrative, parliamentary or judicial proceedings;

(f) use of political speeches as well as extracts of public lectures or similar works or subject-matter to the extent justified by the informatory purpose and provided that the source, including the author's name, is indicated, except where this turns out to be impossible;

(g) use during religious celebrations or official celebrations organised by a public authority;

(h) use of works, such as works of architecture or sculpture, made to be located permanently in public places;

(i) incidental inclusion of a work or other subject-matter in other material;

(j) use for the purpose of advertising the public exhibition or sale of artistic works, to the extent necessary to promote the event, excluding any other commercial use;

(k) use for the purpose of caricature, parody or pastiche;

(l) use in connection with the demonstration or repair of equipment;

(m) use of an artistic work in the form of a building or a drawing or plan of a building for the purposes of reconstructing the building;

(n) use by communication or making available, for the purpose of research or private study, to individual members of the public by dedicated terminals on the premises of establishments referred to in paragraph 2(c) of works and other subject-matter not subject to purchase or licensing terms which are contained in their collections;

(o) use in certain other cases of minor importance where exceptions or limitations already exist under national law, provided that they only concern analogue uses and do not affect the free circulation of goods and services within the Community, without prejudice to the other exceptions and limitations contained in this Article.

4.   Where the Member States may provide for an exception or limitation to the right of reproduction pursuant to paragraphs 2 and 3, they may provide similarly for an exception or limitation to the right of distribution as referred to in Article 4 to the extent justified by the purpose of the authorised act of reproduction.

5.   The exceptions and limitations provided for in paragraphs 1, 2, 3 and 4 shall only be applied in certain special cases which do not conflict with a normal exploitation of the work or other subject-matter and do not unreasonably prejudice the legitimate interests of the rightholder.

CHAPTER III
PROTECTION OF TECHNOLOGICAL MEASURES AND RIGHTS-MANAGEMENT INFORMATION

Article 6 Obligations as to technological measures

1.   Member States shall provide adequate legal protection against the circumvention of any effective technological measures, which the person concerned carries out in the knowledge, or with reasonable grounds to know, that he or she is pursuing that objective.

2.   Member States shall provide adequate legal protection against the manufacture, import, distribution, sale, rental, advertisement for sale or rental, or possession for commercial purposes of devices, products or components or the provision of services which:

(a)   are promoted, advertised or marketed for the purpose of circumvention of, or

(b)   have only a limited commercially significant purpose or use other than to circumvent, or

(c)   are primarily designed, produced, adapted or performed for the purpose of enabling or facilitating the circumvention of,

any effective technological measures.

3.   For the purposes of this Directive, the expression "technological measures" means any technology, device or component that, in the normal course of its operation, is designed to prevent or restrict acts, in respect of works or other subject-matter, which are not authorised by the rightholder of any copyright or any right related to copyright as provided for by law or the sui generis right provided for in Chapter III of Directive 96/9/EC. Technological measures shall be deemed "effective" where the use of a protected work or other subject-matter is controlled by the rightholders through application of an access control or protection process, such as encryption, scrambling or other transformation of the work or other subject-matter or a copy control mechanism, which achieves the protection objective.

4.   Notwithstanding the legal protection provided for in paragraph 1, in the absence of voluntary measures taken by rightholders, including agreements between rightholders and other parties concerned, Member States shall take appropriate measures to ensure that rightholders make available to the beneficiary of an exception or limitation provided for in national law in accordance with Article 5(2)(a), (2)(c), (2)(d), (2)(e), (3)(a), (3)(b) or (3)(e) the means of benefiting from that exception or limitation, to the extent necessary to benefit from that exception or limitation and where that beneficiary has legal access to the protected work or subject-matter concerned.

A Member State may also take such measures in respect of a beneficiary of an exception or limitation provided for in accordance with Article 5(2)(b), unless reproduction for private use has already been made possible by rightholders to the extent necessary to benefit from the exception or limitation concerned and in accordance with the provisions of Article 5(2)(b) and (5), without preventing rightholders from adopting adequate measures regarding the number of reproductions in accordance with these provisions.

The technological measures applied voluntarily by rightholders, including those applied in implementation of voluntary agreements, and technological measures applied in implementation of the measures taken by Member States, shall enjoy the legal protection provided for in paragraph 1.

The provisions of the first and second subparagraphs shall not apply to works or other subject-matter made available to the public on agreed contractual terms in such a way that members of the public may access them from a place and at a time individually chosen by them. When this Article is applied in the context of Directives 92/ 100/EEC and 96/9/EC, this paragraph shall apply *mutatis mutandis*.

Article 7 Obligations concerning rights-management information

1. Member States shall provide for adequate legal protection against any person knowingly performing without authority any of the following acts:
   (a) the removal or alteration of any electronic rights-management information;
   (b) the distribution, importation for distribution, broadcasting, communication or making available to the public of works or other subject-matter protected under this Directive or under Chapter III of Directive 96/9/EC from which electronic rights-management information has been removed or altered without authority,

   if such person knows, or has reasonable grounds to know, that by so doing he is inducing, enabling, facilitating or concealing an infringement of any copyright or any rights related to copyright as provided by law, or of the *sui generis* right provided for in Chapter III of Directive 96/9/EC.

2. For the purposes of this Directive, the expression "rights-management information" means any information provided by rightholders which identifies the work or other subject-matter referred to in this Directive or covered by the *sui generis* right provided for in Chapter III of Directive 96/ 9/EC, the author or any other rightholder, or information about the terms and conditions of use of the work or other subject-matter, and any numbers or codes that represent such information. The first subparagraph shall apply when any of these items of information is associated with a copy of, or appears in connection with the communication to the public of, a work or other subjectmatter referred to in this Directive or covered by the *sui generis* right provided for in Chapter III of Directive 96/9/EC.

CHAPTER IV
COMMON PROVISIONS

Article 8 Sanctions and remedies

1. Member States shall provide appropriate sanctions and remedies in respect of infringements of the rights and obligations set out in this Directive and shall take all the measures necessary to ensure that those sanctions and remedies are applied. The sanctions thus provided for shall be effective, proportionate and dissuasive.
2. Each Member State shall take the measures necessary to ensure that rightholders whose interests are affected by an infringing activity carried out on its territory can bring an action for damages and/or apply for an injunction and, where appropriate, for the seizure of infringing material as well as of devices, products or components referred to in Article 6(2).
3. Member States shall ensure that rightholders are in a position to apply for an injunction against intermediaries whose services are used by a third party to infringe a copyright or related right.

Article 9 Continued application of other legal provisions

This Directive shall be without prejudice to provisions concerning in particular patent rights, trade marks, design rights, utility models, topographies of semi-conductor products, type faces, conditional access, access to cable of broadcasting services, protection of national treasures, legal deposit requirements, laws on restrictive practices and unfair competition, trade secrets, security, confidentiality, data protection and privacy, access to public documents, the law of contract.

Article 10 Application over time

1. The provisions of this Directive shall apply in respect of all works and other subject-matter referred to in this Directive which are, on 22 December 2002, protected by the Member States' legislation in the field of copyright and related rights, or which meet the criteria for protection under the provisions of this Directive or the provisions referred to in Article 1(2).
2. This Directive shall apply without prejudice to any acts concluded and rights acquired before 22 December 2002.

Article 11 Technical adaptations

. . .
2. Article 3(2) of Directive 93/98/EEC shall be replaced by the following
   "2. The rights of producers of phonograms shall expire 50 years after the fixation is made. However, if the phonogram has been lawfully published within this period, the said rights shall expire 50 years from the date of the first lawful publication. If no lawful publication has taken place within the period mentioned in the first sentence, and if the phonogram has

been lawfully communicated to the public within this period, the said rights shall expire 50 years from the date of the first lawful communication to the public.

However, where through the expiry of the term of protection granted pursuant to this paragraph in its version before amendment by Directive 2001/29/EC of the European Parliament and of the Council of 22 May 2001 on the harmonisation of certain aspects of copyright and related rights in the information society the rights of producers of phonograms are no longer protected on 22 December 2002, this paragraph shall not have the effect of protecting those rights anew."

COUNCIL DIRECTIVE 2001/84/EC
(resale right)

CHAPTER I
SCOPE

Article 1 Subject matter of the resale right

1.   Member States shall provide, for the benefit of the author of an original work of art, a resale right, to be defined as an inalienable right, which cannot be waived, even in advance, to receive a royalty based on the sale price obtained for any resale of the work, subsequent to the first transfer of the work by the author.

2.   The right referred to in paragraph 1 shall apply to all acts of resale involving as sellers, buyers or intermediaries art market professionals, such as salesrooms, art galleries and, in general, any dealers in works of art.

3.   Member States may provide that the right referred to in paragraph 1 shall not apply to acts of resale where the seller has acquired the work directly from the author less than three years before that resale and where the resale price does not exceed EUR10 000.

4.   The royalty shall be payable by the seller. Member States may provide that one of the natural or legal persons referred to in paragraph 2 other than the seller shall alone be liable or shall share liability with the seller for payment of the royalty.

Article 2 Works of art to which the resale right relates

1.   For the purposes of this Directive, "original work of art" means works of graphic or plastic art such as pictures, collages, paintings, drawings, engravings, prints, lithographs, sculptures, tapestries, ceramics, glassware and photographs, provided they are made by the artist himself or are copies considered to be original works of art.

2.   Copies of works of art covered by this Directive, which have been made in limited numbers by the artist himself or under his authority, shall be considered to be original works of art for the purposes of this Directive. Such copies will normally have been numbered, signed or otherwise duly authorised by the artist.

CHAPTER II
PARTICULAR PROVISIONS

Article 3 Threshold

1.   It shall be for the Member States to set a minimum sale price from which the sales referred to in Article 1 shall be subject to resale right.

2.   This minimum sale price may not under any circumstances exceed EUR3 000.

Article 4 Rates

1.   The royalty provided for in Article 1 shall be set at the following rates:

(a)   4 % for the portion of the sale price up to EUR 50 000;

(b)   3 % for the portion of the sale price from EUR 50 000,01 to EUR 200 000;

(c)   1 % for the portion of the sale price from EUR 200 000,01 to EUR 350 000;

(d)   0,5 % for the portion of the sale price from EUR 350 000,01 to EUR 500 000;

(e)   0,25 % for the portion of the sale price exceeding EUR 500 000.

However, the total amount of the royalty may not exceed EUR 12 500.

2.   By way of derogation from paragraph 1, Member States may apply a rate of 5 % for the portion of the sale price referred to in paragraph 1(a).

3.   If the minimum sale price set should be lower than EUR3 000, the Member State shall also determine the rate applicable to the portion of the sale price up to EUR3 000; this rate may not be lower than 4 %.

Article 5 Calculation basis

The sale prices referred to in Articles 3 and 4 are net of tax.

Article 6 Persons entitled to receive royalties

1.   The royalty provided for under Article 1 shall be payable to the author of the work and, subject to Article 8(2), after his death to those entitled under him/her.

2.   Member States may provide for compulsory or optional collective management of the royalty provided for under Article 1.

Article 7 Third-country nationals entitled to receive royalties

1.   Member States shall provide that authors who are nationals of third countries and, subject to Article 8(2), their successors in title shall enjoy the resale right in accordance with this Directive and the legislation of the Member State concerned only if legislation in the country of which the author or his/her successor in title is a national permits resale right protection in that country for authors from the Member States and their successors in title.

2.   On the basis of information provided by the Member States, the Commission shall publish as soon as possible an indicative list of those third countries which fulfil the condition set out in paragraph 1. This list shall be kept up to date.

3.   Any Member State may treat authors who are not nationals of a Member State but who have their habitual residence in that Member State in the same way as its own nationals for the purpose of resale right protection.

Article 8 Term of protection of the resale right

1.   The term of protection of the resale right shall correspond to that laid down in Article 1 of Directive 93/98/EEC.

2.   By way of derogation from paragraph 1, those Member States which do not apply the resale right on (the entry into force date referred to in Article 13), shall not be required, for a period expiring not later than 1 January 2010, to apply the resale right for the benefit of those entitled under the artist after his/her death.

3.   A Member State to which paragraph 2 applies may have up to two more years, if necessary to enable the economic operators in that Member State to adapt gradually to the resale right system while maintaining their economic viability, before it is required to apply the resale right for the benefit of those entitled under the artist after his/her death. At least 12 months before the end of the period referred to in paragraph 2, the Member State concerned shall inform the Commission giving its reasons, so that the Commission can give an opinion, after appropriate consultations, within three months following the receipt of such information. If the Member State does not follow the opinion of the Commission, it shall within one month inform the Commission and justify its decision. The notification and justification of the Member State and the opinion of the Commission shall be published in the *Official Journal of the European Communities* and forwarded to the European Parliament.

4.   In the event of the successful conclusion, within the periods referred to in Article 8(2) and (3), of international negotiations aimed at extending the resale right at international level, the Commission shall submit appropriate proposals.

Article 9 Right to obtain information

The Member States shall provide that for a period of three years after the resale, the persons entitled under Article 6 may require from any art market professional mentioned in Article 1(2) to furnish any information that may be necessary in order to secure payment of royalties in respect of the resale.

CHAPTER III
FINAL PROVISIONS

Article 10 Application in time

This Directive shall apply in respect of all original works of art as defined in Article 2 which, on 1 January 2006, are still protected by the legislation of the Member States in the field of copyright or meet the criteria for protection under the provisions of this Directive at that date.

COUNCIL DIRECTIVE 2004/48/EC
(enforcement of intellectual property rights)

CHAPTER I
OBJECTIVE AND SCOPE

Article 1 Subject matter

This Directive concerns the measures, procedures and remedies necessary to ensure the enforcement of intellectual property rights. For the purposes of this Directive, the term «intellectual property rights» includes industrial property rights.

Article 2 Scope

1.   Without prejudice to the means which are or may be provided for in Community or national legislation, in so far as those means may be more favourable for rightholders, the measures, procedures and remedies provided for by this Directive shall apply, in accordance with Article 3, to any infringement of intellectual property rights as provided for by Community law and/or by the national law of the Member State concerned.

2.   This Directive shall be without prejudice to the specific provisions on the enforcement of rights and on exceptions contained in Community legislation concerning copyright and rights related to copyright, notably those found in Directive 91/250/EEC and, in particular, Article 7 thereof or in Directive 2001/29/EC and, in particular, Articles 2 to 6 and Article 8 thereof.

3.   This Directive shall not affect:
   (a) the Community provisions governing the substantive law on intellectual property, Directive 95/46/EC, Directive 1999/93/EC or Directive 2000/31/EC, in general, and Articles 12 to 15 of Directive 2000/31/EC in particular;
   (b) Member States' international obligations and notably the TRIPS Agreement, including those relating to criminal procedures and penalties;
   (c) any national provisions in Member States relating to criminal procedures or penalties in respect of infringement of intellectual property rights.

CHAPTER II
MEASURES, PROCEDURES AND REMEDIES

SECTION 1
GENERAL PROVISIONS

Article 3 General obligation

1.   Member States shall provide for the measures, procedures and remedies necessary to ensure the enforcement of the intellectual property rights covered by this Directive. Those measures, procedures and remedies shall be fair and equitable and shall not be unnecessarily complicated or costly, or entail unreasonable time-limits or unwarranted delays.

2.   Those measures, procedures and remedies shall also be effective, proportionate and dissuasive and shall be applied in such a manner as to avoid the creation of barriers to legitimate trade and to provide for safeguards against their abuse.

Article 4 Persons entitled to apply for the application of the measures, procedures and remedies

Member States shall recognise as persons entitled to seek application of the measures, procedures and remedies referred to in this chapter:

(a)   the holders of intellectual property rights, in accordance with the provisions of the applicable law;

(b)   all other persons authorised to use those rights, in particular licensees, in so far as permitted by and in accordance with the provisions of the applicable law;

(c)   intellectual property collective rights-management bodies which are regularly recognised as having a right to represent holders of intellectual property rights, in so far as permitted by and in accordance with the provisions of the applicable law;

(d)   professional defence bodies which are regularly recognised as having a right to represent holders of intellectual property rights, in so far as permitted by and in accordance with the provisions of the applicable law.

Article 5 Presumption of authorship or ownership

For the purposes of applying the measures, procedures and remedies provided for in this Directive,

(a)   for the author of a literary or artistic work, in the absence of proof to the contrary, to be regarded as such, and consequently to be entitled to institute infringement proceedings, it shall be sufficient for his/her name to appear on the work in the usual manner;

(b)   the provision under (a) shall apply mutatis mutandis to the holders of rights related to copyright with regard to their protected subject matter.

SECTION 2
EVIDENCE

Article 6 Evidence

1.   Member States shall ensure that, on application by a party which has presented reasonably available evidence sufficient to support its claims, and has, in substantiating those claims, specified evidence which lies in the control of the opposing party, the competent judicial authorities may order that such evidence be presented by the opposing party, subject to the protection of confidential information. For the purposes of this paragraph, Member States may provide that a reasonable sample of a substantial number of copies of a work or any other protected object be considered by the competent judicial authorities to constitute reasonable evidence.

2.   Under the same conditions, in the case of an infringement committed on a commercial scale Member States shall take such measures as are necessary to enable the competent judicial authorities to order, where appropriate, on application by a party, the communication of banking, financial or commercial documents under the control of the opposing party, subject to the protection of confidential information.

Article 7 Measures for preserving evidence

1.   Member States shall ensure that, even before the commencement of proceedings on the merits of the case, the competent judicial authorities may, on application by a party who has presented reasonably available evidence to support his/her claims that his/her intellectual property right has been infringed or is about to be infringed, order prompt and effective provisional measures to preserve relevant evidence in respect of the alleged infringement, subject to the protection of confidential information. Such measures may include the detailed description, with or without the taking of samples, or the physical seizure of the infringing goods, and, in appropriate cases, the materials and implements used in the production and/or distribution of these goods and the documents relating thereto. Those measures shall be taken, if necessary without the other party having been heard, in particular where any delay is likely to cause irreparable harm to the rightholder or where there is a demonstrable risk of evidence being destroyed.

Where measures to preserve evidence are adopted without the other party having been heard, the parties affected shall be given notice, without delay after the execution of the measures at the latest. A review, including a right to be heard, shall take place upon request of the parties affected with a view to deciding, within a reasonable period after the notification of the measures, whether the measures shall be modified, revoked or confirmed.

2.   Member States shall ensure that the measures to preserve evidence may be subject to the lodging by the applicant of adequate security or an equivalent assurance intended to ensure compensation for any prejudice suffered by the defendant as provided for in paragraph 4.

3.   Member States shall ensure that the measures to preserve evidence are revoked or otherwise cease to have effect, upon request of the defendant, without prejudice to the damages which may be claimed, if the applicant does not institute, within a reasonable period, proceedings leading to a decision on the merits of the case before the competent judicial authority, the period to be determined by the judicial authority ordering the measures where the law of a Member State so permits or, in the absence of such determination, within a period not exceeding 20 working days or 31 calendar days, whichever is the longer.

4.   Where the measures to preserve evidence are revoked, or where they lapse due to any act or omission by the applicant, or where it is subsequently found that there has been no infringement or threat of infringement of an intellectual property right, the judicial authorities shall have the authority to order the applicant, upon request of the defendant, to provide the defendant appropriate compensation for any injury caused by those measures.

5.   Member States may take measures to protect witnesses' identity.

SECTION 3
RIGHT OF INFORMATION

Article 8 Right of information

1.   Member States shall ensure that, in the context of proceedings concerning an infringement of an intellectual property right and in response to a justified and proportionate request of the claimant, the competent judicial authorities may order that information on the origin and distribution networks of the goods or services which infringe an intellectual property right be provided by the infringer and/or any other person who:
  (a)   was found in possession of the infringing goods on a commercial scale;
  (b)   was found to be using the infringing services on a commercial scale;
  (c)   was found to be providing on a commercial scale services used in infringing activities; or
  (d)   was indicated by the person referred to in point (a), (b) or (c) as being involved in the production, manufacture or distribution of the goods or the provision of the services.

2.   The information referred to in paragraph 1 shall, as appropriate, comprise:
  (a)   the names and addresses of the producers, manufacturers, distributors, suppliers and other previous holders of the goods or services, as well as the intended wholesalers and retailers;
  (b)   information on the quantities produced, manufactured, delivered, received or ordered, as well as the price obtained for the goods or services in question.

3.   Paragraphs 1 and 2 shall apply without prejudice to other statutory provisions which:
  (a)   grant the rightholder rights to receive fuller information;
  (b)   govern the use in civil or criminal proceedings of the information communicated pursuant to this Article;
  (c)   govern responsibility for misuse of the right of information; or
  (d)   afford an opportunity for refusing to provide information which would force the person referred to in paragraph 1 to admit to his/her own participation or that of his/her close relatives in an infringement of an intellectual property right; or
  (e)   govern the protection of confidentiality of information sources or the processing of personal data.

SECTION 4
PROVISIONAL AND PRECAUTIONARY MEASURES

Article 9 Provisional and precautionary measures

1.   Member States shall ensure that the judicial authorities may, at the request of the applicant:
  (a)   issue against the alleged infringer an interlocutory injunction intended to prevent any imminent infringement of an intellectual property right, or to forbid, on a provisional basis and subject, where appropriate, to a recurring penalty payment where provided for by national law, the continuation of the alleged infringements of that right, or to

make such continuation subject to the lodging of guarantees intended to ensure the compensation of the rightholder; an interlocutory injunction may also be issued, under the same conditions, against an intermediary whose services are being used by a third party to infringe an intellectual property right; injunctions against intermediaries whose services are used by a third party to infringe a copyright or a related right are covered by Directive 2001/29/EC;

(b) order the seizure or delivery up of the goods suspected of infringing an intellectual property right so as to prevent their entry into or movement within the channels of commerce.

2. In the case of an infringement committed on a commercial scale, the Member States shall ensure that, if the injured party demonstrates circumstances likely to endanger the recovery of damages, the judicial authorities may order the precautionary seizure of the movable and immovable property of the alleged infringer, including the blocking of his/her bank accounts and other assets. To that end, the competent authorities may order the communication of bank, financial or commercial documents, or appropriate access to the relevant information.

3. The judicial authorities shall, in respect of the measures referred to in paragraphs 1 and 2, have the authority to require the applicant to provide any reasonably available evidence in order to satisfy themselves with a sufficient degree of certainty that the applicant is the rightholder and that the applicant's right is being infringed, or that such infringement is imminent.

4. Member States shall ensure that the provisional measures referred to in paragraphs 1 and 2 may, in appropriate cases, be taken without the defendant having been heard, in particular where any delay would cause irreparable harm to the rightholder. In that event, the parties shall be so informed without delay after the execution of the measures at the latest.

A review, including a right to be heard, shall take place upon request of the defendant with a view to deciding, within a reasonable time after notification of the measures, whether those measures shall be modified, revoked or confirmed.

5. Member States shall ensure that the provisional measures referred to in paragraphs 1 and 2 are revoked or otherwise cease to have effect, upon request of the defendant, if the applicant does not institute, within a reasonable period, proceedings leading to a decision on the merits of the case before the competent judicial authority, the period to be determined by the judicial authority ordering the measures where the law of a Member State so permits or, in the absence of such determination, within a period not exceeding 20 working days or 31 calendar days, whichever is the longer.

6. The competent judicial authorities may make the provisional measures referred to in paragraphs 1 and 2 subject to the lodging by the applicant of adequate security or an equivalent assurance intended to ensure compensation for any prejudice suffered by the defendant as provided for in paragraph 7.

7. Where the provisional measures are revoked or where they lapse due to any act or omission by the applicant, or where it is subsequently found that there has been no infringement or threat of infringement of an intellectual property right, the judicial authorities shall have the authority to order the applicant, upon request of the defendant, to provide the defendant appropriate compensation for any injury caused by those measures.

SECTION 5

MEASURES RESULTING FROM A DECISION ON THE MERITS OF THE CASE

Article 10 Corrective measures

1. Without prejudice to any damages due to the rightholder by reason of the infringement, and without compensation of any sort, Member States shall ensure that the competent judicial authorities may order, at the request of the applicant, that appropriate measures be taken with regard to goods that they have found to be infringing an intellectual property right and, in appropriate cases, with regard to materials and implements principally used in the creation or manufacture of those goods. Such measures shall include:

(a) recall from the channels of commerce;

(b) definitive removal from the channels of commerce; or

(c) destruction.

2. The judicial authorities shall order that those measures be carried out at the expense of the infringer, unless particular reasons are invoked for not doing so.

3.   In considering a request for corrective measures, the need for proportionality between the seriousness of the infringement and the remedies ordered as well as the interests of third parties shall be taken into account.

Article 11 Injunctions

Member States shall ensure that, where a judicial decision is taken finding an infringement of an intellectual property right, the judicial authorities may issue against the infringer an injunction aimed at prohibiting the continuation of the infringement. Where provided for by national law, non-compliance with an injunction shall, where appropriate, be subject to a recurring penalty payment, with a view to ensuring compliance. Member States shall also ensure that rightholders are in a position to apply for an injunction against intermediaries whose services are used by a third party to infringe an intellectual property right, without prejudice to Article 8(3)Z of Directive 2001/29/EC.

Article 12 Alternative measures

Member States may provide that, in appropriate cases and at the request of the person liable to be subject to the measures provided for in this section, the competent judicial authorities may order pecuniary compensation to be paid to the injured party instead of applying the measures provided for in this section if that person acted unintentionally and without negligence, if execution of the measures in question would cause him/her disproportionate harm and if pecuniary compensation to the injured party appears reasonably satisfactory.

SECTION 6
DAMAGES AND LEGAL COSTS

Article 13 Damages

1.   Member States shall ensure that the competent judicial authorities, on application of the injured party, order the infringer who knowingly, or with reasonable grounds to know, engaged in an infringing activity, to pay the rightholder damages appropriate to the actual prejudice suffered by him/her as a result of the infringement.
When the judicial authorities set the damages:
(a)   they shall take into account all appropriate aspects, such as the negative economic consequences, including lost profits, which the injured party has suffered, any unfair profits made by the infringer and, in appropriate cases, elements other than economic factors, such as the moral prejudice caused to the rightholder by the infringement; or
(b)   as an alternative to (a), they may, in appropriate cases, set the damages as a lump sum on the basis of elements such as at least the amount of royalties or fees which would have been due if the infringer had requested authorisation to use the intellectual property right in question.
2.   Where the infringer did not knowingly, or with reasonable grounds know, engage in infringing activity, Member States may lay down that the judicial authorities may order the recovery of profits or the payment of damages, which may be pre-established.

Article 14 Legal costs

Member States shall ensure that reasonable and proportionate legal costs and other expenses incurred by the successful party shall, as a general rule, be borne by the unsuccessful party, unless equity does not allow this.

SECTION 7
PUBLICITY MEASURES

Article 15 Publication of judicial decisions

Member States shall ensure that, in legal proceedings instituted for infringement of an intellectual property right, the judicial authorities may order, at the request of the applicant and at the expense of the infringer, appropriate measures for the dissemination of the information concerning the decision, including displaying the decision and publishing it in full or in part. Member States may provide for other additional publicity measures which are appropriate to the particular circumstances, including prominent advertising.

CHAPTER III
SANCTIONS BY MEMBER STATES

Article 16 Sanctions by Member States

Without prejudice to the civil and administrative measures, procedures and remedies laid down by this Directive, Member States may apply other appropriate sanctions in cases where intellectual property rights have been infringed.

CHAPTER IV
CODES OF CONDUCT AND ADMINISTRATIVE COOPERATION

Article 17 Codes of conduct

Member States shall encourage:

(a)   the development by trade or professional associations or organisations of codes of conduct at Community level aimed at contributing towards the enforcement of the intellectual property rights, particularly by recommending the use on optical discs of a code enabling the identification of the origin of their manufacture;

(b)   the submission to the Commission of draft codes of conduct at national and Community level and of any evaluations of the application of these codes of conduct.

Article 18 Assessment

1.   Three years after the date laid down in Article 20(1), each Member State shall submit to the Commission a report on the implementation of this Directive.
On the basis of those reports, the Commission shall draw up a report on the application of this Directive, including an assessment of the effectiveness of the measures taken, as well as an evaluation of its impact on innovation and the development of the information society. That report shall then be transmitted to the European Parliament, the Council and the European Economic and Social Committee. It shall be accompanied, if necessary and in the light of developments in the Community legal order, by proposals for amendments to this Directive.

2.   Member States shall provide the Commission with all the aid and assistance it may need when drawing up the report referred to in the second subparagraph of paragraph 1.

Article 19 Exchange of information and correspondents

For the purpose of promoting cooperation, including the exchange of information, among Member States and between Member States and the Commission, each Member State shall designate one or more national correspondents for any question relating to the implementation of the measures provided for by this Directive. It shall communicate the details of the national correspondent(s) to the other Member States and to the Commission.

COUNCIL DIRECTIVE 2006/115/EC
(rental right and lending right and certain rights related to copyright)
(codified version)

CHAPTER I
RENTAL AND LENDING RIGHT

Article 1 Object of harmonisation

1.   In accordance with the provisions of this Chapter, Member States shall provide, subject to Article 6, a right to authorise or prohibit the rental and lending of originals and copies of copyright works, and other subject matter as set out in Article 3(1).

2.   The rights referred to in paragraph 1 shall not be exhausted by any sale or other act of distribution of originals and copies of copyright works and other subject matter as set out in Article 3(1).

Article 2 Definitions

1. For the purposes of this Directive the following definitions shall apply:
    (a) "rental" means making available for use, for a limited period of time and for direct or indirect economic or commercial advantage;
    (b) "lending" means making available for use, for a limited period of time and not for direct or indirect economic or commercial advantage, when it is made through establishments which are accessible to the public;
    (c) "film" means a cinematographic or audiovisual work or moving images, whether or not accompanied by sound.
2. The principal director of a cinematographic or audiovisual work shall be considered as its author or one of its authors. Member States may provide for others to be considered as its co-authors.

Article 3 Rightholders and subject matter of rental and lending right

1. The exclusive right to authorise or prohibit rental and lending shall belong to the following:
    (a) the author in respect of the original and copies of his work;
    (b) the performer in respect of fixations of his performance;
    (c) the phonogram producer in respect of his phonograms;
    (d) the producer of the first fixation of a film in respect of the original and copies of his film.
2. This Directive shall not cover rental and lending rights in relation to buildings and to works of applied art.
3. The rights referred to in paragraph 1 may be transferred, assigned or subject to the granting of contractual licences.
4. Without prejudice to paragraph 6, when a contract concerning film production is concluded, individually or collectively, by performers with a film producer, the performer covered by this contract shall be presumed, subject to contractual clauses to the contrary, to have transferred his rental right, subject to Article 5.
5. Member States may provide for a similar presumption as set out in paragraph 4 with respect to authors.
6. Member States may provide that the signing of a contract concluded between a performer and a film producer concerning the production of a film has the effect of authorising rental, provided that such contract provides for an equitable remuneration within the meaning of Article 5. Member States may also provide that this paragraph shall apply mutatis mutandis to the rights included in Chapter II.

Article 4 Rental of computer programs

This Directive shall be without prejudice to Article 4(c) of Council Directive 91/250/EEC of 14 May 1991 on the legal protection of computer programs.

Article 5 Unwaivable right to equitable remuneration

1. Where an author or performer has transferred or assigned his rental right concerning a phonogram or an original or copy of a film to a phonogram or film producer, that author or performer shall retain the right to obtain an equitable remuneration for the rental.
2. The right to obtain an equitable remuneration for rental cannot be waived by authors or performers.
3. The administration of this right to obtain an equitable remuneration may be entrusted to collecting societies representing authors or performers.
4. Member States may regulate whether and to what extent administration by collecting societies of the right to obtain an equitable remuneration may be imposed, as well as the question from whom this remuneration may be claimed or collected.

Article 6 Derogation from the exclusive public lending right

1. Member States may derogate from the exclusive right provided for in Article 1 in respect of public lending, provided that at least authors obtain a remuneration for such lending. Member States shall be free to determine this remuneration taking account of their cultural promotion objectives.
2. Where Member States do not apply the exclusive lending right provided for in Article 1 as regards phonograms, films and computer programs, they shall introduce, at least for authors, a remuneration.

3.   Member States may exempt certain categories of establishments from the payment of the remuneration referred to in paragraphs 1 and 2.

CHAPTER II
RIGHTS RELATED TO COPYRIGHT

Article 7 Fixation right

1.   Member States shall provide for performers the exclusive right to authorise or prohibit the fixation of their performances.
2.   Member States shall provide for broadcasting organisations the exclusive right to authorise or prohibit the fixation of their broadcasts, whether these broadcasts are transmitted by wire or over the air, including by cable or satellite.
3.   A cable distributor shall not have the right provided for in paragraph 2 where it merely retransmits by cable the broadcasts of broadcasting organisations.

Article 8 Broadcasting and communication to the public

1.   Member States shall provide for performers the exclusive right to authorise or prohibit the broadcasting by wireless means and the communication to the public of their performances, except where the performance is itself already a broadcast performance or is made from a fixation.
2.   Member States shall provide a right in order to ensure that a single equitable remuneration is paid by the user, if a phonogram published for commercial purposes, or a reproduction of such phonogram, is used for broadcasting by wireless means or for any communication to the public, and to ensure that this remuneration is shared between the relevant performers and phonogram producers. Member States may, in the absence of agreement between the performers and phonogram producers, lay down the conditions as to the sharing of this remuneration between them.
3.   Member States shall provide for broadcasting organisations the exclusive right to authorise or prohibit the rebroadcasting of their broadcasts by wireless means, as well as the communication to the public of their broadcasts if such communication is made in places accessible to the public against payment of an entrance fee.

Article 9 Distribution right

1.   Member States shall provide the exclusive right to make available to the public, by sale or otherwise, the objects indicated in points (a) to (d), including copies thereof, hereinafter "the distribution right":
       (a)   for performers, in respect of fixations of their performances;
       (b)   for phonogram producers, in respect of their phonograms;
       (c)   for producers of the first fixations of films, in respect of the original and copies of their films;
       (d)   for broadcasting organisations, in respect of fixations of their broadcasts as set out in Article 7(2).
2.   The distribution right shall not be exhausted within the Community in respect of an object as referred to in paragraph 1, except where the first sale in the Community of that object is made by the rightholder or with his consent.
3.   The distribution right shall be without prejudice to the specific provisions of Chapter I, in particular Article 1(2).
4.   The distribution right may be transferred, assigned or subject to the granting of contractual licences.

Article 10 Limitations to rights

1.   Member States may provide for limitations to the rights referred to in this Chapter in respect of:
       (a)   private use;
       (b)   use of short excerpts in connection with the reporting of current events;
       (c)   ephemeral fixation by a broadcasting organisation by means of its own facilities and for its own broadcasts;
       (d)   use solely for the purposes of teaching or scientific research.

2.   Irrespective of paragraph 1, any Member State may provide for the same kinds of limitations with regard to the protection of performers, producers of phonograms, broadcasting organisations and of producers of the first fixations of films, as it provides for in connection with the protection of copyright in literary and artistic works.
        However, compulsory licences may be provided for only to the extent to which they are compatible with the Rome Convention.

3.   The limitations referred to in paragraphs 1 and 2 shall be applied only in certain special cases which do not conflict with a normal exploitation of the subject matter and do not unreasonably prejudice the legitimate interests of the rightholder.

CHAPTER III
COMMON PROVISIONS

Article 11 Application in tune

1.   This Directive shall apply in respect of all copyright works, performances, phonograms, broadcasts and first fixations of films referred to in this Directive which were, on 1 July 1994, still protected by the legislation of the Member States in the field of copyright and related rights or which met the criteria for protection under this Directive on that date.

2.   This Directive shall apply without prejudice to any acts of exploitation performed before 1 July 1994.

3.   Member States may provide that the rightholders are deemed to have given their authorisation to the rental or lending of an object referred to in points (a) to (d) of Article 3(1) which is proven to have been made available to third parties for this purpose or to have been acquired before 1 July 1994.
        However, in particular where such an object is a digital recording, Member States may provide that rightholders shall have a right to obtain an adequate remuneration for the rental or lending of that object.

4.   Member States need not apply the provisions of Article 2(2) to cinematographic or audiovisual works created before 1 July 1994.

5.   This Directive shall, without prejudice to paragraph 3 and subject to paragraph 7, not affect any contracts concluded before 19 November 1992.

6.   Member States may provide, subject to the provisions of paragraph 7, that when rightholders who acquire new rights under the national provisions adopted in implementation of this Directive have, before 1 July 1994, given their consent for exploitation, they shall be presumed to have transferred the new exclusive rights.

7.   For contracts concluded before 1 July 1994, the unwaivable right to an equitable remuneration provided for in Article 5 shall apply only where authors or performers or those representing them have submitted a request to that effect before 1 January 1997. In the absence of agreement between rightholders concerning the level of remuneration, Member States may fix the level of equitable remuneration.

Article 12 Relation between copyright and related rights

Protection of copyright-related rights under this Directive shall leave intact and shall in no way affect the protection of copyright.

Article 14 Repeal

Directive 92/100/EEC is hereby repealed, without prejudice to the obligations of the Member States relating to the time-limits for transposition into national law of the Directives as set out in Part B of Annex I.

References made to the repealed Directive shall be construed as being made to this Directive and should be read in accordance with the correlation table in Annex II.

COUNCIL DIRECTIVE 2006/116/EC
(term of protection of copyright and certain related rights)
(codified version) (as amended by Directive 2011/77/EU)

Article 1 Duration of authors' rights

1.   The rights of an author of a literary or artistic work within the meaning of Article 2 of the Berne Convention shall run for the life of the author and for 70 years after his death, irrespective of the date when the work is lawfully made available to the public.

2.   In the case of a work of joint authorship, the term referred to in paragraph 1 shall be calculated from the death of the last surviving author.

3.   In the case of anonymous or pseudonymous works, the term of protection shall run for 70 years after the work is lawfully made available to the public. However, when the pseudonym adopted by the author leaves no doubt as to his identity, or if the author discloses his identity during the period referred to in the first sentence, the term of protection applicable shall be that laid down in paragraph 1.

4.   Where a Member State provides for particular provisions on copyright in respect of collective works or for a legal person to be designated as the rightholder, the term of protection shall be calculated according to the provisions of paragraph 3, except if the natural persons who have created the work are identified as such in the versions of the work which are made available to the public. This paragraph is without prejudice to the rights of identified authors whose identifiable contributions are included in such works, to which contributions paragraph 1 or 2 shall apply.

5.   Where a work is published in volumes, parts, instalments, issues or episodes and the term of protection runs from the time when the work was lawfully made available to the public, the term of protection shall run for each such item separately.

6.   In the case of works for which the term of protection is not calculated from the death of the author or authors and which have not been lawfully made available to the public within 70 years from their creation, the protection shall terminate.

7.   The term of protection of a musical composition with words shall expire 70 years after the death of the last of the following persons to survive, whether or not those persons are designated as co-authors: the author of the lyrics and the composer of the musical composition, provided that both contributions were specifically created for the respective musical composition with words.

Article 2 Cinematographic or audiovisual works

1.   The principal director of a cinematographic or audiovisual work shall be considered as its author or one of its authors. Member States shall be free to designate other co-authors.

2.   The term of protection of cinematographic or audiovisual works shall expire 70 years after the death of the last of the following persons to survive, whether or not these persons are designated as co-authors: the principal director, the author of the screenplay, the author of the dialogue and the composer of music specifically created for use in the cinematographic or audiovisual work.

Article 3 Duration of related rights

1.   The rights of performers shall expire 50 years after the date of the performance. However,
    —   if a fixation of the performance otherwise than in a phonogram is lawfully published or lawfully communicated to the public within this period, the rights shall expire 50 years from the date of the first such publication or the first such communication to the public, whichever is the earlier,
    —   if a fixation of the performance in a phonogram is lawfully published or lawfully communicated to the public within this period, the rights shall expire 70 years from the date of the first such publication or the first such communication to the public, whichever is the earlier.

2.   The rights of producers of phonograms shall expire 50 years after the fixation is made. However, if the phonogram has been lawfully published within this period, the said rights shall expire 70 years from the date of the first lawful publication. If no lawful publication has

taken place within the period mentioned in the first sentence, and if the phonogram has been lawfully communicated to the public within this period, the said rights shall expire 70 years from the date of the first lawful communication to the public.

However, this paragraph shall not have the effect of protecting anew the rights of producers of phonograms where, through the expiry of the term of protection granted them pursuant to Article 3(2) of Directive 93/98/EEC in its version before amendment by Directive 2001/29/EEC, they were no longer protected on 22 December 2002.

2a.   If, 50 years after the phonogram was lawfully published or, failing such publication, 50 years after it was lawfully communicated to the public, the phonogram producer does not offer copies of the phonogram for sale in sufficient quantity or does not make it available to the public, by wire or wireless means, in such a way that members of the public may access it from a place and at a time individually chosen by them, the performer may terminate the contract by which the performer has transferred or assigned his rights in the fixation of his performance to a phonogram producer (hereinafter a "contract on transfer or assignment"). The right to terminate the contract on transfer or assignment may be exercised if the producer, within a year from the notification by the performer of his intention to terminate the contract on transfer or assignment pursuant to the previous sentence, fails to carry out both of the acts of exploitation referred to in that sentence. This right to terminate may not be waived by the performer. Where a phonogram contains the fixation of the performances of a plurality of performers, they may terminate their contracts on transfer or assignment in accordance with applicable national law. If the contract on transfer or assignment is terminated pursuant to this paragraph, the rights of the phonogram producer in the phonogram shall expire.

2b.   Where a contract on transfer or assignment gives the performer a right to claim a non-recurring remuneration, the performer shall have the right to obtain an annual supplementary remuneration from the phonogram producer for each full year immediately following the 50th year after the phonogram was lawfully published or, failing such publication, the 50th year after it was lawfully communicated to the public. The right to obtain such annual supplementary remuneration may not be waived by the performer.

2c.   The overall amount to be set aside by a phonogram producer for payment of the annual supplementary remuneration referred to in paragraph 2b shall correspond to 20 % of the revenue which the phonogram producer has derived, during the year preceding that for which the said remuneration is paid, from the reproduction, distribution and making available of the phonogram in question, following the 50th year after it was lawfully published or, failing such publication, the 50th year after it was lawfully communicated to the public.

Member States shall ensure that phonogram producers are required on request to provide to performers who are entitled to the annual supplementary remuneration referred to in paragraph 2b any information which may be necessary in order to secure payment of that remuneration.

2d.   Member States shall ensure that the right to obtain an annual supplementary remuneration as referred to in paragraph 2b is administered by collecting societies.

2e.   Where a performer is entitled to recurring payments, neither advance payments nor any contractually defined deductions shall be deducted from the payments made to the performer following the 50th year after the phonogram was lawfully published or, failing such publication, the 50th year after it was lawfully communicated to the public.

3.   The rights of producers of the first fixation of a film shall expire 50 years after the fixation is made. However, if the film is lawfully published or lawfully communicated to the public during this period, the rights shall expire 50 years from the date of the first such publication or the first such communication to the public, whichever is the earlier. The term "film" shall designate a cinematographic or audiovisual work or moving images, whether or not accompanied by sound.

4.   The rights of broadcasting organisations shall expire 50 years after the first transmission of a broadcast, whether this broadcast is transmitted by wire or over the air, including by cable or satellite.

Article 4 Protection of previously unpublished works

Any person who, after the expiry of copyright protection, for the first time lawfully publishes or lawfully communicates to the public a previously unpublished work, shall benefit from a protection equivalent to the economic rights of the author. The term of protection of such rights shall be 25 years from the time when the work was first lawfully published or lawfully communicated to the public.

Article 5 Critical and scientific publications

Member States may protect critical and scientific publications of works which have come into the public domain. The maximum term of protection of such rights shall be 30 years from the time when the publication was first lawfully published.

Article 6 Protection of photographs

Photographs which are original in the sense that they are the author's own intellectual creation shall be protected in accordance with Article 1. No other criteria shall be applied to determine their eligibility for protection. Member States may provide for the protection of other photographs.

Article 7 Protection vis-à-vis third countries

1.   Where the country of origin of a work, within the meaning of the Berne Convention, is a third country, and the author of the work is not a Community national, the term of protection granted by the Member States shall expire on the date of expiry of the protection granted in the country of origin of the work, but may not exceed the term laid down in Article 1.

2.   The terms of protection laid down in Article 3 shall also apply in the case of rightholders who are not Community nationals, provided Member States grant them protection. However, without prejudice to the international obligations of the Member States, the term of protection granted by Member States shall expire no later than the date of expiry of the protection granted in the country of which the rightholder is a national and may not exceed the term laid down in Article 3.

3.   Member States which, on 29 October 1993, in particular pursuant to their international obligations, granted a longer term of protection than that which would result from the provisions of paragraphs 1 and 2 may maintain this protection until the conclusion of international agreements on the term of protection of copyright or related rights.

Article 8 Calculation of terms

The terms laid down in this Directive shall be calculated from the first day of January of the year following the event which gives rise to them.

Article 9 Moral rights

This Directive shall be without prejudice to the provisions of the Member States regulating moral rights.

Article 10 Application in time

1.   Where a term of protection which is longer than the corresponding term provided for by this Directive was already running in a Member State on 1 July 1995, this Directive shall not have the effect of shortening that term of protection in that Member State.

2.   The terms of protection provided for in this Directive shall apply to all works and subject matter which were protected in at least one Member State on the date referred to in paragraph 1, pursuant to national provisions on copyright or related rights, or which meet the criteria for protection under [Council Directive 92/100/EEC of 19 November 1992 on rental right and lending right and on certain rights related to copyright in the field of intellectual property].

3.   This Directive shall be without prejudice to any acts of exploitation performed before the date referred to in paragraph 1. Member States shall adopt the necessary provisions to protect in particular acquired rights of third parties.

4.   Member States need not apply the provisions of Article 2(1) to cinematographic or audiovisual works created before 1 July 1994.

5.   Article 3(1) to (2e) in the version thereof in force on 31 October 2011 shall apply to fixations of performances and phonograms in regard to which the performer and the phonogram producer are still protected, by virtue of those provisions in the version thereof in force on 30 October 2011, as at 1 November 2013 and to fixations of performances and phonograms which come into being after that date.

6.   Article 1(7) shall apply to musical compositions with words of which at least the musical composition or the lyrics are protected in at least one Member State on 1 November 2013, and to musical compositions with words which come into being after that date.

The first subparagraph of this paragraph shall be without prejudice to any acts of exploitation performed before 1 November 2013. Member States shall adopt the necessary provisions to protect, in particular, acquired rights of third parties.

Article 10a Transitional measures

1. In the absence of clear contractual indications to the contrary, a contract on transfer or assignment concluded before 1 November 2013 shall be deemed to continue to produce its effects beyond the moment at which, by virtue of Article 3(1) in the version thereof in force on 30 October 2011, the performer would no longer be protected.
2. Member States may provide that contracts on transfer or assignment which entitle a performer to recurring payments and which are concluded before 1 November 2013 can be modified following the 50th year after the phonogram was lawfully published or, failing such publication, the 50th year after it was lawfully communicated to the public.

Article 11 Notification and communication

1. Member States shall immediately notify the Commission of any governmental plan to grant new related rights, including the basic reasons for their introduction and the term of protection envisaged.
2. Member States shall communicate to the Commission the texts of the provisions of internal law which they adopt in the field governed by this Directive.

Article 12 Repeal

Directive 93/98/EEC is hereby repealed, without prejudice to the obligations of the Member States relating to the time-limits for transposition into national law, as set out in Part B of Annex I, of the Directives, and their application.

References made to the repealed Directive shall be construed as being made to this Directive and should be read in accordance with the correlation table in Annex II.

DIRECTIVE 2009/24/EC
(legal protection of computer programs)

Article 1 Object of protection

1. In accordance with the provisions of this Directive, Member States shall protect computer programs, by copyright, as literary works within the meaning of the Berne Convention for the Protection of Literary and Artistic Works. For the purposes of this Directive, the term "computer programs" shall include their preparatory design material.
2. Protection in accordance with this Directive shall apply to the expression in any form of a computer program. Ideas and principles which underlie any element of a computer program, including those which underlie its interfaces, are not protected by copyright under this Directive.
3. A computer program shall be protected if it is original in the sense that it is the author's own intellectual creation. No other criteria shall be applied to determine its eligibility for protection.
4. The provisions of this Directive shall apply also to programs created before 1 January 1993, without prejudice to any acts concluded and rights acquired before that date.

Article 2 Authorship of computer programs

1. The author of a computer program shall be the natural person or group of natural persons who has created the program or, where the legislation of the Member State permits, the legal person designated as the rightholder by that legislation.

   Where collective works are recognised by the legislation of a Member State, the person considered by the legislation of the Member State to have created the work shall be deemed to be its author.
2. In respect of a computer program created by a group of natural persons jointly, the exclusive rights shall be owned jointly.
3. Where a computer program is created by an employee in the execution of his duties or following the instructions given by his employer, the employer exclusively shall be entitled

to exercise all economic rights in the program so created, unless otherwise provided by contract.

Article 3 Beneficiaries of protection

Protection shall be granted to all natural or legal persons eligible under national copyright legislation as applied to literary works.

Article 4 Restricted acts

1. Subject to the provisions of Articles 5 and 6, the exclusive rights of the rightholder within the meaning of Article 2 shall include the right to do or to authorise:
    (a) the permanent or temporary reproduction of a computer program by any means and in any form, in part or in whole; in so far as loading, displaying, running, transmission or storage of the computer program necessitate such reproduction, such acts shall be subject to authorisation by the rightholder;
    (b) the translation, adaptation, arrangement and any other alteration of a computer program and the reproduction of the results thereof, without prejudice to the rights of the person who alters the program;
    (c) any form of distribution to the public, including the rental, of the original computer program or of copies thereof.
2. The first sale in the Community of a copy of a program by the rightholder or with his consent shall exhaust the distribution right within the Community of that copy, with the exception of the right to control further rental of the program or a copy thereof.

Article 5 Exceptions to the restricted acts

1. In the absence of specific contractual provisions, the acts referred to in points (a) and (b) of Article 4(1) shall not require authorisation by the rightholder where they are necessary for the use of the computer program by the lawful acquirer in accordance with its intended purpose, including for error correction.
2. The making of a back-up copy by a person having a right to use the computer program may not be prevented by contract in so far as it is necessary for that use.
3. The person having a right to use a copy of a computer program shall be entitled, without the authorisation of the rightholder, to observe, study or test the functioning of the program in order to determine the ideas and principles which underlie any element of the program if he does so while performing any of the acts of loading, displaying, running, transmitting or storing the program which he is entitled to do.

Article 6 Decompilation

1. The authorisation of the rightholder shall not be required where reproduction of the code and translation of its form within the meaning of points (a) and (b) of Article 4(1) are indispensable to obtain the information necessary to achieve the interoperability of an independently created computer program with other programs, provided that the following conditions are met:
    (a) those acts are performed by the licensee or by another person having a right to use a copy of a program, or on their behalf by a person authorised to do so;
    (b) the information necessary to achieve interoperability has not previously been readily available to the persons referred to in point (a); and
    (c) those acts are confined to the parts of the original program which are necessary in order to achieve interoperability.
2. The provisions of paragraph 1 shall not permit the information obtained through its application:
    (a) to be used for goals other than to achieve the interoperability of the independently created computer program;
    (b) to be given to others, except when necessary for the interoperability of the independently created computer program; or
    (c) to be used for the development, production or marketing of a computer program substantially similar in its expression, or for any other act which infringes copyright.
3. In accordance with the provisions of the Berne Convention for the protection of Literary and Artistic Works, the provisions of this Article may not be interpreted in such a way as to allow its application to be used in a manner which unreasonably prejudices the rightholder's legitimate interests or conflicts with a normal exploitation of the computer program.

Article 7 Special measures of protection

1.   Without prejudice to the provisions of Articles 4, 5 and 6, Member States shall provide, in accordance with their national legislation, appropriate remedies against a person committing any of the following acts:

    (a)   any act of putting into circulation a copy of a computer program knowing, or having reason to believe, that it is an infringing copy;

    (b)   the possession, for commercial purposes, of a copy of a computer program knowing, or having reason to believe, that it is an infringing copy;

    (c)   any act of putting into circulation, or the possession for commercial purposes of, any means the sole intended purpose of which is to facilitate the unauthorised removal or circumvention of any technical device which may have been applied to protect a computer program.

2.   Any infringing copy of a computer program shall be liable to seizure in accordance with the legislation of the Member State concerned.

3.   Member States may provide for the seizure of any means referred to in point (c) of paragraph 1.

Article 8 Continued application of other legal provisions

The provisions of this Directive shall be without prejudice to any other legal provisions such as those concerning patent rights, trade-marks, unfair competition, trade secrets, protection of semi-conductor products or the law of contract.

Any contractual provisions contrary to Article 6 or to the exceptions provided for in Article 5(2) and (3) shall be null and void.

Article 9 Communication

Member States shall communicate to the Commission the provisions of national law adopted in the field governed by this Directive.

Article 10 Repeal

Directive 91/250/EEC, as amended by the Directive indicated in Annex I, Part A, is repealed, without prejudice to the obligations of the Member States relating to the time-limits for transposition into national law of the Directives set out in Annex I, Part B.

References to the repealed Directive shall be construed as references to this Directive and shall be read in accordance with the correlation table in Annex II.

DIRECTIVE 2012/28/EU
(certain permitted uses of orphan works)

Article 1 Subject-matter and scope

1.   This Directive concerns certain uses made of orphan works by publicly accessible libraries, educational establishments and museums, as well as by archives, film or audio heritage institutions and public-service broadcasting organisations, established in the Member States, in order to achieve aims related to their public-interest missions.

2.   This Directive applies to:

    (a)   works published in the form of books, journals, newspapers, magazines or other writings contained in the collections of publicly accessible libraries, educational establishments or museums as well as in the collections of archives or of film or audio heritage institutions;

    (b)   cinematographic or audiovisual works and phonograms contained in the collections of publicly accessible libraries, educational establishments or museums as well as in the collections of archives or of film or audio heritage institutions; and

    (c)   cinematographic or audiovisual works and phonograms produced by public-service broadcasting organisations up to and including 31 December 2002 and contained in their archives;

    which are protected by copyright or related rights and which are first published in a Member State or, in the absence of publication, first broadcast in a Member State.

3.   This Directive also applies to works and phonograms referred to in paragraph 2 which have never been published or broadcast but which have been made publicly accessible by the organisations referred to in paragraph 1 with the consent of the rightholders, provided that it is reasonable to assume that the rightholders would not oppose the uses referred to in Article 6. Member States may limit the application of this paragraph to works and phonograms which have been deposited with those organisations before 29 October 2014.

4.   This Directive shall also apply to works and other protected subject-matter that are embedded or incorporated in, or constitute an integral part of, the works or phonograms referred to in paragraphs 2 and 3.

5.   This Directive does not interfere with any arrangements concerning the management of rights at national level.

Article 2 Orphan works

1.   A work or a phonogram shall be considered an orphan work if none of the rightholders in that work or phonogram is identified or, even if one or more of them is identified, none is located despite a diligent search for the rightholders having been carried out and recorded in accordance with Article 3.

2.   Where there is more than one rightholder in a work or phonogram, and not all of them have been identified or, even if identified, located after a diligent search has been carried out and recorded in accordance with Article 3, the work or phonogram may be used in accordance with this Directive provided that the rightholders that have been identified and located have, in relation to the rights they hold, authorised the organisations referred to in Article 1(1) to carry out the acts of reproduction and making available to the public covered respectively by Articles 2 and 3 of Directive 2001/29/EC.

3.   Paragraph 2 shall be without prejudice to the rights in the work or phonogram of rightholders that have been identified and located.

4.   Article 5 shall apply mutatis mutandis to the rightholders that have not been identified and located in the works referred to in paragraph 2.

5.   This Directive shall be without prejudice to national provisions on anonymous or pseudonymous works.

Article 3 Diligent search

1.   For the purposes of establishing whether a work or phonogram is an orphan work, the organisations referred to in Article 1(1) shall ensure that a diligent search is carried out in good faith in respect of each work or other protected subject-matter, by consulting the appropriate sources for the category of works and other protected subject-matter in question. The diligent search shall be carried out prior to the use of the work or phonogram.

2.   The sources that are appropriate for each category of works or phonogram in question shall be determined by each Member State, in consultation with rightholders and users, and shall include at least the relevant sources listed in the Annex.

3.   A diligent search shall be carried out in the Member State of first publication or, in the absence of publication, first broadcast, except in the case of cinematographic or audiovisual works the producer of which has his headquarters or habitual residence in a Member State, in which case the diligent search shall be carried out in the Member State of his headquarters or habitual residence.

      In the case referred to in Article 1(3), the diligent search shall be carried out in the Member State where the organisation that made the work or phonogram publicly accessible with the consent of the rightholder is established.

4.   If there is evidence to suggest that relevant information on rightholders is to be found in other countries, sources of information available in those other countries shall also be consulted.

5.   Member States shall ensure that the organisations referred to in Article 1(1) maintain records of their diligent searches and that those organisations provide the following information to the competent national authorities:
      (a)   the results of the diligent searches that the organisations have carried out and which have led to the conclusion that a work or a phonogram is considered an orphan work;
      (b)   the use that the organisations make of orphan works in accordance with this Directive;

(c)   any change, pursuant to Article 5, of the orphan work status of works and phonograms that the organisations use;

(d)   the relevant contact information of the organisation concerned.

6.   Member States shall take the necessary measures to ensure that the information referred to in paragraph 5 is recorded in a single publicly accessible online database established and managed by the Office for Harmonization in the Internal Market ("the Office") in accordance with Regulation (EU) No 386/2012. To that end, they shall forward that information to the Office without delay upon receiving it from the organisations referred to in Article 1(1).

Article 4 Mutual recognition of orphan work status

A work or phonogram which is considered an orphan work according to Article 2 in a Member State shall be considered an orphan work in all Member States. That work or phonogram may be used and accessed in accordance with this Directive in all Member States. This also applies to works and phonograms referred to in Article 2(2) in so far as the rights of the non-identified or non-located rightholders are concerned.

Article 5 End of orphan work status

Member States shall ensure that a rightholder in a work or phonogram considered to be an orphan work has, at any time, the possibility of putting an end to the orphan work status in so far as his rights are concerned.

Article 6 Permitted uses of orphan works

1.   Member States shall provide for an exception or limitation to the right of reproduction and the right of making available to the public provided for respectively in Articles 2 and 3 of Directive 2001/29/EC to ensure that the organisations referred to in Article 1(1) are permitted to use orphan works contained in their collections in the following ways:

(a)   by making the orphan work available to the public, within the meaning of Article 3 of Directive 2001/29/EC;

(b)   by acts of reproduction, within the meaning of Article 2 of Directive 2001/29/EC, for the purposes of digitisation, making available, indexing, cataloguing, preservation or restoration.

2.   The organisations referred to in Article 1(1) shall use an orphan work in accordance with paragraph 1 of this Article only in order to achieve aims related to their public-interest missions, in particular the preservation of, the restoration of, and the provision of cultural and educational access to, works and phonograms contained in their collection. The organisations may generate revenues in the course of such uses, for the exclusive purpose of covering their costs of digitising orphan works and making them available to the public.

3.   Member States shall ensure that the organisations referred to in Article 1(1) indicate the name of identified authors and other rightholders in any use of an orphan work.

4.   This Directive is without prejudice to the freedom of contract of such organisations in the pursuit of their public-interest missions, particularly in respect of public-private partnership agreements.

5.   Member States shall provide that a fair compensation is due to rightholders that put an end to the orphan work status of their works or other protected subject-matter for the use that has been made by the organisations referred to in Article 1(1) of such works and other protected subject-matter in accordance with paragraph 1 of this Article. Member States shall be free to determine the circumstances under which the payment of such compensation may be organised. The level of the compensation shall be determined, within the limits imposed by Union law, by the law of the Member State in which the organisation which uses the orphan work in question is established.

Article 7 Continued application of other legal provisions

This Directive shall be without prejudice to provisions concerning, in particular, patent rights, trade marks, design rights, utility models, the topographies of semi-conductor products, type faces, conditional access, access to cable of broadcasting services, the protection of national treasures, legal deposit requirements, laws on restrictive practices and unfair competition, trade secrets, security, confidentiality, data protection and privacy, access to public documents, the law of contract, and rules on the freedom of the press and freedom of expression in the media.

Article 8 Application in time

1.   This Directive shall apply in respect of all works and phonograms referred to in Article 1 which are protected by the Member States' legislation in the field of copyright on or after 29 October 2014.

2.   This Directive shall apply without prejudice to any acts concluded and rights acquired before 29 October 2014.

Article 9 Transposition

1.   Member States shall bring into force the laws, regulations and administrative provisions necessary to comply with this Directive by 29 October 2014. They shall forthwith communicate to the Commission the text of those provisions.

When Member States adopt those provisions, they shall contain a reference to this Directive or shall be accompanied by such a reference on the occasion of their official publication. The methods of making such reference shall be laid down by Member States.

2.   Member States shall communicate to the Commission the text of the main provisions of national law which they adopt in the field covered by this Directive.

Article 10 Review clause

The Commission shall keep under constant review the development of rights information sources and shall by 29 October 2015, and at annual intervals thereafter, submit a report concerning the possible inclusion in the scope of application of this Directive of publishers and of works or other protected subject-matter not currently included in its scope, and in particular stand-alone photographs and other images.

By 29 October 2015, the Commission shall submit to the European Parliament, the Council and the European Economic and Social Committee a report on the application of this Directive, in the light of the development of digital libraries.

When necessary, in particular to ensure the functioning of the internal market, the Commission shall submit proposals for amendment of this Directive.

A Member State that has valid reasons to consider that the implementation of this Directive hinders one of the national arrangements concerning the management of rights referred to in Article 1(5) may bring the matter to the attention of the Commission together with all relevant evidence. The Commission shall take such evidence into account when drawing up the report referred to in the second paragraph of this Article and when assessing whether it is necessary to submit proposals for amendment of this Directive.

Article 11 Entry into force

This Directive shall enter into force on the day following that of its publication in the Official Journal of the European Union.

ANNEX

The sources referred to in Article 3(2) include the following:
1.   for published books:
      (a)   legal deposit, library catalogues and authority files maintained by libraries and other institutions;
      (b)   the publishers' and authors' associations in the respective country;
      (c)   existing databases and registries, WATCH (Writers, Artists and their Copyright Holders), the ISBN (International Standard Book Number) and databases listing books in print;
      (d)   the databases of the relevant collecting societies, in particular reproduction rights organisations;
      (e)   sources that integrate multiple databases and registries, including VIAF (Virtual International Authority Files) and ARROW (Accessible Registries of Rights Information and Orphan Works);
2.   for newspapers, magazines, journals and periodicals:
      (a)   the ISSN (International Standard Serial Number) for periodical publications;
      (b)   indexes and catalogues from library holdings and collections;
      (c)   legal deposit;
      (d)   the publishers' associations and the authors' and journalists' associations in the respective country;

     (e)   the databases of relevant collecting societies including reproduction rights organisations;

3.   for visual works, including fine art, photography, illustration, design, architecture, sketches of the latter works and other such works that are contained in books, journals, newspapers and magazines or other works:

     (a)   the sources referred to in points (1) and (2);

     (b)   the databases of the relevant collecting societies, in particular for visual arts, and including reproduction rights organisations;

     (c)   the databases of picture agencies, where applicable;

4.   for audiovisual works and phonograms:

     (a)   legal deposit;

     (b)   the producers' associations in the respective country;

     (c)   databases of film or audio heritage institutions and national libraries;

     (d)   databases with relevant standards and identifiers such as ISAN (International Standard Audiovisual Number) for audiovisual material, ISWC (International Standard Music Work Code) for musical works and ISRC (International Standard Recording Code) for phonograms;

     (e)   the databases of the relevant collecting societies, in particular for authors, performers, phonogram producers and audiovisual producers;

     (f)   credits and other information appearing on the work's packaging;

     (g)   databases of other relevant associations representing a specific category of rightholders.

DIRECTIVE 2014/26/EU
on collective management of copyright and related rights and multi-territorial licensing of rights in musical works for online use in the internal market

Article 1 Subject-matter

This Directive lays down requirements necessary to ensure the proper functioning of the management of copyright and related rights by collective management organisations. It also lays down requirements for multi-territorial licensing by collective management organisations of authors' rights in musical works for online use.

Article 2 Scope

1.   Titles I, II, IV and V with the exception of Article 34(2) and Article 38 apply to all collective management organisations established in the Union.

2.   Title III and Article 34(2) and Article 38 apply to collective management organisations established in the Union managing authors' rights in musical works for online use on a multi-territorial basis.

3.   The relevant provisions of this Directive apply to entities directly or indirectly owned or controlled, wholly or in part, by a collective management organisation, provided that such entities carry out an activity which, if carried out by the collective management organisation, would be subject to the provisions of this Directive.

4.   Article 16(1), Articles 18 and 20, points (a), (b), (c), (e), (f) and (g) of Article 21(1) and Articles 36 and 42 apply to all independent management entities established in the Union.

Article 3 Definitions

For the purposes of this Directive, the following definitions shall apply:

(a)   "collective management organisation" means any organisation which is authorised by law or by way of assignment, licence or any other contractual arrangement to manage copyright or rights related to copyright on behalf of more than one rightholder, for the collective benefit of those rightholders, as its sole or main purpose, and which fulfils one or both of the following criteria:

     (i)   it is owned or controlled by its members;

     (ii)   it is organised on a not-for-profit basis;

(b)   "independent management entity" means any organisation which is authorised by law or by way of assignment, licence or any other contractual arrangement to manage copyright or rights related to copyright on behalf of more than one rightholder, for the collective benefit of those rightholders, as its sole or main purpose, and which is:

(i)   neither owned nor controlled, directly or indirectly, wholly or in part, by rightholders; and

(ii)   organised on a for-profit basis;

(c)   "rightholder" means any person or entity, other than a collective management organisation, that holds a copyright or related right or, under an agreement for the exploitation of rights or by law, is entitled to a share of the rights revenue;

(d)   "member" means a rightholder or an entity representing rightholders, including other collective management organisations and associations of rightholders, fulfilling the membership requirements of the collective management organisation and admitted by it;

(e)   "statute" means the memorandum and articles of association, the statute, the rules or documents of constitution of a collective management organisation;

(f)   "general assembly of members" means the body in the collective management organisation wherein members participate and exercise their voting rights, regardless of the legal form of the organisation;

(g)   "director" means:

(i)   where national law or the statute of the collective management organisation provides for a unitary board, any member of the administrative board;

(ii)   where national law or the statute of the collective management organisation provides for a dual board, any member of the management board or the supervisory board;

(h)   "rights revenue" means income collected by a collective management organisation on behalf of rightholders, whether deriving from an exclusive right, a right to remuneration or a right to compensation;

(i)   "management fees" means the amounts charged, deducted or offset by a collective management organisation from rights revenue or from any income arising from the investment of rights revenue in order to cover the costs of its management of copyright or related rights;

(j)   "representation agreement" means any agreement between collective management organisations whereby one collective management organisation mandates another collective management organisation to manage the rights it represents, including an agreement concluded under Articles 29 and 30;

(k)   "user" means any person or entity that is carrying out acts subject to the authorisation of rightholders, remuneration of rightholders or payment of compensation to rightholders and is not acting in the capacity of a consumer;

(l)   "repertoire" means the works in respect of which a collective management organisation manages rights;

(m)   "multi-territorial licence" means a licence which covers the territory of more than one Member State;

(n)   "online rights in musical works" means any of the rights of an author in a musical work provided for under Articles 2 and 3 of Directive 2001/29/EC which are required for the provision of an online service.

TITLE II
COLLECTIVE MANAGEMENT ORGANISATIONS

CHAPTER 1
REPRESENTATION OF RIGHTHOLDERS AND MEMBERSHIP AND ORGANISATION OF COLLECTIVE MANAGEMENT ORGANISATIONS

Article 4 General principles

Member States shall ensure that collective management organisations act in the best interests of the rightholders whose rights they represent and that they do not impose on them any obligations which are not objectively necessary for the protection of their rights and interests or for the effective management of their rights.

Article 5 Rights of rightholders

1.   Member States shall ensure that rightholders have the rights laid down in paragraphs 2 to 8 and that those rights are set out in the statute or membership terms of the collective management organisation.
2.   Rightholders shall have the right to authorise a collective management organisation of their choice to manage the rights, categories of rights or types of works and other subject-matter of their choice, for the territories of their choice, irrespective of the Member State of nationality, residence or establishment of either the collective management organisation or the rightholder. Unless the collective management organisation has objectively justified reasons to refuse management, it shall be obliged to manage such rights, categories of rights or types of works and other subject-matter, provided that their management falls within the scope of its activity.
3.   Rightholders shall have the right to grant licences for non-commercial uses of any rights, categories of rights or types of works and other subject-matter that they may choose.
4.   Rightholders shall have the right to terminate the authorisation to manage rights, categories of rights or types of works and other subject-matter granted by them to a collective management organisation or to withdraw from a collective management organisation any of the rights, categories of rights or types of works and other subject-matter of their choice, as determined pursuant to paragraph 2, for the territories of their choice, upon serving reasonable notice not exceeding six months. The collective management organisation may decide that such termination or withdrawal is to take effect only at the end of the financial year.
5.   If there are amounts due to a rightholder for acts of exploitation which occurred before the termination of the authorisation or the withdrawal of rights took effect, or under a licence granted before such termination or withdrawal took effect, the rightholder shall retain his rights under Articles 12, 13, 18, 20, 28 and 33.
6.   A collective management organisation shall not restrict the exercise of rights provided for under paragraphs 4 and 5 by requiring, as a condition for the exercise of those rights, that the management of rights or categories of rights or types of works and other subject-matter which are subject to the termination or the withdrawal be entrusted to another collective management organisation.
7.   In cases where a rightholder authorises a collective management organisation to manage his rights, he shall give consent specifically for each right or category of rights or type of works and other subject-matter which he authorises the collective management organisation to manage. Any such consent shall be evidenced in documentary form.
8.   A collective management organisation shall inform rightholders of their rights under paragraphs 1 to 7, as well as of any conditions attached to the right set out in paragraph 3, before obtaining their consent to its managing any right or category of rights or type of works and other subject-matter.
       A collective management organisation shall inform those rightholders who have already authorised it of their rights under paragraphs 1 to 7, as well as of any conditions attached to the right set out in paragraph 3, by 10 October 2016.

Article 6 Membership rules of collective management organisations

1.   Member States shall ensure that collective management organisations comply with the rules laid down in paragraphs 2 to 5.
2.   A collective management organisation shall accept rightholders and entities representing rightholders, including other collective management organisations and associations of rightholders, as members if they fulfil the membership requirements, which shall be based on objective, transparent and non-discriminatory criteria. Those membership requirements shall be included in the statute or membership terms of the collective management organisation and shall be made publicly available. In cases where a collective management organisation refuses to accept a request for membership, it shall provide the rightholder with a clear explanation of the reasons for its decision.
3.   The statute of a collective management organisation shall provide for appropriate and effective mechanisms for the participation of its members in the organisation's decision-making process. The representation of the different categories of members in the decision-making process shall be fair and balanced.

4.   A collective management organisation shall allow its members to communicate with it by electronic means, including for the purposes of exercising members' rights.
5.   A collective management organisation shall keep records of its members and shall regularly update those records.

Article 7 Rights of rightholders who are not members of the collective management organisation

1.   Member States shall ensure that collective management organisations comply with the rules laid down in Article 6(4), Article 20, Article 29(2) and Article 33 in respect of rightholders who have a direct legal relationship by law or by way of assignment, licence or any other contractual arrangement with them but are not their members.
2.   Member States may apply other provisions of this Directive to the rightholders referred to in paragraph 1.

Article 8 General assembly of members of the collective management organisation

1.   Member States shall ensure that the general assembly of members is organised in accordance with the rules laid down in paragraphs 2 to 10.
2.   A general assembly of members shall be convened at least once a year.
3.   The general assembly of members shall decide on any amendments to the statute and to the membership terms of the collective management organisation, where those terms are not regulated by the statute.
4.   The general assembly of members shall decide on the appointment or dismissal of the directors, review their general performance and approve their remuneration and other benefits such as monetary and non-monetary benefits, pension awards and entitlements, rights to other awards and rights to severance pay.
      In a collective management organisation with a dual board system, the general assembly of members shall not decide on the appointment or dismissal of members of the management board or approve their remuneration and other benefits where the power to take such decisions is delegated to the supervisory board.
5.   In accordance with the provisions laid down in Chapter 2 of Title II, the general assembly of members shall decide at least on the following issues:
      (a)   the general policy on the distribution of amounts due to rightholders;
      (b)   the general policy on the use of non-distributable amounts;
      (c)   the general investment policy with regard to rights revenue and to any income arising from the investment of rights revenue;
      (d)   the general policy on deductions from rights revenue and from any income arising from the investment of rights revenue;
      (e)   the use of non-distributable amounts;
      (f)   the risk management policy;
      (g)   the approval of any acquisition, sale or hypothecation of immovable property;
      (h)   the approval of mergers and alliances, the setting-up of subsidiaries, and the acquisition of other entities or shares or rights in other entities;
      (i)   the approval of taking out loans, granting loans or providing security for loans.
6.   The general assembly of members may delegate the powers listed in points (f), (g), (h) and (i) of paragraph 5, by a resolution or by a provision in the statute, to the body exercising the supervisory function.
7.   For the purposes of points (a) to (d) of paragraph 5, Member States may require the general assembly of members to determine more detailed conditions for the use of the rights revenue and the income arising from the investment of rights revenue.
8.   The general assembly of members shall control the activities of the collective management organisation by, at least, deciding on the appointment and removal of the auditor and approving the annual transparency report referred to in Article 22.
      Member States may allow alternative systems or modalities for the appointment and removal of the auditor, provided that those systems or modalities are designed to ensure the independence of the auditor from the persons who manage the business of the collective management organisation.

9.   All members of the collective management organisation shall have the right to participate in, and the right to vote at, the general assembly of members. However, Member States may allow for restrictions on the right of the members of the collective management organisation to participate in, and to exercise voting rights at, the general assembly of members, on the basis of one or both of the following criteria:

(a)   duration of membership;

(b)   provided that such criteria are determined and applied in a manner that is fair and proportionate.

The criteria laid down in points (a) and (b) of the first subparagraph shall be included in the statute or the membership terms of the collective management organisation and shall be made publicly available in accordance with Articles 19 and 21.

10.   Every member of a collective management organisation shall have the right to appoint any other person or entity as a proxy holder to participate in, and vote at, the general assembly of members on his behalf, provided that such appointment does not result in a conflict of interest which might occur, for example, where the appointing member and the proxy holder belong to different categories of rightholders within the collective management organisation.

However, Member States may provide for restrictions concerning the appointment of proxy holders and the exercise of the voting rights of the members they represent if such restrictions do not prejudice the appropriate and effective participation of members in the decision-making process of a collective management organisation.

Each proxy shall be valid for a single general assembly of members. The proxy holder shall enjoy the same rights in the general assembly of members as those to which the appointing member would be entitled. The proxy holder shall cast votes in accordance with the instructions issued by the appointing member.

11.   Member States may decide that the powers of the general assembly of members may be exercised by an assembly of delegates elected at least every four years by the members of the collective management organisation, provided that:

(a)   appropriate and effective participation of members in the collective management organisation's decision-making process is ensured; and

(b)   the representation of the different categories of members in the assembly of delegates is fair and balanced.

The rules laid down in paragraphs 2 to 10 shall apply to the assembly of delegates mutatis mutandis.

12.   Member States may decide that where a collective management organisation, by reason of its legal form, does not have a general assembly of members, the powers of that assembly are to be exercised by the body exercising the supervisory function. The rules laid down in paragraphs 2 to 5, 7 and 8 shall apply mutatis mutandis to such body exercising the supervisory function.

13.   Member States may decide that where a collective management organisation has members who are entities representing rightholders, all or some of the powers of the general assembly of members are to be exercised by an assembly of those rightholders. The rules laid down in paragraphs 2 to 10 shall apply mutatis mutandis to the assembly of rightholders.

Article 9 Supervisory function

1.   Member States shall ensure that each collective management organisation has in place a supervisory function for continuously monitoring the activities and the performance of the duties of the persons who manage the business of the organisation.

2.   There shall be fair and balanced representation of the different categories of members of the collective management organisation in the body exercising the supervisory function.

3.   Each person exercising the supervisory function shall make an annual individual statement on conflicts of interest, containing the information referred to in the second subparagraph of Article 10(2), to the general assembly of members.

4.   The body exercising the supervisory function shall meet regularly and shall have at least the following powers:

(a)   to exercise the powers delegated to it by the general assembly of members, including under Article 8(4) and (6);

(b)   to monitor the activities and the performance of the duties of the persons referred to in Article 10, including the implementation of the decisions of the general assembly of members and, in particular, of the general policies listed in points (a) to (d) of Article 8(5).

5. The body exercising the supervisory function shall report on the exercise of its powers to the general assembly of members at least once a year.

Article 10 Obligations of the persons who manage the business of the collective management organisation

1. Member States shall ensure that each collective management organisation takes all necessary measures so that the persons who manage its business do so in a sound, prudent and appropriate manner, using sound administrative and accounting procedures and internal control mechanisms.

2. Member States shall ensure that collective management organisations put in place and apply procedures to avoid conflicts of interest, and where such conflicts cannot be avoided, to identify, manage, monitor and disclose actual or potential conflicts of interest in such a way as to prevent them from adversely affecting the collective interests of the rightholders whom the organisation represents.

    The procedures referred to in the first subparagraph shall include an annual individual statement by each of the persons referred to in paragraph 1 to the general assembly of members, containing the following information:

    (a) any interests in the collective management organisation;

    (b) any remuneration received in the preceding financial year from the collective management organisation, including in the form of pension schemes, benefits in kind and other types of benefits;

    (c) any amounts received in the preceding financial year as a rightholder from the collective management organisation;

    (d) a declaration concerning any actual or potential conflict between any personal interests and those of the collective management organisation or between any obligations owed to the collective management organisation and any duty owed to any other natural or legal person.

CHAPTER 2
MANAGEMENT OF RIGHTS REVENUE

Article 11 Collection and use of rights revenue

1. Member States shall ensure that collective management organisations comply with the rules laid down in paragraphs 2 to 5.

2. A collective management organisation shall be diligent in the collection and management of rights revenue.

3. A collective management organisation shall keep separate in its accounts:

    (a) rights revenue and any income arising from the investment of rights revenue; and

    (b) any own assets it may have and income arising from such assets, from management fees or from other activities.

4. A collective management organisation shall not be permitted to use rights revenue or any income arising from the investment of rights revenue for purposes other than distribution to rightholders, except where it is allowed to deduct or offset its management fees in compliance with a decision taken in accordance with point (d) of Article 8(5) or to use the rights revenue or any income arising from the investment of rights revenue in compliance with a decision taken in accordance with Article 8(5).

5. Where a collective management organisation invests rights revenue or any income arising from the investment of rights revenue, it shall do so in the best interests of the rightholders whose rights it represents, in accordance with the general investment and risk management policy referred to in points (c) and (f) of Article 8(5) and having regard to the following rules:

    (a) where there is any potential conflict of interest, the collective management organisation shall ensure that the investment is made in the sole interest of those rightholders;

    (b) the assets shall be invested in order to ensure the security, quality, liquidity and profitability of the portfolio as a whole;

(c)   the assets shall be properly diversified in order to avoid excessive reliance on any particular asset and accumulations of risks in the portfolio as a whole.

Article 12 Deductions

1.   Member States shall ensure that where a rightholder authorises a collective management organisation to manage his rights, the collective management organisation is required to provide the rightholder with information on management fees and other deductions from the rights revenue and from any income arising from the investment of rights revenue, before obtaining his consent to its managing his rights.

2.   Deductions shall be reasonable in relation to the services provided by the collective management organisation to rightholders, including, where appropriate, the services referred to in paragraph 4, and shall be established on the basis of objective criteria.

3.   Management fees shall not exceed the justified and documented costs incurred by the collective management organisation in managing copyright and related rights.
Member States shall ensure that the requirements applicable to the use and the transparency of the use of amounts deducted or offset in respect of management fees apply to any other deductions made in order to cover the costs of managing copyright and related rights.

4.   Where a collective management organisation provides social, cultural or educational services funded through deductions from rights revenue or from any income arising from the investment of rights revenue, such services shall be provided on the basis of fair criteria, in particular as regards access to, and the extent of, those services.

Article 13 Distribution of amounts due to rightholders

1.   Without prejudice to Article 15(3) and Article 28, Member States shall ensure that each collective management organisation regularly, diligently and accurately distributes and pays amounts due to rightholders in accordance with the general policy on distribution referred to in point (a) of Article 8(5).
Member States shall also ensure that collective management organisations or their members who are entities representing rightholders distribute and pay those amounts to rightholders as soon as possible but no later than nine months from the end of the financial year in which the rights revenue was collected, unless objective reasons relating in particular to reporting by users, identification of rights, rightholders or matching of information on works and other subject-matter with rightholders prevent the collective management organisation or, where applicable, its members from meeting that deadline.

2.   Where the amounts due to rightholders cannot be distributed within the deadline set in paragraph 1 because the relevant rightholders cannot be identified or located and the exception to that deadline does not apply, those amounts shall be kept separate in the accounts of the collective management organisation.

3.   The collective management organisation shall take all necessary measures, consistent with paragraph 1, to identify and locate the rightholders. In particular, at the latest three months after the expiry of the deadline set in paragraph 1, the collective management organisation shall make available information on works and other subject-matter for which one or more rightholders have not been identified or located to:
(a)   the rightholders that it represents or the entities representing rightholders, where such entities are members of the collective management organisation; and
(b)   all collective management organisations with which it has concluded representation agreements.
The information referred to in the first subparagraph shall include, where available, the following:
(a)   the title of the work or other subject-matter;
(b)   the name of the rightholder;
(c)   the name of the relevant publisher or producer; and
(d)   any other relevant information available which could assist in identifying the rightholder.
The collective management organisation shall also verify the records referred to in Article 6(5) and other readily available records. If the abovementioned measures fail to produce results, the collective management organisation shall make that information available to the public at the latest one year after the expiry of the three-month period.

4.   Where the amounts due to rightholders cannot be distributed after three years from the end of the financial year in which the collection of the rights revenue occurred, and provided that the collective management organisation has taken all necessary measures to identify and locate the rightholders referred to in paragraph 3, those amounts shall be deemed non-distributable.

5.   The general assembly of members of a collective management organisation shall decide on the use of the non-distributable amounts in accordance with point (b) of Article 8(5), without prejudice to the right of rightholders to claim such amounts from the collective management organisation in accordance with the laws of the Member States on the statute of limitations of claims.

6.   Member States may limit or determine the permitted uses of non-distributable amounts, inter alia, by ensuring that such amounts are used in a separate and independent way in order to fund social, cultural and educational activities for the benefit of rightholders.

CHAPTER 3
MANAGEMENT OF RIGHTS ON BEHALF OF OTHER COLLECTIVE
MANAGEMENT ORGANISATIONS

Article 14 Rights managed under representation agreements
Member States shall ensure that a collective management organisation does not discriminate against any rightholder whose rights it manages under a representation agreement, in particular with respect to applicable tariffs, management fees, and the conditions for the collection of the rights revenue and distribution of amounts due to rightholders.

Article 15 Deductions and payments in representation agreements
1.   Member States shall ensure that a collective management organisation does not make deductions, other than in respect of management fees, from the rights revenue derived from the rights it manages on the basis of a representation agreement, or from any income arising from the investment of that rights revenue, unless the other collective management organisation that is party to the representation agreement expressly consents to such deductions.

2.   The collective management organisation shall regularly, diligently and accurately distribute and pay amounts due to other collective management organisations.

3.   The collective management organisation shall carry out such distribution and payments to the other collective management organisation as soon as possible but no later than nine months from the end of the financial year in which the rights revenue was collected, unless objective reasons relating in particular to reporting by users, identification of rights, rightholders or matching of information on works and other subject-matter with rightholders prevent the collective management organisation from meeting that deadline.

The other collective management organisation, or, where it has as members entities representing rightholders, those members, shall distribute and pay the amounts due to rightholders as soon as possible but no later than six months from receipt of those amounts, unless objective reasons relating in particular to reporting by users, identification of rights, rightholders or matching of information on works and other subject-matter with rightholders prevent the collective management organisation or, where applicable, its members from meeting that deadline.

CHAPTER 4
RELATIONS WITH USERS

Article 16 Licensing
1.   Member States shall ensure that collective management organisations and users conduct negotiations for the licensing of rights in good faith. Collective management organisations and users shall provide each other with all necessary information.

2.   Licensing terms shall be based on objective and non-discriminatory criteria. When licensing rights, collective management organisations shall not be required to use, as a precedent for other online services, licensing terms agreed with a user where the user is providing a new type of online service which has been available to the public in the Union for less than three years.

Rightholders shall receive appropriate remuneration for the use of their rights. Tariffs for exclusive rights and rights to remuneration shall be reasonable in relation to, inter alia, the economic value of the use of the rights in trade, taking into account the nature and scope of the use of the work and other subject-matter, as well as in relation to the economic value of the service provided by the collective management organisation. Collective management organisations shall inform the user concerned of the criteria used for the setting of those tariffs.

3.   Collective management organisations shall reply without undue delay to requests from users, indicating, inter alia, the information needed in order for the collective management organisation to offer a licence.

Upon receipt of all relevant information, the collective management organisation shall, without undue delay, either offer a licence or provide the user with a reasoned statement explaining why it does not intend to license a particular service.

4.   A collective management organisation shall allow users to communicate with it by electronic means, including, where appropriate, for the purpose of reporting on the use of the licence.

Article 17 Users' obligations

Member States shall adopt provisions to ensure that users provide a collective management organisation, within an agreed or pre-established time and in an agreed or pre-established format, with such relevant information at their disposal on the use of the rights represented by the collective management organisation as is necessary for the collection of rights revenue and for the distribution and payment of amounts due to rightholders. When deciding on the format for the provision of such information, collective management organisations and users shall take into account, as far as possible, voluntary industry standards.

CHAPTER 5

TRANSPARENCY AND REPORTING

Article 18 Information provided to rightholders on the management of their rights

1.   Without prejudice to paragraph 2 of this Article and Article 19 and Article 28(2), Member States shall ensure that a collective management organisation makes available, not less than once a year, to each rightholder to whom it has attributed rights revenue or made payments in the period to which the information relates, at least the following information:

    (a)   any contact details which the rightholder has authorised the collective management organisation to use in order to identify and locate the rightholder;

    (b)   the rights revenue attributed to the rightholder;

    (c)   the amounts paid by the collective management organisation to the rightholder per category of rights managed and per type of use;

    (d)   the period during which the use took place for which amounts were attributed and paid to the rightholder, unless objective reasons relating to reporting by users prevent the collective management organisation from providing this information;

    (e)   deductions made in respect of management fees;

    (f)   deductions made for any purpose other than in respect of management fees, including those that may be required by national law for the provision of any social, cultural or educational services;

    (g)   any rights revenue attributed to the rightholder which is outstanding for any period.

2.   Where a collective management organisation attributes rights revenue and has as members entities which are responsible for the distribution of rights revenue to rightholders, the collective management organisation shall provide the information listed in paragraph 1 to those entities, provided that they do not have that information in their possession. Member States shall ensure that the entities make at least the information listed in paragraph 1 available, not less than once a year, to each rightholder to whom they have attributed rights revenue or made payments in the period to which the information relates.

Article 19 Information provided to other collective management organisations on the management of rights under representation agreements

Member States shall ensure that a collective management organisation makes at least the following information available, not less than once a year and by electronic means, to collective management organisations on whose behalf it manages rights under a representation agreement, for the period to which the information relates:

(a)   the rights revenue attributed, the amounts paid by the collective management organisation per category of rights managed, and per type of use, for the rights it manages under the representation agreement, and any rights revenue attributed which is outstanding for any period;

(b)   deductions made in respect of management fees;

(c)   deductions made for any purpose other than in respect of management fees as referred to in Article 15;

(d)   information on any licences granted or refused with regard to works and other subject-matter covered by the representation agreement;

(e)   resolutions adopted by the general assembly of members in so far as those resolutions are relevant to the management of the rights under the representation agreement.

Article 20 Information provided to rightholders, other collective management organisations and users on request

Without prejudice to Article 25, Member States shall ensure that, in response to a duly justified request, a collective management organisation makes at least the following information available by electronic means and without undue delay to any collective management organisation on whose behalf it manages rights under a representation agreement or to any rightholder or to any user:

(a)   the works or other subject-matter it represents, the rights it manages, directly or under representation agreements, and the territories covered; or

(b)   where, due to the scope of activity of the collective management organisation, such works or other subject-matter cannot be determined, the types of works or of other subject-matter it represents, the rights it manages and the territories covered.

Article 21 Disclosure of information to the public

1.   Member States shall ensure that a collective management organisation makes public at least the following information:

(a)   its statute;

(b)   its membership terms and the terms of termination of authorisation to manage rights, if these are not included in the statute;

(c)   standard licensing contracts and standard applicable tariffs, including discounts;

(d)   the list of the persons referred to in Article 10;

(e)   its general policy on distribution of amounts due to rightholders;

(f)   its general policy on management fees;

(g)   its general policy on deductions, other than in respect of management fees, from rights revenue and from any income arising from the investment of rights revenue, including deductions for the purposes of social, cultural and educational services;

(h)   a list of the representation agreements it has entered into, and the names of the collective management organisations with which those representation agreements have been concluded;

(i)   the general policy on the use of non-distributable amounts;

(j)   the complaint handling and dispute resolution procedures available in accordance with Articles 33, 34 and 35.

2.   The collective management organisation shall publish, and keep up to date, on its public website the information referred to in paragraph 1.

Article 22 Annual transparency report

1.   Member States shall ensure that a collective management organisation, irrespective of its legal form under national law, draws up and makes public an annual transparency report, including the special report referred to in paragraph 3, for each financial year no later than eight months following the end of that financial year.

The collective management organisation shall publish on its website the annual transparency report, which shall remain available to the public on that website for at least five years.

2. The annual transparency report shall contain at least the information set out in the Annex.

3. A special report shall address the use of the amounts deducted for the purposes of social, cultural and educational services and shall contain at least the information set out in point 3 of the Annex.

4. The accounting information included in the annual transparency report shall be audited by one or more persons empowered by law to audit accounts in accordance with Directive 2006/43/EC of the European Parliament and of the Council.

   The audit report, including any qualifications thereto, shall be reproduced in full in the annual transparency report.

   For the purposes of this paragraph, accounting information shall comprise the financial statements referred to in point 1(a) of the Annex and any financial information referred to in points (g) and (h) of point 1 and in point 2 of the Annex.

TITLE III
MULTI-TERRITORIAL LICENSING OF ONLINE RIGHTS IN MUSICAL WORKS BY COLLECTIVE MANAGEMENT ORGANISATIONS

Article 23 Multi-territorial licensing in the internal market

Member States shall ensure that collective management organisations established in their territory comply with the requirements of this Title when granting multi-territorial licences for online rights in musical works.

Article 24 Capacity to process multi-territorial licences

1. Member States shall ensure that a collective management organisation which grants multi-territorial licences for online rights in musical works has sufficient capacity to process electronically, in an efficient and transparent manner, data needed for the administration of such licences, including for the purposes of identifying the repertoire and monitoring its use, invoicing users, collecting rights revenue and distributing amounts due to rightholders.

2. For the purposes of paragraph 1, a collective management organisation shall comply, at least, with the following conditions:

   (a) to have the ability to identify accurately the musical works, wholly or in part, which the collective management organisation is authorised to represent;

   (b) to have the ability to identify accurately, wholly or in part, with respect to each relevant territory, the rights and their corresponding rightholders for each musical work or share therein which the collective management organisation is authorised to represent;

   (c) to make use of unique identifiers in order to identify rightholders and musical works, taking into account, as far as possible, voluntary industry standards and practices developed at international or Union level;

   (d) to make use of adequate means in order to identify and resolve in a timely and effective manner inconsistencies in data held by other collective management organisations granting multi-territorial licences for online rights in musical works.

Article 25 Transparency of multi-territorial repertoire information

1. Member States shall ensure that a collective management organisation which grants multi-territorial licences for online rights in musical works provides to online service providers, to rightholders whose rights it represents and to other collective management organisations, by electronic means, in response to a duly justified request, up-to-date information allowing the identification of the online music repertoire it represents. This shall include:

   (a) the musical works represented;

   (b) the rights represented wholly or in part; and

   (c) the territories covered.

2. The collective management organisation may take reasonable measures, where necessary, to protect the accuracy and integrity of the data, to control their reuse and to protect commercially sensitive information.

Article 26 Accuracy of multi-territorial repertoire information

1. Member States shall ensure that a collective management organisation which grants multi-territorial licences for online rights in musical works has in place arrangements to enable rightholders, other collective management organisations and online service providers to request a correction of the data referred to in the list of conditions under Article 24(2) or the information provided under Article 25, where such rightholders, collective management organisations and online service providers, on the basis of reasonable evidence, believe that the data or the information are inaccurate in respect of their online rights in musical works. Where the claims are sufficiently substantiated, the collective management organisation shall ensure that the data or the information are corrected without undue delay.

2. The collective management organisation shall provide rightholders whose musical works are included in its own music repertoire and rightholders who have entrusted the management of their online rights in musical works to it in accordance with Article 31 with the means of submitting to it in electronic form information concerning their musical works, their rights in those works and the territories in respect of which the rightholders authorise the organisation. When doing so, the collective management organisation and the rightholders shall take into account, as far as possible, voluntary industry standards or practices regarding the exchange of data developed at international or Union level, allowing rightholders to specify the musical work, wholly or in part, the online rights, wholly or in part, and the territories in respect of which they authorise the organisation.

3. Where a collective management organisation mandates another collective management organisation to grant multi-territorial licences for the online rights in musical works under Articles 29 and 30, the mandated collective management organisation shall also apply paragraph 2 of this Article with respect to the rightholders whose musical works are included in the repertoire of the mandating collective management organisation, unless the collective management organisations agree otherwise.

Article 27 Accurate and timely reporting and invoicing

1. Member States shall ensure that a collective management organisation monitors the use of online rights in musical works which it represents, wholly or in part, by online service providers to which it has granted a multi-territorial licence for those rights.

2. The collective management organisation shall offer online service providers the possibility of reporting by electronic means the actual use of online rights in musical works and online service providers shall accurately report the actual use of those works. The collective management organisation shall offer the use of a least one method of reporting which takes into account voluntary industry standards or practices developed at international or Union level for the electronic exchange of such data. The collective management organisation may refuse to accept reporting by the online service provider in a proprietary format if the organisation allows for reporting using an industry standard for the electronic exchange of data.

3. The collective management organisation shall invoice the online service provider by electronic means. The collective management organisation shall offer the use of a least one format which takes into account voluntary industry standards or practices developed at international or Union level. The invoice shall identify the works and rights which are licensed, wholly or in part, on the basis of the data referred to in the list of conditions under Article 24(2), and the corresponding actual uses, to the extent that this is possible on the basis of the information provided by the online service provider and the format used to provide that information. The online service provider may not refuse to accept the invoice because of its format if the collective management organisation is using an industry standard.

4. The collective management organisation shall invoice the online service provider accurately and without delay after the actual use of the online rights in that musical work is reported, except where this is not possible for reasons attributable to the online service provider.

5. The collective management organisation shall have in place adequate arrangements enabling the online service provider to challenge the accuracy of the invoice, including when the online service provider receives invoices from one or more collective management organisations for the same online rights in the same musical work.

Article 28 Accurate and timely payment to rightholders

1.   Without prejudice to paragraph 3, Member States shall ensure that a collective management organisation which grants multi-territorial licences for online rights in musical works distributes amounts due to rightholders accruing from such licences accurately and without delay after the actual use of the work is reported, except where this is not possible for reasons attributable to the online service provider.

2.   Without prejudice to paragraph 3, the collective management organisation shall provide at least the following information to rightholders together with each payment it makes under paragraph 1:

(a)   the period during which the uses took place for which amounts are due to rightholders and the territories in which the uses took place;

(b)   the amounts collected, deductions made and amounts distributed by the collective management organisation for each online right in any musical work which rightholders have authorised the collective management organisation, wholly or in part, to represent;

(c)   the amounts collected for rightholders, deductions made, and amounts distributed by the collective management organisation in respect of each online service provider.

3.   Where a collective management organisation mandates another collective management organisation to grant multi-territorial licences for the online rights in musical works under Articles 29 and 30, the mandated collective management organisation shall distribute the amounts referred to in paragraph 1 accurately and without delay, and shall provide the information referred to in paragraph 2 to the mandating collective management organisation. The mandating collective management organisation shall be responsible for the subsequent distribution of such amounts and the provision of such information to rightholders, unless the collective management organisations agree otherwise.

Article 29 Agreements between collective management organisations for multi-territorial licensing

1.   Member States shall ensure that any representation agreement between collective management organisations whereby a collective management organisation mandates another collective management organisation to grant multi-territorial licences for the online rights in musical works in its own music repertoire is of a non-exclusive nature. The mandated collective management organisation shall manage those online rights on a non-discriminatory basis.

2.   The mandating collective management organisation shall inform its members of the main terms of the agreement, including its duration and the costs of the services provided by the mandated collective management organisation.

3.   The mandated collective management organisation shall inform the mandating collective management organisation of the main terms according to which the latter's online rights are to be licensed, including the nature of the exploitation, all provisions which relate to or affect the licence fee, the duration of the licence, the accounting periods and the territories covered.

Article 30 Obligation to represent another collective management organisation for multi-territorial licensing

1.   Member States shall ensure that where a collective management organisation which does not grant or offer to grant multi-territorial licences for the online rights in musical works in its own repertoire requests another collective management organisation to enter into a representation agreement to represent those rights, the requested collective management organisation is required to agree to such a request if it is already granting or offering to grant multi-territorial licences for the same category of online rights in musical works in the repertoire of one or more other collective management organisations.

2.   The requested collective management organisation shall respond to the requesting collective management organisation in writing and without undue delay.

3.   Without prejudice to paragraphs 5 and 6, the requested collective management organisation shall manage the represented repertoire of the requesting collective management organisation on the same conditions as those which it applies to the management of its own repertoire.

4.   The requested collective management organisation shall include the represented repertoire of the requesting collective management organisation in all offers it addresses to online service providers.

5.   The management fee for the service provided by the requested collective management organisation to the requesting organisation shall not exceed the costs reasonably incurred by the requested collective management organisation.

6.   The requesting collective management organisation shall make available to the requested collective management organisation information relating to its own music repertoire required for the provision of multi-territorial licences for online rights in musical works. Where information is insufficient or provided in a form that does not allow the requested collective management organisation to meet the requirements of this Title, the requested collective management organisation shall be entitled to charge for the costs reasonably incurred in meeting such requirements or to exclude those works for which information is insufficient or cannot be used.

Article 31 Access to multi-territorial licensing
Member States shall ensure that where a collective management organisation does not grant or offer to grant multi-territorial licences for online rights in musical works or does not allow another collective management organisation to represent those rights for such purpose by 10 April 2017, rightholders who have authorised that collective management organisation to represent their online rights in musical works can withdraw from that collective management organisation the online rights in musical works for the purposes of multi-territorial licensing in respect of all territories without having to withdraw the online rights in musical works for the purposes of mono-territorial licensing, so as to grant multi-territorial licences for their online rights in musical works themselves or through any other party they authorise or through any collective management organisation complying with the provisions of this Title.

Article 32 Derogation for online music rights required for radio and television programmes
The requirements under this Title shall not apply to collective management organisations when they grant, on the basis of the voluntary aggregation of the required rights, in compliance with the competition rules under Articles 101 and 102 TFEU, a multi-territorial licence for the online rights in musical works required by a broadcaster to communicate or make available to the public its radio or television programmes simultaneously with or after their initial broadcast as well as any online material, including previews, produced by or for the broadcaster which is ancillary to the initial broadcast of its radio or television programme.

TITLE IV
ENFORCEMENT MEASURES

Article 33 Complaints procedures
1.   Member States shall ensure that collective management organisations make available to their members, and to collective management organisations on whose behalf they manage rights under a representation agreement, effective and timely procedures for dealing with complaints, particularly in relation to authorisation to manage rights and termination or withdrawal of rights, membership terms, the collection of amounts due to rightholders, deductions and distributions.

2.   Collective management organisations shall respond in writing to complaints by members or by collective management organisations on whose behalf they manage rights under a representation agreement. Where the collective management organisation rejects a complaint, it shall give reasons.

Article 34 Alternative dispute resolution procedures
1.   Member States may provide that disputes between collective management organisations, members of collective management organisations, rightholders or users regarding the provisions of national law adopted pursuant to the requirements of this Directive can be submitted to a rapid, independent and impartial alternative dispute resolution procedure.

2.   Member States shall ensure, for the purposes of Title III, that the following disputes relating to a collective management organisation established in their territory which grants or offers to grant multi-territorial licences for online rights in musical works can be submitted to an independent and impartial alternative dispute resolution procedure:
(a)   disputes with an actual or potential online service provider regarding the application of Articles 16, 25, 26 and 27;
(b)   disputes with one or more rightholders regarding the application of Articles 25, 26, 27, 28, 29, 30 and 31;
(c)   disputes with another collective management organisation regarding the application of Articles 25, 26, 27, 28, 29 and 30.

Article 35 Dispute resolution

1.   Member States shall ensure that disputes between collective management organisations and users concerning, in particular, existing and proposed licensing conditions or a breach of contract can be submitted to a court, or if appropriate, to another independent and impartial dispute resolution body where that body has expertise in intellectual property law.
2.   Articles 33 and 34 and paragraph 1 of this Article shall be without prejudice to the right of parties to assert and defend their rights by bringing an action before a court.

Article 36 Compliance

1.   Member States shall ensure that compliance by collective management organisations established in their territory with the provisions of national law adopted pursuant to the requirements laid down in this Directive is monitored by competent authorities designated for that purpose.
2.   Member States shall ensure that procedures exist enabling members of a collective management organisation, rightholders, users, collective management organisations and other interested parties to notify the competent authorities designated for that purpose of activities or circumstances which, in their opinion, constitute a breach of the provisions of national law adopted pursuant to the requirements laid down in this Directive.
3.   Member States shall ensure that the competent authorities designated for that purpose have the power to impose appropriate sanctions or to take appropriate measures where the provisions of national law adopted in implementation of this Directive have not been complied with. Those sanctions and measures shall be effective, proportionate and dissuasive.
    Member States shall notify the Commission of the competent authorities referred to in this Article and in Articles 37 and 38 by 10 April 2016. The Commission shall publish the information received in that regard.

Article 37 Exchange of information between competent authorities

1.   In order to facilitate the monitoring of the application of this Directive, each Member State shall ensure that a request for information received from a competent authority of another Member State, designated for that purpose, concerning matters relevant to the application of this Directive, in particular with regard to the activities of collective management organisations established in the territory of the requested Member State, is responded to without undue delay by the competent authority designated for that purpose, provided that the request is duly justified.
2.   Where a competent authority considers that a collective management organisation established in another Member State but acting within its territory may not be complying with the provisions of the national law of the Member State in which that collective management organisation is established which have been adopted pursuant to the requirements laid down in this Directive, it may transmit all relevant information to the competent authority of the Member State in which the collective management organisation is established, accompanied where appropriate by a request to that authority that it take appropriate action within its competence. The requested competent authority shall provide a reasoned reply within three months.
3.   Matters as referred to in paragraph 2 may also be referred by the competent authority making such a request to the expert group established in accordance with Article 41.

Article 38 Cooperation for the development of multi-territorial licensing

1. The Commission shall foster a regular exchange of information between the competent authorities designated for that purpose in Member States, and between those authorities and the Commission, on the situation and development of multi-territorial licensing.

2. The Commission shall conduct regular consultations with representatives of rightholders, collective management organisations, users, consumers and other interested parties on their experience with the application of the provisions of Title III of this Directive. The Commission shall provide competent authorities with all relevant information that emerges from those consultations, within the framework of the exchange of information provided for in paragraph 1.

3. Member States shall ensure that by 10 October 2017, their competent authorities provide the Commission with a report on the situation and development of multi-territorial licensing in their territory. The report shall include information on, in particular, the availability of multi-territorial licences in the Member State concerned and compliance by collective management organisations with the provisions of national law adopted in implementation of Title III of this Directive, together with an assessment of the development of multi-territorial licensing of online rights in musical works by users, consumers, rightholders and other interested parties.

4. On the basis of the reports received pursuant to paragraph 3 and the information gathered pursuant to paragraphs 1 and 2, the Commission shall assess the application of Title III of this Directive. If necessary, and where appropriate on the basis of a specific report, it shall consider further steps to address any identified problems. That assessment shall cover, in particular, the following:
   (a) the number of collective management organisations meeting the requirements of Title III;
   (b) the application of Articles 29 and 30, including the number of representation agreements concluded by collective management organisations pursuant to those Articles;
   (c) the proportion of repertoire in the Member States which is available for licensing on a multi-territorial basis.

COUNCIL REGULATION (EC) No 6/2002
(Community designs)

TITLE I
GENERAL PROVISIONS

Article 1 Community design

1. A design which complies with the conditions contained in this Regulation is hereinafter referred to as a "Community design".

2. A design shall be protected:
   (a) by an "unregistered Community design", if made available to the public in the manner provided for in this Regulation;
   (b) by a "registered Community design", if registered in the manner provided for in this Regulation.

3. A Community design shall have a unitary character. It shall have equal effect throughout the Community. It shall not be registered, transferred or surrendered or be the subject of a decision declaring it invalid, nor shall its use be prohibited, save in respect of the whole Community. This principle and its implications shall apply unless otherwise provided in this Regulation.

Article 2 Office

The Office for Harmonisation in the Internal Market (Trade Marks and Designs), hereinafter referred to as "the Office", instituted by Council Regulation (EC) No. 40/94 of 20 December 1993 on the Community trade mark, hereinafter referred to as the "Regulation on the Community trade mark", shall carry out the tasks entrusted to it by this Regulation.

TITLE II
THE LAW RELATING TO DESIGNS

SECTION 1
REQUIREMENTS FOR PROTECTION

Article 3 Definitions

For the purposes of this Regulation:

(a)   "design" means the appearance of the whole or a part of a product resulting from the features of, in particular, the lines, contours, colours, shape, texture and/or materials of the product itself and/or its ornamentation;

(b)   "product" means any industrial or handicraft item, including inter alia parts intended to be assembled into a complex product, packaging, get-up, graphic symbols and typographic typefaces, but excluding computer programs;

(c)   "complex product" means a product which is composed of multiple components which can be replaced permitting disassembly and reassembly of the product.

Article 4 Requirements for protection

1.   A design shall be protected by a Community design to the extent that it is new and has individual character.

2.   A design applied to or incorporated in a product which constitutes a component part of a complex product shall only be considered to be new and to have individual character:

(a)   if the component part, once it has been incorporated into the complex product, remains visible during normal use of the latter; and

(b)   to the extent that those visible features of the component part fulfil in themselves the requirements as to novelty and individual character.

3.   "Normal use" within the meaning of paragraph (2)(a) shall mean use by the end user, excluding maintenance, servicing or repair work.

Article 5 Novelty

1.   A design shall be considered to be new if no identical design has been made available to the public:

(a)   in the case of an unregistered Community design, before the date on which the design for which protection is claimed has first been made available to the public;

(b)   in the case of a registered Community design, before the date of filing of the application for registration of the design for which protection is claimed, or, if priority is claimed, the date of priority.

2.   Designs shall be deemed to be identical if their features differ only in immaterial details.

Article 6 Individual character

1.   A design shall be considered to have individual character if the overall impression it produces on the informed user differs from the overall impression produced on such a user by any design which has been made available to the public:

(a)   in the case of an unregistered Community design, before the date on which the design for which protection is claimed has first been made available to the public;

(b)   in the case of a registered Community design, before the date of filing the application for registration or, if a priority is claimed, the date of priority.

2.   In assessing individual character, the degree of freedom of the designer in developing the design shall be taken into consideration.

Article 7 Disclosure

1.   For the purpose of applying Articles 5 and 6, a design shall be deemed to have been made available to the public if it has been published following registration or otherwise, or exhibited, used in trade or otherwise disclosed, before the date referred to in Articles 5(1)(a) and 6(1)(a) or in Articles 5(1)(b) and 6(1)(b), as the case may be, except where these events could not reasonably have become known in the normal course of business to the circles specialised in the sector concerned, operating within the Community. The design shall not, however, be deemed to have been made available to the public for the sole reason that it has been disclosed to a third person under explicit or implicit conditions of confidentiality.

2. A disclosure shall not be taken into consideration for the purpose of applying Articles 5 and 6 and if a design for which protection is claimed under a registered Community design has been made available to the public:

 (a) by the designer, his successor in title, or a third person as a result of information provided or action taken by the designer or his successor in title; and

 (b) during the 12-month period preceding the date of filing of the application or, if a priority is claimed, the date of priority.

3. Paragraph 2 shall also apply if the design has been made available to the public as a consequence of an abuse in relation to the designer or his successor in title.

Article 8 Designs dictated by their technical function and designs of interconnections

1. Community design shall not subsist in features of appearance of a product which are solely dictated by its technical function.

2. A Community design shall not subsist in features of appearance of a product which must necessarily be reproduced in their exact form and dimensions in order to permit the product in which the design is incorporated or to which it is applied to be mechanically connected to or placed in, around or against another product so that either product may perform its function.

3. Notwithstanding paragraph 2, a Community design shall under the conditions set out in Articles 5 and 6 subsist in a design serving the purpose of allowing the multiple assembly or connection of mutually interchangeable products within a modular system.

Article 9 Designs contrary to public policy or morality

A Community design shall not subsist in a design which is contrary to public policy or to accepted principles of morality.

SECTION 2
SCOPE AND TERM OF PROTECTION

Article 10 Scope of protection

1. The scope of the protection conferred by a Community design shall include any design which does not produce on the informed user a different overall impression.

2. In assessing the scope of protection, the degree of freedom of the designer in developing his design shall be taken into consideration.

Article 11 Commencement and term of protection of the unregistered Community design

1. A design which meets the requirements under Section 1 shall be protected by an unregistered Community design for a period of three years as from the date on which the design was first made available to the public within the Community.

2. For the purpose of paragraph 1, a design shall be deemed to have been made available to the public within the Community if it has been published, exhibited, used in trade or otherwise disclosed in such a way that, in the normal course of business, these events could reasonably have become known to the circles specialised in the sector concerned, operating within the Community. The design shall not, however, be deemed to have been made available to the public for the sole reason that it has been disclosed to a third person under explicit or implicit conditions of confidentiality.

Article 12 Commencement and term of protection of the registered Community design

Upon registration by the Office, a design which meets the requirements under Section 1 shall be protected by a registered Community design for a period of five years as from the date of the filing of the application. The right holder may have the term of protection renewed for one or more periods of five years each, up to a total term of 25 years from the date of filing.

Article 13 Renewal

1. Registration of the registered Community design shall be renewed at the request of the right holder or of any person expressly authorised by him, provided that the renewal fee has been paid.

2. . . .

3.   . . .
4.   Renewal shall take effect from the day following the date on which the existing registration expires. The renewal shall be entered in the register.

SECTION 3
RIGHT TO THE COMMUNITY DESIGN

Article 14 Right to the Community design
1.   The right to the Community design shall vest in the designer or his successor in title.
2.   If two or more persons have jointly developed a design, the right to the Community design shall vest in them jointly.
3.   However, where a design is developed by an employee in the execution of his duties or following the instructions given by his employer, the right to the Community design shall vest in the employer, unless otherwise agreed or specified under national law.

Article 15 Claims relating to the entitlement to a Community design
1.   If an unregistered Community design is disclosed or claimed by, or a registered Community design has been applied for or registered in the name of, a person who is not entitled to it under Article 14, the person entitled to it under that provision may, without prejudice to any other remedy which may be open to him, claim to become recognised as the legitimate holder of the Community design.
2.   Where a person is jointly entitled to a Community design, that person may, in accordance with paragraph 1, claim to become recognised as joint holder.
3.   Legal proceedings under paragraphs 1 or 2 shall be barred three years after the date of publication of a registered Community design or the date of disclosure of an unregistered Community design. This provision shall not apply if the person who is not entitled to the Community design was acting in bad faith at the time when such design was applied for or disclosed or was assigned to him.
4.   In the case of a registered Community design, the following shall be entered in the register:
         (a) the mention that legal proceedings under paragraph 1 have been instituted;
         (b) the final decision or any other termination of the proceedings;
         (c) any change in the ownership of the registered Community design resulting from the final decision.

Article 16 Effects of a judgement on entitlement to a registered Community design
1.   Where there is a complete change of ownership of a registered Community design as a result of legal proceedings under Article 15(1), licences and other rights shall lapse upon the entering in the register of the person entitled.
2.   If, before the institution of the legal proceedings under Article 15(1) has been registered, the holder of the registered Community design or a licensee has exploited the design within the Community or made serious and effective preparations to do so, he may continue such exploitation provided that he requests within the period prescribed by the implementing regulation a non-exclusive licence from the new holder whose name is entered in the register. The licence shall be granted for a reasonable period and upon reasonable terms.
3.   Paragraph 2 shall not apply if the holder of the registered Community design or the licensee was acting in bad faith at the time when he began to exploit the design or to make preparations to do so.

Article 17 Presumption in favour of the registered holder of the design
The person in whose name the registered Community design is registered or, prior to registration, the person in whose name the application is filed, shall be deemed to be the person entitled in any proceedings before the Office as well as in any other proceedings.

Article 18 Right of the designer to be cited
The designer shall have the right, in the same way as the applicant for or the holder of a registered Community design, to be cited as such before the Office and in the register. If the design is the result of teamwork, the citation of the team may replace the citation of the individual designers.

SECTION 4
EFFECTS OF THE COMMUNITY DESIGN

Article 19 Rights conferred by the Community design

1. A registered Community design shall confer on its holder the exclusive right to use it and to prevent any third party not having his consent from using it. The aforementioned use shall cover, in particular, the making, offering, putting on the market, importing, exporting or using of a product in which the design is incorporated or to which it is applied, or stocking such a product for those purposes.

2. An unregistered Community design shall, however, confer on its holder the right to prevent the acts referred to in paragraph 1 only if the contested use results from copying the protected design.
   The contested use shall not be deemed to result from copying the protected design if it results from an independent work of creation by a designer who may be reasonably thought not to be familiar with the design made available to the public by the holder.

3. Paragraph 2 shall also apply to a registered Community design subject to deferment of publication as long as the relevant entries in the register and the file have not been made available to the public in accordance with Article 50(4).

Article 20 Limitation of the rights conferred by a Community design

1. The rights conferred by a Community design shall not be exercised in respect of:
   (a) acts done privately and for non-commercial purposes;
   (b) acts done for experimental purposes;
   (c) acts of reproduction for the purpose of making citations or of teaching, provided that such acts are compatible with fair trade practice and do not unduly prejudice the normal exploitation of the design, and that mention is made of the source.

2. In addition, the rights conferred by a Community design shall not be exercised in respect of:
   (a) the equipment on ships and aircraft registered in a third country when these temporarily enter the territory of the Community;
   (b) the importation in the Community of spare parts and accessories for the purpose of repairing such craft;
   (c) the execution of repairs on such craft.

Article 21 Exhaustion of rights

The rights conferred by a Community design shall not extend to acts relating to a product in which a design included within the scope of protection of the Community design is incorporated or to which it is applied, when the product has been put on the market in the Community by the holder of the Community design or with his consent.

Article 22 Rights of prior use in respect of a registered Community design

1. A right of prior use shall exist for any third person who can establish that before the date of filing of the application, or, if a priority is claimed, before the date of priority, he has in good faith commenced use within the Community, or has made serious and effective preparations to that end, of a design included within the scope of protection of a registered Community design, which has not been copied from the latter.

2. The right of prior use shall entitle the third person to exploit the design for the purposes for which its use had been effected, or for which serious and effective preparations had been made, before the filing or priority date of the registered Community design.

3. The right of prior use shall not extend to granting a licence to another person to exploit the design.

4. The right of prior use cannot be transferred except, where the third person is a business, along with that part of the business in the course of which the act was done or the preparations were made.

Article 23 Government use

Any provision in the law of a Member State allowing use of national designs by or for the government may be applied to Community designs, but only to the extent that the use is necessary for essential defence or security needs.

SECTION 5
INVALIDITY

Article 24 Declaration of invalidity

1.   A registered Community design shall be declared invalid on application to the Office in accordance with the procedure in Titles VI and VII or by a Community design court on the basis of a counterclaim in infringement proceedings.
2.   A Community design may be declared invalid even after the Community design has lapsed or has been surrendered.
3.   An unregistered Community design shall be declared invalid by a Community design court on application to such a court or on the basis of a counterclaim in infringement proceedings.

Article 25 Grounds for invalidity

1.   A Community design may be declared invalid only in the following cases:
      (a)   if the design does not correspond to the definition under Article 3(a);
      (b)   if it does not fulfil the requirements of Articles 4 to 9;
      (c)   if, by virtue of a court decision, the right holder is not entitled to the Community design under Article 14;
      (d)   if the Community design is in conflict with a prior design which has been made available to the public after the date of filing of the application or, if priority is claimed, the date of priority of the Community design, and which is protected from a date prior to the said date
            (i)   by a registered Community design or an application for such a design, or
            (ii)   by a registered design right of a Member State, or by an application for such a right, or
            (iii)   by a design right registered under the Geneva Act of the Hague Agreement concerning the international registration of industrial designs, adopted in Geneva on 2 July 1999, hereinafter referred to as "the Geneva Act", which was approved by Council Decision 954/2006 and which has effect in the Community, or by an application for such a right;
      (e)   if a distinctive sign is used in a subsequent design, and Community law or the law of the Member State governing that sign confers on the right holder of the sign the right to prohibit such use;
      (f)   if the design constitutes an unauthorised use of a work protected under the copyright law of a Member State;
      (g)   if the design constitutes an improper use of any of the items listed in Article 6ter of the "Paris Convention" for the Protection of Industrial Property hereafter referred to as the "Paris Convention", or of badges, emblems and escutcheons other than those covered by the said Article 6*ter* and which are of particular public interest in a Member State.
2.   The ground provided for in paragraph (1)(c) may be invoked solely by the person who is entitled to the Community design under Article 14.
3.   The grounds provided for in paragraph (1)(d), (e) and (f) may be invoked solely by the applicant for or holder of the earlier right.
4.   The ground provided for in paragraph (1)(g) may be invoked solely by the person or entity concerned by the use.
5.   Paragraphs 3 and 4 shall be without prejudice to the freedom of Member States to provide that the grounds provided for in paragraphs 1(d) and (g) may also be invoked by the appropriate authority of the Member State in question on its own initiative.
6.   A registered Community design which has been declared invalid pursuant to paragraph (1) (b), (e), (f) or (g) may be maintained in an amended form, if in that form it complies with the requirements for protection and the identity of the design is retained. "Maintenance" in an amended form may include registration accompanied by a partial disclaimer by the holder of the registered Community design or entry in the register of a court decision or a decision by the Office declaring the partial invalidity of the registered Community design.

Article 26 Consequences of invalidity

1.   A Community design shall be deemed not to have had, as from the outset, the effects specified in this Regulation, to the extent that it has been declared invalid.

2. Subject to the national provisions relating either to claims for compensation for damage caused by negligence or lack of good faith on the part of the holder of the Community design, or to unjust enrichment, the retroactive effect of invalidity of the Community design shall not affect:

   (a) any decision on infringement which has acquired the authority of a final decision and been enforced prior to the invalidity decision;

   (b) any contract concluded prior to the invalidity decision, in so far as it has been performed before the decision; however, repayment, to an extent justified by the circumstances, of sums paid under the relevant contract may be claimed on grounds of equity.

TITLE III
COMMUNITY DESIGNS AS OBJECTS OF PROPERTY

Article 27 Dealing with Community designs as national design rights

1. Unless Articles 28, 29, 30, 31 and 32 provide otherwise, a Community design as an object of property shall be dealt with in its entirety, and for the whole area of the Community, as a national design right of the Member State in which:

   (a) the holder has his seat or his domicile on the relevant date; or

   (b) where point (a) does not apply, the holder has an establishment on the relevant date.

2. In the case of a registered Community design, paragraph 1 shall apply according to the entries in the register.

3. In the case of joint holders, if two or more of them fulfil the condition under paragraph 1, the Member State referred to in that paragraph shall be determined:

   (a) in the case of an unregistered Community design, by reference to the relevant joint holder designated by them by common agreement;

   (b) in the case of a registered Community design, by reference to the first of the relevant joint holders in the order in which they are mentioned in the register.

4. Where paragraphs 1, 2 and 3 do not apply, the Member State referred to in paragraph 1 shall be the Member State in which the seat of the Office is situated.

Article 28 Transfer of the registered Community design

The transfer of a registered Community design shall be subject to the following provisions:

   (a) at the request of one of the parties, a transfer shall be entered in the register and published;

   (b) until such time as the transfer has been entered in the register, the successor in title may not invoke the rights arising from the registration of the Community design;

   (c) where there are time limits to be observed in dealings with the Office, the successor in title may make the corresponding statements to the Office once the request for registration of the transfer has been received by the Office;

   (d) all documents which by virtue of Article 66 require notification to the holder of the registered Community design shall be addressed by the Office to the person registered as holder or his representative, if one has been appointed.

Article 29 Rights *in rem* on a registered Community design

1. A registered Community design may be given as security or be the subject of rights *in rem*.

2. On request of one of the parties, the rights mentioned in paragraph 1 shall be entered in the register and published.

Article 30 Levy of execution

1. A registered Community design may be levied in execution.

. . .

Article 31 Insolvency proceedings

1. The only insolvency proceedings in which a Community design may be involved shall be those opened in the Member State within the territory of which the centre of a debtor's main interests is situated.

. . .

Article 32 Licensing

1. A Community design may be licensed for the whole or part of the Community. A licence may be exclusive or non-exclusive.

2.   Without prejudice to any legal proceedings based on the law of contract, the holder may invoke the rights conferred by the Community design against a licensee who contravenes any provision in his licensing contract with regard to its duration, the form in which the design may be used, the range of products for which the licence is granted and the quality of products manufactured by the licensee.

3.   Without prejudice to the provisions of the licensing contract, the licensee may bring proceedings for infringement of a Community design only if the right holder consents thereto. However, the holder of an exclusive licence may bring such proceedings if the right holder in the Community design, having been given notice to do so, does not himself bring infringement proceedings within an appropriate period.

4.   A licensee shall, for the purpose of obtaining compensation for damage suffered by him, be entitled to intervene in an infringement action brought by the right holder in a Community design.

5.   In the case of a registered Community design, the grant or transfer of a licence in respect of such right shall, at the request of one of the parties, be entered in the register and published.

Article 33 Effects vis-à-vis third parties

1.   The effects vis-à-vis third parties of the legal acts referred to in Articles 28, 29, 30 and 32 shall be governed by the law of the Member State determined in accordance with Article 27.

2.   However, as regards registered Community designs, legal acts referred to in Articles 28, 29 and 32 shall only have effect vis-à-vis third parties in all the Member States after entry in the register. Nevertheless, such an act, before it is so entered, shall have effect vis-à-vis third parties who have acquired rights in the registered Community design after the date of that act but who knew of the act at the date on which the rights were acquired.

3.   Paragraph 2 shall not apply to a person who acquires the registered Community design or a right concerning the registered Community design by way of transfer of the whole of the undertaking or by any other universal succession.

4.   Until such time as common rules for the Member States in the field of insolvency enter into force, the effects vis-à-vis third parties of insolvency proceedings shall be governed by the law of the Member State in which such proceedings are first brought under the national law or the regulations applicable in this field.

Article 34 The application for a registered Community design as an object of property

1.   An application for a registered Community design as an object of property shall be dealt with in its entirety, and for the whole area of the Community, as a national design right of the Member State determined in accordance with Article 27.

2.   Articles 28, 29, 30, 31, 32 and 33 shall apply mutatis mutandis to applications for registered Community designs. Where the effect of one of these provisions is conditional upon an entry in the register, that formality shall be performed upon registration of the resulting registered Community design.

TITLE IV

APPLICATION FOR A REGISTERED COMMUNITY DESIGN

SECTION 1

FILING OF APPLICATIONS AND THE CONDITIONS WHICH GOVERN THEM

Article 35 Filing and forwarding of applications

1.   An application for a registered Community design shall be filed, at the option of the applicant:
   (a)   at the Office; or
   (b)   at the central industrial property office of a Member State; or
   (c)   in the Benelux countries, at the Benelux Design Office.
   . . .

Article 36 Conditions with which applications must comply

1.   An application for a registered Community design shall contain:
   (a)   a request for registration;
   (b)   information identifying the applicant;
   (c)   a representation of the design suitable for reproduction. However, if the object of the application is a two-dimensional design and the application contains a request for deferment of publication in accordance with Article 50, the representation of the design may be replaced by a specimen.
2.   The application shall further contain an indication of the products in which the design is intended to be incorporated or to which it is intended to be applied.
3.   In addition, the application may contain:
   (a)   a description explaining the representation or the specimen;
   (b)   a request for deferment of publication of the registration in accordance with Article 50;
   (c)   information identifying the representative if the applicant has appointed one;
   (d)   the classification of the products in which the design is intended to be incorporated or to which it is intended to be applied according to class;
   (e)   the citation of the designer or of the team of designers or a statement under the applicant's responsibility that the designer or the team of designers has waived the right to be cited.
4.   The application shall be subject to the payment of the registration fee and the publication fee. Where a request for deferment under paragraph 3(b) is filed, the publication fee shall be replaced by the fee for deferment of publication.
5.   The application shall comply with the conditions laid down in the implementing regulation.
6.   The information contained in the elements mentioned in paragraph 2 and in paragraph 3(a) and (d) shall not affect the scope of protection of the design as such.

Article 37 Multiple applications

1.   Several designs may be combined in one multiple application for registered Community designs. Except in cases of ornamentation, this possibility is subject to the condition that the products in which the designs are intended to be incorporated or to which they are intended to be applied all belong to the same class of the International Classification for Industrial Designs.
   . . .

Article 38 Date of filing

1.   The date of filing of an application for a registered Community design shall be the date on which documents containing the information specified in Article 36(1) are filed with the Office by the applicant, or, if the application has been filed with the central industrial property office of a Member State or with the Benelux Design Office, with that office.
2.   By derogation from paragraph 1, the date of filing of an application filed with the central industrial property office of a Member State or with the Benelux Design Office and reaching the Office more than two months after the date on which documents containing the information specified in Article 36(1) have been filed shall be the date of receipt of such documents by the Office.

Article 39 Equivalence of Community filing with national filing

An application for a registered Community design which has been accorded a date of filing shall, in the Member States, be equivalent to a regular national filing, including where appropriate the priority claimed for the said application.

Article 40 Classification

For the purpose of this Regulation, use shall be made of the Annex to the Agreement establishing an International Classification for Industrial Designs, signed at Locarno on 8 October 1968.

SECTION 2
PRIORITY

Article 41 Right of priority

1.   A person who has duly filed an application for a design right or for a utility model in or for any State party to the Paris Convention for the Protection of Industrial Property, or to the

Agreement establishing the World Trade Organisation, or his successors in title, shall enjoy, for the purpose of filing an application for a registered Community design in respect of the same design or utility model, a right of priority of six months from the date of filing of the first application.

2.   Every filing that is equivalent to a regular national filing under the national law of the State where it was made or under bilateral or multilateral agreements shall be recognised as giving rise to a right of priority.

3.   "Regular national filing" means any filing that is sufficient to establish the date on which the application was filed, whatever may be the outcome of the application.

4.   A subsequent application for a design which was the subject of a previous first application, and which is filed in or in respect of the same State, shall be considered as the first application for the purpose of determining priority, provided that, at the date of the filing of the subsequent application, the previous application has been withdrawn, abandoned or refused without being open to public inspection and without leaving any rights outstanding, and has not served as a basis for claiming priority. The previous application may not thereafter serve as a basis for claiming a right of priority.

5.   If the first filing has been made in a State which is not a party to the Paris Convention, or to the Agreement establishing the World Trade Organisation, paragraphs 1 to 4 shall apply only in so far as that State, according to published findings, grants, on the basis of a filing made at the Office and subject to conditions equivalent to those laid down in this Regulation, a right of priority having equivalent effect.

Article 42 Claiming priority

An applicant for a registered Community design desiring to take advantage of the priority of a previous application shall file a declaration of priority and a copy of the previous application. If the language of the latter is not one of the languages of the Office, the Office may require a translation of the previous application in one of those languages.

Article 43 Effect of priority right

The effect of the right of priority shall be that the date of priority shall count as the date of the filing of the application for a registered Community design for the purpose of Articles 5, 6, 7, 22, 25(1) (d) and 50(1).

Article 44 Exhibition priority

1.   If an applicant for a registered Community design has disclosed products in which the design is incorporated, or to which it is applied, at an official or officially recognised international exhibition falling within the terms of the Convention on International Exhibitions signed in Paris on 22 November 1928 and last revised on 30 November 1972, he may, if he files the application within a period of six months from the date of the first disclosure of such products, claim a right of priority from that date within the meaning of Article 43.

2.   An applicant who wishes to claim priority pursuant to paragraph 1, under the conditions laid down in the implementing regulation, must file evidence that he has disclosed at an exhibition the products in or to which the design is incorporated or applied.

3.   An exhibition priority granted in a Member State or in a third country does not extend the period of priority laid down in Article 41.

TITLE V
REGISTRATION PROCEDURE

Article 45 Examination as to formal requirements for filing

1.   The Office shall examine whether the application complies with the requirements laid down in Article 36(1) for the accordance of a date of filing.

2.   The Office shall examine whether:
    (a)   the application complies with the other requirements laid down in Article 36(2), (3), (4) and (5) and, in the case of a multiple application, Article 37(1) and (2);
    (b)   the application meets the formal requirements laid down in the implementing regulation for the implementation of Articles 36 and 37;
    (c)   the requirements of Article 77(2) are satisfied;
    (d)   the requirements concerning the claim to priority are satisfied, if a priority is claimed.

3.   The conditions for the examination as to the formal requirements for filing shall be laid down in the implementing regulation.

Article 46 Remediable deficiencies

1.   Where, in carrying out the examination under Article 45, the Office notes that there are deficiencies which may be corrected, the Office shall request the applicant to remedy them within the prescribed period.

2.   If the deficiencies concern the requirements referred to in Article 36(1) and the applicant complies with the Office's request within the prescribed period, the Office shall accord as the date of filing the date on which the deficiencies are remedied. If the deficiencies are not remedied within the prescribed period, the application shall not be dealt with as an application for a registered Community design.

3.   If the deficiencies concern the requirements, including the payment of fees, as referred to in Article 45(2)(a), (b) and (c) and the applicant complies with the Office's request within the prescribed period, the Office shall accord as the date of filing the date on which the application was originally filed. If the deficiencies or the default in payment are not remedied within the prescribed period, the Office shall refuse the application.

4.   If the deficiencies concern the requirements referred to in Article 45(2)(d), failure to remedy them within the prescribed period shall result in the loss of the right of priority for the application.

Article 47 Grounds for non-registrability

1.   If the Office, in carrying out the examination pursuant to Article 45, notices that the design for which protection is sought:
        (a)   does not correspond to the definition under Article 3(a); or
        (b)   is contrary to public policy or to accepted principles of morality, it shall refuse the application.

2.   The application shall not be refused before the applicant has been allowed the opportunity of withdrawing or amending the application or of submitting his observations.

Article 48 Registration

If the requirements that an application for a registered Community design must satisfy have been fulfilled and to the extent that the application has not been refused by virtue of Article 47, the Office shall register the application in the Community design Register as a registered Community design. The registration shall bear the date of filing of the application referred to in Article 38.

Article 49 Publication

Upon registration, the Office shall publish the registered Community design in the Community Designs Bulletin as mentioned in Article 73(1). The contents of the publication shall be set out in the implementing regulation.

TITLE VI
SURRENDER AND INVALIDITY OF THE REGISTERED COMMUNITY DESIGN

Article 51 Surrender

1.   The surrender of a registered Community design shall be declared to the Office in writing by the right holder. It shall not have effect until it has been entered in the register.

2.   If a Community design which is subject to deferment of publication is surrendered it shall be deemed from the outset not to have had the effects specified in this Regulation.

. . .

Article 52 Application for a declaration of invalidity

1.   Subject to Article 25(2), (3), (4) and (5), any natural or legal person, as well as a public authority empowered to do so, may submit to the Office an application for a declaration of invalidity of a registered Community design.

2.   The application shall be filed in a written reasoned statement. It shall not be deemed to have been filed until the fee for an application for a declaration of invalidity has been paid.

. . .

TITLE VII
APPEALS

Article 55 Decisions subject to appeal

1.   An appeal shall lie from decisions of the examiners, the Administration of Trade Marks and Designs and Legal Division and Invalidity Divisions. It shall have suspensive effect.
2.   A decision which does not terminate proceedings as regards one of the parties can only be appealed together with the final decision, unless the decision allows separate appeal.

Article 56 Persons entitled to appeal and to be parties to appeal proceedings

Any party to proceedings adversely affected by a decision may appeal. Any other parties to the proceedings shall be parties to the appeal proceedings as of right.

Article 57 Time limit and form of appeal

Notice of appeal must be filed in writing at the Office within two months after the date of notification of the decision appealed from. The notice shall be deemed to have been filed only when the fee for appeal has been paid. Within four months after the date of notification of the decision, a written statement setting out the grounds of appeal must be filed.

Article 59 Examination of appeals

1.   If the appeal is admissible, the Board of Appeal shall examine whether the appeal is to be allowed.

. . .

Article 61 Actions before the Court of Justice

1.   Actions may be brought before the Court of Justice against decisions of the Boards of Appeal on appeals.
2.   The action may be brought on grounds of lack of competence, infringement of an essential procedural requirement, infringement of the Treaty, of this Regulation or of any rule of law relating to their application or misuse of power.

. . .

SECTION 3
INFORMING THE PUBLIC AND THE OFFICIAL AUTHORITIES OF THE MEMBER STATES

Article 72 Register of Community designs

The Office shall keep a register to be known as the register of Community designs, which shall contain those particulars of which the registration is provided for by this Regulation or by the implementing regulation. The register shall be open to public inspection, except to the extent that Article 50(2) provides otherwise.

TITLE IX
JURISDICTION AND PROCEDURE IN LEGAL ACTIONS RELATING TO COMMUNITY
DESIGNS

SECTION 2
DISPUTES CONCERNING THE INFRINGEMENT AND VALIDITY OF COMMUNITY DESIGNS

Article 80 Community design courts

1.   The Member States shall designate in their territories as limited a number as possible of national courts and tribunals of first and second instance (Community design courts) which shall perform the functions assigned to them by this Regulation.

. . .

Article 81 Jurisdiction over infringement and validity

The Community design courts shall have exclusive jurisdiction:

(a)   for infringement actions and - if they are permitted under national law - actions in respect of threatened infringement of Community designs;
(b)   for actions for declaration of non-infringement of Community designs, if they are permitted under national law;
(c)   for actions for a declaration of invalidity of an unregistered Community design;

(d)   for counterclaims for a declaration of invalidity of a Community design raised in connection with actions under (a).

Article 84 Action or counterclaim for a declaration of invalidity of a Community design

1.   An action or a counterclaim for a declaration of invalidity of a Community design may only be based on the grounds for invalidity mentioned in Article 25.

2.   In the cases referred to in Article 25(2), (3), (4) and (5) the action or the counterclaim may be brought solely by the person entitled under those provisions.

3.   If the counterclaim is brought in a legal action to which the right holder of the Community design is not already a party, he shall be informed thereof and may be joined as a party to the action in accordance with the conditions set out in the law of the Member State where the court is situated.

4.   The validity of a Community design may not be put in issue in an action for a declaration of non-infringement.

Article 85 Presumption of validity—defence as to the merits

1.   In proceedings in respect of an infringement action or an action for threatened infringement of a registered Community design, the Community design court shall treat the Community design as valid. Validity may be challenged only with a counterclaim for a declaration of invalidity. However, a plea relating to the invalidity of a Community design, submitted otherwise than by way of counterclaim, shall be admissible in so far as the defendant claims that the Community design could be declared invalid on account of an earlier national design right, within the meaning of Article 25(1)(d), belonging to him.

2.   In proceedings in respect of an infringement action or an action for threatened infringement of an unregistered Community design, the Community design court shall treat the Community design as valid if the right holder produces proof that the conditions laid down in Article 11 have been met and indicates what constitutes the individual character of his Community design. However, the defendant may contest its validity by way of a plea or with a counterclaim for a declaration of invalidity.

Article 86 Judgements of invalidity

1.   Where in a proceeding before a Community design court the Community design has been put in issue by way of a counterclaim for a declaration of invalidity:

      (a)   if any of the grounds mentioned in Article 25 are found to prejudice the maintenance of the Community design, the court shall declare the Community design invalid;

      (b)   if none of the grounds mentioned in Article 25 is found to prejudice the maintenance of the Community design, the court shall reject the counterclaim.

2.   The Community design court with which a counterclaim for a declaration of invalidity of a registered Community design has been filed shall inform the Office of the date on which the counterclaim was filed. The latter shall record this fact in the register.

3.   The Community design court hearing a counterclaim for a declaration of invalidity of a registered Community design may, on application by the right holder of the registered Community design and after hearing the other parties, stay the proceedings and request the defendant to submit an application for a declaration of invalidity to the Office within a time limit which the court shall determine. If the application is not made within the time limit, the proceedings shall continue; the counterclaim shall be deemed withdrawn. Article 91(3) shall apply.

4.   Where a Community design court has given a judgment which has become final on a counterclaim for a declaration of invalidity of a registered Community design, a copy of the judgment shall be sent to the Office. Any party may request information about such transmission. The Office shall mention the judgment in the register in accordance with the provisions of the implementing regulation.

5.   No counterclaim for a declaration of invalidity of a registered Community design may be made if an application relating to the same subject matter and cause of action, and involving the same parties, has already been determined by the Office in a decision which has become final.

Article 87 Effects of the judgement on invalidity

When it has become final, a judgment of a Community design court declaring a Community design invalid shall have in all the Member States the effects specified in Article 26.

Article 88 Applicable law

1.   The Community design courts shall apply the provisions of this Regulation.
2.   On all matters not covered by this Regulation, a Community design court shall apply its national law, including its private international law.
3.   Unless otherwise provided in this Regulation, a Community design court shall apply the rules of procedure governing the same type of action relating to a national design right in the Member State where it is situated.

Article 89 Sanctions in actions for infringement

1.   Where in an action for infringement or for threatened infringement a Community design court finds that the defendant has infringed or threatened to infringe a Community design, it shall, unless there are special reasons for not doing so, order the following measures:
   (a)   an order prohibiting the defendant from proceeding with the acts which have infringed or would infringe the Community design;
   (b)   an order to seize the infringing products;
   (c)   an order to seize materials and implements predominantly used in order to manufacture the infringing goods, if their owner knew the effect for which such use was intended or if such effect would have been obvious in the circumstances;
   (d)   any order imposing other sanctions appropriate under the circumstances which are provided by the law of the Member State in which the acts of infringement or threatened infringement are committed, including its private international law.
2.   The Community design court shall take such measures in accordance with its national law as are aimed at ensuring that the orders referred to in paragraph 1 are complied with.

Article 92 Jurisdiction of Community design courts of second instance— further appeal

1.   An appeal to the Community design courts of second instance shall lie from judgments of the Community design courts of first instance in respect of proceedings arising from the actions and claims referred to in Article 81.
2.   The conditions under which an appeal may be lodged with a Community design court of second instance shall be determined by the national law of the Member State in which that court is located.
3.   The national rules concerning further appeal shall be applicable in respect of judgments of Community design courts of second instance.

TITLE X
EFFECTS ON THE LAWS OF THE MEMBER STATES

Article 95 Parallel actions on the basis of Community designs and national design rights

1.   Where actions for infringement or for threatened infringement involving the same cause of action and between the same parties are brought before the courts of different Member States, one seized on the basis of a Community design and the other seized on the basis of a national design right providing simultaneous protection, the court other than the court first seized shall of its own motion decline jurisdiction in favour of that court. The court which would be required to decline jurisdiction may stay its proceedings if the jurisdiction of the other court is contested.
2.   The Community design court hearing an action for infringement or threatened infringement on the basis of a Community design shall reject the action if a final judgment on the merits has been given on the same cause of action and between the same parties on the basis of a design right providing simultaneous protection.
3.   The court hearing an action for infringement or for threatened infringement on the basis of a national design right shall reject the action if a final judgment on the merits has been given on the same cause of action and between the same parties on the basis of a Community design providing simultaneous protection.
4.   Paragraphs 1, 2 and 3 shall not apply in respect of provisional measures, including protective measures.

Article 96 Relationship to other forms of protection under national law

1.   The provisions of this Regulation shall be without prejudice to any provisions of Community law or of the law of the Member States concerned relating to unregistered designs, trade marks or other distinctive signs, patents and utility models, typefaces, civil liability and unfair competition.

2.   A design protected by a Community design shall also be eligible for protection under the law of copyright of Member States as from the date on which the design was created or fixed in any form. The extent to which, and the conditions under which, such a protection is conferred, including the level of originality required, shall be determined by each Member State.

TITLE XIA
INTERNATIONAL REGISTRATION OF DESIGNS
SECTION 1
GENERAL PROVISIONS

Article 106a Application of provisions

1.   Unless otherwise specified in this title, this Regulation and any Regulations implementing this Regulation adopted pursuant to Article 109 shall apply, mutatis mutandis, to registrations of industrial designs in the international register maintained by the International Bureau of the World Intellectual Property Organisation (hereinafter referred to as "international registration" and "the International Bureau") designating the Community, under the Geneva Act.

2.   Any recording of an international registration designating the Community in the International Register shall have the same effect as if it had been made in the register of Community designs of the Office, and any publication of an international registration designating the Community in the Bulletin of the International Bureau shall have the same effect as if it had been published in the Community Designs Bulletin.

SECTION 2
INTERNATIONAL REGISTRATIONS DESIGNATING THE COMMUNITY

Article 106b Procedure for filing the international application

International applications pursuant to Article 4(1) of the Geneva Act shall be filed directly at the International Bureau.

Article 106c Designation fees

The prescribed designation fees referred to in Article 7(1) of the Geneva Act are replaced by an individual designation fee.

Article 106d Effects of international registration designating the European Community

1.   An international registration designating the Community shall, from the date of its registration referred to in Article 10(2) of the Geneva Act, have the same effect as an application for a registered Community design.

2.   If no refusal has been notified or if any such refusal has been withdrawn, the international registration of a design designating the Community shall, from the date referred to in paragraph 1, have the same effect as the registration of a design as a registered Community design.

3.   The Office shall provide information on international registrations referred to in paragraph 2, in accordance with the conditions laid down in the Implementing Regulation.

Article 106e Refusal

1.   The Office shall communicate to the International Bureau a notification of refusal not later than six months from the date of publication of the international registration, if in carrying out an examination of an international registration, the Office notices that the design for which protection is sought does not correspond to the definition under Article 3(a), or is contrary to public policy or to accepted principles of morality.

The notification shall state the grounds on which the refusal is based.

2.   The effects of an international registration in the Community shall not be refused before the holder has been allowed the opportunity of renouncing the international registration in respect of the Community or of submitting observations.

3.   The conditions for the examination as to the grounds for refusal shall be laid down in the Implementing Regulation.

Article 106f Invalidation of the effects of an international registration

1.   The effects of an international registration in the Community may be declared invalid partly or in whole in accordance with the procedure in Titles VI and VII or by a Community design court on the basis of a counterclaim in infringement proceedings.

2.   Where the Office is aware of the invalidation, it shall notify it to the International Bureau.

TITLE XII
FINAL PROVISIONS

Article 110 Transitional provisions

1.   Until such time as amendments to this Regulation enter into force on a proposal from the Commission on this subject, protection as a Community design shall not exist for a design which constitutes a component part of a complex product used within the meaning of Article 19(1) for the purpose of the repair of that complex product so as to restore its original appearance.

2.   The proposal from the Commission referred to in paragraph 1 shall be submitted together with, and take into consideration, any changes which the Commission shall propose on the same subject pursuant to Article 18 of Directive 98/71/EC.

Article 110a Provisions relating to the enlargement of the Community

1.   As of the date of accession of Bulgaria, the Czech Republic, Estonia, Croatia, Cyprus, Latvia, Lithuania, Hungary, Malta, Poland, Romania, Slovenia and Slovakia (hereinafter referred to as "new Member State(s)"), a Community design protected or applied for pursuant to this Regulation before their respective date of accession shall be extended to the territory of those Member States in order to have equal effect throughout the Community.

2.   The application for a registered Community design may not be refused on the basis of any of the grounds for non-registrability listed in Article 47(1), if these grounds became applicable merely because of the accession of a new Member State.

3.   A Community design as referred to in paragraph 1 may not be declared invalid pursuant to Article 25(1) if the grounds for invalidity became applicable merely because of the accession of a new Member State.

4.   The applicant or the holder of an earlier right in a new Member State may oppose the use of a Community design falling under Article 25(1) (d), (e) or (f) within the territory where the earlier right is protected. For the purpose of this provision, "earlier right" means a right acquired or applied for in good faith before accession.

5.   Paragraphs 1, 3 and 4 above shall also apply to unregistered Community designs. Pursuant to Article 11, a design which has not been made public within the territory of the Community shall not enjoy protection as an unregistered Community design.

. . .

REGULATION (EU) 2017/1128
(cross-border portability of online content services)

Article 1 Subject matter and scope

1.   This Regulation introduces a common approach in the Union to the cross-border portability of online content services, by ensuring that subscribers to portable online content services which are lawfully provided in their Member State of residence can access and use those services when temporarily present in a Member State other than their Member State of residence.

2.   This Regulation shall not apply to the field of taxation.

Article 2 Definitions

For the purposes of this Regulation, the following definitions apply:

(1) "subscriber" means any consumer who, on the basis of a contract for the provision of an online content service with a provider whether against payment of money or without such payment, is entitled to access and use such service in the Member State of residence;

(2) "consumer" means any natural person who, in contracts covered by this Regulation, is acting for purposes which are outside that person's trade, business, craft or profession;

(3) "Member State of residence" means the Member State, determined on the basis of Article 5, where the subscriber has his or her actual and stable residence;

(4) "temporarily present in a Member State" means being present in a Member State other than the Member State of residence for a limited period of time;

(5) "online content service" means a service as defined in Articles 56 and 57 TFEU that a provider lawfully provides to subscribers in their Member State of residence on agreed terms and online, which is portable and which is:

   (i) an audiovisual media service as defined in point (a) of Article 1 of Directive 2010/13/EU, or

   (ii) a service the main feature of which is the provision of access to, and the use of, works, other protected subject-matter or transmissions of broadcasting organisations, whether in a linear or an on-demand manner;

(6) "portable" means a feature of an online content service whereby subscribers can effectively access and use the online content service in their Member State of residence without being limited to a specific location.

Article 3 Obligation to enable cross-border portability of online content services

1. The provider of an online content service provided against payment of money shall enable a subscriber who is temporarily present in a Member State to access and use the online content service in the same manner as in the Member State of residence, including by providing access to the same content, on the same range and number of devices, for the same number of users and with the same range of functionalities.

2. The provider shall not impose any additional charges on the subscriber for the access to and the use of the online content service pursuant to paragraph 1.

3. The obligation set out in paragraph 1 shall not extend to any quality requirements applicable to the delivery of an online content service that the provider is subject to when providing that service in the Member State of residence, unless otherwise expressly agreed between the provider and the subscriber.

   The provider shall not take any action to reduce the quality of delivery of the online content service when providing the online content service in accordance with paragraph 1.

4. The provider shall, on the basis of the information in its possession, provide the subscriber with information concerning the quality of delivery of the online content service provided in accordance with paragraph 1. The information shall be provided to the subscriber prior to providing the online content service in accordance with paragraph 1 and by means which are adequate and proportionate.

Article 4 Localisation of the provision of, access to and use of online content services

The provision of an online content service under this Regulation to a subscriber who is temporarily present in a Member State, as well as the access to and the use of that service by the subscriber, shall be deemed to occur solely in the subscriber's Member State of residence.

Article 5 Verification of the Member State of residence

1. At the conclusion and upon the renewal of a contract for the provision of an online content service provided against payment of money, the provider shall verify the Member State of residence of the subscriber by using not more than two of the following means of verification and shall ensure that the means used are reasonable, proportionate and effective:

   (a) an identity card, electronic means of identification, in particular those falling under the electronic identification schemes notified in accordance with Regulation (EU) No 910/2014 of the European Parliament and of the Council, or any other valid identity document confirming the subscriber's Member State of residence;

(b)   payment details such as the bank account or credit or debit card number of the subscriber;

(c)   the place of installation of a set top box, a decoder or a similar device used for supply of services to the subscriber;

(d)   the payment by the subscriber of a licence fee for other services provided in the Member State, such as public service broadcasting;

(e)   an internet or telephone service supply contract or any similar type of contract linking the subscriber to the Member State;

(f)   registration on local electoral rolls, if the information concerned is publicly available;

(g)   payment of local taxes, if the information concerned is publicly available;

(h)   a utility bill of the subscriber linking the subscriber to the Member State;

(i)   the billing address or the postal address of the subscriber;

(j)   a declaration by the subscriber confirming the subscriber's address in the Member State;

(k)   an internet protocol (IP) address check, to identify the Member State where the subscriber accesses the online content service.

. . .

4.   The holders of copyright or related rights or those holding any other rights in the content of an online content service may authorise the provision of, access to and use of their content under this Regulation without verification of the Member State of residence. In such cases, the contract between the provider and the subscriber for the provision of an online content service shall be sufficient to determine the subscriber's Member State of residence.

The holders of copyright or related rights or those holding any other rights in the content of an online content service shall be entitled to withdraw the authorisation given pursuant to the first subparagraph subject to giving reasonable notice to the provider.

5.   The contract between the provider and the holders of copyright or related rights or those holding any other rights in the content of an online content service shall not restrict the possibility for such holders of rights to withdraw the authorisation referred to in paragraph 4.

Article 6 Cross-border portability of online content services provided without payment of money

1.   The provider of an online content service provided without payment of money may decide to enable its subscribers who are temporarily present in a Member State to access and use the online content service on condition that the provider verifies the subscriber's Member State of residence in accordance with this Regulation.

2.   The provider shall inform its subscribers, the relevant holders of copyright and related rights and the relevant holders of any other rights in the content of the online content service of its decision to provide the online content service in accordance with paragraph 1, prior to providing that service. The information shall be provided by means which are adequate and proportionate.

3.   This Regulation shall apply to providers that provide an online content service in accordance with paragraph 1.

Article 7 Contractual provisions

1.   Any contractual provisions, including those between providers of online content services and holders of copyright or related rights or those holding any other rights in the content of online content services, as well as those between such providers and their subscribers, which are contrary to this Regulation, including those which prohibit cross-border portability of online content services or limit such portability to a specific time period, shall be unenforceable.

2.   This Regulation shall apply irrespective of the law applicable to contracts concluded between providers of online content services and holders of copyright or related rights or those holding any other rights in the content of online content services, or to contracts concluded between such providers and their subscribers.

Article 8 Protection of personal data

1.   The processing of personal data carried out within the framework of this Regulation including, in particular, for the purposes of verification of the subscriber's Member State of

residence under Article 5, shall be carried out in compliance with Directives 95/46/EC and 2002/58/EC. In particular, the use of the means of verification in accordance with Article 5 and any processing of personal data under this Regulation, shall be limited to what is necessary and proportionate in order to achieve its purpose.

2.	Data collected pursuant to Article 5 shall be used solely for the purpose of verifying the subscriber's Member State of residence. They shall not be communicated, transferred, shared, licensed or otherwise transmitted or disclosed to holders of copyright or related rights or to those holding any other rights in the content of online content services, or to any other third parties.

3.	Data collected pursuant to Article 5 shall not be stored by the provider of an online content service longer than necessary to complete a verification of a subscriber's Member State of residence pursuant to Article 5(1) or (2). On completion of each verification, the data shall be immediately and irreversibly destroyed.

Article 9 Application to existing contracts and rights acquired

1.	This Regulation shall apply also to contracts concluded and rights acquired before the date of its application if they are relevant for the provision of, access to and use of an online content service, in accordance with Articles 3 and 6, after that date.

2.	By 21 May 2018, the provider of an online content service provided against payment of money shall verify, in accordance with this Regulation, the Member State of residence of those subscribers who concluded contracts for the provision of the online content service before that date.

	Within two months of the date upon which the provider of an online content service provided without payment of money first provides the service in accordance with Article 6, the provider shall verify, in accordance with this Regulation, the Member State of residence of those subscribers who concluded contracts for the provision of the online content service before that date.

BERNE CONVENTION FOR THE PROTECTION OF LITERARY AND ARTISTIC WORKS
of September 9, 1886

Article 1
The countries to which this Convention applies constitute a Union for the protection of the rights of authors in their literary and artistic works.

Article 2
(1)	The expression "literary and artistic works" shall include every production in the literary, scientific and artistic domain, whatever may be the mode or form of its expression, such as books, pamphlets and other writings; lectures, addresses, sermons and other works of the same nature; dramatic or dramaticomusical works; choreographic works and entertainments in dumb show; musical compositions with or without words; cinematographic works to which are assimilated works expressed by a process analogous to cinematography; works of drawing, painting, architecture, sculpture, engraving and lithography; photographic works to which are assimilated works expressed by a process analogous to photography; works of applied art; illustrations, maps, plans, sketches and three-dimensional works relative to geography, topography, architecture or science.

(2)	It shall, however, be a matter for legislation in the countries of the Union to prescribe that works in general or any specified categories of works shall not be protected unless they have been fixed in some material form.

(3)	Translations, adaptations, arrangements of music and other alterations of a literary or artistic work shall be protected as original works without prejudice to the copyright in the original work.

(4)	It shall be a matter for legislation in the countries of the Union to determine the protection to be granted to official texts of a legislative, administrative and legal nature, and to official translations of such texts.

(5)   Collections of literary or artistic works such as encyclopaedias and anthologies which, by reason of the selection and arrangement of their contents, constitute intellectual creations shall be protected as such, without prejudice to the copyright in each of the works forming part of such collections.

(6)   The works mentioned in this Article shall enjoy protection in all countries of the Union. This protection shall operate for the benefit of the author and his successors in title.

(7)   Subject to the provisions of Article 7(4) of this Convention, it shall be a matter for legislation in the countries of the Union to determine the extent of the application of their laws to works of applied art and industrial designs and models, as well as the conditions under which such works, designs and models shall be protected. Works protected in the country of origin solely as designs and models shall be entitled in another country of the Union only to such special protection as is granted in that country to designs and models; however, if no such special protection is granted in that country, such works shall be protected as artistic works.

(8)   The protection of this Convention shall not apply to news of the day or to miscellaneous facts having the character of mere items of press information.

Article 2*bis*

(1)   It shall be a matter for legislation in the countries of the Union to exclude, wholly or in part, from the protection provided by the preceding Article political speeches and speeches delivered in the course of legal proceedings.

(2)   It shall also be a matter for legislation in the countries of the Union to determine the conditions under which lectures, addresses and other works of the same nature which are delivered in public may be reproduced by the press, broadcast, communicated to the public by wire and made the subject of public communication as envisaged in Article 11bis(1) of this Convention, when such use is justified by the informatory purpose.

(3)   Nevertheless, the author shall enjoy the exclusive right of making a collection of his works mentioned in the preceding paragraphs.

Article 3

(1)   The protection of this Convention shall apply to:
   (a)   authors who are nationals of one of the countries of the Union, for their works, whether published or not;
   (b)   authors who are not nationals of one of the countries of the Union, for their works first published in one of those countries, or simultaneously in a country outside the Union and in a country of the Union.

(2)   Authors who are not nationals of one of the countries of the Union but who have their habitual residence in one of them shall, for the purposes of this Convention, be assimilated to nationals of that country.

(3)   The expression "published works" means works published with the consent of their authors, whatever may be the means of manufacture of the copies, provided that the availability of such copies has been such as to satisfy the reasonable requirements of the public, having regard to the nature of the work. The performance of a dramatic, dramatico-musical, cinematographic or musical work, the public recitation of a literary work, the communication by wire or the broadcasting of literary or artistic works, the exhibition of a work of art and the construction of a work of architecture shall not constitute publication.

(4)   A work shall be considered as having been published simultaneously in several countries if it has been published in two or more countries within thirty days of its first publication.

Article 4

The protection of this Convention shall apply, even if the conditions of Article 3 are not fulfilled, to:
(a)   authors of cinematographic works the maker of which has his headquarters or habitual residence in one of the countries of the Union;
(b)   authors of works of architecture erected in a country of the Union or of other artistic works incorporated in a building or other structure located in a country of the Union.

Article 5

(1)   Authors shall enjoy, in respect of works for which they are protected under this Convention, in countries of the Union other than the country of origin, the rights which their respective laws do now or may hereafter grant to their nationals, as well as the rights specially granted by this Convention.

(2) The enjoyment and the exercise of these rights shall not be subject to any formality; such enjoyment and such exercise shall be independent of the existence of protection in the country of origin of the work. Consequently, apart from the provisions of this Convention, the extent of protection, as well as the means of redress afforded to the author to protect his rights, shall be governed exclusively by the laws of the country where protection is claimed.

(3) Protection in the country of origin is governed by domestic law. However, when the author is not a national of the country of origin of the work for which he is protected under this Convention, he shall enjoy in that country the same rights as national authors.

(4) The country of origin shall be considered to be:
   (a) in the case of works first published in a country of the Union, that country; in the case of works published simultaneously in several countries of the Union which grant different terms of protection, the country whose legislation grants the shortest term of protection;
   (b) in the case of works published simultaneously in a country outside the Union and in a country of the Union, the latter country;
   (c) in the case of unpublished works or of works first published in a country outside the Union, without simultaneous publication in a country of the Union, the country of the Union of which the author is a national, provided that:
      (i) when these are cinematographic works the maker of which has his headquarters or his habitual residence in a country of the Union, the country of origin shall be that country, and
      (ii) when these are works of architecture erected in a country of the Union or other artistic works incorporated in a building or other structure located in a country of the Union, the country of origin shall be that country.

Article 6

(1) Where any country outside the Union fails to protect in an adequate manner the works of authors who are nationals of one of the countries of the Union, the latter country may restrict the protection given to the works of authors who are, at the date of the first publication thereof, nationals of the other country and are not habitually resident in one of the countries of the Union. If the country of first publication avails itself of this right, the other countries of the Union shall not be required to grant to works thus subjected to special treatment a wider protection than that granted to them in the country of first publication.

(2) No restrictions introduced by virtue of the preceding paragraph shall affect the rights which an author may have acquired in respect of a work published in a country of the Union before such restrictions were put into force.

(3) The countries of the Union which restrict the grant of copyright in accordance with this Article shall give notice thereof to the Director General of the World Intellectual Property Organization (hereinafter designated as "the Director General") by a written declaration specifying the countries in regard to which protection is restricted, and the restrictions to which rights of authors who are nationals of those countries are subjected. The Director General shall immediately communicate this declaration to all the countries of the Union.

Article 6*bis*

(1) Independently of the author's economic rights, and even after the transfer of the said rights, the author shall have the right to claim authorship of the work and to object to any distortion, mutilation or other modification of, or other derogatory action in relation to, the said work, which would be prejudicial to his honor or reputation.

(2) The rights granted to the author in accordance with the preceding paragraph shall, after his death, be maintained, at least until the expiry of the economic rights, and shall be exercisable by the persons or institutions authorized by the legislation of the country where protection is claimed. However, those countries whose legislation, at the moment of their ratification of or accession to this Act, does not provide for the protection after the death of the author of all the rights set out in the preceding paragraph may provide that some of these rights may, after his death, cease to be maintained.

(3) The means of redress for safeguarding the rights granted by this Article shall be governed by the legislation of the country where protection is claimed.

Article 7

(1)   The term of protection granted by this Convention shall be the life of the author and fifty years after his death.

(2)   However, in the case of cinematographic works, the countries of the Union may provide that the term of protection shall expire fifty years after the work has been made available to the public with the consent of the author, or, failing such an event within fifty years from the making of such a work, fifty years after the making.

(3)   In the case of anonymous or pseudonymous works, the term of protection granted by this Convention shall expire fifty years after the work has been lawfully made available to the public. However, when the pseudonym adopted by the author leaves no doubt as to his identity, the term of protection shall be that provided in paragraph (1). If the author of an anonymous or pseudonymous work discloses his identity during the above-mentioned period, the term of protection applicable shall be that provided in paragraph (1). The countries of the Union shall not be required to protect anonymous or pseudonymous works in respect of which it is reasonable to presume that their author has been dead for fifty years.

(4)   It shall be a matter for legislation in the countries of the Union to determine the term of protection of photographic works and that of works of applied art in so far as they are protected as artistic works; however, this term shall last at least until the end of a period of twenty-five years from the making of such a work.

(5)   The term of protection subsequent to the death of the author and the terms provided by paragraphs (2), (3) and (4) shall run from the date of death or of the event referred to in those paragraphs, but such terms shall always be deemed to begin on the first of January of the year following the death or such event.

(6)   The countries of the Union may grant a term of protection in excess of those provided by the preceding paragraphs.

(7)   Those countries of the Union bound by the Rome Act of this Convention which grant, in their national legislation in force at the time of signature of the present Act, shorter terms of protection than those provided for in the preceding paragraphs shall have the right to maintain such terms when ratifying or acceding to the present Act.

(8)   In any case, the term shall be governed by the legislation of the country where protection is claimed; however, unless the legislation of that country otherwise provides, the term shall not exceed the term fixed in the country of origin of the work.

Article 7*bis*

The provisions of the preceding Article shall also apply in the case of a work of joint authorship, provided that the terms measured from the death of the author shall be calculated from the death of the last surviving author.

Article 8

Authors of literary and artistic works protected by this Convention shall enjoy the exclusive right of making and of authorizing the translation of their works throughout the term of protection of their rights in the original works.

Article 9

(1)   Authors of literary and artistic works protected by this Convention shall have the exclusive right of authorizing the reproduction of these works, in any manner or form.

(2)   It shall be a matter for legislation in the countries of the Union to permit the reproduction of such works in certain special cases, provided that such reproduction does not conflict with a normal exploitation of the work and does not unreasonably prejudice the legitimate interests of the author.

(3)   Any sound or visual recording shall be considered as a reproduction for the purposes of this Convention.

Article 10

(1)   It shall be permissible to make quotations from a work which has already been lawfully made available to the public, provided that their making is compatible with fair practice, and their extent does not exceed that justified by the purpose, including quotations from newspaper articles and periodicals in the form of press summaries.

(2)   It shall be a matter for legislation in the countries of the Union, and for special agreements existing or to be concluded between them, to permit the utilization, to the extent justified by the purpose, of literary or artistic works by way of illustration in publications, broadcasts or sound or visual recordings for teaching, provided such utilization is compatible with fair practice.

(3)   Where use is made of works in accordance with the preceding paragraphs of this Article, mention shall be made of the source, and of the name of the author if it appears thereon.

Article 10*bis*

(1)   It shall be a matter for legislation in the countries of the Union to permit the reproduction by the press, the broadcasting or the communication to the public by wire of articles published in newspapers or periodicals on current economic, political or religious topics, and of broadcast works of the same character, in cases in which the reproduction, broadcasting or such communication thereof is not expressly reserved. Nevertheless, the source must always be clearly indicated; the legal consequences of a breach of this obligation shall be determined by the legislation of the country where protection is claimed.

(2)   It shall also be a matter for legislation in the countries of the Union to determine the conditions under which, for the purpose of reporting current events by means of photography, cinematography, broadcasting or communication to the public by wire, literary or artistic works seen or heard in the course of the event may, to the extent justified by the informatory purpose, be reproduced and made available to the public.

Article 11

(1)   Authors of dramatic, dramatico-musical and musical works shall enjoy the exclusive right of authorizing:
 (i)   the public performance of their works, including such public performance by any means or process;
 (ii)   any communication to the public of the performance of their works.

(2)   Authors of dramatic or dramatico-musical works shall enjoy, during the full term of their rights in the original works, the same rights with respect to translations thereof.

Article 11*bis*

(1)   Authors of literary and artistic works shall enjoy the exclusive right of authorizing:
 (i)   the broadcasting of their works or the communication thereof to the public by any other means of wireless diffusion of signs, sounds or images;
 (ii)   any communication to the public by wire or by rebroadcasting of the broadcast of the work, when this communication is made by an organization other than the original one;
 (iii)   the public communication by loudspeaker or any other analogous instrument transmitting, by signs, sounds or images, the broadcast of the work.

(2)   It shall be a matter for legislation in the countries of the Union to determine the conditions under which the rights mentioned in the preceding paragraph may be exercised, but these conditions shall apply only in the countries where they have been prescribed. They shall not in any circumstances be prejudicial to the moral rights of the author, nor to his right to obtain equitable remuneration which, in the absence of agreement, shall be fixed by competent authority.

(3)   In the absence of any contrary stipulation, permission granted in accordance with paragraph (1) of this Article shall not imply permission to record, by means of instruments recording sounds or images, the work broadcast. It shall, however, be a matter for legislation in the countries of the Union to determine the regulations for ephemeral recordings made by a broadcasting organization by means of its own facilities and used for its own broadcasts. The preservation of these recordings in official archives may, on the ground of their exceptional documentary character, be authorized by such legislation.

Article 11*ter*

(1)   Authors of literary works shall enjoy the exclusive right of authorizing:
 (i)   the public recitation of their works, including such public recitation by any means or process;
 (ii)   any communication to the public of the recitation of their works.

(2) Authors of literary works shall enjoy, during the full term of their rights in the original works, the same rights with respect to translations thereof.

Article 12
Authors of literary or artistic works shall enjoy the exclusive right of authorizing adaptations, arrangements and other alterations of their works.

Article 13
(1) Each country of the Union may impose for itself reservations and conditions on the exclusive right granted to the author of a musical work and to the author of any words, the recording of which together with the musical work has already been authorized by the latter, to authorize the sound recording of that musical work, together with such words, if any; but all such reservations and conditions shall apply only in the countries which have imposed them and shall not, in any circumstances, be prejudicial to the rights of these authors to obtain equitable remuneration which, in the absence of agreement, shall be fixed by competent authority.

(2) Recordings of musical works made in a country of the Union in accordance with Article 13(3) of the Conventions signed at Rome on June 2, 1928, and at Brussels on June 26, 1948, may be reproduced in that country without the permission of the author of the musical work until a date two years after that country becomes bound by this Act.

(3) Recordings made in accordance with paragraphs (1) and (2) of this Article and imported without permission from the parties concerned into a country where they are treated as infringing recordings shall be liable to seizure.

Article 14
(1) Authors of literary or artistic works shall have the exclusive right of authorizing:
   (i) the cinematographic adaptation and reproduction of these works, and the distribution of the works thus adapted or reproduced;
   (ii) the public performance and communication to the public by wire of the works thus adapted or reproduced.

(2) The adaptation into any other artistic form of a cinematographic production derived from literary or artistic works shall, without prejudice to the authorization of the author of the cinematographic production, remain subject to the authorization of the authors of the original works.

(3) The provisions of Article 13(1) shall not apply.

Article 14bis
(1) Without prejudice to the copyright in any work which may have been adapted or reproduced, a cinematographic work shall be protected as an original work. The owner of copyright in a cinematographic work shall enjoy the same rights as the author of an original work, including the rights referred to in the preceding Article.

(2) (a) Ownership of copyright in a cinematographic work shall be a matter for legislation in the country where protection is claimed.
   (b) However, in the countries of the Union which, by legislation, include among the owners of copyright in a cinematographic work authors who have brought contributions to the making of the work, such authors, if they have undertaken to bring such contributions, may not, in the absence of any contrary or special stipulation, object to the reproduction, distribution, public performance, communication to the public by wire, broadcasting or any other communication to the public, or to the subtitling or dubbing of texts, of the work.
   (c) The question whether or not the form of the undertaking referred to above should, for the application of the preceding subparagraph (b), be in a written agreement or a written act of the same effect shall be a matter for the legislation of the country where the maker of the cinematographic work has his headquarters or habitual residence. However, it shall be a matter for the legislation of the country of the Union where protection is claimed to provide that the said undertaking shall be in a written agreement or a written act of the same effect. The countries whose legislation so provides shall notify the Director General by means of a written declaration, which will be immediately communicated by him to all the other countries of the Union.

(d) By "contrary or special stipulation" is meant any restrictive condition which is relevant to the aforesaid undertaking.

(3) Unless the national legislation provides to the contrary, the provisions of paragraph (2)(b) above shall not be applicable to authors of scenarios, dialogues and musical works created for the making of the cinematographic work, or to the principal director thereof. However, those countries of the Union whose legislation does not contain rules providing for the application of the said paragraph (2)(b) to such director shall notify the Director General by means of a written declaration, which will be immediately communicated by him to all the other countries of the Union.

Article 14*ter*

(1) The author, or after his death the persons or institutions authorized by national legislation, shall, with respect to original works of art and original manuscripts of writers and composers, enjoy the inalienable right to an interest in any sale of the work subsequent to the first transfer by the author of the work.

(2) The protection provided by the preceding paragraph may be claimed in a country of the Union only if legislation in the country to which the author belongs so permits, and to the extent permitted by the country where this protection is claimed.

(3) The procedure for collection and the amounts shall be matters for determination by national legislation.

Article 15

(1) In order that the author of a literary or artistic work protected by this Convention shall, in the absence of proof to the contrary, be regarded as such, and consequently be entitled to institute infringement proceedings in the countries of the Union, it shall be sufficient for his name to appear on the work in the usual manner. This paragraph shall be applicable even if this name is a pseudonym, where the pseudonym adopted by the author leaves no doubt as to his identity.

(2) The person or body corporate whose name appears on a cinematographic work in the usual manner shall, in the absence of proof to the contrary, be presumed to be the maker of the said work.

(3) In the case of anonymous and pseudonymous works, other than those referred to in paragraph (1) above, the publisher whose name appears on the work shall, in the absence of proof to the contrary, be deemed to represent the author, and in this capacity he shall be entitled to protect and enforce the author's rights. The provisions of this paragraph shall cease to apply when the author reveals his identity and establishes his claim to authorship of the work.

(4) (a) In the case of unpublished works where the identity of the author is unknown, but where there is every ground to presume that he is a national of a country of the Union, it shall be a matter for legislation in that country to designate the competent authority which shall represent the author and shall be entitled to protect and enforce his rights in the countries of the Union.

(b) Countries of the Union which make such designation under the terms of this provision shall notify the Director General by means of a written declaration giving full information concerning the authority thus designated. The Director General shall at once communicate this declaration to all other countries of the Union.

Article 16

(1) Infringing copies of a work shall be liable to seizure in any country of the Union where the work enjoys legal protection.

(2) The provisions of the preceding paragraph shall also apply to reproductions coming from a country where the work is not protected, or has ceased to be protected.

(3) The seizure shall take place in accordance with the legislation of each country.

Article 17

The provisions of this Convention cannot in any way affect the right of the Government of each country of the Union to permit, to control, or to prohibit, by legislation or regulation, the circulation, presentation, or exhibition of any work or production in regard to which the competent authority may find it necessary to exercise that right.

Article 18

(1) This Convention shall apply to all works which, at the moment of its coming into force, have not yet fallen into the public domain in the country of origin through the expiry of the term of protection.

(2) If, however, through the expiry of the term of protection which was previously granted, a work has fallen into the public domain of the country where protection is claimed, that work shall not be protected anew.

(3) The application of this principle shall be subject to any provisions contained in special conventions to that effect existing or to be concluded between countries of the Union. In the absence of such provisions, the respective countries shall determine, each in so far as it is concerned, the conditions of application of this principle.

(4) The preceding provisions shall also apply in the case of new accessions to the Union and to cases in which protection is extended by the application of Article 7 or by the abandonment of reservations.

Article 19

The provisions of this Convention shall not preclude the making of a claim to the benefit of any greater protection which may be granted by legislation in a country of the Union.

Article 20

The Governments of the countries of the Union reserve the right to enter into special agreements among themselves, in so far as such agreements grant to authors more extensive rights than those granted by the Convention, or contain other provisions not contrary to this Convention. The provisions of existing agreements which satisfy these conditions shall remain applicable.

Article 21

(1) Special provisions regarding developing countries are included in the Appendix.

(2) Subject to the provisions of Article 28(1)(b), the Appendix forms an integral part of this Act.

Article 29

(1) Any country outside the Union may accede to this Act and thereby become party to this Convention and a member of the Union. Instruments of accession shall be deposited with the Director General.

. . .

ROME CONVENTION (1961)
International Convention for the protection of performers, producers of phonograms and broadcasting organisations

The Contracting States, moved by the desire to protect the rights of performers, producers of phonograms, and broadcasting organisations,

Have agreed as follows:

Article 1

Protection granted under this Convention shall leave intact and shall in no way affect the protection of copyright in literary and artistic works. Consequently, no provision of this Convention may be interpreted as prejudicing such protection.

Article 2

1. For the purposes of this Convention, national treatment shall mean the treatment accorded by the domestic law of the Contracting State in which protection is claimed:

   (a) to performers who are its nationals, as regards performances taking place, broadcast, or first fixed, on its territory;

   (b) to producers of phonograms who are its nationals, as regards phonograms first fixed or first published on its territory;

   (c) to broadcasting organisations which have their headquarters on its territory, as regards broadcasts transmitted from transmitters situated on its territory.

2.　　National treatment shall be subject to the protection specifically guaranteed, and the limitations specifically provided for, in this Convention.

Article 3
For the purposes of this Convention:
- (a)　"performers" means actors, singers, musicians, dancers, and other persons who act, sing, deliver, declaim, play in, or otherwise perform literary or artistic works;
- (b)　"phonogram" means any exclusively aural fixation of sounds of a performance or of other sounds;
- (c)　"producer of phonograms" means the person who, or the legal entity which, first fixes the sounds of a performance or other sounds;
- (d)　"publication" means the offering of copies of a phonogram to the public in reasonable quantity;
- (e)　"reproduction" means the making of a copy or copies of a fixation;
- (f)　"broadcasting" means the transmission by wireless means for public reception of sounds or of images and sounds;
- (g)　"rebroadcasting" means the simultaneous broadcasting by one broadcasting organisation of the broadcast of another broadcasting organisation.

Article 4
Each Contracting State shall grant national treatment to performers if any of the following conditions is met:
- (a)　the performance takes place in another Contracting State;
- (b)　the performance is incorporated in a phonogram which is protected under Article 5 of this Convention;
- (c)　the performance, not being fixed on a phonogram, is carried by a broadcast which is protected by Article 6 of this Convention.

Article 5
1.　　Each Contracting State shall grant national treatment to producers of phonograms if any of the following conditions is met:
- (a)　the producer of the phonogram is a national of another Contracting State (criterion of nationality);
- (b)　the first fixation of the sound was made in another Contracting State (criterion of fixation);
- (c)　the phonogram was first published in another Contracting State (criterion of publication).

2.　　If a phonogram was first published in a non-contracting State but if it was also published, within thirty days of its first publication, in a Contracting State (simultaneous publication), it shall be considered as first published in the Contracting State.

3.　　By means of a notification deposited with the Secretary-General of the United Nations, any Contracting State may declare that it will not apply the criterion of publication or, alternatively, the criterion of fixation. Such notification may be deposited at the time of ratification, acceptance or accession, or at any time thereafter; in the last case, it shall become effective six months after it has been deposited.

Article 6
1.　　Each Contracting State shall grant national treatment to broadcasting organisations if either of the following conditions is met:
- (a)　the headquarters of the broadcasting organisation is situated in another Contracting State;
- (b)　the broadcast was transmitted from a transmitter situated in another Contracting State.

2.　　By means of a notification deposited with the Secretary-General of the United Nations, any Contracting State may declare that it will protect broadcasts only if the headquarters of the broadcasting organisation is situated in another Contracting State and the broadcast was transmitted from a transmitter situated in the same Contracting State. Such notification may be deposited at the time of ratification, acceptance or accession, or at any time thereafter; in the last case, it shall become effective six months after it has been deposited.

Article 7

1.   The protection provided for performers by this Convention shall include the possibility of preventing:

         (a)   the broadcasting and the communication to the public, without their consent, of their performance, except where the performance used in the broadcasting or the public communication is itself already a broadcast performance or is made from a fixation;

         (b)   the fixation, without their consent, of their unfixed performance;

         (c)   the reproduction, without their consent, of a fixation of their performance:

              (i)   if the original fixation itself was made without their consent;

              (ii)   if the reproduction is made for purposes different from those for which the performers gave their consent;

              (iii)   if the original fixation was made in accordance with the provisions of Article 15, and the reproduction is made for purposes different from those referred to in those provisions.

2.   (1)   If broadcasting was consented to by the performers, it shall be a matter for the domestic law of the Contracting State where protection is claimed to regulate the protection against rebroadcasting, fixation for broadcasting purposes and the reproduction of such fixation for broadcasting purposes.

         (2)   The terms and conditions governing the use by broadcasting organisations of fixations made for broadcasting purposes shall be determined in accordance with the domestic law of the Contracting State where protection is claimed.

         (3)   However, the domestic law referred to in sub-paragraphs (1) and (2) of this paragraph shall not operate to deprive performers of the ability to control, by contract, their relations with broadcasting organisations.

Article 8

Any Contracting State may, by its domestic laws and regulations, specify the manner in which performers will be represented in connection with the exercise of their rights if several of them participate in the same performance.

Article 9

Any Contracting State may, by its domestic laws and regulations, extend the protection provided for in this Convention to artists who do not perform literary or artistic works.

Article 10

Producers of phonograms shall enjoy the right to authorize or prohibit the direct or indirect reproduction of their phonograms.

Article 11

If, as a condition of protecting the rights of producers of phonograms, or of performers, or both, in relation to phonograms, a Contracting State, under its domestic law, requires compliance with formalities, these shall be considered as fulfilled if all the copies in commerce of the published phonogram or their containers bear a notice consisting of the symbol (P), accompanied by the year date of the first publication, placed in such a manner as to give reasonable notice of claim of protection; and if the copies or their containers do not identify the producer or the licensee of the producer (by carrying his name, trade mark or other appropriate designation), the notice shall also include the name of the owner of the rights of the producer; and, furthermore, if the copies or their containers do not identify the principal performers, the notice shall also include the name of the person who, in the country in which the fixation was effected, owns the rights of such performers.

Article 12

If a phonogram published for commercial purposes, or a reproduction of such phonogram, is used directly for broadcasting or for any communication to the public, a single equitable remuneration shall be paid by the user to the performers, or to the producers of the phonograms, or to both. Domestic law may, in the absence of agreement between these parties, lay down the conditions as to the sharing of this remuneration.

Article 13
Broadcasting organisations shall enjoy the right to authorize or prohibit:
(a)   the rebroadcasting of their broadcasts;
(b)   the fixation of their broadcasts;
(c)   the reproduction:
  (i)   of fixations, made without their consent, of their broadcasts;
  (ii)   of fixations, made in accordance with the provisions of Article 15, of their broadcasts, if the reproduction is made for purposes different from those referred to in those provisions;
(d)   the communication to the public of their television broadcasts if such communication is made in places accessible to the public against payment of an entrance fee; it shall be a matter for the domestic law of the State where protection of this right is claimed to determine the conditions under which it may be exercised.

Article 14
The term of protection to be granted under this Convention shall last at least until the end of a period of twenty years computed from the end of the year in which:
(a)   the fixation was made - for phonograms and for performances incorporated therein;
(b)   the performance took place - for performances not incorporated in phonograms;
(c)   the broadcast took place - for broadcasts.

Article 15
1.   Any Contracting State may, in its domestic laws and regulations, provide for exceptions to the protection guaranteed by this Convention as regards:
  (a)   private use;
  (b)   use of short excerpts in connection with the reporting of current events;
  (c)   ephemeral fixation by a broadcasting organisation by means of its own facilities and for its own broadcasts;
  (d)   use solely for the purposes of teaching or scientific research.
2.   Irrespective of paragraph 1 of this Article, any Contracting State may, in its domestic laws and regulations, provide for the same kinds of limitations with regard to the protection of performers, producers of phonograms and broadcasting organisations, as it provides for, in its domestic laws and regulations, in connection with the protection of copyright in literary and artistic works. However, compulsory licences may be provided for only to the extent to which they are compatible with this Convention.

Article 16
1.   Any State, upon becoming party to this Convention, shall be bound by all the obligations and shall enjoy all the benefits thereof. However, a State may at any time, in a notification deposited with the Secretary-General of the United Nations, declare that:
  (a)   as regards Article 12:
    (i)   it will not apply the provisions of that Article;
    (ii)   it will not apply the provisions of that Article in respect of certain uses;
    (iii)   as regards phonograms the producer of which is not a national of another Contracting State, it will not apply that Article;
    (iv)   as regards phonograms the producer of which is a national of another Contracting State, it will limit the protection provided for by that Article to the extent to which, and to the term for which, the latter State grants protection to phonograms first fixed by a national of the State making the declaration; however, the fact that the Contracting State of which the producer is a national does not grant the protection to the same beneficiary or beneficiaries as the State making the declaration shall not be considered as a difference in the extent of the protection;
  (b)   as regards Article 13, it will not apply item (d) of that Article; if a Contracting State makes such a declaration, the other Contracting States shall not be obliged to grant the right referred to in Article 13, item (d), to broadcasting organisations whose headquarters are in that State.
2.   If the notification referred to in paragraph 1 of this Article is made after the date of the deposit of the instrument of ratification, acceptance or accession, the declaration will become effective six months after it has been deposited.

Article 17

Any State which, on October 26, 1961, grants protection to producers of phonograms solely on the basis of the criterion of fixation may, by a notification deposited with the Secretary-General of the United Nations at the time of ratification, acceptance or accession, declare that it will apply, for the purposes of Article 5, the criterion of fixation alone and, for the purposes of paragraph 1 (a)(iii) and (iv) of Article 16, the criterion of fixation instead of the criterion of nationality.

Article 18

Any State which has deposited a notification under paragraph 3 of Article 5, paragraph 2 of Article 6, paragraph 1 of Article 16 or Article 17, may, by a further notification deposited with the Secretary–General of the United Nations, reduce its scope or withdraw it.

Article 19

Notwithstanding anything in this Convention, once a performer has consented to the incorporation of his performance in a visual or audio-visual fixation, Article 7 shall have no further application.

Article 20

1.   This Convention shall not prejudice rights acquired in any Contracting State before the date of coming into force of this Convention for that State.
2.   No Contracting State shall be bound to apply the provisions of this Convention to performances or broadcasts which took place, or to phonograms which were fixed, before the date of coming into force of this Convention for that State.

Article 21

The protection provided for in this Convention shall not prejudice any protection otherwise secured to performers, producers of phonograms and broadcasting organisations.

Article 22

Contracting States reserve the right to enter into special agreements among themselves in so far as such agreements grant to performers, producers of phonograms or broadcasting organisations more extensive rights than those granted by this Convention or contain other provisions not contrary to this Convention.

Article 23

This Convention shall be deposited with the Secretary-General of the United Nations. It shall be open until June 30, 1962, for signature by any State invited to the Diplomatic Conference on the International Protection of Performers, Producers of Phonograms and Broadcasting Organisations which is a party to the Universal Copyright Convention or a member of the International Union for the Protection of Literary and Artistic Works.

Article 24

1.   This Convention shall be subject to ratification or acceptance by the signatory States.
2.   This Convention shall be open for accession by any State invited to the Conference referred to in Article 23, and by any State Member of the United Nations, provided that in either case such State is a party to the Universal Copyright Convention or a member of the International Union for the Protection of Literary and Artistic Works.
3.   Ratification, acceptance or accession shall be effected by the deposit of an instrument to that effect with the Secretary-General of the United Nations.

Article 25

1.   This Convention shall come into force three months after the date of deposit of the sixth instrument of ratification, acceptance or accession.
2.   Subsequently, this Convention shall come into force in respect of each State three months after the date of deposit of its instrument of ratification, acceptance or accession.

Article 26

1.   Each Contracting State undertakes to adopt, in accordance with its Constitution, the measures necessary to ensure the application of this Convention.
2.   At the time of deposit of its instrument of ratification, acceptance or accession, each State must be in a position under its domestic law to give effect to the terms of this Convention.

Article 27

1.   Any State may, at the time of ratification, acceptance or accession, or at any time thereafter, declare by notification addressed to the Secretary-General of the United Nations that this Convention shall extend to all or any of the territories for whose international relations it is responsible, provided that the Universal Copyright Convention or the International Convention for the Protection of Literary and Artistic Works applies to the territory or territories concerned. This notification shall take effect three months after the date of its receipt.

2.   The notifications referred to in paragraph 3 of Article 5, paragraph 2 of Article 6, paragraph 1 of Article 16 and Articles 17 and 18, may be extended to cover all or any of the territories referred to in paragraph 1 of this Article.

Article 28

1.   Any Contracting State may denounce this Convention, on its own behalf or on behalf of all or any of the territories referred to in Article 27.

2.   The denunciation shall be effected by a notification addressed to the Secretary-General of the United Nations and shall take effect twelve months after the date of receipt of the notification.

3.   The right of denunciation shall not be exercised by a Contracting State before the expiry of a period of five years from the date on which the Convention came into force with respect to that State.

4.   A Contracting State shall cease to be a party to this Convention from that time when it is neither a party to the Universal Copyright Convention nor a member of the International Union for the Protection of Literary and Artistic Works.

5.   This Convention shall cease to apply to any territory referred to in Article 27 from that time when neither the Universal Copyright Convention nor the International Convention for the Protection of Literary and Artistic Works applies to that territory.

Article 30

Any dispute which may arise between two or more Contracting States concerning the interpretation or application of this Convention and which is not settled by negotiation shall, at the request of any one of the parties to the dispute, be referred to the International Court of Justice for decision, unless they agree to another mode of settlement.

WIPO COPYRIGHT TREATY (WCT)
(adopted in Geneva on December 20, 1996)

Article 1 Relation to the Berne Convention

(1)   This Treaty is a special agreement within the meaning of Article 20 of the Berne Convention for the Protection of Literary and Artistic Works, as regards Contracting Parties that are countries of the Union established by that Convention. This Treaty shall not have any connection with treaties other than the Berne Convention, nor shall it prejudice any rights and obligations under any other treaties.

(2)   Nothing in this Treaty shall derogate from existing obligations that Contracting Parties have to each other under the Berne Convention for the Protection of Literary and Artistic Works.

(3)   Hereinafter, "Berne Convention" shall refer to the Paris Act of July 24, 1971, of the Berne Convention for the Protection of Literary and Artistic Works.

(4)   Contracting Parties shall comply with Articles 1 to 21 and the Appendix of the Berne Convention.

Article 2 Scope of copyright protection

Copyright protection extends to expressions and not to ideas, procedures, methods of operation or mathematical concepts as such.

Article 3 Application of Articles 2 to 6 of the Berne Convention

Contracting Parties shall apply *mutatis mutandis* the provisions of Articles 2 to 6 of the Berne Convention in respect of the protection provided for in this Treaty.

Article 4 Computer programs

Computer programs are protected as literary works within the meaning of Article 2 of the Berne Convention. Such protection applies to computer programs, whatever may be the mode or form of their expression.

Article 5 Compilations of data (databases)

Compilations of data or other material, in any form, which by reason of the selection or arrangement of their contents constitute intellectual creations, are protected as such. This protection does not extend to the data or the material itself and is without prejudice to any copyright subsisting in the data or material contained in the compilation.

Article 6 Right of distribution

(1)   Authors of literary and artistic works shall enjoy the exclusive right of authorizing the making available to the public of the original and copies of their works through sale or other transfer of ownership.

(2)   Nothing in this Treaty shall affect the freedom of Contracting Parties to determine the conditions, if any, under which the exhaustion of the right in paragraph (1) applies after the first sale or other transfer of ownership of the original or a copy of the work with the authorization of the author.

Article 7 Right of rental

(1)   Authors of
        (i)   computer programs;
        (ii)   cinematographic works; and
        (iii) works embodied in phonograms, as determined in the national law of Contracting Parties, shall enjoy the exclusive right of authorizing commercial rental to the public of the originals or copies of their works.

(2)   Paragraph (1) shall not apply
        (i)   in the case of computer programs, where the program itself is not the essential object of the rental; and
        (ii)   in the case of cinematographic works, unless such commercial rental has led to widespread copying of such works materially impairing the exclusive right of reproduction.

(3)   Notwithstanding the provisions of paragraph (1), a Contracting Party that, on April 15, 1994, had and continues to have in force a system of equitable remuneration of authors for the rental of copies of their works embodied in phonograms may maintain that system provided that the commercial rental of works embodied in phonograms is not giving rise to the material impairment of the exclusive right of reproduction of authors.

Article 8 Right of communication to the public

Without prejudice to the provisions of Articles 11(1)(ii), 11bis(1)(i) and (ii), 11ter(1)(ii), 14(1)(ii) and 14bis(1) of the Berne Convention, authors of literary and artistic works shall enjoy the exclusive right of authorizing any communication to the public of their works, by wire or wireless means, including the making available to the public of their works in such a way that members of the public may access these works from a place and at a time individually chosen by them.

Article 9 Duration of the protection of photographic works

In respect of photographic works, the Contracting Parties shall not apply the provisions of Article 7(4) of the Berne Convention.

Article 10 Limitations and exceptions

(1)   Contracting Parties may, in their national legislation, provide for limitations of or exceptions to the rights granted to authors of literary and artistic works under this Treaty in certain special cases that do not conflict with a normal exploitation of the work and do not unreasonably prejudice the legitimate interests of the author.

(2)   Contracting Parties shall, when applying the Berne Convention, confine any limitations of or exceptions to rights provided for therein to certain special cases that do not conflict with a normal exploitation of the work and do not unreasonably prejudice the legitimate interests of the author.

Article 11 Obligations concerning technological measures

Contracting Parties shall provide adequate legal protection and effective legal remedies against the circumvention of effective technological measures that are used by authors in connection with the exercise of their rights under this Treaty or the Berne Convention and that restrict acts, in respect of their works, which are not authorized by the authors concerned or permitted by law.

Article 12 Obligations concerning rights management information

(1)   Contracting Parties shall provide adequate and effective legal remedies against any person knowingly performing any of the following acts knowing, or with respect to civil remedies having reasonable grounds to know, that it will induce, enable, facilitate or conceal an infringement of any right covered by this Treaty or the Berne Convention:

(i)   to remove or alter any electronic rights management information without authority;

(ii)   to distribute, import for distribution, broadcast or communicate to the public, without authority, works or copies of works knowing that electronic rights management information has been removed or altered without authority.

(2)   As used in this Article, "rights management information" means information which identifies the work, the author of the work, the owner of any right in the work, or information about the terms and conditions of use of the work, and any numbers or codes that represent such information, when any of these items of information is attached to a copy of a work or appears in connection with the communication of a work to the public.

Article 13 Application in time

Contracting Parties shall apply the provisions of Article 18 of the Berne Convention to all protection provided for in this Treaty.

Article 14 Provisions on enforcement of rights

(1)   Contracting Parties undertake to adopt, in accordance with their legal systems, the measures necessary to ensure the application of this Treaty.

(2)   Contracting Parties shall ensure that enforcement procedures are available under their law so as to permit effective action against any act of infringement of rights covered by this Treaty, including expeditious remedies to prevent infringements and remedies which constitute a deterrent to further infringements.

Article 17 Eligibility for becoming party to the Treaty

(1)   Any Member State of WIPO may become party to this Treaty.

. . .

Article 18 Rights and obligations under the Treaty

Subject to any specific provisions to the contrary in this Treaty, each Contracting Party shall enjoy all of the rights and assume all of the obligations under this Treaty.

Article 22 No reservations to the Treaty

No reservation to this Treaty shall be admitted.

WIPO PERFORMANCES AND PHONOGRAMS TREATY
(adopted in Geneva on December 20, 1996)

CHAPTER 1
GENERAL PROVISIONS

Article 1 Relation to other conventions

(1)   Nothing in this Treaty shall derogate from existing obligations that Contracting Parties have to each other under the International Convention for the Protection of Performers, Producers of Phonograms and Broadcasting Organizations done in Rome, October 26, 1961 (hereinafter the "Rome Convention").

(2)   Protection granted under this Treaty shall leave intact and shall in no way affect the protection of copyright in literary and artistic works. Consequently, no provision of this Treaty may be interpreted as prejudicing such protection.

(3)   This Treaty shall not have any connection with, nor shall it prejudice any rights and obligations under, any other treaties.

Article 2 Definitions

For the purposes of this Treaty:

(a)   "performers" are actors, singers, musicians, dancers, and other persons who act, sing, deliver, declaim, play in, interpret, or otherwise perform literary or artistic works or expressions of folklore;

(b)   "phonogram" means the fixation of the sounds of a performance or of other sounds, or of a representation of sounds, other than in the form of a fixation incorporated in a cinematographic or other audiovisual work;

(c)   "fixation" means the embodiment of sounds, or of the representations thereof, from which they can be perceived, reproduced or communicated through a device;

(d)   "producer of a phonogram" means the person, or the legal entity, who or which takes the initiative and has the responsibility for the first fixation of the sounds of a performance or other sounds, or the representations of sounds;

(e)   "publication" of a fixed performance or a phonogram means the offering of copies of the fixed performance or the phonogram to the public, with the consent of the rightholder, and provided that copies are offered to the public in reasonable quantity;

(f)   "broadcasting" means the transmission by wireless means for public reception of sounds or of images and sounds or of the representations thereof; such transmission by satellite is also "broadcasting"; transmission of encrypted signals is "broadcasting" where the means for decrypting are provided to the public by the broadcasting organization or with its consent;

(g)   "communication to the public" of a performance or a phonogram means the transmission to the public by any medium, otherwise than by broadcasting, of sounds of a performance or the sounds or the representations of sounds fixed in a phonogram. For the purposes of Article 15, "communication to the public" includes making the sounds or representations of sounds fixed in a phonogram audible to the public.

Article 3 Beneficiaries of protection under this Treaty

(1)   Contracting Parties shall accord the protection provided under this Treaty to the performers and producers of phonograms who are nationals of other Contracting Parties.

(2)   The nationals of other Contracting Parties shall be understood to be those performers or producers of phonograms who would meet the criteria for eligibility for protection provided under the Rome Convention, were all the Contracting Parties to this Treaty Contracting States of that Convention. In respect of these criteria of eligibility, Contracting Parties shall apply the relevant definitions in Article 2 of this Treaty.

(3)   Any Contracting Party availing itself of the possibilities provided in Article 5(3) of the Rome Convention or, for the purposes of Article 5 of the same Convention, Article 17 thereof shall make a notification as foreseen in those provisions to the Director General of the World Intellectual Property Organization (WIPO).

Article 4 National treatment

(1)   Each Contracting Party shall accord to nationals of other Contracting Parties, as defined in Article 3(2), the treatment it accords to its own nationals with regard to the exclusive rights specifically granted in this Treaty, and to the right to equitable remuneration provided for in Article 15 of this Treaty.

(2)   The obligation provided for in paragraph (1) does not apply to the extent that another Contracting Party makes use of the reservations permitted by Article 15(3) of this Treaty.

CHAPTER II
RIGHTS OF PERFORMERS

Article 5 Moral rights of performers

(1)   Independently of a performer's economic rights, and even after the transfer of those rights, the performer shall, as regards his live aural performances or performances fixed in phonograms, have the right to claim to be identified as the performer of his performances, except where omission is dictated by the manner of the use of the performance, and to object to any distortion, mutilation or other modification of his performances that would be prejudicial to his reputation.

(2)   The rights granted to a performer in accordance with paragraph (1) shall, after his death, be maintained, at least until the expiry of the economic rights, and shall be exercisable by the persons or institutions authorized by the legislation of the Contracting Party where protection is claimed. However, those Contracting Parties whose legislation, at the moment of their ratification of or accession to this Treaty, does not provide for protection after the death of the performer of all rights set out in the preceding paragraph may provide that some of these rights will, after his death, cease to be maintained.

(3)   The means of redress for safeguarding the rights granted under this Article shall be governed by the legislation of the Contracting Party where protection is claimed.

Article 6 Economic rights of performers in their unfixed performances

Performers shall enjoy the exclusive right of authorizing, as regards their performances:

(i)   the broadcasting and communication to the public of their unfixed performances except where the performance is already a broadcast performance; and

(ii)   the fixation of their unfixed performances.

Article 7 Right of reproduction

Performers shall enjoy the exclusive right of authorizing the direct or indirect reproduction of their performances fixed in phonograms, in any manner or form.

Article 8 Right of distribution

(1)   Performers shall enjoy the exclusive right of authorizing the making available to the public of the original and copies of their performances fixed in phonograms through sale or other transfer of ownership.

(2)   Nothing in this Treaty shall affect the freedom of Contracting Parties to determine the conditions, if any, under which the exhaustion of the right in paragraph (1) applies after the first sale or other transfer of ownership of the original or a copy of the fixed performance with the authorization of the performer.

Article 9 Right of rental

(1)   Performers shall enjoy the exclusive right of authorizing the commercial rental to the public of the original and copies of their performances fixed in phonograms as determined in the national law of Contracting Parties, even after distribution of them by, or pursuant to, authorization by the performer.

(2)   Notwithstanding the provisions of paragraph (1), a Contracting Party that, on April 15, 1994, had and continues to have in force a system of equitable remuneration of performers for the rental of copies of their performances fixed in phonograms, may maintain that system provided that the commercial rental of phonograms is not giving rise to the material impairment of the exclusive right of reproduction of performers.

Article 10 Right of making available of fixed performances

Performers shall enjoy the exclusive right of authorizing the making available to the public of their performances fixed in phonograms, by wire or wireless means, in such a way that members of the public may access them from a place and at a time individually chosen by them.

CHAPTER III
RIGHTS OF PRODUCERS OF PHONOGRAMS

Article 11 Right of reproduction

Producers of phonograms shall enjoy the exclusive right of authorizing the direct or indirect reproduction of their phonograms, in any manner or form.

Article 12 Right of distribution

(1)   Producers of phonograms shall enjoy the exclusive right of authorizing the making available to the public of the original and copies of their phonograms through sale or other transfer of ownership.

(2)   Nothing in this Treaty shall affect the freedom of Contracting Parties to determine the conditions, if any, under which the exhaustion of the right in paragraph (1) applies after the first sale or other transfer of ownership of the original or a copy of the phonogram with the authorization of the producer of the phonogram.

Article 13 Right of rental

(1)   Producers of phonograms shall enjoy the exclusive right of authorizing the commercial rental to the public of the original and copies of their phonograms, even after distribution of them, by or pursuant to, authorization by the producer.

(2)   Notwithstanding the provisions of paragraph (1), a Contracting Party that, on April 15, 1994, had and continues to have in force a system of equitable remuneration of producers of phonograms for the rental of copies of their phonograms, may maintain that system provided that the commercial rental of phonograms is not giving rise to the material impairment of the exclusive rights of reproduction of producers of phonograms.

Article 14 Right of making available of phonograms

Producers of phonograms shall enjoy the exclusive right of authorizing the making available to the public of their phonograms, by wire or wireless means, in such a way that members of the public may access them from a place and at a time individually chosen by them.

CHAPTER IV

COMMON PROVISIONS

Article 15 Right to remuneration for broadcasting and communication to the public

(1)   Performers and producers of phonograms shall enjoy the right to a single equitable remuneration for the direct or indirect use of phonograms published for commercial purposes for broadcasting or for any communication to the public.

(2)   Contracting Parties may establish in their national legislation that the single equitable remuneration shall be claimed from the user by the performer or by the producer of a phonogram or by both. Contracting Parties may enact national legislation that, in the absence of an agreement between the performer and the producer of a phonogram, sets the terms according to which performers and producers of phonograms shall share the single equitable remuneration.

(3)   Any Contracting Party may, in a notification deposited with the Director General of WIPO, declare that it will apply the provisions of paragraph (1) only in respect of certain uses, or that it will limit their application in some other way, or that it will not apply these provisions at all.

(4)   For the purposes of this Article, phonograms made available to the public by wire or wireless means in such a way that members of the public may access them from a place and at a time individually chosen by them shall be considered as if they had been published for commercial purposes.

Article 16 Limitations and exceptions

(1)   Contracting Parties may, in their national legislation, provide for the same kinds of limitations or exceptions with regard to the protection of performers and producers of phonograms as they provide for, in their national legislation, in connection with the protection of copyright in literary and artistic works.

(2)   Contracting Parties shall confine any limitations of or exceptions to rights provided for in this Treaty to certain special cases which do not conflict with a normal exploitation of the performance or phonogram and do not unreasonably prejudice the legitimate interests of the performer or of the producer of the phonogram.

Article 17 Term of protection

(1)   The term of protection to be granted to performers under this Treaty shall last, at least, until the end of a period of 50 years computed from the end of the year in which the performance was fixed in a phonogram.

(2)   The term of protection to be granted to producers of phonograms under this Treaty shall last, at least, until the end of a period of 50 years computed from the end of the year in which the phonogram was published, or failing such publication within 50 years from fixation of the phonogram, 50 years from the end of the year in which the fixation was made.

Article 18 Obligations concerning technological measures

Contracting Parties shall provide adequate legal protection and effective legal remedies against the circumvention of effective technological measures that are used by performers or producers of phonograms in connection with the exercise of their rights under this Treaty and that restrict acts, in respect of their performances or phonograms, which are not authorized by the performers or the producers of phonograms concerned or permitted by law.

Article 19 Obligations concerning rights management information

(1)   Contracting Parties shall provide adequate and effective legal remedies against any person knowingly performing any of the following acts knowing, or with respect to civil remedies having reasonable grounds to know, that it will induce, enable, facilitate or conceal an infringement of any right covered by this Treaty:

  (i)   to remove or alter any electronic rights management information without authority;
  (ii)   to distribute, import for distribution, broadcast, communicate or make available to the public, without authority, performances, copies of fixed performances or phonograms knowing that electronic rights management information has been removed or altered without authority.

(2)   As used in this Article, "rights management information" means information which identifies the performer, the performance of the performer, the producer of the phonogram, the phonogram, the owner of any right in the performance or phonogram, or information about the terms and conditions of use of the performance or phonogram, and any numbers or codes that represent such information, when any of these items of information is attached to a copy of a fixed performance or a phonogram or appears in connection with the communication or making available of a fixed performance or a phonogram to the public.

Article 20 Formalities

The enjoyment and exercise of the rights provided for in this Treaty shall not be subject to any formality.

Article 21 Reservations

Subject to the provisions of Article 15(3), no reservations to this Treaty shall be permitted.

Article 22 Application in time

(1)   Contracting Parties shall apply the provisions of Article 18 of the Berne Convention, *mutatis mutandis*, to the rights of performers and producers of phonograms provided for in this Treaty.

(2)   Notwithstanding paragraph (1), a Contracting Party may limit the application of Article 5 of this Treaty to performances which occurred after the entry into force of this Treaty for that Party.

Article 23 Provisions on enforcement of rights

(1)   Contracting Parties undertake to adopt, in accordance with their legal systems, the measures necessary to ensure the application of this Treaty.

(2)   Contracting Parties shall ensure that enforcement procedures are available under their law so as to permit effective action against any act of infringement of rights covered by this Treaty, including expeditious remedies to prevent infringements and remedies which constitute a deterrent to further infringements.

CHAPTER V
ADMINISTRATIVE AND FINAL CLAUSES

Article 24 Assembly

(1)   (a)   The Contracting Parties shall have an Assembly.
        (b)   Each Contracting Party shall be represented by one delegate who may be assisted by alternate delegates, advisors and experts.
        (c)   The expenses of each delegation shall be borne by the Contracting Party that has appointed the delegation. The Assembly may ask WIPO to grant financial assistance to facilitate the participation of delegations of Contracting Parties that arc regarded as developing countries in conformity with the established practice of the General Assembly of the United Nations or that are countries in transition to a market economy.

(2)   (a)   The Assembly shall deal with matters concerning the maintenance and development of this Treaty and the application and operation of this Treaty.

       (b)   The Assembly shall perform the function allocated to it under Article 26(2) in respect of the admission of certain intergovernmental organizations to become party to this Treaty.

       (c)   The Assembly shall decide the convocation of any diplomatic conference for the revision of this Treaty and give the necessary instructions to the Director General of WIPO for the preparation of such diplomatic conference.

(3)   (a)   Each Contracting Party that is a State shall have one vote and shall vote only in its own name.

       (b)   Any Contracting Party that is an intergovernmental organization may participate in the vote, in place of its Member States, with a number of votes equal to the number of its Member States which are party to this Treaty. No such intergovernmental organization shall participate in the vote if any one of its Member States exercises its right to vote and vice versa.

(4)   The Assembly shall meet in ordinary session once every two years upon convocation by the Director General of WIPO.

(5)   The Assembly shall establish its own rules of procedure, including the convocation of extraordinary sessions, the requirements of a quorum and, subject to the provisions of this Treaty, the required majority for various kinds of decisions.

Article 25 International Bureau

The International Bureau of WIPO shall perform the administrative tasks concerning the Treaty.

Article 26 Eligibility for becoming party to the Treaty

(1)   Any Member State of WIPO may become party to this Treaty.

(2)   The Assembly may decide to admit any intergovernmental organization to become party to this Treaty which declares that it is competent in respect of, and has its own legislation binding on all its Member States on, matters covered by this Treaty and that it has been duly authorized, in accordance with its internal procedures, to become party to this Treaty.

(3)   The European Community, having made the declaration referred to in the preceding paragraph in the Diplomatic Conference that has adopted this Treaty, may become party to this Treaty.

Article 27 Rights and obligations under the Treaty

Subject to any specific provisions to the contrary in this Treaty, each Contracting Party shall enjoy all of the rights and assume all of the obligations under this Treaty.

Article 28 Signature of the Treaty

This Treaty shall be open for signature until December 31, 1997, by any Member State of WIPO and by the European Community.

PATENTS ACT 1977
(c. 37)

PART I
NEW DOMESTIC LAW

Patentability

1   Patentable inventions

(1)   A patent may be granted only for an invention in respect of which the following conditions are satisfied, that is to say—

    (a)   the invention is new;

    (b)   it involves an inventive step;

    (c)   it is capable of industrial application;

    (d)   the grant of a patent for it is not excluded by subsections (2) and (3) or section 4A below;

and references in this Act to a patentable invention shall be construed accordingly.

(2)   It is hereby declared that the following (among other things) are not inventions for the purposes of this Act, that is to say, anything which consists of—

(a)   a discovery, scientific theory or mathematical method;

(b)   a literary, dramatic, musical or artistic work or any other aesthetic creation whatsoever;

(c)   a scheme, rule or method for performing a mental act, playing a game or doing business, or a program for a computer;

(d)   the presentation of information;

but the foregoing provision shall prevent anything from being treated as an invention for the purposes of this Act only to the extent that a patent or application for a patent relates to that thing as such.

(3)   A patent shall not be granted for an invention the commercial exploitation of which would be contrary to public policy or morality.

(4)   For the purposes of subsection (3) above exploitation shall not be regarded as contrary to public policy or morality only because it is prohibited by any law in force in the United Kingdom or any part of it.

(5)   The Secretary of State may by order vary the provisions of subsection (2) above for the purpose of maintaining them in conformity with developments in science and technology; and no such order shall be made unless a draft of the order has been laid before, and approved by resolution of, each House of Parliament.

2   Novelty

(1)   An invention shall be taken to be new if it does not form part of the state of the art.

(2)   The state of the art in the case of an invention shall be taken to comprise all matter (whether a product, a process, information about either, or anything else) which has at any time before the priority date of that invention been made available to the public (whether in the United Kingdom or elsewhere) by written or oral description, by use or in any other way.

(3)   The state of the art in the case of an invention to which an application for a patent or a patent relates shall be taken also to comprise matter contained in an application for another patent which was published on or after the priority date of that invention, if the following conditions are satisfied, that is to say—

(a)   that matter was contained in the application for that other patent both as filed and as published; and

(b)   the priority date of that matter is earlier than that of the invention.

(4)   For the purposes of this section the disclosure of matter constituting an invention shall be disregarded in the case of a patent or an application for a patent if occurring later than the beginning of the period of six months immediately preceding the date of filing the application for the patent and either—

(a)   the disclosure was due to, or made in consequence of, the matter having been obtained unlawfully or in breach of confidence by any person—

(i)   from the inventor or from any other person to whom the matter was made available in confidence by the inventor or who obtained it from the inventor because he or the inventor believed that he was entitled to obtain it; or

(ii)   from any other person to whom the matter was made available in confidence by any person mentioned in sub-paragraph (i) above or in this sub-paragraph or who obtained it from any person so mentioned because he or the person from whom he obtained it believed that he was entitled to obtain it;

(b)   the disclosure was made in breach of confidence by any person who obtained the matter in confidence from the inventor or from any other person to whom it was made available, or who obtained it, from the inventor; or

(c)   the disclosure was due to, or made in consequence of the inventor displaying the invention at an international exhibition and the applicant states, on filing the application, that the invention has been so displayed and also, within the prescribed period, files written evidence in support of the statement complying with any prescribed conditions.

(5)   In this section references to the inventor include references to any proprietor of the invention for the time being.

(6)   . . .

3   Inventive step

An invention shall be taken to involve an inventive step if it is not obvious to a person skilled in the art, having regard to any matter which forms part of the state of the art by virtue only of section 2(2) above (and disregarding section 2(3) above).

4   Industrial application

(1)   An invention shall be taken to be capable of industrial application if it can be made or used in any kind of industry, including agriculture.

. . .

4A   Methods of treatment or diagnosis

(1)   A patent shall not be granted for the invention of—

  (a)   a method of treatment of the human or animal body by surgery or therapy, or

  (b)   a method of diagnosis practised on the human or animal body.

(2)   Subsection (1) above does not apply to an invention consisting of a substance or composition for use in any such method.

(3)   In the case of an invention consisting of a substance or composition for use in any such method, the fact that the substance or composition forms part of the state of the art shall not prevent the invention from being taken to be new if the use of the substance or composition in any such method does not form part of the state of the art.

(4)   In the case of an invention consisting of a substance or composition for a specific use in any such method, the fact that the substance or composition forms part of the state of the art shall not prevent the invention from being taken to be new if that specific use does not form part of the state of the art.

5   Priority date

(1)   For the purposes of this Act the priority date of an invention to which an application for a patent relates and also of any matter (whether or not the same as the invention) contained in any such application is, except as provided by the following provisions of this Act, the date of filing the application.

(2)   If in or in connection with an application for a patent (the application in suit) a declaration is made, whether by the applicant or any predecessor in title of his, complying with the relevant requirements of rules and specifying one or more earlier relevant applications for the purposes of this section made by the applicant or a predecessor in title of his and the application in suit has a date of filing during the period allowed under subsection (2A)(a) or (b) below, then—

  (a)   if an invention to which the application in suit relates is supported by matter disclosed in the earlier relevant application or applications, the priority date of that invention shall instead of being the date of filing the application in suit be the date of filing the relevant application in which that matter was disclosed, or, if it was disclosed in more than one relevant application, the earliest of them;

  (b)   the priority date of any matter contained in the application in suit which was also disclosed in the earlier relevant application or applications shall be the date of filing the relevant application in which that matter was disclosed or, if it was disclosed in more than one relevant application, the earliest of them.

(2A) The periods are—

  (a)   the period of twelve months immediately following the date of filing of the earlier specified relevant application, or if there is more than one, of the earliest of them; and

  (b)   where the comptroller has given permission under subsection (2B) below for a late declaration to be made under subsection (2) above, the period commencing immediately after the end of the period allowed under paragraph (a) above and ending at the end of the prescribed period.

(2B) The applicant may make a request to the comptroller for permission to make a late declaration under subsection (2) above.

(2C) The comptroller shall grant a request made under subsection (2B) above if, and only if—

  (a)   the request complies with the relevant requirements of rules; and

(b) the comptroller is satisfied that the applicant's failure to file the application in suit within the period allowed under subsection (2A)(a) above was unintentional.

(3) Where an invention or other matter contained in the application in suit was also disclosed in two earlier relevant applications filed by the same applicant as in the case of the application in suit or a predecessor in title of his and the second of those relevant applications was specified in or in connection with the application in suit, the second of those relevant applications shall, so far as concerns that invention or matter, be disregarded unless—

(a) it was filed in or in respect of the same country as the first; and

(b) not later than the date of filing the second, the first (whether or not so specified) was unconditionally withdrawn, or was abandoned or refused, without—

(i) having been made available to the public (whether in the United Kingdom or elsewhere);

(ii) leaving any rights outstanding; and

(iii) having served to establish a priority date in relation to another application, wherever made.

(4) The foregoing provisions of this section shall apply for determining the priority date of an invention for which a patent has been granted as they apply for determining the priority date of an invention to which an application for that patent relates.

(5) In this section "relevant application" means any of the following applications which has a date of filing, namely—

(a) an application for a patent under this Act;

(aa) an application in or for a country (other than the United Kingdom) which is a member of the World Trade Organisation for protection in respect of an invention which, in accordance with the law of that country or a treaty or international obligation to which it is a party, is equivalent to an application for a patent under this Act;

(b) an application in or for a convention country (specified under section 90 below) for protection in respect of an invention or an application which, in accordance with the law of a convention country or a treaty or international convention to which a convention country is a party, is equivalent to an application for a patent under this Act.

. . .

6 Disclosure of matter, etc., between earlier and later applications

(1) It is hereby declared for the avoidance of doubt that where an application (the application in suit) is made for a patent and a declaration is made in accordance with section 5(2) above in or in connection with that application specifying an earlier relevant application, the application in suit and any patent granted in pursuance of it shall not be invalidated by reason only of relevant intervening acts.

(2) In this section—

"relevant application" has the same meaning as in section 5 above; and

"relevant intervening acts" means acts done in relation to matter disclosed in an earlier relevant application between the dates of the earlier relevant application and the application in suit, as for example, filing another application for the invention for which the earlier relevant application was made, making information available to the public about that invention or that matter or working that invention, but disregarding any application, or the disclosure to the public of matter contained in any application, which is itself to be disregarded for the purposes of section 5(3) above.

Right to apply for and obtain a patent and be mentioned as inventor

7 Right to apply for and obtain a patent

(1) Any person may make an application for a patent either alone or jointly with another.

(2) A patent for an invention may be granted—

(a) primarily to the inventor or joint inventors;

(b) in preference to the foregoing, to any person or persons who, by virtue of any enactment or rule of law, or any foreign law or treaty or international convention, or by virtue of an enforceable term of any agreement entered into with the inventor before the making of the invention, was or were at the time of the making of the invention entitled to the whole of the property in it (other than equitable interests) in the United Kingdom;

(c)   in any event, to the successor or successors in title of any person or persons mentioned in paragraph (a) or (b) above or any person so mentioned and the successor or successors in title of another person so mentioned;

and to no other person.

(3)   In this Act "inventor" in relation to an invention means the actual deviser of the invention and "joint inventor" shall be construed accordingly.

(4)   Except so far as the contrary is established, a person who makes an application for a patent shall be taken to be the person who is entitled under subsection (2) above to be granted a patent and two or more persons who make such an application jointly shall be taken to be the persons so entitled.

8   Determination before grant of questions about entitlement to patents, etc.

(1)   At any time before a patent has been granted for an invention (whether or not an application has been made for it)—

(a)   any person may refer to the comptroller the question whether he is entitled to be granted (alone or with any other persons) a patent for that invention or has or would have any right in or under any patent so granted or any application for such a patent; or

(b)   any of two or more co-proprietors of an application for a patent for that invention may so refer the question whether any right in or under the application should be transferred or granted to any other person;

and the comptroller shall determine the question and may make such order as he thinks fit to give effect to the determination.

(2)   Where a person refers a question relating to an invention under subsection (1)(a) above to the comptroller after an application for a patent for the invention has been filed and before a patent is granted in pursuance of the application, then, unless the application is refused or withdrawn before the reference is disposed of by the comptroller, the comptroller may, without prejudice to the generality of subsection (1) above and subject to subsection (6) below—

(a)   order that the application shall proceed in the name of that person, either solely or jointly with that of any other applicant, instead of in the name of the applicant or any specified applicant;

(b)   where the reference was made by two or more persons, order that the application shall proceed in all their names jointly;

(c)   refuse to grant a patent in pursuance of the application or order the application to be amended so as to exclude any of the matter in respect of which the question was referred;

(d)   make an order transferring or granting any licence or other right in or under the application and give directions to any person for carrying out the provisions of any such order.

(3)   Where a question is referred to the comptroller under subsection (1)(a) above and—

(a)   the comptroller orders an application for a patent for the invention to which the question relates to be so amended;

(b)   any such application is refused under subsection 2(c) above before the comptroller has disposed of the reference (whether the reference was made before or after the publication of the application); or

(c)   any such application is refused under any other provision of this Act or is withdrawn before the comptroller has disposed of the reference, whether the application is refused or withdrawn before or after its publication;

the comptroller may order that any person by whom the reference was made may within the prescribed period make a new application for a patent for the whole or part of any matter comprised in the earlier application or, as the case may be, for all or any of the matter excluded from the earlier application, subject in either case to section 76 below, and in either case that, if such a new application is made, it shall be treated as having been filed on the date of filing the earlier application.

(4) Where a person refers a question under subsection (1)(b) above relating to an application, any order under subsection (1) above may contain directions to any person for transferring or granting any right in or under the application.

(5) If any person to whom directions have been given under subsection (2)(d) or (4) above fails to do anything necessary for carrying out any such directions within 14 days after the date of the directions, the comptroller may, on application made to him by any person in whose favour or on whose reference the directions were given, authorise him to do that thing on behalf of the person to whom the directions were given.

(6) Where on a reference under this section it is alleged that, by virtue of any transaction, instrument or event relating to an invention or an application for a patent, any person other than the inventor or the applicant for the patent has become entitled to be granted (whether alone or with any other persons) a patent for the invention or has or would have any right in or under any patent so granted or any application for any such patent, an order shall not be made under subsection (2)(a), (b) or (d) above on the reference unless notice of the reference is given to the applicant and any such person, except any of them who is a party to the reference.

(7) If it appears to the comptroller on a reference of a question under this section that the question involves matters which would more properly be determined by the court, he may decline to deal with it and, without prejudice to the court's jurisdiction to determine any such question and make a declaration, or any declaratory jurisdiction of the court in Scotland, the court shall have jurisdiction to do so.

(8) No directions shall be given under this section so as to affect the mutual rights or obligations of trustees or of the personal representatives of deceased persons, or their right or obligations as such.

9 Determination after grant of questions referred before grant

If a question with respect to a patent or application is referred by any person to the comptroller under section 8 above, whether before or after the making of an application for the patent, and is not determined before the time when the application is first in order for a grant of a patent in pursuance of the application, that fact shall not prevent the grant of a patent, but on its grant that person shall be treated as having referred to the comptroller under section 37 below any question mentioned in that section which the comptroller thinks appropriate.

10 Handling of application by joint applicants

If any dispute arises between joint applicants for a patent whether or in what manner the application should be proceeded with, the comptroller may, on a request made by any of the parties, give such directions as he thinks fit for enabling the application to proceed in the name of one or more of the parties alone or for regulating the manner in which it shall be proceeded with, or for both those purposes, according as the case may require.

11 Effect of transfer of application under s. 8 or 10

(1) Where an order is made or directions are given under section 8 or 10 above that an application for a patent shall proceed in the name of one or some of the original applicants (whether or not it is also to proceed in the name of some other person), any licences or other rights in or under the application shall, subject to the provisions of the order and any directions under either of those sections, continue in force and be treated as granted by the persons in whose name the application is to proceed.

(2) Where an order is made or directions are given under section 8 above that an application for a patent shall proceed in the name of one or more persons none of whom was an original applicant (on the ground that the original applicant or applicants was or were not entitled to be granted the patent), any licences or other rights in or under the application shall, subject to the provisions of the order and any directions under that section and subject to subsection (3) below, lapse on the registration of that person or those persons as the applicant or applicants or, where the application has not been published, on the making of the order.

(3) If before registration of a reference under section 8 above resulting in the making of any order mentioned in subsection (2) above—

(a) the original applicant or any of the applicants, acting in good faith, worked the invention in question in the United Kingdom or made effective and serious preparations to do so; or

(a)   a licensee of the applicant, acting in good faith, worked the invention in the United Kingdom or made effective and serious preparations to do so;

that or those original applicant or applicants or the licensee shall, on making a request within the prescribed period to the person in whose name the application is to proceed, be entitled to be granted a licence (but not an exclusive licence) to continue working or, as the case may be, to work the invention.

(3A) If, before registration of a reference under section 8 above resulting in the making of an order under subsection (3) of that section, the condition in subsection (3)(a) or (b) above is met, the original applicant or any of the applicants or the licensee shall, on making a request within the prescribed period to the new applicant, be entitled to be granted a licence (but not an exclusive licence) to continue working or, as the case may be, to work the invention so far as it is the subject of the new application.

(4)   A licence under subsection 3 or 3A above shall be granted for a reasonable period and on reasonable terms.

(5)   Where an order is made as mentioned in subsection (2) or (3A) above, the person in whose name the application is to proceed or, as the case may be, who makes the new application or any person claiming that he is entitled to be granted any such licence may refer to the comptroller the question whether the latter is so entitled and whether any such period is or terms are reasonable, and the comptroller shall determine the question and may, if he considers it appropriate, order the grant of such a licence.

12   Determination of questions about entitlement to foreign and convention patents, etc.

(1)   At any time before a patent is granted for an invention in pursuance of an application made under the law of any country other than the United Kingdom or under any treaty or international convention (whether or not that application has been made)—

(a)   any person may refer to the comptroller the question whether he is entitled to be granted (alone or with any other persons) any such patent for that invention or has or would have any right in or under any such patent or an application for such a patent; or

(b)   any of two or more co-proprietors of an application for such a patent for that invention may so refer the question whether any right in or under the application should be transferred or granted to any other person;

and the comptroller shall determine the question so far as he is able to and may make such order as he thinks fit to give effect to the determination.

(2)   If it appears to the comptroller on a reference of a question under this section that the question involves matters which would more properly be determined by the court, he may decline to deal with it and, without prejudice to the court's jurisdiction to determine any such question and make a declaration, or any declaratory jurisdiction of the court in Scotland, the court shall have jurisdiction to do so.

(3)   Subsection (1) above, in its application to a European patent and an application for any such patent, shall have effect subject to section 82 below.

(4)   Section 10 above, except so much of it as enables the comptroller to regulate the manner in which an application is to proceed, shall apply to disputes between joint applicants for any such patent as is mentioned in subsection (1) above as it applies to joint applicants for a patent under this Act.

(5)   Section 11 above shall apply in relation to—

(a)   any orders made under subsection (1) above and any directions given under section 10 above by virtue of subsection (4) above; and

(b)   any orders made and directions given by the relevant convention court with respect to a question corresponding to any question which may be determined under subsection (1) above;

as it applies to orders made and directions given apart from this section under section 8 or 10 above.

(6)   In the following cases, that is to say—

(a)   where an application for a European patent (UK) is refused or withdrawn, or the designation of the United Kingdom in the application is withdrawn, whether before or after publication of the application but before a question relating to the right to the patent has been referred to the comptroller under subsection (1) above or before proceedings relating to that right have begun before the relevant convention court;

(b) where an application has been made for a European patent (UK) and on a reference under subsection (1) above or any such proceedings as are mentioned in paragraph (a) above the comptroller, the court or the relevant convention court determines by a final decision (whether before or after publication of the application) that a person other than the applicant has the right to the patent, but that person requests the European Patent Office that the application for the patent should be refused; or

(c) where an international application for a patent (UK) is withdrawn, or the designation of the United Kingdom in the application is withdrawn, whether before or after the making of any reference under subsection (1) above but after publication of the application;

the comptroller may order that any person (other than the applicant) appearing to him to be entitled to be granted a patent under this Act may within the prescribed period make an application for such a patent for the whole or part of any matter comprised in the earlier application (subject, however, to section 76 below) and that if the application for a patent under this Act is filed, it shall be treated as having been filed on the date of filing the earlier application.

(7) In this section—

(a) references to a patent and an application for a patent include respectively references to protection in respect of an invention and an application which, in accordance with the law of any country other than the United Kingdom or any treaty or international convention, is equivalent to an application for a patent or for such protection; and

(b) a decision shall be taken to be final for the purposes of this section when the time for appealing from it has expired without an appeal being brought or, where an appeal is brought, when it is finally disposed of.

13 Mention of inventor

(1) The inventor or joint inventors of an invention shall have a right to be mentioned as such in any patent granted for the invention and shall also have a right to be so mentioned if possible in any published application for a patent for the invention and, if not so mentioned, a right to be so mentioned in accordance with rules in a prescribed document.

(2) Unless he has already given the Patent Office the information hereinafter mentioned, an applicant for a patent shall within the prescribed period file with the Patent Office a statement—

(a) identifying the person or persons whom he believes to be the inventor or inventors; and

(b) where the applicant is not the sole inventor or the applicants are not the joint inventors, indicating the derivation of his or their right to be granted the patent; and, if he fails to do so, the application shall be taken to be withdrawn.

(3) Where a person has been mentioned as sole or joint inventor in pursuance of this section, any other person who alleges that the former ought not to have been so mentioned may at any time apply to the comptroller for a certificate to that effect, and the comptroller may issue such a certificate; and if he does so, he shall accordingly rectify any undistributed copies of the patent and of any documents prescribed for the purposes of subsection (1) above.

Applications

14 Making of application

(1) Every application for a patent—

(a) shall be made in the prescribed form and shall be filed at the Patent Office in the prescribed manner;

. . .

(1A) Where an application for a patent is made, the fee prescribed for the purposes of this subsection ("the application fee") shall be paid not later than the end of the period prescribed for the purposes of section 15(10)(c) below.

(2)   Every application for a patent shall contain—
     (a)   a request for the grant of a patent;
     (b)   a specification containing a description of the invention, a claim or claims and any drawing referred to in the description or any claim; and
     (c)   an abstract;
     but the foregoing provision shall not prevent an application being initiated by documents complying with section 15(1) below.

(3)   The specification of an application shall disclose the invention in a manner which is clear enough and complete enough for the invention to be performed by a person skilled in the art.

(4)   . . .

(5)   The claim or claims shall—
     (a)   define the matter for which the applicant seeks protection;
     (b)   be clear and concise;
     (c)   be supported by the description; and
     (d)   relate to one invention or to a group of inventions which are so linked as to form a single inventive concept.

(6)   Without prejudice to the generality of subsection (5)(d) above, rules may provide for treating two or more inventions as being so linked as to form a single inventive concept for the purposes of this Act.

(7)   The purpose of the abstract is to give technical information and on publication it shall not form part of the state of the art by virtue of section 2(3) above, and the comptroller may determine whether the abstract adequately fulfils its purpose and, if it does not, may reframe it so that it does.

(8)   . . .

(9)   An application for a patent may be withdrawn at any time before the patent is granted and any withdrawal of such an application may not be revoked.

(10) Subsection (9) above does not affect the power of the comptroller under section 117(1) below to correct an error or mistake in a withdrawal of an application for a patent.

15   Date of filing application

(1)   Subject to the following provisions of this Act, the date of filing an application for a patent shall be taken to be the earliest date on which documents filed at the Patent Office to initiate the application satisfy the following conditions—
     (a)   the documents indicate that a patent is sought;
     (b)   the documents identify the person applying for a patent or contain information sufficient to enable that person to be contacted by the Patent Office; and
     (c)   the documents contain either—
          (i)   something which is or appears to be a description of the invention for which a patent is sought; or
          (ii)   a reference, complying with the relevant requirements of rules, to an earlier relevant application made by the applicant or a predecessor in title of his.

(2)   It is immaterial for the purposes of subsection (1)(c)(i) above—
     (a)   whether the thing is in, or is accompanied by a translation into, a language accepted by the Patent Office in accordance with rules;
     (b)   whether the thing otherwise complies with the other provisions of this Act and with any relevant rules.

(3)   Where documents filed at the Patent Office to initiate an application for a patent satisfy one or more of the conditions specified in subsection (1) above, but do not satisfy all those conditions, the comptroller shall as soon as practicable after the filing of those documents notify the applicant of what else must be filed in order for the application to have a date of filing.

(4)   Where documents filed at the Patent Office to initiate an application for a patent satisfy all the conditions specified in subsection (1) above, the comptroller shall as soon as practicable after the filing of the last of those documents notify the applicant of—
     (a)   the date of filing the application, and
     (b)   the requirements that must be complied with, and the periods within which they are required by this Act or rules to be complied with, if the application is not to be treated as having been withdrawn.

(5) Subsection (6) below applies where—
    (a) an application has a date of filing by virtue of subsection (1) above;
    (b) within the prescribed period the applicant files at the Patent Office—
        (i) a drawing, or
        (ii) part of the description of the invention for which a patent is sought, and
    (c) that drawing or that part of the description was missing from the application at the date of filing.

(6) Unless the applicant withdraws the drawing or the part of the description filed under subsection (5)(b) above ("the missing part") before the end of the prescribed period—
    (a) the missing part shall be treated as included in the application; and
    (b) the date of filing the application shall be the date on which the missing part is filed at the Patent Office.

(7) Subsection (6)(b) above does not apply if—
    (a) on or before the date which is the date of filing the application by virtue of subsection (1) above a declaration is made under section 5(2) above in or in connection with the application;
    (b) the applicant makes a request for subsection (6)(b) above not to apply; and
    (c) the request complies with the relevant requirements of rules and is made within the prescribed period.

(8) Subsections (6) and (7) above do not affect the power of the comptroller under section 117(1) below to correct an error or mistake.

(9) Where, after an application for a patent has been filed and before the patent is granted—
    (a) a new application is filed by the original applicant or his successor in title in accordance with rules in respect of any part of the matter contained in the earlier application, and
    (b) the conditions mentioned in subsection (1) above are satisfied in relation to the new application (without the new application contravening section 76 below),
the new application shall be treated as having, as its date of filing, the date of filing the earlier application.

(10) Where an application has a date of filing by virtue of this section, the application shall be treated as having been withdrawn if any of the following applies—
    (a) the applicant fails to file at the Patent Office, before the end of the prescribed period, one or more claims and the abstract;
    (b) where a reference to an earlier relevant application has been filed as mentioned in subsection (1)(c)(ii) above—
        (i) the applicant fails to file at the Patent Office, before the end of the prescribed period, a description of the invention for which the patent is sought;
        (ii) the applicant fails to file at the Patent Office, before the end of the prescribed period, a copy of the application referred to, complying with the relevant requirements of rules;
    (c) the applicant fails to pay the application fee before the end of the prescribed period;
    (d) the applicant fails, before the end of the prescribed period, to make a request for a search under section 17 below and pay the search fee.

(11) In this section "relevant application" has the meaning given by section 5(5) above.

15A Preliminary examination

(1) The comptroller shall refer an application for a patent to an examiner for a preliminary examination if—
    (a) the application has a date of filing;
    (b) the application has not been withdrawn or treated as withdrawn; and
    (c) the application fee has been paid.

(2) On a preliminary examination of an application the examiner shall—
    (a) determine whether the application complies with those requirements of this Act and the rules which are designated by the rules as formal requirements for the purposes of this Act; and

(b)   determine whether any requirements under section 13(2) or 15(10) above remain to be complied with.

(3)   The examiner shall report to the comptroller his determinations under subsection (2) above.

(4)   If on the preliminary examination of an application it is found that—

   (a)   any drawing referred to in the application, or

   (b)   part of the description of the invention for which the patent is sought,

   is missing from the application, then the examiner shall include this finding in his report under subsection (3) above.

(5)   Subsections (6) to (8) below apply if a report is made to the comptroller under subsection (3) above that not all the formal requirements have been complied with.

(6)   The comptroller shall specify a period during which the applicant shall have the opportunity—

   (a)   to make observations on the report, and

   (b)   to amend the application so as to comply with those requirements (subject to section 76 below).

(7)   The comptroller may refuse the application if the applicant fails to amend the application as mentioned in subsection (6)(b) above before the end of the period specified by the comptroller under that subsection.

(8)   Subsection (7) above does not apply if—

   (a)   the applicant makes observations as mentioned in subsection (6)(a) above before the end of the period specified by the comptroller under that subsection, and

   (b)   as a result of the observations, the comptroller is satisfied that the formal requirements have been complied with.

(9)   If a report is made to the comptroller under subsection (3) above—

   (a)   that any requirement of section 13(2) or 15(10) above has not been complied with;

      or

   (b)   that a drawing or part of the description of the invention has been found to be missing,

   then the comptroller shall notify the applicant accordingly.

16   Publication of application

(1)   Subject to section 22 below, and to any prescribed restrictions, where an application has a date of filing, then, as soon as possible after the end of the prescribed period, the comptroller shall, unless the application is withdrawn or refused before preparations for its publication have been completed by the Patent Office, publish it as filed (including not only the original claims but also any amendments of those claims and new claims subsisting immediately before the completion of those preparations) and he may, if so requested by the applicant, publish it as aforesaid during that period, and in either event shall advertise the fact and date of its publication in the journal.

(2)   The comptroller may omit from the specification of a published application for a patent any matter—

   (a)   which in his opinion disparages any person in a way likely to damage him, or

   (b)   the publication or exploitation of which would in his opinion be generally expected to encourage offensive, immoral or anti-social behaviour.

Examination and search

17   Search

(1)   The comptroller shall refer an application for a patent to an examiner for a search if, and only if—

   (a)   the comptroller has referred the application to an examiner for a preliminary examination under section 15A(1) above;

   (b)   the application has not been withdrawn or treated as withdrawn;

   (c)   before the end of the prescribed period—

      (i)   the applicant makes a request to the Patent Office in the prescribed form for a search; and

      (ii)   the fee prescribed for the search ("the search fee") is paid;

(d) the application includes—
    (i) a description of the invention for which a patent is sought; and
    (ii) one or more claims; and
(e) the description and each of the claims comply with the requirements of rules as to language.

. . .

(4) Subject to subsections (5) and (6) below, on a search requested under this section, the examiner shall make such investigation as in his opinion is reasonably practicable and necessary for him to identify the documents which he thinks will be needed to decide, on a substantive examination under section 18 below, whether the invention for which a patent is sought is new and involves an inventive step.

(5) On any such search the examiner shall determine whether or not the search would serve any useful purpose on the application as for the time being constituted and—
(a) if he determines that it would serve such a purpose in relation to the whole or part of the application, he shall proceed to conduct the search so far as it would serve such a purpose and shall report on the results of the search to the comptroller; and
(b) if he determines that the search would not serve such a purpose in relation to the whole or part of the application, he shall report accordingly to the comptroller; and in either event the applicant shall be informed of the examiner's report.

(6) If it appears to the examiner, either before or on conducting a search under this section, that an application relates to two or more inventions, but that they are not so linked as to form a single inventive concept, he shall initially only conduct a search in relation to the first invention specified in the claims of the application, but may proceed to conduct a search in relation to another invention so specified if the applicant pays the search fee in respect of the application so far as it relates to that other invention.

(7) After a search has been requested under this section for an application the comptroller may at any time refer the application to an examiner for a supplementary search, and subsections (4) and (5) above shall apply in relation to a supplementary search as they apply in relation to any other search under this section.

(8) A reference for a supplementary search in consequence of—
(a) an amendment of the application made by the applicant under section 18(3) or 19(1) below, or
(b) a correction of the application, or of a document filed in connection with the application, under section 117 below,
shall be made only on payment of the prescribed fee, unless the comptroller directs otherwise.

18 Substantive examination and grant or refusal of patent

(1) Where the conditions imposed by section 17(1) above for the comptroller to refer an application to an examiner for search are satisfied and at the time of the request under that subsection or within the prescribed period—
(a) a request is made by the applicant to the Patent Office in the prescribed form for a substantive examination; and
(b) the prescribed fee is paid for the examination;
the comptroller shall refer the application to an examiner for a substantive examination; and if no such request is made or the prescribed fee is not paid within that period, the application shall be treated as having been withdrawn at the end of that period.

(1A) If the examiner forms the view that a supplementary search under section 17 above is required for which a fee is payable, he shall inform the comptroller, who may decide that the substantive examination should not proceed until the fee is paid; and if he so decides, then unless within such period as he may allow—
(a) the fee is paid, or
(b) the application is amended so as to render the supplementary search unnecessary, he may refuse the application.

(2) On a substantive examination of an application the examiner shall investigate, to such extent as he considers necessary in view of any examination carried out under section 15A above and search carried out under section 17 above, whether the application

complies with the requirements of this Act and the rules and shall determine that question and report his determination to the comptroller.

(3)   If the examiner reports that any of those requirements are not complied with, the comptroller shall give the applicant an opportunity within a specified period to make observations on the report and to amend the application so as to comply with those requirements (subject, however, to section 76 below), and if the applicant fails to satisfy the comptroller that those requirements are complied with, or to amend the application so as to comply with them, the comptroller may refuse the application.

(4)   If the examiner reports that the application, whether as originally filed or as amended in pursuance of section 15A above, this section or section 19 below, complies with those requirements at any time before the end of the prescribed period, the comptroller shall notify the applicant of that fact and, subject to subsection (5) and sections 19 and 22 below and on payment within the prescribed period of any fee prescribed for the grant, grant him a patent.

(5)   Where two or more applications for a patent for the same invention having the same priority date are filed by the same applicant or his successor in title, the comptroller may on that ground refuse to grant a patent in pursuance of more than one of the applications.

19   General power to amend application before grant

(1)   At any time before a patent is granted in pursuance of an application the applicant may, in accordance with the prescribed conditions and subject to section 76 below, amend the application of his own volition.

(2)   The comptroller may, without an application being made to him for the purpose, amend the specification and abstract contained in an application for a patent so as to acknowledge a registered trade mark.

20   Failure of application

(1)   If it is not determined that an application for a patent complies before the end of the prescribed period with all the requirements of this Act and the rules, the application shall be treated as having been refused by the comptroller at the end of that period, and section 97 below shall apply accordingly.

(2)   If at the end of that period an appeal to the court is pending in respect of the application or the time within which such an appeal could be brought has not expired, that period—

(a)   where such an appeal is pending, or is brought within the said time or before the expiration of any extension of that time granted (in the case of a first extension) on an application made within that time or (in the case of a subsequent extension) on an application made before the expiration of the last previous extension, shall be extended until such date as the court may determine;

(b)   where no such appeal is pending or is so brought, shall continue until the end of the said time or, if any extension of that time is so granted, until the expiration of the extension or last extension so granted.

20A   Reinstatement of applications

(1)   Subsection (2) below applies where an application for a patent is refused, or is treated as having been refused or withdrawn, as a direct consequence of a failure by the applicant to comply with a requirement of this Act or rules within a period which is—

(a)   set out in this Act or rules, or

(b)   specified by the comptroller.

(2)   Subject to subsection (3) below, the comptroller shall reinstate the application if, and only if—

(a)   the applicant requests him to do so;

(b)   the request complies with the relevant requirements of rules; and

(c)   he is satisfied that the failure to comply referred to in subsection (1) above was unintentional.

(3)   The comptroller shall not reinstate the application if—

(a)   an extension remains available under this Act or rules for the period referred to in subsection (1) above; or

(b) the period referred to in subsection (1) above is set out or specified—

    (i) in relation to any proceedings before the comptroller;

    (ii) for the purposes of section 5(2A)(b) above; or

    (iii) for the purposes of a request under this section or section 117B below.

(4) Where the application was made by two or more persons jointly, a request under subsection (2) above may, with the leave of the comptroller, be made by one or more of those persons without joining the others.

(5) If the application has been published under section 16 above, then the comptroller shall publish notice of a request under subsection (2) above in the prescribed manner.

(6) The reinstatement of an application under this section shall be by order.

(7) If an application is reinstated under this section the applicant shall comply with the requirement referred to in subsection (1) above within the further period specified by the comptroller in the order reinstating the application.

(8) The further period specified under subsection (7) above shall not be less than two months.

(9) If the applicant fails to comply with subsection (7) above the application shall be treated as having been withdrawn on the expiry of the period specified under that subsection.

20B Effect of reinstatement under section 20A

(1) The effect of reinstatement under section 20A of an application for a patent is as follows.

(2) Anything done under or in relation to the application during the period between termination and reinstatement shall be treated as valid.

(3) If the application has been published under section 16 above before its termination anything done during that period which would have constituted an infringement of the rights conferred by publication of the application if the termination had not occurred shall be treated as an infringement of those rights—

    (a) if done at a time when it was possible for the period referred to in section 20A(1) above to be extended, or

    (b) if it was a continuation or repetition of an earlier act infringing those rights.

(4) If the application has been published under section 16 above before its termination and, after the termination and before publication of notice of the request for its reinstatement, a person—

    (a) began in good faith to do an act which would have constituted an infringement of the rights conferred by publication of the application if the termination had not taken place, or

    (b) made in good faith effective and serious preparations to do such an act,

he has the right to continue to do the act or, as the case may be, to do the act, notwithstanding the reinstatement of the application and the grant of the patent; but this right does not extend to granting a licence to another person to do the act.

(4A) The right conferred by subsection (4) does not become exercisable until the end of the period during which a request may be made under this Act, or under the rules, for an extension of the period referred to in section 20A(1).

(5) If the act was done, or the preparations were made, in the course of a business, the person entitled to the right conferred by subsection (4) above may—

    (a) authorise the doing of that act by any partners of his for the time being in that business, and

    (b) assign that right, or transmit it on death (or in the case of a body corporate on its dissolution), to any person who acquires that part of the business in the course of which the act was done or the preparations were made.

(6) Where a product is disposed of to another in exercise of a right conferred by subsection or (5) above, that other and any person claiming through him may deal with the product in the same way as if it had been disposed of by the applicant.

(6A) The above provisions apply in relation to the use of a patented invention for the services of the Crown as they apply in relation to infringement of the rights conferred by publication of the application for a patent (or, as the case may be, infringement of the patent).

"Patented invention" has the same meaning as in section 55 below.

(7)   In this section "termination", in relation to an application, means—
      (a)   the refusal of the application, or
      (b)   the application being treated as having been refused or withdrawn.

21   Observations by third party on patentability

(1)   Where an application for a patent has been published but a patent has not been granted to the applicant, any other person may make observations in writing to the comptroller on the question whether the invention is a patentable invention, stating reasons for the observations, and the comptroller shall consider the observations in accordance with rules.

(2)   It is hereby declared that a person does not become a party to any proceedings under this Act before the comptroller by reason only that he makes observations under this section.

Security and safety

22   Information prejudicial to national security or safety of public

(1)   Where an application for a patent is filed in the Patent Office (whether under this Act or any treaty or international convention to which the United Kingdom is a party and whether before or after the appointed day) and it appears to the comptroller that the application contains information of a description notified to him by the Secretary of State as being information the publication of which might be prejudicial to national security, the comptroller may give directions prohibiting or restricting the publication of that information or its communication to any specified person or description of persons.

(2)   If it appears to the comptroller that any application so filed contains information the publication of which might be prejudicial to the safety of the public, he may give directions prohibiting or restricting the publication of that information or its communication to any specified person or description of persons until the end of a period not exceeding three months from the end of the period prescribed for the purposes of section 16 above.

(3)   While directions are in force under this section with respect to an application—
      (a)   if the application is made under this Act, it may proceed to the stage where it is in order for the grant of a patent, but it shall not be published and that information shall not be so communicated and no patent shall be granted in pursuance of the application;
      (b)   if it is an application for a European patent, it shall not be sent to the European Patent Office; and
      (c)   if it is an international application for a patent, a copy of it shall not be sent to the International Bureau or any international searching authority appointed under the Patent Co-operation Treaty.

(4)   Subsection (3)(b) above shall not prevent the comptroller from sending the European Patent Office any information which it is his duty to send that office under the European Patent Convention.

(5)   Where the comptroller gives directions under this section with respect to any application, he shall give notice of the application and of the directions to the Secretary of State, and the following provisions shall then have effect:—
      (a)   the Secretary of State shall, on receipt of the notice, consider whether the publication of the application or the publication or communication of the information in question would be prejudicial to national security or the safety of the public;
      (b)   if the Secretary of State determines under paragraph (a) above that the publication of the application or the publication or communication of that information would be prejudicial to the safety of the public, he shall notify the comptroller who shall continue his directions under subsection (2) above until they are revoked under paragraph (e) below;
      (c)   if the Secretary of State determines under paragraph (a) above that the publication of the application or the publication or communication of that information would be prejudicial to national security or the safety of the public,

he shall (unless a notice under paragraph (d) below has previously been given by the Secretary of State to the comptroller) reconsider that question during the period of nine months from the date of filing the application and at least once in every subsequent period of twelve months;

(d) if on consideration of an application at any time it appears to the Secretary of State that the publication of the application or the publication or communication of the information contained in it would not, or would no longer, be prejudicial to national security or the safety of the public, he shall give notice to the comptroller to that effect; and

(e) on receipt of such a notice the comptroller shall revoke the directions and may, subject to such conditions (if any) as he thinks fit, extend the time for doing anything required or authorised to be done by or under this Act in connection with the application, whether or not that time has previously expired.

(6) The Secretary of State may do the following for the purpose of enabling him to decide the question referred to in subsection (5)(c) above—

(a) where the application contains information relating to the production or use of atomic energy or research into matters connected with such production or use, he may at any time do one or both of the following, that is to say—

(i) inspect the application and any documents sent to the comptroller in connection with it;

(ii) authorise a government body with responsibility for the production of atomic energy or for research into matters connected with its production or use, or a person appointed by such a government body, to inspect the application and any documents sent to the comptroller in connection with it; and

(b) in any other case, he may at any time after (or, with the applicant's consent, before) the end of the period prescribed for the purposes of section 16 above inspect the application and any such documents;

and where a government body or a person appointed by a government body carries out an inspection which the body or person is authorised to carry out under paragraph (a) above, the body or (as the case may be) the person shall report on the inspection to the Secretary of State as soon as practicable.

(7) Where directions have been given under this section in respect of an application for a patent for an invention and, before the directions are revoked, that prescribed period expires and the application is brought in order for the grant of a patent, then—

(a) if while the directions are in force the invention is worked by (or with the written authorisation of or to the order of) a government department, the provisions of sections 55 to 59 below shall apply as if—

(i) the working were use made by section 55;

(ii) the application had been published at the end of that period; and

(iii) a patent had been granted for the invention at the time the application is brought in order for the grant of a patent (taking the terms of the patent to be those of the application as it stood at the time it was so brought in order); and

(b) if it appears to the Secretary of State that the applicant for the patent has suffered hardship by reason of the continuance in force of the directions, the Secretary of State may, with the consent of the Treasury, make such payment (if any) by way of compensation to the applicant as appears to the Secretary of State and the Treasury to be reasonable having regard to the inventive merit and utility of the invention, the purpose for which it is designed and any other relevant circumstances.

(8) Where a patent is granted in pursuance of an application in respect of which directions have been given under this section, no renewal fees shall be payable in respect of any period during which those directions were in force.

(9) A person who fails to comply with any direction under this section shall be liable—

(a) on summary conviction, to a fine not exceeding the prescribed sum; or

(b) on conviction on indictment, to imprisonment for a term not exceeding two years or a fine, or both.

23   Restrictions on applications abroad by United Kingdom residents

(1)   Subject to the following provisions of this section, no person resident in the United
Kingdom shall, without written authority granted by the comptroller, file or cause to
be filed outside the United Kingdom an application for a patent for an invention if
subsection (1A) below applies to that application, unless—

   (a)   an application for a patent for the same invention has been filed in the Patent
Office (whether before, on or after the appointed day) not less than six weeks
before the application outside the United Kingdom; and

   (b)   either no directions have been given under section 22 above in relation to the
application in the United Kingdom or all such directions have been revoked.

(1A) This subsection applies to an application if—

   (a)   the application contains information which relates to military technology or for
any other reason publication of the information might be prejudicial to national
security; or

   (b)   the application contains information the publication of which might be prejudicial
to the safety of the public.

(2)   Subsection (1) above does not apply to an application for a patent for an invention
for which an application for a patent has first been filed (whether before or after the
appointed day) in a country outside the United Kingdom by a person resident outside
the United Kingdom.

(3)   A person who files or causes to be filed an application for the grant of a patent in
contravention of this section shall be liable—

   (a)   on summary conviction, to a fine not exceeding the prescribed sum; or

   (b)   on conviction on indictment, to imprisonment for a term not exceeding two years
or a fine, or both.

(3A) A person is liable under subsection (3) above only if–

   (a)   he knows that filing the application, or causing it to be filed, would contravene
this section; or

   (b)   he is reckless as to whether filing the application, or causing it to be filed, would
contravene this section.

(4)   In this section—

   (a)   any reference to an application for a patent includes a reference to an application
for other protection for an invention;

   (b)   any reference to either kind of application is a reference to an application under
this Act, under the law of any country other than the United Kingdom or under
any treaty or international convention to which the United Kingdom is a party.

Provisions as to patents after grant

24   Publication and certificate of grant

(1)   As soon as practicable after a patent has been granted under this Act the comptroller
shall publish in the journal a notice that it has been granted.

. . .

(3)   The comptroller shall, at the same time as he publishes a notice under subsection (1)
above in relation to a patent publish the specification of the patent, the names of the
proprietor and (if different) the inventor and any other matters constituting or relating
to the patent which in the comptroller's opinion it is desirable to publish.

(4)   Subsection (3) above shall not require the comptroller to identify as inventor a person
who has waived his right to be mentioned as inventor in any patent granted for the
invention.

25   Term of patent

(1)   A patent granted under this Act shall be treated for the purposes of the following
provisions of this Act as having been granted, and shall take effect, on the date on
which notice of its grant is published in the journal and, subject to subsection (3)
below, shall continue in force until the end of the period of 20 years beginning with
the date of filing the application for the patent or with such other date as may be
prescribed.

. . .

(3)   Where any renewal fee in respect of a patent is not paid by the end of the period prescribed for payment (the "prescribed period") the patent shall cease to have effect at the end of such day, in the final month of that period, as may be prescribed.

(4)   If during the period ending with the sixth month after the month in which the prescribed period ends the renewal fee and any prescribed additional fee are paid, the patent shall be treated for the purposes of this Act as if it had never expired, and accordingly—

    (a)   anything done under or in relation to it during that further period shall be valid;

    (b)   an act which would constitute an infringement of it if it had not expired shall constitute such an infringement; and

    (c)   an act which would constitute the use of the patented invention for the services of the Crown if the patent had not expired shall constitute that use.

26   Patent not to be impugned for lack of unity

No person may in any proceeding object to a patent or to an amendment of a specification of a patent on the ground that the claims contained in the specification of the patent, as they stand or, as the case may be, as proposed to be amended, relate—

(a)   to more than one invention, or

(b)   to a group of inventions which are not so linked as to form a single inventive concept.

27   General power to amend specification after grant

(1)   Subject to the following provisions of this section and to section 76 below, the comptroller may, on an application made by the proprietor of a patent, allow the specification of the patent to be amended subject to such conditions, if any, as he thinks fit.

(2)   No such amendment shall be allowed under this section where there are pending before the court or the comptroller proceedings in which the validity of the patent may be put in issue.

(3)   An amendment of a specification of a patent under this section shall have effect and be deemed always to have had effect from the grant of the patent.

(4)   The comptroller may, without an application being made to him for the purpose, amend the specification of a patent so as to acknowledge a registered trade-mark.

(5)   A person may give notice to the comptroller of his opposition to an application under this section by the proprietor of a patent, and if he does so the comptroller shall notify the proprietor and consider the opposition in deciding whether to grant the application.

(6)   In considering whether or not to allow an application under this section, the comptroller shall have regard to any relevant principles applicable under the European Patent Convention.

28   Restoration of lapsed patents

(1)   Where a patent has ceased to have effect by reason of a failure to pay any renewal fee, an application for the restoration of the patent may be made to the comptroller within the prescribed period.

. . .

(2)   An application under this section may be made by the person who was the proprietor of the patent or by any other person who would have been entitled to the patent if it had not ceased to have effect; and where the patent was held by two or more persons jointly, the application may, with the leave of the comptroller, be made by one or more of them without joining the others.

(2A) Notice of the application shall be published by the comptroller in the prescribed manner.

(3)   If the comptroller is satisfied that the failure of the proprietor of the patent—

    (a)   to pay the renewal fee within the prescribed period; or

    (b)   to pay that fee and any prescribed additional fee within the period of six months immediately following the end of that period,

was unintentional, the comptroller shall by order restore the patent on payment of any unpaid renewal fee and any prescribed additional fee.

. . .

28A   Effect of order for restoration of patent

(1)   The effect of an order for the restoration of a patent is as follows.

(2)   Anything done under or in relation to the patent during the period between expiry and restoration shall be treated as valid.

(3)   Anything done during that period which would have constituted an infringement if the patent had not expired shall be treated as an infringement—

     (a)   if done at a time when it was possible for the patent to be renewed under section 25(4), or

     (b)   if it was a continuation or repetition of an earlier infringing act.

(4)   If after it was no longer possible for the patent to be so renewed, and before publication of notice of the application for restoration, a person—

     (a)   began in good faith to do an act which would have constituted an infringement of the patent if it had not expired, or

     (b)   made in good faith effective and serious preparations to do such an act,

     he has the right to continue to do the act or, as the case may be, to do the act, notwithstanding the restoration of the patent; but this right does not extend to granting a licence to another person to do the act.

(5)   If the act was done, or the preparations were made, in the course of a business, the person entitled to the right conferred by subsection (4) may—

     (a)   authorise the doing of that act by any partners of his for the time being in that business, and

     (b)   assign that right, or transmit it on death (or in the case of a body corporate on its dissolution), to any person who acquires that part of the business in the course of which the act was done or the preparations were made.

(6)   Where a product is disposed of to another in exercise of the rights conferred by subsection (4) or (5), that other and any person claiming through him may deal with the product in the same way as if it had been disposed of by the registered proprietor of the patent.

(7)   The above provisions apply in relation to the use of a patent for the services of the Crown as they apply in relation to infringement of the patent.

29   Surrender of patents

(1)   The proprietor of a patent may at any time by notice given to the comptroller offer to surrender his patent.

(2)   A person may give notice to the comptroller of his opposition to the surrender of a patent under this section, and if he does so the comptroller shall notify the proprietor of the patent and determine the question.

(3)   If the comptroller is satisfied that the patent may properly be surrendered, he may accept the offer and, as from the date when notice of his acceptance is published in the journal, the patent shall cease to have effect, but no action for infringement shall lie in respect of any act done before that date and no right to compensation shall accrue for any use of the patented invention before that date for the services of the Crown.

Property in patents and applications, and registration

30   Nature of, and transactions in, patents and applications for patents

(1)   Any patent or application for a patent is personal property (without being a thing in action), and any patent or any such application and rights in or under it may be transferred, created or granted in accordance with subsections (2) to (7) below.

(2)   Subject to section 36(3) below, any patent or any such application, or any right in it, may be assigned or mortgaged.

(3)   Any patent or any such application or right shall vest by operation of law in the same way as any other personal property and may be vested by an assent of personal representatives.

(4)   Subject to section 36(3) below, a licence may be granted under any patent or any such application for working the invention which is the subject of the patent or the application; and—

     (a)   to the extent that the licence so provides, a sub-licence may be granted under any such licence and any such licence or sub-licence may be assigned or mortgaged; and

      (b)   any such licence or sub-licence shall vest by operation of law in the same way as any other personal property and may be vested by an assent of personal representatives.

(5)   Subsections (2) to (4) above shall have effect subject to the following provisions of this Act.

(6)   Any of the following transactions, that is to say—

      (a)   any assignment or mortgage of a patent or any such application, or any right in a patent or any such application;

      (b)   any assent relating to any patent or any such application or right;

    shall be void unless it is in writing and is signed by or on behalf of the assignor or mortgagor (or, in the case of an assent or other transaction by a personal representative, by or on behalf of the personal representative)

(6A) If a transaction mentioned in subsection (6) above is by a body corporate, references in that subsection to such a transaction being signed by or on behalf of the assignor or mortgagor shall be taken to include references to its being under the seal of the body corporate.

(7)   An assignment of a patent or any such application or a share in it, and an exclusive licence granted under any patent or any such application, may confer on the assignee or licensee the right of the assignor or licensor to bring proceedings by virtue of section 61 or 69 below for a previous infringement or to bring proceedings under section 58 below for a previous act.

31 Nature of, and transactions in, patents and applications for patents in Scotland

(1)   Section 30 above shall not extend to Scotland, but instead the following provisions of this section shall apply there.

(2)   Any patent or application for a patent, and any right in or under any patent or any such application, is incorporeal moveable property, and the provisions of the following subsections and of section 36(3) below shall apply to any grant of licences, assignations and securities in relation to such property.

(3)   Any patent or any such application, or any right in it, may be assigned and security may be granted over a patent or any such application or right.

(4)   A licence may be granted, under any patent or any application for a patent, for working the invention which is the subject of the patent or the application.

(5)   To the extent that any licence granted under subsection (4) above so provides, a sub-licence may be granted under any such licence and any such licence or sub-licence may be assigned and security may be granted over it.

(6)   Any assignation or grant of security under this section may be carried out only by writing subscribed in accordance with the Requirements of Writing (Scotland) Act 1995.

(7)   An assignation of a patent or application for a patent or a share in it, and an exclusive licence granted under any patent or any such application, may confer on the assignee or licensee the right of the assignor or licensor to bring proceedings by virtue of section 61 or 69 below for a previous infringement or to bring proceedings under section 58 below for a previous act.

32 Register of patents etc.

(1)   The comptroller shall maintain the register of patents, which shall comply with rules made by virtue of this section and shall be kept in accordance with such rules.

(2)   Without prejudice to any other provision of this Act or rules, rules may make provision with respect to the following matters, including provision imposing requirements as to any of those matters—

      (a)   the registration of patents and of published applications for patents;

      (b)   the registration of transactions, instruments or events affecting rights in or under patents and applications;

      (ba) the entering on the register of notices concerning opinions issued, or to be issued, under section 74A below;

      (c)   the furnishing to the comptroller of any prescribed documents or description of documents in connection with any matter which is required to be registered;

    (d)   the correction of errors in the register and in any documents filed at the Patent Office in connection with registration; and

    (e)   the publication and advertisement of anything done under this Act or rules in relation to the register.

(2)   Notwithstanding anything in subsection (2)(b) above, no notice of any trust, whether express, implied or constructive, shall be entered in the register and the comptroller shall not be affected by any such notice.

. . .

(5)   Subject to rules, the public shall have a right to inspect the register at the Patent Office at all convenient times.

. . .

(9)   The register shall be prima facie evidence of anything required or authorised by this Act or rules to be registered and in Scotland shall be sufficient evidence of any such thing.

. . .

33   Effect of registration, etc., on rights in patents

(1)   Any person who claims to have acquired the property in a patent or application for a patent by virtue of any transaction, instrument or event to which this section applies shall be entitled as against any other person who claims to have acquired that property by virtue of an earlier transaction, instrument or event to which this section applies if, at the time of the later transaction, instrument or event—

    (a)   the earlier transaction, instrument or event was not registered, or

    (b)   in the case of any application which has not been published, notice of the earlier transaction, instrument or event had not been given to the comptroller, and

    (c)   in any case, the person claiming under the later transaction, instrument or event, did not know of the earlier transaction, instrument or event.

(2)   Subsection (1) above shall apply equally to the case where any person claims to have acquired any right in or under a patent or application for a patent, by virtue of a transaction, instrument or event to which this section applies, and that right is incompatible with any such right acquired by virtue of an earlier transaction, instrument or event to which this section applies.

(3)   This section applies to the following transactions, instruments and events:—

    (a)   the assignment or assignation of a patent or application for a patent, or a right in it;

    (b)   the mortgage of a patent or application or the granting of security over it;

    (c)   the grant, assignment or assignation of a licence or sub-licence, or mortgage of a licence or sub-licence, under a patent or application;

    (d)   the death of the proprietor or one of the proprietors of any such patent or application or any person having a right in or under a patent or application and the vesting by an assent of personal representatives of a patent, application or any such right; and

    (e)   any order or directions of a court or other competent authority—

        (i)   transferring a patent or application or any right in or under it to any person; or

        (ii)   that an application should proceed in the name of any person;

and in either case the event by virtue of which the court or authority had power to make any such order or give any such directions.

(4)   Where an application for the registration of a transaction, instrument or event has been made, but the transaction, instrument or event has not been registered, then, for the purposes of subsection (1)(a) above, registration of the application shall be treated as registration of the transaction, instrument or event.

34   Rectification of register

(1)   The court may, on the application of any person aggrieved, order the register to be rectified by the making, or the variation or deletion, of any entry in it.

(2)   In proceedings under this section the court may determine any question which it may be necessary or expedient to decide in connection with the rectification of the register.

. . .

36   Co-ownership of patents and applications for patents

(1)   Where a patent is granted to two or more persons, each of them shall, subject to any agreement to the contrary, be entitled to an equal undivided share in the patent.

(2)   Where two or more persons are proprietors of a patent, then, subject to the provisions of this section and subject to any agreement to the contrary—

    (a)   each of them shall be entitled, by himself or his agents, to do in respect of the invention concerned, for his own benefit and without the consent of or the need to account to the other or others, any act which would apart from this subsection and section 55 below, amount to an infringement of the patent concerned; and

    (b)   any such act shall not amount to an infringement of the patent concerned.

(3)   Subject to the provisions of sections 8 and 12 above and section 37 below and to any agreement for the time being in force, where two or more persons are proprietors of a patent one of them shall not without the consent of the other or others—

    (a)   amend the specification of the patent or apply for such an amendment to be allowed or for the patent to be revoked, or

    (b)   grant a licence under the patent or assign or mortgage a share in the patent or in Scotland cause or permit security to be granted over it.

(4)   Subject to the provisions of those sections, where two or more persons are proprietors of a patent, anyone else may supply one of those persons with the means, relating to an essential element of the invention, for putting the invention into effect, and the supply of those means by virtue of this subsection shall not amount to an infringement of the patent.

(5)   Where a patented product is disposed of by any of two or more proprietors to any person, that person and any other person claiming through him shall be entitled to deal with the product in the same way as if it had been disposed of by a sole registered proprietor.

(6)   Nothing in subsection (1) or (2) above shall affect the mutual rights or obligations of trustees or of the personal representatives of a deceased person, or their rights or obligations as such.

(7)   The foregoing provisions of this section shall have effect in relation to an application for a patent which is filed as they have effect in relation to a patent and—

    (a)   references to a patent and a patent being granted shall accordingly include references respectively to any such application and to the application being filed; and

    (b)   the reference in subsection (5) above to a patented product shall be construed accordingly.

37   Determination of right to patent after grant

(1)   After a patent has been granted for an invention any person having or claiming a proprietary interest in or under the patent may refer to the comptroller the question—

    (a)   who is or are the true proprietor or proprietors of the patent,

    (b)   whether the patent should have been granted to the person or persons to whom it was granted, or

    (c)   whether any right in or under the patent should be transferred or granted to any other person or persons;

and the comptroller shall determine the question and make such order as he thinks fit to give effect to the determination.

. . .

(4)   Where the comptroller finds on a reference under this section that the patent was granted to a person not entitled to be granted that patent (whether alone or with other persons) and on an application made under section 72 below makes an order on that ground for the conditional or unconditional revocation of the patent, the comptroller may order that the person by whom the application was made or his successor in title may, subject to section 76 below, make a new application for a patent—

    (a)   in the case of unconditional revocation, for the whole of the matter comprised in the specification of that patent; and

    (b)   in the case of conditional revocation, for the matter which in the opinion of the comptroller should be excluded from that specification by amendment under section 75 below;

and where such a new application is made, it shall be treated as having been filed on the date of filing the application for the patent to which the reference relates.

(5)   On any such reference no order shall be made under this section transferring the patent to which the reference relates on the ground that the patent was granted to a person not so entitled, and no order shall be made under subsection (4) above on that ground, if the reference was made the second anniversary of the date of the grant, unless it is shown that any person registered as a proprietor of the patent knew at the time of the grant or, as the case may be, of the transfer of the patent to him that he was not entitled to the patent.

. . .

38   Effect of transfer of patent under s. 37

(1)   Where an order is made under section 37 above that a patent shall be transferred from any person or persons (the old proprietor or proprietors) to one or more persons (whether or not including an old proprietor), then, except in a case falling within subsection (2) below, any licences or other rights granted or created by the old proprietor or proprietors shall, subject to section 33 above and to the provisions of the order, continue in force and be treated as granted by the person or persons to whom the patent is ordered to be transferred (the new proprietor or proprietors).

(2)   Where an order is so made that a patent shall be transferred from the old proprietor or proprietors to one or more persons none of whom was an old proprietor (on the ground that the patent was granted to a person not entitled to be granted the patent), any licences or other rights in or under the patent shall, subject to the provisions of the order and subsection (3) below, lapse on the registration of that person or those persons as the new proprietor or proprietors of the patent.

(3)   Where an order is so made that a patent shall be transferred as mentioned in subsection (2) above or that a person other than an old proprietor may make a new application for a patent and before the reference of the question under that section resulting in the making of any such order is registered, the old proprietor or proprietors or a licensee of the patent, acting in good faith, worked the invention in question in the United Kingdom or made effective and serious preparations to do so, the old proprietor or proprietors or the licensee shall, on making a request to the new proprietor or proprietors or, as the case may be, the new applicant within the prescribed period, be entitled to be granted a licence (but not an exclusive licence) to continue working or, as the case may be, to work the invention, so far as it is the subject of the new application.

. . .

Employees' inventions

39   Right to employees' inventions

(1)   Notwithstanding anything in any rule of law, an invention made by an employee shall, as between him and his employer, be taken to belong to his employer for the purposes of this Act and all other purposes if—

(a)   it was made in the course of the normal duties of the employee or in the course of duties falling outside his normal duties, but specifically assigned to him, and the circumstances in either case were such that an invention might reasonably be expected to result from the carrying out of his duties; or

(b)   the invention was made in the course of the duties of the employee and, at the time of making the invention, because of the nature of his duties and the particular responsibilities arising from the nature of his duties he had a special obligation to further the interests of the employer's undertaking.

(2)   Any other invention made by an employee shall, as between him and his employer, be taken for those purposes to belong to the employee.

(3)   Where by virtue of this section an invention belongs, as between him and his employer, to an employee, nothing done—

(a)   by or on behalf of the employee or any person claiming under him for the purposes of pursuing an application for a patent, or

(b)   by any person for the purpose of performing or working the invention,

shall be taken to infringe any copyright or design right to which, as between him and his employer, his employer is entitled in any model or document relating to the invention.

40   Compensation of employees for certain inventions

(1)   Where it appears to the court or the comptroller on an application made by an employee within the prescribed period that—

(a)   the employee has made an invention belonging to the employer for which a patent has been granted,

(b)   having regard among other things to the size and nature of the employer's undertaking, the invention or the patent for it (or the combination of both) is of outstanding benefit to the employer, and

(c)   by reason of those facts it is just that the employee should be awarded compensation to be paid by the employer,

the court or the comptroller may award him such compensation of an amount determined under section 41 below.

(2)   Where it appears to the court or the comptroller on an application made by an employee within the prescribed period that—

(a)   a patent has been granted for an invention made by and belonging to the employee;

(b)   his rights in the invention, or in any patent or application for a patent for the invention, have since the appointed day been assigned to the employer or an exclusive licence under the patent or application has since the appointed day been granted to the employer;

(c)   the benefit derived by the employee from the contract of assignment, assignation or grant or any ancillary contract ("the relevant contract") is inadequate in relation to the benefit derived by the employer from the invention or the patent for it (or both); and

(d)   by reason of those facts it is just that the employee should be awarded compensation to be paid by the employer in addition to the benefit derived from the relevant contract;

the court or the comptroller may award him such compensation of an amount determined under section 41 below.

(3)   Subsections (1) and (2) above shall not apply to the invention of an employee where a relevant collective agreement provides for the payment of compensation in respect of inventions of the same description as that invention to employees of the same description as that employee.

(4)   Subsection (2) above shall have effect notwithstanding anything in the relevant contract or any agreement applicable to the invention (other than any such collective agreement).

(5)   If it appears to the comptroller on an application under this section that the application involves matters which would more properly be determined by the court, he may decline to deal with it.

(6)   In this section—

"the prescribed period", in relation to proceedings before the court, means the period prescribed by rules of court, and

"relevant collective agreement" means a collective agreement within the meaning of the Trade Union and Labour Relations (Consolidation) Act 1992, made by or on behalf of a trade union to which the employee belongs, and by the employer or an employers' association to which the employer belongs which is in force at the time of the making of the invention.

(7)   References in this section to an invention belonging to an employer or employee are references to it so belonging as between the employer and the employee.

41   Amount of compensation

(1)   An award of compensation to an employee under section 40(1) or (2) above shall be such as will secure for the employee a fair share (having regard to all the circumstances) of the benefit which the employer has derived, or may reasonably be expected to derive, from any of the following—

(a)   the invention in question;

(b)   the patent for the invention;

    (c)   the assignment, assignation or grant of—
        (i)   the property or any right in the invention, or
        (ii)   the property in, or any right in or under, an application for the patent,
    to a person connected with the employer.

(2)   For the purposes of subsection (1) above the amount of any benefit derived or expected to be derived by an employer from the assignment, assignation or grant of—

    (a)   the property in, or any right in or under, a patent for the invention or an application for such a patent; or

    (b)   the property or any right in the invention;

    to a person connected with him shall be taken to be the amount which could reasonably be expected to be so derived by the employer if that person had not been connected with him.

(3)   Where the Crown, United Kingdom Research and Innovation or a Research Council in its capacity as employer assigns or grants the property in, or any right in or under, an invention, patent or application for a patent to a body having among its functions that of developing or exploiting inventions resulting from public research and does so for no consideration or only a nominal consideration, any benefit derived from the invention, patent or application by that body shall be treated for the purposes of the foregoing provisions of this section as so derived by the Crown or, United Kingdom Research and Innovation or the Research Council (as the case may be).
    In this subsection "Research Council" means a body which is a Research Council for the purposes of the Science and Technology Act 1965.

(4)   In determining the fair share of the benefit to be secured for an employee in respect of an invention which has always belonged to an employer, the court or the comptroller shall, among other things, take the following matters into account, that is to say—

    (a)   the nature of the employee's duties, his remuneration and the other advantages he derives or has derived from his employment or has derived in relation to the invention under this Act;

    (b)   the effort and skill which the employee has devoted to making the invention;

    (c)   the effort and skill which any other person has devoted to making the invention jointly with the employee concerned, and the advice and other assistance contributed by any other employee who is not a joint inventor of the invention; and

    (d)   the contribution made by the employer to the making, developing and working of the invention by the provision of advice, facilities and other assistance, by the provision of opportunities and by his managerial and commercial skill and activities.

(5)   In determining the fair share of the benefit to be secured for an employee in respect of an invention which originally belonged to him, the court or the comptroller shall, among other things, take the following matters into account, that is to say—

    (a)   any conditions in a licence or licences granted under this Act or otherwise in respect of the invention or the patent for it;

    (b)   the extent to which the invention was made jointly by the employee with any other person; and

    (c)   the contribution made by the employer to the making, developing and working of the invention as mentioned in subsection (4)(d) above.

(6)   Any order for the payment of compensation under section 40 above may be an order for the payment of a lump sum or for periodical payment, or both.

(7)   Without prejudice to section 12 or section 14 of the Interpretation Act 1978, the refusal of the court or the comptroller to make any such order on an application made by an employee under section 40 above shall not prevent a further application being made under that section by him or any successor in title of his.

(8)   Where the court or the comptroller has made any such order, the court or he may on the application of either the employer or the employee vary or discharge it or suspend any provision of the order and revive any provision so suspended, and

section 40(5) above shall apply to the application as it applies to an application under that section.

. . .

42 Enforceability of contracts relating to employees' inventions

(1) This section applies to any contract (whenever made) relating to inventions made by an employee, being a contract entered into by him—

  (a) with the employer (alone or with another); or

  (b) with some other person at the request of the employer or in pursuance of the employee's contract of employment.

(2) Any term in a contract to which this section applies which diminishes the employee's rights in inventions of any description made by him after the appointed day and the date of the contract, or in or under patents for those inventions or applications for such patents, shall be unenforceable against him to the extent that it diminishes his rights in an invention of that description so made, or in or under a patent for such an invention or an application for any such patent.

(3) Subsection (2) above shall not be construed as derogating from any duty of confidentiality owed to his employer by an employee by virtue of any rule of law or otherwise.

(4) This section applies to any arrangement made with a Crown employee by or on behalf of the Crown as his employer as it applies to any contract made between an employee and an employer other than the Crown, and for the purposes of this section "Crown employee" means a person employed under or for the purposes of a government department or any officer or body exercising on behalf of the Crown functions conferred by any enactment or a person serving in the naval, military or air forces of the Crown.

43 Supplementary

(1) Sections 39 to 42 above shall not apply to an invention made before the appointed day.

(2) Sections 39 to 42 above shall not apply to an invention made by an employee unless at the time he made the invention one of the following conditions was satisfied in his case, that is to say—

  (a) he was mainly employed in the United Kingdom; or

  (b) he was not mainly employed anywhere or his place of employment could not be determined, but his employer had a place of business in the United Kingdom to which the employee was attached, whether or not he was also attached elsewhere.

(3) In sections 39 to 42 above and this section, except so far as the context otherwise requires, references to the making of an invention by an employee are references to his making it alone or jointly with any other person, but do not include references to his merely contributing advice or other assistance in the making of an invention by another employee.

(4) Any references in sections 39 to 42 above to a patent and to a patent being granted are respectively references to a patent or other protection and to its being granted whether under the law of the United Kingdom or the law in force in any other country or under any treaty or international convention.

(5) For the purposes of sections 40 and 41 above the benefit derived or expected to be derived by an employer from an invention or a patent shall, where he dies before any award is made under section 40 above in respect of it, include any benefit derived or expected to be derived from the patent by his personal representatives or by any person in whom it was vested by their assent.

(5A) For the purposes of sections 40 and 41 above the benefit derived or expected to be derived by an employer from an invention shall not include any benefit derived or expected to be derived from the invention after the patent for it has expired or has been surrendered or revoked.

(6) Where an employee dies before an award is made under section 40 above in respect of a patented invention made by him, his personal representatives or their successors in title may exercise his right to make or proceed with an application for compensation under subsection (1) or (2) of that section.

(7) In sections 40 and 41 above and this section "benefit" means benefit in money or money's worth.

Licences of right and compulsory licences

46 Patentee's application for entry in register that licences are available as of right

(1) At any time after the grant of a patent its proprietor may apply to the comptroller for an entry to be made in the register to the effect that licences under the patent are to be available as of right.

(2) Where such an application is made, the comptroller shall give notice of the application to any person registered as having a right in or under the patent and, if satisfied that the proprietor of the patent is not precluded by contract from granting licences under the patent, shall make that entry.

(3) Where such an entry is made in respect of a patent—

(a) any person shall, at any time after the entry is made, be entitled as of right to a licence under the patent on such terms as may be settled by agreement or, in default of agreement, by the comptroller on the application of the proprietor of the patent or the person requiring the licence;

(b) the comptroller may, on the application of the holder of any licence granted under the patent before the entry was made, order the licence to be exchanged for a licence of right on terms so settled;

(c) if in proceedings for infringement of the patent (otherwise than by the importation of any article from a country which is not a member State of the European Union) the defendant or defender undertakes to take a licence on such terms, no injunction or interdict shall be granted against him and the amount (if any) recoverable against him by way of damages shall not exceed double the amount which would have been payable by him as licensee if such a licence on those terms had been granted before the earliest infringement;

(d) if the expiry date in relation to a renewal fee falls after the date of the entry, that fee shall be half the fee which would be payable had the entry not been made.

(3A) An undertaking under subsection (3)(c) above may be given at any time before final order in the proceedings, without any admission of liability.

(3B) For the purposes of subsection (3)(d) above the expiry date in relation to a renewal fee is the day at the end of which, by virtue of section 25(3) above, the patent in question ceases to have effect if that fee is not paid.

(4) The licensee under a licence of right may (unless, in the case of a licence the terms of which are settled by agreement, the licence otherwise expressly provides) request the proprietor of the patent to take proceedings to prevent any infringement of the patent; and if the proprietor refuses or neglects to do so within two months after being so requested, the licensee may institute proceedings for the infringement in his own name as if he were proprietor, making the proprietor a defendant or defender.

(5) A proprietor so added as defendant or defender shall not be liable for any costs or expenses unless he enters an appearance and takes part in the proceedings.

47 Cancellation of entry made under s. 46

(1) At any time after an entry has been made under section 46 above in respect of a patent, the proprietor of the patent may apply to the comptroller for cancellation of the entry.

. . .

(3) Within the prescribed period after an entry has been made under section 46 above in respect of a patent, any person who claims that the proprietor of the patent is, and was at the time of the entry, precluded by a contract in which the claimant is interested from granting licences under the patent may apply to the comptroller for cancellation of the entry.

. . .

48   Compulsory licences: general

(1)   At any time after the expiration of three years, or of such other period as may be prescribed, from the date of the grant of a patent, any person may apply to the comptroller on one or more of the relevant grounds—

   (a)   for a licence under the patent;

   (b)   for an entry to be made in the register to the effect that licences under the patent are to be available as of right; or

   (c)   where the applicant is a government department, for the grant to any person specified in the application of a licence under the patent.

(2)   Subject to sections 48A and 48B below, if he is satisfied that any of the relevant grounds are established, the comptroller may—

   (a)   where the application is under subsection (1)(a) above, order the grant of a licence to the applicant on such terms as the comptroller thinks fit;

   (b)   where the application is under subsection (1)(b) above, make such an entry as is there mentioned;

   (c)   where the application is under subsection (1)(c) above, order the grant of a licence to the person specified in the application on such terms as the comptroller thinks fit.

(3)   An application may be made under this section in respect of a patent even though the applicant is already the holder of a licence under the patent; and no person shall be estopped or barred from alleging any of the matters specified in the relevant grounds by reason of any admission made by him, whether in such a licence or otherwise, or by reason of his having accepted a licence.

(4)   In this section "the relevant grounds" means—

   (a)   in the case of an application made in respect of a patent whose proprietor is a WTO proprietor, the grounds set out in section 48A(1) below;

   (b)   in any other case, the grounds set out in section 48B(1) below.

(5)   A proprietor is a WTO proprietor for the purposes of this section and sections 48A, 48B, 50 and 52 below if—

   (a)   he is a national of, or is domiciled in, a country which is a member of the World Trade Organisation; or

   (b)   he has a real and effective industrial or commercial establishment in such a country.

(6)   . . .

48A   Compulsory licences: WTO proprietors

(1)   In the case of an application made under section 48 above in respect of a patent whose proprietor is a WTO proprietor, the relevant grounds are—

   (a)   where the patented invention is a product, that a demand in the United Kingdom for that product is not being met on reasonable terms;

   (b)   that by reason of the refusal of the proprietor of the patent concerned to grant a licence or licences on reasonable terms—

      (i)   the exploitation in the United Kingdom of any other patented invention which involves an important technical advance of considerable economic significance in relation to the invention for which the patent concerned was granted is prevented or hindered, or

      (ii)   the establishment or development of commercial or industrial activities in the United Kingdom is unfairly prejudiced;

   (c)   that by reason of conditions imposed by the proprietor of the patent concerned on the grant of licences under the patent, or on the disposal or use of the patented product or on the use of the patented process, the manufacture, use or disposal of materials not protected by the patent, or the establishment or development of commercial or industrial activities in the United Kingdom, is unfairly prejudiced.

(2)   No order or entry shall be made under section 48 above in respect of a patent whose proprietor is a WTO proprietor unless—

   (a)   the applicant has made efforts to obtain a licence from the proprietor on reasonable commercial terms and conditions; and

   (b)   his efforts have not been successful within a reasonable period.

(3) No order or entry shall be so made if the patented invention is in the field of semi-conductor technology.

(4) No order or entry shall be made under section 48 above in respect of a patent on the ground mentioned in subsection (1)(b)(i) above unless the comptroller is satisfied that the proprietor of the patent for the other invention is able and willing to grant the proprietor of the patent concerned and his licensees a licence under the patent for the other invention on reasonable terms.

(5) A licence granted in pursuance of an order or entry so made shall not be assigned except to a person to whom the patent for the other invention is also assigned.

(6) A licence granted in pursuance of an order or entry made under section 48 above in respect of a patent whose proprietor is a WTO proprietor—

(a) shall not be exclusive;

(b) shall not be assigned except to a person to whom there is also assigned the part of the enterprise that enjoys the use of the patented invention, or the part of the goodwill that belongs to that part;

(c) shall be predominantly for the supply of the market in the United Kingdom;

(d) shall include conditions entitling the proprietor of the patent concerned to remuneration adequate in the circumstances of the case, taking into account the economic value of the licence; and

(e) shall be limited in scope and in duration to the purpose for which the licence was granted.

48B Compulsory licences: other cases

(1) In the case of an application made under section 48 above in respect of a patent whose proprietor is not a WTO proprietor, the relevant grounds are—

(a) where the patented invention is capable of being commercially worked in the United Kingdom, that it is not being so worked or is not being so worked to the fullest extent that is reasonably practicable;

(b) where the patented invention is a product, that a demand for the product in the United Kingdom—

(i) is not being met on reasonable terms, or

(ii) is being met to a substantial extent by importation from a country which is not a member State;

(c) where the patented invention is capable of being commercially worked in the United Kingdom, that it is being prevented or hindered from being so worked—

(i) where the invention is a product, by the importation of the product from a country which is not a member State,

(ii) where the invention is a process, by the importation from such a country of a product obtained directly by means of the process or to which the process has been applied;

(d) that by reason of the refusal of the proprietor of the patent to grant a licence or licences on reasonable terms—

(i) a market for the export of any patented product made in the United Kingdom is not being supplied, or

(ii) the working or efficient working in the United Kingdom of any other patented invention which makes a substantial contribution to the art is prevented or hindered, or

(iii) the establishment or development of commercial or industrial activities in the United Kingdom is unfairly prejudiced;

(e) that by reason of conditions imposed by the proprietor of the patent on the grant of licences under the patent, or on the disposal or use of the patented product or on the use of the patented process, the manufacture, use or disposal of materials not protected by the patent, or the establishment or development of commercial or industrial activities in the United Kingdom, is unfairly prejudiced.

(2) Where—

(a) an application is made on the ground that the patented invention is not being commercially worked in the United Kingdom or is not being so worked to the fullest extent that is reasonably practicable; and

(b) it appears to the comptroller that the time which has elapsed since the publication in the journal of a notice of the grant of the patent has for any reason been insufficient to enable the invention to be so worked,

he may by order adjourn the application for such period as will in his opinion give sufficient time for the invention to be so worked.

(3) No order or entry shall be made under section 48 above in respect of a patent on the ground mentioned in subsection (1)(a) above if—

(a) the patented invention is being commercially worked in a country which is a member State; and

(b) demand in the United Kingdom is being met by importation from that country.

(4) No entry shall be made in the register under section 48 above on the ground mentioned in subsection (1)(d)(i) above, and any licence granted under section 48 above on that ground shall contain such provisions as appear to the comptroller to be expedient for restricting the countries in which any product concerned may be disposed of or used by the licensee.

(5) No order or entry shall be made under section 48 above in respect of a patent on the ground mentioned in subsection (1)(d)(ii) above unless the comptroller is satisfied that the proprietor of the patent for the other invention is able and willing to grant to the proprietor of the patent concerned and his licensees a licence under the patent for the other invention on reasonable terms.

49 Provisions about licences under s. 48

(1) Where the comptroller is satisfied, on an application made under section 48 above in respect of a patent, that the manufacture, use or disposal of materials not protected by the patent is unfairly prejudiced by reason of conditions imposed by the proprietor of the patent on the grant of licences under the patent, or on the disposal or use of the patented product or the use of the patented process, he may (subject to the provisions of that section) order the grant of licences under the patent to such customers of the applicant as he thinks fit as well as to the applicant.

(2) Where an application under section 48 above is made in respect of a patent by a person who holds a licence under the patent, the comptroller—

(a) may, if he orders the grant of a licence to the applicant, order the existing licence to be cancelled, or

(b) may, instead of ordering the grant of a licence to the applicant, order the existing licence to be amended.

(3) . . .

(4) Section 46(4) and (5) above shall apply to a licence granted in pursuance of an order under section 48 above and to a licence granted by virtue of an entry under that section as it applies to a licence granted by virtue of an entry under section 46 above.

50 Exercise of powers on applications under s. 48

(1) The powers of the comptroller on an application under section 48 above in respect of a patent whose proprietor is not a WTO proprietor shall be exercised with a view to securing the following general purposes:—

(a) that inventions which can be worked on a commercial scale in the United Kingdom and which should in the public interest be so worked shall be worked there without undue delay and to the fullest extent that is reasonably practicable;

(b) that the inventor or other person beneficially entitled to a patent shall receive reasonable remuneration having regard to the nature of the invention;

(c) that the interests of any person for the time being working or developing an invention in the United Kingdom under the protection of a patent shall not be unfairly prejudiced.

(2) Subject to subsection (1) above, the comptroller shall, in determining whether to make an order or entry in pursuance of any application under section 48 above, take account of the following matters, that is to say—

(a) the nature of the invention, the time which has elapsed since the publication in the journal of a notice of the grant of the patent and the measures already taken by the proprietor of the patent or any licensee to make full use of the invention;

(b)   the ability of any person to whom a licence would be granted under the order concerned to work the invention to the public advantage; and

(c)   the risks to be undertaken by that person in providing capital and working the invention if the application for an order is granted,

but shall not be required to take account of matters subsequent to the making of the application.

50A   Powers exercisable following merger and market investigations

(1)   Subsection (2) below applies where—

(a)   section 41(2), 55(2), 66(6), 75(2), 83(2), 138(2), 147(2)[, 147A(2)] or 160(2) of, or paragraph 5(2) or 10(2) of Schedule 7 to, the Enterprise Act 2002 (powers to take remedial action following merger or market investigations) applies;

(b)   the [Competition and Markets Authority] or (as the case may be) the Secretary of State considers that it would be appropriate to make an application under this section for the purpose of remedying, mitigating or preventing a matter which cannot be dealt with under the enactment concerned; and

(c)   the matter concerned involves—

(i)   conditions in licences granted under a patent by its proprietor restricting the use of the invention by the licensee or the right of the proprietor to grant other licences; or

(ii)   a refusal by the proprietor of a patent to grant licences on reasonable terms.

(2)   The [Competition and Markets Authority] or (as the case may be) the Secretary of State may apply to the comptroller to take action under this section.

(3)   Before making an application the [Competition and Markets Authority] or (as the case may be) the Secretary of State shall publish, in such manner as it or he thinks appropriate, a notice describing the nature of the proposed application and shall consider any representations which may be made within 30 days of such publication by persons whose interests appear to it or him to be affected.

(4)   The comptroller may, if it appears to him on an application under this section that the application is made in accordance with this section, by order cancel or modify any condition concerned of the kind mentioned in subsection (1)(c)(i) above or may, instead or in addition, make an entry in the register to the effect that licences under the patent are to be available as of right.

. . .

51   Powers exercisable in consequence of report of Competition and Markets Authority

(1)   Where a report of the Competition and Markets Authority has been laid before Parliament containing conclusions to the effect—

. . .

(c)   on a competition reference, that a person was engaged in an anti-competitive practice which operated or may be expected to operate against the public interest, or

(d)   on a reference under section 11 of the Competition Act 1980 (reference of public bodies and certain other persons), that a person is pursuing a course of conduct which operates against the public interest,

the appropriate Minister or Ministers may apply to the comptroller to take action under this section.

(2)   Before making an application the appropriate Minister or Ministers shall publish, in such manner as he or they think appropriate, a notice describing the nature of the proposed application and shall consider any representations which may be made within 30 days of such publication by persons whose interests appear to him or them to be affected.

(3)   If on an application under this section it appears to the comptroller that the matters specified in the Competition and Markets Authority's report as being those which in the opinion of the Competition and Markets Authority operate, or operated or may be expected to operate, against the public interest include—

(a)   conditions in licences granted under a patent by its proprietor restricting the use of the invention by the licensee or the right of the proprietor to grant other licences, or

(b) a refusal by the proprietor of a patent to grant licences on reasonable terms

he may by order cancel or modify any such condition or may, instead or in addition, make an entry in the register to the effect that licences under the patent are to be available as of right.

(4) In this section "the appropriate Minister or Ministers" means the Minister or Ministers to whom the report of the Competition and Markets Authority was made.

52 Opposition, appeal and arbitration

(1) The proprietor of the patent concerned or any other person wishing to oppose an application under sections 48 to 51 above may, in accordance with rules, give to the comptroller notice of opposition; and the comptroller shall consider any opposition in deciding whether to grant the application.

(2) Where an order or entry has been made under section 48 above in respect of a patent whose proprietor is a WTO proprietor—

(a) the proprietor or any other person may, in accordance with rules, apply to the comptroller to have the order revoked or the entry cancelled on the grounds that the circumstances which led to the making of the order or entry have ceased to exist and are unlikely to recur;

(b) any person wishing to oppose an application under paragraph (a) above may, in accordance with rules, give to the comptroller notice of opposition; and

(c) the comptroller shall consider any opposition in deciding whether to grant the application.

(3) If it appears to the comptroller on an application under subsection (2)(a) above that the circumstances which led to the making of the order or entry have ceased to exist and are unlikely to recur, he may—

(a) revoke the order or cancel the entry; and

(b) terminate any licence granted to a person in pursuance of the order or entry subject to such terms and conditions as he thinks necessary for the protection of the legitimate interests of that person.

. . .

53 Compulsory licences; supplementary provisions

. . .

(3) The comptroller may make an entry in the register under sections 48 to 51 above notwithstanding any contract which would have precluded the entry on the application of the proprietor of the patent under section 46 above.

(4) An entry made in the register under sections 48 to 51 above shall for all purposes have the same effect as an entry made under section 46 above.

(5) No order or entry shall be made in pursuance of an application under sections 48 to 51 above which would be at variance with any treaty or international convention to which the United Kingdom is a party.

Use of patented inventions for services of the Crown

55 Use of patented inventions for services of the Crown

(1) Notwithstanding anything in this Act, any government department and any person authorised in writing by a government department may, for the services of the Crown and in accordance with this section, do any of the following acts in the United Kingdom in relation to a patented invention without the consent of the proprietor of the patent, that is to say—

(a) where the invention is a product, may—

(i) make, use, import or keep the product, or sell or offer to sell it where to do so would be incidental or ancillary to making, using, importing or keeping it; or

(ii) in any event, sell or offer to sell it for foreign defence purposes or for the production or supply of specified drugs and medicines, or dispose or offer to dispose of it (otherwise than by selling it) for any purpose whatever;

(b) where the invention is a process, may use it or do in relation to any product obtained directly by means of the process anything mentioned in paragraph (a) above;

(c)   without prejudice to the foregoing, where the invention or any product obtained directly by means of the invention is a specified drug or medicine, may sell or offer to sell the drug or medicine;

(d)   may supply or offer to supply to any person any of the means, relating to an essential element of the invention, for putting the invention into effect;

(e)   may dispose or offer to dispose of anything which was made, used, imported or kept in the exercise of the powers conferred by this section and which is no longer required for the purpose for which it was made, used, imported or kept (as the case may be),

and anything done by virtue of this subsection shall not amount to an infringement of the patent concerned.

. . .

56   Interpretation, etc., of provisions about Crown use

(1)   Any reference in section 55 above to a patented invention, in relation to any time, is a reference to an invention for which a patent has before that time been, or is subsequently, granted.

(2)   In this Act, except so far as the context otherwise requires, "the services of the Crown" includes—

(a)   the supply of anything for foreign defence purposes;

(b)   the production or supply of specified drugs and medicines; and

(c)   such purposes relating to the production or use of atomic energy or research into matters connected therewith as the Secretary of State thinks necessary or expedient;

and "use for the services of the Crown" shall be construed accordingly.

. . .

57   Rights of third parties in respect of Crown use

(1)   In relation to—

(a)   any use made for the services of the Crown of an invention by a government department, or a person authorised by a government department, by virtue of section 55 above, or

(b)   anything done for the services of the Crown to the order of a government department by the proprietor of a patent in respect of a patented invention or by the proprietor of an application in respect of an invention for which an application for a patent has been filed and is still pending,

the provisions of any licence, assignment, assignation or agreement to which this subsection applies shall be of no effect so far as those provisions restrict or regulate the working of the invention, or the use of any model, document or information relating to it, or provide for the making of payments in respect of, or calculated by reference to, such working or use; and the reproduction or publication of any model or document in connection with the said working or use shall not be deemed to be an infringement of any copyright or design right subsisting in the model or document or of any topography right.

. . .

57A   Compensation for loss of profit

(1)   Where use is made of an invention for the services of the Crown, the government department concerned shall pay—

(a)   to the proprietor of the patent, or

(b)   if there is an exclusive licence in force in respect of the patent, to the exclusive licensee,

compensation for any loss resulting from his not being awarded a contract to supply the patented product or, as the case may be, to perform the patented process or supply a thing made by means of the patented process.

(2)   Compensation is payable only to the extent that such a contract could have been fulfilled from his existing manufacturing or other capacity; but is payable notwithstanding the existence of circumstances rendering him ineligible for the award of such a contract.

(3)   In determining the loss, regard shall be had to the profit which would have been made on such a contract and to the extent to which any manufacturing or other capacity was underused.

(4)   No compensation is payable in respect of any failure to secure contracts to supply the patented product or, as the case may be, to perform the patented process or supply a thing made by means of the patented process, otherwise than for the services of the Crown.

(5)   The amount payable shall, if not agreed between the proprietor or licensee and the government department concerned with the approval of the Treasury, be determined by the court on a reference under section 58, and is in addition to any amount payable under section 55 or 57.

(6)   In this section "the government department concerned", in relation to any use of an invention for the services of the Crown, means the government department by whom or on whose authority the use was made.

(7)   In the application of this section to Northern Ireland, the reference in subsection (5) above to the Treasury shall, where the government department concerned is a department of the Government of Northern Ireland, be construed as a reference to the Department of Finance and Personnel.

58   References of disputes as to Crown use

(1)   Any dispute as to—

    (a)   the exercise by a government department, or a person authorised by a government department, of the powers conferred by section 55 above,

    (b)   terms for the use of an invention for the services of the Crown under that section,

    (c)   the right of any person to receive any part of a payment made in pursuance of subsection (4) of that section, or

    (d)   the right of any person to receive a payment under section 57A,

may be referred to the court by either party to the dispute after a patent has been granted for the invention.

(2)   If in such proceedings any question arises whether an invention has been recorded or tried as mentioned in section 55 above, and the disclosure of any document recording the invention, or of any evidence of the trial thereof, would in the opinion of the department be prejudicial to the public interest, the disclosure may be made confidentially to the other party's legal representative or to an independent expert mutually agreed upon.

(3)   In determining under this section any dispute between a government department and any person as to the terms for the use of an invention for the services of the Crown, the court shall have regard—

    (a)   to any benefit or compensation which that person or any person from whom he derives title may have received or may be entitled to receive directly or indirectly from any government department in respect of the invention in question;

    (b)   to whether that person or any person from whom he derives title has in the court's opinion without reasonable cause failed to comply with a request of the department to use the invention for the services of the Crown on reasonable terms.

. . .

(13)   One of two or more joint proprietors of a patent or application for a patent may without the concurrence of the others refer a dispute to the court under this section, but shall not do so unless the others are made parties to the proceedings; but any of the others made a defendant or defender shall not be liable for any costs or expenses unless he enters an appearance and takes part in the proceedings.

Infringement

60   Meaning of infringement

(1)   Subject to the provisions of this section, a person infringes a patent for an invention if, but only if, while the patent is in force, he does any of the following things in the United Kingdom in relation to the invention without the consent of the proprietor of the patent, that is to say—

    (a)   where the invention is a product, he makes, disposes of, offers to dispose of, uses or imports the product or keeps it whether for disposal or otherwise;

    (b)   where the invention is a process, he uses the process or he offers it for use in the United Kingdom when he knows, or it is obvious to a reasonable person in the circumstances, that its use there without the consent of the proprietor would be an infringement of the patent;

(c)   where the invention is a process, he disposes of, offers to dispose of, uses or imports any product obtained directly by means of that process or keeps any such product whether for disposal or otherwise.

(2) Subject to the following provisions of this section, a person (other than the proprietor of the patent) also infringes a patent for an invention if, while the patent is in force and without the consent of the proprietor, he supplies or offers to supply in the United Kingdom a person other than a licensee or other person entitled to work the invention with any of the means, relating to an essential element of the invention, for putting the invention into effect when he knows, or it is obvious to a reasonable person in the circumstances, that those means are suitable for putting, and are intended to put, the invention into effect in the United Kingdom.

(3) Subsection (2) above shall not apply to the supply or offer of a staple commercial product unless the supply or the offer is made for the purpose of inducing the person supplied or, as the case may be, the person to whom the offer is made to do an act which constitutes an infringement of the patent by virtue of subsection (1) above.

. . .

(5) An act which, apart from this subsection, would constitute an infringement of a patent for an invention shall not do so if—

(a)   it is done privately and for purposes which are not commercial;

(b)   it is done for experimental purposes relating to the subject-matter of the invention;

(c)   it consists of the extemporaneous preparation in a pharmacy of a medicine for an individual in accordance with a prescription given by a registered medical or dental practitioner or consists of dealing with a medicine so prepared;

(d)   it consists of the use, exclusively for the needs of a relevant ship, of a product or process in the body of such a ship or in its machinery, tackle, apparatus or other accessories, in a case where the ship has temporarily or accidentally entered the internal or territorial waters of the United Kingdom;

(e)   it consists of the use of a product or process in the body or operation of a relevant aircraft, hovercraft or vehicle which has temporarily or accidentally entered or is crossing the United Kingdom (including the air space above it and its territorial waters) or the use of accessories for such a relevant aircraft, hovercraft or vehicle;

(f)   it consists of the use of an exempted aircraft which has lawfully entered or is lawfully crossing the United Kingdom as aforesaid or of the importation into the United Kingdom, or the use or storage there, of any part or accessory for such an aircraft.

(g)   it consists of the use by a farmer of the product of his harvest for propagation or multiplication by him on his own holding, where there has been a sale of plant propagating material to the farmer by the proprietor of the patent or with his consent for agricultural use;

(h)   it consists of the use of an animal or animal reproductive material by a farmer for an agricultural purpose following a sale to the farmer, by the proprietor of the patent or with his consent, of breeding stock or other animal reproductive material which constitutes or contains the patented invention.

(i)   it consists of—

(i)   an act done in conducting a study, test or trial which is necessary for and is conducted with a view to the application of paragraphs 1 to 5 of article 13 of Directive 2001/82/EC or paragraphs 1 to 4 of article 10 of Directive 2001/83/ EC, or

(ii)   any other act which is required for the purpose of the application of those paragraphs.

[(j)   it consists of a use referred to in Article 27(c) of the Agreement on a Unified Patent Court;

(k)   subject to subsection (6H), it consists of an act or use referred to in Article 27(k) of the Agreement on a Unified Patent Court.]

(6) For the purposes of subsection (2) above a person who does an act in relation to an invention which is prevented only by virtue of paragraph (a), (b) or (c) of subsection (5) above from constituting an infringement of a patent for the invention shall not be treated as a person entitled to work the invention, but—

- (a) the reference in that subsection to a person entitled to work an invention includes a reference to a person so entitled by virtue of section 55 above, and
- (b) a person who by virtue of section 20B(4) or (5) above or section 28A(4) or (5) above or section 64 below or section 117A(4) or (5) below is entitled to do an act in relation to the invention without it constituting such an infringement shall, so far as concerns that act, be treated as a person entitled to work the invention.

(6A) Schedule A1 contains—
- (a) provisions restricting the circumstances in which subsection (5)(g) applies; and
- (b) provisions which apply where an act would constitute an infringement of a patent but for subsection (5)(g).

(6B) For the purposes of subsection (5)(h), use for an agricultural purpose—
- (a) includes making an animal or animal reproductive material available for the purposes of pursuing the farmer's agricultural activity; but
- (b) does not include sale within the framework, or for the purposes, of a commercial reproduction activity.

(6C) In paragraphs (g) and (h) of subsection (5) "sale" includes any other form of commercialisation.

(6D) For the purposes of subsection (5)(b), anything done in or for the purposes of a medicinal product assessment which would otherwise constitute an infringement of a patent for an invention is to be regarded as done for experimental purposes relating to the subject-matter of the invention.

(6E) In subsection (6D), *"medicinal product assessment"* means any testing, course of testing or other activity undertaken with a view to providing data for any of the following purposes—
- (a) obtaining or varying an authorisation to sell or supply, or offer to sell or supply, a medicinal product (whether in the United Kingdom or elsewhere);
- (b) complying with any regulatory requirement imposed (whether in the United Kingdom or elsewhere) in relation to such an authorisation;
- (c) enabling a government or public authority (whether in the United Kingdom or elsewhere), or a person (whether in the United Kingdom or elsewhere) with functions of—
  - (i) providing health care on behalf of such a government or public authority, or
  - (ii) providing advice to, or on behalf of, such a government or public authority about the provision of health care,

to carry out an assessment of suitability of a medicinal product for human use for the purpose of determining whether to use it, or recommend its use, in the provision of health care.

(6F) In subsection (6E) and this subsection—
"medicinal product" means a medicinal product for human use or a veterinary medicinal product;
"medicinal product for human use" has the meaning given by article 1 of Directive 2001/83/EC;
"veterinary medicinal product" has the meaning given by article 1 of Directive 2001/82/EC.

(6G) Nothing in subsections (6D) to (6F) is to be read as affecting the application of subsection (5)(b) in relation to any act of a kind not falling within subsection (6D).

[(6H) Subsection (5)(k) applies to an act or use in relation to a European patent (UK) or a European patent with unitary effect, but does not apply to an act or use in relation to a patent granted by the comptroller.]

(7) In this section—
"relevant ship" and *"relevant aircraft, hovercraft or vehicle"* mean respectively a ship and an aircraft, hovercraft or vehicle registered in, or belonging to, any country, other than the United Kingdom, which is a party to the Convention for the Protection of Industrial Property signed at Paris on 20th March 1883 or which is a member of the World Trade Organisation; and
"exempted aircraft" means an aircraft to which section 89 of the Civil Aviation Act 1982 (aircraft exempted from seizure in respect of patent claims) applies.

. . .

Note: Words in square brackets will be inserted when the Patents (European Patent with Unitary Effect and Unified Patent Court) Order 2016 comes into force.

61 Proceedings for infringement of patent

(1) Subject to the following provisions of this Part of this Act, civil proceedings may be brought in the court by the proprietor of a patent in respect of any act alleged to infringe the patent and (without prejudice to any other jurisdiction of the court) in those proceedings a claim may be made—

    (a) for an injunction or interdict restraining the defendant or defender from any apprehended act of infringement;

    (b) for an order for him to deliver up or destroy any patented product in relation to which the patent is infringed or any article in which that product is inextricably comprised;

    (c) for damages in respect of the infringement;

    (d) for an account of the profits derived by him from the infringement;

    (e) for a declaration or declarator that the patent is valid and has been infringed by him.

(2) The court shall not, in respect of the same infringement, both award the proprietor of a patent damages and order that he shall be given an account of the profits.

(3) The proprietor of a patent and any other person may by agreement with each other refer to the comptroller the question whether that other person has infringed the patent and on the reference the proprietor of the patent may make any claim mentioned in subsection (1)(c) or (e) above.

(4) Except so far as the context requires, in the following provisions of this Act—

    (a) any reference to proceedings for infringement and the bringing of such proceedings includes a reference to a reference under subsection (3) above and the making of such a reference;

    (b) any reference to a claimant or pursuer includes a reference to the proprietor of the patent; and

    (c) any reference to a defendant or defender includes a reference to any other party to the reference.

(5) If it appears to the comptroller on a reference under subsection (3) above that the question referred to him would more properly be determined by the court, he may decline to deal with it and the court shall have jurisdiction to determine the question as if the reference were proceedings brought in the court.

(6) Subject to the following provisions of this Part of this Act, in determining whether or not to grant any kind of relief claimed under this section and the extent of the relief granted the court or the comptroller shall apply the principles applied by the court in relation to that kind of relief immediately before the appointed day.

. . .

62 Restrictions on recovery of damages for infringement

(1) In proceedings for infringement of a patent damages shall not be awarded, and no order shall be made for an account of profits, against a defendant or defender who proves that at the date of the infringement he was not aware, and had no reasonable grounds for supposing, that the patent existed; and a person shall not be taken to have been so aware or to have had reasonable grounds for so supposing by reason only of the application to a product of the word "patent" or "patented", or any word or words expressing or implying that a patent has been obtained for the product, unless the number of the patent or a relevant internet link accompanied the word or words in question.

(1A) The reference in subsection (1) to a relevant internet link is a reference to an address of a posting on the internet—

    (a) which is accessible to the public free of charge, and

    (b) which clearly associates the product with the number of the patent.

(2) In proceedings for infringement of a patent the court or the comptroller may, if it or he thinks fit, refuse to award any damages or make any such order in respect of an infringement committed during the further period specified in section 25(4) above, but before the payment of the renewal fee and any additional fee prescribed for the purposes of that subsection.

(3) Where an amendment of the specification of a patent has been allowed under any of the provisions of this Act, the court or the comptroller shall, when awarding damages

or making an order for an account of profits in proceedings for an infringement of the patent committed before the decision to allow the amendment, take into account the following—

- (a)   whether at the date of infringement the defendant or defender knew, or had reasonable grounds to know, that he was infringing the patent;
- (b)   whether the specification of the patent as published was framed in good faith and with reasonable skill and knowledge;
- (c)   whether the proceedings are brought in good faith.

63   Relief for infringement of partially valid patent

- (1)   If the validity of a patent is put in issue in proceedings for infringement of the patent and it is found that the patent is only partially valid, the court or the comptroller may, subject to subsection (2) below, grant relief in respect of that part of the patent which is found to be valid and infringed.
- (2)   Where in any such proceedings it is found that a patent is only partially valid, the court or the comptroller shall, when awarding damages, costs or expenses or making an order for an account of profits, take into account the following—
  - (a)   whether at the date of the infringement the defendant or defender knew, or had reasonable grounds to know, that he was infringing the patent;
  - (b)   whether the specification of the patent was framed in good faith and with reasonable skill and knowledge;
  - (c)   whether the proceedings are brought in good faith;

  and any relief granted shall be subject to the discretion of the court or the comptroller as to costs or expenses and as to the date from which damages or an account should be reckoned.
- (3)   As a condition of relief under this section the court or the comptroller may direct that the specification of the patent shall be amended to its or his satisfaction upon an application made for that purpose under section 75 below, and an application may be so made accordingly, whether or not all other issues in the proceedings have been determined.
- (4)   The court or the comptroller may also grant relief under this section in the case of a European patent (UK) on condition that the claims of the patent are limited to its or his satisfaction by the European Patent Office at the request of the proprietor.

64   Right to continue use begun before priority date

- (1)   Where a patent is granted for an invention, a person who in the United Kingdom before the priority date of the invention—
  - (a)   does in good faith an act which would constitute an infringement of the patent if it were in force, or
  - (b)   makes in good faith effective and serious preparations to do such an act,

  has the right to continue to do the act or, as the case may be, to do the act, notwithstanding the grant of the patent; but this right does not extend to granting a licence to another person to do the act.
- (2)   If the act was done, or the preparations were made, in the course of a business, the person entitled to the right conferred by subsection (1) may—
  - (a)   authorise the doing of that act by any partners of his for the time being in that business, and
  - (b)   assign that right, or transmit it on death (or in the case of a body corporate on its dissolution), to any person who acquires that part of the business in the course of which the act was done or the preparations were made.
- (3)   Where a product is disposed of to another in exercise of the rights conferred by subsection (1) or (2), that other and any person claiming through him may deal with the product in the same way as if it had been disposed of by the registered proprietor of the patent.

65   Certificate of contested validity of patent

- (1)   If in any proceedings before the court or the comptroller the validity of a patent to any extent is contested and that patent is found by the court or the comptroller to be wholly or partially valid, the court or the comptroller may certify the finding and the fact that the validity of the patent was so contested.
- (2)   Where a certificate is granted under this section, then, if in any subsequent proceedings before the court or the comptroller for infringement of the patent concerned or for

revocation of the patent a final order or judgment or interlocutor is made or given in favour of the party relying on the validity of the patent as found in the earlier proceedings, that party shall, unless the court or the comptroller otherwise directs, be entitled to his costs or expenses as between solicitor and own client (other than the costs or expenses of any appeal in the subsequent proceedings).

66　Proceedings for infringement by a co-owner

(1) In the application of section 60 above to a patent of which there are two or more joint proprietors the reference to the proprietor shall be construed—

　(a) in relation to any act, as a reference to that proprietor or those proprietors who, by virtue of section 36 above or any agreement referred to in that section, is or are entitled to do that act without its amounting to an infringement; and

　(b) in relation to any consent, as a reference to that proprietor or those proprietors who, by virtue of section 36 above or any such agreement, is or are the proper person or persons to give the requisite consent.

(2) One of two or more joint proprietors of a patent may without the concurrence of the others bring proceedings in respect of an act alleged to infringe the patent, but shall not do so unless the others are made parties to the proceedings; but any of the others made a defendant or defender shall not be liable for any costs or expenses unless he enters an appearance and takes part in the proceedings.

67　Proceedings for infringement by exclusive licensee

(1) Subject to the provisions of this section, the holder of an exclusive licence under a patent shall have the same right as the proprietor of the patent to bring proceedings in respect of any infringement of the patent committed after the date of the licence; and references to the proprietor of the patent in the provisions of this Act relating to infringement shall be construed accordingly.

(2) In awarding damages or granting any other relief in any such proceedings the court or the comptroller shall take into consideration any loss suffered or likely to be suffered by the exclusive licensee as such as a result of the infringement, or, as the case may be, the profits derived from the infringement, so far as it constitutes an infringement of the rights of the exclusive licensee as such.

(3) In any proceedings taken by an exclusive licensee by virtue of this section the proprietor of the patent shall be made a party to the proceedings, but if made a defendant or defender shall not be liable for any costs or expenses unless he enters an appearance and takes part in the proceedings.

68　Effect of non-registration on infringement proceedings

Where by virtue of a transaction, instrument or event to which section 33 above applies a person becomes the proprietor or one of the proprietors or an exclusive licensee of a patent and the patent is subsequently infringed before the transaction, instrument or event is registered, in proceedings for such an infringement, the court or controller shall not award him costs or expenses unless—

(a) the transaction, instrument or event is registered within the period of six months beginning with its date; or

(b) the court or the comptroller is satisfied that it was not practicable to register the transaction, instrument or event before the end of that period and that it was registered as soon as practicable thereafter.

69　Infringement of rights conferred by publication of application

(1) Where an application for a patent for an invention is published, then, subject to subsections (2) and (3) below, the applicant shall have, as from the publication and until the grant of the patent, the same right as he would have had, if the patent had been granted on the date of the publication of the application, to bring proceedings in the court or before the comptroller for damages in respect of any act which would have infringed the patent; and (subject to subsections (2) and (3) below) references in sections 60 to 62 and 66 to 68 above to a patent and the proprietor of a patent shall be respectively construed as including references to any such application and the applicant, and references to a patent being in force, being granted, being valid or existing shall be construed accordingly.

(2) The applicant shall be entitled to bring proceedings by virtue of this section in respect of any act only—
(a) after the patent has been granted; and
(b) if the act would, if the patent had been granted on the date of the publication of the application, have infringed not only the patent, but also the claims (as interpreted by the description and any drawings referred to in the description or claims) in the form in which they were contained in the application immediately before the preparations for its publication were completed by the Patent Office.

(3) Section 62(2) and (3) above shall not apply to an infringement of the rights conferred by this section, but in considering the amount of any damages for such an infringement, the court or the comptroller shall consider whether or not it would have been reasonable to expect, from a consideration of the application as published under section 16 above, that a patent would be granted conferring on the proprietor of the patent protection from an act of the same description as that found to infringe those rights, and if the court or the comptroller finds that it would not have been reasonable, it or he shall reduce the damages to such an amount as it or he thinks just.

Unjustified threats

70 Threats of infringement proceedings

(1) A communication contains a "threat of infringement proceedings" if a reasonable person in the position of a recipient would understand from the communication that—
(a) a patent exists, and
(b) a person intends to bring proceedings (whether in a court in the United Kingdom or elsewhere) against another person for infringement of the patent by—
(i) an act done in the United Kingdom, or
(ii) an act which, if done, would be done in the United Kingdom.

(2) References in this section and in section 70C to a "recipient" include, in the case of a communication directed to the public or a section of the public, references to a person to whom the communication is directed.

70A Actionable threats

(1) Subject to subsections (2) to (5), a threat of infringement proceedings made by any person is actionable by any person aggrieved by the threat.

(2) A threat of infringement proceedings is not actionable if the infringement is alleged to consist of—
(a) where the invention is a product, making a product for disposal or importing a product for disposal, or
(b) where the invention is a process, using a process.

(3) A threat of infringement proceedings is not actionable if the infringement is alleged to consist of an act which, if done, would constitute an infringement of a kind mentioned in subsection (2)(a) or (b).

(4) A threat of infringement proceedings is not actionable if the threat—
(a) is made to a person who has done, or intends to do, an act mentioned in subsection (2)(a) or (b) in relation to a product or process, and
(b) is a threat of proceedings for an infringement alleged to consist of doing anything else in relation to that product or process.

(5) A threat of infringement proceedings which is not an express threat is not actionable if it is contained in a permitted communication.

(6) In sections 70C and 70D "an actionable threat" means a threat of infringement proceedings that is actionable in accordance with this section.

70B Permitted communications

(1) For the purposes of section 70A(5), a communication containing a threat of infringement proceedings is a "permitted communication" if—
(a) the communication, so far as it contains information that relates to the threat, is made for a permitted purpose;
(b) all of the information that relates to the threat is information that—
(i) is necessary for that purpose (see subsection (5)(a) to (c) for some examples of necessary information), and
(ii) the person making the communication reasonably believes is true.

(2) Each of the following is a "permitted purpose"—

    (a) giving notice that a patent exists;

    (b) discovering whether, or by whom, a patent has been infringed by an act mentioned in section 70A(2)(a) or (b);

    (c) giving notice that a person has a right in or under a patent, where another person's awareness of the right is relevant to any proceedings that may be brought in respect of the patent.

(3) The court may, having regard to the nature of the purposes listed in subsection (2)(a) to (c), treat any other purpose as a "permitted purpose" if it considers that it is in the interests of justice to do so.

(4) But the following may not be treated as a "permitted purpose"—

    (a) requesting a person to cease doing, for commercial purposes, anything in relation to a product or process;

    (b) requesting a person to deliver up or destroy a product; or

    (c) requesting a person to give an undertaking relating to a product or process.

(5) If any of the following information is included in a communication made for a permitted purpose, it is information that is "necessary for that purpose" (see subsection (1)(b)(i))—

    (a) a statement that a patent exists and is in force or that an application for a patent has been made;

    (b) details of the patent, or of a right in or under the patent, which—

        (i) are accurate in all material respects, and

        (ii) are not misleading in any material respect; and

    (c) information enabling the identification of the products or processes in respect of which it is alleged that acts infringing the patent have been carried out.

70C Remedies and defences

(1) Proceedings in respect of an actionable threat may be brought against the person who made the threat for—

    (a) a declaration that the threat is unjustified;

    (b) an injunction against the continuance of the threat;

    (c) damages in respect of any loss sustained by the aggrieved person by reason of the threat.

(2) In the application of subsection (1) to Scotland—

    (a) "declaration" means "declarator"; and

    (b) "injunction" means "interdict".

(3) It is a defence for the person who made the threat to show that the act in respect of which proceedings were threatened constitutes (or if done would constitute) an infringement of the patent.

(4) It is a defence for the person who made the threat to show—

    (a) that, despite having taken reasonable steps, the person has not identified anyone who has done an act mentioned in section 70A(2)(a) or (b) in relation to the product or the use of a process which is the subject of the threat; and

    (b) that the person notified the recipient, before or at the time of making the threat, of the steps taken.

70D Professional advisers

(1) Proceedings in respect of an actionable threat may not be brought against a professional adviser (or any person vicariously liable for the actions of that professional adviser) if the conditions in subsection (3) are met.

(2) In this section "professional adviser" means a person who, in relation to the making of the communication containing the threat—

    (a) is acting in a professional capacity in providing legal services or the services of a trade mark attorney or a patent attorney; and

    (b) is regulated in the provision of legal services, or the services of a trade mark attorney or a patent attorney, by one or more regulatory bodies (whether through membership of a regulatory body, the issue of a licence to practise or any other means).

(3) The conditions are that—
  (a) in making the communication the professional adviser is acting on the instructions of another person, and
  (b) when the communication is made the professional adviser identifies the person on whose instructions the adviser is acting.
(4) This section does not affect any liability of the person on whose instructions the professional adviser is acting.
(5) It is for a person asserting that subsection (1) applies to prove (if required) that at the material time—
  (a) the person concerned was acting as a professional adviser, and
  (b) the conditions in subsection (3) were met.

70E Supplementary: pending registration

(1) In sections 70 and 70B references to a patent include references to an application for a patent that has been published under section 16.
(2) Where the threat of infringement proceedings is made after an application has been published (but before grant) the reference in section 70C(3) to "the patent" is to be treated as a reference to the patent as granted in pursuance of that application.

70F Supplementary: proceedings for delivery up etc.

In section 70(1)(b) the reference to proceedings for infringement of a patent includes a reference to proceedings for an order under section 61(1)(b) (order to deliver up or destroy patented products etc) [and proceedings in the Unified Patent Court for an order for delivery up made in accordance with articles 32(1)(c) and 62(3) of the Agreement on a Unified Patent Court].

Note: Words in square brackets will be inserted when the Intellectual Property (Unjustified Threats) Act 2017, s 1(3) comes into force.

Declaration or declarator as to non-infringement

71 Declaration or declarator as to non-infringement

(1) Without prejudice to the court's jurisdiction to make a declaration or declarator apart from this section, a declaration or declarator that an act does not, or a proposed act would not, constitute an infringement of a patent may be made by the court or the comptroller in proceedings between the person doing or proposing to do the act and the proprietor of the patent, notwithstanding that no assertion to the contrary has been made by the proprietor, if it is shown—
  (a) that that person has applied in writing to the proprietor for a written acknowledgment to the effect of the declaration or declarator claimed, and has furnished him with full particulars in writing of the act in question; and
  (b) that the proprietor has refused or failed to give any such acknowledgment.
(2) Subject to section 72(5) below, a declaration made by the comptroller under this section shall have the same effect as a declaration or declarator by the court.

Revocation of patents

72 Power to revoke patents on application

(1) Subject to the following provisions of this Act, the court or the comptroller may by order revoke a patent for an invention on the application of any person (including the proprietor of the patent) on (but only on) any of the following grounds, that is to say—
  (a) the invention is not a patentable invention;
  (b) that the patent was granted to a person who was not entitled to be granted that patent;
  (c) the specification of the patent does not disclose the invention clearly enough and completely enough for it to be performed by a person skilled in the art;
  (d) the matter disclosed in the specification of the patent extends beyond that disclosed in the application for the patent, as filed, or, if the patent was granted on a new application filed under section 8(3), 12 or 37(4) above or as mentioned in section 15(9) above, in the earlier application, as filed;

(e)   the protection conferred by the patent has been extended by an amendment which should not have been allowed.

(2)   An application for the revocation of a patent on the ground mentioned in subsection (1) (b) above—

    (a)   may only be made by a person found by the court in an action for a declaration or declarator, or found by the court or the comptroller on a reference under section 37 above, to be entitled to be granted that patent or to be granted a patent for part of the matter comprised in the specification of the patent sought to be revoked; and

    (b)   may not be made if that action was commenced or that reference was made after the second anniversary of the date of the grant of the patent sought to be revoked, unless it is shown that any person registered as a proprietor of the patent knew at the time of the grant or of the transfer of the patent to him that he was not entitled to the patent.

(3)   . . .

(4)   An order under this section may be an order for the unconditional revocation of the patent or, where the court or the comptroller determines that one of the grounds mentioned in subsection (1) above has been established, but only so as to invalidate the patent to a limited extent, an order that the patent should be revoked unless within a specified time the specification is amended to the satisfaction of the court or the comptroller, as the case may be.

(4A) The reference in subsection (4) above to the specification being amended is to its being amended under section 75 below and also, in the case of a European patent (UK), to its being amended under any provision of the European Patent Convention under which the claims of the patent may be limited by amendment at the request of the proprietor.

(5)   A decision of the comptroller or on appeal from the comptroller shall not estop any party to civil proceedings in which infringement of a patent is in issue from alleging invalidity of the patent on any of the grounds referred to in subsection (1) above, whether or not any of the issues involved were decided in the said decision.

(6)   Where the comptroller refuses to grant an application made to him by any person under this section, no application (otherwise than by way of appeal or by way of putting validity in issue in proceedings for infringement) may be made to the court by that person under this section in relation to the patent concerned, without the leave of the court.

. . .

73   Comptroller's power to revoke patents on his own initiative

(1)   If it appears to the comptroller that an invention for which a patent has been granted formed part of the state of the art by virtue only of section 2(3) above, he may on his own initiative by order revoke the patent, but shall not do so without giving the proprietor of the patent an opportunity of making any observations and of amending the specification of the patent so as to exclude any matter which formed part of the state of the art as aforesaid without contravening section 76 below.

(1A) Where the comptroller issues an opinion under section 74A that section 1(1)(a) or (b) is not satisfied in relation to an invention for which there is a patent, the comptroller may revoke the patent.

(1B) The power under subsection (1A) may not be exercised before—

    (a)   the end of the period in which the proprietor of the patent may apply under the rules (by virtue of section 74B) for a review of the opinion, or

    (b)   if the proprietor applies for a review, the decision on the review is made (or, if there is an appeal against that decision, the appeal is determined).

(1C) The comptroller shall not exercise the power under subsection (1A) without giving the proprietor of the patent an opportunity to make any observations and to amend the specification of the patent without contravening section 76.

(2)   If it appears to the comptroller that a patent under this Act and a European patent (UK) have been granted for the same invention having the same priority date, and that the applications for the patents were filed by the same applicant or his successor in title, he shall give the proprietor of the patent under this Act an opportunity of making observations and of amending the specification of the patent, and if the proprietor

fails to satisfy the comptroller that there are not two patents in respect of the same invention, or to amend the specification so as to prevent there being two patents in respect of the same invention, the comptroller shall revoke the patent.

(3) The comptroller shall not take action under subsection (2) above before—

    (a) the end of the period for filing an opposition to the European patent (UK) under the European Patent Convention, or

    (b) if later, the date on which opposition proceedings are finally disposed of;

and he shall not then take any action if the decision is not to maintain the European patent or if it is amended so that there are not two patents in respect of the same invention.

(4) The comptroller shall not take action under subsection (2) above if the European patent (UK) has been surrendered under section 29(1) above before the date on which by virtue of section 25(1) above the patent under this Act is to be treated as having been granted or, if proceedings for the surrender of the European patent (UK) have been begun before that date, until those proceedings are finally disposed of; and he shall not then take any action if the decision is to accept the surrender of the European patent.

Putting validity in issue

74   Proceedings in which validity of patent may be put in issue

(1) Subject to the following provisions of this section, the validity of a patent may be put in issue—

    (a) by way of defence, in proceedings for infringement of the patent under section 61 above or proceedings under section 69 above for infringement of rights conferred by the publication of an application;

    (b) in proceedings in respect of an actionable threat under section 70A above;

    (c) in proceedings in which a declaration in relation to the patent is sought under section 71 above;

    (d) in proceedings before the court or the comptroller under section 72 above for the revocation of the patent;

    (e) in proceedings under section 58 above.

(2) The validity of a patent may not be put in issue in any other proceedings and, in particular, no proceedings may be instituted (whether under this Act or otherwise) seeking only a declaration as to the validity or invalidity of a patent.

(3) The only grounds on which the validity of a patent may be put in issue (whether in proceedings for revocation under section 72 above or otherwise) are the grounds on which the patent may be revoked under that section.

(4) No determination shall be made in any proceedings mentioned in subsection (1) above on the validity of a patent which any person puts in issue on the ground mentioned in section 72(1)(b) above unless—

    (a) it has been determined in entitlement proceedings commenced by that person or in the proceedings in which the validity of the patent is in issue that the patent should have been granted to him and not some other person; and

    (b) except where it has been so determined in entitlement proceedings, the proceedings in which the validity of the patent is in issue are commenced on or before the second anniversary of the date of the grant of the patent or it is shown that any person registered as a proprietor of the patent knew at the time of the grant or of the transfer of the patent to him that he was not entitled to the patent.

(5) Where the validity of a patent is put in issue by way of defence or counterclaim the court or the comptroller shall, if it or he thinks it just to do so, give the defendant an opportunity to comply with the condition in subsection (4)(a) above.

(6) In subsection (4) above "entitlement proceedings", in relation to a patent, means a reference under[section 37(1) above] on the ground that the patent was granted to a person not entitled to it or proceedings for a declaration or declarator that it was so granted.

(7) Where proceedings with respect to a patent are pending in the court under any provision of this Act mentioned in subsection (1) above, no proceedings may be instituted without the leave of the court before the comptroller with respect to that patent under section 61(3), 69, 71 or 72 above.

(8)   It is hereby declared that for the purposes of this Act the validity of a patent is not put in issue merely because

(a)   the comptroller is considering its validity in order to decide whether to revoke it under section 73 above; or

(b)   its validity is being considered in connection with an opinion under section 74A below or a review of such an opinion.

Opinions by Patent Office

74A   Opinions on matters prescribed in the rules

(1)   The proprietor of a patent or any other person may request the comptroller to issue an opinion on a prescribed matter in relation to the patent.

(2)   Subsection (1) above applies even if the patent has expired or has been surrendered.

(3)   The comptroller shall issue an opinion if requested to do so under subsection (1) above, but shall not do so—

(a)   in such circumstances as may be prescribed, or

(b)   if for any reason he considers it inappropriate in all the circumstances to do so.

(4)   An opinion under this section shall not be binding for any purposes.

(5)   An opinion under this section shall be prepared by an examiner.

(6)   In relation to a decision of the comptroller whether to issue an opinion under this section—

(a)   for the purposes of section 101 below, only the person making the request under subsection (1) above shall be regarded as a party to a proceeding before the comptroller; and

(b)   no appeal shall lie at the instance of any other person.

74B   Reviews of opinions under section 74A

(1)   Rules may make provision for a review before the comptroller, on an application by the proprietor or an exclusive licensee of the patent in question, of an opinion under section 74A above.

(2)   The rules may, in particular–

(a)   prescribe the circumstances in which, and the period within which, an application may be made;

(b)   provide that, in prescribed circumstances, proceedings for a review may not be brought or continued where other proceedings have been brought;

(d)   provide for there to be a right of appeal against a decision made on a review only in prescribed cases.

General provisions as to amendment of patents and applications

75   Amendment of patent in infringement or revocation proceedings

(1)   In any proceedings before the court or the comptroller in which the validity of a patent may be put in issue the court or, as the case may be, the comptroller may, subject to section 76 below, allow the proprietor of the patent to amend the specification of the patent in such manner, and subject to such terms as to advertising the proposed amendment and as to costs, expenses or otherwise, as the court or comptroller thinks fit.

(2)   A person may give notice to the court or the comptroller of his opposition to an amendment proposed by the proprietor of the patent under this section, and if he does so the court or the comptroller shall notify the proprietor and consider the opposition in deciding whether the amendment or any amendment should be allowed.

(3)   An amendment of a specification of a patent under this section shall have effect and be deemed always to have had effect from the grant of the patent.

(4)   Where an application for an order under this section is made to the court, the applicant shall notify the comptroller, who shall be entitled to appear and be heard and shall appear if so directed by the court.

(5)   In considering whether or not to allow an amendment proposed under this section, the court or the comptroller shall have regard to any relevant principles applicable under the European Patent Convention.

76 Amendments of applications and patents not to include added matter

(1) An application for a patent which—

    (a) is made in respect of matter disclosed in an earlier application, or in the specification of a patent which has been granted, and

    (b) discloses additional matter, that is, matter extending beyond that disclosed in the earlier application, as filed, or the application for the patent, as filed,

may be filed under section 8(3), 12 or 37(4) above, or as mentioned in section 15(4) above, but shall not be allowed to proceed unless it is amended so as to exclude the additional matter.

(1A) Where, in relation to an application for a patent—

    (a) a reference to an earlier relevant application has been filed as mentioned in section 15(1)(c)(ii) above; and

    (b) the description filed under section 15(10)(b)(i) above discloses additional matter, that is, matter extending beyond that disclosed in the earlier relevant application,

the application shall not be allowed to proceed unless it is amended so as to exclude the additional matter.

(2) No amendment of an application for a patent shall be allowed under section 17(3), 18(3) or 19(1) if it results in the application disclosing matter extending beyond that disclosed in the application as filed.

(3) No amendment of the specification of a patent shall be allowed under section 27(1), 73 or 75 if it—

    (a) results in the specification disclosing additional matter, or

    (b) extends the protection conferred by the patent.

(4) In subsection (1A) above "relevant application" has the meaning given by section 5(5) above.

76A Biotechnological inventions

(1) Any provision of, or made under, this Act is to have effect in relation to a patent or an application for a patent which concerns a biotechnological invention, subject to the provisions of Schedule A2.

(2) Nothing in this section or Schedule A2 is to be read as affecting the application of any provision in relation to any other kind of patent or application for a patent.

PART II

PROVISIONS ABOUT INTERNATIONAL CONVENTIONS

European patents and patent applications

77 Effect of European patent (UK)

(1) Subject to the provisions of this Act, a European patent (UK) shall, as from the publication of the mention of its grant in the European Patent Bulletin, be treated for the purposes of Parts I and III of this Act as if it were a patent under this Act granted in pursuance of an application made under this Act and as if notice of the grant of the patent had, on the date of that publication, been published under section 24 above in the journal; and—

    (a) the proprietor of a European patent (UK) shall accordingly as respects the United Kingdom have the same rights and remedies, subject to the same conditions, as the proprietor of a patent under this Act;

    (b) references in Parts I and III of this Act to a patent shall be construed accordingly; and

    (c) any statement made and any certificate filed for the purposes of the provision of the convention corresponding to section 2(4)(c) above shall be respectively treated as a statement made and written evidence filed for the purposes of the said paragraph (c).

(2) Subsection (1) above shall not affect the operation in relation to a European patent (UK) of any provisions of the European Patent Convention relating to the amendment or revocation of such a patent in proceedings before the European Patent Office.

(3) Where in the case of a European patent (UK)—

    (a) proceedings for infringement, or proceedings under section 58 above, have been commenced before the court or the comptroller and have not been finally disposed of, and

(b)   it is established in proceedings before the European Patent Office that the patent is only partially valid,

the provisions of section 63 or, as the case may be, of subsections (7) to (9) of section 58 apply as they apply to proceedings in which the validity of a patent is put in issue and in which it is found that the patent is only partially valid.

(4)   Where a European patent (UK) is amended in accordance with the European Patent Convention [or the Agreement on a Unified Patent Court], the amendment shall have effect for the purposes of Parts I and III of this Act as if the specification of the patent had been amended under this Act; but subject to subsection (6)(b) below.

(4A)   Where a European patent (UK) is revoked in accordance with the European Patent Convention [or the Agreement on a Unified Patent Court], the patent shall be treated for the purposes of Parts I and III of this Act as having been revoked under this Act.

(5)   Where—
  (a)   under the European Patent Convention [or the Agreement on a Unified Patent Court] a European patent (UK) is revoked for failure to observe a time limit and is subsequently restored or is revoked by the Board of Appeal and is subsequently restored by the Enlarged Board of Appeal [or is revoked and subsequently restored by the Unified Patent Court]; and
  (b)   between the revocation and publication of the fact that it has been restored a person begins in good faith to do an act which would, apart from section 55 above, constitute an infringement of the patent or makes in good faith effective and serious preparations to do such an act;

he shall have the rights conferred by section 28A(4) and (5) above, and subsections (6) and (7) of that section shall apply accordingly.

(5A)   Where, under the European Patent Convention [or the Agreement on a Unified Patent Court], a European patent (UK) is revoked and subsequently restored (including where it is revoked by the Board of Appeal and subsequently restored by the Enlarged Board of Appeal), any fee that would have been imposed in relation to the patent after the revocation but before the restoration is payable within the prescribed period following the restoration.

(6)   . . .

(7)   Where such a translation is not filed the patent shall be treated as always having been void.

(8)   The comptroller shall publish any translation filed at the Patent Office under subsection (6) above.

[(10) Subsection (1) does not apply and is to be treated as never having applied in respect of a European patent (UK) whose unitary effect is registered by the European Patent Office in the Register for unitary patent protection (see, in particular, the Unitary Patent Regulation).]

. . .

Note: Words in square brackets will be inserted when the Patents (European Patent with Unitary Effect and Unified Patent Court) Order 2016 comes into force.

78   Effect of filing an application for a European patent (UK)

(1)   Subject to the provisions of this Act, an application for a European patent (UK) having a date of filing under the European Patent Convention shall be treated for the purposes of the provisions of this Act to which this section applies as an application for a patent under this Act having that date as its date of filing and having the other incidents listed in subsection (3) below, but subject to the modifications mentioned in the following provisions of this section.

(2)   This section applies to the following provisions of this Act:—
section 2(3) and so much of section 14(7) as relates to section 2(3);
section 5;
section 6;
so much of section 13(3) as relates to an application for and issue of a certificate under that subsection;
sections 30 to 33;
section 36;
sections 55 to 69;
sections 70 to 70F;

section 74, so far as relevant to any of the provisions mentioned above; section 111; and section 125.

(3) The incidents referred to in subsection (1) above in relation to an application for a European patent (UK) are as follows:—

    (a) any declaration of priority made in connection with the application under the European Patent Convention shall be treated for the purposes of this Act as a declaration made under section 5(2) above;

    (b) where a period of time relevant to priority is extended under that convention, the period of twelve months specified in section 5(2) above shall be so treated as altered correspondingly;

    (c) where the date of filing an application is re-dated under that convention to a later date, that date shall be so treated as the date of filing the application;

    (d) the application, if published in accordance with that convention, shall, subject to subsection (7) and section 79 below, be so treated as published under section 16 above;

    (e) any designation of the inventor under that convention or any statement under it indicating the origin of the right to a European patent shall be treated for the purposes of section 13(3) above as a statement filed under section 13(2) above;

    (f) registration of the application in the register of European patents shall be treated as registration under this Act.

(4) Rules under section 32 above may not impose any requirements as to the registration of applications for European patents (UK) but may provide for the registration of copies of entries relating to such applications in the European register of patents.

(5) Subsections (1) to (3) above shall cease to apply to an application for a European patent (UK), except as mentioned in subsection (5A) below, if—

    (a) the application is refused or withdrawn or deemed to be withdrawn, or

    (b) the designation of the United Kingdom in the application is withdrawn or deemed to be withdrawn,

but shall apply again if the rights of the applicant are re-established under the European Patent Convention, as from their re-establishment.

(5A) The occurrence of any of the events mentioned in subsection (5)(a) or (b) shall not affect the continued operation of section 2(3) above in relation to matter contained in an application for a European patent (UK) which by virtue of that provision has become part of the state of the art as regards other inventions; and the occurrence of any event mentioned in subsection (5)(b) shall not prevent matter contained in an application for a European patent (UK) becoming part of the state of the art by virtue of section 2(3) above as regards other inventions where the event occurs before the publication of that application.

(6) Where, between subsections (1) to (3) above ceasing to apply to an application for a European patent (UK) and the re-establishment of the rights of the applicant, a person—

    (a) begins in good faith to do an act which would constitute an infringement of the rights conferred by publication of the application if those subsections then applied, or

    (b) makes in good faith effective and serious preparations to do such an act,

he shall have the right to continue to do the act or, as the case may be, to do the act, notwithstanding subsections (1) to (3) applying again and notwithstanding the grant of the patent.

(6A) Subsections (5) and (6) of section 20B above have effect for the purposes of subsection (6) above as they have effect for the purposes of that section and as if the references to subsection (4) of that section were references to subsection (6) above.

(6B) Subject to subsection (6A) above, the right conferred by subsection (6) above does not extend to granting a licence to another person to do the act in question.

(6C) Subsections (6) to (6B) above apply in relation to the use of a patented invention for the services of the Crown as they apply in relation to an infringement of the rights conferred by publication of the application (or, as the case may be, infringement of the patent). "Patented invention" has the same meaning as in section 55 above.

(7) While this subsection is in force, an application for a European patent (UK) published by the European Patent Office under the European Patent Convention in French or

German shall be treated for the purposes of sections 55 and 69 above as published under section 16 above when a translation into English of the claims of the specification of the application has been filed at and published by the Patent Office and the prescribed fee has been paid, but an applicant—

(a)   may recover a payment by virtue of section 55(5) above in respect of the use of the invention in question before publication of that translation; or

(b)   may bring proceedings by virtue of section 69 above in respect of an act mentioned in that section which is done before publication of that translation;

if before that use or the doing of that act he has sent by post or delivered to the government department who made use or authorised the use of the invention, or, as the case may be, to the person alleged to have done the act, a translation into English of those claims.

. . .

79   Operation of s. 78 in relation to certain European patent applications

(1)   Subject to the following provisions of this section, section 78 above, in its operation in relation to an international application for a patent (UK) which is treated by virtue of the European Patent Convention as an application for a European patent (UK), shall have effect as if any reference in that section to anything done in relation to the application under the European Patent Convention included a reference to the corresponding thing done under the Patent Co-operation Treaty.

(2)   Any such international application which is published under that treaty shall be treated for the purposes of section 2(3) above as published only when a copy of the application has been supplied to the European Patent Office in English, French or German and the relevant fee has been paid under that convention.

(3)   Any such international application which is published under that treaty in a language other than English, French or German shall, subject to section 78(7) above, be treated for the purposes of sections 55 and 69 above as published only when it is re-published in English, French or German by the European Patent Office under that convention.

81   Conversion of European patent applications

(1)   The comptroller may direct that on compliance with the relevant conditions mentioned in subsection (2) below an application for a European patent (UK) shall be treated as an application for a patent under this Act where the application is deemed to be withdrawn under the provisions of the European Patent Convention relating to the time for forwarding applications to the European Patent Office.

(2)   The relevant conditions referred to above are—

(a)   . . .

(b)   that—

(i)   the applicant requests the comptroller within the relevant prescribed period (where the application was filed with the Patent Office) to give a direction under this section, or

(ii)   the central industrial property office of a country which is party to the convention, other than the United Kingdom, with which the application was filed transmits within the relevant prescribed period a request that the application should be converted into an application under this Act, together with a copy of the application; and

(c)   that the applicant within the relevant prescribed period pays the application fee and if the application is in a language other than English, files a translation into English of the application and of any amendments previously made in accordance with the convention.

(3)   Where an application for a European patent falls to be treated as an application for a patent under this Act by virtue of a direction under this section—

(a)   the date which is the date of filing the application under the European Patent Convention shall be treated as its date of filing for the purposes of this Act, but if that date is re-dated under the convention to a later date, that later date shall be treated for those purposes as the date of filing the application;

. . .

88A Implementation of Agreement on a Unified Patent Court

(1) The Secretary of State may by order make provision for giving effect in the United Kingdom to the provisions of the Agreement on a Unified Patent Court made in Brussels on 19 February 2013.

(2) An order under this section may, in particular, make provision—

    (a) to confer jurisdiction on a court, remove jurisdiction from a court or vary the jurisdiction of a court;

    (b) to require the payment of fees.

88B Designation as international organisation of which UK is member

The Unified Patent Court is to be treated for the purposes of section 1 of the International Organisations Act 1968 (organisations of which the United Kingdom is a member) as an organisation to which that section applies.

International applications for patents

89 Effect of international application for patent

(1) An international application for a patent (UK) for which a date of filing has been accorded under the Patent Co-operation Treaty shall, subject to—

section 89A (international and national phases of application), and

section 89B (adaptation of provisions in relation to international application),

be treated for the purposes of Parts I and III of this Act as an application for a patent under this Act.

(2) If the application, or the designation of the United Kingdom in it, is withdrawn or (except as mentioned in subsection (3)) deemed to be withdrawn under the Treaty, it shall be treated as withdrawn under this Act.

(3) An application shall not be treated as withdrawn under this Act if it, or the designation of the United Kingdom in it, is deemed to be withdrawn under the Treaty—

    (a) because of an error or omission in an institution having functions under the Treaty, or

    (b) because, owing to circumstances outside the applicant's control, a copy of the application was not received by the International Bureau before the end of the time limited for that purpose under the Treaty,

or in such other circumstances as may be prescribed.

(4) . . .

(5) If an international application for a patent which designates the United Kingdom is refused a filing date under the Treaty and the comptroller determines that the refusal was caused by an error or omission in an institution having functions under the Treaty, he may direct that the application shall be treated as an application under this Act, having such date of filing as he may direct.

89A International and national phases of application

(1) The provisions of the Patent Co-operation Treaty relating to publication, search, examination and amendment, and not those of this Act, apply to an international application for a patent (UK) during the international phase of the application.

(2) The international phase of the application means the period from the filing of the application in accordance with the Treaty until the national phase of the application begins.

(3) The national phase of the application begins—

    (a) when the prescribed period expires, provided any necessary translation of the application into English has been filed at the Patent Office and the prescribed fee has been paid by the applicant; or

    (b) on the applicant expressly requesting the comptroller to proceed earlier with the national phase of the application, filing at the Patent Office—

        (i) a copy of the application, if none has yet been sent to the Patent Office in accordance with the Treaty, and

        (ii) any necessary translation of the application into English,

    and paying the prescribed fee.

. . .

89B Adaptation of provisions in relation to international application

(1) Where an international application for a patent (UK) is accorded a filing date under the Patent Co-operation Treaty—

    (a) that date, or if the application is re-dated under the Treaty to a later date that later date, shall be treated as the date of filing the application under this Act,

    (b) any declaration of priority made under the Treaty shall be treated as made under section 5(2) above, and where in accordance with the Treaty any extra days are allowed, the period of 12 months allowed under in section 5(2A)(a) above shall be treated as altered accordingly, and

    (c) any statement of the name of the inventor under the Treaty shall be treated as a statement filed under section 13(2) above.

(2) If the application, not having been published under this Act, is published in accordance with the Treaty it shall be treated, for purposes other than those mentioned in subsection (3), as published under section 16 above when the national phase of the application begins, or, if later, when published in accordance with the Treaty.

. . .

PART III

MISCELLANEOUS AND GENERAL

100 Burden of proof in certain cases

(1) If the invention for which a patent is granted is a process for obtaining a new product, the same product produced by a person other than the proprietor of the patent or a licensee of his shall, unless the contrary is proved, be taken in any proceedings to have been obtained by that process.

(2) In considering whether a party has discharged the burden imposed upon him by this section, the court shall not require him to disclose any manufacturing or commercial secrets if it appears to the court that it would be unreasonable to do so.

101 Exercise of comptroller's discretionary powers

Without prejudice to any rule of law, the comptroller shall give any party to a proceeding before him an opportunity of being heard before exercising adversely to that party any discretion vested in the comptroller by this Act or rules.

102 Right of audience, etc. in proceedings before comptroller

(1) A party to proceedings before the comptroller under this Act, or under any treaty or international convention to which the United Kingdom is a party, may appear before the comptroller in person or be represented by any person whom he desires to represent him.

. . .

Offences

109 Falsification of register etc.

If a person makes or causes to be made a false entry in any register kept under this Act, or a writing falsely purporting to be a copy or reproduction of an entry in any such register, or produces or tenders or causes to be produced or tendered in evidence any such writing, knowing the entry or writing to be false, he shall be liable—

(a) on summary conviction, to a fine not exceeding the prescribed sum,

(b) on conviction on indictment, to imprisonment for a term not exceeding two years or a fine, or both.

110 Unauthorised claim of patent rights

(1) If a person falsely represents that anything disposed of by him for value is a patented product he shall, subject to the following provisions of this section, be liable on summary conviction to a fine not exceeding level 3 on the standard scale

(2) For the purposes of subsection (1) above a person who for value disposes of an article having stamped, engraved or impressed on it or otherwise applied to it the word "patent" or "patented" or anything expressing or implying that the article is a patented product, shall be taken to represent that the article is a patented product.

(3) Subsection (1) above does not apply where the representation is made in respect of a product after the patent for that product or, as the case may be, the process in question has expired or been revoked and before the end of a period which is reasonably sufficient to enable the accused to take steps to ensure that the representation is not made (or does not continue to be made).

(4) In proceedings for an offence under this section it shall be a defence for the accused to prove that he used due diligence to prevent the commission of the offence.

111 Unauthorised claim that patent has been applied for

(1) If a person represents that a patent has been applied for in respect of any article disposed of for value by him and—
   (a)   no such application has been made, or
   (b)   any such application has been refused or withdrawn,
   he shall, subject to the following provisions of this section, be liable on summary conviction to a fine not exceeding level 3 on the standard scale.

(2) Subsection (1)(b) above does not apply where the representation is made (or continues to be made) before the expiry of a period which commences with the refusal or withdrawal and which is reasonably sufficient to enable the accused to take steps to ensure that the representation is not made (or does not continue to be made).

(3) For the purposes of subsection (1) above a person who for value disposes of an article having stamped, engraved or impressed on it or otherwise applied to it the words "patent applied for" or "patent pending", or anything expressing or implying that a patent has been applied for in respect of the article, shall be taken to represent that a patent has been applied for in respect of it.

(4) In any proceedings for an offence under this section it shall be a defence for the accused to prove that he used due diligence to prevent the commission of such an offence.

112 Misuse of title "Patent Office"

If any person uses on his place of business, or on any document issued by him, or otherwise, the words "Patent Office" or any other words suggesting that his place of business is, or is officially connected with, the Patent Office, he shall be liable on summary conviction to a fine not exceeding level 4 on the standard scale.

Supplemental

125 Extent of invention

(1) For the purposes of this Act an invention for a patent for which an application has been made or for which a patent has been granted shall, unless the context otherwise requires, be taken to be that specified in a claim of the specification of the application or patent, as the case may be, as interpreted by the description and any drawings contained in that specification, and the extent of the protection conferred by a patent or application for a patent shall be determined accordingly.

(2) It is hereby declared for the avoidance of doubt that where more than one invention is specified in any such claim, each invention may have a different priority date under section 5 above.

(3) The Protocol on the Interpretation of Article 69 of the European Patent Convention (which Article contains a provision corresponding to subsection (1) above) shall, as for the time being in force, apply for the purposes of subsection (1) above as it applies for the purposes of that Article.

125A Disclosure of invention by specification: availability of samples of biological material

(1) Provision may be made by rules prescribing the circumstances in which the specification of an application for a patent, or of a patent, for an invention which involves the use of or concerns biological material is to be treated as disclosing the invention in a manner which is clear enough and complete enough for the invention to be performed by a person skilled in the art.

(2) The rules may in particular require the applicant or patentee—
   (a)   to take such steps as may be prescribed for the purposes of making available to the public samples of the biological material, and

      (b)   not to impose or maintain restrictions on the uses to which such samples may be put, except as may be prescribed.

(3)   The rules may provide that, in such cases as may be prescribed, samples need only be made available to such persons or descriptions of persons as may be prescribed; and the rules may identify a description of persons by reference to whether the comptroller has given his certificate as to any matter.

(4)   An application for revocation of the patent under section 72(1)(c) above may be made if any of the requirements of the rules cease to be complied with.

130 Interpretation

(1)   In this Act, except so far as the context otherwise requires—

"Agreement on a Unified Patent Court" means the Agreement on a Unified Patent Court signed at Brussels on 19th February 2013;

"application fee" means the fee prescribed for the purposes of section 14(1A) above; "application for a European patent (UK)" and subject to section (4A) below "international application for a patent (UK)" each mean an application of the relevant description which, on its date of filing, designates the United Kingdom;

"appointed day", in any provision of this Act, means the day appointed under section 132 below for the coming into operation of that provision;

"biological material" means any material containing genetic information and capable of reproducing itself or being reproduced in a biological system;

"biotechnological invention" means an invention which concerns a product consisting of or containing biological material or a process by means of which biological material is produced, processed or used;

"Community Patent Convention" means the Convention for the European Patent for the Common Market;

"comptroller" means the Comptroller-General of Patents, Designs and Trade Marks;

"Convention on International Exhibitions" means the Convention relating to International Exhibitions signed in Paris on 22nd November 1928, as amended or supplemented by any protocol to that convention which is for the time being in force;

"court" means

(a)   as respects England and Wales, the High Court;

(b)   as respects Scotland, the Court of Session;

(c)   as respects Northern Ireland, the High Court in Northern Ireland; *or the Unified Patent Court, as respects the jurisdiction which it has by virtue of Schedule A4;*

"date of filing" means—

(a)   in relation to an application for a patent made under this Act, the date which is the date of filing that application by virtue of section 15 above; and

(b)   in relation to any other application, the date which, under the law of the country where the application was made or in accordance with the terms of a treaty or convention to which that country is a party, is to be treated as the date of filing that application or is equivalent to the date of filing an application in that country (whatever the outcome of the application);

"designate" in relation to an application or a patent, means designate the country or countries (in pursuance of the European Patent Convention or the Patent Co-operation Treaty) in which protection is sought for the invention which is the subject of the application or patent and includes a reference to a country being treated as designated in pursuance of the convention or treaty;

"electronic communication" has the same meaning as in the Electronic Communications Act 2000;

"employee" means a person who works or (where the employment has ceased) worked under a contract of employment or in employment under or for the purposes of a government department or a person who serves (or served) in the naval, military or air forces of the Crown;

"employer", in relation to an employee, means the person by whom the employee is or was employed;

"European Patent Convention" means the Convention on the Grant of European Patents, "European patent" means a patent granted under that convention, "European patent (UK)" means a European patent designating the United Kingdom, "European Patent Bulletin" means the bulletin of that name published under that convention, and "European Patent Office" means the office of that name established by that convention; *"European patent with unitary effect" has the same meaning as in Article 2 of the Unitary Patent Regulation;*

"exclusive licence" means a licence from the proprietor of or applicant for a patent conferring on the licensee, or on him and persons authorised by him, to the exclusion of all other persons (including the proprietor or applicant), any right in respect of the invention to which the patent or application relates, and "exclusive licensee" and "non-exclusive licence" shall be construed accordingly;

. . .

"formal requirements" means those requirements designated as such by rules made for the purposes of section 15A above;

"international application for a patent" means an application made under the Patent Co-operation Treaty;

"International Bureau" means the secretariat of the World Intellectual Property Organization established by a convention signed at Stockholm on 14th July 1967;

"international exhibition" means an official or officially recognised international exhibition falling within the terms of the Convention on International Exhibitions or falling within the terms of any subsequent treaty or convention replacing that convention;

"inventor" has the meaning assigned to it by section 7 above;

"journal" has the meaning assigned to it by section 123(6) above;

"mortgage", when used as a noun, includes a charge for securing money or money's worth and, when used as a verb, shall be construed accordingly;

"1949 Act" means the Patents Act 1949;

"patent" means a patent under this Act;

. . .

"Patent Co-operation Treaty" means the treaty of that name signed at Washington on 19th June 1970;

"patented invention" means an invention for which a patent is granted and "patented process" shall be construed accordingly;

"patented product" means a product which is a patented invention or, in relation to a patented process, a product obtained directly by means of the process or to which the process has been applied;

"prescribed" and "rules" have the meanings assigned to them by section 123 above;

"priority date" means the date determined as such under section 5 above;

"published" means made available to the public (whether in the United Kingdom or elsewhere) and a document shall be taken to be published under any provision of this Act if it can be inspected as of right at any place in the United Kingdom by members of the public, whether on payment of a fee or not; and "republished" shall be construed accordingly;

"register" and cognate expressions have the meanings assigned to them by section 32 above;

"relevant convention court", in relation to any proceedings under the European Patent Convention, or the Patent Co-operation Treaty, means that court or other body which under that convention or treaty has jurisdiction over those proceedings, including (where it has such jurisdiction) any department of the European Patent Office;

"right", in relation to any patent or application, includes an interest in the patent or application and, without prejudice to the foregoing, any reference to a right in a patent includes a reference to a share in the patent;

"search fee" means the fee prescribed for the purposes of section 17(1) above;

"services of the Crown" and "use for the services of the Crown" have the meanings assigned to them by section 56(2) above, including, as respects any period of emergency within the meaning of section 59 above, the meanings assigned to them by the said section 59.

"Unified Patent Court" means the court established under the Agreement on a Unified Patent Court;

"Unitary Patent Regulation" means Regulation (EU) No. 1257/2012 of the European Parliament and of the Council of 17 December 2012 implementing enhanced cooperation in the area of the creation of unitary patent protection.

(2) Rules may provide for stating in the journal that an exhibition falls within the definition of international exhibition in subsection (1) above and any such statement shall be conclusive evidence that the exhibition falls within that definition.

(3) For the purposes of this Act matter shall be taken to have been disclosed in any relevant application within the meaning of section 5 above or in the specification of a patent if it was either claimed or disclosed (otherwise than by way of disclaimer or acknowledgment of prior art) in that application or specification.

(4) References in this Act to an application for a patent, as filed, are references to such an application in the state it was on the date of filing.

(4A) An international application for a patent is not, by reason of being treated by virtue of the European Patent Convention as an application for a European patent (UK), to be treated also as an international application for a patent (UK).

(5) References in this Act to an application for a patent being published are references to its being published under section 16 above.

(5A) References in this Act to the amendment of a patent or its specification (whether under this Act or by the European Patent Office) include, in particular, limitation of the claims (as interpreted by the description and any drawings referred to in the description or claims).

(6) References in this Act to any of the following conventions, that is to say—
    (a)   The European Patent Convention;
    (b)   The Community Patent Convention;
    (c)   The Patent Co-operation Treaty;
    [(d)   The Agreement on a Unified Patent Court;]
are references to that convention or any other international convention or agreement replacing it, as amended or supplemented by any convention or international agreement (including in either case any protocol or annex), or in accordance with the terms of any such convention or agreement, and include references to any instrument made under any such convention or agreement.

(7) Whereas by a resolution made on the signature of the Community Patent Convention the governments of the member states of the European Economic Community resolved to adjust their laws relating to patents so as (among other things) to bring those laws into conformity with the corresponding provisions of the European Patent Convention, the Community Patent Convention and the Patent Co-operation Treaty, it is hereby declared that the following provisions of this Act, that is to say, sections 1(1) to (4), 2 to 6, 14(3), (5) and (6), 37(5), 54, 60, 69, 72(1) and (2), 74(4), 82, 83, 100 and 125, are so framed as to have, as nearly as practicable, the same effects in the United Kingdom as the corresponding provisions of the European Patent Convention, the Community Patent Convention and the Patent Co-operation Treaty have in the territories to which those Conventions apply.

(8) Nothing in any of sections 1 to 15 of and Schedule 1 to the Arbitration (Scotland) Act 2010 or Part I of the Arbitration Act 1996 applies to any proceedings before the comptroller under this Act.

(9) Except so far as the context otherwise requires, any reference in this Act to any enactment shall be construed as a reference to that enactment as amended or extended by or under any other enactment, including this Act.

Note: Words in italics will be added when SI 2016/388 comes into force.

SCHEDULE A2
BIOTECHNOLOGICAL INVENTIONS

1.   An invention shall not be considered unpatentable solely on the ground that it concerns—
    (a)   a product consisting of or containing biological material; or
    (b)   a process by which biological material is produced, processed or used.

2.   Biological material which is isolated from its natural environment or produced by means of a technical process may be the subject of an invention even if it previously occurred in nature.

3. The following are not patentable inventions—
   (a) the human body, at the various stages of its formation and development, and the simple discovery of one of its elements, including the sequence or partial sequence of a gene;
   (b) processes for cloning human beings;
   (c) processes for modifying the germ line genetic identity of human beings;
   (d) uses of human embryos for industrial or commercial purposes;
   (e) processes for modifying the genetic identity of animals which are likely to cause them suffering without any substantial medical benefit to man or animal, and also animals resulting from such processes;
   (f) any variety of animal or plant or any essentially biological process for the production of animals or plants, not being a micro-biological or other technical process or the product of such a process.

4. Inventions which concern plants or animals may be patentable if the technical feasibility of the invention is not confined to a particular plant or animal variety.

5. An element isolated from the human body or otherwise produced by means of a technical process, including the sequence or partial sequence of a gene, may constitute a patentable invention, even if the structure of that element is identical to that of a natural element.

6. The industrial application of a sequence or partial sequence of a gene must be disclosed in the patent application as filed.

7. The protection conferred by a patent on a biological material possessing specific characteristics as a result of the invention shall extend to any biological material derived from that biological material through propagation or multiplication in an identical or divergent form and possessing those same characteristics.

8. The protection conferred by a patent on a process that enables a biological material to be produced possessing specific characteristics as a result of the invention shall extend to biological material directly obtained through that process and to any other biological material derived from the directly obtained biological material through propagation or multiplication in an identical or divergent form and possessing those same characteristics.

9. The protection conferred by a patent on a product containing or consisting of genetic information shall extend to all material, save as provided for in paragraph 3(a) above, in which the product is incorporated and in which the genetic information is contained and performs its function.

10. The protection referred to in paragraphs 7, 8 and 9 above shall not extend to biological material obtained from the propagation or multiplication of biological material placed on the market by the proprietor of the patent or with his consent, where the multiplication or propagation necessarily results from the application for which the biological material was marketed, provided that the material obtained is not subsequently used for other propagation or multiplication.

11. In this Schedule:
   "essentially biological process" means a process for the production of animals and plants which consists entirely of natural phenomena such as crossing and selection;
   "microbiological process" means any process involving or performed upon or resulting in microbiological material;
   "plant variety" means a plant grouping within a single botanical taxon of the lowest known rank, which grouping can be:
   (a) defined by the expression of the characteristics that results from a given genotype or combination of genotypes; and
   (b) distinguished from any other plant grouping by the expression of at least one of the said characteristics; and
   (c) considered as a unit with regard to its suitability for being propagated unchanged.

SCHEDULE A3
EUROPEAN PATENT WITH UNITARY EFFECT

1 Meaning of "relevant statutory provisions"
In this Schedule "relevant statutory provisions" means—
   (a) the provisions of this Act which, by virtue of paragraph 2, apply in relation to the European patent with unitary effect, and

(b)   the other provisions of this Act which, by virtue of the Unitary Patent Regulation, are to be treated as applying in relation to the European patent with unitary effect (see, in particular, Article 7 of that Regulation).

2   Provisions applied by this Schedule to the European patent with unitary effect

The following provisions of this Act apply in relation to a European patent with unitary effect, subject to paragraphs 3 and 4—

section 48 (compulsory licences: general);

section 48A (compulsory licences: WTO proprietors);

section 48B (compulsory licences: other cases);

section 49 (provisions about licences under section 48);

section 50 (exercise of powers on applications under section 48);

section 50A (powers exercisable following merger and market investigations);

section 51 (powers exercisable in consequence of report of Competition and Markets Authority);

section 52 (opposition, appeal and arbitration);

section 53 (compulsory licences; supplementary provisions);

section 54 (special provisions where patented invention is being worked abroad);

section 55 (use of patented inventions for services of the Crown);

section 56 (interpretation, etc, of provisions about Crown use);

section 57 (rights of third parties in respect of Crown use);

section 57A (compensation for loss of profit);

section 58(1) to (6) and (9A) to (13) (references of disputes as to Crown use);

section 59 (special provisions as to Crown use during emergency);

section 60 (meaning of infringement);

section 64 (right to continue use begun before priority date);

sections 70 to 70F (unjustified threats);

section 73(2) to (4) (Comptroller's power to revoke patents on his own initiative);

section 74A (opinions on matters prescribed in the rules);

section 74B (reviews of opinions under section 74A);

section 76A (biotechnological inventions);

section 77(4) to (5A) (effect of European patent (UK));

section 80(1) (authentic text of European patents and patent applications);

sections 97 to 100 (legal proceedings) so far as they relate to proceedings which do not fall within the exclusive jurisdiction of the Unified Patent Court as set out in paragraph 1 of Schedule A4;

section 101 (exercise of comptroller's discretionary powers);

section 102 (right of audience, &c in proceedings before comptroller);

sections 103 (extension of privilege for communications with solicitors relating to patent proceedings) and 105 (extension of privilege in Scotland for communications relating to patent proceedings) so far as they relate to proceedings before the comptroller;

section 107 (costs and expenses in proceedings before the comptroller);

section 108 (licences granted by order of comptroller);

section 110 (unauthorised claim of patent rights);

section 116 (immunity of department as regards official acts);

section 118 (information about patent applications and patents, and inspection of documents);

section 123 (rules);

section 124 (rules, regulations and orders; supplementary);

section 125 (extent of invention);

section 128A (EU compulsory licences);

section 128B (supplementary protection certificates).

3   Manner of application of relevant statutory provisions

The relevant statutory provisions apply in relation to a European patent with unitary effect in the same way as they apply in relation to a European patent (UK).

. . .

Note: This schedule will be inserted when the Patents (European Patent with Unitary Effect and Unified Patent Court) Order 2016 comes into force. Words in square brackets will be added when the Intellectual Property (Unjustified Threats) Act 2017, s 1(1), (8) comes into force.

SCHEDULE A4
THE UNIFIED PATENT COURT

1 **Jurisdiction**

The Unified Patent Court has exclusive jurisdiction in respect of an Article 32(1) action which relates to—
(a) a European patent with unitary effect, or
(b) a supplementary protection certificate for which the basic patent is a European patent with unitary effect,
(c) subject to paragraph 2—
    (i) a European patent (UK), or
    (ii) a supplementary protection certificate for which the basic patent is a European patent (UK).

. . .

3 **Modifications of law applicable where UPC has jurisdiction**

(1) In the case of an Article 32(1) action relating to—
    (a) a European patent with unitary effect, or
    (b) a European patent (UK),
    the provisions of this Act listed in sub-paragraph (2) do not apply in relation to the action where the Unified Patent Court has jurisdiction in accordance with paragraph 1.

(2) The provisions referred to in sub-paragraph (1) are—
    section 58(7) to (9) (references of disputes as to Crown use);
    section 61 (proceedings for infringement of patent);
    section 62 (restrictions on recovery of damages for infringement);
    section 63 (relief for infringement of partially valid patent);
    section 65 (certificate of contested validity of patent);
    section 66 (proceedings for infringement by a co-owner);
    section 67 (proceedings for infringement by exclusive licensee);
    section 68 (effect of non-registration on infringement proceedings);
    section 69 (infringement of rights conferred by publication of application);
    section 71 (declaration or declarator as to non-infringement);
    section 72 (power to revoke patents on application);
    section 73(1) to (1C) (comptroller's power to revoke patents on his own initiative);
    section 74 (proceedings in which validity of patent may be put in issue);
    section 75 (amendment of patent in infringement or revocation proceedings);
    section 77(3) (effect of European patent (UK)).

(3) In the case of an Article 32(1) action relating to a supplementary protection certificate for which the basic patent is—
    (a) a European patent with unitary effect, or
    (b) a European patent (UK),
    the provisions of this Act listed in sub-paragraph (4) do not apply in relation to the action where the Unified Patent Court has jurisdiction in accordance with paragraph 1.

(4) The provisions referred to in sub-paragraph (3) are—
    section 58(7) to (9) (references of disputes as to Crown use);
    section 61 (proceedings for infringement of patent);
    section 62 (restrictions on recovery of damages for infringement);
    section 63 (relief for infringement of partially valid patent);
    section 65 (certificate of contested validity of patent);
    section 66 (proceedings for infringement by a co-owner);
    section 67 (proceedings for infringement by exclusive licensee);
    section 68 (effect of non-registration on infringement proceedings);
    section 69 (infringement of rights conferred by publication of application);

section 71 (declaration or declarator as to non-infringement);

section 74 (proceedings in which validity of patent may be put in issue);

section 75 (amendment of a patent in infringement or revocation proceedings).

4   Enforcement

(1)   For the purposes of enforcement of a decision or order of the Unified Patent Court—

(a)   the decision or order has the same force and effect,

(b)   proceedings for or with respect to enforcement of the decision or order may be taken, and

(c)   the enforcing court, or in a relevant Northern Ireland case the Enforcement of Judgments Office, has the same powers in relation to the enforcement of the decision or order,

as if the decision or order had originally been made by the enforcing court.

. . .

Note: This schedule will be inserted when the Patents (European Patent with Unitary Effect and Unified Patent Court) Order 2016 comes into force.

CONVENTION ON THE GRANT OF EUROPEAN PATENTS (EUROPEAN PATENT CONVENTION)
of 5 October 1973
As revised . . .

PART I

GENERAL AND INSTITUTIONAL PROVISIONS

CHAPTER 1

GENERAL PROVISIONS

Article 1 European law for the grant of patents

A system of law, common to the Contracting States, for the grant of patents for invention is established by this Convention.

Article 2 European patent

(1)   Patents granted under this Convention shall be called European patents.

(2)   The European patent shall, in each of the Contracting States for which it is granted, have the effect of and be subject to the same conditions as a national patent granted by that State, unless this Convention provides otherwise.

Article 3 Territorial effect

The grant of a European patent may be requested for one or more of the Contracting States.

Article 4 European Patent Organisation

(1)   A European Patent Organisation, hereinafter referred to as the Organisation, is established by this Convention. It shall have administrative and financial autonomy.

(2)   The organs of the Organisation shall be:

(a)   the European Patent Office;

(b)   the Administrative Council.

(3)   The task of the Organisation shall be to grant European patents. This shall be carried out by the European Patent Office supervised by the Administrative Council.

Article 4a Conference of ministers of the Contracting States

A conference of ministers of the Contracting States responsible for patent matters shall meet at least every five years to discuss issues pertaining to the Organisation and to the European patent system.

PART II
SUBSTANTIVE PATENT LAW
CHAPTER 1
PATENTABILITY

Article 52 Patentable inventions

(1) European patents shall be granted for any inventions, in all fields of technology, provided that they are new, involve an inventive step and are susceptible of industrial application.
(2) The following in particular shall not be regarded as inventions within the meaning of paragraph 1:
   (a) discoveries, scientific theories and mathematical methods;
   (b) aesthetic creations;
   (c) schemes, rules and methods for performing mental acts, playing games or doing business, and programs for computers;
   (d) presentations of information.
(3) Paragraph 2 shall exclude the patentability of the subject-matter or activities referred to therein only to the extent to which a European patent application or European patent relates to such subject-matter or activities as such.

Article 53 Exceptions to patentability

European patents shall not be granted in respect of:
(a) inventions the commercial exploitation of which would be contrary to "ordre public" or morality; such exploitation shall not be deemed to be so contrary merely because it is prohibited by law or regulation in some or all of the Contracting States;
(b) plant or animal varieties or essentially biological processes for the production of plants or animals; this provision shall not apply to microbiological processes or the products thereof;
(c) methods for treatment of the human or animal body by surgery or therapy and diagnostic methods practised on the human or animal body; this provision shall not apply to products, in particular substances or compositions, for use in any of these methods.

Article 54 Novelty

(1) An invention shall be considered to be new if it does not form part of the state of the art.
(2) The state of the art shall be held to comprise everything made available to the public by means of a written or oral description, by use, or in any other way, before the date of filing of the European patent application.
(3) Additionally, the content of European patent applications as filed, the dates of filing of which are prior to the date referred to in paragraph 2 and which were published on or after that date, shall be considered as comprised in the state of the art.
(4) Paragraphs 2 and 3 shall not exclude the patentability of any substance or composition, comprised in the state of the art, for use in a method referred to in Article 53(c), provided that its use for any such method is not comprised in the state of the art.
(5) Paragraphs 2 and 3 shall also not exclude the patentability of any substance or composition referred to in paragraph 4 for any specific use in a method referred to in Article 53(c), provided that such use is not comprised in the state of the art.

Article 55 Non-prejudicial disclosures

(1) For the application of Article 54, a disclosure of the invention shall not be taken into consideration if it occurred no earlier than six months preceding the filing of the European patent application and if it was due to, or in consequence of:
   (a) an evident abuse in relation to the applicant or his legal predecessor, or
   (b) the fact that the applicant or his legal predecessor has displayed the invention at an official, or officially recognised, international exhibition falling within the terms of the Convention on international exhibitions signed at Paris on 22 November 1928 and last revised on 30 November 1972.
(2) In the case of paragraph 1(b), paragraph 1 shall apply only if the applicant states, when filing the European patent application, that the invention has been so displayed and files a supporting certificate within the time limit and under the conditions laid down in the Implementing Regulations.

Article 56 Inventive step

An invention shall be considered as involving an inventive step if, having regard to the state of the art, it is not obvious to a person skilled in the art. If the state of the art also includes documents within the meaning of Article 54, paragraph 3, these documents shall not be considered in deciding whether there has been an inventive step.

Article 57 Industrial application

An invention shall be considered as susceptible of industrial application if it can be made or used in any kind of industry, including agriculture.

CHAPTER II

PERSONS ENTITLED TO APPLY FOR AND OBTAIN A EUROPEAN PATENT – MENTION OF THE INVENTOR

Article 58 Entitlement to file a European patent application

A European patent application may be filed by any natural or legal person, or any body equivalent to a legal person by virtue of the law governing it.

Article 59 Multiple applicants

A European patent application may also be filed either by joint applicants or by two or more applicants designating different Contracting States.

Article 60 Right to a European patent

(1)   The right to a European patent shall belong to the inventor or his successor in title. If the inventor is an employee, the right to a European patent shall be determined in accordance with the law of the State in which the employee is mainly employed; if the State in which the employee is mainly employed cannot be determined, the law to be applied shall be that of the State in which the employer has the place of business to which the employee is attached.

(2)   If two or more persons have made an invention independently of each other, the right to a European patent therefor shall belong to the person whose European patent application has the earliest date of filing, provided that this first application has been published.

(3)   In proceedings before the European Patent Office, the applicant shall be deemed to be entitled to exercise the right to a European patent.

Article 61 European patent applications filed by non-entitled persons

(1)   If by a final decision it is adjudged that a person other than the applicant is entitled to the grant of the European patent, that person may, in accordance with the Implementing Regulations:
    (a)   prosecute the European patent application as his own application in place of the applicant;
    (b)   file a new European patent application in respect of the same invention; or
    (c)   request that the European patent application be refused.

(2)   Article 76, paragraph 1, shall apply mutatis mutandis to a new European patent application filed under paragraph 1(b).

Article 62 Right of the inventor to be mentioned

The inventor shall have the right, vis-à-vis the applicant for or proprietor of a European patent, to be mentioned as such before the European Patent Office.

CHAPTER III

EFFECTS OF THE EUROPEAN PATENT AND THE EUROPEAN PATENT APPLICATION

Article 63 Term of the European patent

(1)   The term of the European patent shall be 20 years from the date of filing of the application.

(2)   Nothing in the preceding paragraph shall limit the right of a Contracting State to extend the term of a European patent, or to grant corresponding protection which follows immediately on expiry of the term of the patent, under the same conditions as those applying to national patents:

(a) in order to take account of a state of war or similar emergency conditions affecting that State;

(b) if the subject-matter of the European patent is a product or a process for manufacturing a product or a use of a product which has to undergo an administrative authorisation procedure required by law before it can be put on the market in that State.

(3) Paragraph 2 shall apply mutatis mutandis to European patents granted jointly for a group of Contracting States in accordance with Article 142.

(4) A Contracting State which makes provision for extension of the term or corresponding protection under paragraph 2(b) may, in accordance with an agreement concluded with the Organisation, entrust to the European Patent Office tasks associated with implementation of the relevant provisions.

Article 64 Rights conferred by a European patent

(1) A European patent shall, subject to the provisions of paragraph 2, confer on its proprietor from the date on which the mention of its grant is published in the European Patent Bulletin, in each Contracting State in respect of which it is granted, the same rights as would be conferred by a national patent granted in that State.

(2) If the subject-matter of the European patent is a process, the protection conferred by the patent shall extend to the products directly obtained by such process.

(3) Any infringement of a European patent shall be dealt with by national law.

Article 65 Translation of the European patent

(1) Any Contracting State may, if the European patent as granted, amended or limited by the European Patent Office is not drawn up in one of its official languages, prescribe that the proprietor of the patent shall supply to its central industrial property office a translation of the patent as granted, amended or limited in one of its official languages at his option or, where that State has prescribed the use of one specific official language, in that language. The period for supplying the translation shall end three months after the date on which the mention of the grant, maintenance in amended form or limitation of the European patent is published in the European Patent Bulletin, unless the State concerned prescribes a longer period.

. . .

Article 66 Equivalence of European filing with national filing

A European patent application which has been accorded a date of filing shall, in the designated Contracting States, be equivalent to a regular national filing, where appropriate with the priority claimed for the European patent application.

Article 67 Rights conferred by a European patent application after publication

(1) A European patent application shall, from the date of its publication, provisionally confer upon the applicant the protection provided for by Article 64, in the Contracting States designated in the application.

(2) Any Contracting State may prescribe that a European patent application shall not confer such protection as is conferred by Article 64. However, the protection attached to the publication of the European patent application may not be less than that which the laws of the State concerned attach to the compulsory publication of unexamined national patent applications. In any event, each State shall ensure at least that, from the date of publication of a European patent application, the applicant can claim compensation reasonable in the circumstances from any person who has used the invention in that State in circumstances where that person would be liable under national law for infringement of a national patent.

(3) Any Contracting State which does not have as an official language the language of the proceedings may prescribe that provisional protection in accordance with paragraphs 1 and 2 above shall not be effective until such time as a translation of the claims in one of its official languages at the option of the applicant or, where that State has prescribed the use of one specific official language, in that language:

(a) has been made available to the public in the manner prescribed by national law, or

(b) has been communicated to the person using the invention in the said State.

(4) The European patent application shall be deemed never to have had the effects set out in paragraphs 1 and 2 when it has been withdrawn, deemed to be withdrawn or finally

refused. The same shall apply in respect of the effects of the European patent application in a Contracting State the designation of which is withdrawn or deemed to be withdrawn.

Article 68 Effect of revocation or limitation of the European patent

The European patent application and the resulting European patent shall be deemed not to have had, from the outset, the effects specified in Articles 64 and 67, to the extent that the patent has been revoked or limited in opposition, limitation or revocation proceedings.

Article 69 Extent of protection

(1)   The extent of the protection conferred by a European patent or a European patent application shall be determined by the claims. Nevertheless, the description and drawings shall be used to interpret the claims.

(2)   For the period up to grant of the European patent, the extent of the protection conferred by the European patent application shall be determined by the claims contained in the application as published. However, the European patent as granted or as amended in opposition, limitation or revocation proceedings shall determine retroactively the protection conferred by the application, in so far as such protection is not thereby extended.

Article 70 Authentic text of a European patent application or European patent

(1)   The text of a European patent application or a European patent in the language of the proceedings shall be the authentic text in any proceedings before the European Patent Office and in any Contracting State.

(2)   If, however, the European patent application has been filed in a language which is not an official language of the European Patent Office, that text shall be the application as filed within the meaning of this Convention.

. . .

CHAPTER IV
THE EUROPEAN PATENT APPLICATION AS AN OBJECT OF PROPERTY

Article 71 Transfer and constitution of rights

A European patent application may be transferred or give rise to rights for one or more of the designated Contracting States.

Article 72 Assignment

An assignment of a European patent application shall be made in writing and shall require the signature of the parties to the contract.

Article 73 Contractual licensing

A European patent application may be licensed in whole or in part for the whole or part of the territories of the designated Contracting States.

Article 74 Law applicable

Unless this Convention provides otherwise, the European patent application as an object of property shall, in each designated Contracting State and with effect for such State, be subject to the law applicable in that State to national patent applications.

PART III
THE EUROPEAN PATENT APPLICATION

CHAPTER I
FILING AND REQUIREMENTS OF THE EUROPEAN PATENT APPLICATION

Article 75 Filing of a European patent application

(1)   A European patent application may be filed:
     (a)   with the European Patent Office, or
     (b)   if the law of a Contracting State so permits, and subject to Article 76, paragraph 1, with the central industrial property office or other competent authority of that State. Any application filed in this way shall have the same effect as if it had been filed on the same date with the European Patent Office.

(2)   Paragraph 1 shall not preclude the application of legislative or regulatory provisions which, in any Contracting State:
    (a)   govern inventions which, owing to the nature of their subject-matter, may not be communicated abroad without the prior authorisation of the competent authorities of that State, or
    (b)   prescribe that any application is to be filed initially with a national authority, or make direct filing with another authority subject to prior authorisation.

Article 76 European divisional applications

(1)   A European divisional application shall be filed directly with the European Patent Office in accordance with the Implementing Regulations. It may be filed only in respect of subject-matter which does not extend beyond the content of the earlier application as filed; in so far as this requirement is complied with, the divisional application shall be deemed to have been filed on the date of filing of the earlier application and shall enjoy any right of priority.
(2)   All the Contracting States designated in the earlier application at the time of filing of a European divisional application shall be deemed to be designated in the divisional application.

Article 77 Forwarding of European patent applications

(1)   The central industrial property office of a Contracting State shall forward to the European Patent Office any European patent application filed with it or any other competent authority in that State, in accordance with the Implementing Regulations.
(2)   A European patent application the subject of which has been made secret shall not be forwarded to the European Patent Office.
(3)   A European patent application not forwarded to the European Patent Office in due time shall be deemed to be withdrawn.

Article 78 Requirements of a European patent application

(1)   A European patent application shall contain:
    (a)   a request for the grant of a European patent;
    (b)   a description of the invention;
    (c)   one or more claims;
    (d)   any drawings referred to in the description or the claims;
    (e)   an abstract,
    and satisfy the requirements laid down in the Implementing Regulations.
(2)   A European patent application shall be subject to the payment of the filing fee and the search fee. If the filing fee or the search fee is not paid in due time, the application shall be deemed to be withdrawn.

Article 79 Designation of Contracting States

(1)   All the Contracting States party to this Convention at the time of filing of the European patent application shall be deemed to be designated in the request for grant of a European patent.

. . .

Article 80 Date of filing

The date of filing of a European patent application shall be the date on which the requirements laid down in the Implementing Regulations are fulfilled.

Article 81 Designation of the inventor

The European patent application shall designate the inventor. If the applicant is not the inventor or is not the sole inventor, the designation shall contain a statement indicating the origin of the right to the European patent.

Article 82 Unity of invention

The European patent application shall relate to one invention only or to a group of inventions so linked as to form a single general inventive concept.

Article 83 Disclosure of the invention

The European patent application shall disclose the invention in a manner sufficiently clear and complete for it to be carried out by a person skilled in the art.

Article 84 Claims
The claims shall define the matter for which protection is sought. They shall be clear and concise and be supported by the description.

Article 85 Abstract
The abstract shall serve the purpose of technical information only; it may not be taken into account for any other purpose, in particular for interpreting the scope of the protection sought or applying Article 54, paragraph 3.

CHAPTER II
PRIORITY

Article 87 Priority right
(1)   Any person who has duly filed, in or for:
     (a)   any State party to the Paris Convention for the Protection of Industrial Property, or
     (b)   any Member of the World Trade Organization,
     an application for a patent, a utility model or a utility certificate, or his successor in title, shall enjoy, for the purpose of filing a European patent application in respect of the same invention, a right of priority during a period of twelve months from the date of filing of the first application.
(2)   Every filing that is equivalent to a regular national filing under the national law of the State where it was made or under bilateral or multilateral agreements, including this Convention, shall be recognised as giving rise to a right of priority.
(3)   A regular national filing shall mean any filing that is sufficient to establish the date on which the application was filed, whatever the outcome of the application may be.
(4)   A subsequent application in respect of the same subject-matter as a previous first application and filed in or for the same State shall be considered as the first application for the purposes of determining priority, provided that, at the date of filing the subsequent application, the previous application has been withdrawn, abandoned or refused, without being open to public inspection and without leaving any rights outstanding, and has not served as a basis for claiming a right of priority. The previous application may not thereafter serve as a basis for claiming a right of priority.
(5)   If the first filing has been made with an industrial property authority which is not subject to the Paris Convention for the Protection of Industrial Property or the Agreement Establishing the World Trade Organization, paragraphs 1 to 4 shall apply if that authority, according to a communication issued by the President of the European Patent Office, recognises that a first filing made with the European Patent Office gives rise to a right of priority under conditions and with effects equivalent to those laid down in the Paris Convention.

Article 88 Claiming priority
(1)   An applicant desiring to take advantage of the priority of a previous application shall file a declaration of priority and any other document required, in accordance with the Implementing Regulations.
(2)   Multiple priorities may be claimed in respect of a European patent application, notwithstanding the fact that they originated in different countries. Where appropriate, multiple priorities may be claimed for any one claim. Where multiple priorities are claimed, time limits which run from the date of priority shall run from the earliest date of priority.
(3)   If one or more priorities are claimed in respect of a European patent application, the right of priority shall cover only those elements of the European patent application which are included in the application or applications whose priority is claimed.
(4)   If certain elements of the invention for which priority is claimed do not appear among the claims formulated in the previous application, priority may nonetheless be granted, provided that the documents of the previous application as a whole specifically disclose such elements.

Article 89 Effect of priority right
The right of priority shall have the effect that the date of priority shall count as the date of filing of the European patent application for the purposes of Article 54, paragraphs 2 and 3, and Article 60, paragraph 2.

PART IV
PROCEDURE UP TO GRANT

Article 90 Examination on filing and examination as to formal requirements

(1)   The European Patent Office shall examine, in accordance with the Implementing Regulations, whether the application satisfies the requirements for the accordance of a date of filing.

(2)   If a date of filing cannot be accorded following the examination under paragraph 1, the application shall not be dealt with as a European patent application.

(3)   If the European patent application has been accorded a date of filing, the European Patent Office shall examine, in accordance with the Implementing Regulations, whether the requirements in Articles 14, 78 and 81, and, where applicable, Article 88. paragraph 1, and Article 133, paragraph 2, as well as any other requirement laid down in the Implementing Regulations, have been satisfied.

(4)   Where the European Patent Office in carrying out the examination under paragraphs 1 or 3 notes that there are deficiencies which may be corrected, it shall give the applicant an opportunity to correct them.

(5)   If any deficiency noted in the examination under paragraph 3 is not corrected, the European patent application shall be refused unless a different legal consequence is provided for by this Convention. Where the deficiency concerns the right of priority, this right shall be lost for the application.

Article 92 Drawing up of the European search report

The European Patent Office shall, in accordance with the Implementing Regulations, draw up and publish a European search report in respect of the European patent application on the basis of the claims, with due regard to the description and any drawings.

Article 93 Publication of the European patent application

(1)   The European Patent Office shall publish the European patent application as soon as possible
   (a) after the expiry of a period of eighteen months from the date of filing or, if priority has been claimed, from the date of priority, or
   (b) at the request of the applicant, before the expiry of that period.

(2)   The European patent application shall be published at the same time as the specification of the European patent when the decision to grant the patent becomes effective before the expiry of the period referred to in paragraph 1(a).

Article 94 Examination of the European patent application

(1)   The European Patent Office shall, in accordance with the Implementing Regulations, examine on request whether the European patent application and the invention to which it relates meet the requirements of this Convention. The request shall not be deemed to be filed until the examination fee has been paid.

(2)   If no request for examination has been made in due time, the application shall be deemed to be withdrawn.

(3)   If the examination reveals that the application or the invention to which it relates does not meet the requirements of this Convention, the Examining Division shall invite the applicant, as often as necessary, to file his observations and, subject to Article 123, paragraph 1, to amend the application.

(4)   If the applicant fails to reply in due time to any communication from the Examining Division, the application shall be deemed to be withdrawn.

Article 97 Grant or refusal

(1)   If the Examining Division is of the opinion that the European patent application and the invention to which it relates meet the requirements of this Convention, it shall decide to grant a European patent, provided that the conditions laid down in the Implementing Regulations are fulfilled.

(2)   If the Examining Division is of the opinion that the European patent application or the invention to which it relates does not meet the requirements of this Convention, it shall refuse the application unless this Convention provides for a different legal consequence.

(3)   The decision to grant a European patent shall take effect on the date on which the mention of the grant is published in the European Patent Bulletin.

Article 98 Publication of the specification of the European patent

The European Patent Office shall publish the specification of the European patent as soon as possible after the mention of the grant of the European patent has been published in the European Patent Bulletin

PART V
OPPOSITION AND LIMITATION PROCEDURE

Article 99 Opposition

(1)   Within nine months of the publication of the mention of the grant of the European patent in the European Patent Bulletin, any person may give notice to the European Patent Office of opposition to that patent, in accordance with the Implementing Regulations. Notice of opposition shall not be deemed to have been filed until the opposition fee has been paid.

(2)   The opposition shall apply to the European patent in all the Contracting States in which that patent has effect.

(3)   Opponents shall be parties to the opposition proceedings as well as the proprietor of the patent.

(4)   Where a person provides evidence that in a Contracting State, following a final decision, he has been entered in the patent register of such State instead of the previous proprietor, such person shall, at his request, replace the previous proprietor in respect of such State. Notwithstanding Article 118, the previous proprietor and the person making the request shall not be regarded as joint proprietors unless both so request.

Article 100 Grounds for opposition

Opposition may only be filed on the grounds that:

(a)   the subject-matter of the European patent is not patentable under Articles 52 to 57;

(b)   the European patent does not disclose the invention in a manner sufficiently clear and complete for it to be carried out by a person skilled in the art;

(c)   the subject-matter of the European patent extends beyond the content of the application as filed, or, if the patent was granted on a divisional application or on a new application filed under Article 61, beyond the content of the earlier application as filed.

Article 101 Examination of the opposition – Revocation or maintenance of the European patent

(1)   If the opposition is admissible, the Opposition Division shall examine, in accordance with the Implementing Regulations, whether at least one ground for opposition under Article 100 prejudices the maintenance of the European patent. During this examination, the Opposition Division shall invite the parties, as often as necessary, to file observations on communications from another party or issued by itself.

(2)   If the Opposition Division is of the opinion that at least one ground for opposition prejudices the maintenance of the European patent, it shall revoke the patent. Otherwise, it shall reject the opposition.

(3)   If the Opposition Division is of the opinion that, taking into consideration the amendments made by the proprietor of the European patent during the opposition proceedings, the patent and the invention to which it relates

(a)   meet the requirements of this Convention, it shall decide to maintain the patent as amended, provided that the conditions laid down in the Implementing Regulations are fulfilled;

(b)   do not meet the requirements of this Convention, it shall revoke the patent.

Article 103 Publication of a new specification of the European patent

If the European patent is maintained as amended under Article 101, paragraph 3(a), the European Patent Office shall publish a new specification of the European patent as soon as possible after the mention of the opposition decision has been published in the European Patent Bulletin.

Article 105 Intervention of the assumed infringer

(1)   Any third party may, in accordance with the Implementing Regulations, intervene in opposition proceedings after the opposition period has expired, if the third party proves that

(a)   proceedings for infringement of the same patent have been instituted against him, or

(b)   following a request of the proprietor of the patent to cease alleged infringement, the third party has instituted proceedings for a ruling that he is not infringing the patent.

(2)   An admissible intervention shall be treated as an opposition.

Article 105a Request for limitation or revocation

(1)   At the request of the proprietor, the European patent may be revoked or be limited by an amendment of the claims. The request shall be filed with the European Patent Office in accordance with the Implementing Regulations. It shall not be deemed to have been filed until the limitation or revocation fee has been paid.

(2)   The request may not be filed while opposition proceedings in respect of the European patent are pending.

Article 105b Limitation or revocation of the European patent

(1)   The European Patent Office shall examine whether the requirements laid down in the Implementing Regulations for limiting or revoking the European patent have been met.

(2)   If the European Patent Office considers that the request for limitation or revocation of the European patent meets these requirements, it shall decide to limit or revoke the European patent in accordance with the Implementing Regulations. Otherwise, it shall reject the request.

(3)   The decision to limit or revoke the European patent shall apply to the European patent in all the Contracting States in respect of which it has been granted. It shall take effect on the date on which the mention of the decision is published in the European Patent Bulletin.

Article 105c Publication of the amended specification of the European patent

If the European patent is limited under Article 105b, paragraph 2, the European Patent Office shall publish the amended specification of the European patent as soon as possible after the mention of the limitation has been published in the European Patent Bulletin.

PART VI
APPEALS PROCEDURE

Article 106 Decisions subject to appeal

(1)   An appeal shall lie from decisions of the Receiving Section, Examining Divisions, Opposition Divisions and the Legal Division. It shall have suspensive effect.

(2)   A decision which does not terminate proceedings as regards one of the parties can only be appealed together with the final decision, unless the decision allows a separate appeal.

(3)   The right to file an appeal against decisions relating to the apportionment or fixing of costs in opposition proceedings may be restricted in the Implementing Regulations.

Article 107 Persons entitled to appeal and to be parties to appeal proceedings

Any party to proceedings adversely affected by a decision may appeal. Any other parties to the proceedings shall be parties to the appeal proceedings as of right.

Article 108 Time limit and form

Notice of appeal shall be filed, in accordance with the Implementing Regulations, at the European Patent Office within two months of notification of the decision. Notice of appeal shall not be deemed to have been filed until the fee for appeal has been paid. Within four months of notification of the decision, a statement setting out the grounds of appeal shall be filed in accordance with the Implementing Regulations.

Article 110 Examination of appeals

If the appeal is admissible, the Board of Appeal shall examine whether the appeal is allowable. The examination of the appeal shall be conducted in accordance with the Implementing Regulations.

Article 111 Decision in respect of appeals

(1)   Following the examination as to the allowability of the appeal, the Board of Appeal shall decide on the appeal. The Board of Appeal may either exercise any power within the competence of the department which was responsible for the decision appealed or remit the case to that department for further prosecution.

(2)   If the Board of Appeal remits the case for further prosecution to the department whose decision was appealed, that department shall be bound by the ratio decidendi of the Board of Appeal, in so far as the facts are the same. If the decision under appeal was taken by the Receiving Section, the Examining Division shall also be bound by the ratio decidendi of the Board of Appeal.

Article 112 Decision or opinion of the Enlarged Board of Appeal

(1)   In order to ensure uniform application of the law, or if a point of law of fundamental importance arises:

(a)   the Board of Appeal shall, during proceedings on a case and either of its own motion or following a request from a party to the appeal, refer any question to the Enlarged Board of Appeal if it considers that a decision is required for the above purposes. If the Board of Appeal rejects the request, it shall give the reasons in its final decision;

(b)   the President of the European Patent Office may refer a point of law to the Enlarged Board of Appeal where two Boards of Appeal have given different decisions on that question.

(2)   In the cases referred to in paragraph 1(a) the parties to the appeal proceedings shall be parties to the proceedings before the Board of Appeal.

(3)   The decision of the Enlarged Board of Appeal referred to in paragraph 1(a) shall be binding on the Board of Appeal in respect of the appeal in question.

Article 112a Petition for review by the Enlarged Board of Appeal

(1)   Any party to appeal proceedings adversely affected by the decision of the Board of Appeal may file a petition for review of the decision by the Enlarged Board of Appeal.

(2)   The petition may only be filed on the grounds that:

(a)   a member of the Board of Appeal took part in the decision in breach of Article 24, paragraph 1, or despite being excluded pursuant to a decision under Article 24, paragraph 4;

(b)   the Board of Appeal included a person not appointed as a member of the Boards of Appeal;

(c)   a fundamental violation of Article 113 occurred;

(d)   any other fundamental procedural defect defined in the Implementing Regulations occurred in the appeal proceedings; or (e) a criminal act established under the conditions laid down in the Implementing Regulations may have had an impact on the decision.

(3)   The petition for review shall not have suspensive effect.

(4)   The petition for review shall be filed in a reasoned statement, in accordance with the Implementing Regulations. If based on paragraph 2(a) to (d), the petition shall be filed within two months of notification of the decision of the Board of Appeal. If based on paragraph 2(e), the petition shall be filed within two months of the date on which the criminal act has been established and in any event no later than five years from notification of the decision of the Board of Appeal. The petition shall not be deemed to have been filed until after the prescribed fee has been paid.

(5)   The Enlarged Board of Appeal shall examine the petition for review in accordance with the Implementing Regulations. If the petition is allowable, the Enlarged Board of Appeal shall set aside the decision and shall re-open proceedings before the Boards of Appeal in accordance with the Implementing Regulations.

(6)   Any person who, in a designated Contracting State, has in good faith used or made effective and serious preparations for using an invention which is the subject of a published European patent application or a European patent in the period between the decision of the Board of Appeal and publication in the European Patent Bulletin of the mention of the decision of the Enlarged Board of Appeal on the petition, may without payment continue such use in the course of his business or for the needs thereof.

PART VII
COMMON PROVISIONS
CHAPTER 1
COMMON PROVISIONS GOVERNING PROCEDURE

Article 113 Right to be heard and basis of decisions

(1)   The decisions of the European Patent Office may only be based on grounds or evidence on which the parties concerned have had an opportunity to present their comments.

(2)   The European Patent Office shall examine, and decide upon, the European patent application or the European patent only in the text submitted to it, or agreed, by the applicant or the proprietor of the patent.

Article 114 Examination by the European Patent Office of its own motion

(1)   In proceedings before it, the European Patent Office shall examine the facts of its own motion; it shall not be restricted in this examination to the facts, evidence and arguments provided by the parties and the relief sought.

(2)   The European Patent Office may disregard facts or evidence which are not submitted in due time by the parties concerned.

Article 115 Observations by third parties

In proceedings before the European Patent Office, following the publication of the European patent application, any third party may, in accordance with the Implementing Regulations, present observations concerning the patentability of the invention to which the application or patent relates. That person shall not be a party to the proceedings.

Article 121 Further processing of the European patent application

(1)   If an applicant fails to observe a time limit vis-à-vis the European Patent Office, he may request further processing of the European patent application.

(2)   The European Patent Office shall grant the request, provided that the requirements laid down in the Implementing Regulations are met. Otherwise, it shall reject the request.

(3)   If the request is granted, the legal consequences of the failure to observe the time limit shall be deemed not to have ensued.

(4)   Further processing shall be ruled out in respect of the time limits in Article 87, paragraph 1, Article 108 and Article 112a, paragraph 4, as well as the time limits for requesting further processing or re-establishment of rights. The Implementing Regulations may rule out further processing for other time limits.

Article 122 Re-establishment of rights

(1)   An applicant for or proprietor of a European patent who, in spite of all due care required by the circumstances having been taken, was unable to observe a time limit vis-à-vis the European Patent Office shall have his rights re-established upon request if the non-observance of this time limit has the direct consequence of causing the refusal of the European patent application or of a request, or the deeming of the application to have been withdrawn, or the revocation of the European patent, or the loss of any other right or means of redress.

(2)   The European Patent Office shall grant the request, provided that the conditions of paragraph 1 and any other requirements laid down in the Implementing Regulations are met. Otherwise, it shall reject the request.

(3)   If the request is granted, the legal consequences of the failure to observe the time limit shall be deemed not to have ensued.

(4)   Re-establishment of rights shall be ruled out in respect of the time limit for requesting re-establishment of rights. The Implementing Regulations may rule out re-establishment for other time limits.

(5)   Any person who, in a designated Contracting State, has in good faith used or made effective and serious preparations for using an invention which is the subject of a published European patent application or a European patent in the period between the loss of rights referred to in paragraph 1 and publication in the European Patent Bulletin of the mention of re-establishment of those rights, may without payment continue such use in the course of his business or for the needs thereof.

(6)   Nothing in this Article shall limit the right of a Contracting State to grant re-establishment of rights in respect of time limits provided for in this Convention and to be observed vis-à-vis the authorities of such State.

Article 123 Amendments

(1)   The European patent application or European patent may be amended in proceedings before the European Patent Office, in accordance with the Implementing Regulations. In any event, the applicant shall be given at least one opportunity to amend the application of his own volition.

(2)   The European patent application or European patent may not be amended in such a way that it contains subject-matter which extends beyond the content of the application as filed.

(3)   The European patent may not be amended in such a way as to extend the protection it confers.

Article 124 Information on prior art

(1)   The European Patent Office may, in accordance with the Implementing Regulations, invite the applicant to provide information on prior art taken into consideration in national or regional patent proceedings and concerning an invention to which the European patent application relates.

(2)   If the applicant fails to reply in due time to an invitation under paragraph 1, the European patent application shall be deemed to be withdrawn.

Article 125 Reference to general principles

In the absence of procedural provisions in this Convention, the European Patent Office shall take into account the principles of procedural law generally recognised in the Contracting States.

CHAPTER II
INFORMATION TO THE PUBLIC OR TO OFFICIAL AUTHORITIES

Article 127 European Patent Register

The European Patent Office shall keep a European Patent Register, in which the particulars specified in the Implementing Regulations shall be recorded. No entry shall be made in the European Patent Register before the publication of the European patent application. The European Patent Register shall be open to public inspection.

PART VIII
IMPACT ON NATIONAL LAW

CHAPTER I
CONVERSION INTO A NATIONAL PATENT APPLICATION

Article 135 Request for conversion

(1)   The central industrial property office of a designated Contracting State shall, at the request of the applicant for or proprietor of a European patent, apply the procedure for the grant of a national patent in the following circumstances:
(a)   where the European patent application is deemed to be withdrawn under Article 77, paragraph 3;
(b)   in such other cases as are provided for by the national law, in which the European patent application is refused or withdrawn or deemed to be withdrawn, or the European patent is revoked under this Convention.

(2)   In the case referred to in paragraph 1(a), the request for conversion shall be filed with the central industrial property office with which the European patent application has been filed. That office shall, subject to the provisions governing national security, transmit the request directly to the central industrial property offices of the Contracting States specified therein.

(3)   In the cases referred to in paragraph 1(b), the request for conversion shall be submitted to the European Patent Office in accordance with the Implementing Regulations. It shall not be deemed to be filed until the conversion fee has been paid. The European Patent Office

shall transmit the request to the central industrial property offices of the Contracting States specified therein.

(4)   The effect of the European patent application referred to in Article 66 shall lapse if the request for conversion is not submitted in due time.

CHAPTER II
REVOCATION AND PRIOR RIGHTS

Article 138 Revocation of European patents

(1)   Subject to Article 139, a European patent may be revoked with effect for a Contracting State only on the grounds that:

   (a)   the subject-matter of the European patent is not patentable under Articles 52 to 57;

   (b)   the European patent does not disclose the invention in a manner sufficiently clear and complete for it to be carried out by a person skilled in the art;

   (c)   the subject-matter of the European patent extends beyond the content of the application as filed or, if the patent was granted on a divisional application or on a new application filed under Article 61, beyond the content of the earlier application as filed;

   (d)   the protection conferred by the European patent has been extended; or

   (e)   the proprietor of the European patent is not entitled under Article 60, paragraph 1.

(2)   If the grounds for revocation affect the European patent only in part, the patent shall be limited by a corresponding amendment of the claims and revoked in part.

(3)   In proceedings before the competent court or authority relating to the validity of the European patent, the proprietor of the patent shall have the right to limit the patent by amending the claims. The patent as thus limited shall form the basis for the proceedings.

Article 139 Prior rights and rights arising on the same date

(1)   In any designated Contracting State a European patent application and a European patent shall have with regard to a national patent application and a national patent the same prior right effect as a national patent application and a national patent.

(2)   A national patent application and a national patent in a Contracting State shall have with regard to a European patent designating that Contracting State the same prior right effect as if the European patent were a national patent.

(3)   Any Contracting State may prescribe whether and on what terms an invention disclosed in both a European patent application or patent and a national application or patent having the same date of filing or, where priority is claimed, the same date of priority, may be protected simultaneously by both applications or patents.

PROTOCOL ON THE INTERPRETATION OF ARTICLE 69 OF THE EUROPEAN PATENT CONVENTION
of 5 October 1973
as revised by the Act revising the EPC of 29 November 2000

Article 1 General principles

Article 69 should not be interpreted as meaning that the extent of the protection conferred by a European patent is to be understood as that defined by the strict, literal meaning of the wording used in the claims, the description and drawings being employed only for the purpose of resolving an ambiguity found in the claims. Nor should it be taken to mean that the claims serve only as a guideline and that the actual protection conferred may extend to what, from a consideration of the description and drawings by a person skilled in the art, the patent proprietor has contemplated. On the contrary, it is to be interpreted as defining a position between these extremes which combines a fair protection for the patent proprietor with a reasonable degree of legal certainty for third parties.

Article 2 Equivalents

For the purpose of determining the extent of protection conferred by a European patent, due account shall be taken of any element which is equivalent to an element specified in the claims.

DIRECTIVE 98/44/EC
(legal protection of biotechnological inventions)

CHAPTER I
PATENTABILITY

Article 1
1. Member States shall protect biotechnological inventions under national patent law. They shall, if necessary, adjust their national patent law to take account of the provisions of this Directive.
2. This Directive shall be without prejudice to the obligations of the Member States pursuant to international agreements, and in particular the TRIPs Agreement and the Convention on Biological Diversity.

Article 2
1. For the purposes of this Directive,
   (a) "biological material" means any material containing genetic information and capable of reproducing itself or being reproduced in a biological system;
   (b) "microbiological process" means any process involving or performed upon or resulting in microbiological material.
2. A process for the production of plants or animals is essentially biological if it consists entirely of natural phenomena such as crossing or selection.
3. The concept of "plant variety" is defined by Article 5 of Regulation (EC) No 2100/94.

Article 3
1. For the purposes of this Directive, inventions which are new, which involve an inventive step and which are susceptible of industrial application shall be patentable even if they concern a product consisting of or containing biological material or a process by means of which biological material is produced, processed or used.
2. Biological material which is isolated from its natural environment or produced by means of a technical process may be the subject of an invention even if it previously occurred in nature.

Article 4
1. The following shall not be patentable:
   (a) plant and animal varieties;
   (b) essentially biological processes for the production of plants or animals.
2. Inventions which concern plants or animals shall be patentable if the technical feasibility of the invention is not confined to a particular plant or animal variety.
3. Paragraph 1(b) shall he without prejudice to the patentability of inventions which concern a microbiological or other technical process or a product obtained by means of such a process.

Article 5
1. The human body, at the various stages of its formation and development, and the simple discovery of one of its elements, including the sequence or partial sequence of a gene, cannot constitute patentable inventions.
2. An element isolated from the human body or otherwise produced by means of a technical process, including the sequence or partial sequence of a gene, may constitute a patentable invention, even if the structure of that element is identical to that of a natural element.
3. The industrial application of a sequence or a partial sequence of a gene must be disclosed in the patent application.

Article 6
1. Inventions shall be considered unpatentable where their commercial exploitation would be contrary to *ordre public* or morality; however, exploitation shall not be deemed to be so contrary merely because it is prohibited by law or regulation.

2.   On the basis of paragraph 1, the following, in particular, shall be considered unpatentable:
  (a)   processes for cloning human beings;
  (b)   processes for modifying the germ line genetic identity of human beings;
  (c)   uses of human embryos for industrial or commercial purposes;
  (d)   processes for modifying the genetic identity of animals which are likely to cause them
        suffering without any substantial medical benefit to man or animal, and also animals
        resulting from such processes.

Article 7
The Commission's European Group on Ethics in Science and New Technologies evaluates all ethical aspects of biotechnology.

CHAPTER II
SCOPE OF PROTECTION

Article 8
1.   The protection conferred by a patent on a biological material possessing specific
        characteristics as a result of the invention shall extend to any biological material derived
        from that biological material through propagation or multiplication in an identical or
        divergent form and possessing those same characteristics.
2.   The protection conferred by a patent on a process that enables a biological material to
        be produced possessing specific characteristics as a result of the invention shall extend
        to biological material directly obtained through that process and to any other biological
        material derived from the directly obtained biological material through propagation or
        multiplication in an identical or divergent form and possessing those same characteristics.

Article 9
The protection conferred by a patent on a product containing or consisting of genetic information shall extend to all material, save as provided in Article 5(1), in which the product in incorporated and in which the genetic information is contained and performs its function.

Article 10
The protection referred to in Articles 8 and 9 shall not extend to biological material obtained from the propagation or multiplication of biological material placed on the market in the territory of a Member State by the holder of the patent or with his consent, where the multiplication or propagation necessarily results from the application for which the biological material was marketed, provided that the material obtained is not subsequently used for other propagation or multiplication.

Article 11
1.   By way of derogation from Articles 8 and 9, the sale or other form of commercialisation of
        plant propagating material to a farmer by the holder of the patent or with his consent for
        agricultural use implies authorisation for the farmer to use the product of his harvest for
        propagation or multiplication by him on his own farm, the extent and conditions of this
        derogation corresponding to those under Article 14 of Regulation (EC) No 2100/94.
2.   By way of derogation from Articles 8 and 9, the sale or any other form of commercialisation
        of breeding stock or other animal reproductive material to a farmer by the holder of the
        patent or with his consent implies authorisation for the farmer to use the protected livestock
        for an agricultural purpose. This includes making the animal or other animal reproductive
        material available for the purposes of pursuing his agricultural activity but not sale within
        the framework or for the purpose of a commercial reproduction activity.
3.   The extent and the conditions of the derogation provided for in paragraph 2 shall be
        determined by national laws, regulations and practices.

CHAPTER III
COMPULSORY CROSS-LICENSING

Article 12
1.   Where a breeder cannot acquire or exploit a plant variety right without infringing a prior
        patent, he may apply for a compulsory licence for non-exclusive use of the invention
        protected by the patent inasmuch as the licence is necessary for the exploitation of the

plant variety to be protected, subject to payment of an appropriate royalty. Member States shall provide that, where such a licence is granted, the holder of the patent will be entitled to a cross-licence on reasonable terms to use the protected variety.

2.   Where the holder of a patent concerning a biotechnological invention cannot exploit it without infringing a prior plant variety right, he may apply for a compulsory licence for non-exclusive use of the plant variety protected by that right, subject to payment of an appropriate royalty. Member States shall provide that, where such a licence is granted, the holder of the variety right will be entitled to a cross-licence on reasonable terms to use the protected invention.

3.   Applicants for the licences referred to in paragraphs 1 and 2 must demonstrate that:
   (a)   they have applied unsuccessfully to the holder of the patent or of the plant variety right to obtain a contractual licence;
   (b)   the plant variety or the invention constitutes significant technical progress of considerable economic interest compared with the invention claimed in the patent or the protected plant variety.

4.   Each Member State shall designate the authority or authorities responsible for granting the licence. Where a licence for a plant variety can be granted only by the Community Plant Variety Office, Article 29 of Regulation (EC) No 2100/94 shall apply.

CHAPTER IV
DEPOSIT, ACCESS AND RE-DEPOSIT OF A BIOLOGICAL MATERIAL

Article 13
1.   Where an invention involves the use of or concerns biological material which is not available to the public and which cannot be described in a patent application in such a manner as to enable the invention to be reproduced by a person skilled in the art, the description shall be considered inadequate for the purposes of patent law unless:
   (a)   the biological material has been deposited no later than the date on which the patent application was filed with a recognised depositary institution. At least the international depositary authorities which acquired this status by virtue of Article 7 of the Budapest Treaty of 28 April 1977 on the international recognition of the deposit of micro-organisms for the purposes of patent procedure, hereinafter referred to as the "Budapest Treaty", shall be recognised;
   (b)   the application as filed contains such relevant information as is available to the applicant on the characteristics of the biological material deposited;
   (c)   the patent application states the name of the depository institution and the accession number.

2.   Access to the deposited biological material shall be provided through the supply of a sample:
   (a)   up to the first publication of the patent application, only to those persons who are authorised under national patent law;
   (b)   between the first publication of the application and the granting of the patent, to anyone requesting it or, if the applicant so requests, only to an independent expert;
   (c)   after the patent has been granted, and notwithstanding revocation or cancellation of the patent, to anyone requesting it.

3.   The sample shall be supplied only if the person requesting it undertakes, for the term during which the patent is in force:
   (a)   not to make it or any material derived from it available to third parties; and
   (b)   not to use it or any material derived from it except for experimental purposes, unless the applicant for or proprietor of the patent, as applicable, expressly waives such an undertaking.

4.   At the applicant's request, where an application is refused or withdrawn, access to the deposited material shall be limited to an independent expert for 20 years from the date on which the patent application was filed. In that case, paragraph 3 shall apply.

5.   The applicant's requests referred to in point (b) of paragraph 2 and in paragraph 4 may only be made up to the date on which the technical preparations for publishing the patent application are deemed to have been completed.

Article 14
1.   If the biological material deposited in accordance with Article 13 ceases to be available from the recognised depositary institution, a new deposit of the material shall be permitted on the same terms as those laid down in the Budapest Treaty.
2.   Any new deposit shall be accompanied by a statement signed by the depositor certifying that the newly deposited biological material is the same as that originally deposited.

CHAPTER V
FINAL PROVISIONS

Article 15
1.   Member States shall bring into force the laws, regulations and administrative provisions necessary to comply with this Directive not later than 30 July 2000. They shall forthwith inform the Commission thereof.
      When Member States adopt these measures, they shall contain a reference to this Directive or shall be accompanied by such reference on the occasion of their official publication. The methods of making such reference shall be laid down by Member States.
2.   Member States shall communicate to the Commission the text of the provisions of national law which they adopt in the field covered by this Directive.

Article 16
The Commission shall send the European Parliament and the Council:
(a)   every five years as from the date specified in Article 15(1) a report on any problems encountered with regard to the relationship between this Directive and international agreements on the protection of human rights to which the Member States have acceded;
(b)   within two years of entry into force of this Directive, a report assessing the implications for basic genetic engineering research of failure to publish, or late publication of, papers on subjects which could be patentable;
(c)   annually as from the date specified in Article 15(1), a report on the development and implications of patent law in the field of biotechnology and genetic engineering.

Article 17
This Directive shall enter into force on the day of its publication in the *Official Journal of the European Communities*.

REGULATION No 469/2009
(supplementary protection certificates)

Article 1 Definitions
For the purposes of this Regulation, the following definitions shall apply:
(a)   "medicinal product" means any substance or combination of substances presented for treating or preventing disease in human beings or animals and any substance or combination of substances which may be administered to human beings or animals with a view to making a medical diagnosis or to restoring, correcting or modifying physiological functions in humans or in animals;
(b)   "product" means the active ingredient or combination of active ingredients of a medicinal product;
(c)   "basic patent" means a patent which protects a product as such, a process to obtain a product or an application of a product, and which is designated by its holder for the purpose of the procedure for grant of a certificate;
(d)   "certificate" means the supplementary protection certificate;
(e)   "application for an extension of the duration" means an application for an extension of the duration of the certificate pursuant to Article 13(3) of this Regulation and Article 36 of Regulation (EC) No 1901/2006 of the European Parliament and of the Council of 12 December 2006 on medicinal products for paediatric use.

Article 2 Scope

Any product protected by a patent in the territory of a Member State and subject, prior to being placed on the market as a medicinal product, to an administrative authorisation procedure as laid down in Directive 2001/83/EC of the European Parliament and of the Council of 6 November 2001 on the Community code relating to medicinal products for human use or Directive 2001/82/EC of the European Parliament and of the Council of 6 November 2001 on the Community code relating to veterinary medicinal products may, under the terms and conditions provided for in this Regulation, be the subject of a certificate.

Article 3 Conditions for obtaining a certificate

A certificate shall be granted if, in the Member State in which the application referred to in Article 7 is submitted and at the date of that application:

(a)   the product is protected by a basic patent in force;
(b)   a valid authorisation to place the product on the market as a medicinal product has been granted in accordance with Directive 2001/83/EC or Directive 2001/82/EC, as appropriate;
(c)   the product has not already been the subject of a certificate;
(d)   the authorisation referred to in point (b) is the first authorisation to place the product on the market as a medicinal product.

Article 4 Subject matter of protection

Within the limits of the protection conferred by the basic patent, the protection conferred by a certificate shall extend only to the product covered by the authorisation to place the corresponding medicinal product on the market and for any use of the product as a medicinal product that has been authorised before the expiry of the certificate.

Article 5 Effects of the certificate

Subject to the provisions of Article 4, the certificate shall confer the same rights as conferred by the basic patent and shall be subject to the same limitations and the same obligations.

Article 6 Entitlement to the certificate

The certificate shall be granted to the holder of the basic patent or his successor in title.

Article 7 Application for a certificate

1.   The application for a certificate shall be lodged within six months of the date on which the authorisation referred to in Article 3(b) to place the product on the market as a medicinal product was granted.
2.   Notwithstanding paragraph 1, where the authorisation to place the product on the market is granted before the basic patent is granted, the application for a certificate shall be lodged within six months of the date on which the patent is granted.
3.   The application for an extension of the duration may be made when lodging the application for a certificate or when the application for the certificate is pending and the appropriate requirements of Article 8(1)(d) or Article 8(2), respectively, are fulfilled.
4.   The application for an extension of the duration of a certificate already granted shall be lodged not later than two years before the expiry of the certificate.
5.   Notwithstanding paragraph 4, for five years following the entry into force of Regulation (EC) No 1901/2006, the application for an extension of the duration of a certificate already granted shall be lodged not later than six months before the expiry of the certificate.

Article 8 Content of the application for a certificate

1.   The application for a certificate shall contain:
      (a)   a request for the grant of a certificate, stating in particular:
          (i)   the name and address of the applicant;
          (ii)   if he has appointed a representative, the name and address of the representative;
          (iii)   the number of the basic patent and the title of the invention;
          (iv)   the number and date of the first authorisation to place the product on the market, as referred to in Article 3(b) and, if this authorisation is not the first authorisation for placing the product on the market in the Community, the number and date of that authorisation;
      (b)   a copy of the authorisation to place the product on the market, as referred to in Article 3(b), in which the product is identified, containing in particular the number and date of

the authorisation and the summary of the product characteristics listed in Article 11 of Directive 2001/83/EC or Article 14 of Directive 2001/82/EC;

(c) if the authorisation referred to in point (b) is not the first authorisation for placing the product on the market as a medicinal product in the Community, information regarding the identity of the product thus authorised and the legal provision under which the authorisation procedure took place, together with a copy of the notice publishing the authorisation in the appropriate official publication;

(d) where the application for a certificate includes a request for an extension of the duration:

(i) a copy of the statement indicating compliance with an agreed completed paediatric investigation plan as referred to in Article 36(1) of Regulation (EC) No 1901/2006;

(ii) where necessary, in addition to the copy of the authorisation to place the product on the market as referred to in point (b), proof of possession of authorisations to place the product on the market of all other Member States, as referred to in Article 36(3) of Regulation (EC) No 1901/2006.

2. Where an application for a certificate is pending, an application for an extended duration in accordance with Article 7(3) shall include the particulars referred to in paragraph 1(d) of this Article and a reference to the application for a certificate already filed.

3. The application for an extension of the duration of a certificate already granted shall contain the particulars referred to in paragraph 1(d) and a copy of the certificate already granted.

4. Member States may provide that a fee is to be payable upon application for a certificate and upon application for the extension of the duration of a certificate.

Article 9 Lodging of an application for a certificate

1. The application for a certificate shall be lodged with the competent industrial property office of the Member State which granted the basic patent or on whose behalf it was granted and in which the authorisation referred to in Article 3(b) to place the product on the market was obtained, unless the Member State designates another authority for the purpose.

The application for an extension of the duration of a certificate shall be lodged with the competent authority of the Member State concerned.

2. Notification of the application for a certificate shall be published by the authority referred to in paragraph 1. The notification shall contain at least the following information:

(a) the name and address of the applicant;

(b) the number of the basic patent;

(c) the title of the invention;

(d) the number and date of the authorisation to place the product on the market, referred to in Article 3(b), and the product identified in that authorisation;

(e) where relevant, the number and date of the first authorisation to place the product on the market in the Community;

(f) where applicable, an indication that the application includes an application for an extension of the duration.

3. Paragraph 2 shall apply to the notification of the application for an extension of the duration of a certificate already granted or where an application for a certificate is pending. The notification shall additionally contain an indication of the application for an extended duration of the certificate.

Article 10 Grant of the certificate or rejection of the application for a certificate

1. Where the application for a certificate and the product to which it relates meet the conditions laid down in this Regulation, the authority referred to in Article 9(1) shall grant the certificate.

2. The authority referred to in Article 9(1) shall, subject to paragraph 3, reject the application for a certificate if the application or the product to which it relates does not meet the conditions laid down in this Regulation.

3. Where the application for a certificate does not meet the conditions laid down in Article 8, the authority referred to in Article 9(1) shall ask the applicant to rectify the irregularity, or to settle the fee, within a stated time.

4. If the irregularity is not rectified or the fee is not settled under paragraph 3 within the stated time, the authority shall reject the application.

5.   Member States may provide that the authority referred to in Article 9(1) is to grant certificates without verifying that the conditions laid down in Article 3(c) and (d) are met.
6.   Paragraphs 1 to 4 shall apply *mutatis mutandis* to the application for an extension of the duration.

Article 11 Publication
1.   Notification of the fact that a certificate has been granted shall be published by the authority referred to in Article 9(1). The notification shall contain at least the following information:
    (a)   the name and address of the holder of the certificate;
    (b)   the number of the basic patent;
    (c)   the title of the invention;
    (d)   the number and date of the authorisation to place the product on the market referred to in Article 3(b) and the product identified in that authorisation;
    (e)   where relevant, the number and date of the first authorisation to place the product on the market in the Community;
    (f)   the duration of the certificate.
2.   Notification of the fact that the application for a certificate has been rejected shall be published by the authority referred to in Article 9(1). The notification shall contain at least the information listed in Article 9(2).
3.   Paragraphs 1 and 2 shall apply to the notification of the fact that an extension of the duration of a certificate has been granted or of the fact that the application for an extension has been rejected.

Article 12 Annual fees
Member States may require that the certificate be subject to the payment of annual fees.

Article 13 Duration of the certificate
1.   The certificate shall take effect at the end of the lawful term of the basic patent for a period equal to the period which elapsed between the date on which the application for a basic patent was lodged and the date of the first authorisation to place the product on the market in the Community, reduced by a period of five years.
2.   Notwithstanding paragraph 1, the duration of the certificate may not exceed five years from the date on which it takes effect.
3.   The periods laid down in paragraphs 1 and 2 shall be extended by six months in the case where Article 36 of Regulation (EC) No 1901/2006 applies. In that case, the duration of the period laid down in paragraph 1 of this Article may be extended only once.
4.   Where a certificate is granted for a product protected by a patent which, before 2 January 1993, had its term extended or for which such extension was applied for, under national law, the term of protection to be afforded under this certificate shall be reduced by the number of years by which the term of the patent exceeds 20 years.

Article 14 Expiry of the certificate
The certificate shall lapse:
(a)   at the end of the period provided for in Article 13;
(b)   if the certificate holder surrenders it;
(c)   if the annual fee laid down in accordance with Article 12 is not paid in time;
(d)   if and as long as the product covered by the certificate may no longer be placed on the market following the withdrawal of the appropriate authorisation or authorisations to place on the market in accordance with Directive 2001/83/EC or Directive 2001/82/EC. The authority referred to in Article 9(1) of this Regulation may decide on the lapse of the certificate either of its own motion or at the request of a third party.

Article 15 Invalidity of the certificate
1.   The certificate shall be invalid if:
    (a)   it was granted contrary to the provisions of Article 3;
    (b)   the basic patent has lapsed before its lawful term expires;
    (c)   the basic patent is revoked or limited to the extent that the product for which the certificate was granted would no longer be protected by the claims of the basic patent

or, after the basic patent has expired, grounds for revocation exist which would have justified such revocation or limitation.

2.   Any person may submit an application or bring an action for a declaration of invalidity of the certificate before the body responsible under national law for the revocation of the corresponding basic patent.

Article 16 Revocation of an extension of the duration

1.   The extension of the duration may be revoked if it was granted contrary to the provisions of Article 36 of Regulation (EC) No 1901/2006.

2.   Any person may submit an application for revocation of the extension of the duration to the body responsible under national law for the revocation of the corresponding basic patent.

Article 17 Notification of lapse or invalidity

1.   If the certificate lapses in accordance with point (b), (c) or (d) of Article 14, or is invalid in accordance with Article 15, notification thereof shall be published by the authority referred to in Article 9(1).

2.   If the extension of the duration is revoked in accordance with Article 16, notification thereof shall be published by the authority referred to in Article 9(1).

Article 18 Appeals

The decisions of the authority referred to in Article 9(1) or of the bodies referred to in Articles 15(2) and 16(2) taken under this Regulation shall be open to the same appeals as those provided for in national law against similar decisions taken in respect of national patents.

Article 19 Procedure

1.   In the absence of procedural provisions in this Regulation, the procedural provisions applicable under national law to the corresponding basic patent shall apply to the certificate, unless the national law lays down special procedural provisions for certificates.

2.   Notwithstanding paragraph 1, the procedure for opposition to the granting of a certificate shall be excluded.

Article 20 Additional provisions relating to the enlargement of the Community

Without prejudice to the other provisions of this Regulation, the following provisions shall apply:

(a)   any medicinal product protected by a valid basic patent and for which the first authorisation to place it on the market as a medicinal product was obtained after 1 January 2000 may be granted a certificate in Bulgaria, provided that the application for a certificate was lodged within six months from 1 January 2007;

(b)   any medicinal product protected by a valid basic patent in the Czech Republic and for which the first authorisation to place it on the market as a medicinal product was obtained:

   (i)   in the Czech Republic after 10 November 1999 may be granted a certificate, provided that the application for a certificate was lodged within six months of the date on which the first market authorisation was obtained;

   (ii)   in the Community not earlier than six months prior to 1 May 2004 may be granted a certificate, provided that the application for a certificate was lodged within six months of the date on which the first market authorisation was obtained;

(c)   any medicinal product protected by a valid basic patent and for which the first authorisation to place it on the market as a medicinal product was obtained in Estonia prior to 1 May 2004 may be granted a certificate, provided that the application for a certificate was lodged within six months of the date on which the first market authorisation was obtained or, in the case of those patents granted prior to 1 January 2000, within the six months provided for in the Patents Act of October 1999;

(d)   any medicinal product protected by a valid basic patent and for which the first authorisation to place it on the market as a medicinal product was obtained in Cyprus prior to 1 May 2004 may be granted a certificate, provided that the application for a certificate was lodged within six months of the date on which the first market authorisation was obtained; notwithstanding the above, where the market authorisation was obtained before the grant of the basic patent, the application for a certificate must be lodged within six months of the date on which the patent was granted;

(e)   any medicinal product protected by a valid basic patent and for which the first authorisation to place it on the market as a medicinal product was obtained in Latvia prior to 1 May 2004 may be granted a certificate. In cases where the period provided for in Article 7(1) has expired, the possibility of applying for a certificate shall be open for a period of six months starting no later than 1 May 2004;

(f)   any medicinal product protected by a valid basic patent applied for after 1 February 1994 and for which the first authorisation to place it on the market as a medicinal product was obtained in Lithuania prior to 1 May 2004 may be granted a certificate, provided that the application for a certificate was lodged within six months from 1 May 2004;

(g)   any medicinal product protected by a valid basic patent and for which the first authorisation to place it on the market as a medicinal product was obtained after 1 January 2000 may be granted a certificate in Hungary, provided that the application for a certificate was lodged within six months from 1 May 2004;

(h)   any medicinal product protected by a valid basic patent and for which the first authorisation to place it on the market as a medicinal product was obtained in Malta prior to 1 May 2004 may be granted a certificate. In cases where the period provided for in Article 7(1) has expired, the possibility of applying for a certificate shall be open for a period of six months starting no later than 1 May 2004;

(i)   any medicinal product protected by a valid basic patent and for which the first authorisation to place it on the market as a medicinal product was obtained after 1 January 2000 may be granted a certificate in Poland, provided that the application for a certificate was lodged within six months starting no later than 1 May 2004;

(j)   any medicinal product protected by a valid basic patent and for which the first authorisation to place it on the market as a medicinal product was obtained after 1 January 2000 may be granted a certificate in Romania. In cases where the period provided for in Article 7(1) has expired, the possibility of applying for a certificate shall be open for a period of six months starting no later than 1 January 2007;

(k)   any medicinal product protected by a valid basic patent and for which the first authorisation to place it on the market as a medicinal product was obtained in Slovenia prior to 1 May 2004 may be granted a certificate, provided that the application for a certificate was lodged within six months from 1 May 2004, including in cases where the period provided for in Article 7(1) has expired;

(l)   any medicinal product protected by a valid basic patent and for which the first authorisation to place it on the market as a medicinal product was obtained in Slovakia after 1 January 2000 may be granted a certificate, provided that the application for a certificate was lodged within six months of the date on which the first market authorisation was obtained or within six months of 1 July 2002 if the market authorisation was obtained before that date;

(m)   any medicinal product protected by a valid basic patent and for which the first authorisation to place it on the market as a medicinal product was obtained after 1 January 2003 may be granted a certificate in Croatia, provided that the application for a certificate is lodged within six months from the date of accession.

Article 21 Transitional provisions

1.   This Regulation shall not apply to certificates granted in accordance with the national legislation of a Member State before 2 January 1993 or to applications for a certificate filed in accordance with that legislation before 2 July 1992.

    With regard to Austria, Finland and Sweden, this Regulation shall not apply to certificates granted in accordance with their national legislation before 1 January 1995.

2.   This Regulation shall apply to supplementary protection certificates granted in accordance with the national legislation of the Czech Republic, Estonia, Croatia, Cyprus, Latvia, Lithuania, Malta, Poland, Romania, Slovenia and Slovakia prior to their respective date of accession.

Article 22 Repeal

Regulation (EEC) No 1768/92, as amended by the acts listed in Annex I, is repealed.

References to the repealed Regulation shall be construed as references to this Regulation and shall be read in accordance with the correlation table in Annex II.

REGULATION (EU) No 1257/2012
implementing enhanced cooperation in the area of the creation of unitary patent protection

CHAPTER I
GENERAL PROVISIONS

Article 1 Subject matter

1. This Regulation implements enhanced cooperation in the area of the creation of unitary patent protection, authorised by Decision 2011/167/EU.
2. This Regulation constitutes a special agreement within the meaning of Article 142 of the Convention on the Grant of European Patents of 5 October 1973, as revised on 17 December 1991 and on 29 November 2000 (hereinafter "EPC").

Article 2 Definitions

For the purposes of this Regulation, the following definitions shall apply:
(a) "Participating Member State" means a Member State which participates in enhanced cooperation in the area of the creation of unitary patent protection by virtue of Decision 2011/ 167/EU, or by virtue of a decision adopted in accordance with the second or third subparagraph of Article 331(1) of the TFEU, at the time the request for unitary effect as referred to in Article 9 is made;
(b) "European patent" means a patent granted by the European Patent Office (hereinafter "EPO") under the rules and procedures laid down in the EPC;
(c) "European patent with unitary effect" means a European patent which benefits from unitary effect in the participating Member States by virtue of this Regulation;
(d) "European Patent Register" means the register kept by the EPO under Article 127 of the EPC;
(e) "Register for unitary patent protection" means the register constituting part of the European Patent Register in which the unitary effect and any limitation, licence, transfer, revocation or lapse of a European patent with unitary effect are registered;
(f) "European Patent Bulletin" means the periodical publication provided for in Article 129 of the EPC.

Article 3 European patent with unitary effect

1. A European patent granted with the same set of claims in respect of all the participating Member States shall benefit from unitary effect in the participating Member States provided that its unitary effect has been registered in the Register for unitary patent protection.
   A European patent granted with different sets of claims for different participating Member States shall not benefit from unitary effect.
2. A European patent with unitary effect shall have a unitary character. It shall provide uniform protection and shall have equal effect in all the participating Member States.
   It may only be limited, transferred or revoked, or lapse, in respect of all the participating Member States.
   It may be licensed in respect of the whole or part of the territories of the participating Member States.
3. The unitary effect of a European patent shall be deemed not to have arisen to the extent that the European patent has been revoked or limited.

Article 4 Date of effect

1. A European patent with unitary effect shall take effect in the participating Member States on the date of publication by the EPO of the mention of the grant of the European patent in the European Patent Bulletin.
2. The participating Member States shall take the necessary measures to ensure that, where the unitary effect of a European patent has been registered and extends to their territory, that European patent is deemed not to have taken effect as a national patent in their territory on the date of publication of the mention of the grant in the European Patent Bulletin.

CHAPTER II
EFFECTS OF A EUROPEAN PATENT WITH UNITARY EFFECT

Article 5 Uniform protection

1. The European patent with unitary effect shall confer on its proprietor the right to prevent any third party from committing acts against which that patent provides protection throughout the territories of the participating Member States in which it has unitary effect, subject to applicable limitations.

2. The scope of that right and its limitations shall be uniform in all participating Member States in which the patent has unitary effect.

3. The acts against which the patent provides protection referred to in paragraph 1 and the applicable limitations shall be those defined by the law applied to European patents with unitary effect in the participating Member State whose national law is applicable to the European patent with unitary effect as an object of property in accordance with Article 7.

4. In its report referred to in Article 16(1), the Commission shall evaluate the functioning of the applicable limitations and shall, where necessary, make appropriate proposals.

Article 6 Exhaustion of the rights conferred by a European patent with unitary effect

The rights conferred by a European patent with unitary effect shall not extend to acts concerning a product covered by that patent which arc carried out within the participating Member States in which that patent has unitary effect after that product has been placed on the market in the Union by, or with the consent of, the patent proprietor, unless there are legitimate grounds for the patent proprietor to oppose further commercialisation of the product.

CHAPTER III
A EUROPEAN PATENT WITH UNITARY EFFECT AS AN OBJECT OF PROPERTY

Article 7 Treating a European patent with unitary effect as a national patent

1. A European patent with unitary effect as an object of property shall be treated in its entirety and in all the participating Member States as a national patent of the participating Member State in which that patent has unitary effect and in which, according to the European Patent Register:
   (a) the applicant had his residence or principal place of business on the date of filing of the application for the European patent; or
   (b) where point (a) does not apply, the applicant had a place of business on the date of filing of the application for the European patent.

2. Where two or more persons are entered in the European Patent Register as joint applicants, point (a) of paragraph 1 shall apply to the joint applicant indicated first. Where this is not possible, point (a) of paragraph 1 shall apply to the next joint applicant indicated in the order of entry. Where point (a) of paragraph 1 does not apply to any of the joint applicants, point (b) of paragraph 1 shall apply accordingly.

3. Where no applicant had his residence, principal place of business or place of business in a participating Member State in which that patent has unitary effect for the purposes of paragraphs 1 or 2, the European patent with unitary effect as an object of property shall be treated in its entirety and in all the participating Member States as a national patent of the State where the European Patent Organisation has its headquarters in accordance with Article 6(1) of the EPC.

4. The acquisition of a right may not be dependent on any entry in a national patent register.

Article 8 Licences of right

1. The proprietor of a European patent with unitary effect may file a statement with the EPO to the effect that the proprietor is prepared to allow any person to use the invention as a licensee in return for appropriate consideration.

2. A licence obtained under this Regulation shall be treated as a contractual licence.

CHAPTER IV
INSTITUTIONAL PROVISIONS

Article 9 Administrative tasks in the framework of the European Patent Organisation

1.   The participating Member States shall, within the meaning of Article 143 of the EPC, give the EPO the following tasks, to be carried out in accordance with the internal rules of the EPO:
   (a)   to administer requests for unitary effect by proprietors of European patents;
   (b)   to include the Register for unitary patent protection within the European Patent Register and to administer the Register for unitary patent protection;
   (c)   to receive and register statements on licensing referred to in Article 8, their withdrawal and licensing commitments undertaken by the proprietor of the European patent with unitary effect in international standardisation bodies;
   (d)   to publish the translations referred to in Article 6 of Regulation (EU) No 1260/2012 during the transitional period referred to in that Article;
   (e)   to collect and administer renewal fees for European patents with unitary effect, in respect of the years following the year in which the mention of the grant is published in the European Patent Bulletin; to collect and administer additional fees for late payment of renewal fees where such late payment is made within six months of the due date, as well as to distribute part of the collected renewal fees to the participating Member States;
   (f)   to administer the compensation scheme for the reimbursement of translation costs referred to in Article 5 of Regulation (EU) No 1260/2012;
   (g)   to ensure that a request for unitary effect by a proprietor of a European patent is submitted in the language of the proceedings as defined in Article 14(3) of the EPC no later than one month after the mention of the grant is published in the European Patent Bulletin; and
   (h)   to ensure that the unitary effect is indicated in the Register for unitary patent protection, where a request for unitary effect has been filed and, during the transitional period provided for in Article 6 of Regulation (EU) No 1260/2012, has been submitted together with the translations referred to in that Article, and that the EPO is informed of any limitations, licences, transfers or revocations of European patents with unitary effect.

2.   The participating Member States shall ensure compliance with this Regulation in fulfilling their international obligations undertaken in the EPC and shall cooperate to that end. In their capacity as Contracting States to the EPC, the participating Member States shall ensure the governance and supervision of the activities related to the tasks referred to in paragraph 1 of this Article and shall ensure the setting of the level of renewal fees in accordance with Article 12 of this Regulation and the setting of the share of distribution of the renewal fees in accordance with Article 13 of this Regulation.

To that end they shall set up a select committee of the Administrative Council of the European Patent Organisation (hereinafter "Select Committee") within the meaning of Article 145 of the EPC.

The Select Committee shall consist of the representatives of the participating Member States and a representative of the Commission as an observer, as well as alternates who will represent them in their absence. The members of the Select Committee may be assisted by advisers or experts.

Decisions of the Select Committee shall be taken with due regard for the position of the Commission and in accordance with the rules laid down in Article 35(2) of the EPC.

3.   The participating Member States shall ensure effective legal protection before a competent court of one or several participating Member States against the decisions of the EPO in carrying out the tasks referred to in paragraph 1.

CHAPTER V
FINANCIAL PROVISIONS

Article 10 Principle on expenses

The expenses incurred by the EPO in carrying out the additional tasks given to it, within the meaning of Article 143 of the EPC, by the participating Member States shall be covered by the fees generated by the European patents with unitary effect.

Article 11 Renewal fees

1. Renewal fees for European patents with unitary effect and additional fees for their late payment shall be paid to the European Patent Organisation by the patent proprietor. Those fees shall be due in respect of the years following the year in which the mention of the grant of the European patent which benefits from unitary effect is published in the European Patent Bulletin.
2. A European patent with unitary effect shall lapse if a renewal fee and, where applicable, any additional fee have not been paid in due time.
3. Renewal fees which fall due after receipt of the statement referred to in Article 8(1) shall be reduced.

Article 12 Level of renewal fees

1. Renewal fees for European patents with unitary effect shall be:
   (a) progressive throughout the term of the unitary patent protection;
   (b) sufficient to cover all costs associated with the grant of the European patent and the administration of the unitary patent protection; and
   (c) sufficient, together with the fees to be paid to the European Patent Organisation during the pre-grant stage, to ensure a balanced budget of the European Patent Organisation.
2. The level of the renewal fees shall be set, taking into account, among others, the situation of specific entities such as small and medium-sized enterprises, with the aim of:
   (a) facilitating innovation and fostering the competitiveness of European businesses;
   (b) reflecting the size of the market covered by the patent; and
   (c) being similar to the level of the national renewal fees for an average European patent taking effect in the participating Member States at the time the level of the renewal fees is first set.
3. In order to attain the objectives set out in this Chapter, the level of renewal fees shall be set at a level that:
   (a) is equivalent to the level of the renewal fee to be paid for the average geographical coverage of current European patents;
   (b) reflects the renewal rate of current European patents; and
   (c) reflects the number of requests for unitary effect.

Article 13 Distribution

1. The EPO shall retain 50 per cent of the renewal fees referred to in Article 11 paid for European patents with unitary effect. The remaining amount shall be distributed to the participating Member States in accordance with the share of distribution of the renewal fees set pursuant to Article 9(2).
2. In order to attain the objectives set out in this Chapter, the share of distribution of renewal fees among the participating Member States shall be based on the following fair, equitable and relevant criteria:
   (a) the number of patent applications;
   (b) the size of the market, while ensuring a minimum amount to be distributed to each participating Member State;
   (c) compensation to the participating Member States which have:
       (i) an official language other than one of the official languages of the EPO;
       (ii) a disproportionately low level of patenting activity; and/or
       (iii) acquired membership of the European Patent Organisation relatively recently.

CHAPTER VI

FINAL PROVISIONS

Article 14 Cooperation between the Commission and the EPO

The Commission shall establish a close cooperation through a working agreement with the EPO in the fields covered by this Regulation. This cooperation shall include regular exchanges of views on the functioning of the working agreement and, in particular, on the issue of renewal fees and their impact on the budget of the European Patent Organisation.

Article 15 Application of competition law and the law relating to unfair competition

This Regulation shall be without prejudice to the application of competition law and the law relating to unfair competition.

Article 16 Report on the operation of this Regulation

1.   Not later than three years from the date on which the first European patent with unitary effect takes effect, and every five years thereafter, the Commission shall present to the European Parliament and the Council a report on the operation of this Regulation and, where necessary, make appropriate proposals for amending it.

2.   The Commission shall regularly submit to the European Parliament and the Council reports on the functioning of the renewal fees referred to in Article 11, with particular emphasis on compliance with Article 12.

Article 17 Notification by the participating Member States

1.   The participating Member States shall notify the Commission of the measures adopted in accordance with Article 9 by the date of application of this Regulation.

2.   Each participating Member State shall notify the Commission of the measures adopted in accordance with Article 4(2) by the date of application of this Regulation or, in the case of a participating Member State in which the Unified Patent Court does not have exclusive jurisdiction with regard to European patents with unitary effect on the date of application of this Regulation, by the date from which the Unified Patent Court has such exclusive jurisdiction in that participating Member State.

Article 18 Entry into force and application

1.   This Regulation shall enter into force on the twentieth day following that of its publication in the *Official Journal of the European Union*.

2.   It shall apply from 1 January 2014 or the date of entry into force of the Agreement on a Unified Patent Court (the "Agreement"), whichever is the later.

        By way of derogation from Articles 3(1), 3(2) and 4(1), a European patent for which unitary effect is registered in the Register for unitary patent protection shall have unitary effect only in those participating Member States in which the Unified Patent Court has exclusive jurisdiction with regard to European patents with unitary effect at the date of registration.

3.   Each participating Member State shall notify the Commission of its ratification of the Agreement at the time of deposit of its ratification instrument. The Commission shall publish in the *Official Journal of the European Union* the date of entry into force of the Agreement and a list of the Member States who have ratified the Agreement at the date of entry into force. The Commission shall thereafter regularly update the list of the participating Member States which have ratified the Agreement and shall publish such updated list in the *Official Journal of the European Union*.

4.   The participating Member States shall ensure that the measures referred to in Article 9 are in place by the date of application of this Regulation.

5.   Each participating Member State shall ensure that the measures referred to in Article 4(2) are in place by the date of application of this Regulation or, in the case of a participating Member State in which the Unified Patent Court does not have exclusive jurisdiction with regard to European patents with unitary effect on the date of application of this Regulation, by the date from which the Unified Patent Court has such exclusive jurisdiction in that participating Member State.

6.   Unitary patent protection may be requested for any European patent granted on or after the date of application of this Regulation.

COUNCIL REGULATION (EU) No 1260/2012
implementing enhanced cooperation in the area of the creation of unitary patent protection with regard to the applicable translation arrangements

Article 1 Subject matter

This Regulation implements enhanced cooperation in the area of the creation of unitary patent protection authorised by Decision No 2011/167/EU with regard to the applicable translation arrangements.

Article 2 Definitions

For the purposes of this Regulation: the following definitions shall apply:

(a)   "European patent with unitary effect" means a European patent which benefits from unitary effect in the participating Member States by virtue of Regulation (EU) No 1257/2012;

(b)   "Language of the proceedings" means the language used in the proceedings before the EPO as defined in Article 14(3) of the Convention on the Grant of European Patents of 5 October 1973, as revised on 17 December 1991 and on 29 November 2000 (hereinafter "EPC").

Article 3 Translation arrangements for the European patent with unitary effect

1.   Without prejudice to Articles 4 and 6 of this Regulation, where the specification of a European patent, which benefits from unitary effect has been published in accordance with Article 14(6) of the EPC, no further translations shall be required.

2.   A request for unitary effect as referred to in Article 9 of Regulation (EU) No 1257/2012 shall be submitted in the language of the proceedings.

Article 4 Translation in the event of a dispute

1.   In the event of a dispute relating to an alleged infringement of a European patent with unitary effect, the patent proprietor shall provide at the request and the choice of an alleged infringer, a full translation of the European patent with unitary effect into an official language of either the participating Member State in which the alleged infringement took place or the Member State in which the alleged infringer is domiciled.

2.   In the event of a dispute relating to a European patent with unitary effect, the patent proprietor shall provide in the course of legal proceedings, at the request of a court competent in the participating Member States for disputes concerning European patents with unitary effect, a full translation of the patent into the language used in the proceedings of that court.

3.   The cost of the translations referred to in paragraphs 1 and 2 shall be borne by the patent proprietor.

4.   In the event of a dispute concerning a claim for damages, the court hearing the dispute shall assess and take into consideration, in particular where the alleged infringer is a SME, a natural person or a non-profit organisation, a university or a public research organisation, whether the alleged infringer acted without knowing or without reasonable grounds for knowing, that he was infringing the European patent with unitary effect before having been provided with the translation referred to in paragraph 1.

Article 5 Administration of a compensation scheme

1.   Given the fact that European patent applications may be filed in any language under Article 14(2) of the EPC, the participating Member States shall in accordance with Article 9 of Regulation (EU) No 1257/2012, give, within the meaning of Article 143 of the EPC, the EPO the task of administering a compensation scheme for the reimbursement of all translation costs up to a ceiling, for applicants filing patent applications at the EPO in one of the official languages of the Union that is not an official language of the EPO.

2.   The compensation scheme referred to in paragraph 1 shall be funded through the fees referred to in Article 11 of Regulation (EU) No 1257/2012 and shall be available only for SMEs, natural persons, non-profit organisations, universities and public research organisations having their residence or principal place of business within a Member State.

Article 6 Transitional measures

1.   During a transitional period starting on the date of application of this Regulation a request for unitary effect as referred to in Article 9 of Regulation (EU) No 1257/2012 shall be submitted together with the following:

    (a)   where the language of the proceedings is French or German, a full translation of the specification of the European patent into English; or

    (b)   where the language of the proceedings is English, a full translation of the specification of the European patent into any other official language of the Union.

2.   In accordance with Article 9 of Regulation (EU) No 1257/2012, the participating Member States shall give, within the meaning of Article 143 of the EPC, the EPO the task of publishing the translations referred to in paragraph 1 of this Article as soon as possible after the date of the submission of a request for unitary effect as referred to in Article 9 of Regulation (EU) No 1257/ 2012. The text of such translations shall have no legal effect and shall be for information purposes only.

3.   Six years after the date of application of this Regulation and every two years thereafter, an independent expert committee shall carry out an objective evaluation of the availability of high quality machine translations of patent applications and specifications into all the official languages of the Union as developed by the EPO. This expert committee shall be established by the participating Member States in the framework of the European Patent Organisation and shall be composed of representatives of the EPO and of the non-governmental organisations representing users of the European patent system invited by the Administrative Council of the European Patent Organisation as observers in accordance with Article 30(3) of the EPC.

4.   On the basis of the first of the evaluations referred to in paragraph 3 of this Article and every two years thereafter on the basis of the subsequent evaluations, the Commission shall present a report to the Council and, if appropriate, make proposals for terminating the transitional period.

5.   If the transitional period is not terminated on the basis of a proposal of the Commission, it shall lapse 12 years from the date of application of this Regulation.

. . .

TRADE MARKS ACT 1994
(c. 26)

PART I
REGISTERED TRADE MARKS

Introductory

1   Trade marks

(1)   In this Act a "trade mark" means any sign capable of being represented graphically which is capable of distinguishing goods or services of one undertaking from those of other undertakings.

A trade mark may, in particular, consist of words (including personal names), designs, letters, numerals or the shape of goods or their packaging.

(2)   References in this Act to a trade mark include, unless the context otherwise requires, references to a collective mark (see section 49) or certification mark (see section 50).

2   Registered trade marks

(1)   A registered trade mark is a property right obtained by the registration of the trade mark under this Act and the proprietor of a registered trade mark has the rights and remedies provided by this Act.

(2)   No proceedings lie to prevent or recover damages for the infringement of an unregistered trade mark as such; but nothing in this Act affects the law relating to passing off.

Grounds for refusal of registration

3   Absolute grounds for refusal of registration

(1)   The following shall not be registered—

(a)   signs which do not satisfy the requirements of section 1(1),

(b)   trade marks which are devoid of any distinctive character,

(c)   trade marks which consist exclusively of signs or indications which may serve, in trade, to designate the kind, quality, quantity, intended purpose, value, geographical origin, the time of production of goods or of rendering of services, or other characteristics of goods or services,

(d)   trade marks which consist exclusively of signs or indications which have become customary in the current language or in the bona fide and established practices of the trade:

Provided that, a trade mark shall not be refused registration by virtue of paragraph (b), (c) or (d) above if, before the date of application for registration, it has in fact acquired a distinctive character as a result of the use made of it.

(2) A sign shall not be registered as a trade mark if it consists exclusively of—
   (a)   the shape which results from the nature of the goods themselves,
   (b)   the shape of goods which is necessary to obtain a technical result, or
   (c)   the shape which gives substantial value to the goods.
(3) A trade mark shall not be registered if it is—
   (a)   contrary to public policy or to accepted principles of morality, or
   (b)   of such a nature as to deceive the public (for instance as to the nature, quality or geographical origin of the goods or service).
(4) A trade mark shall not be registered if or to the extent that its use is prohibited in the United Kingdom by any enactment or rule of law or by any provision of EU law.
(5) A trade mark shall not be registered in the cases specified, or referred to, in section 4 (specially protected emblems).
(6) A trade mark shall not be registered if or to the extent that the application is made in bad faith.

4   Specially protected emblems

(1) A trade mark which consists of or contains—
   (a)   the Royal arms, or any of the principal armorial bearings of the Royal arms, or any insignia or device so nearly resembling the Royal arms or any such armorial bearing as to be likely to be mistaken for them or it,
   (b)   a representation of the Royal crown or any of the Royal flags, .
   (c)   a representation of Her Majesty or any member of the Royal family, or any colourable imitation thereof, or
   (d)   words, letters or devices likely to lead persons to think that the applicant either has or recently has had Royal patronage or authorisation,
   shall not be registered unless it appears to the registrar that consent has been given by or on behalf of Her Majesty or, as the case may be, the relevant member of the Royal family.
(2) A trade mark which consists of or contains a representation of—
   (a)   the national flag of the United Kingdom (commonly known as the Union Jack), or
   (b)   the flag of England, Wales, Scotland, Northern Ireland or the Isle of Man,
   shall not be registered if it appears to the registrar that the use of the trade mark would be misleading or grossly offensive.
   Provision may be made by rules identifying the flags to which paragraph (b) applies.
(3) A trade mark shall not be registered in the cases specified in—
   section 57 (national emblems, etc. of Convention countries), or
   section 58 (emblems, etc. of certain international organisations).
(4) Provision may be made by rules prohibiting in such cases as may be prescribed the registration of a trade mark which consists of or contains—
   (a)   arms to which a person is entitled by virtue of a grant of arms by the Crown, or
   (b)   insignia so nearly resembling such arms as to be likely to be mistaken for them,
   unless it appears to the registrar that consent has been given by or on behalf of that person.
   Where such a mark is registered, nothing in this Act shall be construed as authorising its use in any way contrary to the laws of arms.
(5) A trade mark which consists of or contains a controlled representation within the meaning of the Olympic Symbol etc. (Protection) Act 1995 shall not be registered unless it appears to the registrar—
   (a)   that the application is made by the person for the time being appointed under section 1(2) of the Olympic Symbol etc. (Protection) Act 1995 (power of Secretary of State to appoint a person as the proprietor of the Olympics association right), or
   (b)   that consent has been given by or on behalf of the person mentioned in paragraph (a) above.

5   Relative grounds for refusal of registration

(1) A trade mark shall not be registered if it is identical with an earlier trade mark and the goods or services for which the trade mark is applied for are identical with the goods or services for which the earlier trade mark is protected.

(2)   A trade mark shall not be registered if because—

    (a)   it is identical with an earlier trade mark and is to be registered for goods or services similar to those for which the earlier trade mark is protected, or

    (b)   it is similar to an earlier trade mark and is to be registered for goods or services identical with or similar to those for which the earlier trade mark is protected,

    there exists a likelihood of confusion on the part of the public, which includes the likelihood of association with the earlier trade mark.

(3)   A trade mark which—

    (a)   is identical with or similar to an earlier trade mark,

    (b)   . . .

    shall not be registered if, or to the extent that, the earlier trade mark has a reputation in the United Kingdom (or, in the case of a European Union trade mark or international trade mark (EC), in the European Union) and the use of the later mark without due cause would take unfair advantage of, or be detrimental to, the distinctive character or the repute of the earlier trade mark.

(4)   A trade mark shall not be registered if, or to the extent that, its use in the United Kingdom is liable to be prevented—

    (a)   by virtue of any rule of law (in particular, the law of passing off) protecting an unregistered trade mark or other sign used in the course of trade, or

    (b)   by virtue of an earlier right other than those referred to in subsections (1) to (3) or paragraph (a) above, in particular by virtue of the law of copyright, design right or registered designs.

    A person thus entitled to prevent the use of a trade mark is referred to in this Act as the proprietor of an "earlier right" in relation to the trade mark.

(5)   Nothing in this section prevents the registration of a trade mark where the proprietor of the earlier trade mark or other earlier right consents to the registration.

6   Meaning of "earlier trade mark"

(1)   In this Act an "earlier trade mark" means—

    (a)   a registered trade mark, international trade mark (UK) or European Union trade mark or international trade mark (EC) which has a date of application for registration earlier than that of the trade mark in question, taking account (where appropriate) of the priorities claimed in respect of the trade marks,

    (b)   a European Union trade mark or international trade mark (EC) which has a valid claim to seniority from an earlier registered trade mark or international trade mark (UK),

    (ba) a registered trade mark or international trade mark (UK) which—

       (i)   has been converted from a European Union trade mark or international trade mark (EC) which itself had a valid claim to seniority within paragraph (b) from an earlier trade mark, and

       (ii) accordingly has the same claim to seniority, or

    (c)   a trade mark which, at the date of application for registration of the trade mark in question or (where appropriate) of the priority claimed in respect of the application, was entitled to protection under the Paris Convention or the WTO agreement as a well known trade mark.

(2)   References in this Act to an earlier trade mark include a trade mark in respect of which an application for registration has been made and which, if registered, would be an earlier trade mark by virtue of subsection (1)(a) or (b), subject to its being so registered.

(3)   A trade mark within subsection (1)(a) or (b) whose registration expires shall continue to be taken into account in determining the registrability of a later mark for a period of one year after the expiry unless the registrar is satisfied that there was no bona fide use of the mark during the two years immediately preceding the expiry.

6A   Raising of relative grounds in opposition proceedings in case of non-use

(1)   This section applies where—

    (a)   an application for registration of a trade mark has been published,

    (b)   there is an earlier trade mark of a kind falling within section 6(1)(a), or (ba) in relation to which the conditions set out in section 5(1), (2) or (3) obtain, and

(c)   the registration procedure for the earlier trade mark was completed before the start of the period of five years ending with the date of publication.

(2)   In opposition proceedings, the registrar shall not refuse to register the trade mark by reason of the earlier trade mark unless the use conditions are met.

(3)   The use conditions are met if—
   (a)   within the period of five years ending with the date of publication of the application the earlier trade mark has been put to genuine use in the United Kingdom by the proprietor or with his consent in relation to the goods or services for which it is registered, or
   (b)   the earlier trade mark has not been so used, but there are proper reasons for non-use.

(4)   For these purposes—
   (a)   use of a trade mark includes use in a form differing in elements which do not alter the distinctive character of the mark in the form in which it was registered, and
   (b)   use in the United Kingdom includes affixing the trade mark to goods or to the packaging of goods in the United Kingdom solely for export purposes.

(5)   In relation to a European Union trade mark or international trade mark (EC), any reference in subsection (3) or (4) to the United Kingdom shall be construed as a reference to the European Union.

(6)   Where an earlier trade mark satisfies the use conditions in respect of some only of the goods or services for which it is registered, it shall be treated for the purposes of this section as if it were registered only in respect of those goods or services.

(7)   Nothing in this section affects—
   (a)   the refusal of registration on the grounds mentioned in section 3 (absolute grounds for refusal) or section 5(4) (relative grounds of refusal on the basis of an earlier right), or
   (b)   the making of an application for a declaration of invalidity under section 47(2) (application on relative grounds where no consent to registration).

7   Raising of relative grounds in case of honest concurrent use

(1)   This section applies where on an application for the registration of a trade mark it appears to the registrar—
   (a)   that there is an earlier trade mark in relation to which the conditions set out in section 5(1), (2) or (3) obtain, or
   (b)   that there is an earlier right in relation to which the condition set out in section 5(4) is satisfied,
   but the applicant shows to the satisfaction of the registrar that there has been honest concurrent use of the trade mark for which registration is sought.

(2)   In that case the registrar shall not refuse the application by reason of the earlier trade mark or other earlier right unless objection on that ground is raised in opposition proceedings by the proprietor of that earlier trade mark or other earlier right.

(3)   For the purposes of this section "honest concurrent use" means such use in the United Kingdom, by the applicant or with his consent, as would formerly have amounted to honest concurrent use for the purposes of section 12(2) of the Trade Marks Act 1938.

(4)   Nothing in this section affects—
   (a)   the refusal of registration on the grounds mentioned in section 3 (absolute grounds for refusal), or
   (b)   the making of an application for a declaration of invalidity under section 47(2) (application on relative grounds where no consent to registration).

(5)   This section does not apply when there is an order in force under section 8 below.

8   Power to require that relative grounds be raised in opposition proceedings

(1)   The Secretary of State may by order provide that in any case a trade mark shall not be refused registration on a ground mentioned in section 5 (relative grounds for refusal) unless objection on that ground is raised in opposition proceedings by the proprietor of the earlier trade mark or other earlier right.

. . .

Effects of registered trade mark

9   Rights conferred by registered trade mark

(1)   The proprietor of a registered trade mark has exclusive rights in the trade mark which are infringed by use of the trade mark in the United Kingdom without his consent.

       The acts amounting to infringement, if done without the consent of the proprietor, are specified in section 10.

(2)   References in this Act to the infringement of a registered trade mark are to any such infringement of the rights of the proprietor.

(3)   The rights of the proprietor have effect from the date of registration (which in accordance with section 40(3) is the date of filing of the application for registration): Provided that—

       (a)   no infringement proceedings may be begun before the date on which the trade mark is in fact registered; and

       (b)   no offence under section 92 (unauthorised use of trade mark, etc. in relation to goods) is committed by anything done before the date of publication of the registration.

10   Infringement of registered trade mark

(1)   A person infringes a registered trade mark if he uses in the course of trade a sign which is identical with the trade mark in relation to goods or services which are identical with those for which it is registered.

(2)   A person infringes a registered trade mark if he uses in the course of trade a sign where because—

       (a)   the sign is identical with the trade mark and is used in relation to goods or services similar to those for which the trade mark is registered, or

       (b)   the sign is similar to the trade mark and is used in relation to goods or services identical with or similar to those for which the trade mark is registered,

       there exists a likelihood of confusion on the part of the public, which includes the likelihood of association with the trade mark.

(3)   A person infringes a registered trade mark if he uses in the course of trade in relation to goods or services, a sign which—

       (a)   is identical with or similar to the trade mark,

       (b)   . . .

       where the trade mark has a reputation in the United Kingdom and the use of the sign, being without due cause, takes unfair advantage of, or is detrimental to, the distinctive character or the repute of the trade mark.

(4)   For the purposes of this section a person uses a sign if, in particular, he—

       (a)   affixes it to goods or the packaging thereof;

       (b)   offers or exposes goods for sale, puts them on the market or stocks them for those purposes under the sign, or offers or supplies services under the sign;

       (c)   imports or exports goods under the sign; or

       (d)   uses the sign on business papers or in advertising.

(5)   A person who applies a registered trade mark to material intended to be used for labelling or packaging goods, as a business paper, or for advertising goods or services, shall be treated as a party to any use of the material which infringes the registered trade mark if when he applied the mark he knew or had reason to believe that the application of the mark was not duly authorised by the proprietor or a licensee.

(6)   Nothing in the preceding provisions of this section shall be construed as preventing the use of a registered trade mark by any person for the purpose of identifying goods or services as those of the proprietor or a licensee.

       But any such use otherwise than in accordance with honest practices in industrial or commercial matters shall be treated as infringing the registered trade mark if the use without due cause takes unfair advantage of, or is detrimental to, the distinctive character or repute of the trade mark.

11   Limits on effect of registered trade mark

(1)   A registered trade mark is not infringed by the use of another registered trade mark in relation to goods or services for which the latter is registered (but see section 47(6) (effect of declaration of invalidity of registration)).

(2) A registered trade mark is not infringed by—

    (a)   the use by a person of his own name or address,

    (b)   the use of indications concerning the kind, quality, quantity, intended purpose, value, geographical origin, the time of production of goods or of rendering of services, or other characteristics of goods or services, or

    (c)   the use of the trade mark where it is necessary to indicate the intended purpose of a product or service (in particular, as accessories or spare parts),

  provided the use is in accordance with honest practices in industrial or commercial matters.

(3) A registered trade mark is not infringed by the use in the course of trade in a particular locality of an earlier right which applies only in that locality.

  For this purpose an "earlier right" means an unregistered trade mark or other sign continuously used in relation to goods or services by a person or a predecessor in title of his from a date prior to whichever is the earlier of—

    (a)   the use of the first-mentioned trade mark in relation to those goods or services by the proprietor or a predecessor in title of his, or

    (b)   the registration of the first-mentioned trade mark in respect of those goods or services in the name of the proprietor or a predecessor in title of his;

  and an earlier right shall be regarded as applying in a locality if, or to the extent that, its use in that locality is protected by virtue of any rule of law (in particular, the law of passing off).

12 Exhaustion of rights conferred by registered trade mark

(1) A registered trade mark is not infringed by the use of the trade mark in relation to goods which have been put on the market in the European Economic Area under that trade mark by the proprietor or with his consent.

(2) Subsection (1) does not apply where there exist legitimate reasons for the proprietor to oppose further dealings in the goods (in particular, where the condition of the goods has been changed or impaired after they have been put on the market).

13 Registration subject to disclaimer or limitation

(1) An applicant for registration of a trade mark, or the proprietor of a registered trade mark, may—

    (a)   disclaim any right to the exclusive use of any specified element of the trade mark, or

    (b)   agree that the rights conferred by the registration shall be subject to a specified territorial or other limitation;

  and where the registration of a trade mark is subject to a disclaimer or limitation, the rights conferred by section 9 (rights conferred by registered trade mark) are restricted accordingly.

(2) Provision shall be made by rules as to the publication and entry in the register of a disclaimer or limitation.

Infringement proceedings

14 Action for infringement

(1) An infringement of a registered trade mark is actionable by the proprietor of the trade mark.

(2) In an action for infringement all such relief by way of damages, injunctions, accounts or otherwise is available to him as is available in respect of the infringement of any other property right.

15 Order for erasure, etc of offending sign

(1) Where a person is found to have infringed a registered trade mark, the court may make an order requiring him—

    (a)   to cause the offending sign to be erased, removed or obliterated from any infringing goods, material or articles in his possession, custody or control, or

    (b)   if it is not reasonably practicable for the offending sign to be erased, removed or obliterated, to secure the destruction of the infringing goods, material or articles in question.

(2) If an order under subsection (1) is not complied with, or it appears to the court likely that such an order would not be complied with, the court may order that the infringing goods, material or articles be delivered to such person as the court may direct for erasure, removal or obliteration of the sign, or for destruction, as the case may be.

16 Order for delivery up of infringing goods, material or articles

(1) The proprietor of a registered trade mark may apply to the court for an order for the delivery up to him, or such other person as the court may direct, of any infringing goods, material or articles which a person has in his possession, custody or control in the course of a business.

(2) An application shall not be made after the end of the period specified in section 18 (period after which remedy of delivery up not available); and no order shall be made unless the court also makes, or it appears to the court that there are grounds for making, an order under section 19 (order as to disposal of infringing goods, etc.).

(3) A person to whom any infringing goods, material or articles are delivered up in pursuance of an order under this section shall, if an order under section 19 is not made, retain them pending the making of an order, or the decision not to make an order, under that section.

(4) Nothing in this section affects any other power of the court.

17 Meaning of "infringing goods, material or articles"

(1) In this Act the expressions "infringing goods", "infringing material" and "infringing articles" shall be construed as follows.

(2) Goods are "infringing goods", in relation to a registered trade mark, if they or their packaging bear a sign identical or similar to that mark and—
  (a) the application of the sign to the goods or their packaging was an infringement of the registered trade mark, or
  (b) the goods are proposed to be imported into the United Kingdom and the application of the sign in the United Kingdom to them or their packaging would be an infringement of the registered trade mark, or
  (c) the sign has otherwise been used in relation to the goods in such a way as to infringe the registered trade mark.

(3) Nothing in subsection (2) shall be construed as affecting the importation of goods which may lawfully be imported into the United Kingdom by virtue of an enforceable EU right.

(4) Material is "infringing material", in relation to a registered trade mark if it bears a sign identical or similar to that mark and either—
  (a) it is used for labelling or packaging goods, as a business paper, or for advertising goods or services, in such a way as to infringe the registered trade mark, or
  (b) it is intended to be so used and such use would infringe the registered trade mark.

(5) "Infringing articles", in relation to a registered trade mark, means articles—
  (a) which are specifically designed or adapted for making copies of a sign identical or similar to that mark, and
  (b) which a person has in his possession, custody or control, knowing or having reason to believe that they have been or are to be used to produce infringing goods or material.

18 Period after which remedy of delivery up not available

(1) An application for an order under section 16 (order for delivery up of infringing goods, material or articles) may not be made after the end of the period of six years from—
  (a) in the case of infringing goods, the date on which the trade mark was applied to the goods or their packaging,
  (b) in the case of infringing material, the date on which the trade mark was applied to the material, or
  (c) in the case of infringing articles, the date on which they were made,
  except as mentioned in the following provisions.

(2) If during the whole or part of that period the proprietor of the registered trade mark—
  (a) is under a disability, or

(b)   is prevented by fraud or concealment from discovering the facts entitling him to apply for an order,

an application may be made at any time before the end of the period of six years from the date on which he ceased to be under a disability or, as the case may be, could with reasonable diligence have discovered those facts.

(3)   In subsection (2) "disability"—
   (a)   in England and Wales, has the same meaning as in the Limitation Act 1980;
   (b)   in Scotland, means legal disability within the meaning of the Prescription and Limitation (Scotland) Act 1973;
   (c)   in Northern Ireland, has the same meaning as in the Limitation (Northern Ireland) Order 1989.

19   Order as to disposal of infringing goods, material or articles

(1)   Where infringing goods, material or articles have been delivered up in pursuance of an order under section 16, an application may be made to the court—
   (a)   for an order that they be destroyed or forfeited to such person as the court may think fit, or
   (b)   for a decision that no such order should be made.

(2)   In considering what order (if any) should be made, the court shall consider whether other remedies available in an action for infringement of the registered trade mark would be adequate to compensate the proprietor and any licensee and protect their interests.

(3)   Provision shall be made by rules of court as to the service of notice on persons having an interest in the goods, material or articles, and any such person is entitled—
   (a)   to appear in proceedings for an order under this section, whether or not he was served with notice, and
   (b)   to appeal against any order made, whether or not he appeared;

and an order shall not take effect until the end of the period within which notice of an appeal may be given or, if before the end of that period notice of appeal is duly given, until the final determination or abandonment of the proceedings on the appeal.

(4)   Where there is more than one person interested in the goods, material or articles, the court shall make such order as it thinks just.

(5)   If the court decides that no order should be made under this section, the person in whose possession, custody or control the goods, material or articles were before being delivered up is entitled to their return.

(6)   References in this section to a person having an interest in goods, material or articles include any person in whose favour an order could be made—
   (a)   under this section (including that section as applied by regulation 4 of the Community Trade Mark Regulations 2006);
   (b)   under section 24D of the Registered Designs Act 1949;
   (c)   under section 114, 204 or 231 of the Copyright, Designs and Patents Act 1988; or
   (d)   under regulation 1C of the Community Design Regulations 2005.

20   Jurisdiction of sheriff court or county court in Northern Ireland

Proceedings for an order under section 16 (order for delivery up of infringing goods, material or articles) or section 19 (order as to disposal of infringing goods, etc.) may be brought—

(a)   in the sheriff court in Scotland, or

(b)   in a county court in Northern Ireland.

This does not affect the jurisdiction of the Court of Session or the High Court in Northern Ireland.

Unjustified threats

21   Threats of infringement proceedings

(1)   A communication contains a "threat of infringement proceedings" if a reasonable person in the position of a recipient would understand from the communication that—
   (a)   a registered trade mark exists, and

(b)   a person intends to bring proceedings (whether in a court in the United Kingdom or elsewhere) against another person for infringement of the registered trade mark by—

      (i)   an act done in the United Kingdom, or

      (ii)   an act which, if done, would be done in the United Kingdom.

(2)   References in this section and in section 21C to a "recipient" include, in the case of a communication directed to the public or a section of the public, references to a person to whom the communication is directed.

21A Actionable threats

(1)   Subject to subsections (2) to (6), a threat of infringement proceedings made by any person is actionable by any person aggrieved by the threat.

(2)   A threat of infringement proceedings is not actionable if the infringement is alleged to consist of—

    (a)   applying, or causing another person to apply, a sign to goods or their packaging,

    (b)   importing, for disposal, goods to which, or to the packaging of which, a sign has been applied, or

    (c)   supplying services under a sign.

(3)   A threat of infringement proceedings is not actionable if the infringement is alleged to consist of an act which, if done, would constitute an infringement of a kind mentioned in subsection (2)(a), (b) or (c).

(4)   A threat of infringement proceedings is not actionable if the threat—

    (a)   is made to a person who has done, or intends to do, an act mentioned in subsection (2)(a) or (b) in relation to goods or their packaging, and

    (b)   is a threat of proceedings for an infringement alleged to consist of doing anything else in relation to those goods or their packaging.

(5)   A threat of infringement proceedings is not actionable if the threat—

    (a)   is made to a person who has done, or intends to do, an act mentioned in subsection (2)(c) in relation to services, and

    (b)   is a threat of proceedings for an infringement alleged to consist of doing anything else in relation to those services.

(6)   A threat of infringement proceedings which is not an express threat is not actionable if it is contained in a permitted communication.

(7)   In sections 21C and 21D "an actionable threat" means a threat of infringement proceedings that is actionable in accordance with this section.

21B Permitted communications

(1)   For the purposes of section 21A(6), a communication containing a threat of infringement proceedings is a "permitted communication" if—

    (a)   the communication, so far as it contains information that relates to the threat, is made for a permitted purpose;

    (b)   all of the information that relates to the threat is information that—

      (i)   is necessary for that purpose (see subsection (5)(a) to (c) for some examples of necessary information), and

      (ii)   the person making the communication reasonably believes is true.

(2)   Each of the following is a "permitted purpose"—

    (a)   giving notice that a registered trade mark exists;

    (b)   discovering whether, or by whom, a registered trade mark has been infringed by an act mentioned in section 21A(2)(a), (b) or (c);

    (c)   giving notice that a person has a right in or under a registered trade mark, where another person's awareness of the right is relevant to any proceedings that may be brought in respect of the registered trade mark.

(3)   The court may, having regard to the nature of the purposes listed in subsection (2)(a) to (c), treat any other purpose as a "permitted purpose" if it considers that it is in the interests of justice to do so.

(4)   But the following may not be treated as a "permitted purpose"—

    (a)   requesting a person to cease using, in the course of trade, a sign in relation to goods or services,

          (b)   requesting a person to deliver up or destroy goods, or

          (c)   requesting a person to give an undertaking relating to the use of a sign in relation to goods or services.

    (5)   If any of the following information is included in a communication made for a permitted purpose, it is information that is "necessary for that purpose" (see subsection (1)(b)(i))—

          (a)   a statement that a registered trade mark exists and is in force or that an application for the registration of a trade mark has been made;

          (b)   details of the registered trade mark, or of a right in or under the registered trade mark, which—

               (i)   are accurate in all material respects, and

               (ii)   are not misleading in any material respect; and

          (c)   information enabling the identification of the goods or their packaging, or the services, in relation to which it is alleged that the use of a sign constitutes an infringement of the registered trade mark.

21C   Remedies and defences

    (1)   Proceedings in respect of an actionable threat may be brought against the person who made the threat for—

          (a)   a declaration that the threat is unjustified;

          (b)   an injunction against the continuance of the threat;

          (c)   damages in respect of any loss sustained by the aggrieved person by reason of the threat.

    (2)   It is a defence for the person who made the threat to show that the act in respect of which proceedings were threatened constitutes (or if done would constitute) an infringement of the registered trade mark.

    (3)   It is a defence for the person who made the threat to show—

          (a)   that, despite having taken reasonable steps, the person has not identified anyone who has done an act mentioned in section 21A(2)(a), (b) or (c) in relation to the goods or their packaging or the services which are the subject of the threat, and

          (b)   that the person notified the recipient, before or at the time of making the threat, of the steps taken.

21D   Professional advisers

    (1)   Proceedings in respect of an actionable threat may not be brought against a professional adviser (or any person vicariously liable for the actions of that professional adviser) if the conditions in subsection (3) are met.

    (2)   In this section "professional adviser" means a person who, in relation to the making of the communication containing the threat—

          (a)   is acting in a professional capacity in providing legal services or the services of a trade mark attorney or a patent attorney, and

          (b)   is regulated in the provision of legal services, or the services of a trade mark attorney or a patent attorney, by one or more regulatory bodies (whether through membership of a regulatory body, the issue of a licence to practise or any other means).

    (3)   The conditions are that—

          (a)   in making the communication the professional adviser is acting on the instructions of another person, and

          (b)   when the communication is made the professional adviser identifies the person on whose instructions the adviser is acting.

    (4)   This section does not affect any liability of the person on whose instructions the professional adviser is acting.

    (5)   It is for a person asserting that subsection (1) applies to prove (if required) that at the material time—

          (a)   the person concerned was acting as a professional adviser, and

          (b)   the conditions in subsection (3) were met.

21E   Supplementary: pending registration

    (1)   In sections 21 and 21B references to a registered trade mark include references to a trade mark in respect of which an application for registration has been published under section 38.

(2)   Where the threat of infringement proceedings is made after an application for registration has been published (but before registration) the reference in section 21C(2) to "the registered trade mark" is to be treated as a reference to the trade mark registered in pursuance of that application.

21F   Supplementary: proceedings for delivery up etc.

In section 21(1)(b) the reference to proceedings for infringement of a registered trade mark includes a reference to—

(a)   proceedings for an order under section 16 (order for delivery up of infringing goods, material or articles), and

(b)   proceedings for an order under section 19 (order as to disposal of infringing goods, material or articles).

Registered trade mark as object of property

22   Nature of registered trade mark

A registered trade mark is personal property (in Scotland, incorporeal moveable property).

23   Co-ownership of registered trade mark

(1)   Where a registered trade mark is granted to two or more persons jointly, each of them is entitled, subject to any agreement to the contrary, to an equal undivided share in the registered trade mark.

(2)   The following provisions apply where two or more persons are co-proprietors of a registered trade mark, by virtue of subsection (1) or otherwise.

(3)   Subject to any agreement to the contrary, each co-proprietor is entitled, by himself or his agents, to do for his own benefit and without the consent of or the need to account to the other or others, any act which would otherwise amount to an infringement of the registered trade mark.

(4)   One co-proprietor may not without the consent of the other or others—

(a)   grant a licence to use the registered trade mark, or

(b)   assign or charge his share in the registered trade mark (or, in Scotland, cause or permit security to be granted over it).

(5)   Infringement proceedings may be brought by any co-proprietor, but he may not, without the leave of the court, proceed with the action unless the other, or each of the others, is either joined as a plaintiff or added as a defendant.

A co-proprietor who is thus added as a defendant shall not be made liable for any costs in the action unless he takes part in the proceedings.

Nothing in this subsection affects the granting of interlocutory relief on the application of a single co-proprietor.

(6)   Nothing in this section affects the mutual rights and obligations of trustees or personal representatives, or their rights and obligations as such.

24   Assignment, etc. of registered trade mark

(1)   A registered trade mark is transmissible by assignment, testamentary disposition or operation of law in the same way as other personal or moveable property.

It is so transmissible either in connection with the goodwill of a business or independently.

(2)   An assignment or other transmission of a registered trade mark may be partial, that is, limited so as to apply—

(a)   in relation to some but not all of the goods or services for which the trade mark is registered, or

(b)   in relation to use of the trade mark in a particular manner or a particular locality.

(3)   An assignment of a registered trade mark, or an assent relating to a registered trade mark, is not effective unless it is in writing signed by or on behalf of the assignor or, as the case may be, a personal representative.

Except in Scotland, this requirement may be satisfied in a case where the assignor or personal representative is a body corporate by the affixing of its seal.

(4)   The above provisions apply to assignment by way of security as in relation to any other assignment.

(5) A registered trade mark may be the subject of a charge (in Scotland, security) in the same way as other personal or moveable property.

(6) Nothing in this Act shall be construed as affecting the assignment or other transmission of an unregistered trade mark as part of the goodwill of a business.

25   Registration of transactions affecting registered trade mark

(1) On application being made to the registrar by—

(a)   a person claiming to be entitled to an interest in or under a registered trade mark by virtue of a registrable transaction, or

(b)   any other person claiming to be affected by such a transaction,

the prescribed particulars of the transaction shall be entered in the register.

(2) The following are registrable transactions—

(a)   an assignment of a registered trade mark or any right in it;

(b)   the grant of a licence under a registered trade mark;

(c)   the granting of any security interest (whether fixed or floating) over a registered trade mark or any right in or under it;

(d)   the making by personal representatives of an assent in relation to a registered trade mark or any right in or under it;

(e)   an order of a court or other competent authority transferring a registered trade mark or any right in or under it.

(3) Until an application has been made for registration of the prescribed particulars of a registrable transaction—

(a)   the transaction is ineffective as against a person acquiring a conflicting interest in or under the registered trade mark in ignorance of it, and

(b)   a person claiming to be a licensee by virtue of the transaction does not have the protection of section 30 or 31 (rights and remedies of licensee in relation to infringement).

(4) Where a person becomes the proprietor or a licensee of a registered trade mark by virtue of a registrable transaction and the mark is infringed before the prescribed particulars of the transaction are registered, in proceedings for such an infringement, the court shall not award him costs unless—

(a)   an application for registration of the prescribed particulars of the transaction is made before the end of the period of six months beginning with its date, or

(b)   the court is satisfied that it was not practicable for such an application to be made before the end of that period and that an application was made as soon as practicable thereafter.

(5) Provision may be made by rules as to—

(a)   the amendment of registered particulars relating to a licence so as to reflect any alteration of the terms of the licence, and

(b)   the removal of such particulars from the register—

(i)   where it appears from the registered particulars that the licence was granted for a fixed period and that period has expired, or

(ii)   where no such period is indicated and, after such period as may be prescribed, the registrar has notified the parties of his intention to remove the particulars from the register.

(6) Provision may also be made by rules as to the amendment or removal from the register of particulars relating to a security interest on the application of, or with the consent of, the person entitled to the benefit of that interest.

26   Trusts and equities

(1) No notice of any trust (express, implied or constructive) shall be entered in the register; and the registrar shall not be affected by any such notice.

(2) Subject to the provisions of this Act, equities (in Scotland, rights) in respect of a registered trade mark may be enforced in like manner as in respect of other personal or moveable property.

27   Application for registration of trade mark as an object of property

(1) The provisions of sections 22 to 26 (which relate to a registered trade mark as an object of property) apply, with the necessary modifications, in relation to an application for the registration of a trade mark as in relation to a registered trade mark.

(2)   In section 23 (co-ownership of registered trade mark) as it applies in relation to an application for registration the reference in subsection (1) to the granting of the registration shall be construed as a reference to the making of the application.

(3)   In section 25 (registration of transactions affecting registered trade marks) as it applies in relation to a transaction affecting an application for the registration of a trade mark, the references to the entry of particulars in the register, and to the making of an application to register particulars, shall be construed as references to the giving of notice to the registrar of those particulars.

Licensing

28   Licensing of registered trade mark

(1)   A licence to use a registered trade mark may be general or limited.

A limited licence may, in particular, apply—

(a)   in relation to some but not all of the goods or services for which the trade mark is registered, or

(b)   in relation to use of the trade mark in a particular manner or a particular locality.

(2)   A licence is not effective unless it is in writing signed by or on behalf of the grantor.

Except in Scotland, this requirement may be satisfied in a case where the grantor is a body corporate by the affixing of its seal.

(3)   Unless the licence provides otherwise, it is binding on a successor in title to the grantor's interest.

References in this Act to doing anything with, or without, the consent of the proprietor of a registered trade mark shall be construed accordingly.

(4)   Where the licence so provides, a sub-licence may be granted by the licensee; and references in this Act to a licence or licensee include a sub-licence or sub-licensee.

29   Exclusive licences

(1)   In this Act an "exclusive licence" means a licence (whether general or limited) authorising the licensee to the exclusion of all other persons, including the person granting the licence, to use a registered trade mark in the manner authorised by the licence.

The expression "exclusive licensee" shall be construed accordingly.

(2)   An exclusive licensee has the same rights against a successor in title who is bound by the licence as he has against the person granting the licence.

30   General provisions as to rights of licensees in case of infringement

(1)   This section has effect with respect to the rights of a licensee in relation to infringement of a registered trade mark.

The provisions of this section do not apply where or to the extent that, by virtue of section 31(1) below (exclusive licensee having rights and remedies of assignee), the licensee has a right to bring proceedings in his own name.

(2)   A licensee is entitled, unless his licence, or any licence through which his interest is derived, provides otherwise, to call on the proprietor of the registered trade mark to take infringement proceedings in respect of any matter which affects his interests.

(3)   If the proprietor—

(a)   refuses to do so, or

(b)   fails to do so within two months after being called upon,

the licensee may bring the proceedings in his own name as if he were the proprietor.

(4)   Where infringement proceedings are brought by a licensee by virtue of this section, the licensee may not, without the leave of the court, proceed with the action unless the proprietor is either joined as a plaintiff or added as a defendant.

This does not affect the granting of interlocutory relief on an application by a licensee alone.

(5)   A proprietor who is added as a defendant as mentioned in subsection (4) shall not be made liable for any costs in the action unless he takes part in the proceedings.

(6)   In infringement proceedings brought by the proprietor of a registered trade mark any loss suffered or likely to be suffered by licensees shall be taken into account; and the

court may give such directions as it thinks fit as to the extent to which the plaintiff is to hold the proceeds of any pecuniary remedy on behalf of licensees.

(7)   The provisions of this section apply in relation to an exclusive licensee if or to the extent that he has, by virtue of section 31(1), the rights and remedies of an assignee as if he were the proprietor of the registered trade mark.

31   Exclusive licensee having rights and remedies of assignee

(1)   An exclusive licence may provide that the licensee shall have, to such extent as may be provided by the licence, the same rights and remedies in respect of matters occurring after the grant of the licence as if the licence had been an assignment.

Where or to the extent that such provision is made, the licensee is entitled, subject to the provisions of the licence and to the following provisions of this section, to bring infringement proceedings, against any person other than the proprietor, in his own name.

(2)   Any such rights and remedies of an exclusive licensee are concurrent with those of the proprietor of the registered trade mark; and references to the proprietor of a registered trade mark in the provisions of this Act relating to infringement shall be construed accordingly.

(3)   In an action brought by an exclusive licensee by virtue of this section a defendant may avail himself of any defence which would have been available to him if the action had been brought by the proprietor of the registered trade mark.

(4)   Where proceedings for infringement of a registered trade mark brought by the proprietor or an exclusive licensee relate wholly or partly to an infringement in respect of which they have concurrent rights of action, the proprietor or, as the case may be, the exclusive licensee may not, without the leave of the court, proceed with the action unless the other is either joined as a plaintiff or added as a defendant.

This does not affect the granting of interlocutory relief on an application by a proprietor or exclusive licensee alone.

(5)   A person who is added as a defendant as mentioned in subsection (4) shall not be made liable for any costs in the action unless he takes part in the proceedings.

(6)   Where an action for infringement of a registered trade mark is brought which relates wholly or partly to an infringement in respect of which the proprietor and an exclusive licensee have or had concurrent rights of action—

(a)   the court shall in assessing damages take into account—

(i)   the terms of the licence, and

(ii)   any pecuniary remedy already awarded or available to either of them in respect of the infringement;

(b)   no account of profits shall be directed if an award of damages has been made, or an account of profits has been directed, in favour of the other of them in respect of the infringement; and

(c)   the court shall if an account of profits is directed apportion the profits between them as the court considers just, subject to any agreement between them.

The provisions of this subsection apply whether or not the proprietor and the exclusive licensee are both parties to the action; and if they are not both parties the court may give such directions as it thinks fit as to the extent to which the party to the proceedings is to hold the proceeds of any pecuniary remedy on behalf of the other.

(7)   The proprietor of a registered trade mark shall notify any exclusive licensee who has a concurrent right of action before applying for an order under section 16 (order for delivery up); and the court may on the application of the licensee make such order under that section as it thinks fit having regard to the terms of the licence.

(8)   The provisions of subsections (4) to (7) above have effect subject to any agreement to the contrary between the exclusive licensee and the proprietor.

Application for registered trade mark

32   Application for registration

(1)   An application for registration of a trade mark shall be made to the registrar.

(2)   The application shall contain—

(a)   a request for registration of a trade mark,

  (b)   the name and address of the applicant,
  (c)   a statement of the goods or services in relation to which it is sought to register
        the trade mark, and
  (d)   a representation of the trade mark.
(3)   The application shall state that the trade mark is being used, by the applicant or with
      his consent, in relation to those goods or services, or that he has a bona fide intention
      that it should be so used.
(4)   The application shall be subject to the payment of the application fee and such class
      fees as may be appropriate.

33   Date of filing

(1)   The date of filing of an application for registration of a trade mark is the date on
      which documents containing everything required by section 32(2) are furnished to the
      registrar by the applicant.
      If the documents are furnished on different days, the date of filing is the last of those
      days.
(2)   References in this Act to the date of application for registration are to the date of filing
      of the application.

34   Classification of trade marks

(1)   Goods and services shall be classified for the purposes of the registration of trade
      marks according to a prescribed system of classification.
(2)   Any question arising as to the class within which any goods or services fall shall be
      determined by the registrar, whose decision shall be final.

Priority

35   Claim to priority of Convention application

(1)   A person who has duly filed an application for protection of a trade mark in a Convention
      country (a "Convention application"), or his successor in title, has a right to priority, for
      the purposes of registering the same trade mark under this Act for some or all of the
      same goods or services, for a period of six months from the date of filing of the first such
      application.
(2)   If the application for registration under this Act is made within that six-month period—
  (a)   the relevant date for the purposes of establishing which rights take precedence
        shall be the date of filing of the first Convention application, and
  (b)   the registrability of the trade mark shall not be affected by any use of the mark
        in the United Kingdom in the period between that date and the date of the
        application under this Act.
(3)   Any filing which in a Convention country is equivalent to a regular national filing, under
      its domestic legislation or an international agreement, shall be treated as giving rise to
      the right of priority.
      A "regular national filing" means a filing which is adequate to establish the date on
      which the application was filed in that country, whatever may be the subsequent fate
      of the application.
(4)   A subsequent application concerning the same subject as the first Convention
      application, filed in the same Convention country, shall be considered the first
      Convention application (of which the filing date is the starting date of the period of
      priority), if at the time of the subsequent application—
  (a)   the previous application has been withdrawn, abandoned or refused, without
        having been laid open to public inspection and without leaving any rights
        outstanding, and
  (b)   it has not yet served as a basis for claiming a right of priority.
      The previous application may not thereafter serve as a basis for claiming a right of
      priority.
(5)   Provision may be made by rules as to the manner of claiming a right to priority on the
      basis of a Convention application.
(6)   A right to priority arising as a result of a Convention application may be assigned or
      otherwise transmitted, either with the application or independently.

The reference in subsection (1) to the applicant's "successor in title" shall be construed accordingly.

36   Claim to priority from other relevant overseas application

(1)   Her Majesty may by Order in Council make provision for conferring on a person who has duly filed an application for protection of a trade mark in—

    (a)   any of the Channel Islands or a colony, or

    (b)   a country or territory in relation to which Her Majesty's Government in the United Kingdom have entered into a treaty, convention, arrangement or engagement for the reciprocal protection of trade marks,

a right to priority, for the purpose of registering the same trade mark under this Act for some or all of the same goods or services, for a specified period from the date of filing of that application.

(2)   An Order in Council under this section may make provision corresponding to that made by section 35 in relation to Convention countries or such other provision as appears to Her Majesty to be appropriate.

. . .

Registration procedure

37   Examination of application

(1)   The registrar shall examine whether an application for registration of a trade mark satisfies the requirements of this Act (including any requirements imposed by rules).

(2)   . . .

(3)   If it appears to the registrar that the requirements for registration are not met, he shall inform the applicant and give him an opportunity, within such period as the registrar may specify, to make representations or to amend the application.

(4)   If the applicant fails to satisfy the registrar that those requirements are met, or to amend the application so as to meet them, or fails to respond before the end of the specified period, the registrar shall refuse to accept the application.

(5)   If it appears to the registrar that the requirements for registration are met, he shall accept the application.

38   Publication, opposition proceedings and observations

(1)   When an application for registration has been accepted, the registrar shall cause the application to be published in the prescribed manner.

(2)   Any person may, within the prescribed time from the date of the publication of the application, give notice to the registrar of opposition to the registration.

The notice shall be given in writing in the prescribed manner, and shall include a statement of the grounds of opposition.

(3)   Where an application has been published, any person may, at any time before the registration of the trade mark, make observations in writing to the registrar as to whether the trade mark should be registered; and the registrar shall inform the applicant of any such observations.

A person who makes observations does not thereby become a party to the proceedings on the application.

39   Withdrawal, restriction or amendment of application

(1)   The applicant may at any time withdraw his application or restrict the goods or services covered by the application.

If the application has been published, the withdrawal or restriction shall also be published.

(2)   In other respects, an application may be amended, at the request of the applicant, only by correcting—

    (a)   the name or address of the applicant,

    (b)   errors of wording or of copying, or

    (c)   obvious mistakes,

and then only where the correction does not substantially affect the identity of the trade mark or extend the goods or services covered by the application.

(3) Provision shall be made by rules for the publication of any amendment which affects the representation of the trade mark, or the goods or services covered by the application, and for the making of objections by any person claiming to be affected by it.

40 Registration

(1) Where an application has been accepted and—
  (a) no notice of opposition is given within the period referred to in section 38(2), or
  (b) all opposition proceedings are withdrawn or decided in favour of the applicant,
  the registrar shall register the trade mark, unless it appears to him having regard to matters coming to his notice since the application was accepted that the registration requirements (other than those mentioned in section 5(1), (2) or (3)) were not met at that time.

(2) A trade mark shall not be registered unless any fee prescribed for the registration is paid within the prescribed period.
  If the fee is not paid within that period, the application shall be deemed to be withdrawn.

(3) A trade mark when registered shall be registered as of the date of filing of the application for registration; and that date shall be deemed for the purposes of this Act to be the date of registration.

(4) On the registration of a trade mark the registrar shall publish the registration in the prescribed manner and issue to the applicant a certificate of registration.

41 Registration: supplementary provisions

(1) Provision may be made by rules as to—
  (a) the division of an application for the registration of a trade mark into several applications;
  (b) the merging of separate applications or registrations;
  (c) the registration of a series of trade marks.

(2) A series of trade marks means a number of trade marks which resemble each other as to their material particulars and differ only as to matters of a non-distinctive character not substantially affecting the identity of the trade mark.

(3) Rules under this section may include provision as to—
  (a) the circumstances in which, and conditions subject to which, division, merger or registration of a series is permitted, and
  (b) the purposes for which an application to which the rules apply is to be treated as a single application and those for which it is to be treated as a number of separate applications.

Duration, renewal and alteration of registered trade mark

42 Duration of registration

(1) A trade mark shall be registered for a period of ten years from the date of registration.

(2) Registration may be renewed in accordance with section 43 for further periods of ten years.

43 Renewal of registration

(1) The registration of a trade mark may be renewed at the request of the proprietor, subject to payment of a renewal fee.

(2) Provision shall be made by rules for the registrar to inform the proprietor of a registered trade mark, before the expiry of the registration, of the date of expiry and the manner in which the registration may be renewed.

(3) A request for renewal must be made, and the renewal fee paid, before the expiry of the registration.
  Failing this, the request may be made and the fee paid within such further period (of not less than six months) as may be prescribed, in which case an additional renewal fee must also be paid within that period.

(4) Renewal shall take effect from the expiry of the previous registration.

(5) If the registration is not renewed in accordance with the above provisions, the registrar shall remove the trade mark from the register.

Provision may be made by rules for the restoration of the registration of a trade mark which has been removed from the register, subject to such conditions (if any) as may be prescribed.

(6)   The renewal or restoration of the registration of a trade mark shall be published in the prescribed manner.

44   Alteration of registered trade mark

(1)   A registered trade mark shall not be altered in the register, during the period of registration or on renewal.

(2)   Nevertheless, the registrar may, at the request of the proprietor, allow the alteration of a registered trade mark where the mark includes the proprietor's name or address and the alteration is limited to alteration of that name or address and does not substantially affect the identity of the mark.

(3)   Provision shall be made by rules for the publication of any such alteration and the making of objections by any person claiming to be affected by it.

Surrender, revocation and invalidity

45   Surrender of registered trade mark

(1)   A registered trade mark may be surrendered by the proprietor in respect of some or all of the goods or services for which it is registered.

(2)   Provision may be made by rules—

(a)   as to the manner and effect of a surrender, and

(b)   for protecting the interests of other persons having a right in the registered trade mark.

46   Revocation of registration

(1)   The registration of a trade mark may be revoked on any of the following grounds—

(a)   that within the period of five years following the date of completion of the registration procedure it has not been put to genuine use in the United Kingdom, by the proprietor or with his consent, in relation to the goods or services for which it is registered, and there are no proper reasons for non-use;

(b)   that such use has been suspended for an uninterrupted period of five years, and there are no proper reasons for non-use;

(c)   that, in consequence of acts or inactivity of the proprietor, it has become the common name in the trade for a product or service for which it is registered;

(d)   that in consequence of the use made of it by the proprietor or with his consent in relation to the goods or services for which it is registered, it is liable to mislead the public, particularly as to the nature, quality or geographical origin of those goods or services.

(2)   For the purposes of subsection (1) use of a trade mark includes use in a form differing in elements which do not alter the distinctive character of the mark in the form in which it was registered, and use in the United Kingdom includes affixing the trade mark to goods or to the packaging of goods in the United Kingdom solely for export purposes.

(3)   The registration of a trade mark shall not be revoked on the ground mentioned in subsection (1)(a) or (b) if such use as is referred to in that paragraph is commenced or resumed after the expiry of the five year period and before the application for revocation is made:

Provided that, any such commencement or resumption of use after the expiry of the five year period but within the period of three months before the making of the application shall be disregarded unless preparations for the commencement or resumption began before the proprietor became aware that the application might be made.

(4)   An application for revocation may be made by any person, and may be made either to the registrar or to the court, except that—

(a)   if proceedings concerning the trade mark in question are pending in the court, the application must be made to the court; and

(b)   if in any other case the application is made to the registrar, he may at any stage of the proceedings refer the application to the court.

(5) Where grounds for revocation exist in respect of only some of the goods or services for which the trade mark is registered, revocation shall relate to those goods or services only.

(6) Where the registration of a trade mark is revoked to any extent, the rights of the proprietor shall be deemed to have ceased to that extent as from—
  (a) the date of the application for revocation, or
  (b) if the registrar or court is satisfied that the grounds for revocation existed at an earlier date, that date.

47 Grounds for invalidity of registration

(1) The registration of a trade mark may be declared invalid on the ground that the trade mark was registered in breach of section 3 or any of the provisions referred to in that section (absolute grounds for refusal of registration).
Where the trade mark was registered in breach of subsection (1)(b), (c) or (d) of that section, it shall not be declared invalid if, in consequence of the use which has been made of it, it has after registration acquired a distinctive character in relation to the goods or services for which it is registered.

(2) The registration of a trade mark may be declared invalid on the ground—
  (a) that there is an earlier trade mark in relation to which the conditions set out in section 5(1), (2) or (3) obtain, or
  (b) that there is an earlier right in relation to which the condition set out in section 5(4) is satisfied,
unless the proprietor of that earlier trade mark or other earlier right has consented to the registration.

(2A) But the registration of a trade mark may not be declared invalid on the ground that there is an earlier trade mark unless—
  (a) the registration procedure for the earlier trade mark was completed within the period of five years ending with the date of the application for the declaration,
  (b) the registration procedure for the earlier trade mark was not completed before that date, or
  (c) the use conditions are met.

(2B) The use conditions are met if—
  (a) within the period of five years ending with the date of the application for the declaration the earlier trade mark has been put to genuine use in the United Kingdom by the proprietor or with his consent in relation to the goods or services for which it is registered, or
  (b) it has not been so used, but there are proper reasons for non-use.

(2C) For these purposes—
  (a) use of a trade mark includes use in a form differing in elements which do not alter the distinctive character of the mark in the form in which it was registered, and
  (b) use in the United Kingdom includes affixing the trade mark to goods or to the packaging of goods in the United Kingdom solely for export purposes.

(2D) In relation to a European Union trade mark or international trade mark (EC), any reference in subsection (2B) or (2C) to the United Kingdom shall be construed as a reference to the European Union.

(2E) Where an earlier trade mark satisfies the use conditions in respect of some only of the goods or services for which it is registered, it shall be treated for the purposes of this section as if it were registered only in respect of those goods or services.

(2F) Subsection (2A) does not apply where the earlier trade mark is a trade mark within section 6(1)(c).

(3) An application for a declaration of invalidity may be made by any person, and may be made either to the registrar or to the court, except that—
  (a) if proceedings concerning the trade mark in question are pending in the court, the application must be made to the court; and
  (b) if in any other case the application is made to the registrar, he may at any stage of the proceedings refer the application to the court.

(4) In the case of bad faith in the registration of a trade mark, the registrar himself may apply to the court for a declaration of the invalidity of the registration.

(5)   Where the grounds of invalidity exist in respect of only some of the goods or services for which the trade mark is registered, the trade mark shall be declared invalid as regards those goods or services only.

(6)   Where the registration of a trade mark is declared invalid to any extent, the registration shall to that extent be deemed never to have been made:

Provided that this shall not affect transactions past and closed.

48   Effect of acquiescence

(1)   Where the proprietor of an earlier trade mark or other earlier right has acquiesced for a continuous period of five years in the use of a registered trade mark in the United Kingdom, being aware of that use, there shall cease to be any entitlement on the basis of that earlier trade mark or other right—

(a)   to apply for a declaration that the registration of the later trade mark is invalid, or

(b)   to oppose the use of the later trade mark in relation to the goods or services in relation to which it has been so used,

unless the registration of the later trade mark was applied for in bad faith.

(2)   Where subsection (1) applies, the proprietor of the later trade mark is not entitled to oppose the use of the earlier trade mark or, as the case may be, the exploitation of the earlier right, notwithstanding that the earlier trade mark or right may no longer be invoked against his later trade mark.

Collective marks

49   Collective marks

(1)   A collective mark is a mark distinguishing the goods or services of members of the association which is the proprietor of the mark from those of other undertakings.

(2)   The provisions of this Act apply to collective marks subject to the provisions of Schedule 1.

Certification marks

50   Certification marks

(1)   A certification mark is a mark indicating that the goods or services in connection with which it is used are certified by the proprietor of the mark in respect of origin, material, mode of manufacture of goods or performance of services, quality, accuracy or other characteristics.

(2)   The provisions of this Act apply to certification marks subject to the provisions of Schedule 2.

PART II

EUROPEAN UNION TRADE MARKS AND INTERNATIONAL MATTERS

European Union trade marks

51   Meaning of "European Union trade mark"

In this Act—

"European Union trade mark" has the meaning given by Article 1(1) of the European Union Trade Mark Regulation; and

"the European Union Trade Mark Regulation" means Council Regulation (EC) No. 207/2009 of 26 February 2009 on the European Union Trade Mark.

Note: Regulation (EC) 207/2009 has been repealed and replaced by Regulation (EU) 2017/1001.

52   Power to make provision in connection with European Union Trade Mark Regulation

(1)   The Secretary of State may by regulations make such provision as he considers appropriate in connection with the operation of the European Union Trade Mark Regulation.

(2)   Provision may, in particular, be made with respect to—

. . .

(b)   the procedures for determining *a posteriori* the invalidity, or liability to revocation, of the registration of a trade mark from which a European Union trade mark claims seniority;

(c)   the conversion of a European Union trade mark, or an application for a European Union trade mark, into an application for registration under this Act;

(d)   the designation of courts in the United Kingdom having jurisdiction over proceedings arising out of the European Union Trade Mark Regulation.

(3)   Without prejudice to the generality of subsection (1), provision may be made by regulations under this section—

    (a)   applying in relation to a European Union trade mark the provisions of—

        (i)   section 21 to 21F (unjustified threats);

        (ii)   sections 89 to 91 (importation of infringing goods, material or articles); and

        (iii)   sections 92, 93, 95 and 96 (offences); and

    (b)   making in relation to the list of professional representatives maintained in pursuance of Article 93 of the European Union Trade Mark Regulation, and persons on that list, provision corresponding to that made by, or capable of being made under, sections 84 to 88 in relation to the register of trade mark attorneys and registered trade mark attorneys.

(3A)   The reference in subsections (1) and (2)(d) to the European Union Trade Mark Regulation includes a reference to Council Regulation (EC) No 40/94 of 20th December 1993 on the Community trade mark.

(4)   Regulations under this section shall be made by statutory instrument which shall be subject to annulment in pursuance of a resolution of either House of Parliament.

The Madrid Protocol: international registration

53   The Madrid Protocol

In this Act—

"the Madrid Protocol" means the Protocol relating to the Madrid Agreement concerning the International Registration of Marks, adopted at Madrid on 27th June 1989;

"the International Bureau" has the meaning given by Article 2(1) of that Protocol; and

"international trade mark (EC)" means a trade mark which is entitled to protection in the European Union under that Protocol; and

"international trade mark (UK)" means a trade mark which is entitled to protection in the United Kingdom under that Protocol.

54   Power to make provision giving effect to Madrid Protocol

(1)   The Secretary of State may by order make such provision as he thinks fit for giving effect in the United Kingdom to the provisions of the Madrid Protocol.

(2)   Provision may, in particular, be made with respect to—

    (a)   the making of applications for international registrations by way of the Patent Office as office of origin;

    (b)   the procedures to be followed where the basic United Kingdom application or registration fails or ceases to be in force;

    (c)   the procedures to be followed where the Patent Office receives from the International Bureau a request for extension of protection to the United Kingdom;

    (d)   the effects of a successful request for extension of protection to the United Kingdom;

    (e)   the transformation of an application for an international registration, or an international registration, into a national application for registration;

    (f)   the communication of information to the International Bureau;

    (g)   the payment of fees and amounts prescribed in respect of applications for international registrations, extensions of protection and renewals.

(3)   Without prejudice to the generality of subsection (1), provision may be made by regulations under this section applying in relation to an international trade mark (UK) the provisions of—

    (a)   section 21 to 21F (unjustified threats);

    (b)   sections 89 to 91 (importation of infringing goods, material or articles); and

    (c)   sections 92, 93, 95 and 96 (offences).

. . .

The Paris Convention: supplementary provisions

55   The Paris Convention

(1) In this Act—
    (a) "the Paris Convention" means the Paris Convention for the Protection of Industrial Property of March 20th 1883, as revised or amended from time to time, . . .
    (aa) "the WTO agreement" means the Agreement establishing the World Trade Organisation signed at Marrakesh on 15th April 1994 , and
    (b) a "Convention country" means a country, other than the United Kingdom, which is a party to that Convention or to that Agreement.

(2) The Secretary of State may by order make such amendments of this Act, and rules made under this Act, as appear to him appropriate in consequence of any revision or amendment of the Paris Convention or the WTO agreement after the passing of this Act.

. . .

56   Protection of well-known trade marks: Article 6*bis*

(1) References in this Act to a trade mark which is entitled to protection under the Paris Convention or the WTO agreement as a well known trade mark are to a mark which is well-known in the United Kingdom as being the mark of a person who—
    (a) is a national of a Convention country, or
    (b) is domiciled in, or has a real and effective industrial or commercial establishment in, a Convention country,
whether or not that person carries on business, or has any goodwill, in the United Kingdom.
References to the proprietor of such a mark shall be construed accordingly.

(2) The proprietor of a trade mark which is entitled to protection under the Paris Convention or the WTO agreement as a well known trade mark is entitled to restrain by injunction the use in the United Kingdom of a trade mark which, or the essential part of which, is identical or similar to his mark, in relation to identical or similar goods or services, where the use is likely to cause confusion.
This right is subject to section 48 (effect of acquiescence by proprietor of earlier trade mark).

(3) Nothing in subsection (2) affects the continuation of any bona fide use of a trade mark begun before the commencement of this section.

57   National emblems, etc. of Convention countries: Article 6*ter*

(1) A trade mark which consists of or contains the flag of a Convention country shall not be registered without the authorisation of the competent authorities of that country, unless it appears to the registrar that use of the flag in the manner proposed is permitted without such authorisation.

(2) A trade mark which consists of or contains the armorial bearings or any other state emblem of a Convention country which is protected under the Paris Convention[or the WTO agreement] shall not be registered without the authorisation of the competent authorities of that country.

(3) A trade mark which consists of or contains an official sign or hallmark adopted by a Convention country and indicating control and warranty shall not, where the sign or hallmark is protected under the Paris Convention or the WTO agreement, be registered in relation to goods or services of the same, or a similar kind, as those in relation to which it indicates control and warranty, without the authorisation of the competent authorities of the country concerned.

(4) The provisions of this section as to national flags and other state emblems, and official signs or hallmarks, apply equally to anything which from a heraldic point of view imitates any such flag or other emblem, or sign or hallmark.

(5) Nothing in this section prevents the registration of a trade mark on the application of a national of a country who is authorised to make use of a state emblem, or official sign or hallmark, of that country, notwithstanding that it is similar to that of another country.

(6) Where by virtue of this section the authorisation of the competent authorities of a Convention country is or would be required for the registration of a trade mark, those

authorities are entitled to restrain by injunction any use of the mark in the United Kingdom without their authorisation.

58 Emblems, etc. of certain international organisations: Article 6*ter*

(1) This section applies to—
    (a) the armorial bearings, flags or other emblems, and
    (b) the abbreviations and names,
of international intergovernmental organisations of which one or more Convention countries are members.

(2) A trade mark which consists of or contains any such emblem, abbreviation or name which is protected under the Paris Convention or the WTO agreement shall not be registered without the authorisation of the international organisation concerned, unless it appears to the registrar that the use of the emblem, abbreviation or name in the manner proposed—
    (a) is not such as to suggest to the public that a connection exists between the organisation and the trade mark, or
    (b) is not likely to mislead the public as to the existence of a connection between the user and the organisation.

(3) The provisions of this section as to emblems of an international organisation apply equally to anything which from a heraldic point of view imitates any such emblem.

(4) Where by virtue of this section the authorisation of an international organisation is or would be required for the registration of a trade mark, that organisation is entitled to restrain by injunction any use of the mark in the United Kingdom without its authorisation.

(5) Nothing in this section affects the rights of a person whose bona fide use of the trade mark in question began before 4th January 1962 (when the relevant provisions of the Paris Convention entered into force in relation to the United Kingdom).

59 Notification under Article 6*ter* of the Convention

(1) For the purposes of section 57 state emblems of a Convention country (other than the national flag), and official signs or hallmarks, shall be regarded as protected under the Paris Convention only if, or to the extent that—
    (a) the country in question has notified the United Kingdom in accordance with Article 6*ter*(3) of the Convention that it desires to protect that emblem, sign or hallmark,
    (b) the notification remains in force, and
    (c) the United Kingdom has not objected to it in accordance with Article 6*ter*(4) or any such objection has been withdrawn.

(2) For the purposes of section 58 the emblems, abbreviations and names of an international organisation shall be regarded as protected under the Paris Convention only if, or to the extent that—
    (a) the organisation in question has notified the United Kingdom in accordance with Article 6*ter*(3) of the Convention that it desires to protect that emblem, abbreviation or name,
    (b) the notification remains in force, and
    (c) the United Kingdom has not objected to it in accordance with Article 6*ter*(4) or any such objection has been withdrawn.

(3) Notification under Article 6*ter*(3) of the Paris Convention shall have effect only in relation to applications for registration made more than two months after the receipt of the notification.

(4) The registrar shall keep and make available for public inspection by any person, at all reasonable hours and free of charge, a list of—
    (a) the state emblems and official signs or hallmarks, and
    (b) the emblems, abbreviations and names of international organisations,
which are for the time being protected under the Paris Convention by virtue of notification under Article 6*ter*(3).

(5) Any reference in this section to Article 6*ter* of the Paris Convention shall be construed as including a reference to that Article as applied by the WTO agreement.

PART III
ADMINISTRATIVE AND OTHER SUPPLEMENTARY PROVISIONS

The registrar

62   The registrar

In this Act "the registrar" means the Comptroller-General of Patents, Designs and Trade Marks.

The register

63   The register

(1)   The registrar shall maintain a register of trade marks.
       References in this Act to "the register" are to that register; and references to registration (in particular, in the expression "registered trade mark") are, unless the context otherwise requires, to registration in that register.
(2)   There shall be entered in the register in accordance with this Act—
       (a)   registered trade marks,
       (b)   such particulars as may be prescribed of registrable transactions affecting a registered trade mark, and
       (c)   such other matters relating to registered trade marks as may be prescribed.
(3)   The register shall be kept in such manner as may be prescribed, and provision shall in particular be made for—
       (a)   public inspection of the register, and
       (b)   the supply of certified or uncertified copies, or extracts, of entries in the register.

64   Rectification or correction of the register

(1)   Any person having a sufficient interest may apply for the rectification of an error or omission in the register:
       Provided that an application for rectification may not be made in respect of a matter affecting the validity of the registration of a trade mark.
(2)   An application for rectification may be made either to the registrar or to the court, except that—
       (a)   if proceedings concerning the trade mark in question are pending in the court, the application must be made to the court; and
       (b)   if in any other case the application is made to the registrar, he may at any stage of the proceedings refer the application to the court.
(3)   Except where the registrar or the court directs otherwise, the effect of rectification of the register is that the error or omission in question shall be deemed never to have been made.
(4)   The registrar may, on request made in the prescribed manner by the proprietor of a registered trade mark, or a licensee, enter any change in his name or address as recorded in the register.
(5)   The registrar may remove from the register matter appearing to him to have ceased to have effect.

Legal proceedings and appeals

72   Registration to be prima facie evidence of validity

In all legal proceedings relating to a registered trade mark (including proceedings for rectification of the register) the registration of a person as proprietor of a trade mark shall be prima facie evidence of the validity of the original registration and of any subsequent assignment or other transmission of it.

73   Certificate of validity of contested registration

(1)   If in proceedings before the court the validity of the registration of a trade mark is contested and it is found by the court that the trade mark is validly registered, the court may give a certificate to that effect.
(2)   If the court gives such a certificate and in subsequent proceedings—
       (a)   the validity of the registration is again questioned, and
       (b)   the proprietor obtains a final order or judgment in his favour,

he is entitled to his costs as between solicitor and client unless the court directs otherwise. This subsection does not extend to the costs of an appeal in any such proceedings.

75 The court

In this Act, unless the context otherwise requires, "the court" means—

(a) in England and Wales, the High Court or the county court where it has jurisdiction by virtue of an order made under section 1 of the Courts and Legal Services Act 1990,

(aa) in Northern Ireland, the High Court, and

(b) in Scotland, the Court of Session.

76 Appeals from the registrar

(1) An appeal lies from any decision of the registrar under this Act, except as otherwise expressly provided by rules.

For this purpose "decision" includes any act of the registrar in exercise of a discretion vested in him by or under this Act.

(2) Any such appeal may be brought either to an appointed person or to the court.

(3) Where an appeal is made to an appointed person, he may refer the appeal to the court if—

(a) it appears to him that a point of general legal importance is involved,

(b) the registrar requests that it be so referred, or

(c) such a request is made by any party to the proceedings before the registrar in which the decision appealed against was made.

Before doing so the appointed person shall give the appellant and any other party to the appeal an opportunity to make representations as to whether the appeal should be referred to the court.

(4) Where an appeal is made to an appointed person and he does not refer it to the court, he shall hear and determine the appeal and his decision shall be final.

(5) The provisions of sections 68 and 69 (costs and security for costs; evidence) apply in relation to proceedings before an appointed person as in relation to proceedings before the registrar.

(6) In the application of the section to England and Wales, "the court" means the High Court.

77 Persons appointed to hear and determine appeals

(1) For the purposes of section 76 an "appointed person" means a person appointed by the Lord Chancellor to hear and decide appeals under this Act.

. . .

81 The trade marks journal

Provision shall be made by rules for the publication by the registrar of a journal containing particulars of any application for the registration of a trade mark (including a representation of the mark) and such other information relating to trade marks as the registrar thinks fit.

Trade mark agents

82 Recognition of agents

Except as otherwise provided by rules and subject to the Legal Services Act 2007, any act required or authorised by this Act to be done by or to a person in connection with the registration of a trade mark, or any procedure relating to a registered trade mark, may be done by or to an agent authorised by that person orally or in writing.

83 The register of trade mark attorneys

(1) There is to continue to be a register of persons who act as agent for others for the purpose of applying for or obtaining the registration of trade marks.

(2) In this Act a registered trade mark attorney means an individual whose name is entered on the register kept under this section.

(3) The register is to be kept by the Institute of Trade Mark Attorneys.

. . .

83A   Regulation of trade mark attorneys

(1)   The person who keeps the register under section 83 may make regulations which regulate—

    (a)   the keeping of the register and the registration of persons;

    (b)   the carrying on of trade mark agency work by registered persons.

. . .

84   Unregistered persons not to be described as registered trade mark agents

(1)   An individual who is not a registered trade mark attorney shall not—

    (a)   carry on a business (otherwise than in partnership) under any name or other description which contains the words "registered trade mark agent" or registered trade mark attorney; or

    (b)   in the course of a business otherwise describe or hold himself out, or permit himself to be described or held out, as a registered trade mark agent or a registered trade mark attorney.

(2)   A partnership or other unincorporated body shall not—

    (a)   carry on a business under any name or other description which contains the words "registered trade mark agent" or registered trade mark attorney; or

    (b)   in the course of a business otherwise describe or hold itself out, or permit itself to be described or held out, as a firm of registered trade mark agents or registered trade mark attorneys,

unless the partnership or other body is registered in the register kept under section 83.

(3)   A body corporate shall not—

    (a)   carry on a business (otherwise than in partnership) under any name or other description which contains the words "registered trade mark agent" or registered trade mark attorney; or

    (b)   in the course of a business otherwise describe or hold itself out, or permit itself to be described or held out, as a registered trade mark agent or a registered trade mark attorney,

unless the body corporate is registered in the register kept under section 83.

(4)   A person who contravenes this section commits an offence and is liable on summary conviction to a fine not exceeding level 5 on the standard scale; and proceedings for such an offence may be begun at any time within a year from the date of the offence.

86   Use of the term "trade mark attorney"

(1)   No offence is committed under the enactments restricting the use of certain expressions in reference to persons not qualified to act as solicitors by the use of the term "trade mark attorney" in reference to a registered trade mark attorney.

(2)   The enactments referred to in subsection (1) are section 21 of the Solicitors Act 1974, section 31 of the Solicitors (Scotland) Act 1980 and Article 22 of the Solicitors (Northern Ireland) Order 1976.

87   Privilege for communications with registered trade mark agents

(1)   This section applies to—

    (a)   communications as to any matter relating to the protection of any design or trade mark, or as to any matter involving passing off, and

    (b)   documents, material or information relating to any matter mentioned in paragraph (a).

(2)   Where a trade mark attorney acts for a client in relation to a matter mentioned in subsection (1), any communication, document, material or information to which this section applies is privileged from disclosure in like manner as if the trade mark attorney had at all material times been acting as the client's solicitor.

(3)   In subsection (2) "trade mark attorney" means—

    (a)   a registered trade mark attorney, or

    (b)   a partnership entitled to describe itself as a firm of registered trade mark attorneys, or

    (c)   any other unincorporated body or a body corporate entitled to describe itself as a registered trade mark attorney.

Importation of infringing goods, material or articles

89   Infringing goods, material or articles may be treated as prohibited goods

(1)   The proprietor of a registered trade mark, or a licensee, may give notice in writing to the Commissioners of Customs and Excise—

(a)   that he is the proprietor or, as the case may be, a licensee of the registered trade mark,

(b)   that, at a time and place specified in the notice, goods which are, in relation to that registered trade mark, infringing goods, material or articles are expected to arrive in the United Kingdom—

(i)   from outside the European Economic Area, or

(i)   from within that Area but not having been entered for free circulation, and

(c)   that he requests the Commissioners to treat them as prohibited goods.

(2)   When a notice is in force under this section the importation of the goods to which the notice relates, otherwise than by a person for his private and domestic use, is prohibited; but a person is not by reason of the prohibition liable to any penalty other than forfeiture of the goods.

(3)   This section does not apply to goods placed in, or expected to be placed in, one of the situations referred to in Article 1(1), in respect of which an application may be made under Article 5(1), of Council Regulation (EC) No 1383/2003 concerning customs action against goods suspected of infringing certain intellectual property rights and the measures to be taken against goods found to have infringed such rights.

91   Power of Commissioners for Revenue and Customs to disclose information

Where information relating to infringing goods, material or articles has been obtained or is held by the Commissioners for her Majesty's Revenue and Customs for the purposes of, or in connection with, the exercise of functions of Her Majesty's Revenue and Customs in relation to imported goods, the Commissioners may authorise the disclosure of that information for the purpose of facilitating the exercise by any person of any function in connection with the investigation or prosecution of an offence under—

(a)   section 92 below (unauthorised use of trade mark, etc in relation to goods),

(b)   the Trade Descriptions Act 1968,

(c)   the Business Protection from Misleading Marketing Regulations 2008, or

(d)   the Consumer Protection from Unfair Trading Regulations 2008.

Offences

92   Unauthorised use of trade mark, etc. in relation to goods

(1)   A person commits an offence who with a view to gain for himself or another, or with intent to cause loss to another, and without the consent of the proprietor—

(a)   applies to goods or their packaging a sign identical to, or likely to be mistaken for, a registered trade mark, or

(b)   sells or lets for hire, offers or exposes for sale or hire or distributes goods which bear, or the packaging of which bears, such a sign, or

(c)   has in his possession, custody or control in the course of a business any such goods with a view to the doing of anything, by himself or another, which would be an offence under paragraph (b).

(2)   A person commits an offence who with a view to gain for himself or another, or with intent to cause loss to another, and without the consent of the proprietor—

(a)   applies a sign identical to, or likely to be mistaken for, a registered trade mark to material intended to be used—

(i)   for labelling or packaging goods,

(ii)   as a business paper in relation to goods, or

(iii)   for advertising goods, or

(b)   uses in the course of a business material bearing such a sign for labelling or packaging goods, as a business paper in relation to goods, or for advertising goods, or

      (c)   has in his possession, custody or control in the course of a business any such material with a view to the doing of anything, by himself or another, which would be an offence under paragraph (b).

(3)   A person commits an offence who with a view to gain for himself or another, or with intent to cause loss to another, and without the consent of the proprietor—

      (a)   makes an article specifically designed or adapted for making copies of a sign identical to, or likely to be mistaken for, a registered trade mark, or

      (b)   has such an article in his possession, custody or control in the course of a business, knowing or having reason to believe that it has been, or is to be, used to produce goods, or material for labelling or packaging goods, as a business paper in relation to goods, or for advertising goods.

(4)   A person does not commit an offence under this section unless—

      (a)   the goods are goods in respect of which the trade mark is registered, or

      (b)   the trade mark has a reputation in the United Kingdom and the use of the sign takes or would take unfair advantage of, or is or would be detrimental to, the distinctive character or the repute of the trade mark.

(5)   It is a defence for a person charged with an offence under this section to show that he believed on reasonable grounds that the use of the sign in the manner in which it was used, or was to be used, was not an infringement of the registered trade mark.

(6)   A person guilty of an offence under this section is liable—

      (a)   on summary conviction to imprisonment for a term not exceeding six months or a fine not exceeding the statutory maximum, or both;

      (b)   on conviction on indictment to a fine or imprisonment for a term not exceeding ten years, or both.

92A   Search warrants

(1)   Where a justice of the peace (in Scotland, a sheriff or justice of the peace) is satisfied by information on oath given by a constable (in Scotland, by evidence on oath) that there are reasonable grounds for believing—

      (a)   that an offence under section 92 (unauthorised use of trade mark, etc. in relation to goods) has been or is about to be committed in any premises, and

      (b)   that evidence that such an offence has been or is about to be committed is in those premises,

he may issue a warrant authorising a constable to enter and search the premises, using such reasonable force as is necessary.

(2)   The power conferred by subsection (1) does not, in England and Wales, extend to authorising a search for material of the kinds mentioned in section 9(2) of the Police and Criminal Evidence Act 1984 (certain classes of personal or confidential material).

. . .

(4)   In executing a warrant issued under subsection (1) a constable may seize an article if he reasonably believes that it is evidence that any offence under section 92 has been or is about to be committed.

(5)   In this section "premises" includes land, buildings, fixed or moveable structures, vehicles, vessels, aircraft and hovercraft.

93   Enforcement function of local weights and measures authority

(1)   It is the duty of every local weights and measures authority to enforce within their area the provisions of section 92 (unauthorised use of trade mark, etc. in relation to goods).

. . .

94   Falsification of register, etc.

(1)   It is an offence for a person to make, or cause to be made, a false entry in the register of trade marks, knowing or having reason to believe that it is false.

(2)   It is an offence for a person—

      (a)   to make or cause to be made anything falsely purporting to be a copy of an entry in the register, or

      (b)   to produce or tender or cause to be produced or tendered in evidence any such thing,

knowing or having reason to believe that it is false.

    (3)   A person guilty of an offence under this section is liable—

        (a)   on conviction on indictment, to imprisonment for a term not exceeding two years or a fine, or both;

        (b)   on summary conviction, to imprisonment for a term not exceeding six months or a fine not exceeding the statutory maximum, or both.

95 Falsely representing trade mark as registered

    (1)   It is an offence for a person—

        (a)   falsely to represent that a mark is a registered trade mark, or

        (b)   to make a false representation as to the goods or services for which a trade mark is registered

    knowing or having reason to believe that the representation is false.

    (2)   For the purposes of this section, the use in the United Kingdom in relation to a trade mark—

        (a)   of the word "registered", or

        (b)   of any other word or symbol importing a reference (express or implied) to registration,

    shall be deemed to be a representation as to registration under this Act unless it is shown that the reference is to registration elsewhere than in the United Kingdom and that the trade mark is in fact so registered for the goods or services in question.

    (3)   A person guilty of an offence under this section is liable on summary conviction to a fine not exceeding level 3 on the standard scale.

96 Supplementary provisions as to summary proceedings in Scotland

    (1)   Notwithstanding anything in[section 136 of the Criminal Procedure (Scotland) Act 1995], summary proceedings in Scotland for an offence under this Act may be begun at any time within six months after the date on which evidence sufficient in the Lord Advocate's opinion to justify the proceedings came to his knowledge.

    For this purpose a certificate of the Lord Advocate as to the date on which such evidence came to his knowledge is conclusive evidence.

    . . .

Forfeiture of counterfeit goods, etc.

97 Forfeiture: England and Wales or Northern Ireland

    (1)   In England and Wales or Northern Ireland where there has come into the possession of any person in connection with the investigation or prosecution of a relevant offence—

        (a)   goods which, or the packaging of which, bears a sign identical to or likely to be mistaken for a registered trade mark,

        (b)   material bearing such a sign and intended to be used for labelling or packaging goods, as a business paper in relation to goods, or for advertising goods, or

        (c)   articles specifically designed or adapted for making copies of such a sign,

    that person may apply under this section for an order for the forfeiture of the goods, material or articles.

    . . .

    (3)   On an application under this section the court shall make an order for the forfeiture of any goods, material or articles only if it is satisfied that a relevant offence has been committed in relation to the goods, material or articles.

    . . .

    (6)   Subject to subsection (7), where any goods, material or articles are forfeited under this section they shall be destroyed in accordance with such directions as the court may give.

    (7)   On making an order under this section the court may, if it considers it appropriate to do so, direct that the goods, material or articles to which the order relates shall (instead of being destroyed) be released, to such person as the court may specify, on condition that that person—

        (a)   causes the offending sign to be erased, removed or obliterated, and

        (b)   complies with any order to pay costs which has been made against him in the proceedings for the order for forfeiture.

(8) For the purposes of this section a "relevant offence" means—
  (a) an offence under section 92 above (unauthorised use of trade mark, etc. in relation to goods),
  (b) an offence under the Trade Descriptions Act 1968,
  (c) an offence under the Business Protection from Misleading Marketing Regulations 2008,
  (d) an offence under the Consumer Protection from Unfair Trading Regulations 2008, or
  (e) any offence involving dishonesty or deception.

98 Forfeiture: Scotland

(1) In Scotland the court may make an order for the forfeiture of any—
  (a) goods which bear, or the packaging of which bears, a sign identical to or likely to be mistaken for a registered trade mark,
  (b) material bearing such a sign and intended to be used for labelling or packaging goods, as a business paper in relation to goods, or for advertising goods, or
  (c) articles specifically designed or adapted for making copies of such a sign.
. . .
(3) On an application under subsection (2)(a), the court shall make an order for the forfeiture of any goods, material or articles only if it is satisfied that a relevant offence has been committed in relation to the goods, material or articles.
. . .
(12) Subject to subsection (13), goods, material or articles forfeited under this section shall be destroyed in accordance with such directions as the court may give.
(13) On making an order under this section the court may if it considers it appropriate to do so, direct that the goods, material or articles to which the order relates shall (instead of being destroyed) be released, to such person as the court may specify, on condition that that person causes the offending sign to be erased, removed or obliterated.
(14) For the purposes of this section—
  "relevant offence" means—
  (a) an offence under section 92 above (unauthorised use of trade mark, etc. in relation to goods),
  (b) an offence under the Trade Descriptions Act 1968,
  (c) an offence under the Business Protection from Misleading Marketing Regulations 2008,
  (d) an offence under the Consumer Protection from Unfair Trading Regulations 2008, or
  (e) any offence involving dishonesty or deception,
  "the court" means—
  (a) in relation to an order made on an application under subsection (2)(a), the sheriff, and
  (b) in relation to an order made under subsection (2)(b), the court which imposed the penalty.

PART IV
MISCELLANEOUS AND GENERAL PROVISIONS

Miscellaneous

99 Unauthorised use of Royal arms, etc.

(1) A person shall not without the authority of Her Majesty use in connection with any business the Royal arms (or arms so closely resembling the Royal arms as to be calculated to deceive) in such manner as to be calculated to lead to the belief that he is duly authorised to use the Royal arms.
(2) A person shall not without the authority of Her Majesty or of a member of the Royal family use in connection with any business any device, emblem or title in such a manner as to be calculated to lead to the belief that he is employed by, or supplies goods or services to, Her Majesty or that member of the Royal family.
(3) A person who contravenes subsection (1) commits an offence and is liable on summary conviction to a fine not exceeding level 2 on the standard scale.

(4)   Contravention of subsection (1) or (2) may be restrained by injunction in proceedings brought by—

    (a)   any person who is authorised to use the arms, device, emblem or title in question, or

    (b)   any person authorised by the Lord Chamberlain to take such proceedings.

(5)   Nothing in this section affects any right of the proprietor of a trade mark containing any such arms, device, emblem or title to use that trade mark.

100   Burden of proving use of trade mark

If in any civil proceedings under this Act a question arises as to the use to which a registered trade mark has been put, it is for the proprietor to show what use has been made of it.

101   Offences committed by partnerships and bodies corporate

(1)   Proceedings for an offence under this Act alleged to have been committed by a partnership shall be brought against the partnership in the name of the firm and not in that of the partners; but without prejudice to any liability of the partners under subsection (4) below.

(2)   The following provisions apply for the purposes of such proceedings as in relation to a body corporate—

    (a)   any rules of court relating to the service of documents;

    (b)   in England and Wales or Northern Ireland, Schedule 3 to the Magistrates' Courts Act 1980 or Schedule 4 to the Magistrates' Courts (Northern Ireland) Order 1981 (procedure on charge of offence).

(3)   A fine imposed on a partnership on its conviction in such proceedings shall be paid out of the partnership assets.

(4)   Where a partnership is guilty of an offence under this Act, every partner, other than a partner who is proved to have been ignorant of or to have attempted to prevent the commission of the offence, is also guilty of the offence and liable to be proceeded against and punished accordingly.

(5)   Where an offence under this Act committed by a body corporate is proved to have been committed with the consent or connivance of a director, manager, secretary or other similar officer of the body, or a person purporting to act in any such capacity, he as well as the body corporate is guilty of the offence and liable to be proceeded against and punished accordingly.

Interpretation

102   Adaptation of expressions for Scotland

In the application of this Act to Scotland—

"account of profits" means accounting and payment of profits; "accounts" means count, reckoning and payment; "assignment" means assignation;

"costs" means expenses;

"declaration" means declarator;

"defendant" means defender;

"delivery up" means delivery;

"injunction" means interdict;

"interlocutory relief" means interim remedy; and

"plaintiff" means pursuer.

103   Minor definitions

(1)   In this Act—

"business" includes a trade or profession;

"director", in relation to a body corporate whose affairs are managed by its members, means any member of the body;

"infringement proceedings", in relation to a registered trade mark, includes proceedings under section 16 (order for delivery up of infringing goods, etc.);

"publish" means make available to the public, and references to publication—

    (a)   in relation to an application for registration, are to publication under section 38(1), and

(b)   in relation to registration, are to publication under section 40(4);
"statutory provisions" includes provisions of subordinate legislation within the meaning of the Interpretation Act 1978;
"trade" includes any business or profession.

(2) References in this Act to use (or any particular description of use) of a trade mark, or of a sign identical with, similar to, or likely to be mistaken for a trade mark, include use (or that description of use) otherwise than by means of a graphic representation.

(3) References in this Act to an EU instrument include references to any instrument amending or replacing that instrument.

104   Index of defined expressions

In this Act the expressions listed below are defined by or otherwise fall to be construed in accordance with the provisions indicated—

account of profits and accounts (in Scotland)	section 102
appointed person (for purposes of section 76)	section 77
assignment (in Scotland)	section 102
business	section 103(1)
certification mark	section 50(1)
collective mark	section 49(1)
commencement (of this Act)	section 109(2)
Convention country	section 55(1)(b)
costs (in Scotland)	section 102
the court	section 75
date of application	section 33(2)
date of filing	section 33(1)
date of registration	section 40(3)
defendant (in Scotland)	section 102
delivery up (in Scotland)	section 102
director	section 103(1)
earlier right	section 5(4)
earlier trade mark	section 6
European Union trade mark	section 51
European Union Trade Mark Regulation	section 51
exclusive licence and licensee	section 29(1)
infringement (of registered trade mark)	sections 9(1) and (2) and 10
infringement proceedings	section 103(1)
infringing articles	section 17
infringing goods	section 17
infringing material	section 17
injunction (in Scotland)	section 102
interlocutory relief (in Scotland)	section 102
the International Bureau	section 53
international trade mark (EC)	section 53
international trade mark (UK)	section 53
Madrid Protocol	section 53
Paris Convention	section 55(1)(a)
plaintiff (in Scotland)	section 102
prescribed	section 78(1)(b)
protected under the Paris Convention	
—well-known trade marks	section 56(1)
—state emblems and official signs or hallmarks	section 57(1)
—emblems, &c. of international organisations	section 58(2)
publish and references to publication	section 103(1)
register, registered (and related expressions)	section 63(1)
registered trade mark attorney	section 83(2)
registrable transaction	section 25(2)
the registrar	section 62
rules	section 78

statutory provisions   section 103(1)
trade   section 103(1)
trade mark
—generally   section 1(1)
—includes collective mark or certification mark   section 1(2)
United Kingdom (references include Isle of Man)   section 108(2)
use (of trade mark or sign)   section 103(2)
well-known trade mark (under Paris Convention)   section 56(1)

Other general provisions

105 Transitional provisions

The provisions of Schedule 3 have effect with respect to transitional matters, including the treatment of marks registered under the Trade Marks Act 1938, and applications for registration and other proceedings pending under that Act, on the commencement of this Act.

107 Territorial waters and the continental shelf

(1) For the purposes of this Act the territorial waters of the United Kingdom shall be treated as part of the United Kingdom.

(2) This Act applies to things done in the United Kingdom sector of the continental shelf on a structure or vessel which is present there for purposes directly connected with the exploration of the sea bed or subsoil or the exploitation of their natural resources as it applies to things done in the United Kingdom.

(3) The United Kingdom sector of the continental shelf means the areas designated by order under section 1(7) of the Continental Shelf Act 1964.

108 Extent

(1) This Act extends to England and Wales, Scotland and Northern Ireland.

(2) This Act also extends to the Isle of Man, subject to such exceptions and modifications as Her Majesty may specify by Order in Council; and subject to any such Order references in this Act to the United Kingdom shall be construed as including the Isle of Man.

SCHEDULES

SCHEDULE 1
COLLECTIVE MARKS

General

1.   The provisions of this Act apply to collective marks subject to the following provisions.

Signs of which a collective mark may consist

2.   In relation to a collective mark the reference in section 1(1) (signs of which a trade mark may consist) to distinguishing goods or services of one undertaking from those of other undertakings shall be construed as a reference to distinguishing goods or services of members of the association which is the proprietor of the mark from those of other undertakings.

Indication of geographical origin

3.   (1) Notwithstanding section 3(1)(c), a collective mark may be registered which consists of signs or indications which may serve, in trade, to designate the geographical origin of the goods or services.

(2) However, the proprietor of such a mark is not entitled to prohibit the use of the signs or indications in accordance with honest practices in industrial or commercial matters (in particular, by a person who is entitled to use a geographical name).

Mark not to be misleading as to character or significance

4.   (1)   A collective mark shall not be registered if the public is liable to be misled as regards the character or significance of the mark, in particular if it is likely to be taken to be something other than a collective mark.

       (2)   The registrar may accordingly require that a mark in respect of which application is made for registration include some indication that it is a collective mark.
             Notwithstanding section 39(2), an application may be amended so as to comply with any such requirement.

Regulations governing use of collective mark

5.   (1)   An applicant for registration of a collective mark must file with the registrar regulations governing the use of the mark.

       (2)   The regulations must specify the persons authorised to use the mark, the conditions of membership of the association and, where they exist, the conditions of use of the mark, including any sanctions against misuse.
             Further requirements with which the regulations have to comply may be imposed by rules.

Approval of regulations by registrar

6.   (1)   A collective mark shall not be registered unless the regulations governing the use of the mark—
             (a)   comply with paragraph 5(2) and any further requirements imposed by rules, and
             (b)   are not contrary to public policy or to accepted principles of morality.

       (2)   Before the end of the prescribed period after the date of the application for registration of a collective mark, the applicant must file the regulations with the registrar and pay the prescribed fee.
             If he does not do so, the application shall be deemed to be withdrawn.

7.   (1)   The registrar shall consider whether the requirements mentioned in paragraph 6(1) are met.

       (2)   If it appears to the registrar that those requirements are not met, he shall inform the applicant and give him an opportunity, within such period as the registrar may specify, to make representations or to file amended regulations.

       (3)   If the applicant fails to satisfy the registrar that those requirements are met, or to file regulations amended so as to meet them, or fails to respond before the end of the specified period, the registrar shall refuse the application.

       (4)   If it appears to the registrar that those requirements, and the other requirements for registration, are met, he shall accept the application and shall proceed in accordance with section 38 (publication, opposition proceedings and observations).

8.   The regulations shall be published and notice of opposition may be given, and observations may be made, relating to the matters mentioned in paragraph 6(1).
        This is in addition to any other grounds on which the application may be opposed or observations made.

Regulations to be open to inspection

9.   The regulations governing the use of a registered collective mark shall be open to public inspection in the same way as the register.

Amendment of regulations

10.   (1)   An amendment of the regulations governing the use of a registered collective mark is not effective unless and until the amended regulations are filed with the registrar and accepted by him.

       (2)   Before accepting any amended regulations the registrar may in any case where it appears to him expedient to do so cause them to be published.

       (3)   If he does so, notice of opposition may be given, and observations may be made, relating to the matters mentioned in paragraph 6(1).

Infringement: rights of authorised users

11. The following provisions apply in relation to an authorised user of a registered collective mark as in relation to a licensee of a trade mark—
    (a) section 10(5) (definition of infringement: unauthorised application of mark to certain material);
    (b) section 19(2) (order as to disposal of infringing goods, material or articles: adequacy of other remedies);
    (c) section 89 (prohibition of importation of infringing goods, material or articles: request to Commissioners of Customs and Excise).

12. (1) The following provisions (which correspond to the provisions of section 30 (general provisions as to rights of licensees in case of infringement)) have effect as regards the rights of an authorised user in relation to infringement of a registered collective mark.
    (2) An authorised user is entitled, subject to any agreement to the contrary between him and the proprietor, to call on the proprietor to take infringement proceedings in respect of any matter which affects his interests.
    (3) If the proprietor—
        (a) refuses to do so, or
        (b) fails to do so within two months after being called upon,
        the authorised user may bring the proceedings in his own name as if he were the proprietor.
    (4) Where infringement proceedings are brought by virtue of this paragraph, the authorised user may not, without the leave of the court, proceed with the action unless the proprietor is either joined as a plaintiff or added as a defendant.
        This does not affect the granting of interlocutory relief on an application by an authorised user alone.
    (5) A proprietor who is added as a defendant as mentioned in sub-paragraph (4) shall not be made liable for any costs in the action unless he takes part in the proceedings.
    (6) In infringement proceedings brought by the proprietor of a registered collective mark any loss suffered or likely to be suffered by authorised users shall be taken into account; and the court may give such directions as it thinks fit as to the extent to which the plaintiff is to hold the proceeds of any pecuniary remedy on behalf of such users.

Grounds for revocation of registration

13. Apart from the grounds of revocation provided for in section 46, the registration of a collective mark may be revoked on the ground—
    (a) that the manner in which the mark has been used by the proprietor has caused it to become liable to mislead the public in the manner referred to in paragraph 4(1), or
    (b) that the proprietor has failed to observe, or to secure the observance of, the regulations governing the use of the mark, or
    (c) that an amendment of the regulations has been made so that the regulations—
        (i) no longer comply with paragraph 5(2) and any further conditions imposed by rules, or
        (ii) are contrary to public policy or to accepted principles of morality.

Grounds for invalidity of registration

14. Apart from the grounds of invalidity provided for in section 47, the registration of a collective mark may be declared invalid on the ground that the mark was registered in breach of the provisions of paragraph 4(1) or 6(1).

SCHEDULE 2
CERTIFICATION MARKS

General

1. The provisions of this Act apply to certification marks subject to the following provisions.

Signs of which a certification mark may consist

2. In relation to a certification mark the reference in section 1(1) (signs of which a trade mark may consist) to distinguishing goods or services of one undertaking from those of other undertakings shall be construed as a reference to distinguishing goods or services which are certified from those which are not.

Indication of geographical origin

3. (1) Notwithstanding section 3(1)(c), a certification mark may be registered which consists of signs or indications which may serve, in trade, to designate the geographical origin of the goods or services.

   (2) However, the proprietor of such a mark is not entitled to prohibit the use of the signs or indications in accordance with honest practices in industrial or commercial matters (in particular, by a person who is entitled to use a geographical name).

Nature of proprietor's business

4. A certification mark shall not be registered if the proprietor carries on a business involving the supply of goods or services of the kind certified.

Mark not to be misleading as to character or significance

5. (1) A certification mark shall not be registered if the public is liable to be misled as regards the character or significance of the mark, in particular if it is likely to be taken to be something other than a certification mark.

   (2) The registrar may accordingly require that a mark in respect of which application is made for registration include some indication that it is a certification mark. Notwithstanding section 39(2), an application may be amended so as to comply with any such requirement.

Regulations governing use of certification mark

6. (1) An applicant for registration of a certification mark must file with the registrar regulations governing the use of the mark.

   (2) The regulations must indicate who is authorised to use the mark, the characteristics to be certified by the mark, how the certifying body is to test those characteristics and to supervise the use of the mark, the fees (if any) to be paid in connection with the operation of the mark and the procedures for resolving disputes. Further requirements with which the regulations have to comply may be imposed by rules.

Approval of regulations, etc.

7. (1) A certification mark shall not be registered unless—
   (a) the regulations governing the use of the mark—
       (i) comply with paragraph 6(2) and any further requirements imposed by rules, and
       (ii) are not contrary to public policy or to accepted principles of morality, and
   (b) the applicant is competent to certify the goods or services for which the mark is to be registered.

   (2) Before the end of the prescribed period after the date of the application for registration of a certification mark, the applicant must file the regulations with the registrar and pay the prescribed fee. If he does not do so, the application shall be deemed to be withdrawn.

8. (1) The registrar shall consider whether the requirements mentioned in paragraph 7(1) are met.

   (2) If it appears to the registrar that those requirements are not met, he shall inform the applicant and give him an opportunity, within such period as the registrar may specify, to make representations or to file amended regulations.

   (3) If the applicant fails to satisfy the registrar that those requirements are met, or to file

regulations amended so as to meet them, or fails to respond before the end of the specified period, the registrar shall refuse the application.

(4) If it appears to the registrar that those requirements, and the other requirements for registration, are met, he shall accept the application and shall proceed in accordance with section 38 (publication, opposition proceedings and observations).

9. The regulations shall be published and notice of opposition may be given, and observations may be made, relating to the matters mentioned in paragraph 7(1).

This is in addition to any other grounds on which the application may be opposed or observations made.

Regulations to be open to inspection

10. The regulations governing the use of a registered certification mark shall be open to public inspection in the same way as the register.

Amendment of regulations

11. (1) An amendment of the regulations governing the use of a registered certification mark is not effective unless and until the amended regulations are filed with the registrar and accepted by him.

(2) Before accepting any amended regulations the registrar may in any case where it appears to him expedient to do so cause them to be published.

(3) If he does so, notice of opposition may be given, and observations may be made, relating to the matters mentioned in paragraph 7(1).

Consent to assignment of registered certification mark

12. The assignment or other transmission of a registered certification mark is not effective without the consent of the registrar.

Infringement: rights of authorised users

13. The following provisions apply in relation to an authorised user of a registered certification mark as in relation to a licensee of a trade mark—

(a) section 10(5) (definition of infringement: unauthorised application of mark to certain material);

(b) section 19(2) (order as to disposal of infringing goods, material or articles: adequacy of other remedies);

(c) section 89 (prohibition of importation of infringing goods, material or articles: request to Commissioners of Customs and Excise).

14. In infringement proceedings brought by the proprietor of a registered certification mark any loss suffered or likely to be suffered by authorised users shall be taken into account; and the court may give such directions as it thinks fit as to the extent to which the plaintiff is to hold the proceeds of any pecuniary remedy on behalf of such users.

Grounds for revocation of registration

15. Apart from the grounds of revocation provided for in section 46, the registration of a certification mark may be revoked on the ground—

(a) that the proprietor has begun to carry on such a business as is mentioned in paragraph 4,

(b) that the manner in which the mark has been used by the proprietor has caused it to become liable to mislead the public in the manner referred to in paragraph 5(1),

(c) that the proprietor has failed to observe, or to secure the observance of, the regulations governing the use of the mark,

(d) that an amendment of the regulations has been made so that the regulations—

  (i) no longer comply with paragraph 6(2) and any further conditions imposed by rules, or

  (ii) are contrary to public policy or to accepted principles of morality, or

(e) that the proprietor is no longer competent to certify the goods or services for which the mark is registered.

Grounds for invalidity of registration

16.   Apart from the grounds of invalidity provided for in section 47, the registration of a certification mark may be declared invalid on the ground that the mark was registered in breach of the provisions of paragraph 4, 5(1) or 7(1).

GOODS INFRINGING INTELLECTUAL PROPERTY RIGHTS (CUSTOMS) REGULATIONS 2004
(SI 2004 No. 1473)

2   Interpretation

(1)   In these Regulations—

"the 1979 Act" means the Customs and Excise Management Act 1979;

"application" means an application under Article 5 of the Council Regulation; "the Commissioners" means the Commissioners of Customs and Excise;

"the Council Regulation" means Council Regulation (EC) No 1383/2003 concerning customs action against goods suspected of infringing certain intellectual property rights and the measures to be taken against goods found to have infringed such rights;

"the customs and excise Acts" has the meaning given in section 1(1) of the 1979 Act;

"database rights" has the meaning given in regulation 13 of the Copyright and Rights in Databases Regulations 1997;

"decision" means a decision granting an application in accordance with Article 8 of the Council Regulation;

"declarant" has the meaning given in Article 4(18) of Council Regulation (EEC) No 2913/ 1992 establishing the Community Customs Code;

"goods infringing an intellectual property right" has the meaning given in Article 2(1) of the Council Regulation and related expressions shall be construed accordingly;

"publication rights" has the meaning given in regulation 16 of the Copyright and Related Rights Regulations 1996;

"right-holder" has the meaning given in Article 2(2) of the Council Regulation;

"working days" has the meaning given in Article 3(1) of Council Regulation (EEC, Euratom) No 1182/1971 determining the rules applicable to periods, dates and time limits.

(2)   For the purposes of these Regulations, any reference in the Council Regulation to "copyright or related right" is to be construed as a reference to "copyright, rights in performances, publication rights or database rights".

(3)   These Regulations shall apply to goods which fall to be treated by virtue of Article 2 of the Council Regulation as being goods infringing an intellectual property right; but these Regulations shall not apply to any goods in relation to which the Council Regulation does not apply by virtue of Article 3 thereof.

5   Decision to cease to have effect

A decision shall have no further effect where—

(a)   any change, following the making of the application, which takes place in the ownership or authorised use of the intellectual property right specified in the application, is not communicated in writing to the Commissioners; or

(b)   the intellectual property right specified in the application expires.

7   Simplified procedure

(1)   The Commissioners may treat as abandoned for destruction goods which have been suspended from release or detained by virtue of Article 9 of the Council Regulation where the right-holder has informed the Commissioners in writing within the specified period that those goods infringe an intellectual property right and either of the following conditions applies—

     (a)   the right-holder has provided the Commissioners with the written agreement of the declarant, the holder or the owner of the goods ("the interested parties") that the goods may be destroyed; or

     (b)   none of the interested parties has specifically opposed the destruction of the goods within the specified period.

(2)   The Commissioners may not treat the goods as abandoned for destruction where one interested party has given its written agreement as mentioned in regulation 7(1)(a), but either or both of the other interested parties has specifically opposed destruction within the specified period.

(3)   The Commissioners may, at their discretion, accept the written agreement mentioned in regulation 7(1)(a) directly from the interested party.

(4)   Where goods are treated as abandoned for destruction by virtue of paragraph (1)—

     (a)   the right-holder must bear the expense and the responsibility for the destruction of the goods, unless otherwise specified by the Commissioners; and

     (b)   the Commissioners must retain a sample of the goods in such conditions that it can be used if required as evidence in legal proceedings.

(5)   The specified period means ten working days from receipt of the notification to the right-holder provided for in Article 9 of the Council Regulation, or three working days in the case of perishable goods. The Commissioners may, at their discretion, extend this period by a further ten working days.

(6)   A reference in this regulation to the Commissioners is to be construed as a reference to the Secretary of State.

10   Relationship with other powers

Nothing in these Regulations shall be taken to affect—

(a)   any power of the Commissioners conferred otherwise than by any provision of these Regulations to suspend the release of, or detain, any goods; or

(b)   the power of any court to grant any relief, including any power to make an order by way of interim relief.

11   Misuse of information by a right-holder

(1)   Where the Commissioners have reasonable grounds for believing that there has been a misuse of information by a right-holder the Commissioners may suspend the decision in force at the time of the misuse of information, in relation to a relevant intellectual property right, for the remainder of its period of validity.

(2)   Where the Commissioners have reasonable grounds for believing that there has been a further misuse of information within three years of a previous misuse of information by that right-holder the Commissioners may—

     (a)   suspend the decision in force at the time of the further misuse of information, in relation to a relevant intellectual property right, for the remainder of its period of validity; and

     (b)   for a period of up to one year from its expiry, refuse to renew the decision in force at the time of the further misuse of information, or to accept a new application, in relation to a relevant intellectual property right.

(3)   In this regulation—

     (a)   "misuse of information" means the use of information supplied to a right-holder pursuant to the first sub-paragraph of Article 9(3) of the Council Regulation other than for the purposes specified in Articles 10, 11 and 13(1) of the Council Regulation, or pursuant to an enactment or order of a court, and related expressions shall be construed accordingly;

     (b)   "relevant intellectual property right" means any intellectual property right in relation to a suspected infringement of which information was supplied to a right-holder pursuant to the first sub-paragraph of Article 9(3) of the Council Regulation, and in relation to which the Commissioners have reasonable grounds for believing that there has been a misuse of that information.

BUSINESS PROTECTION FROM MISLEADING MARKETING REGULATIONS 2008
(SI 2008 No. 1276)

PART 1
DEFINITIONS AND PROHIBITIONS

1   Citation and commencement

These Regulations may be cited as the Business Protection from Misleading Marketing Regulations 2008 and shall come into force on 26th May 2008.

2   Interpretation

(1)   In these Regulations—

"advertising" means any form of representation which is made in connection with a trade, business, craft or profession in order to promote the supply or transfer of a product and "advertiser" shall be construed accordingly;

"CMA" means the Competition and Markets Authority;

"code owner" means a trader or a body responsible for—

(a)   the formulation and revision of a code of conduct; or

(b)   monitoring compliance with the code by those who have undertaken to be bound by it;

"comparative advertising" means advertising which in any way, either explicitly or by implication, identifies a competitor or a product offered by a competitor;

"court", in relation to England and Wales and Northern Ireland, means a county court or the High Court, and, in relation to Scotland, the sheriff or the Court of Session;

"DETINI" means the Department of Enterprise, Trade and Investment in Northern Ireland;

"enforcement authority" means the CMA, every local weights and measures authority and DETINI and GEMA;

"GEMA" means the Gas and Electricity Markets Authority;

"goods" includes ships, aircraft, animals, things attached to land and growing crops;

"local weights and measures authority" means a local weights and measures authority in Great Britain (within the meaning of section 69 of the Weights and Measures Act 1985);

"premises" includes any place and any stall, vehicle, ship or aircraft;

"product" means any goods or services and includes immovable property, rights and obligations;

"ship" includes any boat and any other description of vessel used in navigation; and

"trader" means any person who is acting for purposes relating to his trade, craft, business or profession and anyone acting in the name of or on behalf of a trader.

(2)   In the application of these Regulations to Scotland for references to an "injunction" or an "interim injunction" there shall be substituted references to an "interdict" or an "interim interdict" respectively.

3   Prohibition of advertising which misleads traders

(1)   Advertising which is misleading is prohibited.

(2)   Advertising is misleading which—

(a)   in any way, including its presentation, deceives or is likely to deceive the traders to whom it is addressed or whom it reaches; and by reason of its deceptive nature, is likely to affect their economic behaviour; or

(b)   for those reasons, injures or is likely to injure a competitor.

(3)   In determining whether advertising is misleading, account shall be taken of all its features, and in particular of any information it contains concerning—

(a)   the characteristics of the product (as defined in paragraph (4));

(b)   the price or manner in which the price is calculated;

(c)   the conditions on which the product is supplied or provided; and

(d)   the nature, attributes and rights of the advertiser (as defined in paragraph (5)).

(4) In paragraph (3)(a) the "characteristics of the product" include—
    (a) availability of the product;
    (b) nature of the product;
    (c) execution of the product;
    (d) composition of the product;
    (e) method and date of manufacture of the product;
    (f) method and date of provision of the product;
    (g) fitness for purpose of the product;
    (h) uses of the product;
    (i) quantity of the product;
    (j) specification of the product;
    (k) geographical or commercial origin of the product;
    (l) results to be expected from use of the product; or
    (m) results and material features of tests or checks carried out on the product.
(5) In paragraph (3)(d) the "nature, attributes and rights" of the advertiser include the advertiser's—
    (a) identity;
    (b) assets;
    (c) qualifications;
    (d) ownership of industrial, commercial or intellectual property rights; or
    (e) awards and distinctions.

4   Comparative advertising

Comparative advertising shall, as far as the comparison is concerned, be permitted only when the following conditions are met—
(a) it is not misleading under regulation 3;
(b) it is not a misleading action under regulation 5 of the Consumer Protection from Unfair Trading Regulations 2008 or a misleading omission under regulation 6 of those Regulations;
(c) it compares products meeting the same needs or intended for the same purpose;
(d) it objectively compares one or more material, relevant, verifiable and representative features of those products, which may include price;
(e) it does not create confusion among traders—
    (i) between the advertiser and a competitor, or
    (ii) between the trade marks, trade names, other distinguishing marks or products of the advertiser and those of a competitor;
(f) it does not discredit or denigrate the trade marks, trade names, other distinguishing marks, products, activities, or circumstances of a competitor;
(g) for products with designation of origin, it relates in each case to products with the same designation;
(h) it does not take unfair advantage of the reputation of a trade mark, trade name or other distinguishing marks of a competitor or of the designation of origin of competing products;
(i) it does not present products as imitations or replicas of products bearing a protected trade mark or trade name.

5   Promotion of misleading advertising and comparative advertising which is not permitted

A code owner shall not promote in a code of conduct—
(a) advertising which is misleading under regulation 3; or
(b) comparative advertising which is not permitted under regulation 4.

PART 2
OFFENCES

6   Misleading advertising

A trader is guilty of an offence if he engages in advertising which is misleading under regulation 3.

7   Penalty for offence under regulation 6

A person guilty of an offence under regulation 6 shall be liable—

(a)   on summary conviction, to a fine not exceeding the statutory maximum; or

(b)   on conviction on indictment, to a fine or imprisonment for a term not exceeding two years or both.

8   Offences committed by bodies of persons

(1)   Where an offence under these Regulations committed by a body corporate is proved—

    (a)   to have been committed with the consent or connivance of an officer of the body, or

    (b)   to be attributable to any neglect on his part,

the officer as well as the body corporate is guilty of the offence and liable to be proceeded against and punished accordingly.

(2)   In paragraph (1) a reference to an officer of a body corporate includes a reference to—

    (a)   a director, manager, secretary or other similar officer; and

    (b)   a person purporting to act as a director, manager, secretary or other similar officer.

(3)   Where an offence under these Regulations committed by a Scottish partnership is proved—

    (a)   to have been committed with the consent or connivance of a partner, or

    (b)   to be attributable to any neglect on his part,

the partner as well as the partnership is guilty of the offence and liable to be proceeded against and punished accordingly.

(4)   In paragraph (3) a reference to a partner includes a person purporting to act as a partner.

9   Offence due to the default of another person

(1)   This regulation applies where a person "X" —

    (a)   commits an offence under regulation 6, or

    (b)   would have committed an offence under regulation 6 but for a defence under regulation 11 or 12,

and the commission of the offence, or of what would have been an offence but for X being able to rely on a defence under regulations 11 or 12, is due to the act or default of some other person "Y".

(2)   Where this regulation applies Y shall be guilty of the offence subject to regulations 11 and 12 whether or not Y is a trader and whether or not Y's act or default is advertising.

(3)   Y may be charged with and convicted of the offence by virtue of paragraph (2) whether or not proceedings are taken against X.

10   Time limit for prosecution

(1)   No proceedings for an offence under these Regulations shall be commenced after—

    (a)   the end of the period of three years beginning with the date of the commission of the offence; or

    (b)   the end of the period of one year beginning with the date of discovery of the offence by the prosecutor,

whichever is earlier.

(2)   For the purposes of paragraph (1)(b) a certificate signed by or on behalf of the prosecutor and stating the date on which the offence was discovered by him shall be conclusive evidence of that fact and a certificate stating that matter and purporting to be so signed shall be treated as so signed unless the contrary is proved.

(3)   Notwithstanding anything in section 127(1) of the Magistrates' Courts Act 1980, an information relating to an offence under these Regulations which is triable by a magistrates' court in England and Wales may be so tried if it is laid at any time before the end of the period of twelve months beginning with the date of the commission of the offence.

(4)   Notwithstanding anything in section 136 of the Criminal Procedure (Scotland) Act 1995 summary proceedings in Scotland for an offence under these Regulations may be commenced at any time before the end of the period of twelve months beginning with the date of the commission of the offence.

(5) For the purposes of paragraph (4), section 136(3) of the Criminal Procedure (Scotland) Act 1995 shall apply as it applies for the purposes of that section.

(6) Notwithstanding anything in Article 19(1) of the Magistrates' Courts (Northern Ireland) Order 1981 a complaint charging an offence under these Regulations which is triable by a magistrates' court in Northern Ireland may be so tried if it is made at any time before the end of the period of twelve months beginning with the date of the commission of the offence.

11 Due diligence defence

(1) In any proceedings against a person for an offence under regulation 6 it is a defence for that person to prove—
    (a) that the commission of the offence was due to—
        (i) a mistake;
        (ii) reliance on information supplied to him by another person;
        (iii) the act or default of another person;
        (iv) an accident; or
        (v) another cause beyond his control;
        and
    (b) that he took all reasonable precautions and exercised all due diligence to avoid the commission of such an offence by himself or any person under his control.

(2) A person shall not be entitled to rely on the defence provided by paragraph (1) by reason of the matters referred to in paragraph (ii) or (iii) of paragraph (1)(a) without the leave of the court unless—
    (a) he has served on the prosecutor a notice in writing giving such information identifying or assisting in the identification of that other person as was in his possession; and
    (b) the notice is served on the prosecutor at least seven clear days before the date of the hearing.

12 Innocent publication defence

In any proceedings against a person for an offence under regulation 6 committed by the publication of advertising it is a defence for that person to prove that—
    (a) he is a person whose business it is to publish or to arrange for the publication of advertising;
    (b) he received the advertising for publication in the ordinary course of business; and
    (c) he did not know and had no reason to suspect that its publication would amount to an offence under regulation 6.

PART 3
ENFORCEMENT

13 Duty and power to enforce

(1) It shall be the duty of every local weights and measures authority and DETINI to enforce these Regulations.

(1A) Each of the following may also enforce these Regulations—
    (a) the CMA;
    (b) GEMA.

(2) Where an enforcement authority is a local weights and measures authority the duty referred to in paragraph (1) shall apply to the enforcement of these Regulations within the authority's area.

(3) Where the enforcement authority is the Department of Enterprise, Trade and Investment in Northern Ireland the duty referred to in paragraph (1) shall apply to the enforcement of these Regulations within Northern Ireland.

(4) In determining how to comply with paragraph (1), or as the case may be, paragraph (1A) every enforcement authority shall have regard to the desirability of encouraging control of advertising which is misleading under regulation 3 and comparative advertising which is not permitted under regulation 4 by such established means as it considers appropriate having regard to all the circumstances of the particular case.

(4A) Nothing in this regulation shall authorise GEMA to bring proceedings for an offence.

14   Notice to CMA of intended prosecution

(1)   Where an enforcement authority is a local weights and measures authority in England and Wales it may bring proceedings for an offence under regulation 6 only if—

(a)   it has notified the CMA of its intention to bring proceedings at least fourteen days before the date on which proceedings are brought; or

(b)   the CMA consents to proceedings being brought in a shorter period.

(2)   The enforcement authority must also notify the CMA of the outcome of the proceedings after they are finally determined.

(3)   Such proceedings are not invalid by reason only of the failure to comply with this regulation.

15   Injunctions to secure compliance with the Regulations

(1)   This regulation applies where an enforcement authority considers that there has been or is likely to be a breach of regulation 3, 4 or 5.

(2)   Where this regulation applies an enforcement authority may, subject to paragraph (3), if it thinks it appropriate to do so, bring proceedings for an injunction (in which proceedings it may also apply for an interim injunction) against any person appearing to it to be concerned or likely to be concerned with the breach.

(3)   Where the enforcement authority is a local weights and measures authority in Great Britain or GEMA it may apply for an injunction only if—

(a)   it has notified the CMA of its intention to apply for an injunction at least fourteen days before the date on which the application is made; or

(b)   the CMA consents to the application for an injunction being made within a shorter period.

(4)   Proceedings referred to in paragraph (2) are not invalid by reason only of the failure to comply with paragraph (3).

16   Undertakings

Where an enforcement authority considers that there has been or is likely to be a breach of regulation 3, 4 or 5 it may accept from the person concerned or likely to be concerned with the breach an undertaking that he will comply with those regulations.

17   Co-ordination

(1)   If more than one local weights and measures authority in Great Britain is contemplating bringing proceedings under regulation 15 in any particular case, the CMA may direct which enforcement authority is to bring the proceedings or decide that only it may do so.

(2)   Where the CMA directs that only it may bring such proceedings it may take into account whether compliance with regulation 3, 4 or 5 could be achieved by other means in deciding whether to bring proceedings.

18   Powers of the court

(1)   The court on an application by an enforcement authority may grant an injunction on such terms as it may think fit to secure compliance with regulation 3, 4 or 5.

(2)   Before granting an injunction the court shall have regard to all the interests involved and in particular the public interest.

(3)   An injunction may relate not only to particular advertising but to any advertising in similar terms or likely to convey a similar impression.

(4)   The court may also require any person against whom an injunction (other than an interim injunction) is granted to publish in such form and manner and to such extent as the court thinks appropriate for the purpose of eliminating any continuing effects of the advertising—

(a)   the injunction; and

(b)   a corrective statement.

(5)   In considering an application for an injunction the court may require the person named in the application to provide evidence as to the accuracy of any factual claim made as part of the advertising of that person if, taking into account the legitimate interests of that person and any other party to the proceedings, it appears appropriate in the circumstances.

(6)   If, having been required under paragraph (5) to provide evidence as to the accuracy of a factual claim, a person—
   (a)   fails to provide such evidence, or .
   (b)   provides evidence as to the accuracy of the factual claim that the court considers inadequate,
   the court may consider that the factual claim is inaccurate.

(7)   The court may grant an injunction even where there is no evidence of proof of actual loss or damage or of intention or negligence on the part of the advertiser.

19   Notifications of undertakings and orders to the CMA

An enforcement authority, other than the CMA, shall notify the CMA—
(a)   of any undertaking given to it under regulation 16;
(b)   of the outcome of any application made by it under regulation 15 and the terms of any order made by the court; and
(c)   of the outcome of any application made by it to enforce a previous order of the court.

20   Publication, information and advice

(1)   The CMA must arrange for the publication, in such form and manner as it considers appropriate, of—
   (a)   details of any undertaking or order notified to it under regulation 19;
   (b)   details of any undertaking given to it under regulation 16;
   (c)   details of any application made by it under regulation 15 and of the terms of any undertaking given to, or order made by, the court;
   (d)   details of any application made by it to enforce a previous order of the court.

(2)   An enforcement authority may arrange for the dissemination, in such form and manner as it considers appropriate, of such information and advice concerning the operation of these Regulations as appear to it to be expedient to give to the public and to all persons likely to be affected by these Regulations.

PART 4
INVESTIGATION POWERS

28   Crown

. . .
(2)   The Crown is not criminally liable as a result of any provision of these Regulations.
(3)   Paragraph (2) does not affect the application of any provision of these Regulations in relation to a person in the public service of the Crown.

29   Validity of agreements

An agreement shall not be void or unenforceable by reason only of a breach of these Regulations.

CONSUMER PROTECTION FROM UNFAIR TRADING REGULATIONS 2008
(SI 2008 No. 1277)

PART 1
GENERAL

1   Citation and commencement

These Regulations may be cited as the Consumer Protection from Unfair Trading Regulations 2008 and shall come into force on 26th May 2008.

2   Interpretation

(1)   In these Regulations
   "average consumer" shall be construed in accordance with paragraphs (2) to (6);
   "business" includes—
   (a)   a trade, craft or profession, and

(b)   the activities of any government department or local or public authority;

"CMA" means the Competition and Markets Authority;

"code of conduct" means an agreement or set of rules (which is not imposed by legal or administrative requirements), which defines the behaviour of traders who undertake to be bound by it in relation to one or more commercial practices or business sectors;

"code owner" means a trader or a body responsible for—

(a)   the formulation and revision of a code of conduct; or

(b)   monitoring compliance with the code by those who have undertaken to be bound by it;

"commercial practice" means any act, omission, course of conduct, representation or commercial communication (including advertising and marketing) by a trader, which is directly connected with the promotion, sale or supply of a product to or from consumers, whether occurring before, during or after a commercial transaction (if any) in relation to a product;

"consumer" means an individual acting for purposes that are wholly or mainly outside that individual's business;

"DETINI" means "the Department of Enterprise, Trade and Investment in Northern Ireland;

"digital content" means data which are produced and supplied in digital form;

"enforcement authority" means the CMA, every local weights and measures authority and DETINI;

"goods" means any tangible moveable items, but that includes water, gas and electricity if and only if they are put up for sale in a limited volume or set quantity;

"invitation to purchase" means a commercial communication which indicates characteristics of the product and the price in a way appropriate to the means of that commercial communication and thereby enables the consumer to make a purchase;

"local weights and measures authority" means a local weights and measures authority in Great Britain (within the meaning of section 69 of the Weights and Measures Act 1985); "materially distort the economic behaviour" means in relation to an average consumer, appreciably to impair the average consumer's ability to make an informed decision thereby causing him to take a transactional decision that he would not have taken otherwise;

"premises" includes any place and any stall, vehicle, ship or aircraft;

"product" means—

(a)   goods,

(b)   a service,

(c)   digital content,

(d)   immoveable property,

(e)   rights or obligations, or

(f)   a product of the kind mentioned in paragraphs (1A) and (1B),

but the application of this definition to Part 4A is subject to regulations 27C and 27D;

"professional diligence" means the standard of special skill and care which a trader may reasonably be expected to exercise towards consumers which is commensurate with either—

(a)   honest market practice in the trader's field of activity, or

(b)   the general principle of good faith in the trader's field of activity;

"ship" includes any boat and any other description of vessel used in navigation;

"trader"—

(a)   means a person acting for purposes relating to that person's business, whether acting personally or through another person acting in the trader's name or on the trader's behalf, and

(b)   except in Part 4A, includes a person acting in the name of or on behalf of a trader;

"transactional decision" means any decision taken by a consumer, whether it is to act or to refrain from acting, concerning—

(a)   whether, how and on what terms to purchase, make payment in whole or in part for, retain or dispose of a product; or

(b)   whether, how and on what terms to exercise a contractual right in relation to a product;

(but the application of this definition to regulations 5 and 7 as they apply for the purposes of Part 4A is subject to regulation 27B(2)).

(1A) A trader ("T") who demands payment from a consumer ("C") in full or partial settlement of C's liabilities or purported liabilities to T is to be treated for the purposes of these Regulations as offering to supply a product to C.

(1B) In such a case the product that T offers to supply comprises the full or partial settlement of those liabilities or purported liabilities.

(2) In determining the effect of a commercial practice on the average consumer where the practice reaches or is addressed to a consumer or consumers account shall be taken of the material characteristics of such an average consumer including his being reasonably well informed, reasonably observant and circumspect.

(3) Paragraphs (4) and (5) set out the circumstances in which a reference to the average consumer shall be read as in addition referring to the average member of a particular group of consumers.

(4) In determining the effect of a commercial practice on the average consumer where the practice is directed to a particular group of consumers, a reference to the average consumer shall be read as referring to the average member of that group.

(5) In determining the effect of a commercial practice on the average consumer—

    (a) where a clearly identifiable group of consumers is particularly vulnerable to the practice or the underlying product because of their mental or physical infirmity, age or credulity in a way which the trader could reasonably be expected to foresee, and

    (b) where the practice is likely to materially distort the economic behaviour only of that group,

a reference to the average consumer shall be read as referring to the average member of that group.

(6) Paragraph (5) is without prejudice to the common and legitimate advertising practice of making exaggerated statements which are not meant to be taken literally.

PART 2
PROHIBITIONS

3 Prohibition of unfair commercial practices

(1) Unfair commercial practices are prohibited.

(2) Paragraphs (3) and (4) set out the circumstances when a commercial practice is unfair.

(3) A commercial practice is unfair if—

    (a) it contravenes the requirements of professional diligence; and

    (b) it materially distorts or is likely to materially distort the economic behaviour of the average consumer with regard to the product.

(4) A commercial practice is unfair if—

    (a) it is a misleading action under the provisions of regulation 5;

    (b) it is a misleading omission under the provisions of regulation 6;

    (c) it is aggressive under the provisions of regulation 7; or

    (d) it is listed in Schedule 1.

4 Prohibition of the promotion of unfair commercial practices

The promotion of any unfair commercial practice by a code owner in a code of conduct is prohibited.

5 Misleading actions

(1) A commercial practice is a misleading action if it satisfies the conditions in either paragraph (2) or paragraph (3).

(2) A commercial practice satisfies the conditions of this paragraph—

    (a) if it contains false information and is therefore untruthful in relation to any of the matters in paragraph (4) or if it or its overall presentation in any way deceives or is likely to deceive the average consumer in relation to any of the matters in that paragraph, even if the information is factually correct; and

    (b) it causes or is likely to cause the average consumer to take a transactional decision he would not have taken otherwise.

(3) A commercial practice satisfies the conditions of this paragraph if—

    (a) it concerns any marketing of a product (including comparative advertising) which creates confusion with any products, trade marks, trade names or other distinguishing marks of a competitor; or

    (b) it concerns any failure by a trader to comply with a commitment contained in a code of conduct which the trader has undertaken to comply with, if—

        (i) the trader indicates in a commercial practice that he is bound by that code of conduct, and

        (ii) the commitment is firm and capable of being verified and is not aspirational,

    and it causes or is likely to cause the average consumer to take a transactional decision he would not have taken otherwise, taking account of its factual context and of all its features and circumstances.

(4) The matters referred to in paragraph (2)(a) are—

    (a) the existence or nature of the product;

    (b) the main characteristics of the product (as defined in paragraph 5);

    (c) the extent of the trader's commitments;

    (d) the motives for the commercial practice;

    (e) the nature of the sales process;

    (f) any statement or symbol relating to direct or indirect sponsorship or approval of the trader or the product;

    (g) the price or the manner in which the price is calculated;

    (h) the existence of a specific price advantage;

    (i) the need for a service, part, replacement or repair;

    (j) the nature, attributes and rights of the trader (as defined in paragraph 6);

    (k) the consumer's rights or the risks he may face.

(5) In paragraph (4)(b), the "main characteristics of the product" include—

    (a) availability of the product;

    (b) benefits of the product;

    (c) risks of the product;

    (d) execution of the product;

    (e) composition of the product;

    (f) accessories of the product;

    (g) after-sale customer assistance concerning the product;

    (h) the handling of complaints about the product;

    (i) the method and date of manufacture of the product;

    (j) the method and date of provision of the product;

    (k) delivery of the product;

    (l) fitness for purpose of the product;

    (m) usage of the product;

    (n) quantity of the product;

    (o) specification of the product;

    (p) geographical or commercial origin of the product;

    (q) results to be expected from use of the product; and

    (r) results and material features of tests or checks carried out on the product.

(6) In paragraph (4)(j), the "nature, attributes and rights" as far as concern the trader include the trader's—

    (a) identity;

    (b) assets;

    (c) qualifications;

    (d) status;

    (e) approval;

    (f) affiliations or connections;

    (g) ownership of industrial, commercial or intellectual property rights; and

    (h) awards and distinctions.

(7) In paragraph (4)(k) "consumer's rights" include rights the consumer may have under sections 19 and 23 or 24 of the Consumer Rights Act 2015.

6   Misleading omissions

(1) A commercial practice is a misleading omission if, in its factual context, taking account of the matters in paragraph (2)—

(a)   the commercial practice omits material information,

(b)   the commercial practice hides material information,

(c)   the commercial practice provides material information in a manner which is unclear, unintelligible, ambiguous or untimely, or

(d)   the commercial practice fails to identify its commercial intent, unless this is already apparent from the context,

and as a result it causes or is likely to cause the average consumer to take a transactional decision he would not have taken otherwise.

(2)   The matters referred to in paragraph (1) are-—

(a)   all the features and circumstances of the commercial practice;

(b)   the limitations of the medium used to communicate the commercial practice (including limitations of space or time); and

(c)   where the medium used to communicate the commercial practice imposes limitations of space or time, any measures taken by the trader to make the information available to consumers by other means.

(3)   In paragraph (1) "material information" means—

(a)   the information which the average consumer needs, according to the context, to take an informed transactional decision; and

(b)   any information requirement which applies in relation to a commercial communication as a result of an EU obligation.

(4)   Where a commercial practice is an invitation to purchase, the following information will be material if not already apparent from the context in addition to any other information which is material information under paragraph (3)—

(a)   the main characteristics of the product, to the extent appropriate to the medium by which the invitation to purchase is communicated and the product;

(b)   the identity of the trader, such as his trading name, and the identity of any other trader on whose behalf the trader is acting;

(c)   the geographical address of the trader and the geographical address of any other trader on whose behalf the trader is acting;

(d)   either—

(i)   the price, including any taxes; or

(ii)   where the nature of the product is such that the price cannot reasonably be calculated in advance, the manner in which the price is calculated;

(e)   where appropriate, either—

(i)   all additional freight, delivery or postal charges; or

(ii)   where such charges cannot reasonably be calculated in advance, the fact that such charges may be payable;

(f)   the following matters where they depart from the requirements of professional diligence—

(i)   arrangements for payment,

(ii)   arrangements for delivery,

(iii)   arrangements for performance,

(iv)   complaint handling policy;

(g)   for products and transactions involving a right of withdrawal or cancellation, the existence of such a right.

7   Aggressive commercial practices

(1)   A commercial practice is aggressive if, in its factual context, taking account of all of its features and circumstances—

(a)   it significantly impairs or is likely significantly to impair the average consumer's freedom of choice or conduct in relation to the product concerned through the use of harassment, coercion or undue influence; and

(b)   it thereby causes or is likely to cause him to take a transactional decision he would not have taken otherwise.

(2)   In determining whether a commercial practice uses harassment, coercion or undue influence account shall be taken of—

(a)   its timing, location, nature or persistence;

(b)   the use of threatening or abusive language or behaviour;

    (c)   the exploitation by the trader of any specific misfortune or circumstance of such gravity as to impair the consumer's judgment, of which the trader is aware, to influence the consumer's decision with regard to the product;

    (d)   any onerous or disproportionate non-contractual barrier imposed by the trader where a consumer wishes to exercise rights under the contract, including rights to terminate a contract or to switch to another product or another trader; and

    (e)   any threat to take any action which cannot legally be taken.

(3) In this regulation—

    (a)   "coercion" includes the use of physical force; and

    (b)   "undue influence" means exploiting a position of power in relation to the consumer so as to apply pressure, even without using or threatening to use physical force, in a way which significantly limits the consumer's ability to make an informed decision.

PART 3
OFFENCES

8   Offences relating to unfair commercial practices

(1) A trader is guilty of an offence if—

    (a)   he knowingly or recklessly engages in a commercial practice which contravenes the requirements of professional diligence under regulation 3(3)(a); and

    (b)   the practice materially distorts or is likely to materially distort the economic behaviour of the average consumer with regard to the product under regulation 3(3)(b).

(2) For the purposes of paragraph (1)(a) a trader who engages in a commercial practice without regard to whether the practice contravenes the requirements of professional diligence shall be deemed recklessly to engage in the practice, whether or not the trader has reason for believing that the practice might contravene those requirements.

9   A trader is guilty of an offence if he engages in a commercial practice which is a misleading action under regulation 5 otherwise than by reason of the commercial practice satisfying the condition in regulation 5(3)(b).

10   A trader is guilty of an offence if he engages in a commercial practice which is a misleading omission under regulation 6.

11   A trader is guilty of an offence if he engages in a commercial practice which is aggressive under regulation 7.

12   A trader is guilty of an offence if he engages in a commercial practice set out in any of paragraphs 1 to 10, 12 to 27 and 29 to 31 of Schedule 1.

13   Penalty for offences

A person guilty of an offence under regulation 8, 9, 10, 11 or 12 shall be liable—

(a) on summary conviction, to a fine not exceeding the statutory maximum; or

(b) on conviction on indictment, to a fine or imprisonment for a term not exceeding two years or both.

14   Time limit for prosecution

(1) No proceedings for an offence under these Regulations shall be commenced after—

    (a)   the end of the period of three years beginning with the date of the commission of the offence, or

    (b)   the end of the period of one year beginning with the date of discovery of the offence by the prosecutor,

whichever is earlier.

(2) For the purposes of paragraph (1)(b) a certificate signed by or on behalf of the prosecutor and stating the date on which the offence was discovered by him shall be conclusive evidence of that fact and a certificate stating that matter and purporting to be so signed shall be treated as so signed unless the contrary is proved.

(3) Notwithstanding anything in section 127(1) of the Magistrates' Courts Act 1980, an information relating to an offence under these Regulations which is triable by a

magistrates' court in England and Wales may be so tried if it is laid at any time before the end of the period of twelve months beginning with the date of the commission of the offence.

(4)   Notwithstanding anything in section 136 of the Criminal Procedure (Scotland) Act 1995 summary proceedings in Scotland for an offence under these Regulations may be commenced at any time before the end of the period of twelve months beginning with the date of the commission of the offence.

(5)   For the purposes of paragraph (4), section 136(3) of the Criminal Procedure (Scotland) Act 1995 shall apply as it applies for the purposes of that subsection.

(6)   Notwithstanding anything in Article 19(1) of the Magistrates' Courts (Northern Ireland) Order 1981 a complaint charging an offence under these Regulations which is triable by a magistrates' court in Northern Ireland may be so tried if it is made at any time before the end of the period of twelve months beginning with the date of the commission of the offence.

15   Offences committed by bodies of persons

(1)   Where an offence under these Regulations committed by a body corporate is proved—

(a)   to have been committed with the consent or connivance of an officer of the body, or

(b)   to be attributable to any neglect on his part,

the officer as well as the body corporate is guilty of the offence and liable to be proceeded against and punished accordingly.

(2)   In paragraph (1) a reference to an officer of a body corporate includes a reference to—

(a)   a director, manager, secretary or other similar officer; and

(b)   a person purporting to act as a director, manager, secretary or other similar officer.

(3)   Where an offence under these Regulations committed by a Scottish partnership is proved—

(a)   to have been committed with the consent or connivance of a partner, or

(b)   to be attributable to any neglect on his part,

the partner as well as the partnership is guilty of the offence and liable to be proceeded against and punished accordingly.

(4)   In paragraph (3) a reference to a partner includes a person purporting to act as a partner.

16   Offence due to the default of another person

(1)   This regulation applies where a person "X"—

(a)   commits an offence under regulation 9, 10, 11 or 12, or

(b)   would have committed an offence under those regulations but for a defence under regulation 17 or 18,

and the commission of the offence, or of what would have been an offence but for X being able to rely on a defence under regulation 17 or 18, is due to the act or default of some other person "Y".

(2)   Where this regulation applies Y is guilty of the offence, subject to regulations 17 and 18, whether or not Y is a trader and whether or not Y's act or default is a commercial practice.

(3)   Y may be charged with and convicted of the offence by virtue of paragraph (2) whether or not proceedings are taken against X.

17   Due diligence defence

(1)   In any proceedings against a person for an offence under regulation 9, 10, 11 or 12 it is a defence for that person to prove—

(a)   that the commission of the offence was due to—

(i)   a mistake;

(ii)   reliance on information supplied to him by another person;

(iii)   the act or default of another person;

(iv)   an accident; or

(v)   another cause beyond his control; and

(b)   that he took all reasonable precautions and exercised all due diligence to avoid the commission of such an offence by himself or any person under his control.

(2)   A person shall not be entitled to rely on the defence provided by paragraph (1) by reason of the matters referred to in paragraph (ii) or (iii) of paragraph (1)(a) without leave of the court unless—

    (a)   he has served on the prosecutor a notice in writing giving such information identifying or assisting in the identification of that other person as was in his possession; and

    (b)   the notice is served on the prosecutor at least seven clear days before the date of the hearing.

18   Innocent publication of advertisement defence

(1)   In any proceedings against a person for an offence under regulation 9, 10, 11 or 12 committed by the publication of an advertisement it shall be a defence for a person to prove that—

    (a)   he is a person whose business it is to publish or to arrange for the publication of advertisements;

    (b)   he received the advertisement for publication in the ordinary course of business; and

    (c)   he did not know and had no reason to suspect that its publication would amount to an offence under the regulation to which the proceedings relate.

(2)   In paragraph (1) "advertisement" includes a catalogue, a circular and a price list.

PART 4

ENFORCEMENT

19   Duty and power to enforce

(1)   It shall be the duty of every local weights and measures authority and DETINI to enforce these Regulations (other than Part 4A).

(1A) The CMA may also enforce these Regulations.

(2)   Where the enforcement authority is a local weights and measures authority the duty referred to in paragraph (1) shall apply to the enforcement of these Regulations within the authority's area.

(3)   Where the enforcement authority is DETINI the duty referred to in paragraph (1) shall apply to the enforcement of these Regulations within Northern Ireland.

(4)   In determining how to comply with paragraph (1), or as the case may be, paragraph (1A), every enforcement authority shall have regard to the desirability of encouraging control of unfair commercial practices by such established means as it considers appropriate having regard to all the circumstances of the particular case.

(5)   Nothing in this regulation shall authorise any enforcement authority to bring proceedings in Scotland for an offence.

PART 5

SUPPLEMENTARY

29   Validity of agreements

Except as provided by Part 4A, an agreement shall not be void or unenforceable by reason only of a breach of these Regulations.

SCHEDULE 1   Regulation 3(4)(d)

COMMERCIAL PRACTICES WHICH ARE IN ALL CIRCUMSTANCES CONSIDERED UNFAIR

1.   Claiming to be a signatory to a code of conduct when the trader is not.

2.   Displaying a trust mark, quality mark or equivalent without having obtained the necessary authorisation.

3.   Claiming that a code of conduct has an endorsement from a public or other body which it does not have.

4.   Claiming that a trader (including his commercial practices) or a product has been approved, endorsed or authorised by a public or private body when the trader, the commercial practices or the product have not or making such a claim without complying with the terms of the approval, endorsement or authorisation.

5.   Making an invitation to purchase products at a specified price without disclosing the existence of any reasonable grounds the trader may have for believing that he will not be able to offer for supply, or to procure another trader to supply, those products or equivalent products at that price for a period that is, and in quantities that are, reasonable having regard to the product, the scale of advertising of the product and the price offered (bait advertising).

6.   Making an invitation to purchase products at a specified price and then—
(a)   refusing to show the advertised item to consumers,
(b)   refusing to take orders for it or deliver it within a reasonable time, or
(c)   demonstrating a defective sample of it,
with the intention of promoting a different product (bait and switch).

7.   Falsely stating that a product will only be available for a very limited time, or that it will only be available on particular terms for a very limited time, in order to elicit an immediate decision and deprive consumers of sufficient opportunity or time to make an informed choice.

8.   Undertaking to provide after-sales service to consumers with whom the trader has communicated prior to a transaction in a language which is not an official language of the EEA State where the trader is located and then making such service available only in another language without clearly disclosing this to the consumer before the consumer is committed to the transaction.

9.   Stating or otherwise creating the impression that a product can legally be sold when it cannot.

10.   Presenting rights given to consumers in law as a distinctive feature of the trader's offer.

11.   Using editorial content in the media to promote a product where a trader has paid for the promotion without making that clear in the content or by images or sounds clearly identifiable by the consumer (advertorial).

12.   Making a materially inaccurate claim concerning the nature and extent of the risk to the personal security of the consumer or his family if the consumer does not purchase the product.

13.   Promoting a product similar to a product made by a particular manufacturer in such a manner as deliberately to mislead the consumer into believing that the product is made by that same manufacturer when it is not.

14.   Establishing, operating or promoting a pyramid promotional scheme where a consumer gives consideration for the opportunity to receive compensation that is derived primarily from the introduction of other consumers into the scheme rather than from the sale or consumption of products.

15.   Claiming that the trader is about to cease trading or move premises when he is not.

16.   Claiming that products are able to facilitate winning in games of chance.

17.   Falsely claiming that a product is able to cure illnesses, dysfunction or malformations.

18.   Passing on materially inaccurate information on market conditions or on the possibility of finding the product with the intention of inducing the consumer to acquire the product at conditions less favourable than normal market conditions.

19.   Claiming in a commercial practice to offer a competition or prize promotion without awarding the prizes described or a reasonable equivalent.

20.   Describing a product as "gratis", "free", "without charge" or similar if the consumer has to pay anything other than the unavoidable cost of responding to the commercial practice and collecting or paying for delivery of the item.

21.   Including in marketing material an invoice or similar document seeking payment which gives the consumer the impression that he has already ordered the marketed product when he has not.

22.   Falsely claiming or creating the impression that the trader is not acting for purposes relating to his trade, business, craft or profession, or falsely representing oneself as a consumer.

23.   Creating the false impression that after-sales service in relation to a product is available in an EEA State other than the one in which the product is sold.

24.   Creating the impression that the consumer cannot leave the premises until a contract is formed.

25.   Conducting personal visits to the consumer's home ignoring the consumer's request to leave or not to return, except in circumstances and to the extent justified to enforce a contractual obligation.

26.   Making persistent and unwanted solicitations by telephone, fax, e-mail or other remote media except in circumstances and to the extent justified to enforce a contractual obligation.

27.   Requiring a consumer who wishes to claim on an insurance policy to produce documents which could not reasonably be considered relevant as to whether the claim was valid, or failing systematically to respond to pertinent correspondence, in order to dissuade a consumer from exercising his contractual rights.

28.   Including in an advertisement a direct exhortation to children to buy advertised products or persuade their parents or other adults to buy advertised products for them.

29.   Demanding immediate or deferred payment for or the return or safekeeping of products supplied by the trader, but not solicited by the consumer . . .

30.   Explicitly informing a consumer that if he does not buy the product or service, the trader's job or livelihood will be in jeopardy.

31.   Creating the false impression that the consumer has already won, will win, or will on doing a particular act win, a prize or other equivalent benefit, when in fact either—
         (a)   there is no prize or other equivalent benefit, or
         (b)   taking any action in relation to claiming the prize or other equivalent benefit is subject to the consumer paying money or incurring a cost.

DIRECTIVE 2008/95/EC
(trade marks)

Article 1 Scope
This Directive shall apply to every trade mark in respect of goods or services which is the subject of registration or of an application in a Member State for registration as an individual trade mark, a collective mark or a guarantee or certification mark, or which is the subject of a registration or an application for registration in the Benelux Office for Intellectual Property or of an international registration having effect in a Member State.

Article 2 Signs of which a trade mark may consist
A trade mark may consist of any signs capable of being represented graphically, particularly words, including personal names, designs, letters, numerals, the shape of goods or of their packaging, provided that such signs are capable of distinguishing the goods or services of one undertaking from those of other undertakings.

Article 3 Grounds for refusal or invalidity
1.   The following shall not be registered or, if registered, shall be liable to be declared invalid:
         (a)   signs which cannot constitute a trade mark;
         (b)   trade marks which are devoid of any distinctive character;
         (c)   trade marks which consist exclusively of signs or indications which may serve, in trade, to designate the kind, quality, quantity, intended purpose, value, geographical origin, or the time of production of the goods or of rendering of the service, or other characteristics of the goods or services;
         (d)   trade marks which consist exclusively of signs or indications which have become customary in the current language or in the bona fide and established practices of the trade;
         (e)   signs which consist exclusively of:
             (i)   the shape which results from the nature of the goods themselves;
             (ii)   the shape of goods which is necessary to obtain a technical result;
             (iii)   the shape which gives substantial value to the goods;
         (f)   trade marks which are contrary to public policy or to accepted principles of morality;
         (g)   trade marks which are of such a nature as to deceive the public, for instance as to the nature, quality or geographical origin of the goods or service;

(h) trade marks which have not been authorised by the competent authorities and are to be refused or invalidated pursuant to Article 6 ter of the Paris Convention for the Protection of Industrial Property, hereinafter referred to as the "Paris Convention".

2. Any Member State may provide that a trade mark shall not be registered or, if registered, shall be liable to be declared invalid where and to the extent that:

(a) the use of that trade mark may be prohibited pursuant to provisions of law other than trade mark law of the Member State concerned or of the Community;

(b) the trade mark covers a sign of high symbolic value, in particular a religious symbol;

(c) the trade mark includes badges, emblems and escutcheons other than those covered by Article 6 ter of the Paris Convention and which are of public interest, unless the consent of the competent authority to their registration has been given in conformity with the legislation of the Member State;

(d) the application for registration of the trade mark was made in bad faith by the applicant.

3. A trade mark shall not be refused registration or be declared invalid in accordance with paragraph 1(b), (c) or (d) if, before the date of application for registration and following the use which has been made of it, it has acquired a distinctive character. Any Member State may in addition provide that this provision shall also apply where the distinctive character was acquired after the date of application for registration or after the date of registration.

4. Any Member State may provide that, by derogation from paragraphs 1, 2 and 3, the grounds of refusal of registration or invalidity in force in that State prior to the date of entry into force of the provisions necessary to comply with Directive 89/104/EEC, shall apply to trade marks for which application has been made prior to that date.

Article 4 Further grounds for refusal or invalidity concerning conflicts with earlier rights

1. A trade mark shall not be registered or, if registered, shall be liable to be declared invalid:

(a) if it is identical with an earlier trade mark, and the goods or services for which the trade mark is applied for or is registered are identical with the goods or services for which the earlier trade mark is protected;

(b) if because of its identity with, or similarity to, the earlier trade mark and the identity or similarity of the goods or services covered by the trade marks, there exists a likelihood of confusion on the part of the public; the likelihood of confusion includes the likelihood of association with the earlier trade mark.

2. "Earlier trade marks" within the meaning of paragraph 1 means:

(a) trade marks of the following kinds with a date of application for registration which is earlier than the date of application for registration of the trade mark, taking account, where appropriate, of the priorities claimed in respect of those trade marks;

(i) Community trade marks;

(ii) trade marks registered in the Member State or, in the case of Belgium, Luxembourg or the Netherlands, at the Benelux Office for Intellectual Property;

(iii) trade marks registered under international arrangements which have effect in the Member State;

(b) Community trade marks which validly claim seniority, in accordance with Council Regulation (EC) No 40/94 of 20 December 1993 on the Community trade mark, from a trade mark referred to in (a)(ii) and (iii), even when the latter trade mark has been surrendered or allowed to lapse;

(c) applications for the trade marks referred to in points (a) and (b), subject to their registration;

(d) trade marks which, on the date of application for registration of the trade mark, or, where appropriate, of the priority claimed in respect of the application for registration of the trade mark, are well known in a Member State, in the sense in which the words "well known" are used in Article 6 bis of the Paris Convention.

3. A trade mark shall furthermore not be registered or, if registered, shall be liable to be declared invalid if it is identical with, or similar to, an earlier Community trade mark within the meaning of paragraph 2 and is to be, or has been, registered for goods or services which are not similar to those for which the earlier Community trade mark is registered, where the earlier Community trade mark has a reputation in the Community and where the use of the later

trade mark without due cause would take unfair advantage of, or be detrimental to, the distinctive character or the repute of the earlier Community trade mark.

4. Any Member State may, in addition, provide that a trade mark shall not be registered or, if registered, shall be liable to be declared invalid where, and to the extent that:

   (a) the trade mark is identical with, or similar to, an earlier national trade mark within the meaning of paragraph 2 and is to be, or has been, registered for goods or services which are not similar to those for which the earlier trade mark is registered, where the earlier trade mark has a reputation in the Member State concerned and where the use of the later trade mark without due cause would take unfair advantage of, or be detrimental to, the distinctive character or the repute of the earlier trade mark;

   (b) rights to a non-registered trade mark or to another sign used in the course of trade were acquired prior to the date of application for registration of the subsequent trade mark, or the date of the priority claimed for the application for registration of the subsequent trade mark, and that non-registered trade mark or other sign confers on its proprietor the right to prohibit the use of a subsequent trade mark;

   (c) the use of the trade mark may be prohibited by virtue of an earlier right other than the rights referred to in paragraph 2 and point (b) of this paragraph and in particular:

      (i) a right to a name;

      (ii) a right of personal portrayal;

      (iii) a copyright;

      (iv) an industrial property right;

   (d) the trade mark is identical with, or similar to, an earlier collective trade mark conferring a right which expired within a period of a maximum of three years preceding application;

   (e) the trade mark is identical with, or similar to, an earlier guarantee or certification mark conferring a right which expired within a period preceding application the length of which is fixed by the Member State;

   (f) the trade mark is identical with, or similar to, an earlier trade mark which was registered for identical or similar goods or services and conferred on them a right which has expired for failure to renew within a period of a maximum of two years preceding application, unless the proprietor of the earlier trade mark gave his agreement for the registration of the later mark or did not use his trade mark;

   (g) the trade mark is liable to be confused with a mark which was in use abroad on the filing date of the application and which is still in use there, provided that at the date of the application the applicant was acting in bad faith.

5. The Member States may permit that in appropriate circumstances registration need not be refused or the trade mark need not be declared invalid where the proprietor of the earlier trade mark or other earlier right consents to the registration of the later trade mark.

6. Any Member State may provide that, by derogation from paragraphs 1 to 5, the grounds for refusal of registration or invalidity in force in that State prior to the date of the entry into force of the provisions necessary to comply with Directive 89/104/EEC, shall apply to trade marks for which application has been made prior to that date.

Article 5 Rights conferred by a trade mark

1. The registered trade mark shall confer on the proprietor exclusive rights therein. The proprietor shall be entitled to prevent all third parties not having his consent from using in the course of trade:

   (a) any sign which is identical with the trade mark in relation to goods or services which are identical with those for which the trade mark is registered;

   (b) any sign where, because of its identity with, or similarity to, the trade mark and the identity or similarity of the goods or services covered by the trade mark and the sign, there exists a likelihood of confusion on the part of the public; the likelihood of confusion includes the likelihood of association between the sign and the trade mark.

2. Any Member State may also provide that the proprietor shall be entitled to prevent all third parties not having his consent from using in the course of trade any sign which is identical with, or similar to, the trade mark in relation to goods or services which are not similar to those for which the trade mark is registered, where the latter has a reputation in the Member State and where use of that sign without due cause takes unfair advantage of, or is detrimental to, the distinctive character or the repute of the trade mark.

3.	The following, inter alia, may be prohibited under paragraphs 1 and 2:
	(a)	affixing the sign to the goods or to the packaging thereof;
	(b)	offering the goods, or putting them on the market or stocking them for these purposes under that sign, or offering or supplying services thereunder;
	(c)	importing or exporting the goods under the sign;
	(d)	using the sign on business papers and in advertising.
4.	Where, under the law of the Member State, the use of a sign under the conditions referred to in paragraph 1(b) or paragraph 2 could not be prohibited before the date of entry into force of the provisions necessary to comply with Directive 89/104/EEC in the Member State concerned, the rights conferred by the trade mark may not be relied on to prevent the continued use of the sign.
5.	Paragraphs 1 to 4 shall not affect provisions in any Member State relating to the protection against the use of a sign other than for the purposes of distinguishing goods or services, where use of that sign without due cause takes unfair advantage of, or is detrimental to, the distinctive character or the repute of the trade mark.

Article 6 Limitation of the effects of a trade mark
1.	The trade mark shall not entitle the proprietor to prohibit a third party from using, in the course of trade:
	(a)	his own name or address;
	(b)	indications concerning the kind, quality, quantity, intended purpose, value, geographical origin, the time of production of goods or of rendering of the service, or other characteristics of goods or services;
	(c)	the trade mark where it is necessary to indicate the intended purpose of a product or service, in particular as accessories or spare parts; provided he uses them in accordance with honest practices in industrial or commercial matters.
2.	The trade mark shall not entitle the proprietor to prohibit a third party from using, in the course of trade, an earlier right which only applies in a particular locality if that right is recognised by the laws of the Member State in question and within the limits of the territory in which it is recognised.

Article 7 Exhaustion of the rights conferred by a trade mark
1.	The trade mark shall not entitle the proprietor to prohibit its use in relation to goods which have been put on the market in the Community under that trade mark by the proprietor or with his consent.
2.	Paragraph 1 shall not apply where there exist legitimate reasons for the proprietor to oppose further commercialisation of the goods, especially where the condition of the goods is changed or impaired after they have been put on the market.

Article 8 Licensing
1.	A trade mark may be licensed for some or all of the goods or services for which it is registered and for the whole or part of the Member State concerned. A licence may be exclusive or non-exclusive.
2.	The proprietor of a trade mark may invoke the rights conferred by that trade mark against a licensee who contravenes any provision in his licensing contract with regard to:
	(a)	its duration;
	(b)	the form covered by the registration in which the trade mark may be used;
	(c)	the scope of the goods or services for which the licence is granted;
	(d)	the territory in which the trade mark may be affixed; or 3
	(e)	the quality of the goods manufactured or of the services provided by the licensee.

Article 9 Limitation in consequence of acquiescence
1.	Where, in a Member State, the proprietor of an earlier trade mark as referred to in Article 4(2) has acquiesced, for a period of five successive years, in the use of a later trade mark registered in that Member State while being aware of such use, he shall no longer be entitled on the basis of the earlier trade mark either to apply for a declaration that the later trade mark is invalid or to oppose the use of the later trade mark in respect of the goods or services for which the later trade mark has been used, unless registration of the later trade mark was applied for in bad faith.

2.   Any Member State may provide that paragraph 1 shall apply mutatis mutandis to the proprietor of an earlier trade mark referred to in Article 4(4)(a) or an other earlier right referred to in Article 4(4)(b) or (c).

3.   In the cases referred to in paragraphs 1 and 2, the proprietor of a later registered trade mark shall not be entitled to oppose the use of the earlier right, even though that right may no longer be invoked against the later trade mark.

Article 10 Use of trade marks

1.   If, within a period of five years following the date of the completion of the registration procedure, the proprietor has not put the trade mark to genuine use in the Member State in connection with the goods or services in respect of which it is registered, or if such use has been suspended during an uninterrupted period of five years, the trade mark shall be subject to the sanctions provided for in this Directive, unless there are proper reasons for non-use. The following shall also constitute use within the meaning of the first subparagraph:

   (a)   use of the trade mark in a form differing in elements which do not alter the distinctive character of the mark in the form in which it was registered;

   (b)   affixing of the trade mark to goods or to the packaging thereof in the Member State concerned solely for export purposes.

2.   Use of the trade mark with the consent of the proprietor or by any person who has authority to use a collective mark or a guarantee or certification mark shall be deemed to constitute use by the proprietor.

3.   In relation to trade marks registered before the date of entry into force in the Member State concerned of the provisions necessary to comply with Directive 89/104/EEC:

   (a)   where a provision in force prior to that date attached sanctions to non-use of a trade mark during an uninterrupted period, the relevant period of five years mentioned in the first subparagraph of paragraph 1 shall be deemed to have begun to run at the same time as any period of nonuse which is already running at that date;

   (b)   where there was no use provision in force prior to that date, the periods of five years mentioned in the first subparagraph of paragraph 1 shall be deemed to run from that date at the earliest.

Article 11 Sanctions for non-use of a trade mark in legal or administrative proceedings

1.   A trade mark may not be declared invalid on the ground that there is an earlier conflicting trade mark if the latter does not fulfil the requirements of use set out in Article 10(1) and (2), or in Article 10(3), as the case may be.

2.   Any Member State may provide that registration of a trade mark may not be refused on the ground that there is an earlier conflicting trade mark if the latter does not fulfil the requirements of use set out in Article 10(1) and (2) or in Article 10(3), as the case may be.

3.   Without prejudice to the application of Article 12, where a counter-claim for revocation is made, any Member State may provide that a trade mark may not be successfully invoked in infringement proceedings if it is established as a result of a plea that the trade mark could be revoked pursuant to Article 12(1).

4.   If the earlier trade mark has been used in relation to part only of the goods or services for which it is registered, it shall, for purposes of applying paragraphs 1, 2 and 3, be deemed to be registered in respect only of that part of the goods or services.

Article 12 Grounds for revocation

1.   A trade mark shall be liable to revocation if, within a continuous period of five years, it has not been put to genuine use in the Member State in connection with the goods or services in respect of which it is registered, and there are no proper reasons for non-use.

   However, no person may claim that the proprietor's rights in a trade mark should be revoked where, during the interval between expiry of the five-year period and filing of the application for revocation, genuine use of the trade mark has been started or resumed.

   The commencement or resumption of use within a period of three months preceding the filing of the application for revocation which began at the earliest on expiry of the continuous period of five years of non-use shall be disregarded where preparations for the commencement or resumption occur only after the proprietor becomes aware that the application for revocation may be filed.

2.   Without prejudice to paragraph 1, a trade mark shall be liable to revocation if, after the date on which it was registered:
   (a) in consequence of acts or inactivity of the proprietor, it has become the common name in the trade for a product or service in respect of which it is registered;
   (b) in consequence of the use made of it by the proprietor of the trade mark or with his consent in respect of the goods or services for which it is registered, it is liable to mislead the public, particularly as to the nature, quality or geographical origin of those goods or services.

Article 13 Grounds for refusal or revocation or invalidity relating to only some of the goods or services

Where grounds for refusal of registration or for revocation or invalidity of a trade mark exist in respect of only some of the goods or services for which that trade mark has been applied for or registered, refusal of registration or revocation or invalidity shall cover those goods or services only.

Article 14 Establishment a posteriori of invalidity or revocation of a trade mark

Where the seniority of an earlier trade mark which has been surrendered or allowed to lapse is claimed for a Community trade mark, the invalidity or revocation of the earlier trade mark may be established a posteriori.

Article 15 Special provisions in respect of collective marks, guarantee marks and certification marks

1.   Without prejudice to Article 4, Member States whose laws authorise the registration of collective marks or of guarantee or certification marks may provide that such marks shall not be registered, or shall be revoked or declared invalid, on grounds additional to those specified in Articles 3 and 12 where the function of those marks so requires.
2.   By way of derogation from Article 3(1)(c), Member States may provide that signs or indications which may serve, in trade, to designate the geographical origin of the goods or services may constitute collective, guarantee or certification marks. Such a mark does not entitle the proprietor to prohibit a third party from using in the course of trade such signs or indications, provided he uses them in accordance with honest practices in industrial or commercial matters; in particular, such a mark may not be invoked against a third party who is entitled to use a geographical name.

Note: This directive will be replaced by Directive 2015/2436, which comes into force on 15/01/2019.

DIRECTIVE (EU) 2015/2436
(trade marks)

CHAPTER 1
GENERAL PROVISIONS

Article 1 Scope

This Directive applies to every trade mark in respect of goods or services which is the subject of registration or of an application for registration in a Member State as an individual trade mark, a guarantee or certification mark or a collective mark, or which is the subject of a registration or an application for registration in the Benelux Office for Intellectual Property or of an international registration having effect in a Member State.

Article 2 Definitions

For the purpose of this Directive, the following definitions apply:
(a) "office" means the central industrial property office of the Member State or the Benelux Office for Intellectual Property, entrusted with the registration of trade marks;
(b) "register" means the register of trade marks kept by an office.

CHAPTER 2
SUBSTANTIVE LAW ON TRADE MARKS

SECTION 1
SIGNS OF WHICH A TRADE MARK MAY CONSIST

Article 3 Signs of which a trade mark may consist

A trade mark may consist of any signs, in particular words, including personal names, or designs, letters, numerals, colours, the shape of goods or of the packaging of goods, or sounds, provided that such signs are capable of:

(a)   distinguishing the goods or services of one undertaking from those of other undertakings; and

(b)   being represented on the register in a manner which enables the competent authorities and the public to determine the clear and precise subject matter of the protection afforded to its proprietor.

SECTION 2
GROUNDS FOR REFUSAL OR INVALIDITY

Article 4 Absolute grounds for refusal or invalidity

1.   The following shall not be registered or, if registered, shall be liable to be declared invalid:

(a)   signs which cannot constitute a trade mark;

(b)   trade marks which are devoid of any distinctive character;

(c)   trade marks which consist exclusively of signs or indications which may serve, in trade, to designate the kind, quality, quantity, intended purpose, value, geographical origin, or the time of production of the goods or of rendering of the service, or other characteristics of the goods or services;

(d)   trade marks which consist exclusively of signs or indications which have become customary in the current language or in the bona fide and established practices of the trade;

(e)   signs which consist exclusively of:

(i)   the shape, or another characteristic, which results from the nature of the goods themselves;

(ii)   the shape, or another characteristic, of goods which is necessary to obtain a technical result;

(iii)   the shape, or another characteristic, which gives substantial value to the goods;

(f)   trade marks which are contrary to public policy or to accepted principles of morality;

(g)   trade marks which are of such a nature as to deceive the public, for instance, as to the nature, quality or geographical origin of the goods or service;

(h)   trade marks which have not been authorised by the competent authorities and are to be refused or invalidated pursuant to Article 6ter of the Paris Convention;

(i)   trade marks which are excluded from registration pursuant to Union legislation or the national law of the Member State concerned, or to international agreements to which the Union or the Member State concerned is party, providing for protection of designations of origin and geographical indications;

(j)   trade marks which are excluded from registration pursuant to Union legislation or international agreements to which the Union is party, providing for protection of traditional terms for wine;

(k)   trade marks which are excluded from registration pursuant to Union legislation or international agreements to which the Union is party, providing for protection of traditional specialities guaranteed;

(l)   trade marks which consist of, or reproduce in their essential elements, an earlier plant variety denomination registered in accordance with Union legislation or the national law of the Member State concerned, or international agreements to which the Union or the Member State concerned is party, providing protection for plant variety rights, and which are in respect of plant varieties of the same or closely related species.

2.   A trade mark shall be liable to be declared invalid where the application for registration of the trade mark was made in bad faith by the applicant. Any Member State may also provide that such a trade mark is not to be registered.

3.   Any Member State may provide that a trade mark is not to be registered or, if registered, is liable to be declared invalid where and to the extent that:
        (a)   the use of that trade mark may be prohibited pursuant to provisions of law other than trade mark law of the Member State concerned or of the Union;
        (b)   the trade mark includes a sign of high symbolic value, in particular a religious symbol
        (c)   the trade mark includes badges, emblems and escutcheons other than those covered by Article 6*ter* of the Paris Convention and which are of public interest, unless the consent of the competent authority to their registration has been given in conformity with the law of the Member State.

4.   A trade mark shall not be refused registration in accordance with paragraph 1(b), (c) or (d) if, before the date of application for registration, following the use which has been made of it, it has acquired a distinctive character. A trade mark shall not be declared invalid for the same reasons if, before the date of application for a declaration of invalidity, following the use which has been made of it, it has acquired a distinctive character.

5.   Any Member State may provide that paragraph 4 is also to apply where the distinctive character was acquired after the date of application for registration but before the date of registration.

Article 5 Relative grounds for refusal or invalidity

1.   A trade mark shall not be registered or, if registered, shall be liable to be declared invalid where:
        (a)   it is identical with an earlier trade mark, and the goods or services for which the trade mark is applied for or is registered are identical with the goods or services for which the earlier trade mark is protected;
        (b)   because of its identity with, or similarity to, the earlier trade mark and the identity or similarity of the goods or services covered by the trade marks, there exists a likelihood of confusion on the part of the public; the likelihood of confusion includes the likelihood of association with the earlier trade mark.

2.   "Earlier trade marks" within the meaning of paragraph 1 means:
        (a)   trade marks of the following kinds with a date of application for registration which is earlier than the date of application for registration of the trade mark, taking account, where appropriate, of the priorities claimed in respect of those trade marks:
              (i)   EU trade marks;
              (ii)   trade marks registered in the Member State concerned or, in the case of Belgium, Luxembourg or the Netherlands, at the Benelux Office for Intellectual Property;
              (iii) trade marks registered under international arrangements which have effect in the Member State concerned;
        (b)   EU trade marks which validly claim seniority, in accordance with Regulation (EC) No 207/2009, of a trade mark referred to in points (a)(ii) and (iii), even when the latter trade mark has been surrendered or allowed to lapse;
        (c)   applications for the trade marks referred to in points (a) and (b), subject to their registration;
        (d)   trade marks which, on the date of application for registration of the trade mark, or, where appropriate, of the priority claimed in respect of the application for registration of the trade mark, are well known in the Member State concerned, in the sense in which the words 'well-known' are used in Article 6bis of the Paris Convention.

3.   Furthermore, a trade mark shall not be registered or, if registered, shall be liable to be declared invalid where:
        (a)   it is identical with, or similar to, an earlier trade mark irrespective of whether the goods or services for which it is applied or registered are identical with, similar to or not similar to those for which the earlier trade mark is registered, where the earlier trade mark has a reputation in the Member State in respect of which registration is applied for or in which the trade mark is registered or, in the case of an EU trade mark, has a reputation in the Union and the use of the later trade mark without due cause would take unfair advantage of, or be detrimental to, the distinctive character or the repute of the earlier trade mark;
        (b)   an agent or representative of the proprietor of the trade mark applies for registration thereof in his own name without the proprietor's authorisation, unless the agent or representative justifies his action;

(c)   and to the extent that, pursuant to Union legislation or the law of the Member State concerned providing for protection of designations of origin and geographical indications:

    (i)   an application for a designation of origin or a geographical indication had already been submitted in accordance with Union legislation or the law of the Member State concerned prior to the date of application for registration of the trade mark or the date of the priority claimed for the application, subject to its subsequent registration;

    (ii)   that designation of origin or geographical indication confers on the person authorised under the relevant law to exercise the rights arising therefrom the right to prohibit the use of a subsequent trade mark.

4.   Any Member State may provide that a trade mark is not to be registered or, if registered, is liable to be declared invalid where, and to the extent that:

(a)   rights to a non-registered trade mark or to another sign used in the course of trade were acquired prior to the date of application for registration of the subsequent trade mark, or the date of the priority claimed for the application for registration of the subsequent trade mark, and that non-registered trade mark or other sign confers on its proprietor the right to prohibit the use of a subsequent trade mark;

(b)   the use of the trade mark may be prohibited by virtue of an earlier right, other than the rights referred to in paragraph 2 and point (a) of this paragraph, and in particular:

    (i)   a right to a name;

    (ii)   a right of personal portrayal;

    (iii) a copyright;

    (iv)   an industrial property right;

(c)   the trade mark is liable to be confused with an earlier trade mark protected abroad, provided that, at the date of the application, the applicant was acting in bad faith.

5.   The Member States shall ensure that in appropriate circumstances there is no obligation to refuse registration or to declare a trade mark invalid where the proprietor of the earlier trade mark or other earlier right consents to the registration of the later trade mark.

6.   Any Member State may provide that, by way of derogation from paragraphs 1 to 5, the grounds for refusal of registration or invalidity in force in that Member State prior to the date of the entry into force of the provisions necessary to comply with Directive 89/104/EEC are to apply to trade marks for which an application has been made prior to that date.

Article 6 Establishment *a posteriori* of invalidity or revocation of a trade mark

Where the seniority of a national trade mark or of a trade mark registered under international arrangements having effect in the Member State, which has been surrendered or allowed to lapse, is claimed for an EU trade mark, the invalidity or revocation of the trade mark providing the basis for the seniority claim may be established *a posteriori*, provided that the invalidity or revocation could have been declared at the time the mark was surrendered or allowed to lapse. In such a case, the seniority shall cease to produce its effects.

Article 7 Grounds for refusal or invalidity relating to only some of the goods or services

Where grounds for refusal of registration or for invalidity of a trade mark exist in respect of only some of the goods or services for which that trade mark has been applied or registered, refusal of registration or invalidity shall cover those goods or services only.

Article 8 Lack of distinctive character or of reputation of an earlier trade mark precluding a declaration of invalidity of a registered trade mark

An application for a declaration of invalidity on the basis of an earlier trade mark shall not succeed at the date of application for invalidation if it would not have been successful at the filing date or the priority date of the later trade mark for any of the following reasons:

(a)   the earlier trade mark, liable to be declared invalid pursuant to Article 4(1)(b), (c) or (d), had not yet acquired a distinctive character as referred to in Article 4(4);

(b)   the application for a declaration of invalidity is based on Article 5(1)(b) and the earlier trade mark had not yet become sufficiently distinctive to support a finding of likelihood of confusion within the meaning of Article 5(1)(b);

(c)   the application for a declaration of invalidity is based on Article 5(3)(a) and the earlier trade mark had not yet acquired a reputation within the meaning of Article 5(3)(a).

Article 9 Preclusion of a declaration of invalidity due to acquiescence

1.   Where, in a Member State, the proprietor of an earlier trade mark as referred to in Article 5(2) or Article 5(3)(a) has acquiesced, for a period of five successive years, in the use of a later trade mark registered in that Member State while being aware of such use, that proprietor shall no longer be entitled on the basis of the earlier trade mark to apply for a declaration that the later trade mark is invalid in respect of the goods or services for which the later trade mark has been used, unless registration of the later trade mark was applied for in bad faith.

2.   Member States may provide that paragraph 1 of this Article is to apply to the proprietor of any other earlier right referred to in Article 5(4)(a) or (b).

3.   In the cases referred to in paragraphs 1 and 2, the proprietor of a later registered trade mark shall not be entitled to oppose the use of the earlier right, even though that right may no longer be invoked against the later trade mark.

SECTION 3
RIGHTS CONFERRED AND LIMITATIONS

Article 10 Rights conferred by a trade mark

1.   The registration of a trade mark shall confer on the proprietor exclusive rights therein.

2.   Without prejudice to the rights of proprietors acquired before the filing date or the priority date of the registered trade mark, the proprietor of that registered trade mark shall be entitled to prevent all third parties not having his consent from using in the course of trade, in relation to goods or services, any sign where:

(a)   the sign is identical with the trade mark and is used in relation to goods or services which are identical with those for which the trade mark is registered;

(b)   the sign is identical with, or similar to, the trade mark and is used in relation to goods or services which are identical with, or similar to, the goods or services for which the trade mark is registered, if there exists a likelihood of confusion on the part of the public; the likelihood of confusion includes the likelihood of association between the sign and the trade mark;

(c)   the sign is identical with, or similar to, the trade mark irrespective of whether it is used in relation to goods or services which are identical with, similar to, or not similar to, those for which the trade mark is registered, where the latter has a reputation in the Member State and where use of that sign without due cause takes unfair advantage of, or is detrimental to, the distinctive character or the repute of the trade mark.

3.   The following, in particular, may be prohibited under paragraph 2:

(a)   affixing the sign to the goods or to the packaging thereof;

(b)   offering the goods or putting them on the market, or stocking them for those purposes, under the sign, or offering or supplying services thereunder;

(c)   importing or exporting the goods under the sign;

(d)   using the sign as a trade or company name or part of a trade or company name;

(e)   using the sign on business papers and in advertising;

(f)   using the sign in comparative advertising in a manner that is contrary to Directive 2006/114/EC.

4.   Without prejudice to the rights of proprietors acquired before the filing date or the priority date of the registered trade mark, the proprietor of that registered trade mark shall also be entitled to prevent all third parties from bringing goods, in the course of trade, into the Member State where the trade mark is registered, without being released for free circulation there, where such goods, including the packaging thereof, come from third countries and bear without authorisation a trade mark which is identical with the trade mark registered in respect of such goods, or which cannot be distinguished in its essential aspects from that trade mark.

The entitlement of the trade mark proprietor pursuant to the first subparagraph shall lapse if, during the proceedings to determine whether the registered trade mark has been infringed, initiated in accordance with Regulation (EU) No 608/2013, evidence is provided by the declarant or the holder of the goods that the proprietor of the registered trade mark is not entitled to prohibit the placing of the goods on the market in the country of final destination.

5.   Where, under the law of a Member State, the use of a sign under the conditions referred to in paragraph 2 (b) or (c) could not be prohibited before the date of entry into force of the

provisions necessary to comply with Directive 89/104/EEC in the Member State concerned, the rights conferred by the trade mark may not be relied on to prevent the continued use of the sign.

6.   Paragraphs 1, 2, 3 and 5 shall not affect provisions in any Member State relating to the protection against the use of a sign other than use for the purposes of distinguishing goods or services, where use of that sign without due cause takes unfair advantage of, or is detrimental to, the distinctive character or the repute of the trade mark.

Article 11 The right to prohibit preparatory acts in relation to the use of packaging or other means

Where the risk exists that the packaging, labels, tags, security or authenticity features or devices, or any other means to which the trade mark is affixed, could be used in relation to goods or services and that use would constitute an infringement of the rights of the proprietor of a trade mark under Article 10(2) and (3), the proprietor of that trade mark shall have the right to prohibit the following acts if carried out in the course of trade:

(a)   affixing a sign identical with, or similar to, the trade mark on packaging, labels, tags, security or authenticity features or devices, or any other means to which the mark may be affixed;

(b)   offering or placing on the market, or stocking for those purposes, or importing or exporting, packaging, labels, tags, security or authenticity features or devices, or any other means to which the mark is affixed.

Article 12 Reproduction of trade marks in dictionaries

If the reproduction of a trade mark in a dictionary, encyclopaedia or similar reference work, in print or electronic form, gives the impression that it constitutes the generic name of the goods or services for which the trade mark is registered, the publisher of the work shall, at the request of the proprietor of the trade mark, ensure that the reproduction of the trade mark is, without delay, and in the case of works in printed form at the latest in the next edition of the publication, accompanied by an indication that it is a registered trade mark.

Article 13 Prohibition of the use of a trade mark registered in the name of an agent or representative

1.   Where a trade mark is registered in the name of the agent or representative of a person who is the proprietor of that trade mark, without the proprietor's consent, the latter shall be entitled to do either or both of the following:
(a)   oppose the use of the trade mark by his agent or representative;
(b)   demand the assignment of the trade mark in his favour.

2.   Paragraph 1 shall not apply where the agent or representative justifies his action.

Article 14 Limitation of the effects of a trade mark

1.   A trade mark shall not entitle the proprietor to prohibit a third party from using, in the course of trade:
(a)   the name or address of the third party, where that third party is a natural person;
(b)   signs or indications which are not distinctive or which concern the kind, quality, quantity, intended purpose, value, geographical origin, the time of production of goods or of rendering of the service, or other characteristics of goods or services;
(c)   the trade mark for the purpose of identifying or referring to goods or services as those of the proprietor of that trade mark, in particular, where the use of the trade mark is necessary to indicate the intended purpose of a product or service, in particular as accessories or spare parts.

2.   Paragraph 1 shall only apply where the use made by the third party is in accordance with honest practices in industrial or commercial matters.

3.   A trade mark shall not entitle the proprietor to prohibit a third party from using, in the course of trade, an earlier right which only applies in a particular locality, if that right is recognised by the law of the Member State in question and the use of that right is within the limits of the territory in which it is recognised.

Article 15 Exhaustion of the rights conferred by a trade mark

1.   A trade mark shall not entitle the proprietor to prohibit its use in relation to goods which have been put on the market in the Union under that trade mark by the proprietor or with the proprietor's consent.

2.   Paragraph 1 shall not apply where there exist legitimate reasons for the proprietor to oppose further commercialisation of the goods, especially where the condition of the goods is changed or impaired after they have been put on the market.

Article 16 Use of trade marks

1.   If, within a period of five years following the date of the completion of the registration procedure, the proprietor has not put the trade mark to genuine use in the Member State in connection with the goods or services in respect of which it is registered, or if such use has been suspended during a continuous five-year period, the trade mark shall be subject to the limits and sanctions provided for in Article 17, Article 19(1), Article 44(1) and (2), and Article 46(3) and (4), unless there are proper reasons for non-use.

2.   Where a Member State provides for opposition proceedings following registration, the five-year period referred to in paragraph 1 shall be calculated from the date when the mark can no longer be opposed or, in the event that an opposition has been lodged, from the date when a decision terminating the opposition proceedings became final or the opposition was withdrawn.

3.   With regard to trade marks registered under international arrangements and having effect in the Member State, the five-year period referred to in paragraph 1 shall be calculated from the date when the mark can no longer be rejected or opposed. Where an opposition has been lodged or when an objection on absolute or relative grounds has been notified, the period shall be calculated from the date when a decision terminating the opposition proceedings or a ruling on absolute or relative grounds for refusal became final or the opposition was withdrawn.

4.   The date of commencement of the five-year period, as referred to in paragraphs 1 and 2, shall be entered in the register.

5.   The following shall also constitute use within the meaning of paragraph 1:

(a)   use of the trade mark in a form differing in elements which do not alter the distinctive character of the mark in the form in which it was registered, regardless of whether or not the trade mark in the form as used is also registered in the name of the proprietor;

(b)   affixing of the trade mark to goods or to the packaging thereof in the Member State concerned solely for export purposes.

6.   Use of the trade mark with the consent of the proprietor shall be deemed to constitute use by the proprietor.

Article 17 Non-use as defence in infringement proceedings

The proprietor of a trade mark shall be entitled to prohibit the use of a sign only to the extent that the proprietor's rights are not liable to be revoked pursuant to Article 19 at the time the infringement action is brought. If the defendant so requests, the proprietor of the trade mark shall furnish proof that, during the five-year period preceding the date of bringing the action, the trade mark has been put to genuine use as provided in Article 16 in connection with the goods or services in respect of which it is registered and which are cited as justification for the action, or that there are proper reasons for non-use, provided that the registration procedure of the trade mark has at the date of bringing the action been completed for not less than five years.

Article 18 Intervening right of the proprietor of a later registered trade mark as defence in infringement proceedings

1.   In infringement proceedings, the proprietor of a trade mark shall not be entitled to prohibit the use of a later registered mark where that later trade mark would not be declared invalid pursuant to Article 8, Article 9(1) or (2) or Article 46(3).

2.   In infringement proceedings, the proprietor of a trade mark shall not be entitled to prohibit the use of a later registered EU trade mark where that later trade mark would not be declared invalid pursuant to Article 53(1), (3) or (4), 54(1) or (2) or 57(2) of Regulation (EC) No 207/2009.

3.   Where the proprietor of a trade mark is not entitled to prohibit the use of a later registered trade mark pursuant to paragraph 1 or 2, the proprietor of that later registered trade mark shall not be entitled to prohibit the use of the earlier trade mark in infringement proceedings, even though that earlier right may no longer be invoked against the later trade mark.

SECTION 4
REVOCATION OF TRADE MARK RIGHTS

Article 19 Absence of genuine use as ground for revocation

1.   A trade mark shall be liable to revocation if, within a continuous five-year period, it has not been put to genuine use in the Member State in connection with the goods or services in respect of which it is registered, and there are no proper reasons for non-use.
2.   No person may claim that the proprietor's rights in a trade mark should be revoked where, during the interval between expiry of the five-year period and filing of the application for revocation, genuine use of the trade mark has been started or resumed.
3.   The commencement or resumption of use within the three-month period preceding the filing of the application for revocation which began at the earliest on expiry of the continuous five-year period of non-use shall be disregarded where preparations for the commencement or resumption occur only after the proprietor becomes aware that the application for revocation may be filed.

Article 20 Trade mark having become generic or misleading indication as grounds for revocation

A trade mark shall be liable to revocation if, after the date on which it was registered:
(a)   as a result of acts or inactivity of the proprietor, it has become the common name in the trade for a product or service in respect of which it is registered;
(b)   as a result of the use made of it by the proprietor of the trade mark or with the proprietor's consent in respect of the goods or services for which it is registered, it is liable to mislead the public, particularly as to the nature, quality or geographical origin of those goods or services.

Article 21 Revocation relating to only some of the goods or services

Where grounds for revocation of a trade mark exist in respect of only some of the goods or services for which that trade mark has been registered, revocation shall cover those goods or services only.

SECTION 5
TRADE MARKS AS OBJECTS OF PROPERTY

Article 22 Transfer of registered trade marks

1.   A trade mark may be transferred, separately from any transfer of the undertaking, in respect of some or all of the goods or services for which it is registered.
2.   A transfer of the whole of the undertaking shall include the transfer of the trade mark except where there is agreement to the contrary or circumstances clearly dictate otherwise. This provision shall apply to the contractual obligation to transfer the undertaking.
3.   Member States shall have procedures in place to allow for the recordal of transfers in their registers.

Article 23 Rights *in rem*

1.   A trade mark may, independently of the undertaking, be given as security or be the subject of rights *in rem*.
2.   Member States shall have procedures in place to allow for the recordal of rights *in rem* in their registers.

Article 24 Levy of execution

1.   A trade mark may be levied in execution.
2.   Member States shall have procedures in place to allow for the recordal of levy of execution in their registers.

Article 25 Licensing

1.   A trade mark may be licensed for some or all of the goods or services for which it is registered and for the whole or part of the Member State concerned. A licence may be exclusive or non-exclusive.
2.   The proprietor of a trade mark may invoke the rights conferred by that trade mark against a licensee who contravenes any provision in his licensing contract with regard to:

(a)   its duration;
(b)   the form covered by the registration in which the trade mark may be used;
(c)   the scope of the goods or services for which the licence is granted;
(d)   the territory in which the trade mark may be affixed; or
(e)   the quality of the goods manufactured or of the services provided by the licensee.
3.   Without prejudice to the provisions of the licensing contract, the licensee may bring proceedings for infringement of a trade mark only if its proprietor consents thereto. However, the holder of an exclusive licence may bring such proceedings if the proprietor of the trade mark, after formal notice, does not himself bring infringement proceedings within an appropriate period.
4.   A licensee shall, for the purpose of obtaining compensation for damage suffered by him, be entitled to intervene in infringement proceedings brought by the proprietor of the trade mark.
5.   Member States shall have procedures in place to allow for the recordal of licences in their registers.

Article 26 Applications for a trade mark as an object of property
Articles 22 to 25 shall apply to applications for trade marks.

SECTION 6
GUARANTEE OR CERTIFICATION MARKS AND COLLECTIVE MARKS

Article 27 Definitions
For the purposes of this Directive, the following definitions apply:
(a)   "guarantee or certification mark" means a trade mark which is described as such when the mark is applied for and is capable of distinguishing goods or services which are certified by the proprietor of the mark in respect of material, mode of manufacture of goods or performance of services, quality, accuracy or other characteristics, from goods and services which are not so certified;
(b)   "collective mark" means a trade mark which is described as such when the mark is applied for and is capable of distinguishing the goods or services of the members of an association which is the proprietor of the mark from the goods or services of other undertakings.

Article 28 Guarantee or certification marks
1.   Member States may provide for the registration of guarantee or certification marks.
2.   Any natural or legal person, including institutions, authorities and bodies governed by public law, may apply for guarantee or certification marks provided that such person does not carry on a business involving the supply of goods or services of the kind certified.
   Member States may provide that a guarantee or certification mark is not to be registered unless the applicant is competent to certify the goods or services for which the mark is to be registered.
3.   Member States may provide that guarantee or certification marks are not to be registered, or are to be revoked or declared invalid, on grounds other than those specified in Articles 4, 19 and 20, where the function of those marks so requires.
4.   By way of derogation from Article 4(1)(c), Member States may provide that signs or indications which may serve, in trade, to designate the geographical origin of the goods or services may constitute guarantee or certification marks. Such a guarantee or certification mark shall not entitle the proprietor to prohibit a third party from using in the course of trade such signs or indications, provided that third party uses them in accordance with honest practices in industrial or commercial matters. In particular, such a mark may not be invoked against a third party who is entitled to use a geographical name.
5.   The requirements laid down in Article 16 shall be satisfied where genuine use of a guarantee or certification mark in accordance with Article 16 is made by any person who has the authority to use it.

Article 29 Collective marks
1.   Member States shall provide for the registration of collective marks.
2.   Associations of manufacturers, producers, suppliers of services or traders, which, under the terms of the law governing them, have the capacity in their own name to have rights and

obligations, to make contracts or accomplish other legal acts, and to sue and be sued, as well as legal persons governed by public law, may apply for collective marks.

3. By way of derogation from Article 4(1)(c), Member States may provide that signs or indications which may serve, in trade, to designate the geographical origin of the goods or services may constitute collective marks. Such a collective mark shall not entitle the proprietor to prohibit a third party from using, in the course of trade, such signs or indications, provided that third party uses them in accordance with honest practices in industrial or commercial matters. In particular, such a mark may not be invoked against a third party who is entitled to use a geographical name.

Article 30 Regulations governing use of a collective mark

1. An applicant for a collective mark shall submit the regulations governing its use to the office.

2. The regulations governing use shall specify at least the persons authorised to use the mark, the conditions of membership of the association and the conditions of use of the mark, including sanctions. The regulations governing use of a mark referred to in Article 29(3) shall authorise any person whose goods or services originate in the geographical area concerned to become a member of the association which is the proprietor of the mark, provided that the person fulfils all the other conditions of the regulations.

Article 31 Refusal of an application

1. In addition to the grounds for refusal of a trade mark application provided for in Article 4, where appropriate with the exception of Article 4(1)(c) concerning signs or indications which may serve, in trade, to designate the geographical origin of the goods or services, and Article 5,and without prejudice to the right of an office not to undertake examination *ex officio* of relative grounds, an application for a collective mark shall be refused where the provisions of point (b) of Article 27, Article 29 or Article 30 are not satisfied, or where the regulations governing use of that collective mark are contrary to public policy or to accepted principles of morality.

2. An application for a collective mark shall also be refused if the public is liable to be misled as regards the character or the significance of the mark, in particular if it is likely to be taken to be something other than a collective mark.

3. An application shall not be refused if the applicant, as a result of amendment of the regulations governing use of the collective mark, meets the requirements referred to in paragraphs 1 and 2.

Article 32 Use of collective marks

The requirements of Article 16 shall be satisfied where genuine use of a collective mark in accordance with that Article is made by any person who has authority to use it.

Article 33 Amendments to the regulations governing use of a collective mark

1. The proprietor of a collective mark shall submit to the office any amended regulations governing use.

2. Amendments to the regulations governing use shall be mentioned in the register unless the amended regulations do not satisfy the requirements of Article 30 or involve one of the grounds for refusal referred to in Article 31.

3. For the purposes of this Directive, amendments to the regulations governing use shall take effect only from the date of entry of the mention of those amendments in the register.

Article 34 Persons entitled to bring an action for infringement

1. Article 25(3) and (4) shall apply to every person who has the authority to use a collective mark.

2. The proprietor of a collective mark shall be entitled to claim compensation on behalf of persons who have authority to use the mark where those persons have sustained damage as a result of unauthorised use of the mark.

Article 35 Additional grounds for revocation

In addition to the grounds for revocation provided for in Articles 19 and 20, the rights of the proprietor of a collective mark shall be revoked on the following grounds:

(a)   the proprietor does not take reasonable steps to prevent the mark being used in a manner that is incompatible with the conditions of use laid down in the regulations governing use, including any amendments thereto mentioned in the register;

(b)   the manner in which the mark has been used by authorised persons has caused it to become liable to mislead the public in the manner referred to in Article 31(2);

(c)   an amendment to the regulations governing use of the mark has been mentioned in the register in breach of Article 33(2), unless the proprietor of the mark, by further amending the regulations governing use, complies with the requirements of that Article.

Article 36 Additional grounds for invalidity

In addition to the grounds for invalidity provided for in Article 4, where appropriate with the exception of Article 4(1)(c) concerning signs or indications which may serve, in trade, to designate the geographical origin of the goods or services, and Article 5, a collective mark which is registered in breach of Article 31 shall be declared invalid unless the proprietor of the mark, by amending the regulations governing use, complies with the requirements of Article 31.

. . .

SECTION 3
DURATION AND RENEWAL OF REGISTRATION

Article 48 Duration of registration

1.   Trade marks shall be registered for a period of 10 years from the date of filing of the application.

2.   Registration may be renewed in accordance with Article 49 for further 10-year periods.

Article 49 Renewal

1.   Registration of a trade mark shall be renewed at the request of the proprietor of the trade mark or any person authorised to do so by law or by contract, provided that the renewal fees have been paid. Member States may provide that receipt of payment of the renewal fees is to be deemed to constitute such a request.

2.   The office shall inform the proprietor of the trade mark of the expiry of the registration at least six months before the said expiry. The office shall not be held liable if it fails to give such information.

3.   The request for renewal shall be submitted and the renewal fees shall be paid within a period of at least six months immediately preceding the expiry of the registration. Failing that, the request may be submitted within a further period of six months immediately following the expiry of the registration or of the subsequent renewal thereof. The renewal fees and an additional fee shall be paid within that further period.

4.   Where the request is submitted or the fees paid in respect of only some of the goods or services for which the trade mark is registered, registration shall be renewed for those goods or services only.

5.   Renewal shall take effect from the day following the date on which the existing registration expires. The renewal shall be recorded in the register.

. . .

CHAPTER 5

Article 55 Repeal

Directive 2008/95/EC is repealed with effect from 15 January 2019, without prejudice to the obligations of the Member States relating to the time limit for the transposition into national law of Directive 89/104/EEC set out in Part B of Annex I to Directive 2008/95/EC.

References to the repealed Directive shall be construed as references to this Directive and shall be read in accordance with the correlation table in the Annex.

Article 56 Entry into Force

This Directive shall enter into force on the twentieth day following that of its publication in the *Official Journal of the European Union*.

Articles 1, 7, 15, 19, 20, 21 and 54 to 57 shall apply from 15 January 2019.

DIRECTIVE (EU) 2016/943
(trade secrets)

CHAPTER I
SUBJECT MATTER AND SCOPE

Article 1 Subject matter and scope

1.   This Directive lays down rules on the protection against the unlawful acquisition, use and disclosure of trade secrets.

   Member States may, in compliance with the provisions of the TFEU, provide for more far-reaching protection against the unlawful acquisition, use or disclosure of trade secrets than that required by this Directive, provided that compliance with Articles 3, 5, 6, Article 7(1), Article 8, the second subparagraph of Article 9(1), Article 9(3) and (4), Article 10(2), Articles 11, 13 and Article 15(3) is ensured.

2.   This Directive shall not affect:
   (a)   the exercise of the right to freedom of expression and information as set out in the Charter, including respect for the freedom and pluralism of the media;
   (b)   the application of Union or national rules requiring trade secret holders to disclose, for reasons of public interest, information, including trade secrets, to the public or to administrative or judicial authorities for the performance of the duties of those authorities;
   (c)   the application of Union or national rules requiring or allowing Union institutions and bodies or national public authorities to disclose information submitted by businesses which those institutions, bodies or authorities hold pursuant to, and in compliance with, the obligations and prerogatives set out in Union or national law;
   (d)   the autonomy of social partners and their right to enter into collective agreements, in accordance with Union law and national laws and practices.

3.   Nothing in this Directive shall be understood to offer any ground for restricting the mobility of employees. In particular, in relation to the exercise of such mobility, this Directive shall not offer any ground for:
   (a)   limiting employees' use of information that does not constitute a trade secret as defined in point (1) of Article 2;
   (b)   limiting employees' use of experience and skills honestly acquired in the normal course of their employment;
   (c)   imposing any additional restrictions on employees in their employment contracts other than restrictions imposed in accordance with Union or national law.

Article 2 Definitions

For the purposes of this Directive, the following definitions apply:

(1)   "trade secret" means information which meets all of the following requirements:
   (a)   it is secret in the sense that it is not, as a body or in the precise configuration and assembly of its components, generally known among or readily accessible to persons within the circles that normally deal with the kind of information in question;
   (b)   it has commercial value because it is secret;
   (c)   it has been subject to reasonable steps under the circumstances, by the person lawfully in control of the information, to keep it secret;

(2)   "trade secret holder" means any natural or legal person lawfully controlling a trade secret;

(3)   "infringer" means any natural or legal person who has unlawfully acquired, used or disclosed a trade secret;

(4)   "infringing goods" means goods, the design, characteristics, functioning, production process or marketing of which significantly benefits from trade secrets unlawfully acquired, used or disclosed.

CHAPTER II
ACQUISITION, USE AND DISCLOSURE OF TRADE SECRETS

Article 3 Lawful acquisition, use and disclosure of trade secrets

1. The acquisition of a trade secret shall be considered lawful when the trade secret is obtained by any of the following means:
   (a) independent discovery or creation;
   (b) observation, study, disassembly or testing of a product or object that has been made available to the public or that is lawfully in the possession of the acquirer of the information who is free from any legally valid duty to limit the acquisition of the trade secret;
   (c) exercise of the right of workers or workers' representatives to information and consultation in accordance with Union law and national laws and practices;
   (d) any other practice which, under the circumstances, is in conformity with honest commercial practices.
2. The acquisition, use or disclosure of a trade secret shall be considered lawful to the extent that such acquisition, use or disclosure is required or allowed by Union or national law.

Article 4 Unlawful acquisition, use and disclosure of trade secrets

1. Member States shall ensure that trade secret holders are entitled to apply for the measures, procedures and remedies provided for in this Directive in order to prevent, or obtain redress for, the unlawful acquisition, use or disclosure of their trade secret.
2. The acquisition of a trade secret without the consent of the trade secret holder shall be considered unlawful, whenever carried out by:
   (a) unauthorised access to, appropriation of, or copying of any documents, objects, materials, substances or electronic files, lawfully under the control of the trade secret holder, containing the trade secret or from which the trade secret can be deduced;
   (b) any other conduct which, under the circumstances, is considered contrary to honest commercial practices.
3. The use or disclosure of a trade secret shall be considered unlawful whenever carried out, without the consent of the trade secret holder, by a person who is found to meet any of the following conditions:
   (a) having acquired the trade secret unlawfully;
   (b) being in breach of a confidentiality agreement or any other duty not to disclose the trade secret;
   (c) being in breach of a contractual or any other duty to limit the use of the trade secret.
4. The acquisition, use or disclosure of a trade secret shall also be considered unlawful whenever a person, at the time of the acquisition, use or disclosure, knew or ought, under the circumstances, to have known that the trade secret had been obtained directly or indirectly from another person who was using or disclosing the trade secret unlawfully within the meaning of paragraph 3.
5. The production, offering or placing on the market of infringing goods, or the importation, export or storage of infringing goods for those purposes, shall also be considered an unlawful use of a trade secret where the person carrying out such activities knew, or ought, under the circumstances, to have known that the trade secret was used unlawfully within the meaning of paragraph 3.

Article 5 Exceptions

Member States shall ensure that an application for the measures, procedures and remedies provided for in this Directive is dismissed where the alleged acquisition, use or disclosure of the trade secret was carried out in any of the following cases:
(a) for exercising the right to freedom of expression and information as set out in the Charter, including respect for the freedom and pluralism of the media;
(b) for revealing misconduct, wrongdoing or illegal activity, provided that the respondent acted for the purpose of protecting the general public interest;
(c) disclosure by workers to their representatives as part of the legitimate exercise by those representatives of their functions in accordance with Union or national law, provided that such disclosure was necessary for that exercise;
(d) for the purpose of protecting a legitimate interest recognised by Union or national law.

CHAPTER III
MEASURES, PROCEDURES AND REMEDIES
SECTION 1
GENERAL PROVISIONS

Article 6 General obligation

1. Member States shall provide for the measures, procedures and remedies necessary to ensure the availability of civil redress against the unlawful acquisition, use and disclosure of trade secrets.
2. The measures, procedures and remedies referred to in paragraph 1 shall:
   (a) be fair and equitable;
   (b) not be unnecessarily complicated or costly, or entail unreasonable time-limits or unwarranted delays; and
   (c) be effective and dissuasive.

Article 7 Proportionality and abuse of process

1. The measures, procedures and remedies provided for in this Directive shall be applied in a manner that:
   (a) is proportionate;
   (b) avoids the creation of barriers to legitimate trade in the internal market; and
   (c) provides for safeguards against their abuse.
2. Member States shall ensure that competent judicial authorities may, upon the request of the respondent, apply appropriate measures as provided for in national law, where an application concerning the unlawful acquisition, use or disclosure of a trade secret is manifestly unfounded and the applicant is found to have initiated the legal proceedings abusively or in bad faith. Such measures may, as appropriate, include awarding damages to the respondent, imposing sanctions on the applicant or ordering the dissemination of information concerning a decision as referred to in Article 15.
   Member States may provide that measures as referred to in the first subparagraph are dealt with in separate legal proceedings.

Article 8 Limitation period

1. Member States shall, in accordance with this Article, lay down rules on the limitation periods applicable to substantive claims and actions for the application of the measures, procedures and remedies provided for in this Directive.
   The rules referred to in the first subparagraph shall determine when the limitation period begins to run, the duration of the limitation period and the circumstances under which the limitation period is interrupted or suspended.
2. The duration of the limitation period shall not exceed 6 years.

Article 9 Preservation of confidentiality of trade secrets in the course of legal proceedings

1. Member States shall ensure that the parties, their lawyers or other representatives, court officials, witnesses, experts and any other person participating in legal proceedings relating to the unlawful acquisition, use or disclosure of a trade secret, or who has access to documents which form part of those legal proceedings, are not permitted to use or disclose any trade secret or alleged trade secret which the competent judicial authorities have, in response to a duly reasoned application by an interested party, identified as confidential and of which they have become aware as a result of such participation or access. In that regard, Member States may also allow competent judicial authorities to act on their own initiative.
   The obligation referred to in the first subparagraph shall remain in force after the legal proceedings have ended. However, such obligation shall cease to exist in any of the following circumstances:
   (a) where the alleged trade secret is found, by a final decision, not to meet the requirements set out in point (1) of Article 2; or
   (b) where over time, the information in question becomes generally known among or readily accessible to persons within the circles that normally deal with that kind of information.

2. Member States shall also ensure that the competent judicial authorities may, on a duly reasoned application by a party, take specific measures necessary to preserve the confidentiality of any trade secret or alleged trade secret used or referred to in the course of legal proceedings relating to the unlawful acquisition, use or disclosure of a trade secret. Member States may also allow competent judicial authorities to take such measures on their own initiative.

The measures referred to in the first subparagraph shall at least include the possibility:

(a) of restricting access to any document containing trade secrets or alleged trade secrets submitted by the parties or third parties, in whole or in part, to a limited number of persons;

(b) of restricting access to hearings, when trade secrets or alleged trade secrets may be disclosed, and the corresponding record or transcript of those hearings to a limited number of persons;

(c) of making available to any person other than those comprised in the limited number of persons referred to in points (a) and (b) a non-confidential version of any judicial decision, in which the passages containing trade secrets have been removed or redacted.

The number of persons referred to in points (a) and (b) of the second subparagraph shall be no greater than necessary in order to ensure compliance with the right of the parties to the legal proceedings to an effective remedy and to a fair trial, and shall include, at least, one natural person from each party and the respective lawyers or other representatives of those parties to the legal proceedings.

3. When deciding on the measures referred to in paragraph 2 and assessing their proportionality, the competent judicial authorities shall take into account the need to ensure the right to an effective remedy and to a fair trial, the legitimate interests of the parties and, where appropriate, of third parties, and any potential harm for either of the parties, and, where appropriate, for third parties, resulting from the granting or rejection of such measures.

. . .

SECTION 2
PROVISIONAL AND PRECAUTIONARY MEASURES

Article 10 Provisional and precautionary measures

1. Member States shall ensure that the competent judicial authorities may, at the request of the trade secret holder, order any of the following provisional and precautionary measures against the alleged infringer:

(a) the cessation of or, as the case may be, the prohibition of the use or disclosure of the trade secret on a provisional basis;

(b) the prohibition of the production, offering, placing on the market or use of infringing goods, or the importation, export or storage of infringing goods for those purposes;

(c) the seizure or delivery up of the suspected infringing goods, including imported goods, so as to prevent their entry into, or circulation on, the market.

2. Member States shall ensure that the judicial authorities may, as an alternative to the measures referred to in paragraph 1, make the continuation of the alleged unlawful use of a trade secret subject to the lodging of guarantees intended to ensure the compensation of the trade secret holder. Disclosure of a trade secret in return for the lodging of guarantees shall not be allowed.

Article 11 Conditions of application and safeguards

1. Member States shall ensure that the competent judicial authorities have, in respect of the measures referred to in Article 10, the authority to require the applicant to provide evidence that may reasonably be considered available in order to satisfy themselves with a sufficient degree of certainty that:

(a) a trade secret exists;

(b) the applicant is the trade secret holder; and

(c) the trade secret has been acquired unlawfully, is being unlawfully used or disclosed, or unlawful acquisition, use or disclosure of the trade secret is imminent.

2.   Member States shall ensure that in deciding on the granting or rejection of the application and assessing its proportionality, the competent judicial authorities shall be required to take into account the specific circumstances of the case, including, where appropriate:

        (a)   the value and other specific features of the trade secret;

        (b)   the measures taken to protect the trade secret;

        (c)   the conduct of the respondent in acquiring, using or disclosing the trade secret;

        (d)   the impact of the unlawful use or disclosure of the trade secret;

        (e)   the legitimate interests of the parties and the impact which the granting or rejection of the measures could have on the parties;

        (f)   the legitimate interests of third parties;

        (g)   the public interest; and

        (h)   the safeguard of fundamental rights.

3.   Member States shall ensure that the measures referred to in Article 10 are revoked or otherwise cease to have effect, upon the request of the respondent, if:

        (a)   the applicant does not institute legal proceedings leading to a decision on the merits of the case before the competent judicial authority, within a reasonable period determined by the judicial authority ordering the measures where the law of a Member State so permits or, in the absence of such determination, within a period not exceeding 20 working days or 31 calendar days, whichever is the longer; or

        (b)   the information in question no longer meets the requirements of point (1) of Article 2, for reasons that cannot be attributed to the respondent.

4.   Member States shall ensure that the competent judicial authorities may make the measures referred to in Article 10 subject to the lodging by the applicant of adequate security or an equivalent assurance intended to ensure compensation for any prejudice suffered by the respondent and, where appropriate, by any other person affected by the measures.

5.   Where the measures referred to in Article 10 are revoked on the basis of point (a) of paragraph 3 of this Article, where they lapse due to any act or omission by the applicant, or where it is subsequently found that there has been no unlawful acquisition, use or disclosure of the trade secret or threat of such conduct, the competent judicial authorities shall have the authority to order the applicant, upon the request of the respondent or of an injured third party, to provide the respondent, or the injured third party, appropriate compensation for any injury caused by those measures.

       Member States may provide that the request for compensation referred to in the first subparagraph is dealt with in separate legal proceedings.

SECTION 3

MEASURES RESULTING FROM A DECISION ON THE MERITS OF THE CASE

Article 12 Injunctions and corrective measures

1.   Member States shall ensure that, where a judicial decision taken on the merits of the case finds that there has been unlawful acquisition, use or disclosure of a trade secret, the competent judicial authorities may, at the request of the applicant, order one or more of the following measures against the infringer:

        (a)   the cessation of or, as the case may be, the prohibition of the use or disclosure of the trade secret;

        (b)   the prohibition of the production, offering, placing on the market or use of infringing goods, or the importation, export or storage of infringing goods for those purposes;

        (c)   the adoption of the appropriate corrective measures with regard to the infringing goods;

        (d)   the destruction of all or part of any document, object, material, substance or electronic file containing or embodying the trade secret or, where appropriate, the delivery up to the applicant of all or part of those documents, objects, materials, substances or electronic files.

2.   The corrective measures referred to in point (c) of paragraph 1 shall include:

        (a)   recall of the infringing goods from the market;

        (b)   depriving the infringing goods of their infringing quality;

        (c)   destruction of the infringing goods or, where appropriate, their withdrawal from the market, provided that the withdrawal does not undermine the protection of the trade secret in question.

3.   Member States may provide that, when ordering the withdrawal of the infringing goods from the market, their competent judicial authorities may order, at the request of the trade secret holder, that the goods be delivered up to the holder or to charitable organisations.

4.   The competent judicial authorities shall order that the measures referred to in points (c) and (d) of paragraph 1 be carried out at the expense of the infringer, unless there are particular reasons for not doing so. Those measures shall be without prejudice to any damages that may be due to the trade secret holder by reason of the unlawful acquisition, use or disclosure of the trade secret.

Article 13 Conditions of application, safeguards and alternative measures

1.   Member States shall ensure that, in considering an application for the adoption of the injunctions and corrective measures provided for in Article 12 and assessing their proportionality, the competent judicial authorities shall be required to take into account the specific circumstances of the case, including, where appropriate:
    (a)   the value or other specific features of the trade secret;
    (b)   the measures taken to protect the trade secret;
    (c)   the conduct of the infringer in acquiring, using or disclosing the trade secret;
    (d)   the impact of the unlawful use or disclosure of the trade secret;
    (e)   the legitimate interests of the parties and the impact which the granting or rejection of the measures could have on the parties;
    (f)   the legitimate interests of third parties;
    (g)   the public interest; and
    (h)   the safeguard of fundamental rights.
    Where the competent judicial authorities limit the duration of the measures referred to in points (a) and (b) of Article 12(1), such duration shall be sufficient to eliminate any commercial or economic advantage that the infringer could have derived from the unlawful acquisition, use or disclosure of the trade secret.

2.   Member States shall ensure that the measures referred to in points (a) and (b) of Article 12(1) are revoked or otherwise cease to have effect, upon the request of the respondent, if the information in question no longer meets the requirements of point (1) of Article 2 for reasons that cannot be attributed directly or indirectly to the respondent.

3.   Member States shall provide that, at the request of the person liable to be subject to the measures provided for in Article 12, the competent judicial authority may order pecuniary compensation to be paid to the injured party instead of applying those measures if all the following conditions are met:
    (a)   the person concerned at the time of use or disclosure neither knew nor ought, under the circumstances, to have known that the trade secret was obtained from another person who was using or disclosing the trade secret unlawfully;
    (b)   execution of the measures in question would cause that person disproportionate harm; and
    (c)   pecuniary compensation to the injured party appears reasonably satisfactory.
    Where pecuniary compensation is ordered instead of the measures referred to in points (a) and (b) of Article 12(1), it shall not exceed the amount of royalties or fees which would have been due, had that person requested authorisation to use the trade secret in question, for the period of time for which use of the trade secret could have been prohibited.

Article 14 Damages

1.   Member States shall ensure that the competent judicial authorities, upon the request of the injured party, order an infringer who knew or ought to have known that he, she or it was engaging in unlawful acquisition, use or disclosure of a trade secret, to pay the trade secret holder damages appropriate to the actual prejudice suffered as a result of the unlawful acquisition, use or disclosure of the trade secret.
    Member States may limit the liability for damages of employees towards their employers for the unlawful acquisition, use or disclosure of a trade secret of the employer where they act without intent.

2.   When setting the damages referred to in paragraph 1, the competent judicial authorities shall take into account all appropriate factors, such as the negative economic consequences, including lost profits, which the injured party has suffered, any unfair profits made by the infringer and, in appropriate cases, elements other than economic factors, such as

the moral prejudice caused to the trade secret holder by the unlawful acquisition, use or disclosure of the trade secret.

Alternatively, the competent judicial authorities may, in appropriate cases, set the damages as a lump sum on the basis of elements such as, at a minimum, the amount of royalties or fees which would have been due had the infringer requested authorisation to use the trade secret in question.

. . .

Article 19 Transposition

1.   Member States shall bring into force the laws, regulations and administrative provisions necessary to comply with this Directive by 9 June 2018. They shall immediately communicate the text of those measures to the Commission.

. . .

REGULATION (EU) No 608/2013
concerning customs enforcement of intellectual property rights

CHAPTER I
SUBJECT MATTER, SCOPE AND DEFINITIONS

Article 1 Subject matter and scope

1.   This Regulation sets out the conditions and procedures for action by the customs authorities where goods suspected of infringing an intellectual property right are, or should have been, subject to customs supervision or customs control within the customs territory of the Union in accordance with Council Regulation (EEC) No 2913/92 of 12 October 1992 establishing the Community Customs Code, particularly goods in the following situations:
    (a)   when declared for release for free circulation, export or re-export;
    (b)   when entering or leaving the customs territory of the Union;
    (c)   when placed under a suspensive procedure or in a free zone or free warehouse.
2.   In respect of the goods subject to customs supervision or customs control, and without prejudice to Articles 17 and 18, the customs authorities shall carry out adequate customs controls and shall take proportionate identification measures as provided for in Article 13(1) and Article 72 of Regulation (EEC) No 2913/92 in accordance with risk analysis criteria with a view to preventing acts in breach of intellectual property laws applicable in the territory of the Union and in order to cooperate with third countries on the enforcement of intellectual property rights.
3.   This Regulation shall not apply to goods that have been released for free circulation under the end-use regime.
4.   This Regulation shall not apply to goods of a non-commercial nature contained in travellers' personal luggage.
5.   This Regulation shall not apply to goods that have been manufactured with the consent of the right-holder or to goods manufactured, by a person duly authorised by a right-holder to manufacture a certain quantity of goods, in excess of the quantities agreed between that person and the right-holder.
6.   This Regulation shall not affect national or Union law on intellectual property or the laws of the Member States in relation to criminal procedures.

Article 2 Definitions

For the purposes of this Regulation:
    (1)   "intellectual property right" means:
        (a)   a trade mark;
        (b)   a design;
        (c)   a copyright or any related right as provided for by national or Union law;
        (d)   a geographical indication;
        (e)   a patent as provided for by national or Union law;

(f)　a supplementary protection certificate for medicinal products as provided for in Regulation (EC) No 469/2009 of the European Parliament and of the Council of 6 May 2009 concerning the supplementary protection certificate for medicinal products;

(g)　a supplementary protection certificate for plant protection products as provided for in Regulation (EC) No 1610/96 of the European Parliament and of the Council of 23 July 1996 concerning the creation of a supplementary protection certificate for plant protection products;

(h)　a Community plant variety right as provided for in Council Regulation (EC) No 2100/94 of 27 July 1994 on Community plant variety rights;

(i)　a plant variety right as provided for by national law;

(j)　a topography of semiconductor product as provided for by national or Union law;

(k)　a utility model in so far as it is protected as an intellectual property right by national or Union law;

(l)　a trade name in so far as it is protected as an exclusive intellectual property right by national or Union law;

(2)　"trade mark" means:

(a)　a Community trade mark as provided for in Council Regulation (EC) No 207/2009 of 26 February 2009 on the Community trade mark;

(b)　a trade mark registered in a Member State, or, in the case of Belgium, Luxembourg or the Netherlands, at the Benelux Office for Intellectual Property;

(c)　a trade mark registered under international arrangements which has effect in a Member State or in the Union;

(3)　"design" means:

(a)　a Community design as provided for in Council Regulation (EC) No 6/2002 of 12 December 2001 on Community designs;

(b)　a design registered in a Member State, or, in the case of Belgium, Luxembourg or the Netherlands, at the Benelux Office for Intellectual Property;

(c)　a design registered under international arrangements which has effect in a Member State or in the Union;

(4)　"geographical indication" means:

(a)　a geographical indication or designation of origin protected for agricultural products and foodstuff as provided for in Regulation (EU) No 1151/2012 of the European Parliament and of the Council of 21 November 2012 on quality schemes for agricultural products and foodstuffs;

(b)　a designation of origin or geographical indication for wine as provided for in Council Regulation (EC) No 1234/2007 of 22 October 2007 establishing a common organisation of agricultural markets and on specific provisions for certain agricultural products (Single CMO Regulation);

(c)　a geographical designation for aromatised drinks based on wine products as provided for in Council Regulation (EEC) No 1601/91 of 10 June 1991 laying down general rules on the definition, description and presentation of aromatized wines, aromatized wine-based drinks and aromatized wine-product cocktails;

(d)　a geographical indication of spirit drinks as provided for in Regulation (EC) No 110/2008 of the European Parliament and of the Council of 15 January 2008 on the definition, description, presentation, labelling and the protection of geographical indications of spirit drinks;

(e)　a geographical indication for products not falling under points (a) to (d) in so far as it is established as an exclusive intellectual property right by national or Union law;

(f)　a geographical indication as provided for in Agreements between the Union and third countries and as such listed in those Agreements;

(5)　"counterfeit goods" means:

(a)　goods which are the subject of an act infringing a trade mark in the Member State where they are found and bear without authorisation a sign which is identical to the trade mark validly registered in respect of the same type of goods, or which cannot be distinguished in its essential aspects from such a trade mark;

    (b)   goods which are the subject of an act infringing a geographical indication in the Member State where they are found and, bear or are described by, a name or term protected in respect of that geographical indication;

    (c)   any packaging, label, sticker, brochure, operating instructions, warranty document or other similar item, even if presented separately, which is the subject of an act infringing a trade mark or a geographical indication, which includes a sign, name or term which is identical to a validly registered trade mark or protected geographical indication, or which cannot be distinguished in its essential aspects from such a trade mark or geographical indication, and which can be used for the same type of goods as that for which the trade mark or geographical indication has been registered;

(6) "pirated goods" means goods which are the subject of an act infringing a copyright or related right or a design in the Member State where the goods are found and which are, or contain copies, made without the consent of the holder of a copyright or related right or a design, or of a person authorised by that holder in the country of production;

(7) "goods suspected of infringing an intellectual property right" means goods with regard to which there are reasonable indications that, in the Member State where those goods are found, they are prima facie:

    (a)   goods which are the subject of an act infringing an intellectual property right in that Member State;

    (b)   devices, products or components which are primarily designed, produced or adapted for the purpose of enabling or facilitating the circumvention of any technology, device or component that, in the normal course of its operation, prevents or restricts acts in respect of works which are not authorised by the holder of any copyright or any right related to copyright and which relate to an act infringing those rights in that Member State;

    (c)   any mould or matrix which is specifically designed or adapted for the manufacture of goods infringing an intellectual property right, if such moulds or matrices relate to an act infringing an intellectual property right in that Member State;

(8) "right-holder" means the holder of an intellectual property right;

(9) "application" means a request made to the competent customs department for customs authorities to take action with respect to goods suspected of infringing an intellectual property right;

(10) "national application" means an application requesting the customs authorities of a Member State to take action in that Member State;

(11) "Union application" means an application submitted in one Member State and requesting the customs authorities of that Member State and of one or more other Member States to take action in their respective Member States;

(12) "applicant" means the person or entity in whose name an application is submitted;

(13) "holder of the decision" means the holder of a decision granting an application;

(14) "holder of the goods" means the person who is the owner of the goods suspected of infringing an intellectual property right or who has a similar right of disposal, or physical control, over such goods;

(15) "declarant" means the declarant as defined in point (18) of Article 4 of Regulation (EEC) No 2913/92;

(16) "destruction" means the physical destruction, recycling or disposal of goods outside commercial channels, in such a way as to preclude damage to the holder of the decision;

(17) "customs territory of the Union" means the customs territory of the Community as defined in Article 3 of Regulation (EEC) No 2913/92;

(18) "release of the goods" means the release of the goods as defined in point (20) of Article 4 of Regulation (EEC) No 2913/92;

(19) "small consignment" means a postal or express courier consignment, which:

    (a)   contains three units or less;

        or

    (b)   has a gross weight of less than two kilograms.

For the purpose of point (a), 'units' means goods as classified under the Combined Nomenclature in accordance with Annex I to Council Regulation (EEC) No 2658/87 of 23 July 1987 on the tariff and statistical nomenclature and on the Common Customs

Tariff if unpackaged, or the package of such goods intended for retail sale to the ultimate consumer.

For the purpose of this definition, separate goods falling in the same Combined Nomenclature code shall be considered as different units and goods presented as sets classified in one Combined Nomenclature code shall be considered as one unit;

(20) "perishable goods" means goods considered by customs authorities to deteriorate by being kept for up to 20 days from the date of their suspension of release or detention;

(21) 'exclusive licence" means a licence (whether general or limited) authorising the licensee to the exclusion of all other persons, including the person granting the licence, to use an intellectual property right in the manner authorised by the licence.

CHAPTER II
APPLICATIONS

SECTION 1
SUBMISSION OF APPLICATIONS

Article 3 Entitlement to submit an application

The following persons and entities shall, to the extent they are entitled to initiate proceedings, in order to determine whether an intellectual property right has been infringed, in the Member State or Member States where the customs authorities are requested to take action, be entitled to submit:

(1) a national or a Union application:
  (a) right-holders;
  (b) intellectual property collective rights management bodies as referred to in point (c) of Article 4(1) of Directive 2004/48/EC of the European Parliament and of the Council of 29 April 2004 on the enforcement of intellectual property rights;
  (c) professional defence bodies as referred to in point (d) of Article 4(1) of Directive 2004/48/EC;
  (d) groups within the meaning of point (2) of Article 3, and Article 49(1) of Regulation (EU) No 1151/2012, groups of producers within the meaning of Article 118e of Regulation (EC) No 1234/2007 or similar groups of producers provided for in Union law governing geographical indications representing producers of products with a geographical indication or representatives of such groups, in particular Regulations (EEC) No 1601/91 and (EC) No 110/2008 and operators entitled to use a geographical indication as well as inspection bodies or authorities competent for such a geographical indication;

(2) a national application:
  (a) persons or entities authorised to use intellectual property rights, which have been authorised formally by the right-holder to initiate proceedings in order to determine whether the intellectual property right has been infringed;
  (b) groups of producers provided for in the legislation of the Member States governing geographical indications representing producers of products with geographical indications or representatives of such groups and operators entitled to use a geographical indication, as well as inspection bodies or authorities competent for such a geographical indication;

(3) a Union application: holders of exclusive licenses covering the entire territory of two or more Member States, where those licence holders have been authorised formally in those Member States by the right-holder to initiate proceedings in order to determine whether the intellectual property right has been infringed.

Article 4 Intellectual property rights covered by Union applications

A Union application may be submitted only with respect to intellectual property rights based on Union law producing effects throughout the Union.

Article 5 Submission of applications

1.   Each Member State shall designate the customs department competent to receive and process applications ('competent customs department'). The Member State shall inform the Commission accordingly and the Commission shall make public a list of competent customs departments designated by the Member States.

2.   Applications shall be submitted to the competent customs department. The applications shall be completed using the form referred to in Article 6 and shall contain the information required therein.

3.   Where an application is submitted after notification by the customs authorities of the suspension of the release or detention of the goods in accordance with Article 18(3), that application shall comply with the following:

    (a) it is submitted to the competent customs department within four working days of the notification of the suspension of the release or detention of the goods;

    (b) it is a national application;

    (c) it contains the information referred to in Article 6(3). The applicant may, however, omit the information referred to in point (g), (h) or (i) of that paragraph.

4.   Except in the circumstances referred to in point (3) of Article 3, only one national application and one Union application may be submitted per Member State for the same intellectual property right protected in that Member State. In the circumstances referred to in point (3) of Article 3, more than one Union application shall be allowed.

5.   Where a Union application is granted for a Member State already covered by another Union application granted to the same applicant and for the same intellectual property right, the customs authorities of that Member State shall take action on the basis of the Union application first granted. They shall inform the competent customs department of the Member State where any subsequent Union application was granted, which shall, amend or revoke the decision granting that subsequent Union application.

6.   Where computerised systems are available for the purpose of receiving and processing applications, applications as well as attachments shall be submitted using electronic data-processing techniques. Member States and the Commission shall develop, maintain and employ such systems in accordance with the multi-annual strategic plan referred to in Article 8(2) of Decision No 70/2008/EC of the European Parliament and of the Council of 15 January 2008 on a paperless customs environment for customs and trade.

. . .

Article 11 Period during which the customs authorities are to take action

1.   When granting an application, the competent customs department shall specify the period during which the customs authorities are to take action.

    That period shall begin on the day the decision granting the application takes effect, pursuant to Article 10, and shall not exceed one year from the day following the date of adoption.

Article 12 Extension of the period during which the customs authorities are to take action

1.   On expiry of the period during which the customs authorities are to take action, and subject to the prior discharge by the holder of the decision of any debt owed to the customs authorities under this Regulation, the competent customs department which adopted the initial decision may, at the request of the holder of the decision, extend that period.

. . .

CHAPTER III

ACTION BY THE CUSTOMS AUTHORITIES

SECTION 1

SUSPENSION OF THE RELEASE OR DETENTION OF GOODS SUSPECTED OF INFRINGING AN INTELLECTUAL PROPERTY RIGHT

Article 17 Suspension of the release or detention of the goods following the grant of an application

1.   Where the customs authorities identify goods suspected of infringing an intellectual property right covered by a decision granting an application, they shall suspend the release of the goods or detain them.

2.   Before suspending the release of or detaining the goods, the customs authorities may ask the holder of the decision to provide them with any relevant information with respect

to the goods. The customs authorities may also provide the holder of the decision with information about the actual or estimated quantity of goods, their actual or presumed nature and images thereof, as appropriate.

. . .

Article 18 Suspension of the release or detention of the goods before the grant of an application

1. Where the customs authorities identify goods suspected of infringing an intellectual property right, which are not covered by a decision granting an application, they may, except for in the case of perishable goods, suspend the release of those goods or detain them.
2. Before suspending the release of or detaining the goods suspected of infringing an intellectual property right, the customs authorities may, without disclosing any information other than the actual or estimated quantity of goods, their actual or presumed nature and images thereof, as appropriate, request any person or entity potentially entitled to submit an application concerning the alleged infringement of the intellectual property rights to provide them with any relevant information.

. . .

Article 19 Inspection and sampling of goods whose release has been suspended or which have been detained

1. The customs authorities shall give the holder of the decision and the declarant or the holder of the goods the opportunity to inspect the goods whose release has been suspended or which have been detained.

. . .

Article 21 Permitted use of certain information by the holder of the decision

Where the holder of the decision has received the information referred to in Article 17(4), Article 18(5), Article 19 or Article 26(8), he may disclose or use that information only for the following purposes:

(a) to initiate proceedings to determine whether an intellectual property right has been infringed and in the course of such proceedings;
(b) in connection with criminal investigations related to the infringement of an intellectual property right and undertaken by public authorities in the Member State where the goods are found;
(c) to initiate criminal proceedings and in the course of such proceedings;
(d) to seek compensation from the infringer or other persons;
(e) to agree with the declarant or the holder of the goods that the goods be destroyed in accordance with Article 23(1);
(f) to agree with the declarant or the holder of the goods of the amount of the guarantee referred to in point (a) of Article 24(2).

Article 22 Sharing of information and data between customs authorities

1. Without prejudice to applicable provisions on data protection in the Union and for the purpose of contributing to eliminating international trade in goods infringing intellectual property rights, the Commission and the customs authorities of the Member States may share certain data and information available to them with the relevant authorities in third countries according to the practical arrangements referred to in paragraph 3.

. . .

SECTION 2
DESTRUCTION OF GOODS, INITIATION OF PROCEEDINGS AND EARLY
RELEASE OF GOODS

Article 23 Destruction of goods and initiation of proceedings

1. Goods suspected of infringing an intellectual property right may be destroyed under customs control, without there being any need to determine whether an intellectual property right has been infringed under the law of the Member State where the goods are found, where all of the following conditions are fulfilled:
   (a) the holder of the decision has confirmed in writing to the customs authorities, within 10 working days, or three working days in the case of perishable goods, of notification

of the suspension of the release or the detention of the goods, that, in his conviction, an intellectual property right has been infringed;

(b) the holder of the decision has confirmed in writing to the customs authorities, within 10 working days, or three working days in the case of perishable goods, of notification of the suspension of the release or the detention of the goods, his agreement to the destruction of the goods;

(c) the declarant or the holder of the goods has confirmed in writing to the customs authorities, within 10 working days, or three working days in the case of perishable goods, of notification of the suspension of the release or the detention of the goods, his agreement to the destruction of the goods. Where the declarant or the holder of the goods has not confirmed his agreement to the destruction of the goods nor notified his opposition thereto to the customs authorities, within those deadlines, the customs authorities may deem the declarant or the holder of the goods to have confirmed his agreement to the destruction of those goods.

The customs authorities shall grant the release of the goods or put an end to their detention, immediately after completion of all customs formalities, where within the periods referred to in points (a) and (b) of the first subparagraph, they have not received both the written confirmation from the holder of the decision that, in his conviction, an intellectual property right has been infringed and his agreement to destruction, unless those authorities have been duly informed about the initiation of proceedings to determine whether an intellectual property right has been infringed.

. . .

Article 25 Goods for destruction

1. Goods to be destroyed under Article 23 or 26 shall not be:

(a) released for free circulation, unless customs authorities, with the agreement of the holder of the decision, decide that it is necessary in the event that the goods are to be recycled or disposed of outside commercial channels, including for awareness-raising, training and educational purposes. The conditions under which the goods can be released for free circulation shall be determined by the customs authorities;

(b) brought out of the customs territory of the Union;

(c) exported;

(d) re-exported;

(e) placed under a suspensive procedure;

(f) placed in a free zone or free warehouse.

. . .

REGULATION (EU) 2017/1001
(European Union trade mark)

CHAPTER I
GENERAL PROVISIONS

Article 1 EU trade mark

1. A trade mark for goods or services which is registered in accordance with the conditions contained in this Regulation and in the manner herein provided is hereinafter referred to as a "European Union trade mark ("EU trade mark")".

2. An EU trade mark shall have a unitary character. It shall have equal effect throughout the Union: it shall not be registered, transferred or surrendered or be the subject of a decision revoking the rights of the proprietor or declaring it invalid, nor shall its use be prohibited, save in respect of the whole Union. This principle shall apply unless otherwise provided for in this Regulation.

Article 2 Office

1. A European Union Intellectual Property Office ("the Office") is established.

2. All references in Union law to the Office for Harmonization in the Internal Market (Trade Marks and Designs) shall be read as references to the Office.

Article 3 Capacity to act

For the purpose of implementing this Regulation, companies or firms and other legal bodies shall be regarded as legal persons if, under the terms of the law governing them, they have the capacity in their own name to have rights and obligations of all kinds, to make contracts or accomplish other legal acts, and to sue and be sued.

CHAPTER II
THE LAW RELATING TO TRADE MARKS

SECTION 1
DEFINITION OF AN EU TRADE MARK AND OBTAINING AN EU TRADE MARK

Article 4 Signs of which an EU trade mark may consist

An EU trade mark may consist of any signs, in particular words, including personal names, or designs, letters, numerals, colours, the shape of goods or of the packaging of goods, or sounds, provided that such signs are capable of:

(a) distinguishing the goods or services of one undertaking from those of other undertakings; and

(b) being represented on the Register of European Union trade marks ("the Register"), in a manner which enables the competent authorities and the public to determine the clear and precise subject matter of the protection afforded to its proprietor.

Article 5 Persons who can be proprietors of EU trade marks

Any natural or legal person, including authorities established under public law, may be the proprietor of an EU trade mark.

Article 6 Means whereby an EU trade mark is obtained

An EU trade mark shall be obtained by registration.

Article 7 Absolute grounds for refusal

1. The following shall not be registered:

   (a) signs which do not conform to the requirements of Article 4;

   (b) trade marks which are devoid of any distinctive character;

   (c) trade marks which consist exclusively of signs or indications which may serve, in trade, to designate the kind, quality, quantity, intended purpose, value, geographical origin or the time of production of the goods or of rendering of the service, or other characteristics of the goods or service;

   (d) trade marks which consist exclusively of signs or indications which have become customary in the current language or in the bona fide and established practices of the trade;

   (e) signs which consist exclusively of:

      (i) the shape, or another characteristic, which results from the nature of the goods themselves;

      (ii) the shape, or another characteristic, of goods which is necessary to obtain a technical result;

      (iii) the shape, or another characteristic, which gives substantial value to the goods;

   (f) trade marks which are contrary to public policy or to accepted principles of morality;

   (g) trade marks which are of such a nature as to deceive the public, for instance as to the nature, quality or geographical origin of the goods or service;

   (h) trade marks which have not been authorised by the competent authorities and are to be refused pursuant to Article 6ter of the Paris Convention for the Protection of Industrial Property ("Paris Convention");

   (i) trade marks which include badges, emblems or escutcheons other than those covered by Article 6ter of the Paris Convention and which are of particular public interest, unless the consent of the competent authority to their registration has been given;

   (j) trade marks which are excluded from registration, pursuant to Union legislation or national law or to international agreements to which the Union or the Member State concerned is party, providing for protection of designations of origin and geographical indications;

(k)   trade marks which are excluded from registration pursuant to Union legislation or international agreements to which the Union is party, providing for protection of traditional terms for wine;

(l)   trade marks which are excluded from registration pursuant to Union legislation or international agreements to which the Union is party, providing for protection of traditional specialities guaranteed;

(m)   trade marks which consist of, or reproduce in their essential elements, an earlier plant variety denomination registered in accordance with Union legislation or national law, or international agreements to which the Union or the Member State concerned is a party, providing for protection of plant variety rights, and which are in respect of plant varieties of the same or closely related species.

2.   Paragraph 1 shall apply notwithstanding that the grounds of non-registrability obtain in only part of the Union.

3.   Paragraph 1(b), (c) and (d) shall not apply if the trade mark has become distinctive in relation to the goods or services for which registration is requested as a consequence of the use which has been made of it.

Article 8 Relative grounds for refusal

1.   Upon opposition by the proprietor of an earlier trade mark, the trade mark applied for shall not be registered:

(a)   if it is identical with the earlier trade mark and the goods or services for which registration is applied for are identical with the goods or services for which the earlier trade mark is protected;

(b)   if, because of its identity with, or similarity to, the earlier trade mark and the identity or similarity of the goods or services covered by the trade marks there exists a likelihood of confusion on the part of the public in the territory in which the earlier trade mark is protected; the likelihood of confusion includes the likelihood of association with the earlier trade mark.

2.   For the purposes of paragraph 1, "earlier trade mark" means:

(a)   trade marks of the following kinds with a date of application for registration which is earlier than the date of application for registration of the EU trade mark, taking account, where appropriate, of the priorities claimed in respect of those trade marks:

(i)   EU trade marks;

(ii)   trade marks registered in a Member State, or, in the case of Belgium, the Netherlands or Luxembourg, at the Benelux Office for Intellectual Property;

(iii) trade marks registered under international arrangements which have effect in a Member State;

(iv)   trade marks registered under international arrangements which have effect in the Union;

(b)   applications for the trade marks referred to in point (a), subject to their registration;

(c)   trade marks which, on the date of application for registration of the EU trade mark, or, where appropriate, of the priority claimed in respect of the application for registration of the EU trade mark, are well known in a Member State, in the sense in which the words "well known" are used in Article 6bis of the Paris Convention.

3.   Upon opposition by the proprietor of the trade mark, a trade mark shall not be registered where an agent or representative of the proprietor of the trade mark applies for registration thereof in his own name without the proprietor's consent, unless the agent or representative justifies his action.

4.   Upon opposition by the proprietor of a non-registered trade mark or of another sign used in the course of trade of more than mere local significance, the trade mark applied for shall not be registered where and to the extent that, pursuant to Union legislation or the law of the Member State governing that sign:

(a)   rights to that sign were acquired prior to the date of application for registration of the EU trade mark, or the date of the priority claimed for the application for registration of the EU trade mark;

(b)   that sign confers on its proprietor the right to prohibit the use of a subsequent trade mark.

5.   Upon opposition by the proprietor of a registered earlier trade mark within the meaning of paragraph 2, the trade mark applied for shall not be registered where it is identical with,

or similar to, an earlier trade mark, irrespective of whether the goods or services for which it is applied are identical with, similar to or not similar to those for which the earlier trade mark is registered, where, in the case of an earlier EU trade mark, the trade mark has a reputation in the Union or, in the case of an earlier national trade mark, the trade mark has a reputation in the Member State concerned, and where the use without due cause of the trade mark applied for would take unfair advantage of, or be detrimental to, the distinctive character or the repute of the earlier trade mark.

6.   Upon opposition by any person authorised under the relevant law to exercise the rights arising from a designation of origin or a geographical indication, the trade mark applied for shall not be registered where and to the extent that, pursuant to the Union legislation or national law providing for the protection of designations of origin or geographical indications:

(i)   an application for a designation of origin or a geographical indication had already been submitted, in accordance with Union legislation or national law, prior to the date of application for registration of the EU trade mark or the date of the priority claimed for the application, subject to its subsequent registration;

(ii)   that designation of origin or geographical indication confers the right to prohibit the use of a subsequent trade mark.

SECTION 2
EFFECTS OF AN EU TRADE MARK

Article 9 Rights conferred by an EU trade mark

1.   The registration of an EU trade mark shall confer on the proprietor exclusive rights therein.

2.   Without prejudice to the rights of proprietors acquired before the filing date or the priority date of the EU trade mark, the proprietor of that EU trade mark shall be entitled to prevent all third parties not having his consent from using in the course of trade, in relation to goods or services, any sign where:

(a)   the sign is identical with the EU trade mark and is used in relation to goods or services which are identical with those for which the EU trade mark is registered;

(b)   the sign is identical with, or similar to, the EU trade mark and is used in relation to goods or services which are identical with, or similar to, the goods or services for which the EU trade mark is registered, if there exists a likelihood of confusion on the part of the public; the likelihood of confusion includes the likelihood of association between the sign and the trade mark;

(c)   the sign is identical with, or similar to, the EU trade mark irrespective of whether it is used in relation to goods or services which are identical with, similar to or not similar to those for which the EU trade mark is registered, where the latter has a reputation in the Union and where use of that sign without due cause takes unfair advantage of, or is detrimental to, the distinctive character or the repute of the EU trade mark.

3.   The following, in particular, may be prohibited under paragraph 2:

(a)   affixing the sign to the goods or to the packaging of those goods;

(b)   offering the goods, putting them on the market, or stocking them for those purposes under the sign, or offering or supplying services thereunder;

(c)   importing or exporting the goods under the sign;

(d)   using the sign as a trade or company name or part of a trade or company name;

(e)   using the sign on business papers and in advertising;

(f)   using the sign in comparative advertising in a manner that is contrary to Directive 2006/114/EC.

4.   Without prejudice to the rights of proprietors acquired before the filing date or the priority date of the EU trade mark, the proprietor of that EU trade mark shall also be entitled to prevent all third parties from bringing goods, in the course of trade, into the Union without being released for free circulation there, where such goods, including packaging, come from third countries and bear without authorisation a trade mark which is identical with the EU trade mark registered in respect of such goods, or which cannot be distinguished in its essential aspects from that trade mark.

The entitlement of the proprietor of an EU trade mark pursuant to the first subparagraph shall lapse if, during the proceedings to determine whether the EU trade mark has been infringed, initiated in accordance with Regulation (EU) No 608/2013, evidence is provided by the declarant or the holder of the goods that the proprietor of the EU trade mark is not entitled to prohibit the placing of the goods on the market in the country of final destination.

Article 10 Right to prohibit preparatory acts in relation to the use of packaging or other means

Where the risk exists that the packaging, labels, tags, security or authenticity features or devices or any other means to which the mark is affixed could be used in relation to goods or services and such use would constitute an infringement of the rights of the proprietor of an EU trade mark under Article 9(2) and (3), the proprietor of that trade mark shall have the right to prohibit the following acts if carried out in the course of trade:

    (a)   affixing a sign identical with, or similar to, the EU trade mark on packaging, labels, tags, security or authenticity features or devices or any other means to which the mark may be affixed;

    (b)   offering or placing on the market, or stocking for those purposes, or importing or exporting, packaging, labels, tags, security or authenticity features or devices or any other means to which the mark is affixed.

Article 11 Date from which rights against third parties prevail

1.   The rights conferred by an EU trade mark shall prevail against third parties from the date of publication of the registration of the trade mark.

2.   Reasonable compensation may be claimed in respect of acts occurring after the date of publication of an EU trade mark application, where those acts would, after publication of the registration of the trade mark, be prohibited by virtue of that publication.

3.   A court seised of a case shall not decide upon the merits of that case until the registration has been published.

Article 12 Reproduction of an EU trade mark in a dictionary

If the reproduction of an EU trade mark in a dictionary, encyclopaedia or similar reference work gives the impression that it constitutes the generic name of the goods or services for which the trade mark is registered, the publisher of the work shall, at the request of the proprietor of the EU trade mark, ensure that the reproduction of the trade mark at the latest in the next edition of the publication is accompanied by an indication that it is a registered trade mark.

Article 13 Prohibition of the use of an EU trade mark registered in the name of an agent or representative

Where an EU trade mark is registered in the name of the agent or representative of a person who is the proprietor of that trade mark, without the proprietor's authorisation, the latter shall be entitled to oppose the use of his mark by his agent or representative if he has not authorised such use, unless the agent or representative justifies his action.

Article 14 Limitation of the effects of an EU trade mark

1.   An EU trade mark shall not entitle the proprietor to prohibit a third party from using, in the course of trade:

    (a)   the name or address of the third party, where that third party is a natural person;

    (b)   signs or indications which are not distinctive or which concern the kind, quality, quantity, intended purpose, value, geographical origin, the time of production of goods or of rendering of the service, or other characteristics of the goods or services;

    (c)   the EU trade mark for the purpose of identifying or referring to goods or services as those of the proprietor of that trade mark, in particular, where the use of that trade mark is necessary to indicate the intended purpose of a product or service, in particular as accessories or spare parts.

2.   Paragraph 1 shall only apply where the use made by the third party is in accordance with honest practices in industrial or commercial matters.

Article 15 Exhaustion of the rights conferred by an EU trade mark

1.   An EU trade mark shall not entitle the proprietor to prohibit its use in relation to goods which have been put on the market in the European Economic Area under that trade mark by the proprietor or with his consent.

2.   Paragraph 1 shall not apply where there exist legitimate reasons for the proprietor to oppose further commercialisation of the goods, especially where the condition of the goods is changed or impaired after they have been put on the market.

Article 16 Intervening right of the proprietor of a later registered trade mark as a defence in infringement proceedings

1.   In infringement proceedings, the proprietor of an EU trade mark shall not be entitled to prohibit the use of a later registered EU trade mark where that later trade mark would not be declared invalid pursuant to Article 60(1), (3) or (4), Article 61(1) or (2), or Article 64(2) of this Regulation.

2.   In infringement proceedings, the proprietor of an EU trade mark shall not be entitled to prohibit the use of a later registered national trade mark where that later registered national trade mark would not be declared invalid pursuant to Article 8 or Article 9(1) or (2), or Article 46(3) of Directive (EU) 2015/2436 of the European Parliament and of the Council.

3.   Where the proprietor of an EU trade mark is not entitled to prohibit the use of a later registered trade mark pursuant to paragraph 1 or 2, the proprietor of that later registered trade mark shall not be entitled to prohibit the use of that earlier EU trade mark in infringement proceedings.

Article 17 Complementary application of national law relating to infringement

1.   The effects of EU trade marks shall be governed solely by the provisions of this Regulation. In other respects, infringement of an EU trade mark shall be governed by the national law relating to infringement of a national trade mark in accordance with the provisions of Chapter X.

2.   This Regulation shall not prevent actions concerning an EU trade mark being brought under the law of Member States relating in particular to civil liability and unfair competition.

3.   The rules of procedure to be applied shall be determined in accordance with the provisions of Chapter X.

SECTION 3

USE OF AN EU TRADE MARK

Article 18 Use of an EU trade mark

1.   If, within a period of five years following registration, the proprietor has not put the EU trade mark to genuine use in the Union in connection with the goods or services in respect of which it is registered, or if such use has been suspended during an uninterrupted period of five years, the EU trade mark shall be subject to the sanctions provided for in this Regulation, unless there are proper reasons for non-use.

The following shall also constitute use within the meaning of the first subparagraph:

(a)   use of the EU trade mark in a form differing in elements which do not alter the distinctive character of the mark in the form in which it was registered, regardless of whether or not the trade mark in the form as used is also registered in the name of the proprietor;

(b)   affixing of the EU trade mark to goods or to the packaging thereof in the Union solely for export purposes.

2.   Use of the EU trade mark with the consent of the proprietor shall be deemed to constitute use by the proprietor.

SECTION 4

EU TRADE MARKS AS OBJECTS OF PROPERTY

Article 19 Dealing with EU trade marks as national trade marks

1.   Unless Articles 20 to 28 provide otherwise, an EU trade mark as an object of property shall be dealt with in its entirety, and for the whole area of the Union, as a national trade mark registered in the Member State in which, according to the Register:

(a)   the proprietor has his seat or his domicile on the relevant date;

(b)   where point (a) does not apply, the proprietor has an establishment on the relevant date.

2.   In cases which are not provided for by paragraph 1, the Member State referred to in that paragraph shall be the Member State in which the seat of the Office is situated.

3.   If two or more persons are mentioned in the Register as joint proprietors, paragraph 1 shall apply to the joint proprietor first mentioned; failing this, it shall apply to the subsequent joint proprietors in the order in which they are mentioned. Where paragraph 1 does not apply to any of the joint proprietors, paragraph 2 shall apply.

Article 20 Transfer

1.   An EU trade mark may be transferred, separately from any transfer of the undertaking, in respect of some or all of the goods or services for which it is registered.

2.   A transfer of the whole of the undertaking shall include the transfer of the EU trade mark except where, in accordance with the law governing the transfer, there is agreement to the contrary or circumstances clearly dictate otherwise. This provision shall apply to the contractual obligation to transfer the undertaking.

3.   Without prejudice to paragraph 2, an assignment of the EU trade mark shall be made in writing and shall require the signature of the parties to the contract, except when it is a result of a judgment; otherwise it shall be void.

4.   On request of one of the parties a transfer shall be entered in the Register and published.

5.   An application for registration of a transfer shall contain information to identify the EU trade mark, the new proprietor, the goods and services to which the transfer relates, as well as documents duly establishing the transfer in accordance with paragraphs 2 and 3. The application may further contain, where applicable, information to identify the representative of the new proprietor.

6.   The Commission shall adopt implementing acts specifying:
(a)   the details to be contained in the application for registration of a transfer;
(b)   the kind of documentation required to establish a transfer, taking account of the agreements given by the registered proprietor and the successor in title;
(c)   the details of how to process applications for partial transfers, ensuring that the goods and services in the remaining registration and the new registration do not overlap and that a separate file, including a new registration number, is established for the new registration.

Those implementing acts shall be adopted in accordance with the examination procedure referred to in Article 207(2).

7.   Where the conditions applicable to the registration of a transfer, as laid down in paragraphs 1, 2 and 3, or in the implementing acts referred to in paragraph 6, are not fulfilled, the Office shall notify the applicant of the deficiencies. If the deficiencies are not remedied within a period to be specified by the Office, it shall reject the application for registration of the transfer.

8.   A single application for registration of a transfer may be submitted for two or more trade marks, provided that the registered proprietor and the successor in title are the same in each case.

9.   Paragraphs 5 to 8 shall also apply to applications for EU trade marks.

10.   In the case of a partial transfer, any application made by the original proprietor pending with regard to the original registration shall be deemed to be pending with regard to the remaining registration and the new registration. Where such application is subject to the payment of fees and those fees have been paid by the original proprietor, the new proprietor shall not be liable to pay any additional fees with regard to such application.

11.   As long as the transfer has not been entered in the Register, the successor in title may not invoke the rights arising from the registration of the EU trade mark.

12.   Where there are time limits to be observed vis-à-vis the Office, the successor in title may make the corresponding statements to the Office once the request for registration of the transfer has been received by the Office.

13.   All documents which require notification to the proprietor of the EU trade mark in accordance with Article 98 shall be addressed to the person registered as proprietor.

Article 21 Transfer of a trade mark registered in the name of an agent

1.   Where an EU trade mark is registered in the name of the agent or representative of a person who is the proprietor of that trade mark, without the proprietor's authorisation, the latter shall be entitled to demand the assignment of the EU trade mark in his favour, unless such agent or representative justifies his action.

2.   The proprietor may submit a request for assignment pursuant to paragraph 1 of this Article to the following:
  (a) the Office, pursuant to Article 60(1)(b), instead of an application for a declaration of invalidity;
  (b) a European Union trade mark court ("EU trade mark court") as referred to in Article 123, instead of a counterclaim for a declaration of invalidity based on Article 128(1).

Article 22 Rights *in rem*
1.   An EU trade mark may, independently of the undertaking, be given as security or be the subject of rights *in rem*.
2.   At the request of one of the parties, the rights referred to in paragraph 1 or the transfer of those rights shall be entered in the Register and published.
3.   An entry in the Register effected pursuant to paragraph 2 shall be cancelled or modified at the request of one of the parties.

Article 23 Levy of execution
1.   An EU trade mark may be levied in execution.
2.   As regards the procedure for levy of execution in respect of an EU trade mark, the courts and authorities of the Member States determined in accordance with Article 19 shall have exclusive jurisdiction.
3.   On request of one the parties, the levy of execution shall be entered in the Register and published.
4.   An entry in the Register effected pursuant to paragraph 3 shall be cancelled or modified at the request of one of the parties.

Article 24 Insolvency proceedings
1.   The only insolvency proceedings in which an EU trade mark may be involved are those opened in the Member State in the territory of which the debtor has his centre of main interests.
      However, where the debtor is an insurance undertaking or a credit institution as defined in Directive 2009/138/EC of the European Parliament and of the Council and Directive 2001/24/EC of the European Parliament and of the Council, respectively, the only insolvency proceedings in which an EU trade mark may be involved are those opened in the Member State where that undertaking or institution has been authorised.
2.   In the case of joint proprietorship of an EU trade mark, paragraph 1 shall apply to the share of the joint proprietor.
3.   Where an EU trade mark is involved in insolvency proceedings, on request of the competent national authority an entry to this effect shall be made in the Register and published in the European Union Trade Marks Bulletin referred to in Article 116.

Article 25 Licensing
1.   An EU trade mark may be licensed for some or all of the goods or services for which it is registered and for the whole or part of the Union. A licence may be exclusive or non-exclusive.
2.   The proprietor of an EU trade mark may invoke the rights conferred by that trade mark against a licensee who contravenes any provision in his licensing contract with regard to:
  (a) its duration;
  (b) the form covered by the registration in which the trade mark may be used;
  (c) the scope of the goods or services for which the licence is granted;
  (d) the territory in which the trade mark may be affixed; or
  (e) the quality of the goods manufactured or of the services provided by the licensee.
3.   Without prejudice to the provisions of the licensing contract, the licensee may bring proceedings for infringement of an EU trade mark only if its proprietor consents thereto. However, the holder of an exclusive licence may bring such proceedings if the proprietor of the trade mark, after formal notice, does not himself bring infringement proceedings within an appropriate period.
4.   A licensee shall, for the purpose of obtaining compensation for damage suffered by him, be entitled to intervene in infringement proceedings brought by the proprietor of the EU trade mark.
5.   On request of one of the parties the grant or transfer of a licence in respect of an EU trade mark shall be entered in the Register and published.
6.   An entry in the Register effected pursuant to paragraph 5 shall be cancelled or modified at the request of one of the parties.

Article 26 Procedure for entering licences and other rights in the Register

1. Article 20(5) and (6) and the rules adopted pursuant to it and Article 20(8) shall apply *mutatis mutandis* to the registration of a right *in rem* or transfer of a right *in rem* as referred to in Article 22(2), the levy of execution as referred to in Article 23(3), the involvement in insolvency proceedings as referred to in Article 24(3), as well as to the registration of a licence or transfer of a licence as referred to in Article 25(5), subject to the following:

    (a) the requirement relating to the identification of goods and services to which the transfer relates shall not apply in respect of a request for registration of a right *in rem*, of a levy of execution or of insolvency proceedings;

    (b) the requirement relating to the documents proving the transfer shall not apply where the request is made by the proprietor of the EU trade mark.

2. The application for registration of the rights referred to in paragraph 1 shall not be deemed to have been filed until the required fee has been paid.

3. The application for registration of a licence may contain a request to record a licence in the Register as one or more of the following:

    (a) an exclusive licence;

    (b) a sub-licence in the event that the licence is granted by a licensee whose licence is recorded in the Register;

    (c) a licence limited to only part of the goods or services for which the mark is registered;

    (d) a licence limited to part of the Union;

    (e) a temporary licence.

    Where a request is made to record the licence as a licence listed in points (c), (d) and (e) of the first subparagraph, the application for registration of a licence shall indicate the goods and services, the part of the Union and the time period for which the licence is granted.

4. Where the conditions applicable to registration, as laid down in Articles 22 to 25, in paragraphs 1 and 3 of this Article and in the other applicable rules adopted pursuant to this Regulation, are not fulfilled, the Office shall notify the applicant of the deficiency. If the deficiency is not corrected within a period specified by the Office, it shall reject the application for registration.

5. Paragraphs 1 and 3 shall apply *mutatis mutandis* to applications for EU trade marks.

Article 27 Effects vis-à-vis third parties

1. Legal acts referred to in Articles 20, 22 and 25 concerning an EU trade mark shall have effects vis-à-vis third parties in all the Member States only after entry in the Register. Nevertheless, such an act, before it is so entered, shall have effect vis-à-vis third parties who have acquired rights in the trade mark after the date of that act but who knew of the act at the date on which the rights were acquired.

2. Paragraph 1 shall not apply in the case of a person who acquires the EU trade mark or a right concerning the EU trade mark by way of transfer of the whole of the undertaking or by any other universal succession.

3. The effects vis-à-vis third parties of the legal acts referred to in Article 23 shall be governed by the law of the Member State determined in accordance with Article 19.

4. Until such time as common rules for the Member States in the field of bankruptcy enter into force, the effects vis-à-vis third parties of bankruptcy or similar proceedings shall be governed by the law of the Member State in which such proceedings are first brought within the meaning of national law or of conventions applicable in this field.

Article 28 The application for an EU trade mark as an object of property

Articles 19 to 27 shall apply to applications for EU trade marks.

Article 29 Procedure for cancelling or modifying the entry in the Register of licences and other rights

1. A registration effected under Article 26(1) shall be cancelled or modified at the request of one of the persons concerned.

2. The application shall contain the registration number of the EU trade mark concerned and the particulars of the right for which registration is requested to be cancelled or modified.

3. The application for cancellation of a licence, a right *in rem* or an enforcement measure shall not be deemed to have been filed until the required fee has been paid.

4. The application shall be accompanied by documents showing that the registered right no longer exists or that the licensee or the holder of another right consents to the cancellation or modification of the registration.

5. Where the requirements for cancellation or modification of the registration are not satisfied, the Office shall notify the applicant of the deficiency. If the deficiency is not corrected within a period to be specified by the Office, it shall reject the application for cancellation or modification of the registration.

6. Paragraphs 1 to 5 of this Article shall apply *mutatis mutandis* to entries made in the files pursuant to Article 26(5).

CHAPTER III
APPLICATION FOR EU TRADE MARKS

SECTION 1
FILING OF APPLICATIONS AND THE CONDITIONS WHICH GOVERN THEM

Article 30 Filing of applications

1. An application for an EU trade mark shall be filed at the Office.

. . .

Article 31 Conditions with which applications must comply

1. An application for an EU trade mark shall contain:
   (a) a request for the registration of an EU trade mark;
   (b) information identifying the applicant;
   (c) a list of the goods or services in respect of which the registration is requested;
   (d) a representation of the mark, which satisfies the requirements set out in Article 4(b).

. . .

Article 32 Date of filing

The date of filing of an EU trade mark application shall be the date on which the documents containing the information specified in Article 31(1) are filed with the Office by the applicant, subject to payment of the application fee within one month of filing those documents.

Article 33 Designation and classification of goods and services

1. Goods and services in respect of which trade mark registration is applied for shall be classified in conformity with the system of classification established by the Nice Agreement Concerning the International Classification of Goods and Services for the Purposes of the Registration of Marks of 15 June 1957 ("the Nice Classification").

2. The goods and services for which the protection of the trade mark is sought shall be identified by the applicant with sufficient clarity and precision to enable the competent authorities and economic operators, on that sole basis, to determine the extent of the protection sought.

3. For the purposes of paragraph 2, the general indications included in the class headings of the Nice Classification or other general terms may be used, provided that they comply with the requisite standards of clarity and precision set out in this Article.

4. The Office shall reject an application in respect of indications or terms which are unclear or imprecise, where the applicant does not suggest an acceptable wording within a period set by the Office to that effect.

5. The use of general terms, including the general indications of the class headings of the Nice Classification, shall be interpreted as including all the goods or services clearly covered by the literal meaning of the indication or term. The use of such terms or indications shall not be interpreted as comprising a claim to goods or services which cannot be so understood.

6. Where the applicant requests registration for more than one class, the applicant shall group the goods and services according to the classes of the Nice Classification, each group being preceded by the number of the class to which that group of goods or services belongs, and shall present them in the order of the classes.

7.   Goods and services shall not be regarded as being similar to each other on the ground that they appear in the same class under the Nice Classification. Goods and services shall not be regarded as being dissimilar from each other on the ground that they appear in different classes under the Nice Classification.

. . .

9.   Where the register is amended, the exclusive rights conferred by the EU trade mark under Article 9 shall not prevent a third party from continuing to use a trade mark in relation to goods or services where and to the extent that the use of the trade mark for those goods or services:

(a)   commenced before the register was amended; and

(b)   did not infringe the proprietor's rights based on the literal meaning of the record of the goods and services in the register at that time.

In addition, the amendment of the list of goods or services recorded in the register shall not give the proprietor of the EU trade mark the right to oppose or to apply for a declaration of invalidity of a later trade mark where and to the extent that:

(a)   the later trade mark was either in use, or an application had been made to register the trade mark, for goods or services before the register was amended; and

(b)   the use of the trade mark in relation to those goods or services did not infringe, or would not have infringed, the proprietor's rights based on the literal meaning of the record of the goods and services in the register at that time.

SECTION 2
PRIORITY

Article 34 Right of priority

1.   A person who has duly filed an application for a trade mark in or in respect of any State party to the Paris Convention or to the Agreement establishing the World Trade Organisation, or his successors in title, shall enjoy, for the purpose of filing an EU trade mark application for the same trade mark in respect of goods or services which are identical with or contained within those for which the application has been filed, a right of priority during a period of six months from the date of filing of the first application.

2.   Every filing that is equivalent to a regular national filing under the national law of the State where it was made or under bilateral or multilateral agreements shall be recognised as giving rise to a right of priority.

3.   By a regular national filing is meant any filing that is sufficient to establish the date on which the application was filed, whatever may be the outcome of the application.

4.   A subsequent application for a trade mark which was the subject of a previous first application in respect of the same goods or services and which is filed in or in respect of the same State shall be considered as the first application for the purposes of determining priority, provided that, at the date of filing of the subsequent application, the previous application has been withdrawn, abandoned or refused, without being open to public inspection and without leaving any rights outstanding, and has not served as a basis for claiming a right of priority. The previous application may not thereafter serve as a basis for claiming a right of priority.

5.   If the first filing has been made in a State which is not a party to the Paris Convention or to the Agreement establishing the World Trade Organisation, paragraphs 1 to 4 shall apply only in so far as that State, according to published findings, grants, on the basis of the first filing made at the Office and subject to conditions equivalent to those laid down in this Regulation, a right of priority having equivalent effect. The Executive Director shall, where necessary, request the Commission to consider enquiring as to whether a State within the meaning of the first sentence accords that reciprocal treatment. If the Commission determines that reciprocal treatment in accordance with the first sentence is accorded, it shall publish a communication to that effect in the *Official Journal of the European Union*.

6.   Paragraph 5 shall apply from the date of publication in the *Official Journal of the European Union* of the communication determining that reciprocal treatment is accorded, unless the communication states an earlier date from which it is applicable. It shall cease to apply from

the date of publication in the *Official Journal of the European Union* of a communication of the Commission to the effect that reciprocal treatment is no longer accorded, unless the communication states an earlier date from which it is applicable.

7.   Communications as referred to in paragraphs 5 and 6 shall also be published in the Official Journal of the Office.

Article 35 Claiming priority

1.   Priority claims shall be filed together with the EU trade mark application and shall include the date, number and country of the previous application. The documentation in support of priority claims shall be filed within three months of the filing date.

. . .

Article 36 Effect of priority right

The right of priority shall have the effect that the date of priority shall count as the date of filing of the EU trade mark application for the purposes of establishing which rights take precedence.

Article 37 Equivalence of Union filing with national filing

An EU trade mark application which has been accorded a date of filing shall, in the Member States, be equivalent to a regular national filing, where appropriate with the priority claimed for the EU trade mark application.

SECTION 3
EXHIBITION PRIORITY

Article 38 Exhibition priority

1.   If an applicant for an EU trade mark has displayed goods or services under the mark applied for, at an official or officially recognised international exhibition falling within the terms of the Convention relating to international exhibitions signed at Paris on 22 November 1928 and last revised on 30 November 1972, he may, if he files the application within a period of six months of the date of the first display of the goods or services under the mark applied for, claim a right of priority from that date within the meaning of Article 36. The priority claim shall be filed together with the EU trade mark application.

2.   An applicant who wishes to claim priority pursuant to paragraph 1 shall file evidence of the display of goods or services under the mark applied for within three months of the filing date.

3.   An exhibition priority granted in a Member State or in a third country shall not extend the period of priority laid down in Article 34.

. . .

SECTION 4
SENIORITY OF A NATIONAL TRADE MARK

Article 39 Claiming seniority of a national trade mark in an application for an EU trade mark or subsequent to the filing of the application

1.   The proprietor of an earlier trade mark registered in a Member State, including a trade mark registered in the Benelux countries, or registered under international arrangements having effect in a Member State, who applies for an identical trade mark for registration as an EU trade mark for goods or services which are identical with or contained within those for which the earlier trade mark has been registered, may claim for the EU trade mark the seniority of the earlier trade mark in respect of the Member State in or for which it is registered.

2.   Seniority claims shall either be filed together with the EU trade mark application or within two months of the filing date of the application, and shall include the Member State or Member States in or for which the mark is registered, the number and the filing date of the relevant registration, and the goods and services for which the mark is registered. …

3.   Seniority shall have the sole effect under this Regulation that, where the proprietor of the EU trade mark surrenders the earlier trade mark or allows it to lapse, he shall be deemed to continue to have the same rights as he would have had if the earlier trade mark had continued to be registered.

4.   The seniority claimed for the EU trade mark shall lapse where the earlier trade mark the seniority of which is claimed is declared to be invalid or revoked. Where the earlier trade mark is revoked, the seniority shall lapse provided that the revocation takes effect prior to the filing date or priority date of that EU trade mark.

. . .

Article 40 Claiming seniority of a national trade mark after registration of an EU trade mark

1.   The proprietor of an EU trade mark who is the proprietor of an earlier identical trade mark registered in a Member State, including a trade mark registered in the Benelux countries or of an earlier identical trade mark, with an international registration effective in a Member State, for goods or services which are identical to those for which the earlier trade mark has been registered, or contained within them, may claim the seniority of the earlier trade mark in respect of the Member State in or for which it was registered.

. . .

CHAPTER IV
REGISTRATION PROCEDURE

SECTION 1
EXAMINATION OF APPLICATIONS

Article 41 Examination of the conditions of filing

1.   The Office shall examine whether:
  (a)   the EU trade mark application satisfies the requirements for the accordance of a date of filing in accordance with Article 32;
  (b)   the EU trade mark application complies with the conditions and requirements referred to in Article 31(3);
  (c)   where appropriate, the class fees have been paid within the prescribed period.

. . .

Article 42 Examination as to absolute grounds for refusal

1.   Where, under Article 7, a trade mark is ineligible for registration in respect of some or all of the goods or services covered by the EU trade mark application, the application shall be refused as regards those goods or services.

2.   The application shall not be refused before the applicant has been allowed the opportunity to withdraw or amend the application or to submit his observations. To this effect, the Office shall notify the applicant of the grounds for refusing registration and shall specify a period within which he may withdraw or amend the application or submit his observations. Where the applicant fails to overcome the grounds for refusing registration, the Office shall refuse registration in whole or in part.

SECTION 2
SEARCH

Article 43 Search report

1.   The Office shall, at the request of the applicant for the EU trade mark when filing the application, draw up a European Union search report ("EU search report") citing those earlier EU trade marks or EU trade mark applications discovered which may be invoked under Article 8 against the registration of the EU trade mark applied for.

. . .

SECTION 3

PUBLICATION OF THE APPLICATION

Article 44 Publication of the application

1. If the conditions which the application for an EU trade mark is required to satisfy have been fulfilled, the application shall be published for the purposes of Article 46 to the extent that it has not been refused pursuant to Article 42. The publication of the application shall be without prejudice to information already made available to the public otherwise in accordance with this Regulation or acts adopted pursuant to this Regulation.

2. Where, after publication, the application is refused pursuant to Article 42, the decision that it has been refused shall be published upon becoming final.

. . .

SECTION 4

OBSERVATIONS BY THIRD PARTIES AND OPPOSITION

Article 45 Observations by third parties

1. Any natural or legal person and any group or body representing manufacturers, producers, suppliers of services, traders or consumers may submit to the Office written observations, explaining on which grounds, under Articles 5 and 7, the trade mark should not be registered *ex officio*.

    Persons and groups or bodies as referred to in the first subparagraph shall not be parties to the proceedings before the Office.

2. Third party observations shall be submitted before the end of the opposition period or, where an opposition against the trade mark has been filed, before the final decision on the opposition is taken.

3. The submission referred to in paragraph 1 shall be without prejudice to the right of the Office to re-open the examination of absolute grounds on its own initiative at any time before registration, where appropriate.

4. The observations referred to in paragraph 1 shall be communicated to the applicant who may comment on them.

Article 46 Opposition

1. Within a period of three months following the publication of an EU trade mark application, notice of opposition to registration of the trade mark may be given on the grounds that it may not be registered under Article 8:
    (a) by the proprietors of earlier trade marks referred to in Article 8(2) as well as licensees authorised by the proprietors of those trade marks, in respect of Article 8(1) and (5);
    (b) by the proprietors of trade marks referred to in Article 8(3);
    (c) by the proprietors of earlier marks or signs referred to in Article 8(4) and by persons authorised under the relevant national law to exercise these rights;
    (d) by the persons authorised under the relevant Union legislation or national law to exercise the rights referred to in Article 8(6).

2. Notice of opposition to registration of the trade mark may also be given, subject to the conditions laid down in paragraph 1, in the event of the publication of an amended application in accordance with the second sentence of Article 49(2).

3. Opposition shall be expressed in writing, and shall specify the grounds on which it is made. It shall not be considered as duly entered until the opposition fee has been paid.

4. Within a period to be fixed by the Office, the opponent may submit facts, evidence and arguments in support of his case.

. . .

SECTION 5

WITHDRAWAL, RESTRICTION, AMENDMENT AND DIVISION OF THE APPLICATION

Article 49 Withdrawal, restriction and amendment of the application

1.   The applicant may at any time withdraw his EU trade mark application or restrict the list of goods or services contained therein. Where the application has already been published, the withdrawal or restriction shall also be published.

2.   In other respects, an EU trade mark application may be amended, upon request of the applicant, only by correcting the name and address of the applicant, errors of wording or of copying, or obvious mistakes, provided that such correction does not substantially change the trade mark or extend the list of goods or services. Where the amendments affect the representation of the trade mark or the list of goods or services and are made after publication of the application, the trade mark application shall be published as amended.

. . .

Article 50 Division of the application

1.   The applicant may divide the application by declaring that some of the goods or services included in the original application will be the subject of one or more divisional applications. The goods or services in the divisional application shall not overlap with the goods or services which remain in the original application or those which are included in other divisional applications.

. . .

SECTION 6

REGISTRATION

Article 51 Registration

1.   Where an application meets the requirements set out in this Regulation and where no notice of opposition has been given within the period referred to in Article 46(1) or where any opposition entered has been finally disposed of by withdrawal, rejection or other disposition, the trade mark and the particulars referred to in Article 111(2) shall be recorded in the Register. The registration shall be published.

. . .

CHAPTER V

DURATION, RENEWAL, ALTERATION AND DIVISION OF EU TRADE MARKS

Article 52 Duration of registration

EU trade marks shall be registered for a period of 10 years from the date of filing of the application. Registration may be renewed in accordance with Article 53 for further periods of 10 years.

Article 53 Renewal

1.   Registration of the EU trade mark shall be renewed at the request of the proprietor of the EU trade mark or any person expressly authorised by him, provided that the fees have been paid.

2.   The Office shall inform the proprietor of the EU trade mark, and any person having a registered right in respect of the EU trade mark, of the expiry of the registration at least six months before the said expiry. Failure to give such information shall not involve the responsibility of the Office and shall not affect the expiry of the registration.

. . .

6.   Renewal shall take effect from the day following the date on which the existing registration expires. The renewal shall be registered.

. . .

Article 54 Alteration

1. The EU trade mark shall not be altered in the Register during the period of registration or on renewal thereof.
2. Nevertheless, where the EU trade mark includes the name and address of the proprietor, any alteration thereof not substantially affecting the identity of the trade mark as originally registered may be registered at the request of the proprietor.

. . .

Article 56 Division of the registration

1. The proprietor of the EU trade mark may divide the registration by declaring that some of the goods or services included in the original registration will be the subject of one or more divisional registrations. The goods or services in the divisional registration shall not overlap with the goods or services which remain in the original registration or those which are included in other divisional registrations.

. . .

7. The divisional registration shall preserve the filing date and any priority date and seniority date of the original registration.

. . .

CHAPTER VI
SURRENDER, REVOCATION AND INVALIDITY

SECTION 1
SURRENDER

Article 57 Surrender

1. An EU trade mark may be surrendered in respect of some or all of the goods or services for which it is registered.

. . .

SECTION 2
GROUNDS FOR REVOCATION

Article 58 Grounds for revocation

1. The rights of the proprietor of the EU trade mark shall be declared to be revoked on application to the Office or on the basis of a counterclaim in infringement proceedings:
    (a) if, within a continuous period of five years, the trade mark has not been put to genuine use in the Union in connection with the goods or services in respect of which it is registered, and there are no proper reasons for non-use; however, no person may claim that the proprietor's rights in an EU trade mark should be revoked where, during the interval between expiry of the five-year period and filing of the application or counterclaim, genuine use of the trade mark has been started or resumed; the commencement or resumption of use within a period of three months preceding the filing of the application or counterclaim which began at the earliest on expiry of the continuous period of five years of non-use shall, however, be disregarded where preparations for the commencement or resumption occur only after the proprietor becomes aware that the application or counterclaim may be filed;
    (b) if, in consequence of acts or inactivity of the proprietor, the trade mark has become the common name in the trade for a product or service in respect of which it is registered;
    (c) if, in consequence of the use made of the trade mark by the proprietor of the trade mark or with his consent in respect of the goods or services for which it is registered, the trade mark is liable to mislead the public, particularly as to the nature, quality or geographical origin of those goods or services.

2.   Where the grounds for revocation of rights exist in respect of only some of the goods or services for which the EU trade mark is registered, the rights of the proprietor shall be declared to be revoked in respect of those goods or services only.

SECTION 3
GROUNDS FOR INVALIDITY

Article 59 Absolute grounds for invalidity

1.   An EU trade mark shall be declared invalid on application to the Office or on the basis of a counterclaim in infringement proceedings:

   (a)   where the EU trade mark has been registered contrary to the provisions of Article 7;

   (b)   where the applicant was acting in bad faith when he filed the application for the trade mark.

2.   Where the EU trade mark has been registered in breach of the provisions of Article 7(1)(b), (c) or (d), it may nevertheless not be declared invalid if, in consequence of the use which has been made of it, it has after registration acquired a distinctive character in relation to the goods or services for which it is registered.

3.   Where the ground for invalidity exists in respect of only some of the goods or services for which the EU trade mark is registered, the trade mark shall be declared invalid as regards those goods or services only.

Article 60 Relative grounds for invalidity

1.   An EU trade mark shall be declared invalid on application to the Office or on the basis of a counterclaim in infringement proceedings:

   (a)   where there is an earlier trade mark as referred to in Article 8(2) and the conditions set out in paragraph 1 or 5 of that Article are fulfilled;

   (b)   where there is a trade mark as referred to in Article 8(3) and the conditions set out in that paragraph are fulfilled;

   (c)   where there is an earlier right as referred to in Article 8(4) and the conditions set out in that paragraph are fulfilled;

   (d)   where there is an earlier designation of origin or geographical indication as referred to in Article 8(6) and the conditions set out in that paragraph are fulfilled.

   All the conditions referred to in the first subparagraph shall be fulfilled at the filing date or the priority date of the EU trade mark.

2.   An EU trade mark shall also be declared invalid on application to the Office or on the basis of a counterclaim in infringement proceedings where the use of such trade mark may be prohibited pursuant to another earlier right under the Union legislation or national law governing its protection, and in particular:

   (a)   a right to a name;

   (b)   a right of personal portrayal;

   (c)   a copyright;

   (d)   an industrial property right.

3.   An EU trade mark may not be declared invalid where the proprietor of a right referred to in paragraph 1 or 2 consents expressly to the registration of the EU trade mark before submission of the application for a declaration of invalidity or the counterclaim.

4.   Where the proprietor of one of the rights referred to in paragraph 1 or 2 has previously applied for a declaration that an EU trade mark is invalid or made a counterclaim in infringement proceedings, he may not submit a new application for a declaration of invalidity or lodge a counterclaim on the basis of another of the said rights which he could have invoked in support of his first application or counterclaim.

5.   Article 59(3) shall apply.

Article 61 Limitation in consequence of acquiescence

1.   Where the proprietor of an EU trade mark has acquiesced, for a period of five successive years, in the use of a later EU trade mark in the Union while being aware of such use, he shall no longer be entitled on the basis of the earlier trade mark to apply for a declaration that the later trade mark is invalid in respect of the goods or services for which the later

trade mark has been used, unless registration of the later EU trade mark was applied for in bad faith.

2. Where the proprietor of an earlier national trade mark as referred to in Article 8(2) or of another earlier sign referred to in Article 8(4) has acquiesced, for a period of five successive years, in the use of a later EU trade mark in the Member State in which the earlier trade mark or the other earlier sign is protected while being aware of such use, he shall no longer be entitled on the basis of the earlier trade mark or of the other earlier sign to apply for a declaration that the later trade mark is invalid in respect of the goods or services for which the later trade mark has been used, unless registration of the later EU trade mark was applied for in bad faith.

3. In the cases referred to in paragraphs 1 and 2, the proprietor of a later EU trade mark shall not be entitled to oppose the use of the earlier right, even though that right may no longer be invoked against the later EU trade mark.

SECTION 4
CONSEQUENCES OF REVOCATION AND INVALIDITY

Article 62 Consequences of revocation and invalidity

1. The EU trade mark shall be deemed not to have had, as from the date of the application for revocation or of the counterclaim, the effects specified in this Regulation, to the extent that the rights of the proprietor have been revoked. An earlier date, on which one of the grounds for revocation occurred, may be fixed in the decision at the request of one of the parties.

2. The EU trade mark shall be deemed not to have had, as from the outset, the effects specified in this Regulation, to the extent that the trade mark has been declared invalid.

3. Subject to the national provisions relating either to claims for compensation for damage caused by negligence or lack of good faith on the part of the proprietor of the trade mark, or to unjust enrichment, the retroactive effect of revocation or invalidity of the trade mark shall not affect:

   (a) any decision on infringement which has acquired the authority of a final decision and been enforced prior to the revocation or invalidity decision;

   (b) any contract concluded prior to the revocation or invalidity decision, in so far as it has been performed before that decision; however, repayment, to an extent justified by the circumstances, of sums paid under the relevant contract may be claimed on grounds of equity.

SECTION 5
PROCEEDINGS IN THE OFFICE IN RELATION TO REVOCATION OR INVALIDITY

Article 63 Application for revocation or for a declaration of invalidity

1. An application for revocation of the rights of the proprietor of an EU trade mark or for a declaration that the trade mark is invalid may be submitted to the Office:

   (a) where Articles 58 and 59 apply, by any natural or legal person and any group or body set up for the purpose of representing the interests of manufacturers, producers, suppliers of services, traders or consumers, which, under the terms of the law governing it, has the capacity in its own name to sue and be sued;

   (b) where Article 60(1) applies, by the persons referred to in Article 46(1);

   (c) where Article 60(2) applies, by the owners of the earlier rights referred to in that provision or by the persons who are entitled under Union legislation or the law of the Member State concerned to exercise the rights in question.

2. The application shall be filed in a written reasoned statement. It shall not be deemed to have been filed until the fee has been paid.

3. An application for revocation or for a declaration of invalidity shall be inadmissible where an application relating to the same subject matter and cause of action, and involving the same parties, has been adjudicated on its merits, either by the Office or by an EU trade mark court as referred to in Article 123, and the decision of the Office or that court on that application has acquired the authority of a final decision.

Article 64 Examination of the application

1.   On the examination of the application for revocation of rights or for a declaration of invalidity, the Office shall invite the parties, as often as necessary, to file observations, within a period to be fixed by the Office, on communications from the other parties or issued by itself.

2.   If the proprietor of the EU trade mark so requests, the proprietor of an earlier EU trade mark, being a party to the invalidity proceedings, shall furnish proof that, during the period of five years preceding the date of the application for a declaration of invalidity, the earlier EU trade mark has been put to genuine use in the Union in connection with the goods or services in respect of which it is registered and which the proprietor of that earlier trade mark cites as justification for his application, or that there are proper reasons for non-use, provided that the earlier EU trade mark has at that date been registered for not less than five years. If, at the date on which the EU trade mark application was filed or at the priority date of the EU trade mark application, the earlier EU trade mark had been registered for not less than five years, the proprietor of the earlier EU trade mark shall furnish proof that, in addition, the conditions set out in Article 47(2) were satisfied at that date. In the absence of proof to this effect, the application for a declaration of invalidity shall be rejected. If the earlier EU trade mark has been used only in relation to part of the goods or services for which it is registered, it shall, for the purpose of the examination of the application for a declaration of invalidity, be deemed to be registered in respect of that part of the goods or services only.

3.   Paragraph 2 shall apply to earlier national trade marks referred to in Article 8(2)(a), by substituting use in the Member State in which the earlier national trade mark is protected for use in the Union.

. . .

5.   If the examination of the application for revocation of rights or for a declaration of invalidity reveals that the trade mark should not have been registered in respect of some or all of the goods or services for which it is registered, the rights of the proprietor of the EU trade mark shall be revoked or it shall be declared invalid in respect of those goods or services. Otherwise the application for revocation of rights or for a declaration of invalidity shall be rejected.

. . .

CHAPTER VII
APPEALS

Article 66 Decisions subject to appeal

1.   An appeal shall lie from decisions of any of the decision-making instances of the Office listed in points (a) to (d) of Article 159, and, where appropriate, point (f) of that Article. Those decisions shall take effect only as from the date of expiration of the appeal period referred to in Article 68. The filing of the appeal shall have suspensive effect.

2.   A decision which does not terminate proceedings as regards one of the parties can only be appealed together with the final decision, unless the decision allows separate appeal.

Article 67 Persons entitled to appeal and to be parties to appeal proceedings

Any party to proceedings adversely affected by a decision may appeal. Any other parties to the proceedings shall be parties to the appeal proceedings as of right.

Article 68 Time limit and form of appeal

1.   Notice of appeal shall be filed in writing at the Office within two months of the date of notification of the decision. The notice shall be deemed to have been filed only when the fee for appeal has been paid. It shall be filed in the language of the proceedings in which the decision subject to appeal was taken. Within four months of the date of notification of the decision, a written statement setting out the grounds of appeal shall be filed.

2.   In *inter partes* proceedings, the defendant may, in his response, seek a decision annulling or altering the contested decision on a point not raised in the appeal. Such submissions shall cease to have effect should the appellant discontinue the proceedings.

Article 69 Revision of decisions in ex parte cases

1.   If the party which has lodged the appeal is the sole party to the procedure, and if the department whose decision is contested considers the appeal to be admissible and well founded, the department shall rectify its decision.

. . .

Article 70 Examination of appeals

1.   If the appeal is admissible, the Board of Appeal shall examine whether the appeal is allowable.

. . .

Article 71 Decisions in respect of appeals

1.   Following the examination as to the allowability of the appeal, the Board of Appeal shall decide on the appeal. The Board of Appeal may either exercise any power within the competence of the department which was responsible for the decision appealed or remit the case to that department for further prosecution.

. . .

Article 72 Actions before the Court of Justice

1.   Actions may be brought before the General Court against decisions of the Boards of Appeal in relation to appeals.
2.   The action may be brought on grounds of lack of competence, infringement of an essential procedural requirement, infringement of the TFEU, infringement of this Regulation or of any rule of law relating to their application or misuse of power.
3.   The General Court shall have jurisdiction to annul or to alter the contested decision.

. . .

CHAPTER VIII
SPECIFIC PROVISIONS ON EUROPEAN UNION COLLECTIVE MARKS AND
CERTIFICATION MARKS

SECTION 1
EU COLLECTIVE MARKS

Article 74 EU collective marks

1.   A European Union collective mark ("EU collective mark") shall be an EU trade mark which is described as such when the mark is applied for and is capable of distinguishing the goods or services of the members of the association which is the proprietor of the mark from those of other undertakings. Associations of manufacturers, producers, suppliers of services, or traders which, under the terms of the law governing them, have the capacity in their own name to have rights and obligations of all kinds, to make contracts or accomplish other legal acts, and to sue and be sued, as well as legal persons governed by public law, may apply for EU collective marks.
2.   By way of derogation from Article 7(1)(c), signs or indications which may serve, in trade, to designate the geographical origin of the goods or services may constitute EU collective marks within the meaning of paragraph 1. An EU collective mark shall not entitle the proprietor to prohibit a third party from using in the course of trade such signs or indications, provided that he uses them in accordance with honest practices in industrial or commercial matters; in particular, such a mark shall not be invoked against a third party who is entitled to use a geographical name.
3.   Chapters I to VII and IX to XIV shall apply to EU collective marks to the extent that this section does not provide otherwise.

Article 75 Regulations governing use of an EU collective mark

1.   An applicant for an EU collective mark shall submit regulations governing use within two months of the date of filing.

2.   The regulations governing use shall specify the persons authorised to use the mark, the conditions of membership of the association and, where they exist, the conditions of use of the mark, including sanctions. The regulations governing use of a mark referred to in Article 74(2) shall authorise any person whose goods or services originate in the geographical area concerned to become a member of the association which is the proprietor of the mark.

. . .

Article 76 Refusal of the application

1.   In addition to the grounds for refusal of an EU trade mark application provided for in Articles 41 and 42, an application for an EU collective mark shall be refused where the provisions of Articles 74 or 75 are not satisfied, or where the regulations governing use are contrary to public policy or to accepted principles of morality.
2.   An application for an EU collective mark shall also be refused if the public is liable to be misled as regards the character or the significance of the mark, in particular if it is likely to be taken to be something other than a collective mark.
3.   An application shall not be refused if the applicant, as a result of amendment of the regulations governing use, meets the requirements of paragraphs 1 and 2.

Article 77 Observations by third parties

Where written observations on an EU collective mark are submitted to the Office pursuant to Article 45, those observations may also be based on the particular grounds on which the application for an EU collective mark should be refused pursuant to Article 76.

Article 78 Use of marks

Use of an EU collective mark by any person who has authority to use it shall satisfy the requirements of this Regulation, provided that the other conditions which this Regulation imposes with regard to the use of EU trade marks are fulfilled.

. . .

Article 80 Persons who are entitled to bring an action for infringement

1.   The provisions of Article 25(3) and (4) concerning the rights of licensees shall apply to every person who has authority to use an EU collective mark.
2.   The proprietor of an EU collective mark shall be entitled to claim compensation on behalf of persons who have authority to use the mark where they have sustained damage in consequence of unauthorised use of the mark.

Article 81 Grounds for revocation

Apart from the grounds for revocation provided for in Article 58, the rights of the proprietor of an EU collective mark shall be revoked on application to the Office or on the basis of a counterclaim in infringement proceedings, if:

(a)   the proprietor does not take reasonable steps to prevent the mark being used in a manner incompatible with the conditions of use, where these exist, laid down in the regulations governing use, amendments to which have, where appropriate, been mentioned in the Register;
(b)   the manner in which the mark has been used by the proprietor has caused it to become liable to mislead the public in the manner referred to in Article 76(2);
(c)   an amendment to the regulations governing use of the mark has been mentioned in the Register in breach of the provisions of Article 79(2), unless the proprietor of the mark, by further amending the regulations governing use, complies with the requirements of those provisions.

Article 82 Grounds for invalidity

Apart from the grounds for invalidity provided for in Articles 59 and 60, an EU collective mark which is registered in breach of the provisions of Article 76 shall be declared invalid on application to the Office or on the basis of a counterclaim in infringement proceedings, unless the proprietor of the mark, by amending the regulations governing use, complies with the requirements of those provisions.

SECTION 2
EU CERTIFICATION MARKS

Article 83 EU certification marks

1.   An EU certification mark shall be an EU trade mark which is described as such when the mark is applied for and is capable of distinguishing goods or services which are certified by the proprietor of the mark in respect of material, mode of manufacture of goods or performance of services, quality, accuracy or other characteristics, with the exception of geographical origin, from goods and services which are not so certified.

2.   Any natural or legal person, including institutions, authorities and bodies governed by public law, may apply for EU certification marks provided that such person does not carry on a business involving the supply of goods or services of the kind certified.

3.   Chapters I to VII and IX to XIV shall apply to EU certification marks to the extent that this Section does not provide otherwise.

Article 84 Regulations governing use of an EU certification mark

1.   An applicant for an EU certification mark shall submit regulations governing the use of the EU certification mark within two months of the date of filing.

2.   The regulations governing use shall specify the persons authorised to use the mark, the characteristics to be certified by the mark, how the certifying body is to test those characteristics and to supervise the use of the mark. Those regulations shall also specify the conditions of use of the mark, including sanctions.

. . .

Article 85 Refusal of the application

1.   In addition to the grounds for refusal of an EU trade mark application provided for in Articles 41 and 42, an application for an EU certification mark shall be refused where the conditions set out in Articles 83 and 84 are not satisfied, or where the regulations governing use are contrary to public policy or to accepted principles of morality.

2.   An application for an EU certification mark shall also be refused if the public is liable to be misled as regards the character or the significance of the mark, in particular if it is likely to be taken to be something other than a certification mark.

3.   An application shall not be refused if the applicant, as a result of an amendment of the regulations governing use, meets the requirements of paragraphs 1 and 2.

Article 86 Observations by third parties

Where written observations on an EU certification mark are submitted to the Office pursuant to Article 45, those observations may also be based on the particular grounds on which the application for an EU certification mark should be refused pursuant to Article 85.

Article 87 Use of the EU certification mark

Use of an EU certification mark by any person who has authority to use it pursuant to the regulations governing use referred to in Article 84 shall satisfy the requirements of this Regulation, provided that the other conditions laid down in this Regulation with regard to the use of EU trade marks are fulfilled.

. . .

Article 89 Transfer

By way of derogation from Article 20(1), an EU certification mark may only be transferred to a person who meets the requirements of Article 83(2).

Article 90 Persons who are entitled to bring an action for infringement

1.   Only the proprietor of an EU certification mark, or any person specifically authorised by him to that effect, shall be entitled to bring an action for infringement.

2.   The proprietor of an EU certification mark shall be entitled to claim compensation on behalf of persons who have authority to use the mark where they have sustained damage as a consequence of unauthorised use of the mark.

Article 91 Grounds for revocation

In addition to the grounds for revocation provided for in Article 58, the rights of the proprietor of an EU certification mark shall be revoked on application to the Office or on the basis of a counterclaim in infringement proceedings, where any of the following conditions is fulfilled:

(a) the proprietor no longer complies with the requirements set out in Article 83(2);

(b) the proprietor does not take reasonable steps to prevent the EU certification mark being used in a manner that is incompatible with the conditions of use laid down in the regulations governing use, amendments to which have, where appropriate, been mentioned in the Register;

(c) the manner in which the EU certification mark has been used by the proprietor has caused it to become liable to mislead the public in the manner referred to in Article 85(2);

(d) an amendment to the regulations governing use of the EU certification mark has been mentioned in the Register in breach of Article 88(2), unless the proprietor of the mark, by further amending the regulations governing use, complies with the requirements of that Article.

Article 92 Grounds for invalidity

In addition to the grounds for invalidity provided for in Articles 59 and 60, an EU certification mark which is registered in breach of Article 85 shall be declared invalid on application to the Office or on the basis of a counterclaim in infringement proceedings, unless the proprietor of the EU certification mark, by amending the regulations governing use, complies with the requirements of Article 85.

Article 93 Conversion

Without prejudice to Article 139(2), conversion of an application for an EU certification mark or of a registered EU certification mark shall not take place where the national law of the Member State concerned does not provide for the registration of guarantee or certification marks pursuant to Article 28 of Directive (EU) 2015/2436.

. . .

Article 101 Time limits

1. Time limits shall be laid down in terms of full years, months, weeks or days. Calculation shall start on the day following the day on which the relevant event occurred. The duration of time limits shall be no less than one month and no more than six months.

. . .

Article 104 Restitutio in integrum

1. The applicant for or proprietor of an EU trade mark or any other party to proceedings before the Office who, in spite of all due care required by the circumstances having been taken, was unable to comply with a time limit vis-à-vis the Office shall, upon application, have his rights re-established if the obstacle to compliance has the direct consequence, by virtue of the provisions of this Regulation, of causing the loss of any right or means of redress.

2. The application shall be filed in writing within two months of the removal of the obstacle to compliance with the time limit. The omitted act shall be completed within this period. The application shall only be admissible within the year immediately following the expiry of the unobserved time limit. In the case of non-submission of the request for renewal of registration or of non-payment of a renewal fee, the further period of six months provided in the third sentence of Article 53(3) shall be deducted from the period of one year.

. . .

6. Where the applicant for or proprietor of an EU trade mark has his rights re-established, he may not invoke his rights vis-à-vis a third party who, in good faith, has put goods on the market or supplied services under a sign which is identical with, or similar to, the EU trade mark in the course of the period between the loss of rights in the application or in the EU trade mark and publication of the mention of re-establishment of those rights.

7. A third party who may avail himself of the provisions of paragraph 6 may bring third party proceedings against the decision re-establishing the rights of the applicant for or proprietor of an EU trade mark within a period of two months as from the date of publication of the mention of re-establishment of those rights.

. . .

SECTION 3

INFORMATION WHICH MAY BE MADE AVAILABLE TO THE PUBLIC AND TO THE AUTHORITIES OF THE MEMBER STATES

Article 111 Register of EU trade marks

1. The Office shall keep a Register of EU trade marks which it shall keep up to date.

. . .

9. All the data, including personal data, concerning the entries in paragraphs 2 and 3 shall be considered to be of public interest and may be accessed by any third party. For reasons of legal certainty, the entries in the Register shall be kept for an indefinite period of time.

. . .

CHAPTER X

JURISDICTION AND PROCEDURE IN LEGAL ACTIONS RELATING TO EU TRADE MARKS

SECTION 1

APPLICATION OF UNION RULES ON JURISDICTION AND THE RECOGNITION AND ENFORCEMENT OF JUDGMENTS IN CIVIL AND COMMERCIAL MATTERS

Article 122 Application of Union rules on jurisdiction and the recognition and enforcement of judgments in civil and commercial matters

1. Unless otherwise specified in this Regulation, the Union rules on jurisdiction and the recognition and enforcement of judgments in civil and commercial matters shall apply to proceedings relating to EU trade marks and applications for EU trade marks, as well as to proceedings relating to simultaneous and successive actions on the basis of EU trade marks and national trade marks.

SECTION 2

DISPUTES CONCERNING THE INFRINGEMENT AND VALIDITY OF EU TRADE MARKS

. . .

Article 124 Jurisdiction over infringement and validity

The EU trade mark courts shall have exclusive jurisdiction:

(a) for all infringement actions and — if they are permitted under national law — actions in respect of threatened infringement relating to EU trade marks;
(b) for actions for declaration of non-infringement, if they are permitted under national law;
(c) for all actions brought as a result of acts referred to in Article 11(2);
(d) for counterclaims for revocation or for a declaration of invalidity of the EU trade mark pursuant to Article 128.

Article 125 International jurisdiction

1. Subject to the provisions of this Regulation as well as to any provisions of Regulation (EU) No 1215/2012 applicable by virtue of Article 122, proceedings in respect of the actions and claims referred to in Article 124 shall be brought in the courts of the Member State in which the defendant is domiciled or, if he is not domiciled in any of the Member States, in which he has an establishment.
2. If the defendant is neither domiciled nor has an establishment in any of the Member States, such proceedings shall be brought in the courts of the Member State in which the plaintiff is domiciled or, if he is not domiciled in any of the Member States, in which he has an establishment.
3. If neither the defendant nor the plaintiff is so domiciled or has such an establishment, such proceedings shall be brought in the courts of the Member State where the Office has its seat.
4. Notwithstanding the provisions of paragraphs 1, 2 and 3:
(a) Article 25 of Regulation (EU) No 1215/2012 shall apply if the parties agree that a different EU trade mark court shall have jurisdiction;
(b) Article 26 of Regulation (EU) No 1215/2012 shall apply if the defendant enters an appearance before a different EU trade mark court.

5.   Proceedings in respect of the actions and claims referred to in Article 124, with the exception of actions for a declaration of non-infringement of an EU trade mark, may also be brought in the courts of the Member State in which the act of infringement has been committed or threatened, or in which an act referred to in Article 11(2) has been committed.

Article 126 Extent of jurisdiction

1.   An EU trade mark court whose jurisdiction is based on Article 125(1) to (4) shall have jurisdiction in respect of:
   (a)   acts of infringement committed or threatened within the territory of any of the Member States;
   (b)   acts referred to in Article 11(2) committed within the territory of any of the Member States.
2.   An EU trade mark court whose jurisdiction is based on Article 125(5) shall have jurisdiction only in respect of acts committed or threatened within the territory of the Member State in which that court is situated.

Article 127 Presumption of validity — Defence as to the merits

1.   The EU trade mark courts shall treat the EU trade mark as valid unless its validity is put in issue by the defendant with a counterclaim for revocation or for a declaration of invalidity.
2.   The validity of an EU trade mark may not be put in issue in an action for a declaration of non-infringement.
3.   In the actions referred to in points (a) and (c) of Article 124, a plea relating to revocation of the EU trade mark submitted otherwise than by way of a counterclaim shall be admissible where the defendant claims that the EU trade mark could be revoked for lack of genuine use at the time the infringement action was brought.

Article 128 Counterclaims

1.   A counterclaim for revocation or for a declaration of invalidity may only be based on the grounds for revocation or invalidity mentioned in this Regulation.
2.   An EU trade mark court shall reject a counterclaim for revocation or for a declaration of invalidity if a decision taken by the Office relating to the same subject matter and cause of action and involving the same parties has already become final.
3.   If the counterclaim is brought in a legal action to which the proprietor of the trade mark is not already a party, he shall be informed thereof and may be joined as a party to the action in accordance with the conditions set out in national law.
4.   The EU trade mark court with which a counterclaim for revocation or for a declaration of invalidity of the EU trade mark has been filed shall not proceed with the examination of the counterclaim, until either the interested party or the court has informed the Office of the date on which the counterclaim was filed. The Office shall record that information in the Register. If an application for revocation or for a declaration of invalidity of the EU trade mark had already been filed before the Office before the counterclaim was filed, the court shall be informed thereof by the Office and stay the proceedings in accordance with Article 132(1) until the decision on the application is final or the application is withdrawn.
5.   Article 64(2) to (5) shall apply.
6.   Where an EU trade mark court has given a judgment which has become final on a counterclaim for revocation or for a declaration of invalidity of an EU trade mark, a copy of the judgment shall be sent to the Office without delay, either by the court or by any of the parties to the national proceedings. The Office or any other interested party may request information about such transmission. The Office shall mention the judgment in the Register and shall take the necessary measures to comply with its operative part.
7.   The EU trade mark court hearing a counterclaim for revocation or for a declaration of invalidity may stay the proceedings on application by the proprietor of the EU trade mark and after hearing the other parties and may request the defendant to submit an application for revocation or for a declaration of invalidity to the Office within a time limit which it shall determine. If the application is not made within the time limit, the proceedings shall continue; the counterclaim shall be deemed withdrawn. Article 132(3) shall apply.

Article 129 Applicable law

1.   The EU trade mark courts shall apply the provisions of this Regulation.
2.   On all trade mark matters not covered by this Regulation, the relevant EU trade mark court shall apply the applicable national law.

3.   Unless otherwise provided for in this Regulation, an EU trade mark court shall apply the rules of procedure governing the same type of action relating to a national trade mark in the Member State in which the court is located.

Article 130 Sanctions

1.   Where an EU trade mark court finds that the defendant has infringed or threatened to infringe an EU trade mark, it shall, unless there are special reasons for not doing so, issue an order prohibiting the defendant from proceeding with the acts which infringed or would infringe the EU trade mark. It shall also take such measures in accordance with its national law as are aimed at ensuring that this prohibition is complied with.

2.   The EU trade mark court may also apply measures or orders available under the applicable law which it deems appropriate in the circumstances of the case.

. . .

Article 133 Jurisdiction of EU trade mark courts of second instance — Further appeal

1.   An appeal to the EU trade mark courts of second instance shall lie from judgments of the EU trade mark courts of first instance in respect of proceedings arising from the actions and claims referred to in Article 124.

2.   The conditions under which an appeal may be lodged with an EU trade mark court of second instance shall be determined by the national law of the Member State in which that court is located.

3.   The national rules concerning further appeal shall be applicable in respect of judgments of EU trade mark courts of second instance.

SECTION 3
OTHER DISPUTES CONCERNING EU TRADE MARKS

Article 134 Supplementary provisions on the jurisdiction of national courts other than EU trade mark courts

1.   Within the Member State whose courts have jurisdiction under Article 122(1) those courts shall have jurisdiction for actions other than those referred to in Article 124, which would have jurisdiction *ratione loci* and *ratione materiae* in the case of actions relating to a national trade mark registered in that State.

2.   Actions relating to an EU trade mark, other than those referred to in Article 124, for which no court has jurisdiction under Article 122(1) and paragraph 1 of this Article may be heard before the courts of the Member State in which the Office has its seat.

Article 135 Obligation of the national court

A national court which is dealing with an action relating to an EU trade mark, other than the action referred to in Article 124, shall treat the EU trade mark as valid.

CHAPTER XI
EFFECTS ON THE LAWS OF THE MEMBER STATES

. . .

SECTION 2
APPLICATION OF NATIONAL LAWS FOR THE PURPOSE OF PROHIBITING THE USE OF
EU TRADE MARKS

Article 137 Prohibition of use of EU trade marks

1.   This Regulation shall, unless otherwise provided for, not affect the right existing under the laws of the Member States to invoke claims for infringement of earlier rights within the meaning of Article 8 or Article 60(2) in relation to the use of a later EU trade mark. Claims for infringement of earlier rights within the meaning of Article 8(2) and (4) may, however, no longer be invoked if the proprietor of the earlier right may no longer apply for a declaration that the EU trade mark is invalid in accordance with Article 61(2).

2.   This Regulation shall, unless otherwise provided for, not affect the right to bring proceedings under the civil, administrative or criminal law of a Member State or under provisions of Union law for the purpose of prohibiting the use of an EU trade mark to the extent that the use of a national trade mark may be prohibited under the law of that Member State or under Union law.

Article 138 Prior rights applicable to particular localities

1.   The proprietor of an earlier right which only applies to a particular locality may oppose the use of the EU trade mark in the territory where his right is protected in so far as the law of the Member State concerned so permits.

2.   Paragraph 1 shall cease to apply if the proprietor of the earlier right has acquiesced in the use of the EU trade mark in the territory where his right is protected for a period of five successive years, being aware of such use, unless the EU trade mark was applied for in bad faith.

3.   The proprietor of the EU trade mark shall not be entitled to oppose use of the right referred to in paragraph 1 even though that right may no longer be invoked against the EU trade mark.

SECTION 3
CONVERSION INTO A NATIONAL TRADE MARK APPLICATION

Article 139 Request for the application of national procedure

1.   The applicant for or proprietor of an EU trade mark may request the conversion of his EU trade mark application or EU trade mark into a national trade mark application:

    (a)   to the extent that the EU trade mark application is refused, withdrawn, or deemed to be withdrawn;

    (b)   to the extent that the EU trade mark ceases to have effect.

. . .

CHAPTER XIII
INTERNATIONAL REGISTRATION OF MARKS

SECTION I
GENERAL PROVISIONS

Article 182 Application of provisions

Unless otherwise specified in this chapter, this Regulation and the acts adopted pursuant to this Regulation shall apply to applications for international registrations under the Madrid Protocol ("international applications"), based on an application for an EU trade mark or on an EU trade mark and to registrations of marks in the international register maintained by the International Bureau of the World Intellectual Property Organisation ("international registrations' and 'the International Bureau", respectively) designating the Union.

. . .

SECTION 2
INTERNATIONAL REGISTRATIONS DESIGNATING THE UNION

Article 189 Effects of international registrations designating the Union

1.   An international registration designating the Union shall, from the date of its registration pursuant to Article 3(4) of the Madrid Protocol or from the date of the subsequent designation of the Union pursuant to Article 3ter(2) of the Madrid Protocol, have the same effect as an application for an EU trade mark.

. . .

Article 191 Seniority claimed in an international application

1.   The applicant for an international registration designating the Union may claim, in the international application, the seniority of an earlier trade mark registered in a Member State, including a trade mark registered in the Benelux countries, or registered under international arrangements having effect in a Member State, as provided for in Article 39.

. . .

MADRID AGREEMENT CONCERNING THE INTERNATIONAL REGISTRATION OF MARKS
of April 14, 1891, as revised
and as amended on September 28, 1979

Article 1

(1)   The countries to which this Agreement applies constitute a Special Union for the International registration of marks.

(2)   Nationals of any of the contracting countries may, in all the other countries party to this Agreement, secure protection for their marks applicable to goods or services, registered in the country of origin, by filing the said marks at the International Bureau of Intellectual Property (hereinafter designated as "the International Bureau") referred to in the Convention establishing the World Intellectual Property Organization (hereinafter designated as "the Organization"), through the intermediary of the Office of the said country of origin.

(3)   Shall be considered the country of origin the country of the Special Union where the applicant has a real and effective industrial or commercial establishment; if he has no such establishment in a country of the Special Union, the country of the Special Union where he has his domicile; if he has no domicile within the Special Union but is a national of a country of the Special Union, the country of which he is a national.

Article 2

Nationals of countries not having acceded to this Agreement who, within the territory of the Special Union constituted by the said Agreement, satisfy the conditions specified in Article 3 of the Paris Convention for the Protection of Industrial Property shall be treated in the same manner as nationals of the contracting countries.

Article 3

(1)   Every application for international registration must be presented on the form prescribed by the Regulations; the Office of the country of origin of the mark shall certify that the particulars appearing in such application correspond to the particulars in the national register, and shall mention the dates and numbers of the filing and registration of the mark in the country of origin and also the date of the application for international registration.

(2)   The applicant must indicate the goods or services in respect of which protection of the mark is claimed and also, if possible, the corresponding class or classes according to the classification established by the Nice Agreement concerning the International Classification of Goods and Services for the Purposes of the Registration of Marks. If the applicant does not give such indication, the International Bureau shall classify the goods or services in the appropriate classes of the said classification. The indication of classes given by the applicant shall be subject to control by the International Bureau, which shall exercise the said control in association with the national Office. In the event of disagreement between the national Office and the International Bureau, the opinion of the latter shall prevail.

(3)   If the applicant claims color as a distinctive feature of his mark, he shall be required:

1.   to state the fact, and to file with his application a notice specifying the color or the combination of colors claimed;

2.   to append to his application copies in color of the said mark, which shall be attached to the notification given by the International Bureau. The number of such copies shall be fixed by the Regulations.

(4)   The International Bureau shall register immediately the marks filed in accordance with Article 1. The registration shall bear the date of the application for international registration in the country of origin, provided that the application has been received by the International Bureau within a period of two months from that date. If the application has not been received within that period, the International Bureau shall record it as at the date on which it received the said application. The International Bureau shall notify such registration without delay to the Offices concerned. Registered marks shall be published in a periodical journal issued by the International Bureau, on the basis of the particulars contained in the application for registration. In the case of marks comprising a figurative element or a special form of writing, the Regulations shall determine whether a printing block must be supplied by the applicant.

(5)   With a view to the publicity to be given in the contracting countries to registered marks, each Office shall receive from the International Bureau a number of copies of the said publication free of charge and a number of copies at a reduced price, in proportion to the number of units mentioned in Article 16(4)(a) of the Paris Convention for the Protection of Industrial Property, under the conditions fixed by the Regulations. Such publicity shall be deemed in all the contracting countries to be sufficient, and no other publicity may be required of the applicant.

Article 3*bis*

(1)   Any contracting country may, at any time, notify the Director General of the Organization (hereinafter designated as "the Director General") in writing that the protection resulting from the international registration shall extend to that country only at the express request of the proprietor of the mark.

(2)   Such notification shall not take effect until six months after the date of the communication thereof by the Director General to the other contracting countries.

Article 3*ter*

(1)   Any request for extension of the protection resulting from the international registration to a country which has availed itself of the right provided for in Article 3*bis* must be specially mentioned in the application referred to in Article 3(1).

(2)   Any request for territorial extension made subsequently to the international registration must be presented through the intermediary of the Office of the country of origin on a form prescribed by the Regulations. It shall be immediately registered by the International Bureau, which shall notify it without delay to the Office or Offices concerned. It shall be published in the periodical journal issued by the International Bureau. Such territorial extension shall be effective from the date on which it has been recorded in the International Register; it shall cease to be valid on the expiration of the international registration of the mark to which it relates.

Article 4

(1)   From the date of the registration so effected at the International Bureau in accordance with the provisions of Articles 3 and 3ter, the protection of the mark in each of the contracting countries concerned shall be the same as if the mark had been filed therein direct. The indication of classes of goods or services provided for in Article 3 shall not bind the contracting countries with regard to the determination of the scope of the protection of the mark.

(2)   Every mark which has been the subject of an international registration shall enjoy the right of priority provided for by Article 4 of the Paris Convention for the Protection of Industrial Property, without requiring compliance with the formalities prescribed in Section D of that Article.

Article 4*bis*

(1)   When a mark already filed in one or more of the contracting countries is later registered by the International Bureau in the name of the same proprietor or his successor in title, the international registration shall be deemed to have replaced the earlier national registrations, without prejudice to any rights acquired by reason of such earlier registrations.

(2)   The national Office shall, upon request, be required to take note in its registers of the international registration.

Article 5

(1)   In countries where the legislation so authorizes, Offices notified by the International Bureau of the registration of a mark or of a request for extension of protection made in accordance with Article 3*ter* shall have the right to declare that protection cannot be granted to such mark in their territory. Any such refusal can be based only on the grounds which would apply, under the Paris Convention for the Protection of Industrial Property, in the case of a mark filed for national registration. However, protection may not be refused, even partially, by reason only that national legislation would not permit registration except in a limited number of classes or for a limited number of goods or services.

(2)   Offices wishing to exercise such right must give notice of their refusal to the International Bureau, together with a statement of all grounds, within the period prescribed by their

domestic law and, at the latest, before the expiration of one year from the date of the international registration of the mark or of the request for extension of protection made in accordance with Article 3ter.

(3)   The International Bureau shall, without delay, transmit to the Office of the country of origin and to the proprietor of the mark, or to his agent if an agent has been mentioned to the Bureau by the said Office, one of the copies of the declaration of refusal so notified. The interested party shall have the same remedies as if the mark had been filed by him direct in the country where protection is refused.

(4)   The grounds for refusing a mark shall be communicated by the International Bureau to any interested party who may so request.

(5)   Offices which, within the aforesaid maximum period of one year, have not communicated to the International Bureau any provisional or final decision of refusal with regard to the registration of a mark or a request for extension of protection shall lose the benefit of the right provided for in paragraph (1) of this Article with respect to the mark in question.

(6)   Invalidation of an international mark may not be pronounced by the competent authorities without the proprietor of the mark having, in good time, been afforded the opportunity of defending his rights. Invalidation shall be notified to the International Bureau.

Article 5bis

Documentary evidence of the legitimacy of the use of certain elements incorporated in a mark, such as armorial bearings, escutcheons, portraits, honorary distinctions, titles, trade names, names of persons other than the name of the applicant, or other like inscriptions, which might be required by the Offices of the contracting countries shall be exempt from any legalization or certification other than that of the Office of the country of origin.

Article 5ter

(1)   The International Bureau shall issue to any person applying therefor, subject to a fee fixed by the Regulations, a copy of the entries in the Register relating to a specific mark.

(2)   The International Bureau may also, upon payment, undertake searches for anticipation among international marks.

(3)   Extracts from the International Register requested with a view to their production in one of the contracting countries shall be exempt from all legalization.

Article 6

(1)   Registration of a mark at the International Bureau is effected for twenty years, with the possibility of renewal under the conditions specified in Article 7.

(2)   Upon expiration of a period of five years from the date of the international registration, such registration shall become independent of the national mark registered earlier in the country of origin, subject to the following provisions.

(3)   The protection resulting from the international registration, whether or not it has been the subject of a transfer, may no longer be invoked, in whole or in part, if, within five years from the date of the international registration, the national mark, registered earlier in the country of origin in accordance with Article 1, no longer enjoys, in whole or in part, legal protection in that country. This provision shall also apply when legal protection has later ceased as the result of an action begun before the expiration of the period of five years.

(4)   In the case of voluntary or ex officio cancellation, the Office of the country of origin shall request the cancellation of the mark at the International Bureau, and the latter shall effect the cancellation. In the case of judicial action, the said Office shall send to the International Bureau, ex officio or at the request of the plaintiff, a copy of the complaint or any other documentary evidence that an action has begun, and also of the final decision of the court; the Bureau shall enter notice thereof in the International Register.

Article 7

(1)   Any registration may be renewed for a period of twenty years from the expiration of the preceding period, by payment only of the basic fee and, where necessary, of the supplementary and complementary fees provided for in Article 8(2).

(2)   Renewal may not include any change in relation to the previous registration in its latest form.

(3)   The first renewal effected under the provisions of the Nice Act of June 15, 1957, or of this Act, shall include an indication of the classes of the International Classification to which the registration relates.

(4)	Six months before the expiration of the term of protection, the International Bureau shall, by sending an unofficial notice, remind the proprietor of the mark and his agent of the exact date of expiration.

(5)	Subject to the payment of a surcharge fixed by the Regulations, a period of grace of six months shall be granted for renewal of the international registration.

Article 8

(1)	The Office of the country of origin may fix, at its own discretion, and collect, for its own benefit, a national fee which it may require from the proprietor of the mark in respect of which international registration or renewal is applied for.

(2)	Registration of a mark at the International Bureau shall be subject to the advance payment of an international fee . . .

Article 8*bis*

The person in whose name the international registration stands may at any time renounce protection in one or more of the contracting countries by means of a declaration filed with the Office of his own country, for communication to the International Bureau, which shall notify accordingly the countries in respect of which renunciation has been made. Renunciation shall not be subject to any fee.

Article 9

(1)	The Office of the country of the person in whose name the international registration stands shall likewise notify the International Bureau of all annulments, cancellations, renunciations, transfers, and other changes made in the entry of the mark in the national register, if such changes also affect the international registration.

(2)	The Bureau shall record those changes in the International Register, shall notify them in turn to the Offices of the contracting countries, and shall publish them in its journal.

(3)	A similar procedure shall be followed when the person in whose name the international registration stands requests a reduction of the list of goods or services to which the registration applies.

(4)	Such transactions may be subject to a fee, which shall be fixed by the Regulations.

(5)	The subsequent addition of new goods or services to the said list can be obtained only by filing a new application as prescribed in Article 3.

(6)	The substitution of one of the goods or services for another shall be treated as an addition.

Article 9*bis*

(1)	When a mark registered in the International Register is transferred to a person established in a contracting country other than the country of the person in whose name the international registration stands, the transfer shall be notified to the International Bureau by the Office of the latter country. The International Bureau shall record the transfer, shall notify the other Offices thereof, and shall publish it in its journal. If the transfer has been effected before the expiration of a period of five years from the international registration, the International Bureau shall seek the consent of the Office of the country of the new proprietor, and shall publish, if possible, the date and registration number of the mark in the country of the new proprietor.

(2)	No transfer of a mark registered in the International Register for the benefit of a person who is not entitled to file an international mark shall be recorded.

(3)	When it has not been possible to record a transfer in the International Register, either because the country of the new proprietor has refused its consent or because the said transfer has been made for the benefit of a person who is not entitled to apply for international registration, the Office of the country of the former proprietor shall have the right to demand that the International Bureau cancel the mark in its Register.

Article 9*ter*

(1)	If the assignment of an international mark for part only of the registered goods or services is notified to the International Bureau, the Bureau shall record it in its Register. Each of the contracting countries shall have the right to refuse to recognize the validity of such assignment if the goods or services included in the part so assigned are similar to those in respect of which the mark remains registered for the benefit of the assignor.

(2)   The International Bureau shall likewise record the assignment of an international mark in respect of one or several of the contracting countries only.

(3)   If, in the above cases, a change occurs in the country of the proprietor, the Office of the country to which the new proprietor belongs shall, if the international mark has been transferred before the expiration of a period of five years from the international registration, give its consent as required by Article 9*bis*.

(4)   The provisions of the foregoing paragraphs shall apply subject to Article 6quater of the Paris Convention for the Protection of Industrial Property.

Article 9*quater*

(1)   If several countries of the Special Union agree to effect the unification of their domestic legislations on marks, they may notify the Director General:

   (a)   that a common Office shall be substituted for the national Office of each of them, and
   (b)   that the whole of their respective territories shall be deemed to be a single country for the purposes of the application of all or part of the provisions preceding this Article.

(2)   Such notification shall not take effect until six months after the date of the communication thereof by the Director General to the other contracting countries.

Article 10

(1)   (a)   The Special Union shall have an Assembly consisting of those countries which have ratified or acceded to this Act.

   . . .

Article 11

(1)   (a)   International registration and related duties, as well as all other administrative tasks concerning the Special Union, shall be performed by the International Bureau.

   . . .

Article 14

(1)   Any country of the Special Union which has signed this Act may ratify it, and, if it has not signed it, may accede to it.

(2)   (a)   Any country outside the Special Union which is party to the Paris Convention for the Protection of Industrial Property may accede to this Act and thereby become a member of the Special Union.

   (b)   As soon as the International Bureau is informed that such a country has acceded to this Act, it shall address to the Office of that country, in accordance with Article 3, a collective notification of the marks which, at that time, enjoy international protection.

   (c)   Such notification shall, of itself, ensure to the said marks the benefits of the foregoing provisions in the territory of the said country, and shall mark the commencement of the period of one year during which the Office concerned may make the declaration provided for in Article 5.

   (d)   However, any such country may, in acceding to this Act, declare that, except in the case of international marks which have already been the subject in that country of an earlier identical national registration still in force, and which shall be immediately recognized upon the request of the interested parties, application of this Act shall be limited to marks registered from the date on which its accession enters into force.

   (e)   Such declaration shall dispense the International Bureau from making the collective notification referred to above. The International Bureau shall notify only those marks in respect of which it receives, within a period of one year from the accession of the new country, a request, with the necessary particulars, to take advantage of the exception provided for in subparagraph (d).

   (f)   The International Bureau shall not make the collective notification to such countries as declare, in acceding to this Act, that they are availing themselves of the right provided for in Article 3*bis*. The said countries may also declare at the same time that the application of this Act shall be limited to marks registered from the day on which their accessions enter into force; however, such limitation shall not affect international marks which have already been the subject of an earlier identical national registration in those countries, and which could give rise to requests for extension of protection made and notified in accordance with Articles 3*ter* and 8(2)(c).

(g)   Registrations of marks which have been the subject of one of the notifications provided for in this paragraph shall be regarded as replacing registrations effected direct in the new contracting country before the date of entry into force of its accession.

. . .

(7)   The provisions of Article 24 of the Paris Convention for the Protection of Industrial Property shall apply to this Agreement.

Article 16

. . .

(2)   Countries outside the Special Union which become party to this Act shall apply it to international registrations effected at the International Bureau through the intermediary of the national Office of any country of the Special Union not party to this Act, provided that such registrations satisfy, with respect to the said countries, the requirements of this Act. With regard to international registrations effected at the International Bureau through the intermediary of the national Offices of the said countries outside the Special Union which become party to this Act, such countries recognize that the aforesaid country of the Special Union may demand compliance with the requirements of the most recent Act to which it is party.

PROTOCOL
relating to the Madrid Agreement concerning the international registration of marks, adopted at
Madrid on 27 June 1989 (as amended on 12 November, 2007)

Article 1 Membership in the Madrid Union

The States party to this Protocol (hereinafter referred to as the contracting States), even where they are not party to the Madrid Agreement concerning the international registration of marks as revised at Stockholm in 1967 and as amended in 1979 (hereinafter referred to as the Madrid (Stockholm) Agreement), and the organisations referred to in Article 14(1)(b) which are party to this Protocol (hereinafter referred to as the contracting organisations) shall be members of the same Union of which countries party to the Madrid (Stockholm) Agreement are members. Any reference in this Protocol to "contracting parties" shall be construed as a reference to both contracting States and contracting organisations.

Article 2 Securing protection through international registration

1.   Where an application for the registration of a mark has been filed with the office of a contracting party, or where a mark has been registered in the register of the office of a contracting party, the person in whose name that application (hereinafter referred to as the basic application) or that registration (hereinafter referred to as the basic registration) stands may, subject to the provisions of this Protocol, secure protection for his mark in the territory of the contracting parties, by obtaining the registration of that mark in the register of the International Bureau of the World Intellectual Property Organisation (hereinafter referred to as "the international registration", "the International Register", "the International Bureau" and the "Organisation", respectively), provided that:

     (i)   where the basic application has been filed with the office of a contracting State or where the basic registration has been made by such an office, the person in whose name that application or registration stands is a national of that contracting State, or is domiciled, or has a real and effective industrial or commercial establishment, in the said contracting State;

     (ii)   where the basic application has been filed with the office of a contracting organisation or where the basic registration has been made by such an office, the person in whose name that application or registration stands is a national of a State member of that contracting organisation, or is domiciled, or has a real and effective industrial or commercial establishment, in the territory of the said contracting organisation.

2.   The application for international registration (hereinafter referred to as the international application) shall be filed with the International Bureau through the intermediary of the

office with which the basic application was filed or by which the basic registration was made (hereinafter referred to as the office of origin), as the case may be.

3.   Any reference in this Protocol to an "office" or an "office of a contracting party" shall be construed as a reference to the office that is in charge, on behalf of a contracting party, of the registration of marks, and any reference in this Protocol to "marks" shall be construed as a reference to trade marks and service marks.

4.   For the purposes of this Protocol, "territory of a contracting party" means, where the contracting party is a State, the territory of that State and, where the contracting party is an intergovernmental organisation, the territory in which the constituting treaty of that intergovernmental organisation applies.

Article 3 International application

1.   Every international application under this Protocol shall be presented on the form prescribed by the regulations. The office of origin shall certify that the particulars appearing in the international application correspond to the particulars appearing, at the time of the certification, in the basic application or basic registration, as the case may be. Furthermore, the said office shall indicate:
   (i)   in the case of a basic application, the date and number of that application;
   (ii)   in the case of a basic registration, the date and number of that registration as well as the date and number of the application from which the basic registration resulted. The office of origin shall also indicate the date of the international application.

2.   The applicant must indicate the goods and services in respect of which protection of the mark is claimed and also, if possible, the corresponding class or classes according to the classification established by the Nice Agreement concerning the international classification of goods and services for the purposes of the registration of marks. If the applicant does not give such indication, the International Bureau shall classify the goods and services in the appropriate classes of the said classification. The indication of classes given by the applicant shall be subject to control by the International Bureau, which shall exercise the said control in association with the office of origin. In the event of disagreement between the said office and the International Bureau, the opinion of the latter shall prevail.

3.   If the applicant claims colour as a distinctive feature of his mark, he shall be required:
   (i)   to state the fact, and to file with his international application a notice specifying the colour or the combination of colours claimed;
   (ii)   to append to his international application copies in colour of the said mark, which shall be attached to the notifications given by the International Bureau, the number of such copies shall be fixed by the regulations.

4.   The International Bureau shall register immediately the marks filed in accordance with Article 2. The international registration shall bear the date on which the international application was received in the office of origin, provided that the international application has been received by the International Bureau within a period of two months from that date. If the international application has not been received within that period, the international registration shall bear the date on which the said international application was received by the International Bureau. The International Bureau shall notify the international registration without delay to the offices concerned. Marks registered in the International Register shall be published in a periodical gazette issued by the International Bureau, on the basis of the particulars contained in the international application.

5.   With a view to the publicity to be given to marks registered in the International Register, each office shall receive from the International Bureau a number of copies of the said gazette free of charge and a number of copies at a reduced price, under the conditions fixed by the assembly referred to in Article 10 (hereinafter referred to as the assembly). Such publicity shall be deemed to be sufficient for the purposes of all the contracting parties, and no other publicity may be required of the holder of the international registration.

Article 3bis Territorial effect

The protection resulting from the international registration shall extend to any contracting party only at the request of the person who files the international application or who is the holder of the international registration. However, no such request can be made with respect to the contracting party whose office is the office of origin.

Article 3ter Request for "territorial extension"

1.   Any request for extension of the protection resulting from the international registration to any contracting party shall be specially mentioned in the international application.

2.   A request for territorial extension may also be made subsequently to the international registration. Any such request shall be presented on the form prescribed by the regulations. It shall be immediately recorded by the International Bureau, which shall notify such recordal without delay to the office or offices concerned. Such recordal shall be published in the periodical gazette of the International Bureau. Such territorial extension shall be effective from the date on which it has been recorded in the International Register; it shall cease to be valid on the expiry of the international registration to which it relates.

Article 4 Effects of international registration

1.   (a)   From the date of the registration or recordal effected in accordance with the provisions of Articles 3 and 3ter, the protection of the mark in each of the contracting parties concerned shall be the same as if the mark had been deposited direct with the office of that contracting party. If no refusal has been notified to the International Bureau in accordance with Article 5(1) and (2) or if a refusal notified in accordance with the said Article has been withdrawn subsequently, the protection of the mark in the contracting party concerned shall, as from the said date, be the same as if the mark had been registered by the office of that contracting party.

      (b)   The indication of classes of goods and services provided for in Article 3 shall not bind the contracting parties with regard to the determination of the scope of the protection of the mark.

2.   Every international registration shall enjoy the right of priority provided for by Article 4 of the Paris Convention for the protection of industrial property, without it being necessary to comply with the formalities prescribed in section D of that Article.

Article 4bis Replacement of a national or regional registration by an international registration

1.   Where a mark that is the subject of a national or regional registration in the office of a contracting party is also the subject of an international registration and both registrations stand in the name of the same person, the international registration is deemed to replace the national or regional registration, without prejudice to any rights acquired by virtue of the latter, provided that:

      (i)   the protection resulting from the international registration extends to the said contracting party under Article 3ter(1) or (2);

      (ii)   all the goods and services listed in the national or regional registration are also listed in the international registration in respect of the said contracting party;

      (iii) such extension takes effect after the date of the national or regional registration.

2.   The office referred to in paragraph 1 shall, upon request, be required to take note in its register of the international registration.

Article 5 Refusal and invalidation of effects of international registration in respect of certain contracting parties

1.   Where the applicable legislation so authorises, any office of a contracting party which has been notified by the International Bureau of an extension to that contracting party, under Article 3ter(1) or (2), of the protection resulting from the international registration shall have the right to declare in a notification of refusal that protection cannot be granted in the said contracting party to the mark which is the subject of such extension. Any such refusal can be based only on the grounds which would apply, under the Paris Convention for the protection of industrial property, in the case of a mark deposited direct with the office which notifies the refusal. However, protection may not be refused, even partially, by reason only that the applicable legislation would permit registration only in a limited number of classes or for a limited number of goods or services.

2.   (a)   Any office wishing to exercise such right shall notify its refusal to the International Bureau, together with a statement of all grounds, within the period prescribed by the law applicable to that office and at the latest, subject to subparagraphs (b) and (c), before the expiry of one year from the date on which the notification of the extension referred to in paragraph 1 has been sent to that office by the International Bureau.

(b) Notwithstanding subparagraph (a), any contracting party may declare that, for international registrations made under this Protocol, the time limit of one year referred to in subparagraph (a) is replaced by 18 months.

(c) Such declaration may also specify that, when a refusal of protection may result from an opposition to the granting of protection, such refusal may be notified by the office of the said contracting party to the International Bureau after the expiry of the 18-month time limit. Such an office may, with respect to any given international registration, notify a refusal of protection after the expiry of the 18-month time limit, but only if:

    (i) it has, before the expiry of the 18-month time limit, informed the International Bureau of the possibility that oppositions may be filed after the expiry of the 18-month time limit; and

    (ii) the notification of the refusal based on an opposition is made within a time limit of one month from the expiry of the opposition period and, in any case, not later than seven months from the date on which the opposition period begins.

(d) Any declaration under subparagraphs (b) or (c) may be made in the instruments referred to in Article 14(2), and the effective date of the declaration shall be the same as the date of entry into force of this Protocol with respect to the State or intergovernmental organisation having made the declaration. Any such declaration may also be made later, in which case the declaration shall have effect three months after its receipt by the Director-General of the organisation (hereinafter referred to as the Director-General), or at any later date indicated in the declaration, in respect of any international registration whose date is the same as or is later than the effective date of the declaration.

(e) Upon the expiry of a period of 10 years from the entry into force of this Protocol, the Assembly shall examine the operation of the system established by subparagraphs (a) to (d). Thereafter, the provisions of the said subparagraphs may be modified by a unanimous decision of the Assembly.

3. The International Bureau shall, without delay, transmit one of the copies of the notification of refusal to the holder of the international registration. The said holder shall have the same remedies as if the mark had been deposited by him direct with the office which has notified its refusal. Where the International Bureau has received information under paragraph 2(c)(i), it shall, without delay, transmit the said information to the holder of the international registration.

4. The grounds for refusing a mark shall be communicated by the International Bureau to any interested party who may so request.

5. Any office which has not notified, with respect to a given international registration, any provisional or final refusal to the International Bureau in accordance with paragraphs 1 and 2 shall, with respect to that international registration, lose the benefit of the right provided for in paragraph 1.

6. Invalidation, by the competent authorities of a contracting party, of the effects, in the territory of that contracting party, of an international registration may not be pronounced without the holder of such international registration having, in good time, been afforded the opportunity of defending his rights. Invalidation shall be notified to the International Bureau.

Article 5*bis* Documentary evidence of legitimacy of use of certain elements of the mark

Documentary evidence of the legitimacy of the use of certain elements incorporated in a mark, such as armorial bearings, escutcheons, portraits, honorary distinctions, titles, trade names, names of persons other than the name of the applicant, or other like inscriptions, which might be required by the offices of the contracting parties, shall be exempt from any legalisation as well as from any certification other than that of the office of origin.

Article 5*ter* Copies of entries in the International Register; searches for anticipations; extracts from the International Register

1. The International Bureau shall issue to any person applying therefor, upon the payment of a fee fixed by the regulations, a copy of the entries in the International Register concerning a specific mark.

2.   The International Bureau may also, upon payment, undertake searches for anticipations among marks that are the subject of international registrations.
3.   Extracts from the International Register requested with a view to their production in one of the contracting parties shall be exempt from any legalisation.

Article 6 Period of validity of international registration; dependence and independence of international registration

1.   Registration of a mark at the International Bureau is effected for 10 years, with the possibility of renewal under the conditions specified in Article 7.
2.   Upon expiry of a period of five years from the date of the international registration, such registration shall become independent of the basic application or the registration resulting therefrom, or of the basic registration, as the case may be, subject to the following provisions.
3.   The protection resulting from the international registration, whether or not it has been the subject of a transfer, may no longer be invoked if, before the expiry of five years from the date of the international registration, the basic application or the registration resulting therefrom, or the basic registration, as the case may be, has been withdrawn, has lapsed, has been renounced or has been the subject of a final decision of rejection, revocation, cancellation or invalidation, in respect of all or some of the goods and services listed in the international registration. The same applies if:
        (i)   an appeal against a decision refusing the effects of the basic application;
        (ii)   an action requesting the withdrawal of the basic application or the revocation, cancellation or invalidation of the registration resulting from the basic application or of the basic registration; or
        (iii) an opposition to the basic application
        results, after the expiry of the five-year period, in a final decision of rejection, revocation, cancellation or invalidation, or ordering the withdrawal, of the basic application, or the registration resulting therefrom, or the basic registration, as the case may be, provided that such appeal, action or opposition had begun before the expiry of the said period. The same also applies if the basic application is withdrawn, or the registration resulting from the basic application or the basic registration is renounced, after the expiry of the five-year period, provided that, at the time of the withdrawal or renunciation, the said application or registration was the subject of a proceeding referred to in item (i), (ii) or (iii) and that such proceeding had begun before the expiry of the said period.
4.   The office of origin shall, as prescribed in the regulations, notify the International Bureau of the facts and decisions relevant under paragraph 3, and the International Bureau shall, as prescribed in the regulations, notify the interested parties and effect any publication accordingly. The office of origin shall, where applicable, request the International Bureau to cancel, to the extent applicable, the international registration, and the International Bureau shall proceed accordingly.

Article 7 Renewal of international registration

1.   Any international registration may be renewed for a period of 10 years from the expiry of the preceding period, by the mere payment of the basic fee and, subject to Article 8(7), of the supplementary and complementary fees provided for in Article 8(2).
2.   Renewal may not bring about any change in the international registration in its latest form.
3.   Six months before the expiry of the term of protection, the International Bureau shall, by sending an unofficial notice, remind the holder of the international registration and his representative, if any, of the exact date of expiry.
4.   Subject to the payment of a surcharge fixed by the regulations, a period of grace of six months shall be allowed for renewal of the international registration.

Article 8 Fees for international application and registration

1.   The office of origin may fix, at its own discretion, and collect, for its own benefit, a fee which it may require from the applicant for international registration or from the holder of the international registration in connection with the filing of the international application or the renewal of the international registration.
2.   Registration of a mark at the International Bureau shall be subject to the advance payment of an international fee which shall, subject to the provisions of paragraph 7(a), include:
        (i)   a basic fee;

(ii)   a supplementary fee for each class of the international classification, beyond three, into which the goods or services to which the mark is applied will fall;

(iii)   a complementary fee for any request for extension of protection under Article 3ter.

3.   However, the supplementary fee specified in paragraph 2(ii) may, without prejudice to the date of the international registration, be paid within the period fixed by the regulations if the number of classes of goods or services has been fixed or disputed by the International Bureau. If, upon expiry of the said period, the supplementary fee has not been paid or the list of goods or services has not been reduced to the required extent by the applicant, the international application shall be deemed to have been abandoned.

4.   The annual product of the various receipts from international registration, with the exception of the receipts derived from the fees mentioned in paragraph 2(ii) and (iii), shall be divided equally among the contracting parties by the International Bureau, after deduction of the expenses and charges necessitated by the implementation of this Protocol.

5.   The amounts derived from the supplementary fees provided for in paragraph 2(ii) shall be divided, at the expiry of each year, among the interested contracting parties in proportion to the number of marks for which protection has been applied for in each of them during that year, this number being multiplied, in the case of contracting parties which make an examination, by a coefficient which shall be determined by the regulations.

6.   The amounts derived from the complementary fees provided for in paragraph 2(iii) shall be divided according to the same rules as those provided for in paragraph 5.

7.   (a)   Any contracting party may declare that, in connection with each international registration in which it is mentioned under Article 3ter, and in connection with the renewal of any such international registration, it wants to receive, instead of a share in the revenue produced by the supplementary and complementary fees, a fee (hereinafter referred to as the individual fee) whose amount shall be indicated in the declaration, and can be changed in further declarations, but may not be higher than the equivalent of the amount which the said contracting party's office would be entitled to receive from an applicant for a 10-year registration, or from the holder of a registration for a 10-year renewal of that registration, of the mark in the register of the said office, the said amount being diminished by the savings resulting from the international procedure. Where such an individual fee is payable:

(i)   no supplementary fees referred to in paragraph 2(ii) shall be payable if only contracting parties which have made a declaration under this subparagraph are mentioned under Article 3ter; and

(ii)   no complementary fee referred to in paragraph 2(iii) shall be payable in respect of any contracting party which has made a declaration under this subparagraph.

(b)   Any declaration under subparagraph (a) may be made in the instruments referred to in Article 14(2), and the effective date of the declaration shall be the same as the date of entry into force of this Protocol with respect to the State or intergovernmental organisation having made the declaration. Any such declaration may also be made later, in which case the declaration shall have effect three months after its receipt by the Director-General, or at any later date indicated in the declaration, in respect of any international registration whose date is the same as or is later than the effective date of the declaration.

Article 9 Recordal of change in the ownership of an international registration

At the request of the person in whose name the international registration stands, or at the request of an interested office made ex officio or at the request of an interested person, the International Bureau shall record in the International Register any change in the ownership of that registration, in respect of all or some of the contracting parties in whose territories the said registration has effect and in respect of all or some of the goods and services has effect and in respect of all or some of the goods and services listed in the registration, provided that the new holder is a person who, under Article 2(1), is entitled to file international applications.

Article 9bis Recordal of certain matters concerning an international registration

The International Bureau shall record in the International Register:

(i)   any change in the name or address of the holder of the international registration;

(ii)   the appointment of a representative of the holder of the international registration and any other relevant fact concerning such representative;

(iii)   any limitation, in respect of all or some of the contracting parties, of the goods and services listed in the international registration;

(iv)   any renunciation, cancellation or invalidation of the international registration in respect of all or some of the contracting parties;

(v)   any other relevant fact, identified in the regulations, concerning the rights in a mark that is the subject of an international registration.

. . .

Article 9*quater* Common office of several contracting States

1.   If several contracting States agree to effect the unification of their domestic legislation on marks, they may notify the Director-General
         (i)   that a common office shall be substituted for the national office of each of them, and
         (ii)   that the whole of their respective territories shall be deemed to be a single State for the purposes of the application of all or part of the provisions preceding this Article as well as the provisions of Articles 9*quinquies* and 9*sexies*.

2.   Such notification shall not take effect until three months after the date of the communication thereof by the Director-General to the other contracting parties.

Article 9*quinquies* Transformation of an international registration into national or regional applications

Where, in the event that the international registration is cancelled at the request of the office of origin under Article 6(4), in respect of all or some of the goods and services listed in the said registration, the person who was the holder of the international registration files an application for the registration of the same mark with the office of any of the contracting parties in the territory of which the international registration had effect, that application shall be treated as if it had been filed on the date of the international registration according to Article 3(4) or on the date of recordal of the territorial extension according to Article 3ter(2) and, if the international registration enjoyed priority, shall enjoy the same priority, provided that:

(i)   such application is filed within three months from the date on which the international registration was cancelled;

(ii)   the goods and services listed in the application are in fact covered by the list of goods and services contained in the international registration in respect of the contracting party concerned; and

(iii)   such application complies with all the requirements of the applicable law, including the requirements concerning fees.

Article 9*sexies*
Relations between States party to both this Protocol and the Madrid (Stockholm) Agreement

(1)   (a)   This Protocol alone shall be applicable as regards the mutual relations of States party to both this Protocol and the Madrid (Stockholm) Agreement.
         (b)   Notwithstanding subparagraph (a), a declaration made under Article 5(2)(b), Article 5(2)(c) or Article 8(7) of this Protocol, by a State party to both this Protocol and the Madrid (Stockholm) Agreement, shall have no effect in the relations with another State party to both this Protocol and the Madrid (Stockholm) Agreement.

(2)   The Assembly shall, after the expiry of a period of three years from September 1, 2008, review the application of paragraph (1)(b) and may, at any time thereafter, either repeal it or restrict its scope, by a three-fourths majority. In the vote of the Assembly, only those States which are party to both the Madrid (Stockholm) Agreement and this Protocol shall have the right to participate.

Article 10 Assembly

1.   (a)   The contracting parties shall be members of the same Assembly as the countries party to the Madrid (Stockholm) Agreement.
         (b)   Each contracting party shall be represented in that Assembly by one delegate, who may be assisted by alternate delegates, advisors, and experts.
         . . .

2.	The Assembly shall, in addition to the functions which it has under the Madrid (Stockholm) Agreement, also:
   (i)	deal with all matters concerning the implementation of this Protocol;
   (ii)	give directions to the International Bureau concerning the preparation for conferences of revision of this Protocol, due account being taken of any comments made by those countries of the Union which are not party to this Protocol;
   (iii)	adopt and modify the provisions of the regulations concerning the implementation of this Protocol;
   (iv)	perform such other functions as are appropriate under this Protocol.

. . .

Article 11 International Bureau

1.	International registration and related duties, as well as all other administrative tasks, under or concerning this Protocol, shall be performed by the International Bureau.
2.	(a)	The International Bureau shall, in accordance with the directions of the Assembly, make the preparations for the conferences of revision of this Protocol.
   (b)	The International Bureau may consult with intergovernmental and international non-governmental organisations concerning preparations for such conferences of revision.
   (c)	The Director-General and persons designated by him shall take part, without the right to vote, in the discussions at such conferences of revision.
3.	The International Bureau shall carry out any other tasks assigned to it in relation to this Protocol.

Article 13 Amendment of certain Articles of the Protocol

1.	Proposals for the amendment of Articles 10, 11, 12, and the present Article, may be initiated by any contracting party, or by the Director-General. Such proposals shall be communicated by the Director-General to the contracting parties at least six months in advance of their consideration by the Assembly.
2.	Amendments to the Articles referred to in paragraph 1 shall be adopted by the Assembly. Adoption shall require three-fourths of the votes cast, provided that any amendment to Article 10, and to the present paragraph, shall require four-fifths of the votes casts.
3.	Any amendment to the Articles referred to in paragraph 1 shall enter into force one month after written notification of acceptance, effected in accordance with their respective constitutional processes, have been received by the Director-General from three-fourths of those States and intergovernmental organisations which, at the time the amendment was adopted, were members of the Assembly and had the right to vote on the amendment. Any amendment to the said Articles thus accepted shall bind all the States and intergovernmental organisations which are contracting parties at the time the amendment enters into force, or which become contracting parties at a subsequent date.

Article 14 Becoming party to the Protocol; entry into force

1.	(a)	Any State that is a party to the Paris Convention for the protection of industrial property may become party to this Protocol.
   (b)	Furthermore, any intergovernmental organisation may also become party to this Protocol where the following conditions are fulfilled:
      (i)	at least one of the member States of that organisation is a party to the Paris Convention for the protection of industrial property;
      (ii)	that organisation has a regional office for the purposes of registering marks with effect in the territory of the organisation, provided that such office is not the subject of a notification under Article 9quater.
2.	Any State or organisation referred to in paragraph 1 may sign this Protocol. Any such State or organisation may, if it has signed this Protocol, deposit an instrument of ratification, acceptance or approval of this Protocol or, if it has not signed this Protocol, deposit an instrument of accession to this Protocol.
3.	The instruments referred to in paragraph 2 shall be deposited with the Director-General.

. . .

5.	Any State or organisation referred to in paragraph 1 may, when depositing its instrument of ratification, acceptance or approval of, or accession to, this Protocol, declare that the protection resulting from any international registration effected under this Protocol before the date of entry into force of this Protocol with respect to it cannot be extended to it.

Article 15 Denunciation

1. This Protocol shall remain in force without limitation as to time.
2. Any contracting party may denounce this Protocol by notification addressed to the Director-General.

. . .

JOINT RECOMMENDATION CONCERNING PROVISIONS ON THE PROTECTION OF WELL-KNOWN MARKS
adopted by
the Assembly of the Paris Union for the Protection of Industrial Property and
the General Assembly of the World Intellectual Property Organization (WIPO) September 20 to 29, 1999
World Intellectual Property Organization Geneva 2000

Joint Recommendation

The Assembly of the Paris Union for the Protection of Industrial Property and the General Assembly of the World Intellectual Property Organization (WIPO),

Taking into account the provisions of the Paris Convention for the Protection of Industrial Property relative to the protection of well-known marks;

Recommend that each Member State may consider the use of any of the provisions adopted by the Standing Committee on the Law of Trademarks, Industrial Designs and Geographical Indications (SCT) at its second session, second part, as guidelines for the protection for well-known marks;

It is further recommended to each Member State of the Paris Union or of WIPO which is also a member of a regional intergovernmental organization that has competence in the area of registration of trademarks, to bring to the attention of that organization the possibility of protecting well-known marks in accordance, mutatis mutandis, with the provisions contained herein.

Provisions follow.

Article 1 Definitions

For the purposes of these Provisions:

(i) Member State means a State member of the Paris Union for the Protection of Industrial Property and/or of the World Intellectual Property Organization;

(ii) Office means any agency entrusted by a Member State with the registration of marks;

(iii) competent authority means an administrative, judicial or quasi-judicial authority of a Member State which is competent for determining whether a mark is a well-known mark, or for enforcing the protection of well-known marks;

(iv) business identifier means any sign used to identify a business of a natural person, a legal person, an organization or an association;

(v) domain name means an alphanumeric string that corresponds to a numerical address on the Internet.

PART I
DETERMINATION OF WELL-KNOWN MARKS

Article 2 Determination of whether a mark is a well-known mark in a Member State

(1) [*Factors for Consideration*]

(a) In determining whether a mark is a well-known mark, the competent authority shall take into account any circumstances from which it may be inferred that the mark is well known.

(b) In particular, the competent authority shall consider information submitted to it with respect to factors from which it may be inferred that the mark is, or is not, well known, including, but not limited to, information concerning the following:

1. the degree of knowledge or recognition of the mark in the relevant sector of the public;

2.   the duration, extent and geographical area of any use of the mark;

3.   the duration, extent and geographical area of any promotion of the mark, including advertising or publicity and the presentation, at fairs or exhibitions, of the goods and/or services to which the mark applies;

4.   the duration and geographical area of any registrations, and/or any applications for registration, of the mark, to the extent that they reflect use or recognition of the mark;

5.   the record of successful enforcement of rights in the mark, in particular, the extent to which the mark was recognized as well known by competent authorities;

6.   the value associated with the mark.

(c)   The above factors, which are guidelines to assist the competent authority to determine whether the mark is a well-known mark, are not pre-conditions for reaching that determination. Rather, the determination in each case will depend upon the particular circumstances of that case. In some cases all of the factors may be relevant. In other cases some of the factors may be relevant. In still other cases none of the factors may be relevant, and the decision may be based on additional factors that are not listed in subparagraph (b), above. Such additional factors may be relevant, alone, or in combination with one or more of the factors listed in subparagraph (b), above.

(2)   [*Relevant Sector of the Public*]

(a)   Relevant sectors of the public shall include, but shall not necessarily be limited to:

(i)   actual and/or potential consumers of the type of goods and/or services to which the mark applies;

(ii)   persons involved in channels of distribution of the type of goods and/or services to which the mark applies;

(iii)   business circles dealing with the type of goods and/or services to which the mark applies.

(b)   Where a mark is determined to be well known in at least one relevant sector of the public in a Member State, the mark shall be considered by the Member State to be a well-known mark.

(c)   Where a mark is determined to be known in at least one relevant sector of the public in a Member State, the mark may be considered by the Member State to be a well-known mark.

(d)   A Member State may determine that a mark is a well-known mark, even if the mark is not well known or, if the Member States applies subparagraph (c), known, in any relevant sector of the public of the Member State.

(3)   [*Factors Which Shall Not Be Required*]

(a)   A Member State shall not require, as a condition for determining whether a mark is a well-known mark:

(i)   that the mark has been used in, or that the mark has been registered or that an application for registration of the mark has been filed in or in respect of, the Member State;

(ii)   that the mark is well known in, or that the mark has been registered or that an application for registration of the mark has been filed in or in respect of, any jurisdiction other than the Member State; or

(iii)   that the mark is well known by the public at large in the Member State.

(b)   Notwithstanding subparagraph (a)(ii), a Member State may, for the purpose of applying paragraph (2)(d), require that the mark be well known in one or more jurisdictions other than the Member State.

PART II

SCOPE OF PROTECTION

Article 3 Protection of well-known marks; bad faith

(1)   [*Protection of Well-Known Marks*] A Member State shall protect a well-known mark against conflicting marks, business identifiers and domain names, at least with effect from the time when the mark has become well known in the Member State.

(2)   [*Consideration of Bad Faith*] Bad faith may be considered as one factor among others in assessing competing interests in applying Part II of these Provisions.

Article 4 Conflicting marks

(1)   [*Conflicting Marks*]

    (a)   A mark shall be deemed to be in conflict with a well-known mark where that mark, or an essential part thereof, constitutes a reproduction, an imitation, a translation, or a transliteration, liable to create confusion, of the well-known mark, if the mark, or an essential part thereof, is used, is the subject of an application for registration, or is registered, in respect of goods and/or services which are identical or similar to the goods and/or services to which the well-known mark applies.

    (b)   Irrespective of the goods and/or services for which a mark is used, is the subject of an application for registration, or is registered, that mark shall be deemed to be in conflict with a well-known mark where the mark, or an essential part thereof, constitutes a reproduction, an imitation, a translation, or a transliteration of the well-known mark, and where at least one of the following conditions is fulfilled:

       (i)   the use of that mark would indicate a connection between the goods and/or services for which the mark is used, is the subject of an application for registration, or is registered, and the owner of the well-known mark, and would be likely to damage his interests;

       (ii)   the use of that mark is likely to impair or dilute in an unfair manner the distinctive character of the well-known mark;

       (iii)   the use of that mark would take unfair advantage of the distinctive character of the well-known mark.

    (c)   Notwithstanding Article 2(3)(a)(iii), for the purpose of applying paragraph (1)(b)(ii) and (iii), a Member State may require that the well-known mark be well known by the public at large.

    (d)   Notwithstanding paragraphs (2) to (4), a Member State shall not be required to apply:

       (i)   paragraph (1)(a) to determine whether a mark is in conflict with a well-known mark, if the mark was used or registered, or an application for its registration was filed, in or in respect of the Member State, in respect of goods and/or services which are identical or similar to the goods and/or services to which the well-known mark applies, before the well-known mark became well known in the Member State;

       (ii)   paragraph (1)(b) to determine whether a mark is in conflict with a well-known mark, to the extent that the mark was used, was the subject of an application for registration, or was registered, in or in respect of the Member State, for particular goods and/or services, before the well-known mark became well known in the Member State;

       except where the mark has been used or registered, or the application for its registration has been filed, in bad faith.

(2)   [*Opposition Procedures*] If the applicable law allows third parties to oppose the registration of a mark, a conflict with a well-known mark under paragraph (1)(a) shall constitute a ground for opposition.

(3)   [*Invalidation Procedures*]

    (a)   The owner of a well-known mark shall be entitled to request, during a period which shall not be less than five years beginning from the date on which the fact of registration was made known to the public by the Office, the invalidation, by a decision of the competent authority, of the registration of a mark which is in conflict with the well-known mark.

    (b)   If the registration of a mark may be invalidated by a competent authority on its own initiative, a conflict with a well-known mark shall, during a period which shall not be less than five years beginning from the date on which the fact of registration was made known to the public by the Office, be a ground for such invalidation.

(4)   [*Prohibition of Use*] The owner of a well-known mark shall be entitled to request the prohibition, by a decision of the competent authority, of the use of a mark which is in conflict with the well-known mark. Such request shall be admissible for a period which shall not be less than five years beginning from the time the owner of the well-known mark had knowledge of the use of the conflicting mark.

(5)   [*No Time Limit in Case of Registration or Use in Bad Faith*]

    (a)   Notwithstanding paragraph (3), a Member State may not prescribe any time limit for requesting the invalidation of the registration of a mark which is in conflict with a well-known mark if the conflicting mark was registered in bad faith.

(b) Notwithstanding paragraph (4), a Member State may not prescribe any time limit for requesting the prohibition of the use of a mark which is in conflict with a well-known mark if the conflicting mark was used in bad faith.

(c) In determining bad faith for the purposes of this paragraph, the competent authority shall take into consideration whether the person who obtained the registration of or used the mark which is in conflict with a well-known mark had, at the time when the mark was used or registered, or the application for its registration was filed, knowledge of, or reason to know of, the well-known mark.

(6) [*No Time Limit in Case of Registration Without Use*] Notwithstanding paragraph (3), a Member State may not prescribe any time limit for requesting the invalidation of the registration of a mark which is in conflict with a well-known mark, if that mark was registered, but never used.

Article 5 Conflicting business identifiers

(1) [*Conflicting Business Identifiers*]

(a) A business identifier shall be deemed to be in conflict with a well-known mark where that business identifier, or an essential part thereof, constitutes a reproduction, an imitation, a translation, or a transliteration of the well-known mark, and where at least one of the following conditions is fulfilled:

(i) the use of the business identifier would indicate a connection between the business for which it is used and the owner of the well-known mark, and would be likely to damage his interests;

(ii) the use of the business identifier is likely to impair or dilute in an unfair manner the distinctive character of the well-known mark;

(iii) the use of the business identifier would take unfair advantage of the distinctive character of the well-known mark.

(b) Notwithstanding Article 2(3)(iii), for the purposes of applying paragraph (1)(a)(ii) and (iii), a Member State may require that the well-known mark be well known to the public at large.

(c) A Member State shall not be required to apply subparagraph (a) to determine whether a business identifier is in conflict with a well-known mark, if that business identifier was used or registered, or an application for its registration was filed, in or in respect of the Member State, before the well-known mark became well known in or in respect of the Member State, except where the business identifier was used or registered, or the application for its registration was filed, in bad faith.

(2) [*Prohibition of Use*] The owner of a well-known mark shall be entitled to request the prohibition, by a decision of the competent authority, of the use of a business identifier which is in conflict with the well-known mark. Such request shall be admissible for a period which shall not be less than five years beginning from the time the owner of the well-known mark had knowledge of the use of the conflicting business identifier.

(3) [*No Time Limit in Case of Registration or Use in Bad Faith*]

(a) Notwithstanding paragraph (2), a Member State may not prescribe any time limit for requesting the prohibition of the use of a business identifier which is in conflict with a well-known mark if the conflicting business identifier was used in bad faith.

(b) In determining bad faith for the purposes of this paragraph, the competent authority shall consider whether the person who obtained the registration of or used the business identifier which is in conflict with a well-known mark had, at the time when the business identifier was used or registered, or the application for its registration was filed, knowledge of, or reason to know of, the well-known mark.

Article 6 Conflicting domain names

(1) [*Conflicting Domain Names*] A domain name shall be deemed to be in conflict with a well-known mark at least where that domain name, or an essential part thereof, constitutes a reproduction, an imitation, a translation, or a transliteration of the well-known mark, and the domain name has been registered or used in bad faith.

(2) [*Cancellation; Transfer*] The owner of a well-known mark shall be entitled to request, by a decision of the competent authority, that the registrant of the conflicting domain name cancel the registration, or transfer it to the owner of the well-known mark.

JOINT RECOMMENDATION CONCERNING PROVISIONS ON THE PROTECTION OF MARKS, AND OTHER INDUSTRIAL PROPERTY RIGHTS IN SIGNS, ON THE INTERNET

Adopted by the Assembly of the Paris Union for the Protection of Industrial Property and the General Assembly of the World Intellectual Property Organization (WIPO) at the Thirty-Sixth Series of Meetings of the Assemblies of the Member States of WIPO September 24 to October 3, 2001

Joint Recommendation

The Assembly of the Paris Union for the Protection of Industrial Property and the General Assembly of the World Intellectual Property Organization (WIPO);

Taking into account the provisions of the Paris Convention for the Protection of Industrial Property;

Recommend that each Member State may consider the use of any of the provisions adopted by the Standing Committee on the Law of Trademarks, Industrial Designs and Geographical Indications (SCT) at its sixth session, as guidelines concerning the protection of marks, and other industrial property rights in signs, on the Internet;

It is further recommended to each Member State of the Paris Union or of WIPO which is also a member of a regional intergovernmental organization that has competence in the area of registration of trademarks, to bring these provisions to the attention of that organization.

Provisions follow.

Preamble

Recognizing that the present provisions are intended to facilitate the application of existing laws relating to marks and other industrial property rights in signs, and existing laws relating to unfair competition, to the use of signs on the Internet;

Recognizing that Member States will apply, wherever possible, existing laws relating to marks and other industrial property rights in signs, and existing laws relating to unfair competition, to the use of signs on the Internet, directly or by analogy;

Recognizing that a sign used on the Internet is simultaneously and immediately accessible irrespective of territorial location;

The present provisions are intended to be applied in the context of determining whether, under the applicable law of a Member State, use of a sign on the Internet has contributed to the acquisition, maintenance or infringement of a mark or other industrial property right in the sign, or whether such use constitutes an act of unfair competition, and in the context of determining remedies.

PART I GENERAL

Article 1 Abbreviated expressions

For the purposes of these Provisions, unless expressly stated otherwise:

(i)   "Member State" means a State member of the Paris Union for the Protection of Industrial Property, of the World Intellectual Property Organization, or of both;

(ii)   "Right" means an industrial property right in a sign under the applicable law, whether registered or unregistered;

(iii)   "Act of unfair competition" means any act of competition contrary to honest business practices in industrial or commercial matters as defined in Article 10*bis* of the Paris Convention for the Protection of Industrial Property, signed in Paris on March 20, 1883, as revised and amended;

(iv)   "Competent authority" means an administrative, judicial or quasi-judicial authority of a Member State which is competent for determining whether a right has been acquired, maintained or infringed, for determining remedies, or for determining whether an act of competition constitutes an act of unfair competition, as the case may be;

(v)   "Remedies" means the remedies which a competent authority of a Member State can impose under the applicable law, as a result of an action for the infringement of a right or an act of unfair competition;

(vi)   "Internet" refers to an interactive medium for communication which contains information that is simultaneously and immediately accessible irrespective of territorial location to members of the public from a place and at a time individually chosen by them;

(vii)   except where the context indicates otherwise, words in the singular include the plural, and vice versa, and masculine personal pronouns include the feminine.

PART II
USE OF A SIGN ON THE INTERNET

Article 2 Use of a sign on the Internet in a Member State

Use of a sign on the Internet shall constitute use in a Member State for the purposes of these provisions, only if the use has a commercial effect in that Member State as described in Article 3.

Article 3 Factors for determining commercial effect in a Member State

(1)   *[Factors]* In determining whether use of a sign on the Internet has a commercial effect in a Member State, the competent authority shall take into account all relevant circumstances. Circumstances that may be relevant include, but are not limited to:

(a)   circumstances indicating that the user of the sign is doing, or has undertaken significant plans to do, business in the Member State in relation to goods or services which are identical or similar to those for which the sign is used on the Internet.

(b)   the level and character of commercial activity of the user in relation to the Member State, including:

(i)   whether the user is actually serving customers located in the Member State or has entered into other commercially motivated relationships with persons located in the Member State;

(ii)   whether the user has stated, in conjunction with the use of the sign on the Internet, that he does not intend to deliver the goods or services offered to customers located in the Member State and whether he adheres to his stated intent;

(iii)   whether the user offers post-sales activities in the Member State, such as warranty or service;

(iv)   whether the user undertakes further commercial activities in the Member State which are related to the use of the sign on the Internet but which are not carried out over the Internet.

(c)   the connection of an offer of goods or services on the Internet with the Member State, including:

(i)   whether the goods or services offered can be lawfully delivered in the Member State;

(ii)   whether the prices are indicated in the official currency of the Member State.

(d)   the connection of the manner of use of the sign on the Internet with the Member State, including:

(i)   whether the sign is used in conjunction with means of interactive contact which are accessible to Internet users in the Member State;

(ii)   whether the user has indicated, in conjunction with the use of the sign, an address, telephone number or other means of contact in the Member State;

(iii)   whether the sign is used in connection with a domain name which is registered under the ISO Standard country code 3166 Top Level Domain referring to the Member State;

(iv)   whether the text used in conjunction with the use of the sign is in a language predominantly used in the Member State;

(v)   whether the sign is used in conjunction with an Internet location which has actually been visited by Internet users located in the Member State.

(e)   the relation of the use of the sign on the Internet with a right in that sign in the Member State, including:

(i)   whether the use is supported by that right;

(ii)   whether, where the right belongs to another, the use would take unfair advantage of, or unjustifiably impair, the distinctive character or the reputation of the sign that is the subject of that right.

(2)   *[Relevance of Factors]* The above factors, which are guidelines to assist the competent authority to determine whether the use of a sign has produced a commercial effect in a Member State, are not pre-conditions for reaching that determination. Rather, the determination in each case will depend upon the particular circumstances of that case. In some cases all of the factors may be relevant. In other cases some of the factors may

be relevant. In still other cases none of the factors may be relevant, and the decision may be based on additional factors that are not listed in paragraph (1), above. Such additional factors may be relevant, alone, or in combination with one or more of the factors listed in paragraph (1), above.

Article 4 Bad faith

(1)   [*Bad Faith*] For the purposes of applying these provisions, any relevant circumstance shall be considered in determining whether a sign was used in bad faith, or whether a right was acquired in bad faith.

(2)   [*Factors*] In particular, the competent authority shall take into consideration, *inter alia*:

(i)   whether the person who used the sign or acquired the right in the sign had knowledge of a right in an identical or similar sign belonging to another, or could not have reasonably been unaware of that right, at the time when the person first used the sign, acquired the right or filed an application for acquisition of the right, whichever is earlier, and

(ii)   whether the use of the sign would take unfair advantage of, or unjustifiably impair, the distinctive character or the reputation of the sign that is the subject of the other right.

PART III

ACQUISITION AND MAINTENANCE OF RIGHTS IN SIGNS

Article 5 Use of a sign on the Internet and acquisition and maintenance of rights

Use of a sign on the Internet in a Member State, including forms of use that are made possible by technological advances, shall in every case be taken into consideration for determining whether the requirements under the applicable law of the Member State for acquiring or maintaining a right in the sign have been met.

PART IV

INFRINGEMENT AND LIABILITY

Article 6 Use of a sign on the Internet, infringement of rights and acts of unfair competition

Use of a sign on the Internet, including forms of use that are made possible by technological advances, shall be taken into consideration for determining whether a right under the applicable law of a Member State has been infringed, or whether the use amounts to an act of unfair competition under the law of that Member State, only if that use constitutes use of the sign on the Internet in that Member State.

Article 7 Liability for infringement and acts of unfair competition under the applicable law

Except where otherwise provided for in these provisions, there shall be liability in a Member State under the applicable law when a right is infringed, or an act of unfair competition is committed, through use of a sign on the Internet in that Member State.

Article 8 Exceptions and limitations under the applicable law

A Member State shall apply the exceptions to liability, and the limitations to the scope of rights, existing under the applicable law when applying these provisions to the use of a sign on the Internet in that Member State.

PART V

NOTICE AND AVOIDANCE OF CONFLICT

Article 9 Use prior to notification of infringement

If the use of a sign on the Internet in a Member State is alleged to infringe a right in that Member State, the user of that sign shall not be held liable for such infringement prior to receiving a notification of infringement, if:

(i)   the user owns a right in the sign in another Member State or uses the sign with the consent of the owner of such a right, or is permitted to use the sign, in the manner in which it is

being used on the Internet, under the law of another Member State to which the user has a close connection;
(ii)   any acquisition of a right in the sign, and any use of the sign, has not been in bad faith; and
(iii)   the user has provided, in conjunction with the use of the sign on the Internet, information reasonably sufficient to contact him by mail, e-mail or telefacsimile.

Article 10 Use after notification of infringement

If the user referred to in Article 9 has received a notification that his use infringes another right, he shall not be held liable if he
(i)   indicates to the person sending the notification that he owns a right in the sign in another Member State, or uses the sign with the consent of the owner of such a right, or that he is permitted to use the sign, in the manner in which it is being used on the Internet, under the law of another Member State to which he has a close connection;
(ii)   gives relevant details of that right or permitted use; and
(iii)   expeditiously takes reasonable measures which are effective to avoid a commercial effect in the Member State referred to in the notification, or to avoid infringement of the right referred to in the notification.

Article 11 Notification under Articles 9 and 10

The notification under Articles 9 and 10 shall be effective if it is sent by the owner of a right or his representative, by mail, e-mail or telefacsimile, and indicates, in the language, or in one of the languages, used in conjunction with the use of the sign on the Internet, the following:
(i)   the right which is alleged to be infringed;
(ii)   the identity of the owner of that right and information reasonably sufficient to contact him or his representative by mail, e-mail or telefacsimile;
(iii)   the Member State in which that right is protected;
(iv)   relevant details of such protection allowing the user to assess the existence, nature and scope of that right; and
(v)   the use that is claimed to infringe that right.

Article 12 Disclaimer as a measure under Article 10

Member States shall accept, inter alia, a disclaimer, by a user referred to in Article 9, as a reasonable and effective measure under Article 10, if:
(i)   the disclaimer includes a clear and unambiguous statement in conjunction with the use of the sign, to the effect that the user has no relationship with the owner of the right which is alleged to be infringed, and does not intend to deliver the goods or services offered to customers located in a particular Member State where the right is protected;
(ii)   the disclaimer is written in the language or in the languages used in conjunction with the use of the sign on the Internet;
(iii)   the user inquires, before the delivery of the goods or services, whether customers are located in the Member State referred to in item (i); and
(iv)   the user in fact refuses delivery to customers who have indicated that they are located in that Member State.

PART VI
REMEDIES

Article 13 Remedy proportionate to commercial effect

(1)   The remedies provided for the infringement of rights or for acts of unfair competition in a Member State, through use of a sign on the Internet in that Member State, shall be proportionate to the commercial effect of the use in that Member State.
(2)   The competent authority shall balance the interests, rights and circumstances involved.
(3)   The user of the sign shall, upon request, be given the opportunity to propose an effective remedy for consideration by the competent authority, prior to a decision on the merits of the case.

Article 14 Limitations of use of a sign on the Internet

(1)   In determining remedies, the competent authority shall take into account limitations of use by imposing reasonable measures designed:
(i)   to avoid a commercial effect in the Member State, or
(ii)   to avoid infringement of the right or to avoid the act of unfair competition.

(2)   The measures referred to in paragraph (1) may include, inter alia:
  (a)   a clear and unambiguous statement in conjunction with the use of the sign on the Internet, to the effect that the user has no relationship with the owner of the infringed right or the person affected by the act of unfair competition, written in the language or in the languages used in conjunction with the use of the sign on the Internet, and any other language indicated by the competent authority;
  (b)   a clear and unambiguous statement in conjunction with the use of the sign on the Internet to the effect that the user does not intend to deliver the goods or services offered to customers located in a particular Member State, written in the language or in the languages used in conjunction with the use of the sign on the Internet, and any other language indicated by the competent authority;
  (c)   an obligation to inquire, before the delivery of the goods or services, whether customers are located in that Member State, and to refuse delivery to customers who have indicated that they are located in that Member State;
  (d)   gateway web pages.

Article 15 Limitation on prohibition to use a sign on the Internet

(1)   Where the use of a sign on the Internet in a Member State infringes a right, or amounts to an act of unfair competition, under the laws of that Member State, the competent authority of the Member State should avoid, wherever possible, imposing a remedy that would have the effect of prohibiting any future use of the sign on the Internet.
(2)   The competent authority shall not, in any case, impose a remedy that would prohibit future use of the sign on the Internet, where
  (i)   the user owns a right in the sign in another Member State, uses the sign with the consent of the owner of such a right, or is permitted to use the sign, in the manner in which it is being used on the Internet, under the law of another Member State to which the user has a close connection; and
  (ii) any acquisition of a right in the sign, and any use of the sign, has not been in bad faith.

INTERNATIONAL CLASSIFICATION OF GOODS AND SERVICES UNDER THE NICE AGREEMENT, 11TH EDN, 2018 VERSION

Goods

Class 1:   Chemicals for use in industry, science and photography, as well as in agriculture, horticulture and forestry; unprocessed artificial resins, unprocessed plastics; fire extinguishing and fire prevention compositions; tempering and soldering preparations; substances for tanning animal skins and hides; adhesives for use in industry; putties and other paste fillers; compost, manures, fertilizers; biological preparations for use in industry and science.

Class 2:   Paints, varnishes, lacquers; preservatives against rust and against deterioration of wood; colorants, dyes; inks for printing, marking and engraving; raw natural resins; metals in foil and powder form for use in painting, decorating, printing and art.

Class 3:   Non-medicated cosmetics and toiletry preparations; non-medicated dentifrices; perfumery, essential oils; bleaching preparations and other substances for laundry use; cleaning, polishing, scouring and abrasive preparations.

Class 4:   Industrial oils and greases, wax; lubricants; dust absorbing, wetting and binding compositions; fuels and illuminants; candles and wicks for lighting.

Class 5:   Pharmaceutical, medical and veterinary preparations; sanitary preparations for medical purposes; dietetic food and substances adapted for medical or veterinary use, food for babies; dietary supplements for humans and animals, plasters, materials for dressings; material for stopping teeth, dental wax; disinfectants; preparations for destroying vermin; fungicides, herbicides.

Class 6:   Common metals and their alloys, ores; metal materials for building and construction; transportable buildings of metal; non-electric cables and wires of common metal; small items of metal hardware; metal containers for storage or transport; safes.

Class 7:   Machines and machine tools, power-operated tools; motors and engines, except for land vehicles; machine coupling and transmission components, except for land vehicles; agricultural implements, other than hand-operated hand tools; incubators for eggs, automatic vending machines.

Class 8:	Hand tools and implements, hand-operated; cutlery; side arms, except firearms; razors.
Class 9:	Scientific, nautical, surveying, photographic, cinematographic, optical, weighing, measuring, signalling, checking (supervision), life-saving and teaching apparatus and instruments; apparatus and instruments for conducting, switching, transforming, accumulating, regulating or controlling electricity; apparatus for recording, transmission or reproduction of sound or images; magnetic data carriers, recording discs; compact discs, DVDs and other digital recording media; mechanisms for coin-operated apparatus; cash registers, calculating machines, data processing equipment, computers; computer software, fire-extinguishing apparatus.
Class 10:	Surgical, medical, dental and veterinary apparatus and instruments, artificial limbs, eyes and teeth; orthopedic articles; suture materials; therapeutic and assistive devices adapted for the disabled; massage apparatus; apparatus, devices and articles for nursing infants; sexual activity apparatus, devices and articles.
Class 11:	Apparatus for lighting, heating, steam generating, cooking, refrigerating, drying, ventilating, water supply and sanitary purposes.
Class 12:	Vehicles; apparatus for locomotion by land, air or water.
Class 13:	Firearms; ammunition and projectiles; explosives; fireworks.
Class 14:	Precious metals and their alloys; jewellery, precious and semi-precious stones; horological and chronometric instruments.
Class 15:	Musical instruments.
Class 16:	Paper and cardboard; printed matter; bookbinding material; photographs; stationery and office requisites, except furniture; adhesives for stationery or household purposes; drawing materials and materials for artists; paintbrushes; instructional and teaching materials; plastic sheets, films and bags for wrapping and packaging; printers' type, printing blocks.
Class 17:	Unprocessed and semi-processed rubber, gutta-percha, gum, asbestos, mica and substitutes for all these materials; plastics and resins in extruded form for use in manufacture; packing, stopping and insulating materials; flexible pipes, tubes and hoses, not of metal.
Class 18:	Leather and imitations of leather; animal skins and hides; luggage and carrying bags; umbrellas and parasols; walking sticks; whips, harness and saddlery; collars, leashes and clothing for animals.
Class 19:	Building materials (non-metallic); non-metallic rigid pipes for building; asphalt, pitch and bitumen; non-metallic transportable buildings; monuments, not of metal.
Class 20:	Furniture, mirrors, picture frames; containers, not of metal, for storage or transport; unworked or semi-worked bone, horn, whalebone or mother-of-pearl; shells; meerschaum; yellow amber.
Class 21:	Household or kitchen utensils and containers; cookware and tableware, except forks, knives and spoons; combs and sponges; brushes, except paintbrushes; brush-making materials; articles for cleaning purposes; unworked or semi-worked glass, except building glass; glassware, porcelain and earthenware.
Class 22:	Ropes and string; nets; tents and tarpaulins; awnings of textile or synthetic materials; sails; sacks for the transport and storage of materials in bulk; padding, cushioning and stuffing materials, except of paper, cardboard, rubber or plastics; raw fibrous textile materials and substitutes therefor.
Class 23:	Yarns and threads, for textile use.
Class 24:	Textiles and substitutes for textiles; household linen; curtains of textile or plastic.
Class 25:	Clothing, footwear, headgear.
Class 26:	Lace and embroidery, ribbons and braid; buttons, hooks and eyes, pins and needles; artificial flowers; hair decorations; false hair.
Class 27:	Carpets, rugs, mats and matting, linoleum and other materials for covering existing floors; wall hangings (non-textile).
Class 28:	Games, toys and playthings; video game apparatus; gymnastic and sporting articles; decorations for Christmas trees.
Class 29:	Meat, fish, poultry and game; meat extracts; preserved, frozen, dried and cooked fruits and vegetables; jellies, jams, compotes; eggs, milk and milk products; oils and fats for food.

Class 30:　　Coffee, tea, cocoa and artificial coffee; rice; tapioca and sago; flour and preparations made from cereals; bread, pastry and confectionery; edible ices; sugar, honey, treacle; yeast, baking-powder; salt; mustard; vinegar, sauces (condiments); spices; ice (frozen water).

Class 31:　　Raw and unprocessed agricultural, aquacultural, horticultural and forestry products; raw and unprocessed grains and seeds; fresh fruits and vegetables, fresh herbs; natural plants and flowers; bulbs, seedlings and seeds for planting; live animals; foodstuffs and beverages for animals; malt.

Class 32:　　Beers; mineral and aerated waters and other non-alcoholic drinks; fruit beverages and fruit juices; syrups and other preparations for making beverages.

Class 33:　　Alcoholic beverages (except beers).

Class 34:　　Tobacco; smokers' articles; matches.

Services

Class 35:　　Advertising; business management; business administration; office functions.

Class 36:　　Insurance; financial affairs; monetary affairs; real estate affairs.

Class 37:　　Building construction; repair; installation services.

Class 38:　　Telecommunications.

Class 39:　　Transport; packaging and storage of goods; travel arrangement.

Class 40:　　Treatment of materials.

Class 41:　　Education; providing of training; entertainment; sporting and cultural activities.

Class 42:　　Scientific and technological services and research and design relating thereto; industrial analysis and research services; design and development of computer hardware and software.

Class 43:　　Services for providing food and drink; temporary accommodation.

Class 44:　　Medical services; veterinary services; hygienic and beauty care for human beings or animals; agriculture, horticulture and forestry services.

Class 45:　　Legal services; security services for the physical protection of tangible property and individuals; personal and social services rendered by others to meet the needs of individuals.

DIGITAL ECONOMY ACT 2010
(c. 24)

OFCOM reports

1　OFCOM reports on infrastructure, internet domain names etc

(1)　In Chapter 1 of Part 2 of the Communications Act 2003 (electronic communications networks and services), after section 134 insert—

. . .

"Reports on internet domain names

134C　OFCOM reports on internet domain names

(1)　OFCOM must, if requested to do so by the Secretary of State—

(a)　prepare a report on matters specified by the Secretary of State relating to internet domain names, and

(b)　send the report to the Secretary of State as soon as practicable.

(2)　The specified matters may, in particular, include matters relating to—

(a)　the allocation and registration of internet domain names, and

(b)　the misuse of internet domain names.

(3)　OFCOM must publish every report under this section—

(a)　as soon as practicable after they send it to the Secretary of State, and

(b)　in such manner as they consider appropriate for bringing it to the attention of persons who, in their opinion, are likely to have an interest in it.

(4)   OFCOM may exclude information from a report when it is published under subsection (3) if they consider that it is information that they could refuse to disclose in response to a request under the Freedom of Information Act 2000."

(2)   In section 135(3) of that Act (information required for purposes of Chapter 1 functions), after paragraph (ib) insert—

"(ic) preparing a report under section 134A;

(id) preparing a report under section 134C;".

Online infringement of copyright

3   Obligation to notify subscribers of reported infringements

After section 124 of the Communications Act 2003 insert—

"Online infringement of copyright: obligations of internet service providers

124A Obligation to notify subscribers of copyright infringement reports

(1)   This section applies if it appears to a copyright owner that—

    (a)   a subscriber to an internet access service has infringed the owner's copyright by means of the service; or

    (b)   a subscriber to an internet access service has allowed another person to use the service, and that other person has infringed the owner's copyright by means of the service.

(2)   The owner may make a copyright infringement report to the internet service provider who provided the internet access service if a code in force under section 124C or 124D (an "initial obligations code") allows the owner to do so.

(3)   A "copyright infringement report" is a report that—

    (a)   states that there appears to have been an infringement of the owner's copyright;

    (b)   includes a description of the apparent infringement;

    (c)   includes evidence of the apparent infringement that shows the subscriber's IP address and the time at which the evidence was gathered;

    (d)   is sent to the internet service provider within the period of 1 month beginning with the day on which the evidence was gathered; and

    (e)   complies with any other requirement of the initial obligations code.

(4)   An internet service provider who receives a copyright infringement report must notify the subscriber of the report if the initial obligations code requires the provider to do so.

(5)   A notification under subsection (4) must be sent to the subscriber within the period of 1 month beginning with the day on which the provider receives the report.

(6)   A notification under subsection (4) must include—

    (a)   a statement that the notification is sent under this section in response to a copyright infringement report;

    (b)   the name of the copyright owner who made the report;

    (c)   a description of the apparent infringement;

    (d)   evidence of the apparent infringement that shows the subscriber's IP address and the time at which the evidence was gathered;

    (e)   information about subscriber appeals and the grounds on which they may be made;

    (f)   information about copyright and its purpose;

    (g)   advice, or information enabling the subscriber to obtain advice, about how to obtain lawful access to copyright works;

    (h)   advice, or information enabling the subscriber to obtain advice, about steps that a subscriber can take to protect an internet access service from unauthorised use; and

      (i)   anything else that the initial obligations code requires the notification to include.

(7)   For the purposes of subsection (6)(h) the internet service provider must take into account the suitability of different protection for subscribers in different circumstances.

(8)   The things that may be required under subsection (6)(i), whether in general or in a particular case, include in particular—

      (a)   a statement that information about the apparent infringement may be kept by the internet service provider;

      (b)   a statement that the copyright owner may require the provider to disclose which copyright infringement reports made by the owner to the provider relate to the subscriber;

      (c)   a statement that, following such a disclosure, the copyright owner may apply to a court to learn the subscriber's identity and may bring proceedings against the subscriber for copyright infringement; and

      (d)   where the requirement for the provider to send the notification arises partly because of a report that has already been the subject of a notification under subsection (4), a statement that the number of copyright infringement reports relating to the subscriber may be taken into account for the purposes of any technical measures.

(9)   In this section "notify", in relation to a subscriber, means send a notification to the electronic or postal address held by the internet service provider for the subscriber (and sections 394 to 396 do not apply)."

4   Obligation to provide infringement lists to copyright owners

After section 124A of the Communications Act 2003 insert—

"124B Obligation to provide copyright infringement lists to copyright owners

(1)   An internet service provider must provide a copyright owner with a copyright infringement list for a period if—

      (a)   the owner requests the list for that period; and

      (b)   an initial obligations code requires the internet service provider to provide it.

(2)   A "copyright infringement list" is a list that—

      (a)   sets out, in relation to each relevant subscriber, which of the copyright infringement reports made by the owner to the provider relate to the subscriber, but

      (b)   does not enable any subscriber to be identified.

(3)   A subscriber is a "relevant subscriber" in relation to a copyright owner and an internet service provider if copyright infringement reports made by the owner to the provider in relation to the subscriber have reached the threshold set in the initial obligations code."

5   Approval of code about the initial obligations

After section 124B of the Communications Act 2003 insert—

"124C Approval of code about the initial obligations

(1)   The obligations of internet service providers under sections 124A and 124B are the "initial obligations".

(2)   If it appears to OFCOM —

      (a)   that a code has been made by any person for the purpose of regulating the initial obligations; and

      (b)   that it would be appropriate for them to approve the code for that purpose,

    they may by order approve it, with effect from the date given in the order.

(3)   The provision that may be contained in a code and approved under this section includes provision that—

      (a)   specifies conditions that must be met for rights and obligations under the copyright infringement provisions or the code to apply in a particular case;

(b)   requires copyright owners or internet service providers to provide any information or assistance that is reasonably required to determine whether a condition under paragraph (a) is met.

(4)   The provision mentioned in subsection (3) (a) may, in particular, specify that a right or obligation does not apply in relation to a copyright owner unless the owner has made arrangements with an internet service provider regarding—

    (a)   the number of copyright infringement reports that the owner may make to the provider within a particular period; and

    (b)   payment in advance of a contribution towards meeting costs incurred by the provider.

(5)   The provision mentioned in subsection (3)(a) may also, in particular, provide that—

    (a)   except as provided by the code, rights and obligations do not apply in relation to an internet service provider unless the number of copyright infringement reports the provider receives within a particular period reaches a threshold set in the code; and

    (b)   if the threshold is reached, rights or obligations apply with effect from the date when it is reached or from a later time.

(6)   OFCOM must not approve a code under this section unless satisfied that it meets the criteria set out in section 124E.

(7)   Not more than one approved code may have effect at a time.

(8)   OFCOM must keep an approved code under review.

(9)   OFCOM may by order, at any time, for the purpose mentioned in subsection (2)—

    (a)   approve modifications that have been made to an approved code; or

    (b)   withdraw their approval from an approved code, with effect from the date given in the order, and must do so if the code ceases to meet the criteria set out in section 124E.

(10)   The consent of the Secretary of State is required for the approval of a code or the modification of an approved code.

(11)   An order made by OFCOM under this section approving a code or modification must set out the code or modification.

(12)   Section 403 applies to the power of OFCOM to make an order under this section.

(13)   A statutory instrument containing an order made by OFCOM under this section is subject to annulment in pursuance of a resolution of either House of Parliament."

6   Initial obligations code by OFCOM in the absence of an approved code

After section 124C of the Communications Act 2003 insert—

"124D Initial obligations code by OFCOM in the absence of an approved code

(1)   For any period when sections 124A and 124B are in force but for which there is no approved initial obligations code under section 124C, OFCOM must by order make a code for the purpose of regulating the initial obligations.

(2)   OFCOM may but need not make a code under subsection (1) for a time before the end of—

    (a)   the period of six months beginning with the day on which sections 124A and 124B come into force, or

    (b)   such longer period as the Secretary of State may specify by notice to OFCOM.

(3)   The Secretary of State may give a notice under subsection (2)(b) only if it appears to the Secretary of State that it is not practicable for OFCOM to make a code with effect from the end of the period mentioned in subsection (2)(a) or any longer period for the time being specified under subsection (2)(b).

(4)   A code under this section may do any of the things mentioned in section 124C(3) to (5).

(5)   A code under this section may also—

  (a)   confer jurisdiction with respect to any matter (other than jurisdiction to determine appeals by subscribers) on OFCOM themselves;

  (b)   provide for OFCOM, in exercising such jurisdiction, to make awards of compensation, to direct the reimbursement of costs, or to do both;

  (c)   provide for OFCOM to enforce, or to participate in the enforcement of, any awards or directions made under the code;

  (d)   make other provision for the enforcement of such awards and directions;

  (e)   establish a body corporate, with the capacity to make its own rules and establish its own procedures, for the purpose of determining subscriber appeals;

  (f)   provide for a person with the function of determining subscriber appeals to enforce, or to participate in the enforcement of, any awards or directions made by the person;

  (g)   make other provision for the enforcement of such awards and directions; and

  (h)   make other provision for the purpose of regulating the initial obligations.

(6)   OFCOM must not make a code under this section unless they are satisfied that it meets the criteria set out in section 124E.

(7)   OFCOM must—

  (a)   keep a code under this section under review; and (b) by order make any amendment of it that is necessary to ensure that while it is in force it continues to meet the criteria set out in section 124E.

(8)   The consent of the Secretary of State is required for the making or amendment by OFCOM of a code under this section.

(9)   Section 403 applies to the power of OFCOM to make an order under this section.

(10) A statutory instrument containing an order made by OFCOM under this section is subject to annulment in pursuance of a resolution of either House of Parliament."

7   **Contents of initial obligations code**
After section 124D of the Communications Act 2003 insert—

"124E Contents of initial obligations code

(1)   The criteria referred to in sections 124C(6) and 124D(6) are—

  (a)   that the code makes the required provision about copyright infringement reports (see subsection (2));

  (b)   that it makes the required provision about the notification of subscribers (see subsections (3) and (4));

  (c)   that it sets the threshold applying for the purposes of determining who is a relevant subscriber within the meaning of section 124B(3) (see subsections (5) and (6));

  (d)   that it makes provision about how internet service providers are to keep information about subscribers;

  (e)   that it limits the time for which they may keep that information;

  (f)   that it makes any provision about contributions towards meeting costs that is required to be included by an order under section 124M;

  (g)   that the requirements concerning administration and enforcement are met in relation to the code (see subsections (7) and (8));

  (h)   that the requirements concerning subscriber appeals are met in relation to the code (see section 124K);

(i) that the provisions of the code are objectively justifiable in relation to the matters to which it relates;

(j) that those provisions are not such as to discriminate unduly against particular persons or against a particular description of persons;

(k) that those provisions are proportionate to what they are intended to achieve; and

(l) that, in relation to what those provisions are intended to achieve, they are transparent.

(2) The required provision about copyright infringement reports is provision that specifies—

(a) requirements as to the means of obtaining evidence of infringement of copyright for inclusion in a report;

(b) the standard of evidence that must be included; and

(c) the required form of the report.

(3) The required provision about the notification of subscribers is provision that specifies, in relation to a subscriber in relation to whom an internet service provider receives one or more copyright infringement reports—

(a) requirements as to the means by which the provider identifies the subscriber;

(b) which of the reports the provider must notify the subscriber of; and (c) requirements as to the form, contents and means of the notification in each case.

(4) The provision mentioned in subsection (3) must not permit any copyright infringement report received by an internet service provider more than 12 months before the date of a notification of a subscriber to be taken into account for the purposes of the notification.

(5) The threshold applying in accordance with subsection (1)(c) may, subject to subsection (6), be set by reference to any matter, including in particular one or more of—

(a) the number of copyright infringement reports;

(b) the time within which the reports are made; and

(c) the time of the apparent infringements to which they relate.

(6) The threshold applying in accordance with subsection (1)(c) must operate in such a way that a copyright infringement report received by an internet service provider more than 12 months before a particular date does not affect whether the threshold is met on that date; and a copyright infringement list provided under section 124B must not take into account any such report.

(7) The requirements concerning administration and enforcement are—

(a) that OFCOM have, under the code, the functions of administering and enforcing it, including the function of resolving owner-provider disputes;

(b) that there are adequate arrangements under the code for OFCOM to obtain any information or assistance from internet service providers or copyright owners that OFCOM reasonably require for the purposes of administering and enforcing the code; and

(c) that there are adequate arrangements under the code for the costs incurred by OFCOM in administering and enforcing the code to be met by internet service providers and copyright owners.

(8) The provision mentioned in subsection (7) may include, in particular—

(a) provision for the payment, to a person specified in the code, of a penalty not exceeding the maximum penalty for the time being specified in section 124L(2);

(b) provision requiring a copyright owner to indemnify an internet service provider for any loss or damage resulting from the owner's failure to comply with the code or the copyright infringement provisions.

(9)   In this section "owner-provider dispute" means a dispute that—

(a)   is between persons who are copyright owners or internet service providers; and

(b)   relates to an act or omission in relation to an initial obligation or an initial obligations code."

8   Progress reports

After section 124E of the Communications Act 2003 insert—

"124F Progress reports

(1)   OFCOM must prepare the following reports for the Secretary of State about the infringement of copyright by subscribers to internet access services.

(2)   OFCOM must prepare a full report for—

(a)   the period of 12 months beginning with the first day on which there is an initial obligations code in force; and

(b)   each successive period of 12 months.

(3)   OFCOM must prepare an interim report for—

(a)   the period of 3 months beginning with the first day on which there is an initial obligations code in force; and

(b)   each successive period of 3 months, other than one ending at the same time as a period of 12 months under subsection (2).

But this is subject to any direction by the Secretary of State under subsection (4).

(4)   The Secretary of State may direct that subsection (3) no longer applies, with effect from the date given in the direction.

(5)   A full report under this section must include—

(a)   an assessment of the current level of subscribers' use of internet access services to infringe copyright;

(b)   a description of the steps taken by copyright owners to enable subscribers to obtain lawful access to copyright works;

(c)   a description of the steps taken by copyright owners to inform, and change the attitude of, members of the public in relation to the infringement of copyright;

(d)   an assessment of the extent of the steps mentioned in paragraphs (b) and (c);

(e)   an assessment of the extent to which copyright owners have made copyright infringement reports;

(f)   an assessment of the extent to which they have brought legal proceedings against subscribers in relation to whom such reports have been made;

(g)   an assessment of the extent to which any such proceedings have been against subscribers in relation to whom a substantial number of reports have been made; and

(h)   anything else that the Secretary of State directs OFCOM to include in the report.

(6)   An interim report under this section must include—

(a)   the assessments mentioned in subsection (5) (a), (e) and (f); and (b) anything else that the Secretary of State directs OFCOM to include in the report.

(7)   OFCOM must send a report prepared under this section to the Secretary of State as soon as practicable after the end of the period for which it is prepared.

(8)   OFCOM must publish every full report under this section—

(a)   as soon as practicable after they send it to the Secretary of State, and

(b)   in such manner as they consider appropriate for bringing it to the attention of persons who, in their opinion, are likely to have an interest in it.

(9) OFCOM may exclude information from a report when it is published under subsection (8) if they consider that it is information that they could refuse to disclose in response to a request under the Freedom of Information Act 2000."

9 Obligations to limit internet access: assessment and preparation

After section 124F of the Communications Act 2003 insert—

"124G Obligations to limit internet access: assessment and preparation

(1) The Secretary of State may direct OFCOM to—

    (a) assess whether one or more technical obligations should be imposed on internet service providers;

    (b) take steps to prepare for the obligations;

    (c) provide a report on the assessment or steps to the Secretary of State.

(2) A "technical obligation", in relation to an internet service provider, is an obligation for the provider to take a technical measure against some or all relevant subscribers to its service for the purpose of preventing or reducing infringement of copyright by means of the internet.

(3) A "technical measure" is a measure that—

    (a) limits the speed or other capacity of the service provided to a subscriber;

    (b) prevents a subscriber from using the service to gain access to particular material, or limits such use;

    (c) suspends the service provided to a subscriber; or

    (d) limits the service provided to a subscriber in another way.

(4) A subscriber to an internet access service is "relevant" if the subscriber is a relevant subscriber, within the meaning of section 124B(3), in relation to the provider of the service and one or more copyright owners.

(5) The assessment and steps that the Secretary of State may direct OFCOM to carry out or take under subsection (1) include, in particular—

    (a) consultation of copyright owners, internet service providers, subscribers or any other person;

    (b) an assessment of the likely efficacy of a technical measure in relation to a particular type of internet access service; and

    (c) steps to prepare a proposed technical obligations code.

(6) Internet service providers and copyright owners must give OFCOM any assistance that OFCOM reasonably require for the purposes of complying with any direction under this section.

(7) The Secretary of State must lay before Parliament any direction under this section.

(8) OFCOM must publish every report under this section—

    (a) as soon as practicable after they send it to the Secretary of State, and (b) in such manner as they consider appropriate for bringing it to the attention of persons who, in their opinion, are likely to have an interest in it.

(9) OFCOM may exclude information from a report when it is published under subsection (8) if they consider that it is information that they could refuse to disclose in response to a request under the Freedom of Information Act 2000."

10 Obligations to limit internet access

After section 124G of the Communications Act 2003 insert—

"124H Obligations to limit internet access

(1) The Secretary of State may by order impose a technical obligation on internet service providers if—

    (a) OFCOM have assessed whether one or more technical obligations should be imposed on internet service providers; and

      (b)   taking into account that assessment, reports prepared by OFCOM under section 124F, and any other matter that appears to the Secretary of State to be relevant, the Secretary of State considers it appropriate to make the order.

(2)   No order may be made under this section within the period of 12 months beginning with the first day on which there is an initial obligations code in force.

(3)   An order under this section must specify the date from which the technical obligation is to have effect, or provide for it to be specified.

(4)   The order may also specify—
      (a)   the criteria for taking the technical measure concerned against a subscriber;
      (b)   the steps to be taken as part of the measure and when they are to be taken.

(5)   No order is to be made under this section unless—
      (a)   the Secretary of State has complied with subsections (6) to (10), and
      (b)   a draft of the order has been laid before Parliament and approved by a resolution of each House.

(6)   If the Secretary of State proposes to make an order under this section, the Secretary of State must lay before Parliament a document that—
      (a)   explains the proposal, and
      (b)   sets it out in the form of a draft order.

(7)   During the period of 60 days beginning with the day on which the document was laid under subsection (6) ("the 60-day period"), the Secretary of State may not lay before Parliament a draft order to give effect to the proposal (with or without modifications).

(8)   In preparing a draft order under this section to give effect to the proposal, the Secretary of State must have regard to any of the following that are made with regard to the draft order during the 60-day period—
      (a)   any representations, and
      (b)   any recommendations of a committee of either House of Parliament charged with reporting on the draft order.

(9)   When laying before Parliament a draft order to give effect to the proposal (with or without modifications), the Secretary of State must also lay a document that explains any changes made to the proposal contained in the document laid before Parliament under subsection (6).

(10) In calculating the 60-day period, no account is to be taken of any time during which Parliament is dissolved or prorogued or during which either House is adjourned for more than 4 days."

11   Code by OFCOM about obligations to limit internet access

After section 124H of the Communications Act 2003 insert—

"124I Code by OFCOM about obligations to limit internet access

(1)   For any period during which there are one or more technical obligations in force under section 124H, OFCOM must by order make a technical obligations code for the purpose of regulating those obligations.

(2)   The code may be made separately from, or in combination with, any initial obligations code under section 124D.

(3)   A code under this section may—
      (a)   do any of the things mentioned in section 124C(3) to (5) or section 124D(5)(a) to (g); and
      (b)   make other provision for the purpose of regulating the technical obligations.

(4)   OFCOM must not make a code under this section unless they are satisfied that it meets the criteria set out in section 124J.

(5)   OFCOM must—
      (a)   keep a code under this section under review; and

(b)   by order make any amendment of it that is necessary to ensure that while it is in force it continues to meet the criteria set out in section 124J.

(6)   The consent of the Secretary of State is required for the making or amendment by OFCOM of a code under this section.

(7)   Section 403 applies to the power of OFCOM to make an order under this section.

(8)   A statutory instrument containing an order made by OFCOM under this section is subject to annulment in pursuance of a resolution of either House of Parliament."

12   Contents of code about obligations to limit internet access

After section 124I of the Communications Act 2003 insert—

"124J Contents of code about obligations to limit internet access

(1)   The criteria referred to in section 124I(4) are—
   (a)   that the requirements concerning enforcement and related matters are met in relation to the code (see subsections (2) and (3));
   (b)   that the requirements concerning subscriber appeals are met in relation to the code (see section 124K);
   (c)   that it makes any provision about contributions towards meeting costs that is required to be included by an order under section 124M;
   (d)   that it makes any other provision that the Secretary of State requires it to make;
   (e)   that the provisions of the code are objectively justifiable in relation to the matters to which it relates;
   (f)   that those provisions are not such as to discriminate unduly against particular persons or against a particular description of persons;
   (g)   that those provisions are proportionate to what they are intended to achieve; and
   (h)   that, in relation to what those provisions are intended to achieve, they are transparent.

(2)   The requirements concerning enforcement and related matters are—
   (a)   that OFCOM have, under the code, the functions of administering and enforcing it, including the function of resolving owner-provider disputes;
   (b)   that there are adequate arrangements under the code for OFCOM to obtain any information or assistance from internet service providers or copyright owners that OFCOM reasonably require for the purposes of administering and enforcing the code; and
   (c)   that there are adequate arrangements under the code for the costs incurred by OFCOM in administering and enforcing the code to be met by internet service providers and copyright owners.

(3)   The provision made concerning enforcement and related matters may also (unless the Secretary of State requires otherwise) include, in particular—
   (a)   provision for the payment, to a person specified in the code, of a penalty not exceeding the maximum penalty for the time being specified in section 124L(2);
   (b)   provision requiring a copyright owner to indemnify an internet service provider for any loss or damage resulting from the owner's infringement or error in relation to the code or the copyright infringement provisions.

(4)   In this section "owner-provider dispute" means a dispute that—
   (a)   is between persons who are copyright owners or internet service providers; and
   (b)   relates to an act or omission in relation to a technical obligation or a technical obligations code."

13   Subscriber appeals

After section 124J of the Communications Act 2003 insert—

"124K Subscriber appeals

(1)   The requirements concerning subscriber appeals are—

    (a)   for the purposes of section 124E(1)(h), the requirements of subsections (2) to (8); and

    (b)   for the purposes of section 124J(1)(b), the requirements of subsections (2) to (11).

(2)   The requirements of this subsection are—

    (a)   that the code confers on subscribers the right to bring a subscriber appeal and, in the case of a technical obligations code, a further right of appeal to the First-tier Tribunal;

    (b)   that there is a person who, under the code, has the function of determining subscriber appeals;

    (c)   that that person is for practical purposes independent (so far as determining subscriber appeals is concerned) of internet service providers, copyright owners and OFCOM; and

    (d)   that there are adequate arrangements under the code for the costs incurred by that person in determining subscriber appeals to be met by internet service providers, copyright owners and the subscriber concerned.

(3)   The code must provide for the grounds of appeal (so far as an appeal relates to, or to anything done by reference to, a copyright infringement report) to include the following—

    (a)   that the apparent infringement to which the report relates was not an infringement of copyright;

    (b)   that the report does not relate to the subscriber's IP address at the time of the apparent infringement.

(4)   The code must provide for the grounds of appeal to include contravention by the copyright owner or internet service provider of the code or of an obligation regulated by the code.

(5)   The code must provide that an appeal on any grounds must be determined in favour of the subscriber unless the copyright owner or internet service provider shows that, as respects any copyright infringement report to which the appeal relates or by reference to which anything to which the appeal relates was done (or, if there is more than one such report, as respects each of them)—

    (a)   the apparent infringement was an infringement of copyright, and

    (b)   the report relates to the subscriber's IP address at the time of that infringement.

(6)   The code must provide that, where a ground mentioned in subsection (3) is relied on, the appeal must be determined in favour of the subscriber if the subscriber shows that—

    (a)   the act constituting the apparent infringement to which the report relates was not done by the subscriber, and

    (b)   the subscriber took reasonable steps to prevent other persons infringing copyright by means of the internet access service.

(7)   The powers of the person determining subscriber appeals must include power—

    (a)   to secure so far as practicable that a subscriber is not prejudiced for the purposes of the copyright infringement provisions by an act or omission in respect of which an appeal is determined in favour of the subscriber;

    (b)   to make an award of compensation to be paid by a copyright owner or internet service provider to a subscriber affected by such an act or omission; and

    (c)   where the appeal is determined in favour of the subscriber, to direct the copyright owner or internet service provider to reimburse the reasonable costs of the subscriber.

(8) The code must provide that the power to direct the reimbursement of costs under subsection (7)(c) is to be exercised to award reasonable costs to a subscriber whose appeal is successful, unless the person deciding the appeal is satisfied that it would be unjust to give such a direction having regard to all the circumstances including the conduct of the parties before and during the proceedings.

(9) In the case of a technical obligations code, the powers of the person determining subscriber appeals must include power—

    (a) on an appeal in relation to a technical measure or proposed technical measure—

        (i) to confirm the measure;

        (ii) to require the measure not to be taken or to be withdrawn;

        (iii) to substitute any other technical measure that the internet service provider has power to take;

    (b) to exercise the power mentioned in paragraph (a) (ii) or (iii) where an appeal is not upheld but the person determining it is satisfied that there are exceptional circumstances that justify the exercise of the power;

    (c) to take any steps that OFCOM could take in relation to the act or omission giving rise to the technical measure; and

    (d) to remit the decision whether to confirm the technical measure, or any matter relating to that decision, to OFCOM.

(10) In the case of a technical obligations code, the code must make provision—

    (a) enabling a determination of a subscriber appeal to be appealed to the First-tier Tribunal, including on grounds that it was based on an error of fact, wrong in law or unreasonable;

    (b) giving the First-tier Tribunal, in relation to an appeal to it, the powers mentioned in subsections (7) and (9); and

    (c) in relation to recovery of costs awarded by the Tribunal.

(11) In the case of a technical obligations code, the code must include provision to secure that a technical measure is not taken against a subscriber until—

    (a) the period for bringing a subscriber appeal, or any further appeal to the First-tier Tribunal, in relation to the proposed measure has ended (or the subscriber has waived the right to appeal); and

    (b) any such subscriber appeal or further appeal has been determined, abandoned or otherwise disposed of."

14 Enforcement of obligations

After section 124K of the Communications Act 2003 insert—

"124L Enforcement of obligations

(1) Sections 94 to 96 apply in relation to a contravention of an initial obligation or a technical obligation, or a contravention of an obligation under section 124G(6), as they apply in relation to a contravention of a condition set out under section 45.

(2) The amount of the penalty imposed under section 96 as applied by this section is to be such amount not exceeding £250,000 as OFCOM determine to be—

    (a) appropriate; and

    (b) proportionate to the contravention in respect of which it is imposed.

(3) In making that determination OFCOM must have regard to—

    (a) any representations made to them by the internet service provider or copyright owner on whom the penalty is imposed;

    (b) any steps taken by the provider or owner towards complying with the obligations contraventions of which have been notified to the provider or owner under section 94 (as applied); and

    (c) any steps taken by the provider or owner for remedying the consequences of those contraventions.

(4) The Secretary of State may by order amend this section so as to substitute a different maximum penalty for the maximum penalty for the time being specified in subsection (2).

(5)   No order is to be made containing provision authorised by subsection (4)
      unless a draft of the order has been laid before Parliament and approved
      by a resolution of each House."

. . .

16   Interpretation and consequential provision

(1)   After section 124M of the Communications Act 2003 insert—

"124N Interpretation

In sections 124A to 124M and this section—

"apparent infringement", in relation to a copyright infringement report,
means the infringement of copyright that the report states appears to
have taken place;

"copyright infringement list" has the meaning given in section 124B(2);

"copyright infringement provisions" means sections 124A to 124M and
this section;

"copyright infringement report" has the meaning given in section 124A(3);

"copyright owner" means—

(a)   a copyright owner within the meaning of Part 1 of the Copyright,
      Designs and Patents Act 1988 (see section 173 of that Act); or

(b)   someone authorised by that person to act on the person's behalf;
      "copyright work" has the same meaning as in Part 1 of the Copyright,
Designs and Patents Act 1988 (see section 1(2) of that Act);

"initial obligations" has the meaning given in section 124C(1);

"initial obligations code" has the meaning given in section 124A(2);

"internet access service" means an electronic communications service
that—

(a)   is provided to a subscriber;

(b)   consists entirely or mainly of the provision of access to the internet;
      and

(c)   includes the allocation of an IP address or IP addresses to the
      subscriber to enable that access;

"internet service provider" means a person who provides an internet
access service;

"IP address" means an internet protocol address;

"subscriber", in relation to an internet access service, means a person
who—

(a)   receives the service under an agreement between the person and
      the provider of the service; and

(b)   does not receive it as a communications provider;

"subscriber appeal" means—

(a)   in relation to an initial obligations code, an appeal by a subscriber
      on grounds specified in the code in relation to—

      (i)   the making of a copyright infringement report;

      (ii)   notification under section 124A(4);

      (iii) the inclusion or proposed inclusion of an entry in a copyright
             infringement list; or

      (iv)   any other act or omission in relation to an initial obligation or
             an initial obligations code;

(b)   in relation to a technical obligations code, an appeal by a subscriber
      on grounds specified in the code in relation to—

      (i)   the proposed taking of a technical measure; or

      (ii)   any other act or omission in relation to a technical obligation
             or a technical obligations code;

"technical measure" has the meaning given in section 124G(3);

"technical obligation" has the meaning given in section 124G(2);

"technical obligations code" means a code in force under section 124I."

(2)   In section 135(3) of that Act (information required for purposes of Chapter 1 functions), after paragraph (i) insert—

"(ia)   preparing a report under section 124F;

(ib)   carrying out an assessment, taking steps or providing a report under section 124G;".

(3)   In Schedule 8 to that Act (decisions not subject to appeal to the Competition Appeal Tribunal), after paragraph 9 insert—

"9A   A decision relating to any of sections 124A to 124N or to anything done under them."

Powers in relation to internet domain registries

19   Powers in relation to internet domain registries

After section 124N of the Communications Act 2003 insert—

"Powers in relation to internet domain registries

124O   Notification of failure in relation to internet domain registry

(1)   This section applies where the Secretary of State—

(a)   is satisfied that a serious relevant failure in relation to a qualifying internet domain registry is taking place or has taken place, and

(b)   wishes to exercise the powers under section 124P or 124R.

(2)   The Secretary of State must notify the internet domain registry, specifying the failure and a period during which the registry has the opportunity to make representations to the Secretary of State.

(3)   There is a relevant failure in relation to a qualifying internet domain registry if—

(a)   the registry, or any of its registrars or end-users, engages in prescribed practices that are unfair or involve the misuse of internet domain names, or

(b)   the arrangements made by the registry for dealing with complaints in connection with internet domain names do not comply with prescribed requirements.

(4)   A relevant failure is serious, for the purposes of this section, if it has adversely affected or is likely adversely to affect—

(a)   the reputation or availability of electronic communications networks or electronic communications services provided in the United Kingdom or a part of the United Kingdom, or

(b)   the interests of consumers or members of the public in the United Kingdom or a part of the United Kingdom.

(5)   In subsection (3) "prescribed" means prescribed by regulations made by the Secretary of State.

(6)   Before making regulations under subsection (3) the Secretary of State must consult such persons as the Secretary of State considers appropriate.

(7)   In this section and sections 124P to 124R—

"end-user", in relation to a qualifying internet domain registry, means a person who has been or wants to be allocated an internet domain name that is or would be included in the register maintained by the registry;

"qualifying internet domain registry" means a relevant body that—

(a)   maintains a relevant register of internet domain names, and

(b)   operates a computer program or server that forms part of the system that enables the names included in the register to be used to access internet protocol addresses or other information by means of the internet;

"registrar", in relation to a qualifying internet domain registry, means a person authorised by the registry to act on behalf of end-users in connection with the registration of internet domain names;

"relevant body" means a company formed and registered under the Companies Act 2006 or a limited liability partnership; "relevant register of internet domain names" means a register of—

(a) the names of second level internet domains that form part of the same UK-related top level internet domain, or

(b) the names of third level internet domains that form part of the same UK-related second level internet domain;

"second level internet domain" means an internet domain indicated by the last two elements of an internet domain name;

"third level internet domain" means an internet domain indicated by the last three elements of an internet domain name;

"top level internet domain" means an internet domain indicated by the last element of an internet domain name.

(8) An internet domain is "UK-related" if, in the opinion of the Secretary of State, the last element of its name is likely to cause users of the internet, or a class of such users, to believe that the domain and its sub-domains are connected with the United Kingdom or a part of the United Kingdom."

Note: Not yet in force.

46 Extent

(1) This Act extends to England and Wales, Scotland and Northern Ireland.

. . .

DISPUTE RESOLUTION SERVICE POLICY (2016)

1 Definitions

Abusive Registration means a Domain Name which either:

i. was registered or otherwise acquired in a manner which, at the time when the registration or acquisition took place, took unfair advantage of or was unfairly detrimental to the Complainant's Rights; OR

ii. is being or has been used in a manner which has taken unfair advantage of or was unfairly detrimental to the Complainant's Rights;

Complainant means a third party who asserts to us the elements set out in paragraph 2.1 or, if there are multiple complainants, the "lead complainant" (see Procedure paragraph 4.2.1);

Days means unless otherwise stated any day other than Saturday, Sunday or any Bank or public holiday in England and Wales;

Decision means any decision reached by an Expert and where applicable includes the summary decision, full decision and the decision of an appeal panel;

Dispute Resolution Service or DRS means the service provided by us according to this Policy;

Domain Name means any registered .UK domain name administered by us which is the subject of dispute between the Parties in accordance with this Policy;

Expert means the expert we appoint under paragraph 10.5 or 12.1;

Expert Review Group means the panel of expert reviewers who will provide peer review of Decisions and from which appeal panel appointments will be drawn under paragraph 20.7;

Fee Schedule means the list of fees that we charge for the services we provide, including the fees for a summary, full or appeal decision, and which is set out in full on our website;

Mediation means impartial mediation which we conduct to facilitate a resolution acceptable to both Parties;

Party means a Complainant or Respondent and "Parties" has a corresponding meaning;

Policy means this document;

Respondent means the person (including a legal person) in whose name or on whose behalf a Domain Name is registered;

Reverse Domain Name Hijacking means using the DRS in bad faith in an attempt to deprive a Respondent of a Domain Name;

Rights means rights enforceable by the Complainant, whether under English law or otherwise, and may include rights in descriptive terms which have acquired a secondary meaning;

we means Nominet UK (company no. 3203859) whose registered office is at Minerva House, Edmund Halley Road, Oxford Science Park, Oxford OX4 4DQ and "us" and "our" have corresponding meanings.

2 Dispute to which the DRS applies

2.1 A Respondent must submit to proceedings under the DRS if a Complainant asserts to us, according to the Policy, that:

2.1.1 The Complainant has Rights in respect of a name or mark which is identical or similar to the Domain Name; and

2.1.2 The Domain Name, in the hands of the Respondent, is an Abusive Registration

2.2 The Complainant is required to prove to the Expert that both elements are present on the balance of probabilities

3 Communication

3.1 We will send a complaint (see paragraph 4) to the Respondent by using, in our discretion, any of the following means:

3.1.1 sending the complaint by post or email to the Respondent at the contact details shown as the registrant or other contacts in our domain name register database entry for the Domain Name;

3.1.2 sending the complaint in electronic form (including attachments to the extent available in that form) by email to;

3.1.2.1 postmaster@<theDomainName>;or

3.1.2.2 if the Domain Name resolves to an active webpage (other than a generic page which we conclude is maintained by a registrar for parking Domain Names), to any email address shown or email links on that web page so far as this is practicable; or

3.1.3 sending the complaint to any addresses provided to us by the Complainant under paragraph 4.3.4 so far as this is practicable.

. . .

4 The complaint

4.1 Any person or entity may submit a complaint to us in accordance with this Policy. . . .

4.2 More than one person or entity may jointly make a complaint. . . .

4.3 The Complainant must send the complaint to us using the online electronic forms on our web site (except to the extent not available for attachments or if other exceptional circumstances apply, in which case an alternative method may be agreed by us). The complaint shall:—

4.3.1 not exceed 5000 words (not including the text set out in annexes);

4.3.2 submit annexes (with clear and descriptive file names) purely for the purposes of submitting evidence to support the arguments raised in the complaint. Annexes must not be used to circumvent the word limit set out in paragraph 4.3.1 above;

4.3.3 specify whether the Complainant wishes to be contacted directly or through an authorised representative, and set out the email address, telephone number and postal address which should be used;

4.3.4 set out any of the Respondent's contact details which are known to the Complainant;

4.3.5 specify the Domain Name and the name or mark which is identical or similar to the Domain Name and in which the Complainant asserts it has Rights;

4.3.6 describe in accordance with this Policy the grounds on which the complaint is made including in particular: what Rights the Complainant asserts in the name or mark; why the Domain Name should be considered to be an Abusive Registration in the hands of the Respondent; and discuss any applicable aspects of paragraph 5 of this Policy, as well as any other grounds which support the Complainant's assertion;

4.3.7 specify whether the Complainant is seeking to have the Domain Name transferred, suspended or cancelled;

4.3.8 tell us whether any legal proceedings have been commenced or terminated in connection with the Domain Name;

4.3.9 state that the Complainant will submit to the exclusive jurisdiction of the English courts with respect to any legal proceedings seeking to reverse the effect of a Decision requiring the suspension, cancellation or transfer of a Domain Name registration, and that the Complainant agrees that any such legal proceedings will be governed by English law.

. . .

4.5 The complaint may relate to more than one Domain Name, provided that each of those Domain Names are registered in the name of the Respondent.

5   Evidence of Abusive Registration

5.1   A non-exhaustive list of factors which may be evidence that the Domain Name is an Abusive Registration is as follows:

5.1.1   Circumstances indicating that the Respondent has registered or otherwise acquired the Domain Name primarily:

5.1.1.1 for the purposes of selling, renting or otherwise transferring the Domain Name to the Complainant or to a competitor of the Complainant, for valuable consideration in excess of the Respondent's documented out-of-pocket costs directly associated with acquiring or using the Domain Name;

5.1.1.2 as a blocking registration against a name or mark in which the Complainant has Rights; or

5.1.1.3 for the purpose of unfairly disrupting the business of the Complainant;

5.1.2   Circumstances indicating that the Respondent is using or threatening to use the Domain Name in a way which has confused or is likely to confuse people or businesses into believing that the Domain Name is registered to, operated or authorised by, or otherwise connected with the Complainant;

5.1.3   The Complainant can demonstrate that the Respondent is engaged in a pattern of registrations where the Respondent is the registrant of domain names (under .UK or otherwise) which correspond to well known names or trademarks in which the Respondent has no apparent rights, and the Domain Name is part of that pattern;

5.1.4   It is independently verified that the Respondent has given false contact details to us;

5.1.5   The Domain Name was registered as a result of a relationship between the Complainant and the Respondent, and the Complainant:

5.1.5.1 has been using the Domain Name registration exclusively; and

5.1.5.2 paid for the registration and/or renewal of the Domain Name registration;

5.1.6   The Domain Name is an exact match (within the limitations of the character set permissible in domain names) for the name or mark in which the Complainant has Rights, the Complainant's mark has a reputation and the Respondent has no reasonable justification for having registered the Domain Name.

5.2   Failure on the Respondent's part to use the Domain Name for the purposes of email or a web site is not in itself evidence that the Domain Name is an Abusive Registration.

5.3   There shall be a presumption of Abusive Registration if the Complainant proves that the Respondent has been found to have made an Abusive Registration in three (3) or more DRS cases in the two (2) years before the complaint was filed. This presumption can be rebutted (see paragraphs 8.1.4 and 8.3).

6   Notification of Complaint

6.1   We will check that the complaint complies with this Policy and, if so, we will forward it to the Respondent together with our Notification of Complaint letter within three (3) Days of our receipt of the complaint.

. . .

7   The response

7.1   Any response to the complaint must be submitted to us within fifteen (15) Days of the date of commencement of proceedings under the DRS.

7.2   Within three (3) Days following our receipt of the response, we will forward the response to the Complainant.

7.3   The Respondent must send the response to us using the online electronic forms on our web site . . . The response shall:

7.3.1   not exceed 5000 words (not including the text set out in annexes);

7.3.2   submit annexes (with clear and descriptive file names) purely for the purposes of submitting evidence to support the arguments raised in the response. Annexes must not be used to circumvent the word limit set out in paragraph 7.3.1 above;

7.3.3   include any grounds the Respondent wishes to rely upon to rebut the Complainant's assertions under paragraph 4.3.6 above including any relevant factors set out in paragraph 5 of the Policy;

7.3.4   specify whether the Respondent wishes to be contacted directly or through a Representative, and set out the email address, telephone number and postal address which should be used;

7.3.5   tell us whether any legal proceedings have been commenced or terminated in connection with the Domain Name;

. . .

8 How the Respondent may demonstrate in its response that the Domain Name is not an Abusive Registration

8.1 A non-exhaustive list of factors which may be evidence that the Domain Name is not an Abusive Registration is as follows:

8.1.1 Before being aware of the Complainant's cause for complaint (not necessarily the "complaint" under the DRS), the Respondent has:

8.1.1.1 used or made demonstrable preparations to use the Domain Name or a domain name which is similar to the Domain Name in connection with a genuine offering of goods or services;

8.1.1.2 been commonly known by the name or legitimately connected with a mark which is identical or similar to the Domain Name; or

8.1.1.3 made legitimate non-commercial or fair use of the Domain Name.

8.1.2 The Domain Name is generic or descriptive and the Respondent is making fair use of it;

8.1.3 In relation to paragraph 5.1.5; that the Respondent's holding of the Domain Name is consistent with an express term of a written agreement entered into by the Parties; or

8.1.4 In relation to paragraphs 5.1.3 and/or 5.3; that the Domain Name is not part of a wider pattern or series of registrations because the Domain Name is of a significantly different type or character to the other domain names registered by the Respondent.

8.2 Fair use may include sites operated solely in tribute to or in criticism of a person or business.

8.3 If paragraph 5.3 applies, to succeed the Respondent must rebut the presumption by proving in the Response that the registration of the Domain Name is not an Abusive Registration.

8.4 Trading in domain names for profit, and holding a large portfolio of domain names, are of themselves lawful activities. The Expert will review each case on its merits.

8.5 Sale of traffic (i.e. connecting domain names to parking pages and earning click-per-view revenue) is not of itself objectionable under this Policy. However, the Expert will take into account:

8.5.1 the nature of the Domain Name;

8.5.2 the nature of the advertising links on any parking page associated with the Domain Name; and

8.5.3 that the use of the Domain Name is ultimately the Respondent's responsibility.

9 Complainant's reply

9.1 Within five (5) Days of receiving the response from us, the Complainant may submit a reply to the Respondent's response, which shall not exceed 2000 words (not including annexes). . . If the Complainant does not submit a reply to us within five (5) Days the dispute will proceed to Mediation.

. . .

9.3 If an Expert is appointed and the reply extends to other matters, the Expert may declare it inadmissible to the extent that it deals with matters going beyond those newly raised in the Respondent's response. To the extent that the Expert intends to take note of any new material, the Expert should invite the Respondent to file a further submission in response to that material and such further submission shall not exceed 2000 words (not including annexes).

10 Mediation

10.1 Within three (3) Days of our receipt of the Complainant's reply (or the expiry of the deadline for the Complainant to submit a reply), we will begin to conduct Mediation. . . . No Mediation will occur if the Respondent does not file a response.

10.2 Negotiations conducted between the Parties during Mediation (including any information obtained from or in connection to negotiations) shall be confidential as between the Parties and us, and will not be disclosed to the Expert. Neither we nor any Party may reveal details of such negotiations to any third parties unless a court of competent jurisdiction orders disclosure, or we or either Party are required to do so by applicable laws or regulations, or the Parties mutually agree to such disclosure. Neither Party shall use any information gained during Mediation for any ulterior or collateral purpose or include it in any submission likely to be seen by any Expert, judge or arbitrator in this dispute or any later dispute or litigation.

10.3   If the Parties reach a settlement during Mediation then the existence, nature and terms of the settlement shall be confidential, unless the Parties specifically agree otherwise or a court of competent jurisdiction orders otherwise.

. . .

10.5   If the Parties do not achieve an acceptable resolution through Mediation within ten (10) Days, we will send notice to the Parties that we will appoint an Expert subject to the Complainant paying the applicable fee within the time limit specified in paragraph 13.2.

. . .

12   Decisions in the absence of a response

. . .

12.2   If the Complainant does not opt for either a full or a summary decision by paying the applicable fee within ten (10) Days of receipt of the notice that the DRS process has reached the decision stage, we will deem the complaint to be withdrawn.

12.3   The Complainant shall not be prevented from submitting a new complaint to us if a complaint is withdrawn under paragraph 12.2.

. . .

12.5   The Expert will only grant a request for summary decision where he or she is satisfied that:

12.5.1   We have sent the complaint to the Respondent in accordance with paragraphs 3 and 6 of this Policy;

12.5.2   The Complainant has, to the Expert's reasonable satisfaction, shown that he or she has Rights in respect of a name or mark which is identical or similar to the Domain Name and the Domain Name is an Abusive Registration; and

12.5.3   No other factors apply which would make a summary decision unconscionable in all the circumstances.

13   Full Decisions: Appointment of the Expert

13.1   If the Respondent has submitted a response, and an acceptable resolution has not been found through Mediation, we will notify the Parties that either the Complainant or Respondent can apply for a full decision.

13.2   If we do not receive within ten (10) Days of receipt of the notice referred to in paragraph 10.5 above a request from the Complainant to refer the matter to an Expert, together with the applicable fee, the Respondent may elect to pay for a full decision.

13.3   If we do not receive the Respondent's request to refer the matter to an Expert together with the applicable fee within ten (10) Days of the Respondent's receipt of the notice, we will deem the complaint to be withdrawn and the Complainant shall not be prevented from submitting a new complaint to us in relation to the same Domain Name and Respondent.

14   Timing of Decision

14.1   Within five (5) Days of our receipt of the applicable fee from the Complainant or Respondent, we will appoint an Expert from our list. . . .

. . .

18   Expert Decision

18.1   The Expert will decide a complaint on the basis of the Parties' submissions and this Policy. It is the Parties' responsibility to explain all the relevant background facts and other circumstances applicable to the dispute in their submissions, and to support those submissions with appropriate evidence. In the ordinary course an Expert will not perform any research into a dispute or check the parties' assertions, However an Expert may (in their entire discretion) check any material which is generally available in the public domain.

18.2   An Expert may be in possession of relevant information which is not in the case papers, and upon which he or she wishes to rely for the purposes of the Decision. In this event, the Expert will inform the Parties that he or she holds such relevant information and invite them to make submissions.

. . .

18.7   If, after considering the submissions, the Expert finds that the complaint was Reverse Domain Name Hijacking, the Expert shall state this finding in the Decision.

18.8   If the Complainant is found on three separate occasions within a 2-year period to have been Reverse Domain Name Hijacking, Nominet will not accept any further complaints from that Complainant for a period of 2 years.

19   Notification and publication
19.1   Within three (3) Days of our receipt of a Decision from the Expert we will communicate the Decision to the Parties and will publish the Decision in full on our web site.

. . .

19.3   If the Expert makes a Decision that a Domain Name registration should be cancelled, suspended or transferred, we will implement that Decision by making any necessary changes to our domain name register database after ten (10) Days of the date that the Parties were notified, unless, we receive from either Party:

19.3.1   an appeal or statement of intention to appeal complying with paragraph 20, in which case we will take no further action in respect of the Domain Name until the appeal is concluded; or

19.3.2   official documentation showing that the Party has issued and served (or in the case of service outside England and Wales, commenced the process of serving) legal proceedings against the other Party in respect of the Domain Name. In this case, we will take no further action in respect of the Domain Name unless we receive;

19.3.2.1 evidence which satisfies us that the Parties have reached a settlement; or

19.3.2.2 evidence which satisfies us that such proceedings have been dismissed, withdrawn or are otherwise concluded.

20   Appeal
20.1   Either Party shall have the right to appeal a Decision . . .

20.3   An appeal notice should not exceed 1000 words, should set out detailed grounds and reasons for the appeal, but shall contain no new evidence or annexes.

20.4   Within three (3) Days of our receipt of the:

20.4.1   statement of the intention to appeal and deposit; or

20.4.2   appeal notice and the full fee,
          we will forward the statement of intention to appeal or appeal notice (as the case may be) to the other Party.

20.5   Within ten (10) Days of receiving the appeal notice from us, the other Party may submit to us an appeal response (paragraph 20.6).

20.6   An appeal response must not exceed 1000 words, should set out detailed grounds and reasons why the appeal should be rejected but should contain no new evidence or annexes.

20.7   Following the filing of an appeal response (or the expiry of the deadline to do so) we will appoint an appeal panel of three members of the Expert Review Group. . . .

20.8   The appeal panel will consider appeals on the basis of a full review of the matter and may review procedural matters. . . .

20.13   The operation of the DRS will not prevent either the Complainant or the Respondent from submitting the dispute to a court of competent jurisdiction.

21   Repeat complaints
21.1   If a complaint has reached the Decision stage on a previous occasion it may not be reconsidered (but it may be appealed, see paragraph 20) by an Expert. If the Expert finds that a complaint is a resubmission of an earlier complaint that had reached the decision stage, he or she shall reject the complaint without examining it.

21.2   In determining whether a complaint is a resubmission of an earlier complaint, or contains a material difference that justifies a re-hearing the Expert shall consider the following questions:

21.2.1   Are the Complainant, the Respondent and the domain name in issue the same as in the earlier case?

21.2.2   Does the substance of the complaint relate to acts that occurred prior to or subsequent to the close of submissions in the earlier case?

21.2.3   If the substance of the complaint relates to acts that occurred prior to the close of submissions in the earlier case, are there any exceptional grounds for the rehearing or reconsideration, bearing in mind the need to protect the integrity and smooth operation of the DRS;

21.2.4   If the substance of the complaint relates to acts that occurred subsequent to the close of submissions in the earlier decision, acts on which the re-filed complaint is based should not be, in substance, the same as the acts on which the previous complaint was based.

21.3   A non-exhaustive list of examples which may be exceptional enough to justify a re-hearing under paragraph 21.2.3 include:

21.3.1 serious misconduct on the part of the Expert, a Party, witness or lawyer;

21.3.2 false evidence having been offered to the Expert;

21.3.3 the discovery of credible and material evidence which could not have been reasonably foreseen or known for the Complainant to have included it in the evidence in support of the earlier complaint;

21.3.4 a breach of natural justice; and

21.3.5 the avoidance of an unconscionable result.

. . .

23   Other action by us

23.1   We will not cancel, transfer, activate, deactivate or otherwise change any Domain Name registration except as set out in paragraph 19 above and as provided under paragraphs X of the Terms and Conditions.

. . .

25   Effect of court proceedings

25.1   If it is brought to our attention that legal proceedings relating to the Domain Name(s) are issued in a court of competent jurisdiction, and have been served, we will suspend the DRS dispute pending the outcome of those legal proceedings.

25.2   A Party must promptly notify us if it initiates legal proceedings in a court of competent jurisdiction relating to the Domain Name during the course of proceedings under the DRS.

. . .

ELECTRONIC COMMERCE (EC DIRECTIVE) REGULATIONS 2002
(SI 2002 No. 2013)

2   Interpretation

(1) In these Regulations and in the Schedule—

"commercial communication" means a communication, in any form, designed to promote, directly or indirectly, the goods, services or image of any person pursuing a commercial, industrial or craft activity or exercising a regulated profession, other than a communication—

(a) consisting only of information allowing direct access to the activity of that person including a geographic address, a domain name or an electronic mail address; or

(b) relating to the goods, services or image of that person provided that the communication has been prepared independently of the person making it (and for this purpose, a communication prepared without financial consideration is to be taken to have been prepared independently unless the contrary is shown);

"the Commission" means the Commission of the European Communities;

"consumer" means any natural person who is acting for purposes other than those of his trade, business or profession;

"coordinated field" means requirements applicable to information society service providers or information society services, regardless of whether they are of a general nature or specifically designed for them, and covers requirements with which the service provider has to comply in respect of—

(a) the taking up of the activity of an information society service, such as requirements concerning qualifications, authorisation or notification, and

(b) the pursuit of the activity of an information society service, such as requirements concerning the behaviour of the service provider, requirements regarding the quality or content of the service including those applicable to advertising and contracts, or requirements concerning the liability of the service provider,

but does not cover requirements such as those applicable to goods as such, to the delivery of goods or to services not provided by electronic means;

"the Directive" means Directive 2000/31/EC of the European Parliament and of the Council of 8 June 2000 on certain legal aspects of information society services, in particular electronic commerce, in the Internal Market (Directive on electronic commerce);

"EEA Agreement" means the Agreement on the European Economic Area signed at Oporto on 2 May 1992 as adjusted by the Protocol signed at Brussels on 17 March 1993; "enactment" includes an enactment comprised in Northern Ireland legislation and comprised in, or an instrument made under, an Act of the Scottish Parliament; "enforcement action" means any form of enforcement action including, in particular—

(a) in relation to any legal requirement imposed by or under any enactment, any action taken with a view to or in connection with imposing any sanction (whether criminal or otherwise) for failure to observe or comply with it; and

(b) in relation to a permission or authorisation, anything done with a view to removing or restricting that permission or authorisation;

"enforcement authority" does not include courts but, subject to that, means any person who is authorised, whether by or under an enactment or otherwise, to take enforcement action;

"established service provider" means a service provider who is a national of a member State or a company or firm as mentioned in Article 54 of the Treaty and who effectively pursues an economic activity by virtue of which he is a service provider using a fixed establishment in a member State for an indefinite period, but the presence and use of the technical means and technologies required to provide the information society service do not, in themselves, constitute an establishment of the provider; in cases where it cannot be determined from which of a number of places of establishment a given service is provided, that service is to be regarded as provided from the place of establishment where the provider has the centre of his activities relating to that service; references to a service provider being established or to the establishment of a service provider shall be construed accordingly;

"information society services" (which is summarised in recital 17 of the Directive as covering "any service normally provided for remuneration, at a distance, by means of electronic equipment for the processing (including digital compression) and storage of data, and at the individual request of a recipient of a service") has the meaning set out in Article 2(a) of the Directive, (which refers to Article 1(2) of Directive 98/34/EC of the European Parliament and of the Council of 22 June 1998 laying down a procedure for the provision of information in the field of technical standards and regulations, as amended by Directive 98/48/EC of 20 July 1998);

"member State" includes a State which is a contracting party to the EEA Agreement; "recipient of the service" means any person who, for professional ends or otherwise, uses an information society service, in particular for the purposes of seeking information or making it accessible;

"regulated profession" means any profession within the meaning of either Article 1(d) of Council Directive 89/48/EEC of 21 December 1988 on a general system for the recognition of higher-education diplomas awarded on completion of professional education and training of at least three years' duration or of Article 1(f) of Council Directive 92/51/EEC of 18 June 1992 on a second general system for the recognition of professional education and training to supplement Directive 89/48/EEC;

"service provider" means any person providing an information society service; "the Treaty" means the Treaty on the Functioning of the European Union.

(2) In regulation 4 and 5, "requirement" means any legal requirement under the law of the United Kingdom, or any part of it, imposed by or under any enactment or otherwise.

(3) Terms used in the Directive other than those in paragraph (1) above shall have the same meaning as in the Directive.

6   General information to be provided by a person providing an information society service

(1) A person providing an information society service shall make available to the recipient of the service and any relevant enforcement authority, in a form and manner which is easily, directly and permanently accessible, the following information—

(a) the name of the service provider;

(b) the geographic address at which the service provider is established;

(c) the details of the service provider, including his electronic mail address, which make it possible to contact him rapidly and communicate with him in a direct and effective manner;

(d) where the service provider is registered in a trade or similar register available to the public, details of the register in which the service provider is entered and his registration number, or equivalent means of identification in that register;

(e) where the provision of the service is subject to an authorisation scheme, the particulars of the relevant supervisory authority;

(f) where the service provider exercises a regulated profession—

    (i) the details of any professional body or similar institution with which the service provider is registered;

    (ii) his professional title and the member State where that title has been granted;

    (iii) a reference to the professional rules applicable to the service provider in the member State of establishment and the means to access them; and

. . .

(2) Where a person providing an information society service refers to prices, these shall be indicated clearly and unambiguously and, in particular, shall indicate whether they are inclusive of tax and delivery costs.

7 Commercial communications

A service provider shall ensure that any commercial communication provided by him and which constitutes or forms part of an information society service shall—

(a) be clearly identifiable as a commercial communication;

(b) clearly identify the person on whose behalf the commercial communication is made;

(c) clearly identify as such any promotional offer (including any discount, premium or gift) and ensure that any conditions which must be met to qualify for it are easily accessible, and presented clearly and unambiguously; and

(d) clearly identify as such any promotional competition or game and ensure that any conditions for participation are easily accessible and presented clearly and unambiguously.

8 Unsolicited commercial communications

A service provider shall ensure that any unsolicited commercial communication sent by him by electronic mail is clearly and unambiguously identifiable as such as soon as it is received.

9 Information to be provided where contracts are concluded by electronic means

(1) Unless parties who are not consumers have agreed otherwise, where a contract is to be concluded by electronic means a service provider shall, prior to an order being placed by the recipient of a service, provide to that recipient in a clear, comprehensible and unambiguous manner the information set out in (a) to (d) below—

(a) the different technical steps to follow to conclude the contract;

(b) whether or not the concluded contract will be filed by the service provider and whether it will be accessible;

(c) the technical means for identifying and correcting input errors prior to the placing of the order; and

(d) the languages offered for the conclusion of the contract.

(2) Unless parties who are not consumers have agreed otherwise, a service provider shall indicate which relevant codes of conduct he subscribes to and give information on how those codes can be consulted electronically.

(3) Where the service provider provides terms and conditions applicable to the contract to the recipient, the service provider shall make them available to him in a way that allows him to store and reproduce them.

(4) The requirements of paragraphs (1) and (2) above shall not apply to contracts concluded exclusively by exchange of electronic mail or by equivalent individual communications.

10 Other information requirements

Regulations 6, 7, 8 and 9(1) have effect in addition to any other information requirements in legislation giving effect to EU law.

11   Placing of the order

(1)   Unless parties who are not consumers have agreed otherwise, where the recipient of the service places his order through technological means, a service provider shall—

    (a)   acknowledge receipt of the order to the recipient of the service without undue delay and by electronic means; and

    (b)   make available to the recipient of the service appropriate, effective and accessible technical means allowing him to identify and correct input errors prior to the placing of the order.

(2)   For the purposes of paragraph (1)(a) above—

    (a)   the order and the acknowledgement of receipt will be deemed to be received when the parties to whom they are addressed are able to access them; and

    (b)   the acknowledgement of receipt may take the form of the provision of the service paid for where that service is an information society service.

(3)   The requirements of paragraph (1) above shall not apply to contracts concluded exclusively by exchange of electronic mail or by equivalent individual communications.

12   Meaning of the term "order"

Except in relation to regulation 9(1)(c) and regulation 11(1)(b) where "order" shall be the contractual offer, "order" may be but need not be the contractual offer for the purposes of regulations 9 and 11.

13   Liability of the service provider

The duties imposed by regulations 6, 7, 8, 9(1) and 11(1)(a) shall be enforceable, at the suit of any recipient of a service, by an action against the service provider for damages for breach of statutory duty.

14   Compliance with Regulation 9(3)

Where on request a service provider has failed to comply with the requirement in regulation 9(3), the recipient may seek an order from any court having jurisdiction in relation to the contract requiring that service provider to comply with that requirement.

15   Right to rescind contract

Where a person—

(a)   has entered into a contract to which these Regulations apply, and

(b)   the service provider has not made available means of allowing him to identify and correct input errors in compliance with regulation 11(1)(b),

he shall be entitled to rescind the contract unless any court having jurisdiction in relation to the contract in question orders otherwise on the application of the service provider.

17   Mere conduit

(1)   Where an information society service is provided which consists of the transmission in a communication network of information provided by a recipient of the service or the provision of access to a communication network, the service provider (if he otherwise would) shall not be liable for damages or for any other pecuniary remedy or for any criminal sanction as a result of that transmission where the service provider—

    (a)   did not initiate the transmission;

    (b)   did not select the receiver of the transmission; and

    (c)   did not select or modify the information contained in the transmission.

(2)   The acts of transmission and of provision of access referred to in paragraph (1) include the automatic, intermediate and transient storage of the information transmitted where:

    (a)   this takes place for the sole purpose of carrying out the transmission in the communication network, and

    (b)   the information is not stored for any period longer than is reasonably necessary for the transmission.

18   Caching

Where an information society service is provided which consists of the transmission in a communication network of information provided by a recipient of the service, the service provider (if he otherwise would) shall not be liable for damages or for any other pecuniary remedy or for any criminal sanction as a result of that transmission where—

(a)   the information is the subject of automatic, intermediate and temporary storage where that storage is for the sole purpose of making more efficient onward transmission of the information to other recipients of the service upon their request, and

(b)   the service provider—

    (i)   does not modify the information;

    (ii)   complies with conditions on access to the information;

    (iii)   complies with any rules regarding the updating of the information, specified in a manner widely recognised and used by industry;

    (iv)   does not interfere with the lawful use of technology, widely recognised and used by industry, to obtain data on the use of the information; and

    (v)   acts expeditiously to remove or to disable access to the information he has stored upon obtaining actual knowledge of the fact that the information at the initial source of the transmission has been removed from the network, or access to it has been disabled, or that a court or an administrative authority has ordered such removal or disablement.

19   Hosting

Where an information society service is provided which consists of the storage of information provided by a recipient of the service, the service provider (if he otherwise would) shall not be liable for damages or for any other pecuniary remedy or for any criminal sanction as a result of that storage where—

(a)   the service provider—

    (i)   does not have actual knowledge of unlawful activity or information and, where a claim for damages is made, is not aware of facts or circumstances from which it would have been apparent to the service provider that the activity or information was unlawful; or

    (ii)   upon obtaining such knowledge or awareness, acts expeditiously to remove or to disable access to the information, and

(b)   the recipient of the service was not acting under the authority or the control of the service provider.

20   Protection of rights

(1)   Nothing in regulations 17, 18 and 19 shall—

    (a)   prevent a person agreeing different contractual terms; or

    (b)   affect the rights of any party to apply to a court for relief to prevent or stop infringement of any rights.

(2)   Any power of an administrative authority to prevent or stop infringement of any rights shall continue to apply notwithstanding regulations 17, 18 and 19.

21   Defence in Criminal Proceedings: burden of proof

(1)   This regulation applies where a service provider charged with an offence in criminal proceedings arising out of any transmission, provision of access or storage falling within regulation 17, 18 or 19 relies on a defence under any of regulations 17, 18 and 19.

(2)   Where evidence is adduced which is sufficient to raise an issue with respect to that defence, the court or jury shall assume that the defence is satisfied unless the prosecution proves beyond reasonable doubt that it is not.

22   Notice for the purposes of actual knowledge

In determining whether a service provider has actual knowledge for the purposes of regulations 18(b)(v) and 19(a)(i), a court shall take into account all matters which appear to it in the particular circumstances to be relevant and, among other things, shall have regard to—

(a)   whether a service provider has received a notice through a means of contact made available in accordance with regulation 6(1)(c), and

(b)   the extent to which any notice includes—

    (i)   the full name and address of the sender of the notice;

    (ii)   details of the location of the information in question; and

    (iii)   details of the unlawful nature of the activity or information in question.

RULES FOR UNIFORM DOMAIN NAME DISPUTE RESOLUTION POLICY
(as Approved by ICANN on 28 September 2013)

Administrative proceedings for the resolution of disputes under the Uniform Dispute Resolution Policy adopted by ICANN shall be governed by these Rules and also the Supplemental Rules of the Provider administering the proceedings, as posted on its web site.

1   Definitions

In these Rules:

Complainant means the party initiating a complaint concerning a domain-name registration.

ICANN refers to the Internet Corporation for Assigned Names and Numbers.

Lock means a set of measures that a registrar applies to a domain name, which prevents at a minimum any modification to the registrant and registrar information by the Respondent, but does not affect the resolution of the domain name or the renewal of the domain name.

Mutual Jurisdiction means a court jurisdiction at the location of either (a) the principal office of the Registrar (provided the domain-name holder has submitted in its Registration Agreement to that jurisdiction for court adjudication of disputes concerning or arising from the use of the domain name) or (b) the domain-name holder's address as shown for the registration of the domain name in Registrar's Whois database at the time the complaint is submitted to the Provider.

Panel means an administrative panel appointed by a Provider to decide a complaint concerning a domain-name registration.

Panelist means an individual appointed by a Provider to be a member of a Panel.

Party means a Complainant or a Respondent.

Pendency means the time period from the moment a UDRP complaint has been submitted by the Complainant to the UDRP Provider to the time the UDRP decision has been implemented or the UDRP complaint has been terminated.

Policy means the Uniform Domain Name Dispute Resolution Policy that is incorporated by reference and made a part of the Registration Agreement.

Provider means a dispute-resolution service provider approved by ICANN. A list of such Providers appears at www.icann.org/udrp/approved-providers.htm.

Registrar means the entity with which the Respondent has registered a domain name that is the subject of a complaint.

Registration Agreement means the agreement between a Registrar and a domain-name holder.

Respondent means the holder of a domain-name registration against which a complaint is initiated.

Reverse Domain Name Hijacking means using the Policy in bad faith to attempt to deprive a registered domain-name holder of a domain name.

Supplemental Rules means the rules adopted by the Provider administering a proceeding to supplement these Rules. Supplemental Rules shall not be inconsistent with the Policy or these Rules and shall cover such topics as fees, word and page limits and guidelines, file size and format modalities, the means for communicating with the Provider and the Panel, and the form of cover sheets.

Written Notice means hardcopy notification by the Provider to the Respondent of the commencement of an administrative proceeding under the Policy which shall inform the respondent that a complaint has been filed against it, and which shall state that the Provider has electronically transmitted the complaint including any annexes to the Respondent by the means specified herein. Written notice does not include a hardcopy of the complaint itself or of any annexes.

2   Communications

(a)   When forwarding a complaint, including any annexes, electronically to the Respondent, it shall be the Provider's responsibility to employ reasonably available means calculated to achieve actual notice to Respondent. Achieving actual notice, or employing the following measures to do so, shall discharge this responsibility:

(i)   sending Written Notice of the complaint to all postal-mail and facsimile addresses

           (A)   shown in the domain name's registration data in Registrar's Whois database for the registered domain-name holder, the technical contact, and the administrative contact and (B) supplied by Registrar to the Provider for the registration's billing contact; and

    (ii)   sending the complaint, including any annexes, in electronic form by e-mail to:

           (A)   the e-mail addresses for those technical, administrative, and billing contacts;

           (B)   postmaster@\<the contested domain name>; and

           (C)   if the domain name (or "www." followed by the domain name) resolves to an active web page (other than a generic page the Provider concludes is maintained by a registrar or ISP for parking domain-names registered by multiple domain-name holders), any e- mail address shown or e-mail links on that web page; and

    (iii)   sending the complaint, including any annexes, to any e-mail address the Respondent has notified the Provider it prefers and, to the extent practicable, to all other e-mail addresses provided to the Provider by Complainant under Paragraph 3(b)(v).

. . .

(c)   Any communication to the Provider or the Panel shall be made by the means and in the manner (including, where applicable, the number of copies) stated in the Provider's Supplemental Rules.

(d)   Communications shall be made in the language prescribed in Paragraph 11.

. . .

(g)   Except as otherwise provided in these Rules, all time periods calculated under these Rules to begin when a communication is made shall begin to run on the earliest date that the communication is deemed to have been made in accordance with Paragraph 2(f).

. . .

3   The complaint

(a)   Any person or entity may initiate an administrative proceeding by submitting a complaint in accordance with the Policy and these Rules to any Provider approved by ICANN. (Due to capacity constraints or for other reasons, a Provider's ability to accept complaints may be suspended at times. In that event, the Provider shall refuse the submission. The person or entity may submit the complaint to another Provider.)

(b)   The complaint including any annexes shall be submitted in electronic form and shall

    . . .

    (vi)   Specify the domain name(s) that is/are the subject of the complaint;

    (vii)   Identify the Registrar(s) with whom the domain name(s) is/are registered at the time the complaint is filed;

    (viii)   Specify the trademark(s) or service mark(s) on which the complaint is based and, for each mark, describe the goods or services, if any, with which the mark is used (Complainant may also separately describe other goods and services with which it intends, at the time the complaint is submitted, to use the mark in the future.);

    (ix)   Describe, in accordance with the Policy, the grounds on which the complaint is made including, in particular,

           (1)   the manner in which the domain name(s) is/are identical or confusingly similar to a trademark or service mark in which the Complainant has rights; and

           (2)   why the Respondent (domain-name holder) should be considered as having no rights or legitimate interests in respect of the domain name(s) that is/are the subject of the complaint; and

           (3)   why the domain name(s) should be considered as having been registered and being used in bad faith

    . . .

    (x)   Specify, in accordance with the Policy, the remedies sought;

    . . .

    (xiii)   State that Complainant will submit, with respect to any challenges to a decision in the administrative proceeding canceling or transferring the domain name, to the jurisdiction of the courts in at least one specified Mutual Jurisdiction;

    . . .

(c)   The complaint may relate to more than one domain name, provided that the domain names are registered by the same domain-name holder.

4   Notification of complaint

(a)   The Provider shall submit a verification request to the Registrar. The verification request will include a request to Lock the domain name.

(b)   Within two (2) business days of receiving the Provider's verification request, the Registrar shall provide the information requested in the verification request and confirm that a Lock of the domain name has been applied. The Registrar shall not notify the Respondent of the proceeding until the Lock status has been applied. The Lock shall remain in place through the remaining Pendency of the UDRP proceeding. . .

. . .

5   The response

(a)   Within twenty (20) days of the date of commencement of the administrative proceeding the Respondent shall submit a response to the Provider.

(b)   The Respondent may expressly request an additional four (4) calendar days in which to respond to the complaint, and the Provider shall automatically grant the extension and notify the Parties thereof.

(c)   The response, including any annexes, shall be submitted in electronic form and shall:

   (i)   Respond specifically to the statements and allegations contained in the complaint and include any and all bases for the Respondent (domain-name holder) to retain registration and use of the disputed domain name. . .

   (ii)   Provide the name, postal and e-mail addresses, and the telephone and telefax numbers of the Respondent (domain-name holder) and of any representative authorized to act for the Respondent in the administrative proceeding;

   (iii)   Specify a preferred method for communications. . .

(e)   At the request of the Respondent, the Provider may, in exceptional cases, extend the period of time for the filing of the response. The period may also be extended by written stipulation between the Parties, provided the stipulation is approved by the Provider.

(f)   If a Respondent does not submit a response, in the absence of exceptional circumstances, the Panel shall decide the dispute based upon the complaint.

13   In-Person Hearings

There shall be no in-person hearings (including hearings by teleconference, videoconference, and web conference), unless the Panel determines, in its sole discretion and as an exceptional matter, that such a hearing is necessary for deciding the complaint.

14   Default

(a)   In the event that a Party, in the absence of exceptional circumstances, does not comply with any of the time periods established by these Rules or the Panel, the Panel shall proceed to a decision on the complaint.

(b)   If a Party, in the absence of exceptional circumstances, does not comply with any provision of, or requirement under, these Rules or any request from the Panel, the Panel shall draw such inferences therefrom as it considers appropriate.

15   Panel decisions

(a)   A Panel shall decide a complaint on the basis of the statements and documents submitted and in accordance with the Policy, these Rules and any rules and principles of law that it deems applicable.

(b)   In the absence of exceptional circumstances, the Panel shall forward its decision on the complaint to the Provider within fourteen (14) days of its appointment pursuant to Paragraph 6.

(c)   In the case of a three-member Panel, the Panel's decision shall be made by a majority.

(d)   The Panel's decision shall be in writing, provide the reasons on which it is based, indicate the date on which it was rendered and identify the name(s) of the Panelist(s).

(e)   Panel decisions and dissenting opinions shall normally comply with the guidelines as to length set forth in the Provider's Supplemental Rules. Any dissenting opinion shall accompany the majority decision. If the Panel concludes that the dispute is not within the scope of Paragraph 4(a) of the Policy, it shall so state. If after considering the submissions the Panel finds that the complaint was brought in bad faith, for example in an attempt at Reverse Domain Name Hijacking or was brought primarily to harass the domain-name holder, the Panel shall declare in its decision that the complaint was brought in bad faith and constitutes an abuse of the administrative proceeding.

17   Settlement or other grounds for termination

(a)   If, before the Panel's decision, the Parties agree on a settlement, the Panel shall terminate the administrative proceeding . . .

(b)   If, before the Panel's decision is made, it becomes unnecessary or impossible to continue the administrative proceeding for any reason, the Panel shall terminate the administrative proceeding, unless a Party raises justifiable grounds for objection within a period of time to be determined by the Panel.

18   Effect of court proceedings

(a)   In the event of any legal proceedings initiated prior to or during an administrative proceeding in respect of a domain-name dispute that is the subject of the complaint, the Panel shall have the discretion to decide whether to suspend or terminate the administrative proceeding, or to proceed to a decision.

(b)   In the event that a Party initiates any legal proceedings during the pendency of an administrative proceeding in respect of a domain-name dispute that is the subject of the complaint, it shall promptly notify the Panel and the Provider. See Paragraph 8 above.

UNIFORM DOMAIN NAME DISPUTE RESOLUTION POLICY
(as Approved by ICANN on 24 October, 1999)

1   Purpose

This Uniform Domain Name Dispute Resolution Policy (the "Policy") has been adopted by the Internet Corporation for Assigned Names and Numbers ("ICANN"), is incorporated by reference into your Registration Agreement, and sets forth the terms and conditions in connection with a dispute between you and any party other than us (the registrar) over the registration and use of an Internet domain name registered by you. Proceedings under Paragraph 4 of this Policy will be conducted according to the Rules for Uniform Domain Name Dispute Resolution Policy (the "Rules of Procedure"), which are available at www.icann.org/udrp/udrp-rules-24oct99.htm, and the selected administrative-dispute-resolution service provider's supplemental rules.

2   Your representations

By applying to register a domain name, or by asking us to maintain or renew a domain name registration, you hereby represent and warrant to us that (a) the statements that you made in your Registration Agreement are complete and accurate; (b) to your knowledge, the registration of the domain name will not infringe upon or otherwise violate the rights of any third party; (c) you are not registering the domain name for an unlawful purpose; and (d) you will not knowingly use the domain name in violation of any applicable laws or regulations. It is your responsibility to determine whether your domain name registration infringes or violates someone else's rights.

3   Cancellations, transfers, and changes

We will cancel, transfer or otherwise make changes to domain name registrations under the following circumstances:

a.   subject to the provisions of Paragraph 8, our receipt of written or appropriate electronic instructions from you or your authorized agent to take such action;

b.   our receipt of an order from a court or arbitral tribunal, in each case of competent jurisdiction, requiring such action; and/or

c.   our receipt of a decision of an Administrative Panel requiring such action in any administrative proceeding to which you were a party and which was conducted under this Policy or a later version of this Policy adopted by ICANN. (See Paragraph 4(i) and (k) below.)

We may also cancel, transfer or otherwise make changes to a domain name registration in accordance with the terms of your Registration Agreement or other legal requirements.

4   Mandatory administrative proceeding

This Paragraph sets forth the type of disputes for which you are required to submit to a mandatory administrative proceeding. These proceedings will be conducted before one of the administrative-dispute-resolution service providers listed at www.icann.org/udrp/approved-providers.htm (each, a "Provider").

a.   **Applicable Disputes.** You are required to submit to a mandatory administrative proceeding in the event that a third party (a "complainant") asserts to the applicable Provider, in compliance with the Rules of Procedure, that

    (i)   your domain name is identical or confusingly similar to a trademark or service mark in which the complainant has rights; and

    (ii)   you have no rights or legitimate interests in respect of the domain name; and

    (iii)   your domain name has been registered and is being used in bad faith.

In the administrative proceeding, the complainant must prove that each of these three elements are present.

b.   **Evidence of Registration and Use in Bad Faith.** For the purposes of Paragraph 4(a)(iii), the following circumstances, in particular but without limitation, if found by the Panel to be present, shall be evidence of the registration and use of a domain name in bad faith:

    (i)   circumstances indicating that you have registered or you have acquired the domain name primarily for the purpose of selling, renting, or otherwise transferring the domain name registration to the complainant who is the owner of the trademark or service mark or to a competitor of that complainant, for valuable consideration in excess of your documented out-of-pocket costs directly related to the domain name; or

    (ii)   you have registered the domain name in order to prevent the owner of the trademark or service mark from reflecting the mark in a corresponding domain name, provided that you have engaged in a pattern of such conduct; or

    (iii)   you have registered the domain name primarily for the purpose of disrupting the business of a competitor; or

    (iv)   by using the domain name, you have intentionally attempted to attract, for commercial gain, Internet users to your web site or other on-line location, by creating a likelihood of confusion with the complainant's mark as to the source, sponsorship, affiliation, or endorsement of your web site or location or of a product or service on your web site or location.

c.   **How to Demonstrate Your Rights to and Legitimate Interests in the Domain Name in Responding to a Complaint.** When you receive a complaint, you should refer to Paragraph 5 of the Rules of Procedure in determining how your response should be prepared. Any of the following circumstances, in particular but without limitation, if found by the Panel to be proved based on its evaluation of all evidence presented, shall demonstrate your rights or legitimate interests to the domain name for purposes of Paragraph 4(a)(ii):

    (i)   before any notice to you of the dispute, your use of, or demonstrable preparations to use, the domain name or a name corresponding to the domain name in connection with a bona fide offering of goods or services; or

    (ii)   you (as an individual, business, or other organization) have been commonly known by the domain name, even if you have acquired no trademark or service mark rights; or

    (iii)   you are making a legitimate noncommercial or fair use of the domain name, without intent for commercial gain to misleadingly divert consumers or to tarnish the trademark or service mark at issue.

d.   **Selection of Provider.** The complainant shall select the Provider from among those approved by ICANN by submitting the complaint to that Provider. The selected Provider will administer the proceeding, except in cases of consolidation as described in Paragraph 4(f).

e.   **Initiation of Proceeding and Process and Appointment of Administrative Panel.** The Rules of Procedure state the process for initiating and conducting a proceeding and for appointing the panel that will decide the dispute (the "Administrative Panel").

f. **Consolidation.** In the event of multiple disputes between you and a complainant, either you or the complainant may petition to consolidate the disputes before a single Administrative Panel. This petition shall be made to the first Administrative Panel appointed to hear a pending dispute between the parties. This Administrative Panel may consolidate before it any or all such disputes in its sole discretion, provided that the disputes being consolidated are governed by this Policy or a later version of this Policy adopted by ICANN.

g. **Fees.** All fees charged by a Provider in connection with any dispute before an Administrative Panel pursuant to this Policy shall be paid by the complainant, except in cases where you elect to expand the Administrative Panel from one to three panelists as provided in Paragraph 5(b)(iv) of the Rules of Procedure, in which case all fees will be split evenly by you and the complainant.

h. **Our Involvement in Administrative Proceedings.** We do not, and will not, participate in the administration or conduct of any proceeding before an Administrative Panel. In addition, we will not be liable as a result of any decisions rendered by the Administrative Panel.

i. **Remedies.** The remedies available to a complainant pursuant to any proceeding before an Administrative Panel shall be limited to requiring the cancellation of your domain name or the transfer of your domain name registration to the complainant.

j. **Notification and Publication.** The Provider shall notify us of any decision made by an Administrative Panel with respect to a domain name you have registered with us. All decisions under this Policy will be published in full over the Internet, except when an Administrative Panel determines in an exceptional case to redact portions of its decision.

k. **Availability of Court Proceedings.** The mandatory administrative proceeding requirements set forth in Paragraph 4 shall not prevent either you or the complainant from submitting the dispute to a court of competent jurisdiction for independent resolution before such mandatory administrative proceeding is commenced or after such proceeding is concluded. If an Administrative Panel decides that your domain name registration should be canceled or transferred, we will wait ten (10) business days (as observed in the location of our principal office) after we are informed by the applicable Provider of the Administrative Panel's decision before implementing that decision. We will then implement the decision unless we have received from you during that ten (10) business day period official documentation (such as a copy of a complaint, file-stamped by the clerk of the court) that you have commenced a lawsuit against the complainant in a jurisdiction to which the complainant has submitted under Paragraph 3(b)(xiii) of the Rules of Procedure. (In general, that jurisdiction is either the location of our principal office or of your address as shown in our Whois database. See Paragraphs 1 and 3(b)(xiii) of the Rules of Procedure for details.) If we receive such documentation within the ten (10) business day period, we will not implement the Administrative Panel's decision, and we will take no further action, until we receive (i) evidence satisfactory to us of a resolution between the parties; (ii) evidence satisfactory to us that your lawsuit has been dismissed or withdrawn; or (iii) a copy of an order from such court dismissing your lawsuit or ordering that you do not have the right to continue to use your domain name.

5   All other disputes and litigation

All other disputes between you and any party other than us regarding your domain name registration that are not brought pursuant to the mandatory administrative proceeding provisions of Paragraph 4 shall be resolved between you and such other party through any court, arbitration or other proceeding that may be available.

6   Our involvement in disputes

We will not participate in any way in any dispute between you and any party other than us regarding the registration and use of your domain name. You shall not name us as a party or otherwise include us in any such proceeding. In the event that we are named as a party in any such proceeding, we reserve the right to raise any and all defenses deemed appropriate, and to take any other action necessary to defend ourselves.

7   **Maintaining the status quo**

We will not cancel, transfer, activate, deactivate, or otherwise change the status of any domain name registration under this Policy except as provided in Paragraph 3 above.

8   **Transfers during a dispute**

a. **Transfers of a Domain Name to a New Holder**. You may not transfer your domain name registration to another holder (i) during a pending administrative proceeding brought pursuant to Paragraph 4 or for a period of fifteen (15) business days (as observed in the location of our principal place of business) after such proceeding is concluded; or (ii) during a pending court proceeding or arbitration commenced regarding your domain name unless the party to whom the domain name registration is being transferred agrees, in writing, to be bound by the decision of the court or arbitrator. We reserve the right to cancel any transfer of a domain name registration to another holder that is made in violation of this subparagraph.

b. **Changing Registrars**. You may not transfer your domain name registration to another registrar during a pending administrative proceeding brought pursuant to Paragraph 4 or for a period of fifteen (15) business days (as observed in the location of our principal place of business) after such proceeding is concluded. You may transfer administration of your domain name registration to another registrar during a pending court action or arbitration, provided that the domain name you have registered with us shall continue to be subject to the proceedings commenced against you in accordance with the terms of this Policy. In the event that you transfer a domain name registration to us during the pendency of a court action or arbitration, such dispute shall remain subject to the domain name dispute policy of the registrar from which the domain name registration was transferred.

9   **Policy modifications**

We reserve the right to modify this Policy at any time with the permission of ICANN. We will post our revised Policy at least thirty (30) calendar days before it becomes effective. Unless this Policy has already been invoked by the submission of a complaint to a Provider, in which event the version of the Policy in effect at the time it was invoked will apply to you until the dispute is over, all such changes will be binding upon you with respect to any domain name registration dispute, whether the dispute arose before, on or after the effective date of our change. In the event that you object to a change in this Policy, your sole remedy is to cancel your domain name registration with us, provided that you will not be entitled to a refund of any fees you paid to us. The revised Policy will apply to you until you cancel your domain name registration.

INTELLECTUAL PROPERTY (UNJUSTIFIED THREATS) ACT 2017

3   **European Union trade marks**

(1) Regulation 6 of the Community Trade Mark Regulations 2006 (unjustified threats of infringement proceedings) is amended as follows.

(2) In paragraph (1), for "section 21" substitute "sections 21 to 21D and section 21F".

(3) After paragraph (1) insert—

"(1A) In the application of sections 21 and 21B in relation to a European Union trade mark, references to a registered trade mark are to be treated as references to a European Union trade mark in respect of which an application has been published in accordance with Article 39 of the European Union Trade Mark Regulation.

(1B) In the application of section 21C in relation to a European Union trade mark in a case where the threat of infringement proceedings is made after an application has been published (but before registration) the reference in section 21C(2) to "the registered trade mark" is to be treated as a reference to the European Union trade mark registered in pursuance of that application."

(4) For paragraph (2) substitute—

"(2) In the application of sections 21 and 21B in relation to an international trade mark (EC), references to a registered trade mark are to be treated as references to an international trade mark (EC) in respect of which particulars of an international registration designating the European Union have been published in accordance with Article 152 of the European Union Trade Mark Regulation.

(3)   In the application of section 21C in relation to an international trade mark (EC) in a case where the threat of infringement proceedings is made after particulars have been published (but before registration) the reference in section 21C(2) to "the registered trade mark" is to be treated as a reference to the international trade mark (EC) registered in pursuance of those particulars."

(5) For the heading substitute "Unjustified threats".

PARIS CONVENTION FOR THE PROTECTION OF INDUSTRIAL PROPERTY
of March 20, 1883
as amended on September 28, 1979

Article 1 Establishment of the Union; scope of industrial property

(1)   The countries to which this Convention applies constitute a Union for the protection of industrial property.

(2)   The protection of industrial property has as its object patents, utility models, industrial designs, trademarks, service marks, trade names, indications of source or appellations of origin, and the repression of unfair competition.

(3)   Industrial property shall be understood in the broadest sense and shall apply not only to industry and commerce proper, but likewise to agricultural and extractive industries and to all manufactured or natural products, for example, wines, grain, tobacco leaf, fruit, cattle, minerals, mineral waters, beer, flowers, and flour.

(4)   Patents shall include the various kinds of industrial patents recognized by the laws of the countries of the Union, such as patents of importation, patents of improvement, patents and certificates of addition, etc.

Article 2 National treatment for nationals of countries of the Union

(1)   Nationals of any country of the Union shall, as regards the protection of industrial property, enjoy in all the other countries of the Union the advantages that their respective laws now grant, or may hereafter grant, to nationals; all without prejudice to the rights specially provided for by this Convention. Consequently, they shall have the same protection as the latter, and the same legal remedy against any infringement of their rights, provided that the conditions and formalities imposed upon nationals are complied with.

(2)   However, no requirement as to domicile or establishment in the country where protection is claimed may be imposed upon nationals of countries of the Union for the enjoyment of any industrial property rights.

(3)   The provisions of the laws of each of the countries of the Union relating to judicial and administrative procedure and to jurisdiction, and to the designation of an address for service or the appointment of an agent, which may be required by the laws on industrial property are expressly reserved.

Article 3 Same treatment for certain categories of persons as for nationals of countries of the Union

Nationals of countries outside the Union who are domiciled or who have real and effective industrial or commercial establishments in the territory of one of the countries of the Union shall be treated in the same manner as nationals of the countries of the Union.

Article 4A to I Patents, utility models, industrial designs, marks, inventors' certificates: right of priority G. Patents: division of the application

A.   (1) Any person who has duly filed an application for a patent, or for the registration of a utility model, or of an industrial design, or of a trademark, in one of the countries of the Union, or his successor in title, shall enjoy, for the purpose of filing in the other countries, a right of priority during the periods hereinafter fixed.

(2) Any filing that is equivalent to a regular national filing under the domestic legislation of any country of the Union or under bilateral or multilateral treaties concluded between countries of the Union shall be recognized as giving rise to the right of priority.

(3) By a regular national filing is meant any filing that is adequate to establish the date on which the application was filed in the country concerned, whatever may be the subsequent fate of the application.

B.   Consequently, any subsequent filing in any of the other countries of the Union before the expiration of the periods referred to above shall not be invalidated by reason of any acts accomplished in the interval, in particular, another filing, the publication or exploitation of the invention, the putting on sale of copies of the design, or the use of the mark, and such acts cannot give rise to any third-party right or any right of personal possession. Rights acquired by third parties before the date of the first application that serves as the basis for the right of priority are reserved in accordance with the domestic legislation of each country of the Union

C.   (1) The periods of priority referred to above shall be twelve months for patents and utility models, and six months for industrial designs and trademarks.

(2) These periods shall start from the date of filing of the first application; the day of filing shall not be included in the period.

(3) If the last day of the period is an official holiday, or a day when the Office is not open for the filing of applications in the country where protection is claimed, the period shall be extended until the first following working day.

(4) A subsequent application concerning the same subject as a previous first application within the meaning of paragraph (2), above, filed in the same country of the Union shall be considered as the first application, of which the filing date shall be the starting point of the period of priority, if, at the time of filing the subsequent application, the said previous application has been withdrawn, abandoned, or refused, without having been laid open to public inspection and without leaving any rights outstanding, and if it has not yet served as a basis for claiming a right of priority. The previous application may not thereafter serve as a basis for claiming a right of priority.

D.   (1) Any person desiring to take advantage of the priority of a previous filing shall be required to make a declaration indicating the date of such filing and the country in which it was made. Each country shall determine the latest date on which such declaration must be made.

(2) These particulars shall be mentioned in the publications issued by the competent authority, and in particular in the patents and the specifications relating thereto.

(3) The countries of the Union may require any person making a declaration of priority to produce a copy of the application (description, drawings, etc.) previously filed. The copy, certified as correct by the authority which received such application, shall not require any authentication, and may in any case be filed, without fee, at any time within three months of the filing of the subsequent application. They may require it to be accompanied by a certificate from the same authority showing the date of filing, and by a translation.

(4) No other formalities may be required for the declaration of priority at the time of filing the application. Each country of the Union shall determine the consequences of failure to comply with the formalities prescribed by this Article, but such consequences shall in no case go beyond the loss of the right of priority.

(5) Subsequently, further proof may be required.
Any person who avails himself of the priority of a previous application shall be required to specify the number of that application; this number shall be published as provided for by paragraph (2), above.

E.   (1) Where an industrial design is filed in a country by virtue of a right of priority based on the filing of a utility model, the period of priority shall be the same as that fixed for industrial designs.

(2) Furthermore, it is permissible to file a utility model in a country by virtue of a right of priority based on the filing of a patent application, and vice versa.

F.   No country of the Union may refuse a priority or a patent application on the ground that the applicant claims multiple priorities, even if they originate in different countries, or on the ground that an application claiming one or more priorities contains one or more elements that were not included in the application or applications whose priority is claimed, provided that, in both cases, there is unity of invention within the meaning of the law of the country. With respect to the elements not included in the application or applications whose priority is claimed, the filing of the subsequent application shall give rise to a right of priority under ordinary conditions.

G.   (1)   If the examination reveals that an application for a patent contains more than one invention, the applicant may divide the application into a certain number of divisional applications and preserve as the date of each the date of the initial application and the benefit of the right of priority, if any.

        (2)   The applicant may also, on his own initiative, divide a patent application and preserve as the date of each divisional application the date of the initial application and the benefit of the right of priority, if any. Each country of the Union shall have the right to determine the conditions under which such division shall be authorized.

H.   Priority may not be refused on the ground that certain elements of the invention for which priority is claimed do not appear among the claims formulated in the application in the country of origin, provided that the application documents as a whole specifically disclose such elements.

I.   (1)   Applications for inventors' certificates filed in a country in which applicants have the right to apply at their own option either for a patent or for an inventor's certificate shall give rise to the right of priority provided for by this Article, under the same conditions and with the same effects as applications for patents.

        (2)   In a country in which applicants have the right to apply at their own option either for a patent or for an inventor's certificate, an applicant for an inventor's certificate shall, in accordance with the provisions of this Article relating to patent applications, enjoy a right of priority based on an application for a patent, a utility model, or an inventor's certificate.

Article 4*bis* Patents: independence of patents obtained for the same invention in different countries

(1)   Patents applied for in the various countries of the Union by nationals of countries of the Union shall be independent of patents obtained for the same invention in other countries, whether members of the Union or not.

(2)   The foregoing provision is to be understood in an unrestricted sense, in particular, in the sense that patents applied for during the period of priority are independent, both as regards the grounds for nullity and forfeiture, and as regards their normal duration.

(3)   The provision shall apply to all patents existing at the time when it comes into effect.

(4)   Similarly, it shall apply, in the case of the accession of new countries, to patents in existence on either side at the time of accession.

(5)   Patents obtained with the benefit of priority shall, in the various countries of the Union, have a duration equal to that which they would have, had they been applied for or granted without the benefit of priority.

Article 4*ter* Patents: mention of the inventor in the patent
The inventor shall have the right to be mentioned as such in the patent.

Article 4*quater* Patents: patentability in case of restrictions of sale by law
The grant of a patent shall not be refused and a patent shall not be invalidated on the ground that the sale of the patented product or of a product obtained by means of a patented process is subject to restrictions or limitations resulting from the domestic law.

Article 5A. Patents: importation of articles; failure to work or insufficient working; compulsory licenses
B. Industrial designs: failure to work; importation of articles
C. Marks: failure to use; different forms; use by co-proprietors
D. Patents, utility models, marks, industrial designs: marking

A.   (1)   Importation by the patentee into the country where the patent has been granted of articles manufactured in any of the countries of the Union shall not entail forfeiture of the patent.

(2) Each country of the Union shall have the right to take legislative measures providing for the grant of compulsory licenses to prevent the abuses which might result from the exercise of the exclusive rights conferred by the patent, for example, failure to work.

(3) Forfeiture of the patent shall not be provided for except in cases where the grant of compulsory licenses would not have been sufficient to prevent the said abuses. No proceedings for the forfeiture or revocation of a patent may be instituted before the expiration of two years from the grant of the first compulsory license.

(4) A compulsory license may not be applied for on the ground of failure to work or insufficient working before the expiration of a period of four years from the date of filing of the patent application or three years from the date of the grant of the patent, whichever period expires last; it shall be refused if the patentee justifies his inaction by legitimate reasons. Such a compulsory license shall be non-exclusive and shall not be transferable, even in the form of the grant of a sub-license, except with that part of the enterprise or goodwill which exploits such license.

(5) The foregoing provisions shall be applicable, mutatis mutandis, to utility models.

B. The protection of industrial designs shall not, under any circumstance, be subject to any forfeiture, either by reason of failure to work or by reason of the importation of articles corresponding to those which are protected.

C. (1) If, in any country, use of the registered mark is compulsory, the registration may be cancelled only after a reasonable period, and then only if the person concerned does not justify his inaction.

(2) Use of a trademark by the proprietor in a form differing in elements which do not alter the distinctive character of the mark in the form in which it was registered in one of the countries of the Union shall not entail invalidation of the registration and shall not diminish the protection granted to the mark.

(3) Concurrent use of the same mark on identical or similar goods by industrial or commercial establishments considered as co-proprietors of the mark according to the provisions of the domestic law of the country where protection is claimed shall not prevent registration or diminish in any way the protection granted to the said mark in any country of the Union,

provided that such use does not result in misleading the public and is not contrary to the public interest.

D. No indication or mention of the patent, of the utility model, of the registration of the trademark, or of the deposit of the industrial design, shall be required upon the goods as a condition of recognition of the right to protection.

Article 5*bis* All industrial property rights: period of grace for the payment of fees for the maintenance of rights; patents: restoration

(1) A period of grace of not less than six months shall be allowed for the payment of the fees prescribed for the maintenance of industrial property rights, subject, if the domestic legislation so provides, to the payment of a surcharge.

(2) The countries of the Union shall have the right to provide for the restoration of patents which have lapsed by reason of non-payment of fees.

Article 5*ter* Patents: patented devices forming part of vessels, aircraft, or land vehicles

In any country of the Union the following shall not be considered as infringements of the rights of a patentee:

(i) the use on board vessels of other countries of the Union of devices forming the subject of his patent in the body of the vessel, in the machinery, tackle, gear and other accessories, when such vessels temporarily or accidentally enter the waters of the said country, provided that such devices are used there exclusively for the needs of the vessel;

(ii) the use of devices forming the subject of the patent in the construction or operation of aircraft or land vehicles of other countries of the Union, or of accessories of such aircraft or land vehicles, when those aircraft or land vehicles temporarily or accidentally enter the said country.

Article 5*quater* Patents: importation of products manufactured by a process patented in the importing country

When a product is imported into a country of the Union where there exists a patent protecting a process of manufacture of the said product, the patentee shall have all the rights, with regard to the imported product, that are accorded to him by the legislation of the country of importation, on the basis of the process patent, with respect to products manufactured in that country.

Article 5*quinquies* Industrial designs

Industrial designs shall be protected in all the countries of the Union.

Article 6 Marks: conditions of registration; independence of protection of same mark in different countries

(1)   The conditions for the filing and registration of trademarks shall be determined in each country of the Union by its domestic legislation.

(2)   However, an application for the registration of a mark filed by a national of a country of the Union in any country of the Union may not be refused, nor may a registration be invalidated, on the ground that filing, registration, or renewal, has not been effected in the country of origin.

(3)   A mark duly registered in a country of the Union shall be regarded as independent of marks registered in the other countries of the Union, including the country of origin.

Article 6*bis* Marks: well-known marks

(1)   The countries of the Union undertake, ex officio if their legislation so permits, or at the request of an interested party, to refuse or to cancel the registration, and to prohibit the use, of a trademark which constitutes a reproduction, an imitation, or a translation, liable to create confusion, of a mark considered by the competent authority of the country of registration or use to be well known in that country as being already the mark of a person entitled to the benefits of this Convention and used for identical or similar goods. These provisions shall also apply when the essential part of the mark constitutes a reproduction of any such well-known mark or an imitation liable to create confusion therewith.

(2)   A period of at least five years from the date of registration shall be allowed for requesting the cancellation of such a mark. The countries of the Union may provide for a period within which the prohibition of use must be requested.

(3)   No time limit shall be fixed for requesting the cancellation or the prohibition of the use of marks registered or used in bad faith.

Article 6*ter* Marks: prohibitions concerning state emblems, official hallmarks, and emblems of intergovernmental organizations

(1)   (a)   The countries of the Union agree to refuse or to invalidate the registration, and to prohibit by appropriate measures the use, without authorization by the competent authorities, either as trademarks or as elements of trademarks, of armorial bearings, flags, and other State emblems, of the countries of the Union, official signs and hallmarks indicating control and warranty adopted by them, and any imitation from a heraldic point of view.

      (b)   The provisions of subparagraph (a), above, shall apply equally to armorial bearings, flags, other emblems, abbreviations, and names, of international intergovernmental organizations of which one or more countries of the Union are members, with the exception of armorial bearings, flags, other emblems, abbreviations, and names, that are already the subject of international agreements in force, intended to ensure their protection.

      (c)   No country of the Union shall be required to apply the provisions of subparagraph (b), above, to the prejudice of the owners of rights acquired in good faith before the entry into force, in that country, of this Convention. The countries of the Union shall not be required to apply the said provisions when the use or registration referred to in subparagraph (a), above, is not of such a nature as to suggest to the public that a connection exists between the organization concerned and the armorial bearings, flags, emblems, abbreviations, and names, or if such use or registration is probably not of such a nature as to mislead the public as to the existence of a connection between the user and the organization.

(2)   Prohibition of the use of official signs and hallmarks indicating control and warranty shall apply solely in cases where the marks in which they are incorporated are intended to be used on goods of the same or a similar kind.

(3)   (a) For the application of these provisions, the countries of the Union agree to communicate reciprocally, through the intermediary of the International Bureau, the list of State emblems, and official signs and hallmarks indicating control and warranty, which they desire, or may hereafter desire, to place wholly or within certain limits under the protection of this Article, and all subsequent modifications of such list. Each country of the Union shall in due course make available to the public the lists so communicated. Nevertheless such communication is not obligatory in respect of flags of States.

        (b) The provisions of subparagraph (b) of paragraph (1) of this Article shall apply only to such armorial bearings, flags, other emblems, abbreviations, and names, of international intergovernmental organizations as the latter have communicated to the countries of the Union through the intermediary of the International Bureau.

(4)   Any country of the Union may, within a period of twelve months from the receipt of the notification, transmit its objections, if any, through the intermediary of the International Bureau, to the country or international intergovernmental organization concerned.

(5)   In the case of State flags, the measures prescribed by paragraph (1), above, shall apply solely to marks registered after November 6, 1925.

(6)   In the case of State emblems other than flags, and of official signs and hallmarks of the countries of the Union, and in the case of armorial bearings, flags, other emblems, abbreviations, and names, of international intergovernmental organizations, these provisions shall apply only to marks registered more than two months after receipt of the communication provided for in paragraph (3), above.

(7)   In cases of bad faith, the countries shall have the right to cancel even those marks incorporating State emblems, signs, and hallmarks, which were registered before November 6, 1925.

(8)   Nationals of any country who are authorized to make use of the State emblems, signs, and hallmarks, of their country may use them even if they are similar to those of another country.

(9)   The countries of the Union undertake to prohibit the unauthorized use in trade of the State armorial bearings of the other countries of the Union, when the use is of such a nature as to be misleading as to the origin of the goods.

(10)   The above provisions shall not prevent the countries from exercising the right given in paragraph (3) of Article 6quinquies, Section B, to refuse or to invalidate the registration of marks incorporating, without authorization, armorial bearings, flags, other State emblems, or official signs and hallmarks adopted by a country of the Union, as well as the distinctive signs of international intergovernmental organizations referred to in paragraph (1), above.

Article 6*quater* Marks: assignment of marks

(1)   When, in accordance with the law of a country of the Union, the assignment of a mark is valid only if it takes place at the same time as the transfer of the business or goodwill to which the mark belongs, it shall suffice for the recognition of such validity that the portion of the business or goodwill located in that country be transferred to the assignee, together with the exclusive right to manufacture in the said country, or to sell therein, the goods bearing the mark assigned.

(2)   The foregoing provision does not impose upon the countries of the Union any obligation to regard as valid the assignment of any mark the use of which by the assignee would, in fact, be of such a nature as to mislead the public, particularly as regards the origin, nature, or essential qualities, of the goods to which the mark is applied.

Article 6*quinquies* Marks: Protection of marks registered in one country of the Union in the other countries of the Union

A.   (1) Every trademark duly registered in the country of origin shall be accepted for filing and protected as is in the other countries of the Union, subject to the reservations indicated in this Article. Such countries may, before proceeding to final registration, require the production of a certificate of registration in the country of origin, issued by the competent authority. No authentication shall be required for this certificate.

        (2) Shall be considered the country of origin the country of the Union where the applicant has a real and effective industrial or commercial establishment, or, if he has no such

establishment within the Union, the country of the Union where he has his domicile, or, if he has no domicile within the Union but is a national of a country of the Union, the country of which he is a national.

B. Trademarks covered by this Article may be neither denied registration nor invalidated except in the following cases:

  (i) when they are of such a nature as to infringe rights acquired by third parties in the country where protection is claimed;

  (ii) when they are devoid of any distinctive character, or consist exclusively of signs or indications which may serve, in trade, to designate the kind, quality, quantity, intended purpose, value, place of origin, of the goods, or the time of production, or have become customary in the current language or in the bona fide and established practices of the trade of the country where protection is claimed;

  (iii) when they are contrary to morality or public order and, in particular, of such a nature as to deceive the public. It is understood that a mark may not be considered contrary to public order for the sole reason that it does not conform to a provision of the legislation on marks, except if such provision itself relates to public order.

  This provision is subject, however, to the application of Article 10bis.

C. (1) In determining whether a mark is eligible for protection, all the factual circumstances must be taken into consideration, particularly the length of time the mark has been in use.

  (2) No trademark shall be refused in the other countries of the Union for the sole reason that it differs from the mark protected in the country of origin only in respect of elements that do not alter its distinctive character and do not affect its identity in the form in which it has been registered in the said country of origin.

D. No person may benefit from the provisions of this Article if the mark for which he claims protection is not registered in the country of origin.

E. However, in no case shall the renewal of the registration of the mark in the country of origin involve an obligation to renew the registration in the other countries of the Union in which the mark has been registered.

F. The benefit of priority shall remain unaffected for applications for the registration of marks filed within the period fixed by Article 4, even if registration in the country of origin is effected after the expiration of such period.

Article 6*sexies* Marks: service marks

The countries of the Union undertake to protect service marks. They shall not be required to provide for the registration of such marks.

Article 6*septies* Marks: registration in the name of the agent or representative of the proprietor without the latter's authorization

(1) If the agent or representative of the person who is the proprietor of a mark in one of the countries of the Union applies, without such proprietor's authorization, for the registration of the mark in his own name, in one or more countries of the Union, the proprietor shall be entitled to oppose the registration applied for or demand its cancellation or, if the law of the country so allows, the assignment in his favor of the said registration, unless such agent or representative justifies his action.

(2) The proprietor of the mark shall, subject to the provisions of paragraph (1), above, be entitled to oppose the use of his mark by his agent or representative if he has not authorized such use.

(3) Domestic legislation may provide an equitable time limit within which the proprietor of a mark must exercise the rights provided for in this Article.

Article 7 Marks: nature of the goods to which the mark is applied

The nature of the goods to which a trademark is to be applied shall in no case form an obstacle to the registration of the mark.

Article 7*bis* Marks: collective marks

(1) The countries of the Union undertake to accept for filing and to protect collective marks belonging to associations the existence of which is not contrary to the law of the country of origin, even if such associations do not possess an industrial or commercial establishment.

(2)   Each country shall be the judge of the particular conditions under which a collective mark shall be protected and may refuse protection if the mark is contrary to the public interest.

(3)   Nevertheless, the protection of these marks shall not be refused to any association the existence of which is not contrary to the law of the country of origin, on the ground that such association is not established in the country where protection is sought or is not constituted according to the law of the latter country.

Article 8 Trade names

A trade name shall be protected in all the countries of the Union without the obligation of filing or registration, whether or not it forms part of a trademark.

Article 9 Marks, trade names: seizure, on importation, etc., of goods unlawfully bearing a mark or trade name

(1)   All goods unlawfully bearing a trademark or trade name shall be seized on importation into those countries of the Union where such mark or trade name is entitled to legal protection.

(2)   Seizure shall likewise be effected in the country where the unlawful affixation occurred or in the country into which the goods were imported.

(3)   Seizure shall take place at the request of the public prosecutor, or any other competent authority, or any interested party, whether a natural person or a legal entity, in conformity with the domestic legislation of each country.

(4)   The authorities shall not be bound to effect seizure of goods in transit.

(5)   If the legislation of a country does not permit seizure on importation, seizure shall be replaced by prohibition of importation or by seizure inside the country.

(6)   If the legislation of a country permits neither seizure on importation nor prohibition of importation nor seizure inside the country, then, until such time as the legislation is modified accordingly, these measures shall be replaced by the actions and remedies available in such cases to nationals under the law of such country.

Article 10 False indications: seizure, on importation, etc., of goods bearing false indications as to their source or the identity of the producer

(1)   The provisions of the preceding Article shall apply in cases of direct or indirect use of a false indication of the source of the goods or the identity of the producer, manufacturer, or merchant.

(2)   Any producer, manufacturer, or merchant, whether a natural person or a legal entity, engaged in the production or manufacture of or trade in such goods and established either in the locality falsely indicated as the source, or in the region where such locality is situated, or in the country falsely indicated, or in the country where the false indication of source is used, shall in any case be deemed an interested party.

Article 10*bis* Unfair competition

(1)   The countries of the Union are bound to assure to nationals of such countries effective protection against unfair competition.

(2)   Any act of competition contrary to honest practices in industrial or commercial matters constitutes an act of unfair competition.

(3)   The following in particular shall be prohibited:

  (i)   all acts of such a nature as to create confusion by any means whatever with the establishment, the goods, or the industrial or commercial activities, of a competitor;

  (ii)   false allegations in the course of trade of such a nature as to discredit the establishment, the goods, or the industrial or commercial activities, of a competitor;

  (iii)   indications or allegations the use of which in the course of trade is liable to mislead the public as to the nature, the manufacturing process, the characteristics, the suitability for their purpose, or the quantity, of the goods.

Article 10*ter* Marks, trade names, false indications, unfair competition: remedies, right to sue

(1)   The countries of the Union undertake to assure to nationals of the other countries of the Union appropriate legal remedies effectively to repress all the acts referred to in Articles 9, 10, and 10bis.

(2)   They undertake, further, to provide measures to permit federations and associations representing interested industrialists, producers, or merchants, provided that the existence of such federations and associations is not contrary to the laws of their countries, to take action in the courts or before the administrative authorities, with a view to the repression of the acts referred to in Articles 9, 10, and 10bis, in so far as the law of the country in which protection is claimed allows such action by federations and associations of that country.

Article 11 Inventions, utility models, industrial designs, marks: temporary protection at certain international exhibitions

(1)   The countries of the Union shall, in conformity with their domestic legislation, grant temporary protection to patentable inventions, utility models, industrial designs, and trademarks, in respect of goods exhibited at official or officially recognized international exhibitions held in the territory of any of them.

(2)   Such temporary protection shall not extend the periods provided by Article 4. If, later, the right of priority is invoked, the authorities of any country may provide that the period shall start from the date of introduction of the goods into the exhibition.

(3)   Each country may require, as proof of the identity of the article exhibited and of the date of its introduction, such documentary evidence as it considers necessary.

Article 12 Special national industrial property services

(1)   Each country of the Union undertakes to establish a special industrial property service and a central office for the communication to the public of patents, utility models, industrial designs, and trademarks.

(2)   This service shall publish an official periodical journal. It shall publish regularly:
   (a)   the names of the proprietors of patents granted, with a brief designation of the inventions patented;
   (b)   the reproductions of registered trademarks.

Article 13 Assembly of the Union

(1)   (a)   The Union shall have an Assembly consisting of those countries of the Union which are bound by Articles 13 to 17.
   (b)   The Government of each country shall be represented by one delegate, who may be assisted by alternate delegates, advisors, and experts.
   (c)   The expenses of each delegation shall be borne by the Government which has appointed it.
   . . .

AGREEMENT ON TRADE-RELATED ASPECTS OF INTELLECTUAL PROPERTY RIGHTS

Members,

Desiring to reduce distortions and impediments to international trade, and taking into account the need to promote effective and adequate protection of intellectual property rights, and to ensure that measures and procedures to enforce intellectual property rights do not themselves become barriers to legitimate trade;

Recognizing, to this end, the need for new rules and disciplines concerning:

(a)   the applicability of the basic principles of GATT 1994 and of relevant international intellectual property agreements or conventions;

(b)   the provision of adequate standards and principles concerning the availability, scope and use of trade-related intellectual property rights;

(c)   the provision of effective and appropriate means for the enforcement of trade-related intellectual property rights, taking into account differences in national legal systems;

(d)   the provision of effective and expeditious procedures for the multilateral prevention and settlement of disputes between governments; and

(e)   transitional arrangements aiming at the fullest participation in the results of the negotiations;

Recognizing the need for a multilateral framework of principles, rules and disciplines dealing with international trade in counterfeit goods;

Recognizing that intellectual property rights are private rights;

Recognizing the underlying public policy objectives of national systems for the protection of intellectual property, including developmental and technological objectives;

Recognizing also the special needs of the least-developed country Members in respect of maximum flexibility in the domestic implementation of laws and regulations in order to enable them to create a sound and viable technological base;

Emphasizing the importance of reducing tensions by reaching strengthened commitments to resolve disputes on trade-related intellectual property issues through multilateral procedures;

Desiring to establish a mutually supportive relationship between the WTO and the World Intellectual Property Organization (referred to in this Agreement as "WIPO") as well as other relevant international organizations;

Hereby agree as follows:

PART I

GENERAL PROVISIONS AND BASIC PRINCIPLES

Article 1 Nature and scope of obligations

1.   Members shall give effect to the provisions of this Agreement. Members may, but shall not be obliged to, implement in their law more extensive protection than is required by this Agreement, provided that such protection does not contravene the provisions of this Agreement. Members shall be free to determine the appropriate method of implementing the provisions of this Agreement within their own legal system and practice.

2.   For the purposes of this Agreement, the term "intellectual property" refers to all categories of intellectual property that are the subject of Sections 1 through 7 of Part II.

3.   Members shall accord the treatment provided for in this Agreement to the nationals of other Members. In respect of the relevant intellectual property right, the nationals of other Members shall be understood as those natural or legal persons that would meet the criteria for eligibility for protection provided for in the Paris Convention (1967), the Berne Convention (1971), the Rome Convention and the Treaty on Intellectual Property in Respect of Integrated Circuits, were all Members of the WTO members of those conventions. Any Member availing itself of the possibilities provided in paragraph 3 of Article 5 or paragraph 2 of Article 6 of the Rome Convention shall make a notification as foreseen in those provisions to the Council for Trade-Related Aspects of Intellectual Property Rights (the "Council for TRIPS").

Article 2 Intellectual Property Conventions

1.   In respect of Parts II, III and IV of this Agreement, Members shall comply with Articles 1 through 12, and Article 19, of the Paris Convention (1967).

2.   Nothing in Parts I to IV of this Agreement shall derogate from existing obligations that Members may have to each other under the Paris Convention, the Berne Convention, the Rome Convention and the Treaty on Intellectual Property in Respect of Integrated Circuits.

Article 3 National treatment

1.   Each Member shall accord to the nationals of other Members treatment no less favourable than that it accords to its own nationals with regard to the protection of intellectual property, subject to the exceptions already provided in, respectively, the Paris Convention (1967), the Berne Convention (1971), the Rome Convention or the Treaty on Intellectual Property in Respect of Integrated Circuits. In respect of performers, producers of phonograms and broadcasting organizations, this obligation only applies in respect of the rights provided under this Agreement. Any Member availing itself of the possibilities provided in Article 6 of the Berne Convention (1971) or paragraph 1(b) of Article 16 of the Rome Convention shall make a notification as foreseen in those provisions to the Council for TRIPS.

2.   Members may avail themselves of the exceptions permitted under paragraph 1 in relation to judicial and administrative procedures, including the designation of an address for service or the appointment of an agent within the jurisdiction of a Member, only where such exceptions are necessary to secure compliance with laws and regulations which are not inconsistent with the provisions of this Agreement and where such practices are not applied in a manner which would constitute a disguised restriction on trade.

Article 4 Most-favoured-nation treatment

With regard to the protection of intellectual property, any advantage, favour, privilege or immunity granted by a Member to the nationals of any other country shall be accorded immediately and unconditionally to the nationals of all other Members. Exempted from this obligation are any advantage, favour, privilege or immunity accorded by a Member:

(a)   deriving from international agreements on judicial assistance or law enforcement of a general nature and not particularly confined to the protection of intellectual property;

(b)   granted in accordance with the provisions of the Berne Convention (1971) or the Rome Convention authorizing that the treatment accorded be a function not of national treatment but of the treatment accorded in another country;

(c)   in respect of the rights of performers, producers of phonograms and broadcasting organizations not provided under this Agreement;

(d)   deriving from international agreements related to the protection of intellectual property which entered into force prior to the entry into force of the WTO Agreement, provided that such agreements are notified to the Council for TRIPS and do not constitute an arbitrary or unjustifiable discrimination against nationals of other Members.

Article 5 Multilateral agreements on acquisition or maintenance of protection

The obligations under Articles 3 and 4 do not apply to procedures provided in multilateral agreements concluded under the auspices of WIPO relating to the acquisition or maintenance of intellectual property rights.

Article 6 Exhaustion

For the purposes of dispute settlement under this Agreement, subject to the provisions of Articles 3 and 4 nothing in this Agreement shall be used to address the issue of the exhaustion of intellectual property rights.

Article 7 Objectives

The protection and enforcement of intellectual property rights should contribute to the promotion of technological innovation and to the transfer and dissemination of technology, to the mutual advantage of producers and users of technological knowledge and in a manner conducive to social and economic welfare, and to a balance of rights and obligations.

Article 8 Principles

1.   Members may, in formulating or amending their laws and regulations, adopt measures necessary to protect public health and nutrition, and to promote the public interest in sectors of vital importance to their socio-economic and technological development, provided that such measures are consistent with the provisions of this Agreement.

2.   Appropriate measures, provided that they are consistent with the provisions of this Agreement, may be needed to prevent the abuse of intellectual property rights by right holders or the resort to practices which unreasonably restrain trade or adversely affect the international transfer of technology.

PART II

STANDARDS CONCERNING THE AVAILABILITY, SCOPE AND USE OF INTELLECTUAL
PROPERTY RIGHTS

SECTION 1:
COPYRIGHT AND RELATED RIGHTS

Article 9 Relation to the Berne Convention

1.   Members shall comply with Articles 1 through 21 of the Berne Convention (1971) and the Appendix thereto. However, Members shall not have rights or obligations under this Agreement in respect of the rights conferred under Article 6bis of that Convention or of the rights derived therefrom.

2.   Copyright protection shall extend to expressions and not to ideas, procedures, methods of operation or mathematical concepts as such.

Article 10 Computer programs and compilations of data

1.   Computer programs, whether in source or object code, shall be protected as literary works under the Berne Convention (1971).

2.   Compilations of data or other material, whether in machine readable or other form, which by reason of the selection or arrangement of their contents constitute intellectual creations shall be protected as such. Such protection, which shall not extend to the data or material itself, shall be without prejudice to any copyright subsisting in the data or material itself.

Article 11 Rental rights

In respect of at least computer programs and cinematographic works, a Member shall provide authors and their successors in title the right to authorize or to prohibit the commercial rental to the public of originals or copies of their copyright works. A Member shall be excepted from this obligation in respect of cinematographic works unless such rental has led to widespread copying of such works which is materially impairing the exclusive right of reproduction conferred in that Member on authors and their successors in title. In respect of computer programs, this obligation does not apply to rentals where the program itself is not the essential object of the rental.

Article 12 Term of protection

Whenever the term of protection of a work, other than a photographic work or a work of applied art, is calculated on a basis other than the life of a natural person, such term shall be no less than 50 years from the end of the calendar year of authorized publication, or, failing such authorized publication within 50 years from the making of the work, 50 years from the end of the calendar year of making.

Article 13 Limitations and exceptions

Members shall confine limitations or exceptions to exclusive rights to certain special cases which do not conflict with a normal exploitation of the work and do not unreasonably prejudice the legitimate interests of the right holder.

Article 14 Protection of performers, producers of phonograms (sound recordings) and broadcasting organizations

1.   In respect of a fixation of their performance on a phonogram, performers shall have the possibility of preventing the following acts when undertaken without their authorization: the fixation of their unfixed performance and the reproduction of such fixation. Performers shall also have the possibility of preventing the following acts when undertaken without their authorization: the broadcasting by wireless means and the communication to the public of their live performance.

2.   Producers of phonograms shall enjoy the right to authorize or prohibit the direct or indirect reproduction of their phonograms.

3.   Broadcasting organizations shall have the right to prohibit the following acts when undertaken without their authorization: the fixation, the reproduction of fixations, and the rebroadcasting by wireless means of broadcasts, as well as the communication to the public of television broadcasts of the same. Where Members do not grant such rights to broadcasting organizations, they shall provide owners of copyright in the subject matter of broadcasts with the possibility of preventing the above acts, subject to the provisions of the Berne Convention (1971).

4.   The provisions of Article 11 in respect of computer programs shall apply mutatis mutandis to producers of phonograms and any other right holders in phonograms as determined in a Member's law. If on 15 April 1994 a Member has in force a system of equitable remuneration of right holders in respect of the rental of phonograms, it may maintain such system provided that the commercial rental of phonograms is not giving rise to the material impairment of the exclusive rights of reproduction of right holders.

5.   The term of the protection available under this Agreement to performers and producers of phonograms shall last at least until the end of a period of 50 years computed from the end of the calendar year in which the fixation was made or the performance took place. The term of protection granted pursuant to paragraph 3 shall last for at least 20 years from the end of the calendar year in which the broadcast took place.

6.   Any Member may, in relation to the rights conferred under paragraphs 1, 2 and 3, provide for conditions, limitations, exceptions and reservations to the extent permitted by the Rome Convention. However, the provisions of Article 18 of the Berne Convention (1971) shall also apply, mutatis mutandis, to the rights of performers and producers of phonograms in phonograms.

SECTION 2:
TRADEMARKS

Article 15 Protectable subject matter

1.   Any sign, or any combination of signs, capable of distinguishing the goods or services of one undertaking from those of other undertakings, shall be capable of constituting a trademark. Such signs, in particular words including personal names, letters, numerals, figurative elements and combinations of colours as well as any combination of such signs, shall be eligible for registration as trademarks. Where signs are not inherently capable of distinguishing the relevant goods or services, Members may make registrability depend on distinctiveness acquired through use. Members may require, as a condition of registration, that signs be visually perceptible.

2.   Paragraph 1 shall not be understood to prevent a Member from denying registration of a trademark on other grounds, provided that they do not derogate from the provisions of the Paris Convention (1967).

3.   Members may make registrability depend on use. However, actual use of a trademark shall not be a condition for filing an application for registration. An application shall not be refused solely on the ground that intended use has not taken place before the expiry of a period of three years from the date of application.

4.   The nature of the goods or services to which a trademark is to be applied shall in no case form an obstacle to registration of the trademark.

5.   Members shall publish each trademark either before it is registered or promptly after it is registered and shall afford a reasonable opportunity for petitions to cancel the registration. In addition, Members may afford an opportunity for the registration of a trademark to be opposed.

Article 16 Rights conferred

1.   The owner of a registered trademark shall have the exclusive right to prevent all third parties not having the owner's consent from using in the course of trade identical or similar signs for goods or services which are identical or similar to those in respect of which the trademark is registered where such use would result in a likelihood of confusion. In case of the use of an identical sign for identical goods or services, a likelihood of confusion shall be presumed. The rights described above shall not prejudice any existing prior rights, nor shall they affect the possibility of Members making rights available on the basis of use.

2.   Article 6bis of the Paris Convention (1967) shall apply, mutatis mutandis, to services. In determining whether a trademark is well-known, Members shall take account of the knowledge of the trademark in the relevant sector of the public, including knowledge in the Member concerned which has been obtained as a result of the promotion of the trademark.

3.   Article 6bis of the Paris Convention (1967) shall apply, mutatis mutandis, to goods or services which are not similar to those in respect of which a trademark is registered, provided that use of that trademark in relation to those goods or services would indicate a connection between those goods or services and the owner of the registered trademark and provided that the interests of the owner of the registered trademark are likely to be damaged by such use.

Article 17 Exceptions

Members may provide limited exceptions to the rights conferred by a trademark, such as fair use of descriptive terms, provided that such exceptions take account of the legitimate interests of the owner of the trademark and of third parties.

Article 18 Term of protection

Initial registration, and each renewal of registration, of a trademark shall be for a term of no less than seven years. The registration of a trademark shall be renewable indefinitely.

Article 19 Requirement of use

1.   If use is required to maintain a registration, the registration may be cancelled only after an uninterrupted period of at least three years of non-use, unless valid reasons based on the existence of obstacles to such use are shown by the trademark owner. Circumstances arising independently of the will of the owner of the trademark which constitute an

obstacle to the use of the trademark, such as import restrictions on or other government requirements for goods or services protected by the trademark, shall be recognized as valid reasons for non-use.

2. When subject to the control of its owner, use of a trademark by another person shall be recognized as use of the trademark for the purpose of maintaining the registration.

Article 20 Other requirements

The use of a trademark in the course of trade shall not be unjustifiably encumbered by special requirements, such as use with another trademark, use in a special form or use in a manner detrimental to its capability to distinguish the goods or services of one undertaking from those of other undertakings. This will not preclude a requirement prescribing the use of the trademark identifying the undertaking producing the goods or services along with, but without linking it to, the trademark distinguishing the specific goods or services in question of that undertaking.

Article 21 Licensing and assignment

Members may determine conditions on the licensing and assignment of trademarks, it being understood that the compulsory licensing of trademarks shall not be permitted and that the owner of a registered trademark shall have the right to assign the trademark with or without the transfer of the business to which the trademark belongs.

SECTION 3:
GEOGRAPHICAL INDICATIONS

Article 22 Protection of geographical indications

1. Geographical indications are, for the purposes of this Agreement, indications which identify a good as originating in the territory of a Member, or a region or locality in that territory, where a given quality, reputation or other characteristic of the good is essentially attributable to its geographical origin.

2. In respect of geographical indications, Members shall provide the legal means for interested parties to prevent:
   (a) the use of any means in the designation or presentation of a good that indicates or suggests that the good in question originates in a geographical area other than the true place of origin in a manner which misleads the public as to the geographical origin of the good;
   (b) any use which constitutes an act of unfair competition within the meaning of Article 10bis of the Paris Convention (1967).

3. A Member shall, ex officio if its legislation so permits or at the request of an interested party, refuse or invalidate the registration of a trademark which contains or consists of a geographical indication with respect to goods not originating in the territory indicated, if use of the indication in the trademark for such goods in that Member is of such a nature as to mislead the public as to the true place of origin.

4. The protection under paragraphs 1, 2 and 3 shall be applicable against a geographical indication which, although literally true as to the territory, region or locality in which the goods originate, falsely represents to the public that the goods originate in another territory.

Article 23 Additional protection for geographical indications for wines and spirits

1. Each Member shall provide the legal means for interested parties to prevent use of a geographical indication identifying wines for wines not originating in the place indicated by the geographical indication in question or identifying spirits for spirits not originating in the place indicated by the geographical indication in question, even where the true origin of the goods is indicated or the geographical indication is used in translation or accompanied by expressions such as "kind", "type", "style", "imitation" or the like.

2. The registration of a trademark for wines which contains or consists of a geographical indication identifying wines or for spirits which contains or consists of a geographical indication identifying spirits shall be refused or invalidated, ex officio if a Member's legislation so permits or at the request of an interested party, with respect to such wines or spirits not having this origin.

3.   In the case of homonymous geographical indications for wines, protection shall be accorded to each indication, subject to the provisions of paragraph 4 of Article 22. Each Member shall determine the practical conditions under which the homonymous indications in question will be differentiated from each other, taking into account the need to ensure equitable treatment of the producers concerned and that consumers are not misled.

4.   In order to facilitate the protection of geographical indications for wines, negotiations shall be undertaken in the Council for TRIPS concerning the establishment of a multilateral system of notification and registration of geographical indications for wines eligible for protection in those Members participating in the system.

Article 24 International negotiations; exceptions

1.   Members agree to enter into negotiations aimed at increasing the protection of individual geographical indications under Article 23. The provisions of paragraphs 4 through 8 below shall not be used by a Member to refuse to conduct negotiations or to conclude bilateral or multilateral agreements. In the context of such negotiations, Members shall be willing to consider the continued applicability of these provisions to individual geographical indications whose use was the subject of such negotiations.

2.   The Council for TRIPS shall keep under review the application of the provisions of this Section; the first such review shall take place within two years of the entry into force of the WTO Agreement. Any matter affecting the compliance with the obligations under these provisions may be drawn to the attention of the Council, which, at the request of a Member, shall consult with any Member or Members in respect of such matter in respect of which it has not been possible to find a satisfactory solution through bilateral or plurilateral consultations between the Members concerned. The Council shall take such action as may be agreed to facilitate the operation and further the objectives of this Section.

3.   In implementing this Section, a Member shall not diminish the protection of geographical indications that existed in that Member immediately prior to the date of entry into force of the WTO Agreement.

4.   Nothing in this Section shall require a Member to prevent continued and similar use of a particular geographical indication of another Member identifying wines or spirits in connection with goods or services by any of its nationals or domiciliaries who have used that geographical indication in a continuous manner with regard to the same or related goods or services in the territory of that Member either (a) for at least 10 years preceding 15 April 1994 or (b) in good faith preceding that date.

5.   Where a trademark has been applied for or registered in good faith, or where rights to a trademark have been acquired through use in good faith either:
   (a)   before the date of application of these provisions in that Member as defined in Part VI; or
   (b)   before the geographical indication is protected in its country of origin;
   measures adopted to implement this Section shall not prejudice eligibility for or the validity of the registration of a trademark, or the right to use a trademark, on the basis that such a trademark is identical with, or similar to, a geographical indication.

6.   Nothing in this Section shall require a Member to apply its provisions in respect of a geographical indication of any other Member with respect to goods or services for which the relevant indication is identical with the term customary in common language as the common name for such goods or services in the territory of that Member. Nothing in this Section shall require a Member to apply its provisions in respect of a geographical indication of any other Member with respect to products of the vine for which the relevant indication is identical with the customary name of a grape variety existing in the territory of that Member as of the date of entry into force of the WTO Agreement.

7.   A Member may provide that any request made under this Section in connection with the use or registration of a trademark must be presented within five years after the adverse use of the protected indication has become generally known in that Member or after the date of registration of the trademark in that Member provided that the trademark has been published by that date, if such date is earlier than the date on which the adverse use became generally known in that Member, provided that the geographical indication is not used or registered in bad faith.

8.   The provisions of this Section shall in no way prejudice the right of any person to use, in the course of trade, that person's name or the name of that person's predecessor in business, except where such name is used in such a manner as to mislead the public.

9.   There shall be no obligation under this Agreement to protect geographical indications which are not or cease to be protected in their country of origin, or which have fallen into disuse in that country.

SECTION 4:
INDUSTRIAL DESIGNS

Article 25 Requirements for protection

1.   Members shall provide for the protection of independently created industrial designs that are new or original. Members may provide that designs are not new or original if they do not significantly differ from known designs or combinations of known design features. Members may provide that such protection shall not extend to designs dictated essentially by technical or functional considerations.

2.   Each Member shall ensure that requirements for securing protection for textile designs, in particular in regard to any cost, examination or publication, do not unreasonably impair the opportunity to seek and obtain such protection. Members shall be free to meet this obligation through industrial design law or through copyright law.

Article 26 Protection

1.   The owner of a protected industrial design shall have the right to prevent third parties not having the owner's consent from making, selling or importing articles bearing or embodying a design which is a copy, or substantially a copy, of the protected design, when such acts are undertaken for commercial purposes.

2.   Members may provide limited exceptions to the protection of industrial designs, provided that such exceptions do not unreasonably conflict with the normal exploitation of protected industrial designs and do not unreasonably prejudice the legitimate interests of the owner of the protected design, taking account of the legitimate interests of third parties.

3.   The duration of protection available shall amount to at least 10 years.

SECTION 5:
PATENTS

Article 27 Patentable subject matter

1.   Subject to the provisions of paragraphs 2 and 3, patents shall be available for any inventions, whether products or processes, in all fields of technology, provided that they are new, involve an inventive step and are capable of industrial application. Subject to paragraph 4 of Article 65, paragraph 8 of Article 70 and paragraph 3 of this Article, patents shall be available and patent rights enjoyable without discrimination as to the place of invention, the field of technology and whether products are imported or locally produced.

2.   Members may exclude from patentability inventions, the prevention within their territory of the commercial exploitation of which is necessary to protect ordre public or morality, including to protect human, animal or plant life or health or to avoid serious prejudice to the environment, provided that such exclusion is not made merely because the exploitation is prohibited by their law.

3.   Members may also exclude from patentability:
        (a)   diagnostic, therapeutic and surgical methods for the treatment of humans or animals;
        (b)   plants and animals other than micro-organisms, and essentially biological processes for the production of plants or animals other than non-biological and microbiological processes. However, Members shall provide for the protection of plant varieties either by patents or by an effective sui generis system or by any combination thereof. The provisions of this subparagraph shall be reviewed four years after the date of entry into force of the WTO Agreement.

Article 28 Rights conferred

1.   A patent shall confer on its owner the following exclusive rights:
        (a)   where the subject matter of a patent is a product, to prevent third parties not having the owner's consent from the acts of: making, using, offering for sale, selling, or importing for these purposes that product;

(b)   where the subject matter of a patent is a process, to prevent third parties not having the owner's consent from the act of using the process, and from the acts of: using, offering for sale, selling, or importing for these purposes at least the product obtained directly by that process.

2.   Patent owners shall also have the right to assign, or transfer by succession, the patent and to conclude licensing contracts.

Article 29 Conditions on patent applicants

1.   Members shall require that an applicant for a patent shall disclose the invention in a manner sufficiently clear and complete for the invention to be carried out by a person skilled in the art and may require the applicant to indicate the best mode for carrying out the invention known to the inventor at the filing date or, where priority is claimed, at the priority date of the application.

2.   Members may require an applicant for a patent to provide information concerning the applicant's corresponding foreign applications and grants.

Article 30 Exceptions to rights conferred

Members may provide limited exceptions to the exclusive rights conferred by a patent, provided that such exceptions do not unreasonably conflict with a normal exploitation of the patent and do not unreasonably prejudice the legitimate interests of the patent owner, taking account of the legitimate interests of third parties.

Article 31 Other use without authorization of the right holder

Where the law of a Member allows for other use of the subject matter of a patent without the authorization of the right holder, including use by the government or third parties authorized by the government, the following provisions shall be respected:

(a)   authorization of such use shall be considered on its individual merits;

(b)   such use may only be permitted if, prior to such use, the proposed user has made efforts to obtain authorization from the right holder on reasonable commercial terms and conditions and that such efforts have not been successful within a reasonable period of time. This requirement may be waived by a Member in the case of a national emergency or other circumstances of extreme urgency or in cases of public non-commercial use. In situations of national emergency or other circumstances of extreme urgency, the right holder shall, nevertheless, be notified as soon as reasonably practicable. In the case of public non-commercial use, where the government or contractor, without making a patent search, knows or has demonstrable grounds to know that a valid patent is or will be used by or for the government, the right holder shall be informed promptly;

(c)   the scope and duration of such use shall be limited to the purpose for which it was authorized, and in the case of semi-conductor technology shall only be for public non-commercial use or to remedy a practice determined after judicial or administrative process to be anti-competitive;

(d)   such use shall be non-exclusive;

(e)   such use shall be non-assignable, except with that part of the enterprise or goodwill which enjoys such use;

(f)   any such use shall be authorized predominantly for the supply of the domestic market of the Member authorizing such use;

(g)   authorization for such use shall be liable, subject to adequate protection of the legitimate interests of the persons so authorized, to be terminated if and when the circumstances which led to it cease to exist and are unlikely to recur. The competent authority shall have the authority to review, upon motivated request, the continued existence of these circumstances;

(h)   the right holder shall be paid adequate remuneration in the circumstances of each case, taking into account the economic value of the authorization;

(i)   the legal validity of any decision relating to the authorization of such use shall be subject to judicial review or other independent review by a distinct higher authority in that Member;

(j)   any decision relating to the remuneration provided in respect of such use shall be subject to judicial review or other independent review by a distinct higher authority in that Member;

(k)   Members are not obliged to apply the conditions set forth in subparagraphs (b) and (f) where such use is permitted to remedy a practice determined after judicial or administrative process to be anti-competitive. The need to correct anti-competitive practices may be taken into account in determining the amount of remuneration in such cases. Competent authorities shall have the authority to refuse termination of authorization if and when the conditions which led to such authorization are likely to recur;

(l)   where such use is authorized to permit the exploitation of a patent ("the second patent") which cannot be exploited without infringing another patent ("the first patent"), the following additional conditions shall apply:

  (i)   the invention claimed in the second patent shall involve an important technical advance of considerable economic significance in relation to the invention claimed in the first patent;

  (ii)   the owner of the first patent shall be entitled to a cross-licence on reasonable terms to use the invention claimed in the second patent; and

  (iii)   the use authorized in respect of the first patent shall be non-assignable except with the assignment of the second patent.

Article 31*bis*

1.   The obligations of an exporting Member under Article 31(f) shall not apply with respect to the grant by it of a compulsory licence to the extent necessary for the purposes of production of a pharmaceutical product(s) and its export to an eligible importing Member(s) in accordance with the terms set out in paragraph 2 of the Annex to this Agreement.

2.   Where a compulsory licence is granted by an exporting Member under the system set out in this Article and the Annex to this Agreement, adequate remuneration pursuant to Article 31(h) shall be paid in that Member taking into account the economic value to the importing Member of the use that has been authorized in the exporting Member. Where a compulsory licence is granted for the same products in the eligible importing Member, the obligation of that Member under Article 31(h) shall not apply in respect of those products for which remuneration in accordance with the first sentence of this paragraph is paid in the exporting Member.

3.   With a view to harnessing economies of scale for the purposes of enhancing purchasing power for, and facilitating the local production of, pharmaceutical products: where a developing or least developed country WTO Member is a party to a regional trade agreement within the meaning of Article XXIV of the GATT 1994 and the Decision of 28 November 1979 on Differential and More Favourable Treatment Reciprocity and Fuller Participation of Developing Countries (L/4903), at least half of the current membership of which is made up of countries presently on the United Nations list of least developed countries, the obligation of that Member under Article 31(f) shall not apply to the extent necessary to enable a pharmaceutical product produced or imported under a compulsory licence in that Member to be exported to the markets of those other developing or least developed country parties to the regional trade agreement that share the health problem in question. It is understood that this will not prejudice the territorial nature of the patent rights in question.

4.   Members shall not challenge any measures taken in conformity with the provisions of this Article and the Annex to this Agreement under subparagraphs 1(b) and 1(c) of Article XXIII of GATT 1994.

5.   This Article and the Annex to this Agreement are without prejudice to the rights, obligations and flexibilities that Members have under the provisions of this Agreement other than paragraphs (f) and (h) of Article 31, including those reaffirmed by the Declaration on the TRIPS Agreement and Public Health (WT/MIN(01)/DEC/2), and to their interpretation. They are also without prejudice to the extent to which pharmaceutical products produced under a compulsory licence can be exported under the provisions of Article 31(f).

Article 32 Revocation/forfeiture

An opportunity for judicial review of any decision to revoke or forfeit a patent shall be available.

Article 33 Term of protection

The term of protection available shall not end before the expiration of a period of twenty years counted from the filing date.

Article 34 Process patents: burden of proof

1.   For the purposes of civil proceedings in respect of the infringement of the rights of the owner referred to in paragraph 1(b) of Article 28, if the subject matter of a patent is a

process for obtaining a product, the judicial authorities shall have the authority to order the defendant to prove that the process to obtain an identical product is different from the patented process. Therefore, Members shall provide, in at least one of the following circumstances, that any identical product when produced without the consent of the patent owner shall, in the absence of proof to the contrary, be deemed to have been obtained by the patented process:

(a)   if the product obtained by the patented process is new;

(b)   if there is a substantial likelihood that the identical product was made by the process and the owner of the patent has been unable through reasonable efforts to determine the process actually used.

2.   Any Member shall be free to provide that the burden of proof indicated in paragraph 1 shall be on the alleged infringer only if the condition referred to in subparagraph (a) is fulfilled or only if the condition referred to in subparagraph (b) is fulfilled.

3.   In the adduction of proof to the contrary, the legitimate interests of defendants in protecting their manufacturing and business secrets shall be taken into account.

SECTION 6:
LAYOUT-DESIGNS (TOPOGRAPHIES) OF INTEGRATED CIRCUITS

Article 35 Relation to the IPIC Treaty

Members agree to provide protection to the layout-designs (topographies) of integrated circuits (referred to in this Agreement as "layout-designs") in accordance with Articles 2 through 7 (other than paragraph 3 of Article 6), Article 12 and paragraph 3 of Article 16 of the Treaty on Intellectual Property in Respect of Integrated Circuits and, in addition, to comply with the following provisions.

Article 36 Scope of the protection

Subject to the provisions of paragraph 1 of Article 37, Members shall consider unlawful the follow-ing acts if performed without the authorization of the right holder: importing, selling, or otherwise distributing for commercial purposes a protected layout-design, an integrated circuit in which a protected layout-design is incorporated, or an article incorporating such an integrated circuit only in so far as it continues to contain an unlawfully reproduced layout-design.

Article 37 Acts not requiring the authorization of the right holder

1.   Notwithstanding Article 36, no Member shall consider unlawful the performance of any of the acts referred to in that Article in respect of an integrated circuit incorporating an unlawfully reproduced layout-design or any article incorporating such an integrated circuit where the person performing or ordering such acts did not know and had no reasonable ground to know, when acquiring the integrated circuit or article incorporating such an integrated circuit, that it incorporated an unlawfully reproduced layout-design. Members shall provide that, after the time that such person has received sufficient notice that the layout-design was unlawfully reproduced, that person may perform any of the acts with respect to the stock on hand or ordered before such time, but shall be liable to pay to the right holder a sum equivalent to a reasonable royalty such as would be payable under a freely negotiated licence in respect of such a layout-design.

2.   The conditions set out in subparagraphs (a) through (k) of Article 31 shall apply *mutatis mutandis* in the event of any non-voluntary licensing of a layout-design or of its use by or for the government without the authorization of the right holder.

Article 38 Term of protection

1.   In Members requiring registration as a condition of protection, the term of protection of layout-designs shall not end before the expiration of a period of 10 years counted from the date of filing an application for registration or from the first commercial exploitation wherever in the world it occurs.

2.   In Members not requiring registration as a condition for protection, layout-designs shall be protected for a term of no less than 10 years from the date of the first commercial exploitation wherever in the world it occurs.

3.   Notwithstanding paragraphs 1 and 2, a Member may provide that protection shall lapse 15 years after the creation of the layout-design.

SECTION 7:
PROTECTION OF UNDISCLOSED INFORMATION

Article 39

1. In the course of ensuring effective protection against unfair competition as provided in Article 10bis of the Paris Convention (1967), Members shall protect undisclosed information in accordance with paragraph 2 and data submitted to governments or governmental agencies in accordance with paragraph 3.

2. Natural and legal persons shall have the possibility of preventing information lawfully within their control from being disclosed to, acquired by, or used by others without their consent in a manner contrary to honest commercial practices so long as such information:
   (a) is secret in the sense that it is not, as a body or in the precise configuration and assembly of its components, generally known among or readily accessible to persons within the circles that normally deal with the kind of information in question;
   (b) has commercial value because it is secret; and
   (c) has been subject to reasonable steps under the circumstances, by the person lawfully in control of the information, to keep it secret.

3. Members, when requiring, as a condition of approving the marketing of pharmaceutical or of agricultural chemical products which utilize new chemical entities, the submission of undisclosed test or other data, the origination of which involves a considerable effort, shall protect such data against unfair commercial use. In addition, Members shall protect such data against disclosure, except where necessary to protect the public, or unless steps are taken to ensure that the data are protected against unfair commercial use.

SECTION 8:
CONTROL OF ANTI-COMPETITIVE PRACTICES IN CONTRACTUAL LICENCES

Article 40

1. Members agree that some licensing practices or conditions pertaining to intellectual property rights which restrain competition may have adverse effects on trade and may impede the transfer and dissemination of technology.

2. Nothing in this Agreement shall prevent Members from specifying in their legislation licensing practices or conditions that may in particular cases constitute an abuse of intellectual property rights having an adverse effect on competition in the relevant market. As provided above, a Member may adopt, consistently with the other provisions of this Agreement, appropriate measures to prevent or control such practices, which may include for example exclusive grantback conditions, conditions preventing challenges to validity and coercive package licensing, in the light of the relevant laws and regulations of that Member.

3. Each Member shall enter, upon request, into consultations with any other Member which has cause to believe that an intellectual property right owner that is a national or domiciliary of the Member to which the request for consultations has been addressed is undertaking practices in violation of the requesting Member's laws and regulations on the subject matter of this Section, and which wishes to secure compliance with such legislation, without prejudice to any action under the law and to the full freedom of an ultimate decision of either Member. The Member addressed shall accord full and sympathetic consideration to, and shall afford adequate opportunity for, consultations with the requesting Member, and shall cooperate through supply of publicly available non-confidential information of relevance to the matter in question and of other information available to the Member, subject to domestic law and to the conclusion of mutually satisfactory agreements concerning the safeguarding of its confidentiality by the requesting Member.

4. A Member whose nationals or domiciliaries are subject to proceedings in another Member concerning alleged violation of that other Member's laws and regulations on the subject matter of this Section shall, upon request, be granted an opportunity for consultations by the other Member under the same conditions as those foreseen in paragraph 3.

PART III

ENFORCEMENT OF INTELLECTUAL PROPERTY RIGHTS

SECTION 1:

GENERAL OBLIGATIONS

Article 41

1. Members shall ensure that enforcement procedures as specified in this Part are available under their law so as to permit effective action against any act of infringement of intellectual property rights covered by this Agreement, including expeditious remedies to prevent infringements and remedies which constitute a deterrent to further infringements. These procedures shall be applied in such a manner as to avoid the creation of barriers to legitimate trade and to provide for safeguards against their abuse.

2. Procedures concerning the enforcement of intellectual property rights shall be fair and equitable. They shall not be unnecessarily complicated or costly, or entail unreasonable time-limits or unwarranted delays.

3. Decisions on the merits of a case shall preferably be in writing and reasoned. They shall be made available at least to the parties to the proceeding without undue delay. Decisions on the merits of a case shall be based only on evidence in respect of which parties were offered the opportunity to be heard.

4. Parties to a proceeding shall have an opportunity for review by a judicial authority of final administrative decisions and, subject to jurisdictional provisions in a Member's law concerning the importance of a case, of at least the legal aspects of initial judicial decisions on the merits of a case. However, there shall be no obligation to provide an opportunity for review of acquittals in criminal cases.

5. It is understood that this Part does not create any obligation to put in place a judicial system for the enforcement of intellectual property rights distinct from that for the enforcement of law in general, nor does it affect the capacity of Members to enforce their law in general. Nothing in this Part creates any obligation with respect to the distribution of resources as between enforcement of intellectual property rights and the enforcement of law in general.

SECTION 2:

CIVIL AND ADMINISTRATIVE PROCEDURES AND REMEDIES

Article 42 Fair and equitable procedures

Members shall make available to right holders civil judicial procedures concerning the enforcement of any intellectual property right covered by this Agreement. Defendants shall have the right to written notice which is timely and contains sufficient detail, including the basis of the claims. Parties shall be allowed to be represented by independent legal counsel, and procedures shall not impose overly burdensome requirements concerning mandatory personal appearances. All parties to such procedures shall be duly entitled to substantiate their claims and to present all relevant evidence. The procedure shall provide a means to identify and protect confidential information, unless this would be contrary to existing constitutional requirements.

Article 43 Evidence

1. The judicial authorities shall have the authority, where a party has presented reasonably available evidence sufficient to support its claims and has specified evidence relevant to substantiation of its claims which lies in the control of the opposing party, to order that this evidence be produced by the opposing party, subject in appropriate cases to conditions which ensure the protection of confidential information.

2. In cases in which a party to a proceeding voluntarily and without good reason refuses access to, or otherwise does not provide necessary information within a reasonable period, or significantly impedes a procedure relating to an enforcement action, a Member may accord judicial authorities the authority to make preliminary and final determinations, affirmative or negative, on the basis of the information presented to them, including the complaint or the allegation presented by the party adversely affected by the denial of access to information, subject to providing the parties an opportunity to be heard on the allegations or evidence.

Article 44 Injunctions

1. The judicial authorities shall have the authority to order a party to desist from an infringement, inter alia to prevent the entry into the channels of commerce in their jurisdiction of imported goods that involve the infringement of an intellectual property right, immediately after customs clearance of such goods. Members are not obliged to accord such authority in respect of protected subject matter acquired or ordered by a person prior to knowing or having reasonable grounds to know that dealing in such subject matter would entail the infringement of an intellectual property right.

2. Notwithstanding the other provisions of this Part and provided that the provisions of Part II specifically addressing use by governments, or by third parties authorized by a government, without the authorization of the right holder are complied with, Members may limit the remedies available against such use to payment of remuneration in accordance with subparagraph (h) of Article 31. In other cases, the remedies under this Part shall apply or, where these remedies are inconsistent with a Member's law, declaratory judgments and adequate compensation shall be available.

Article 45 Damages

1. The judicial authorities shall have the authority to order the infringer to pay the right holder damages adequate to compensate for the injury the right holder has suffered because of an infringement of that person's intellectual property right by an infringer who knowingly, or with reasonable grounds to know, engaged in infringing activity.

2. The judicial authorities shall also have the authority to order the infringer to pay the right holder expenses, which may include appropriate attorney's fees. In appropriate cases, Members may authorize the judicial authorities to order recovery of profits and/or payment of pre-established damages even where the infringer did not knowingly, or with reasonable grounds to know, engage in infringing activity.

Article 46 Other remedies

In order to create an effective deterrent to infringement, the judicial authorities shall have the authority to order that goods that they have found to be infringing be, without compensation of any sort, disposed of outside the channels of commerce in such a manner as to avoid any harm caused to the right holder, or, unless this would be contrary to existing constitutional requirements, destroyed. The judicial authorities shall also have the authority to order that materials and implements the predominant use of which has been in the creation of the infringing goods be, without compensation of any sort, disposed of outside the channels of commerce in such a manner as to minimize the risks of further infringements. In considering such requests, the need for proportionality between the seriousness of the infringement and the remedies ordered as well as the interests of third parties shall be taken into account. In regard to counterfeit trademark goods, the simple removal of the trademark unlawfully affixed shall not be sufficient, other than in exceptional cases, to permit release of the goods into the channels of commerce.

Article 47 Right of information

Members may provide that the judicial authorities shall have the authority, unless this would be out of proportion to the seriousness of the infringement, to order the infringer to inform the right holder of the identity of third persons involved in the production and distribution of the infringing goods or services and of their channels of distribution.

Article 48 Indemnification of the defendant

1. The judicial authorities shall have the authority to order a party at whose request measures were taken and who has abused enforcement procedures to provide to a party wrongfully enjoined or restrained adequate compensation for the injury suffered because of such abuse. The judicial authorities shall also have the authority to order the applicant to pay the defendant expenses, which may include appropriate attorney's fees.

2. In respect of the administration of any law pertaining to the protection or enforcement of intellectual property rights, Members shall only exempt both public authorities and officials from liability to appropriate remedial measures where actions are taken or intended in good faith in the course of the administration of that law.

Article 49 Administrative procedures

To the extent that any civil remedy can be ordered as a result of administrative procedures on the merits of a case, such procedures shall conform to principles equivalent in substance to those set forth in this Section.

SECTION 3:
PROVISIONAL MEASURES

Article 50

1.   The judicial authorities shall have the authority to order prompt and effective provisional measures:

    (a)   to prevent an infringement of any intellectual property right from occurring, and in particular to prevent the entry into the channels of commerce in their jurisdiction of goods, including imported goods immediately after customs clearance;

    (b)   to preserve relevant evidence in regard to the alleged infringement.

2.   The judicial authorities shall have the authority to adopt provisional measures inaudita altera parte where appropriate, in particular where any delay is likely to cause irreparable harm to the right holder, or where there is a demonstrable risk of evidence being destroyed.

3.   The judicial authorities shall have the authority to require the applicant to provide any reasonably available evidence in order to satisfy themselves with a sufficient degree of certainty that the applicant is the right holder and that the applicant's right is being infringed or that such infringement is imminent, and to order the applicant to provide a security or equivalent assurance sufficient to protect the defendant and to prevent abuse.

4.   Where provisional measures have been adopted inaudita altera parte, the parties affected shall be given notice, without delay after the execution of the measures at the latest. A review, including a right to be heard, shall take place upon request of the defendant with a view to deciding, within a reasonable period after the notification of the measures, whether these measures shall be modified, revoked or confirmed.

5.   The applicant may be required to supply other information necessary for the identification of the goods concerned by the authority that will execute the provisional measures.

6.   Without prejudice to paragraph 4, provisional measures taken on the basis of paragraphs 1 and 2 shall, upon request by the defendant, be revoked or otherwise cease to have effect, if proceedings leading to a decision on the merits of the case are not initiated within a reasonable period, to be determined by the judicial authority ordering the measures where a Member's law so permits or, in the absence of such a determination, not to exceed 20 working days or 31 calendar days, whichever is the longer.

7.   Where the provisional measures are revoked or where they lapse due to any act or omission by the applicant, or where it is subsequently found that there has been no infringement or threat of infringement of an intellectual property right, the judicial authorities shall have the authority to order the applicant, upon request of the defendant, to provide the defendant appropriate compensation for any injury caused by these measures.

8.   To the extent that any provisional measure can be ordered as a result of administrative procedures, such procedures shall conform to principles equivalent in substance to those set forth in this Section.

SECTION 4:
SPECIAL REQUIREMENTS RELATED TO BORDER MEASURES

Article 51 Suspension of release by customs authorities

Members shall, in conformity with the provisions set out below, adopt procedures to enable a right holder, who has valid grounds for suspecting that the importation of counterfeit trademark or pirated copyright goods may take place, to lodge an application in writing with competent authorities, administrative or judicial, for the suspension by the customs authorities of the release into free circulation of such goods. Members may enable such an application to be made in respect of goods which involve other infringements of intellectual property rights, provided that the requirements of this Section are met. Members may also provide for corresponding procedures concerning the suspension by the customs authorities of the release of infringing goods destined for exportation from their territories.

Article 52 Application

Any right holder initiating the procedures under Article 51 shall be required to provide adequate evidence to satisfy the competent authorities that, under the laws of the country of importation, there is prima facie an infringement of the right holder's intellectual property right and to supply a sufficiently detailed description of the goods to make them readily recognizable by the customs authorities. The competent authorities shall inform the applicant within a reasonable period whether they have accepted the application and, where determined by the competent authorities, the period for which the customs authorities will take action.

Article 53 Security or equivalent assurance

1. The competent authorities shall have the authority to require an applicant to provide a security or equivalent assurance sufficient to protect the defendant and the competent authorities and to prevent abuse. Such security or equivalent assurance shall not unreasonably deter recourse to these procedures.

2. Where pursuant to an application under this Section the release of goods involving industrial designs, patents, layout-designs or undisclosed information into free circulation has been suspended by customs authorities on the basis of a decision other than by a judicial or other independent authority, and the period provided for in Article 55 has expired without the granting of provisional relief by the duly empowered authority, and provided that all other conditions for importation have been complied with, the owner, importer, or consignee of such goods shall be entitled to their release on the posting of a security in an amount sufficient to protect the right holder for any infringement. Payment of such security shall not prejudice any other remedy available to the right holder, it being understood that the security shall be released if the right holder fails to pursue the right of action within a reasonable period of time.

Article 54 Notice of suspension

The importer and the applicant shall be promptly notified of the suspension of the release of goods according to Article 51.

Article 55 Duration of suspension

If, within a period not exceeding 10 working days after the applicant has been served notice of the suspension, the customs authorities have not been informed that proceedings leading to a decision on the merits of the case have been initiated by a party other than the defendant, or that the duly empowered authority has taken provisional measures prolonging the suspension of the release of the goods, the goods shall be released, provided that all other conditions for importation or exportation have been complied with; in appropriate cases, this time-limit may be extended by another 10 working days. If proceedings leading to a decision on the merits of the case have been initiated, a review, including a right to be heard, shall take place upon request of the defendant with a view to deciding, within a reasonable period, whether these measures shall be modified, revoked or confirmed. Notwithstanding the above, where the suspension of the release of goods is carried out or continued in accordance with a provisional judicial measure, the provisions of paragraph 6 of Article 50 shall apply.

Article 56 Indemnification of the importer and of the owner of the goods

Relevant authorities shall have the authority to order the applicant to pay the importer, the consignee and the owner of the goods appropriate compensation for any injury caused to them through the wrongful detention of goods or through the detention of goods released pursuant to Article 55.

Article 57 Right of Inspection and Information

Without prejudice to the protection of confidential information, Members shall provide the competent authorities the authority to give the right holder sufficient opportunity to have any goods detained by the customs authorities inspected in order to substantiate the right holder's claims. The competent authorities shall also have authority to give the importer an equivalent opportunity to have any such goods inspected. Where a positive determination has been made on the merits of a case, Members may provide the competent authorities the authority to inform the right holder of the names and addresses of the consignor, the importer and the consignee and of the quantity of the goods in question.

Article 58 Ex officio action

Where Members require competent authorities to act upon their own initiative and to suspend the release of goods in respect of which they have acquired *prima facie* evidence that an intellectual property right is being infringed:

(a)   the competent authorities may at any time seek from the right holder any information that may assist them to exercise these powers;

(b)   the importer and the right holder shall be promptly notified of the suspension. Where the importer has lodged an appeal against the suspension with the competent authorities, the suspension shall be subject to the conditions, *mutatis mutandis*, set out at Article 55;

(c)   Members shall only exempt both public authorities and officials from liability to appropriate remedial measures where actions are taken or intended in good faith.

Article 59 Remedies

Without prejudice to other rights of action open to the right holder and subject to the right of the defendant to seek review by a judicial authority, competent authorities shall have the authority to order the destruction or disposal of infringing goods in accordance with the principles set out in Article 46. In regard to counterfeit trademark goods, the authorities shall not allow the re-exportation of the infringing goods in an unaltered state or subject them to a different customs procedure, other than in exceptional circumstances.

Article 60 De minimis imports

Members may exclude from the application of the above provisions small quantities of goods of a non-commercial nature contained in travellers' personal luggage or sent in small consignments.

SECTION 5:
CRIMINAL PROCEDURES

Article 61

Members shall provide for criminal procedures and penalties to be applied at least in cases of wilful trademark counterfeiting or copyright piracy on a commercial scale. Remedies available shall include imprisonment and/or monetary fines sufficient to provide a deterrent, consistently with the level of penalties applied for crimes of a corresponding gravity. In appropriate cases, remedies available shall also include the seizure, forfeiture and destruction of the infringing goods and of any materials and implements the predominant use of which has been in the commission of the offence. Members may provide for criminal procedures and penalties to be applied in other cases of infringement of intellectual property rights, in particular where they are committed wilfully and on a commercial scale.

PART IV
ACQUISITION AND MAINTENANCE OF INTELLECTUAL PROPERTY RIGHTS AND
RELATED *INTER-PARTES* PROCEDURES

Article 62

1.   Members may require, as a condition of the acquisition or maintenance of the intellectual property rights provided for under Sections 2 through 6 of Part II, compliance with reasonable procedures and formalities. Such procedures and formalities shall be consistent with the provisions of this Agreement.

2.   Where the acquisition of an intellectual property right is subject to the right being granted or registered, Members shall ensure that the procedures for grant or registration, subject to compliance with the substantive conditions for acquisition of the right, permit the granting or registration of the right within a reasonable period of time so as to avoid unwarranted curtailment of the period of protection.

3.   Article 4 of the Paris Convention (1967) shall apply *mutatis mutandis* to service marks.

4.   Procedures concerning the acquisition or maintenance of intellectual property rights and, where a Member's law provides for such procedures, administrative revocation and inter partes procedures such as opposition, revocation and cancellation, shall be governed by the general principles set out in paragraphs 2 and 3 of Article 41.

5. Final administrative decisions in any of the procedures referred to under paragraph 4 shall be subject to review by a judicial or quasi-judicial authority. However, there shall be no obligation to provide an opportunity for such review of decisions in cases of unsuccessful opposition or administrative revocation, provided that the grounds for such procedures can be the subject of invalidation procedures.

PART V
DISPUTE PREVENTION AND SETTLEMENT

Article 63 Transparency

1. Laws and regulations, and final judicial decisions and administrative rulings of general application, made effective by a Member pertaining to the subject matter of this Agreement (the availability, scope, acquisition, enforcement and prevention of the abuse of intellectual property rights) shall be published, or where such publication is not practicable made publicly available, in a national language, in such a manner as to enable governments and right holders to become acquainted with them. Agreements concerning the subject matter of this Agreement which are in force between the government or a governmental agency of a Member and the government or a governmental agency of another Member shall also be published.

2. Members shall notify the laws and regulations referred to in paragraph 1 to the Council for TRIPS in order to assist that Council in its review of the operation of this Agreement. The Council shall attempt to minimize the burden on Members in carrying out this obligation and may decide to waive the obligation to notify such laws and regulations directly to the Council if consultations with WIPO on the establishment of a common register containing these laws and regulations are successful. The Council shall also consider in this connection any action required regarding notifications pursuant to the obligations under this Agreement stemming from the provisions of Article 6ter of the Paris Convention (1967).

3. Each Member shall be prepared to supply, in response to a written request from another Member, information of the sort referred to in paragraph 1. A Member, having reason to believe that a specific judicial decision or administrative ruling or bilateral agreement in the area of intellectual property rights affects its rights under this Agreement, may also request in writing to be given access to or be informed in sufficient detail of such specific judicial decisions or administrative rulings or bilateral agreements.

4. Nothing in paragraphs 1, 2 and 3 shall require Members to disclose confidential information which would impede law enforcement or otherwise be contrary to the public interest or would prejudice the legitimate commercial interests of particular enterprises, public or private.

Article 64 Dispute settlement

1. The provisions of Articles XXII and XXIII of GATT 1994 as elaborated and applied by the Dispute Settlement Understanding shall apply to consultations and the settlement of disputes under this Agreement except as otherwise specifically provided herein.

2. Subparagraphs 1(b) and 1(c) of Article XXIII of GATT 1994 shall not apply to the settlement of disputes under this Agreement for a period of five years from the date of entry into force of the WTO Agreement.

3. During the time period referred to in paragraph 2, the Council for TRIPS shall examine the scope and modalities for complaints of the type provided for under subparagraphs 1(b) and 1(c) of Article XXIII of GATT 1994 made pursuant to this Agreement, and submit its recommendations to the Ministerial Conference for approval. Any decision of the Ministerial Conference to approve such recommendations or to extend the period in paragraph 2 shall be made only by consensus, and approved recommendations shall be effective for all Members without further formal acceptance process.

PART VI
TRANSITIONAL ARRANGEMENTS

Article 65 Transitional arrangements

1. Subject to the provisions of paragraphs 2, 3 and 4, no Member shall be obliged to apply the provisions of this Agreement before the expiry of a general period of one year following the date of entry into force of the WTO Agreement.

2. A developing country Member is entitled to delay for a further period of four years the date of application, as defined in paragraph 1, of the provisions of this Agreement other than Articles 3, 4 and 5.

3. Any other Member which is in the process of transformation from a centrally-planned into a market, free-enterprise economy and which is undertaking structural reform of its intellectual property system and facing special problems in the preparation and implementation of intellectual property laws and regulations, may also benefit from a period of delay as foreseen in paragraph 2.

4. To the extent that a developing country Member is obliged by this Agreement to extend product patent protection to areas of technology not so protectable in its territory on the general date of application of this Agreement for that Member, as defined in paragraph 2, it may delay the application of the provisions on product patents of Section 5 of Part II to such areas of technology for an additional period of five years.

5. A Member availing itself of a transitional period under paragraphs 1, 2, 3 or 4 shall ensure that any changes in its laws, regulations and practice made during that period do not result in a lesser degree of consistency with the provisions of this Agreement.

Article 66 Least-developed country members

1. In view of the special needs and requirements of least-developed country Members, their economic, financial and administrative constraints, and their need for flexibility to create a viable technological base, such Members shall not be required to apply the provisions of this Agreement, other than Articles 3, 4 and 5, for a period of 10 years from the date of application as defined under paragraph 1 of Article 65. The Council for TRIPS shall, upon duly motivated request by a least-developed country Member, accord extensions of this period.

2. Developed country Members shall provide incentives to enterprises and institutions in their territories for the purpose of promoting and encouraging technology transfer to least-developed country Members in order to enable them to create a sound and viable technological base.

Article 67 Technical Cooperation

In order to facilitate the implementation of this Agreement, developed country Members shall provide, on request and on mutually agreed terms and conditions, technical and financial cooperation in favour of developing and least-developed country Members. Such cooperation shall include assistance in the preparation of laws and regulations on the protection and enforcement of intellectual property rights as well as on the prevention of their abuse, and shall include support regarding the establishment or reinforcement of domestic offices and agencies relevant to these matters, including the training of personnel.

PART VII
INSTITUTIONAL ARRANGEMENTS; FINAL PROVISIONS

Article 68 Council for Trade-Related Aspects of Intellectual Property Rights

The Council for TRIPS shall monitor the operation of this Agreement and, in particular, Members' compliance with their obligations hereunder, and shall afford Members the opportunity of consulting on matters relating to the trade-related aspects of intellectual property rights. It shall carry out such other responsibilities as assigned to it by the Members, and it shall, in particular, provide any assistance requested by them in the context of dispute settlement procedures. In carrying out its functions, the Council for TRIPS may consult with and seek information from any source it deems appropriate. In consultation with WIPO, the Council shall seek to establish, within one year of its first meeting, appropriate arrangements for cooperation with bodies of that Organization.

Article 69 International cooperation

Members agree to cooperate with each other with a view to eliminating international trade in goods infringing intellectual property rights. For this purpose, they shall establish and notify contact points in their administrations and be ready to exchange information on trade in infringing goods. They shall, in particular, promote the exchange of information and cooperation between customs authorities with regard to trade in counterfeit trademark goods and pirated copyright goods.

Article 70 Protection of existing subject matter

1.   This Agreement does not give rise to obligations in respect of acts which occurred before the date of application of the Agreement for the Member in question.

2.   Except as otherwise provided for in this Agreement, this Agreement gives rise to obligations in respect of all subject matter existing at the date of application of this Agreement for the Member in question, and which is protected in that Member on the said date, or which meets or comes subsequently to meet the criteria for protection under the terms of this Agreement. In respect of this paragraph and paragraphs 3 and 4, copyright obligations with respect to existing works shall be solely determined under Article 18 of the Berne Convention (1971), and obligations with respect to the rights of producers of phonograms and performers in existing phonograms shall be determined solely under Article 18 of the Berne Convention (1971) as made applicable under paragraph 6 of Article 14 of this Agreement.

3.   There shall be no obligation to restore protection to subject matter which on the date of application of this Agreement for the Member in question has fallen into the public domain.

4.   In respect of any acts in respect of specific objects embodying protected subject matter which become infringing under the terms of legislation in conformity with this Agreement, and which were commenced, or in respect of which a significant investment was made, before the date of acceptance of the WTO Agreement by that Member, any Member may provide for a limitation of the remedies available to the right holder as to the continued performance of such acts after the date of application of this Agreement for that Member. In such cases the Member shall, however, at least provide for the payment of equitable remuneration.

5.   A Member is not obliged to apply the provisions of Article 11 and of paragraph 4 of Article 14 with respect to originals or copies purchased prior to the date of application of this Agreement for that Member.

6.   Members shall not be required to apply Article 31, or the requirement in paragraph 1 of Article 27 that patent rights shall be enjoyable without discrimination as to the field of technology, to use without the authorization of the right holder where authorization for such use was granted by the government before the date this Agreement became known.

7.   In the case of intellectual property rights for which protection is conditional upon registration, applications for protection which are pending on the date of application of this Agreement for the Member in question shall be permitted to be amended to claim any enhanced protection provided under the provisions of this Agreement. Such amendments shall not include new matter.

8.   Where a Member does not make available as of the date of entry into force of the WTO Agreement patent protection for pharmaceutical and agricultural chemical products commensurate with its obligations under Article 27, that Member shall:

(a)   notwithstanding the provisions of Part VI, provide as from the date of entry into force of the WTO Agreement a means by which applications for patents for such inventions can be filed;

(b)   apply to these applications, as of the date of application of this Agreement, the criteria for patentability as laid down in this Agreement as if those criteria were being applied on the date of filing in that Member or, where priority is available and claimed, the priority date of the application; and

(c)   provide patent protection in accordance with this Agreement as from the grant of the patent and for the remainder of the patent term, counted from the filing date in accordance with Article 33 of this Agreement, for those of these applications that meet the criteria for protection referred to in subparagraph (b).

9.   Where a product is the subject of a patent application in a Member in accordance with paragraph 8(a), exclusive marketing rights shall be granted, notwithstanding the provisions

of Part VI, for a period of five years after obtaining marketing approval in that Member or until a product patent is granted or rejected in that Member, whichever period is shorter, provided that, subsequent to the entry into force of the WTO Agreement, a patent application has been filed and a patent granted for that product in another Member and marketing approval obtained in such other Member.

Article 71 Review and amendment

1.   The Council for TRIPS shall review the implementation of this Agreement after the expiration of the transitional period referred to in paragraph 2 of Article 65. The Council shall, having regard to the experience gained in its implementation, review it two years after that date, and at identical intervals thereafter. The Council may also undertake reviews in the light of any relevant new developments which might warrant modification or amendment of this Agreement.

2.   Amendments merely serving the purpose of adjusting to higher levels of protection of intellectual property rights achieved, and in force, in other multilateral agreements and accepted under those agreements by all Members of the WTO may be referred to the Ministerial Conference for action in accordance with paragraph 6 of Article X of the WTO Agreement on the basis of a consensus proposal from the Council for TRIPS.

Article 72 Reservations

Reservations may not be entered in respect of any of the provisions of this Agreement without the consent of the other Members.

Article 73 Security exceptions

Nothing in this Agreement shall be construed:

(a)   to require a Member to furnish any information the disclosure of which it considers contrary to its essential security interests; or

(b)   to prevent a Member from taking any action which it considers necessary for the protection of its essential security interests;

    (i)   relating to fissionable materials or the materials from which they are derived;

    (ii)   relating to the traffic in arms, ammunition and implements of war and to such traffic in other goods and materials as is carried on directly or indirectly for the purpose of supplying a military establishment;

    (iii)   taken in time of war or other emergency in international relations; or

(c)   to prevent a Member from taking any action in pursuance of its obligations under the United Nations Charter for the maintenance of international peace and security.

INDEX